To Sarah, Dan, Justin, and Megan
for continuing to support us
and for understanding our absences
while working on this text.

Teaching Students with Mild Disabilities at the Secondary Level

Edward J. Sabornie
North Carolina State University

Laurie U. deBettencourt
Appalachian State University

Merrill,
an imprint of Prentice Hall
Upper Saddle River, New Jersey   Columbus, Ohio

Library of Congress Cataloging-in-Publication Data

Sabornie, Edward James.
Teaching students with mild disabilities at the secondary level / Edward J. Sabornie, Laurie U. deBettencourt.
p. cm.
Includes bibliographical references (p.) and indexes.
ISBN 0-02-404991-3 (pbk.)
1. Learning disabled youth—Education (Secondary)—United States. 2. Problem youth—Education (Secondary)—United States. 3. Mentally handicapped youth—Education (Secondary)—United States. I. DeBettencourt, Laurie Ungerleider. II. Title.
LC4705.S23 1997
371.92′82—dc20

96-30241
CIP

Cover art: E. Degginger/H. Armstrong Roberts, Inc.
Editor: Ann Castel Davis
Production Editor: Sheryl Glicker Langner
Photo Researcher: Angela Jenkins
Design Coordinator: Jill E. Bonar
Text Designer: STELLARViSIONs
Cover Designer: Brian Deep
Production Manager: Laura Messerly
Electronic Text Management: Marilyn Wilson Phelps, Matthew Williams, Karen L. Bretz, Tracey Ward
Director of Marketing: Kevin Flanagan
Advertising/Marketing Coordinator: Julie Shough

This book was set in Clearface by Prentice Hall and was printed and bound by Quebecor Printing/Book Press. The cover was printed by Phoenix Color Corp.

© 1997 by Prentice-Hall, Inc.
Simon & Schuster/A Viacom Company
Upper Saddle River, New Jersey 07458

Photo credits: pp. xviii, 100, 232, 274 by Anne Vega/Merrill; pp. 22, 338 by Anthony Magnacca; p. 130 by Anthony Magnacca/Merrill; pp. 50, 200, 296 by Scott Cunningham/Merrill; p. 70 by Larry Hamill/Merrill; p. 154 by Barbara Schwartz/Merrill

Printed in the United States of America

10 9 8 7 6 5 4 3

ISBN: 0-02-404991-3

Prentice-Hall International (UK) Limited, *London*
Prentice-Hall of Australia Pty. Limited, *Sydney*
Prentice-Hall of Canada, Inc., *Toronto*
Prentice-Hall Hispanoamericana, S. A., *Mexico*
Prentice-Hall of India Private Limited, *New Delhi*
Prentice-Hall of Japan, Inc., *Tokyo*
Simon & Schuster Asia Pte. Ltd., *Singapore*
Editora Prentice-Hall do Brasil, Ltda., *Rio de Janeiro*

Preface

Purpose

In comparison to elementary-level students, adolescents with mild disabilities have traditionally been overlooked in most methods-oriented texts. At best, effective secondary-level methods of instruction have been addressed with very little detail. This text, which comprehensively covers methods and materials that teachers should use while instructing adolescents with mild disabilities, focuses on ways to address learning and behavioral problems that are typical of such adolescents (i.e., learning disabilities, behavioral disorders, and mild mental retardation). The content is grounded in methods that have been validated in research, but it is presented in a style that is easily understood by teachers serving adolescents. A cross-categorical focus is provided in the text, where specific methods found to be effective with all types of youth with mild disabilities are discussed. Moreover, methods found to be effective only with specific groups of adolescents with mild disabilities (e.g., cognitive learning strategies with students identified as learning disabled) are also included.

Audience

This text is designed for the purpose of disseminating instructionally relevant information to pre-service and in-service special and general education teachers of secondary-level students. Our goal was to provide a definitive source of information or reference of practical and proven methods. We recognize that many adolescents with mild disabilities are educated primarily in the mainstream classroom and we support the collaborative instructional model within all instructional areas. This text is intended to assist all educators and parents in the preparation of adolescents with mild disabilities for their roles in modern society.

Organization of the Text

The first part of the text, "Special Education and Adolescence," focuses on the nature of adolescents and special education, in particular the characteristics of secondary-level students with mild disabilities. Part Two, "Instructional Methods," provides specific content area instructional methods. The final section, "Current and Future Instructional Issues," focuses on current and future instructional issues, such as transition and postsecondary preparation.

Features

For the reader's convenience, a consistent format is used throughout. Several distinctive features are included that will benefit the reader:

- Each chapter begins with a list of objectives, followed by an introduction. Before reading the chapter the reader knows the key points to be learned and emphasized, as well as the focus of the chapter.

- Each chapter addresses how teachers of adolescents with mild disabilities can use the material in general education classrooms, in addition to special education settings. Because most adolescents with mild disabilities are currently being served in general education classrooms, the text has a broader appeal and a wider audience.

- At the end of each chapter a summary of the key points and a list of the key terms are included.

- An appendix provides a list of resources for the consumer and a reader's guide for additional content exploration.

- An instructor's manual is available that includes an outline of each chapter, sample multiple-choice questions, and essay test questions.

ACKNOWLEDGMENTS

We are grateful to the following reviewers for their helpful suggestions: Kathy Peca, Eastern New Mexico University; Jeanne B. Repetto, University of Florida; Ernest Rose, Montana State University at Billings; Diane T. Woodrum, West Virginia University; and Eleanor B. Wright, University of North Carolina at Wilmington.

At Merrill/Prentice Hall, we are grateful to Ann Castel Davis and Sheryl Langner for their assistance and patience during this project.

We also want to thank all the secondary-level educators, students, and the parents of students who have given us feedback and encouragement during the making of this text.

Contents

Part 1   *Special Education and Adolescence*

1   Introduction to Programming for Adolescents with Mild Disabilities   1

Factors Influencing Development of Secondary
Education Programs   2

*Definitions and Characteristics of Individuals
    with Mild Disabilities   3*
Legislative Foundations   7
Regular Education's Curricular Emphasis   9
*General and Special Education
    Teacher Preparation   10*

Educational Program Models at the Secondary Level   11

Basic Skills Model   11
The Tutorial Model   12
The Compensatory Model   13
The Vocational Model   13
The Functional Skills Model   13
Learning Strategies Model   13

Issues and Trends in Secondary Education
of Youth with Mild Disabilities   14

Full Inclusion of Adolescents with Mild Disabilities   14
*Dropout Phenomenon Among Adolescents
    with Disabilities   14*
*Adolescent Dilemmas and Their
    Effect on Schooling   17*

2   Adolescence and Its Characteristics   2

Rationale   24

Theories of Adolescence   25

G. Stanley Hall's Views   26
Sigmund Freud's Theories   27
Erickson's Theory of Identity Development   27

Peter Blos's Views   28
Lewin's Theory   29
Havinghurst's Developmental Tasks of Adolescence   30
Piaget's Cognitive Theory of Adolescence   31
Kohlberg's Views on Adolescent Morality   31
Selman's Theory of Social Cognition   32
Elkind's Theory of Adolescent Egocentrism   33
Sullivan's Theory of Adolescent Interpersonal
Development   34

Adolescent Development   35

Physical Development   35
Cognitive Development   37
Psychological and Other Disorders of Adolescence   38

Applications to Adolescents with Disabilities   43

3   Characteristics of Secondary-Level Students with Mild Disabilities   50

Background   52

Personal Characteristics   53

General Demographics   53

Intellectual and Academic Traits   57

Academically-Related Characteristics   58

Behavioral Characteristics   61

Depression   62
Suicide   63
Juvenile Delinquency   63
Other Problem Behaviors During Adolescence   65

Part *2*   *Instructional Methods*

4   Effective Instruction and Behavior Management Techniques   70

Effective Instruction   72

Defining Behaviors   72
Effective Teaching Behaviors   73
Direct Instruction   74

Classroom Management at the Secondary Level   78

Measuring Behavior: Direct Observation   79
Increasing Behaviors in the Classroom   84
Decreasing Behaviors in the Classroom   88

Self-Management of Behavior and Generalization
Techniques with Adolescents   *92*

**5   Reading Instruction for Adolescents
with Mild Disabilities   100**

Students with Mild Disabilities and Reading Problems   102

Teaching Reading as a Complex Process   102
Importance of Functional Reading Skills for
Adolescents with Mild Disabilities   103

Assessment of Reading Skills at the Secondary Level   104

Why Assess Reading?   105
How Does One Assess Reading?   105
Using Standardized, Criterion-Referenced, and
Diagnostic Tests: Selected Instruments   106
Using Informal Reading Assessment Procedures   108

Reading Instruction at the Secondary Level   114

Vocabulary Development   114
Comprehension Instruction   117
Critical Features of Reading Instruction   120

Selected Commercial Reading Curricula for Adolescents
with Reading Difficulties   120

Selected Computer Software for Reading Instruction
at the Secondary Level   121

Special Considerations in Reading Instruction of Adolescents
with Mild Disabilities in Mainstream Classrooms   122

Importance of Motivation for Learning   122
Importance of Teaching Reading
Skills for Generalization   123
Adaptations to Mainstream Classrooms   123

**6   Written Language Instruction for
Adolescents with Mild Disabilities   130**

Students with Mild Disabilities and Written Language Problems 132

Teaching Written Language as a Complex Process   133
Importance of Functional Writing Skills for
Adolescents with Mild Disabilities   133

Assessment of Written Language Skills at the Secondary Level 134

Using Standardized Criterion-Referenced and Diagnostic
Tests: Selected Instruments   134
Using Informal Written Language Assessment
Procedures   136

Written Language Instruction at the Secondary Level   139

Instruction Using Cognitive Models   140

Instruction Using Reciprocal Peer Editing   145

Concluding Comments on Instruction   146

Selected Commercial Written Language Curricula for Adolescents with Written Language Difficulties   147

Selected Computer Software for Written Language Instruction at the Secondary Level   147

Special Considerations in Written Language Instruction of Adolescents with Mild Disabilities in Mainstream Classrooms   148

7   Teaching Mathematics to Adolescents with Mild Disabilities   154

Assessing Math Skills   157

Standardized, Criterion-Referenced, and Diagnostic Tests   157

Informal Assessment Procedures   159

Research-Validated Math Instruction: Adolescents with Mental Retardation   162

Research-Validated Math Instruction: Adolescents with Learning Disabilities   165

Functional Math Instruction   168

Mathematical Process Instruction   173

Math Instruction via Cognitive Strategies   176

Commercial Mathematics Curricula for Adolescents   183

Mathematics Instruction of Adolescents with Mild Disabilities in Regular Classes   190

Additional Considerations in Math Instruction   192

8   Cognitive Strategy Training and Study Skills Instruction   200

Teaching Cognitive Strategy Training at the Secondary Level   202

Impetus for Developing Cognitive Strategy Training Procedures   203

Distinction Between Cognitive Strategy Training and Study Skills Training   204

Assessment of Cognitive Learning Strategies   207

Using Standardized, Criterion-Referenced and Diagnostic Tests: Selected Instruments   208

Using Informal Study Skills and Cognitive Strategy Assessment Procedures   209

Development of a Cognitive Learning Strategies Curriculum   212
   Selection of Strategy Content   213
   Design of Strategy Content   213
   Usefulness of Learning Strategies   214
   Instruction of Learning Strategies   214
Specific Examples of Cognitive Learning Strategies   215
   Reading   215
   Written Language   216
   Mathematics   218
   Study Skills   219
Generalization of Strategy Training   225
   Adaptations to Mainstream Classrooms   226

9   Social Skills Instruction   232
Rationale for Social Skills Instruction   234
   Definitions   235
Assessment Procedures   238
   Direct Observation   238
   Direct Observation Recording Procedures   239
   Sociometry   243
   Teacher Rating Scales   247
Intervention Methods   249
   Social Skill Training Curricula   250
   Noncommercial Social Skills Training Procedures   256
   Social Skills Training for Employment   260
   Teaching Social Skills in Regular Classrooms   262
   Important Considerations in the
      Teaching of Social Skills   264

Part *3*   *Current and Future Instructional Issues*

10   Improving Adaptability of Adolescents with Mild Disabilities in Secondary Classrooms   274
Issues and Dilemmas in Mainstream
Secondary Classrooms   276
   Curriculum Express Instruction   276
   Standards for Graduation   277
   Grading Practices at the Secondary Level   278
Students with Mild Disabilities and the Curricular
Demands of Secondary School   280

Effective Content-Area Instruction   280

    Advance Organizers   282
    Visual Displays   283
    Study Guides   285
    Mnemonic Devices   285
    Audio Recordings   286
    Computer-Assisted Instruction   286
    Peer-Mediated Instruction   286
    School Survival Skills   287

Collaboration at the Secondary Level   289

11   Transition-Related Instruction   296

Rationale and Introduction   298

    Definitions   299
    Transition: Employment Issues   304
    Transition: Collateral Areas   307

Assessment for Transition Programming   308

Career Education in the Transition Process   317

Community-Based Instruction at the Secondary Level   322

Role of the Educator in the Transition Process   325

    Curriculum   326
    Interagency Cooperation   327
    Other Issues in Transition Programming   328

12   Education of Students with Mild Disabilities in Postsecondary Programs   338

Impetus for Studying Postsecondary Training with Persons with Mild Disabilities   340

Postsecondary-Level Educational Programs for Adults with Mild Disabilities   341

    Legal Foundations for Postsecondary
        Educational Programs   341
    Diversity and Scope of Programs   342
    Specific Two-Year and Four-Year
        College Programs   344
    Technical Education and Vocational Rehabilitation
        Programs   345
    Supported Employment Models   347

Assessment Issues   347

Preparing Students for Postsecondary Training   348

*Specific Guidelines for Preparing Students
for Postsecondary Training   349*

Review of Commercial Curriculum Guides for
Postsecondary Institutions   352

Issues at the Postsecondary Level   353

Administrative Considerations   354
Service Delivery Issues   354
Technological Issues   355

Training and Research Needs   356

Appendix   361

Name Index   365

Subject Index   372

1

Introduction to Programming for Adolescents with Mild Disabilities

Objectives

After reading this chapter, the reader should be able to:

1. define students with mild disabilities (i.e., learning disabilities, mild mental retardation, mild emotional disabilities, and traumatic brain injury);

2. describe characteristics of adolescents with mild disabilities;

3. identify legislation that has contributed to service delivery to adolescents with disabilities;

4. discuss factors that have influenced secondary programming for students with mild disabilities;

5. discuss several program options currently available to secondary students with mild disabilities;

6. identify factors that increase the likelihood of dropout among students with mild disabilities.

Programming for secondary students with mild disabilities is currently one of the fastest-growing areas of service delivery in special education. Many students with learning difficulties continue to need special education at the secondary level. The purpose of this chapter is to introduce the concept of programming for students with mild disabilities at the secondary level by first, defining students with mild disabilities; second, discussing the legislative actions that have led to the current services provided at the secondary level; third, identifying program models currently available for adolescents with mild disabilities; and last, discussing briefly recent research relevant to secondary-age students with mild disabilities. In essence, the chapter will serve as an introduction to the chapters that follow.

Factors Influencing Development of Secondary Education Programs

The vast majority of secondary students with mild disabilities receive their education in public secondary schools (Gajar, Goodman, & McAfee, 1993; Wagner, 1990). Public secondary schools attracted a great deal of negative attention in the 1980s with the publication of *A Nation at Risk* (National Commission on Excellence in Education, 1983), which warned that "the educational foundations of our society are presently being eroded by a rising tide of mediocrity that threatens our very future as a Nation and a people" (p. 5).

In response to the criticisms discussed in *A Nation at Risk* and other studies of that time, several reforms were implemented across the country at the secondary level. One such reform was to make high school more rigorous. Students are required in many states to pass a minimum competency test (MCT) as a requirement for graduation (Vitello, 1988). There is some concern for many students with disabilities that the added pressure to prepare them for such a required test is in conflict with their individual educational program (IEP). Many school districts are also increasing requirements for graduation. This shift to a more rigorous academic curriculum increases the pressure for students with mild disabilities.

Another reform of the 1980s made schools more accountable. (Teachers are pressured to demonstrate that all their students are learning at a rate that is acceptable to the district.) Many students who are more difficult to teach and do not learn at such a rate are having difficulty managing in the mainstream classroom (Donahoe & Zigmond, 1990). As a result, many drop out.

The basic agenda of the 1980s reform movement and the 1990s federal reform legislation, Goals 2000: Educate America Act (U.S. Senate, 1993), has been to increase the academic press of the schools, to increase achievement in core subjects, to increase students' higher-order thinking skills, and to better prepare our secondary students for the world of work (Zigmond, 1990). Shriner, Ysseldyke, and Thurlow (1994) suggest the recent rhetoric surrounding increasing the standards emphasizes that high content standards are important for *all* students. Unfortunately, studies have suggested that for students with mild disabilities to be successful, fundamental changes in instruction in the secondary regular classrooms are necessary (e.g., Baker & Zigmond, 1990; Zigmond, 1990).

Frequently, the secondary curriculum is departmentalized by content area and regular class instruction is provided in an array of subjects by different instructors. Thus the basic setting demands differ quite drastically from elementary or middle school. The change in method of instructional organization adds to the problems of adolescents with mild disabilities (Espin & Deno, 1993b); that is, changing classes (and content) every 45 minutes is often difficult for these students, who lack organizational and short-term memory skills. Students are required frequently to: (a) read many different content-area assignments independently over a short period of time, (b) take notes in each class, (c) keep each class material- and time-organized, and (d) write various papers synthesizing their research and thoughts. Ellett's (1993) survey of teachers suggests that the following student skills are necessary in regular secondary classrooms: following directions in

Figure 1.1
Secondary setting demands

> Reading skills need to be especially automatic and fluent.
> Teachers rely heavily on the lecture method.
> Teachers use few advance organizers.
> Students are required to take notes.
> Feedback and reinforcement is low frequency.
> Written tests and essays are common.
> Students are required to integrate concept formation, language, memory, and attention in altogether new blends.

class, coming to class prepared with materials, using class time wisely, and making up assignments and tests. Many students with mild disabilities do not have these skills and have not been prepared for the instructional changes and, as a result, have great difficulty with these demands. (See Figure 1.1 for a list of secondary setting demands).

The developmental changes and the social pressures of adolescence also add to these problems. Adolescence is marked by dramatic physical, psychological, and social changes brought about by biological maturation and societal and cultural expectations. The challenges of adolescence are even more formidable for the student with serious learning and/or behavioral problems.

The legal requirements for classification categories for special education assistance compound the above-mentioned challenges. Adolescents are undoubtedly aware of stigmatizing labels; and special education labels and/or grouping by categories can present very difficult problems. However, to receive federal and state funding for special education assistance, such classification labels are required (Masters, Mori, & Mori, 1993).

Definitions and Characteristics of Individuals with Mild Disabilities

The legal requirements for classification categories for special education that exist at the elementary level also exist at the secondary level. In 1975, Congress passed PL 94-142, the Education for All Handicapped Children Act, which outlined the entire foundation on which current special education practice rests. The law specifically described all of the categories of disabilities that make students eligible to receive special education. In 1990, Congress passed PL 101-476, the Individuals with Disabilities Education Act, a reauthorization of PL 94-142. This law continues to uphold the major provisions of PL 94-142, and it also adds significantly to the provisions for very young children with disabilities and for students preparing to leave secondary school (Ysseldyke, Algozzine, & Thurlow, 1992). One other change was the addition of two new categories of disability: autism and traumatic brain injury. Current federal definitions of students with mild disabilities include learning disabilities (LD), educable mentally retarded (EMR), emotionally disturbed (ED), and the 1990 addition of traumatic brain injury (TBI). Attention deficit disorder/attention deficit hyperactivity disorder (ADD/ADHD) is not a disability category recognized by the federal government, but because an increasing number of students are identified as ADD or ADHD and may be served under the "other health impaired" category, we discuss the definition in the following section.

Definitions

Specific learning disability is a broad term and has been defined by many. According to Public Law 94-142, specific **learning disability (LD)** means:

> a disorder in one or more of the basic psychological processes involved in understanding or using language, spoken or written, which may manifest itself in an imperfect ability to listen, think, speak, read, write, spell or do mathematical calculations. The term includes such conditions as perceptual handicap, brain injury, minimal brain dysfunction, dyslexia and developmental aphasia. The term does not include children who have learning problems which are primarily the result of visual, hearing, or motor handicaps, of mental retardation, or of environmental, cultural or economic disadvantage. (U.S. Office of Education, 1977, p. 42478)

Local school districts are obligated to determine learning disability eligibility based upon the above definition. Other definitions have been proposed by other organizations (e.g., the National Joint Committee on Learning Disabilities), but the federal definition remains the most widely used in public education (Masters et al., 1993).

The definition of **emotional disturbance (ED)** is also incorporated into Public Law 94-142 (U.S. Office of Education, 1977) and concentrates on the severe end of the continuum:

> (i) the term means a condition exhibiting one or more of the following characteristics over a long period of time and to a marked degree, which adversely affects educational performance, (a) an inability to learn which cannot be explained by intellectual, sensory, or health factors; (b) an inability to build or maintain satisfactory interpersonal relationships with peers and teachers; (c) inappropriate types of behavior or feelings under normal circumstances; (d) a general pervasive mood of unhappiness or depression; or (e) a tendency to develop physical symptoms or fears associated with personal or school problems. (ii) the term includes children who are schizophrenic or autistic. The term does not include children who are socially maladjusted, unless it is determined that they are seriously emotionally disturbed. (Section 121a.5, p. 42478)

Although other definitions have been proposed that provide more guidance regarding educational needs (e.g., Kauffman, 1989), school systems are faced with the requirement to use the federal definition for classification services.

The most widely accepted definition of **mental retardation (MR)** is the definition proposed by the American Association on Mental Retardation (AAMR) and revised by Grossman in 1983. This revised definition is included in Public Law 94-142:

> Mental retardation refers to significantly subaverage general intellectual functioning existing concurrently with deficits in adaptive behavior, and manifested during the developmental period . . . significantly subaverage refers to performance which is two or more standard deviations from the mean or average of the test. (Grossman, 1983, p. 11)

Mental retardation is classified most frequently by severity. There are four categories: mild, moderate, severe, and profound. The distinction between the severity levels is primarily determined through the use of scores on intelligence tests as well as indicators of maladaptive behavior (Hardman, Drew, Egan, & Wolf, 1996). The AAMR (Grossman, 1983) refers to individuals with mild retardation as those with an IQ in the range of 55 to 70. Individuals with mild mental retardation comprise approximately 90% of the estimated prevalence of individuals with mental retardation.

In 1992, a new definition of mental retardation was developed that represents a shift away from conceptualizations of mental retardation as an inherent trait or a permanent state of being to a description of the individual's present functioning and the environmental supports needed to improve it.

shift in meaning for MR

> Mental retardation refers to substantial limitations in present functioning. It is characterized by significantly subaverage intellectual functioning, existing concurrently with related limitations in two or more of the following applicable adaptive skill areas: communication, self-care, home living, social skills, community use, self-direction, health and safety, functional academics, leisure, and work. Mental retardation manifests before age 18.
>
> The following four assumptions are essential to the application of the definition:
>
> 1. Valid assessment considers cultural and linguistic diversity as well as differences in communication and behavioral factors;
>
> 2. The existence of limitations in adaptive skills occurs within the context of community environments typical of the individual's age peers and is indexed to the person's individualized needs for supports;
>
> 3. Specific adaptive limitations often coexist with strengths in other adaptive skills or other personal capabilities; and
>
> 4. With appropriate supports over a sustained period, the life functioning of the person with mental retardation will generally improve. (Luckasson et al., 1992, p. 1)

The position of the Council for Exceptional Children's Division on Mental Retardation and Developmental Disabilities (CEC MRDD) on the AAMR 1992 definition is one of cautious support. In an official position statement, CEC MRDD praised the new definition for focusing on the needs of individuals rather than on degrees of deficiency residing within the person with mental retardation. However, the statement notes that the changes required by and the implications of the new definition are so profound that they will require the most careful consideration before they are implemented in special education practices (Smith, 1994).

Traumatic brain injury (TBI) is included as a new category in Public Law 101-476 (the reaffirmation of PL 94-142) and refers to a set of individuals who have suffered an insult to the brain and need special education and related services. The Education of the Handicapped Amendments of 1990 (PL 101-476) defined traumatic brain injury as the following:

TBI

> an insult to the brain, not of a degenerative or congenital nature but caused by an external physical force, that may produce a diminished or altered state of consciousness, which results in impairment of cognitive abilities or physical functioning. It can also

result in the disturbance of behavioral or emotional functioning. These impairments may be either temporary or permanent and cause partial or total functional disability or psychosocial maladjustment. (p. 1103)

Each year, between 400,000 and 500,000 individuals are treated for a traumatic brain injury; approximately 40% percent of these cases are children (Savage, 1987). The prevalence of brain injuries takes a dramatic jump during the adolescent years (Hardman et al., 1996).

Attention deficit (the inability to attend to a task) and hyperactivity (high rates of purposeless movement) are frequently cited as characteristics of children with learning disabilities (Heward, 1996). The term frequently used to describe this combination of behavioral traits is *attention deficit disorder* (ADD).

Children are diagnosed as having ADD according to criteria found in the *Diagnostic and Statistical Manual of Mental Disorders* (DSM-IV) (American Psychiatric Association, 1994), which refers to the condition as attention deficit/hyperactivity disorder or ADHD:

> the essential feature of attention deficit/hyperactivity disorder is a persistent pattern of inattention and/or hyperactivity-impulsivity that is more frequent and severe than is typically observed in individuals at a comparable level of development. (APA, 1994, p. 78)

To diagnose ADD, a physician must determine that a child consistently displays six or more symptoms of either inattention or hyperactivity impulsivity for a period of at least six months.

The Office of Special Education and Rehabilitative Services (OSERS) of the U.S. Department of Education issued a policy memorandum stating that although children with ADD are not automatically mandated to receive special education services, they can be served under the "other health impaired" category if limited alertness negatively affects academic performance (Davila, Williams, & MacDonald, 1991).

Characteristics

Students with mild disabilities are extremely heterogeneous and bring to the educational process widely varied abilities and disabilities (Wagner, 1990). Individual characteristics vary widely, yet there are some common characteristics among the many adolescents with mild disabilities (Mercer, 1993):

> *Academic deficits* (poor academic achievement)   Deshler, Warner, Schumaker, and Alley (1983) suggest achievement levels in reading in the high 3rd-grade level to 5th-grade levels and in mathematics average performance at the 5th- to 6th-grade levels.

> *Cognitive deficits* (delayed or deficit executive functioning)   Torgesen (1982) and others have suggested that students with mild disabilities approach academic tasks passively. Many have memory and attention problems that hinder their ability to master academic content (Hallahan & Kauffman, 1994).

> *Social skill deficits* (difficulty in social situations)   Students with mild disabilities are generally less well liked than their peers and less accepted (Gresham, 1981;

Schumaker, Sheldon-Wildgen, & Sherman, 1980). They also have difficulties establishing relationships with their peers (Sabornie, Kauffman, & Cullinan, 1990).

Study skill deficits (difficulty in study skills and test taking) Many students with mild disabilities have problems in test taking and study skills. They make little use of cognitive learning strategies, but when provided with a format for interacting with the material, they have proven to be more successful (Clark, Deshler, Schumaker, Alley, & Warner, 1984).

Motivation problems (often passive learner)   Students with mild disabilities exhibit a learned helplessness (they attribute academic success to factors beyond their control) (Aponich & Dembo, 1983). They have been characterized as being inactive or passive learners (Torgesen, 1977).

Masters et al. (1993) characterize most adolescents with mild disabilities as having "chronic low achievement in academic subjects, particularly reading, mathematics, and writing, inadequate study skills, poorly developed self-concept, low self-esteem, deficiencies in social skills and interpersonal relationships, deficiencies in problem-solving strategies and behaviors, deficiencies in decision-making skills, deficiencies in planning and organizational skills" (p. 3).

The characteristics of adolescents with mild disabilities are diverse. Therefore, instructional opportunities should address individual strengths and weaknesses. The legislative events that serve as a backdrop to current instructional opportunities for and service delivery to adolescents with mild disabilities are discussed in the next section.

Legislative Foundations

The 1970s and the 1980s witnessed several landmark court decisions that led to increased legislation in favor of individuals with disabilities (see Figure 1.2 for a listing of legislative actions). In 1973, Congress passed the Vocational Rehabilitation Act, which serves as a civil rights law for individuals with disabilities. **Section 504 of the Rehabilitation Act** specifically stated:

> No otherwise qualified handicapped individual in the United States . . . shall, solely by reason of his handicap, be excluded from the participation in, be denied the benefits of, or be subjected to discrimination under any program or activity receiving Federal financial assistance.

Section 504 provided all students with a right to access to a public education curriculum, extracurricular activities, and instructional and curricular adaptations. Two years later, Public Law 94-142, the Education for All Handicapped Children Act of 1975, was passed; it was the most comprehensive law ever enacted on behalf of children and youth with disabilities. Figure 1.3 outlines the provisions provided by this legislation.

In 1976, Public Law 94-482 Education Amendments increased funding for vocational education programs with 10% designated for persons who are disabled. Seven

Figure 1.2
Legislative actions of the 1970s and
1980s

1973	Rehabilitation Act, PL 93-112, Section 504
	Comprehensive Employment and Training Act (CETA), PL 93-203
1975	Education for All Handicapped Children Act, PL 94-142
1976	Education Amendments of Vocational Education Act, PL 94-482
1983	Education of the Handicapped Act Amendments, PL 98-199
1984	Carl D. Perkins Vocational Education Act, PL 98-524
1990	Amendments to the Education of the Handicapped Act, PL 101-476
	Americans with Disabilities Act of 1990, PL 101-336

years later, Section 626 of the 1983 amendments entitled "Secondary Education and Transitional Services for Handicapped Youth" authorized $6.6 million annually in grants and contracts for the purpose of supporting and coordinating educational and service programs designed to assist handicapped youth in the transition from secondary to post-secondary education, employment, and services (Gajar et al., 1993, p. 30).

In 1984, the Carl D. Perkins Vocational and Technical Education Act was signed into law. The act was designed to:

> assure individuals who are inadequately served under vocational education programs access to quality vocational education programs, especially individuals who are disadvantaged, who are handicapped, men and women who are entering non-traditional occupations, adults who are in need of training and retraining, individuals who are single parents or homemakers, individuals with limited English proficiency, and individuals who are incarcerated in correctional institutions. (Public Law 98-524, 98 Stat. 2435)

Figure 1.3
Provisions of PL 94-142, Education for All Handicapped Children Act

- development of child identification procedures
- providing special education in the least restrictive environment
- ensuring nondiscriminatory testing
- ensuring due process procedures
- writing of individualized education program for each child
- related services (i.e., transportation, speech therapy, psychological services, physical and occupational therapy, recreation and medical services) needed to benefit from education are to be provided

In 1990, Public Law 101-476, the Education of Handicapped Act Amendments of 1990, later renamed the **Individuals with Disabilities Education Act (IDEA)**, reaffirmed the basic provisions outlined in Public Law 94-142 and initiated several other changes:

- The categories of children with disabilities were expanded to include autism and traumatic brain injury.
- Definition of special education was expanded to include instruction in all settings, including the workplace and training centers.
- Transition objectives must be included on IEPs no later than age 16 for students with disabilities.
- Related services were expanded to include rehabilitation counseling and social work services.
- The issue of special education to students with attention deficit disorders was to be studied by the U.S. Department of Education.

These changes went into effect on October 30, 1990, and the law was to be reviewed again by Congress in 1995, but delays in Congress have put the review into 1996 or later. Also in 1990, a second legislation was enacted that would have great impact on students with disabilities, Public Law 101-336, the **Americans with Disabilities Act** (ADA). This legislation prohibits discrimination in employment, public accommodations, and transportation, and it provides for telecommunications relay services. The ADA directly influences the transition concerns of young adults with mild disabilities. Employers, public service providers, agencies, and businesses cannot discriminate or deny access to services for this population. In addition to covering all individuals with physical and mental impairments, the ADA also includes individuals with AIDS and those affected with HIV.

Regular Education's Curricular Emphasis

Students with mild disabilities spend most of their time fully included in regular education classes with an average of 70% to 75% of instructional time in regular classrooms (U.S. Department of Education, 1994, 1992; Wagner, 1990). Unfortunately, there is often little accommodation made for such students; they are frequently expected to keep up in regular classes without special help (Zigmond & Baker, 1995; Wagner, 1990).

Suggested accommodations that may be made consist of the following: (a) alternative grading policies; (b) direct instruction provided by a "special educator" (e.g., counseling, tutoring); (c) indirect instruction (e.g., consultation services provided to the regular educator by the special education professionals; in-service training) (Wagner, 1990). Although these accommodations are made at some secondary schools, in most cases accommodations beyond special education instruction are provided infrequently (Zigmond & Baker, 1995; Wagner, 1990).

For students with learning difficulties, the question of appropriate instructional programming is much more complex than for secondary students without academic problems (Espin & Deno, 1993a). As Zigmond (1990) suggests, these students enter secondary school trailing behind their peers in basic skills and leave without significant improvement in such skills. Without some accommodations, many of them opt to leave the system (deBettencourt, Zigmond, & Thornton, 1989; Zigmond & Thornton, 1985).

Secondary-school staff members have a number of options from which to choose to formulate programs for secondary-age students with disabilities (Espin & Deno, 1993a). Mercer and Mercer (1989) identified five program options: (a) academic remediation; (b) regular coursework with supportive instruction; (c) functional living skills; (d) career-related instruction; and (e) learning strategies. Zigmond (1990) described two major program options that differ in terms of amount of "special education" time that is provided. Laurie, Buchwach, Silverman, and Zigmond (1978) recommended that special and regular teachers follow a problem-solving sequence in developing an effective instructional program for students with disabilities at the secondary level, such as:

1. Determine the requirements for "making it" in the regular class.
2. Specify the course requirements that the student is not satisfying.
3. Identify factors hindering the student's performance.
4. Brainstorm possible classroom modifications.
5. Select a plan of action.
6. Implement the plan.
7. Evaluate the plan.

Some accommodations must be made in the regular classroom environment at the secondary level for students with mild disabilities to be successful. "It is not sufficient to simply begin placing students in mainstream content classrooms and hope for the best; an effective collaborative relationship between the content and special education teachers needs to be developed" (Nolet & Tindal, 1993, p. 38).

General and Special Education Teacher Preparation

Part of the issue of successful accommodations may be solved by preparing general education teachers to work with a more diverse student body. The data provided by the National Longitudinal Study confirm the contention of the U.S. Department of Education regarding "the compelling importance of regular education instructors in the secondary school preparation of students with disabilities" (U.S. Department of Education, 1992).

Shifts in education are occurring—individual planning, curriculum alignment, and cooperative learning. Designing instruction for all students that is relevant to their individual needs is forcing many teachers to refocus their instructional planning process. General educators are finding the need to understand the unique learning needs and styles of students with mild disabilities, and special educators are finding the need to develop a thorough understanding of the general education classes in which students with disabilities may receive their instruction. "Special educators must be part of the ongoing dialogue in general education that will lead to reform of curriculum, school organization, and professional development. . . . The price for coming to the general education reform table must not be abandonment of our special education commitment to providing extra to those in special need" (Zigmond & Baker, 1995, p. 248).

A new relationship between special education and general education teachers is needed. The content-area teacher brings to the relationship expertise associated with content knowledge of the particular domain; the special education teacher in turn brings pedagogical expertise related to methods for designing instruction, classroom management, and motivational strategies effective with at-risk learners (Nolet & Tindal, 1993). This new relationship should also encourage teacher training institutions to change their preparation programs.

Educational Program Models at the Secondary Level

Most youth with disabilities attend comprehensive secondary schools whose student bodies are primarily students without disabilities (Wagner & Shaver, 1989). There are a variety of program models currently available for students with disabilities. Zigmond and Sansone (1986) discuss an illustrative, although not necessarily exhaustive, list of secondary program options or approaches available for students with mild disabilities along a two-dimensional framework. The temporal dimension represents the extent to which the student spends class time with special education teachers in a designated special setting. The second dimension designates the degree to which the curriculum and program content are unique or different from the regular classroom curriculum and program content (Figure 1.4).

Zigmond and Sansone (1986) plotted several of the current program options within their two-dimensional framework, which helps to clarify the range of program options currently predominant in secondary-school settings. Several of the program options plotted on Zigmond and Sansone's framework and readily found in the literature will be described briefly in the following sections.

Basic Skills Model

The *basic skills* option (Alley & Deshler, 1979) provides developmental or remedial instruction for basic academic skill deficits. This approach tries to prepare the student for reentering the mainstream of regular education by emphasizing instruction in functional mathematics, reading, and written language. Competency in basic literacy and numeracy is viewed as a necessity for independent functioning during and after high school.

In 1979, Deshler, Lowrey, and Alley (1979) found that 45% of the secondary learning disabilities programs emphasized basic skills remediation. "Although additional studies are necessary, initial indications are that the amount of gain received from rather intensive basic skills remedial programming in junior and senior high, at least for students with learning disabilities, may not justify the time spent on such training" (Masters et al., 1993, p. 148). This remedial approach may not be the best preparation for the world after high school. There is also the belief that the range of skills covered is too narrow for secondary-level students.

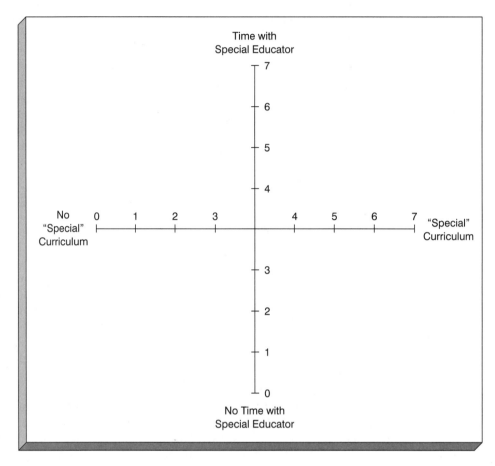

Figure 1.4
Framework for categorizing program options at the secondary level
Source: From "Designing a Program for the Learning Disabled Adolescent" by N. Zigmond and J. Sansone, 1986, *Remedial and Special Education, 7*(5), p. 14. Copyright 1986 by PRO-ED, Inc. Reprinted by permission.

The Tutorial Model

The goal of the *tutorial* model is to assist students with disabilities in meeting the academic demands of the regular education program (Sabatino & Mann, 1982). The tutorial approach provides assistance with specific academic course content. The instructional goals are defined by the course of study each student pursues in regular education. There is some concern that special education teachers are often not trained in the subject matter in which they are providing assistance (Sabatino & Mann, 1982). Cline and Billingsley (1991) found that 41% of the teachers who responded to their survey indicated that they were providing instruction in courses that they were not certified to teach.

The Compensatory Model

The *compensatory* model's goal is to continue student progress by altering tasks to substitute stronger skills for weaker ones. Usually, as students get older the remedial approach may change to a compensatory model, and the modifications may lead to modified performance standards and graduation requirements. The compensatory approach requires marked acceptance by instructional personnel in order to be implemented.

The Vocational Model

The *vocational* model's goal is to prepare students for employment. It emphasizes instruction in job- and career-related skills and supervised on-the-job experiences as part of the school day. When the prospect of employment becomes a concern, the decision is made to set aside academic goals and focus on independent and successful employment skills. The effectiveness is usually measured by initial placement into a job after completion of high school. The vocational curriculum may be provided by general educators; if so, there is some concern that regular vocational training in schools may be too difficult for adolescents with disabilities (Sitlington, 1981).

The Functional Skills Model

The *functional* curricular model's goal is to equip students with the ability to function in society and to cope with the immediate demands of daily living. The regular curriculum of the high school is deemed inappropriate for some students, so they are assigned to special education teachers the entire day and are taught a different curriculum more suited to their needs. Real-life situations are used to train students, and they may vary depending on the degree of disability. Job-related skills and vocational training are the central components. Disadvantages include that the curriculum may be too restrictive and possible underdevelopment of student strengths may occur (Alley & Deshler, 1979).

Learning Strategies Model

The *learning strategies* model's goal is to teach students how to learn rather than what to learn (Deshler & Schumaker, 1986; Deshler, Ellis, & Lenz, 1996). Task-specific strategies, techniques, rules, or principles are developed and taught to the student following a series of steps (see Chapter 8 on Cognitive Strategies). Students are encouraged to use the strategies for task demands in the mainstream setting.

Many of the program models or approaches, as described here, have advantages and disadvantages. However, it is important to note that the newness of secondary programs for students with mild disabilities is shown in the fact that methods texts that address elementary-level students with disabilities are in their third, and even fourth, printings, while textbooks that address secondary populations with mild disabilities are just beginning to appear.

Issues and Trends in Secondary Education of Youth with Mild Disabilities

Unsuccessful experiences of secondary students with and without mild disabilities has become a national concern (Gajar et al., 1993). Underachievement, lack of appropriate educational programming and support systems, limited interagency involvement, and high school dropout rates have all contributed to unsuccessful adult experiences for individuals with disabilities (Gajar et al., 1993; Owings & Stockling, 1985; Wagner, 1990).

Full Inclusion of Adolescents with Mild Disabilities

Few professionals would question the appropriateness of including adolescents with disabilities in general education high school classes. However, considerable debate continues about which students should be part of the general education and how much time students should spend there. There is also much discussion regarding who has the primary responsibility for teaching content to students with mild disabilities and where and how this should be accomplished.

Quality, fully-inclusive programming for adolescents with mild disabilities requires that teachers work together as a well-orchestrated team (Zigmond & Baker, 1995). Content-area teachers and special educators bring different emphases to the educational team on the behalf of students with special needs. The content-area teacher is in a perfect position to prompt students to use strategies that the special educator has taught them (Deshler & Putnam, 1996). He or she can also model strategies that may help all the students in the class to learn the subject matter.

However, the realities of teaching in today's secondary schools include the following: teachers must cover large amounts of content; there is a great deal of academic diversity among students; and there are few opportunities for cooperative study, planning, and teaching. But inclusion can be successful at the secondary level when significant support services are provided to teachers and students (Bulgren & Lenz, 1996). To facilitate inclusion of students with special needs, Bulgren and Lenz suggest the following support services: (a) group instruction embeds prompts and teaching for all students to learn and use strategies; (b) content-area learning is guided by routines that compensate for students' poor strategies and involve students in the learning process; (c) additional support is made available by support classroom teachers to help students learn and apply specific and general learning strategies; and (d) collaboration and teaming with a focus on enhanced student learning occurs frequently between regular and special education teachers (p. 420). When teachers enhance the delivery of content to all students, full inclusion of students with mild disabilities will be successful.

Dropout Phenomenon Among Adolescents with Disabilities

The dropout phenomenon is a major problem confronting all of public education (Gajar et al., 1993). Discussion of the problem among regular and special educators is complicated by a lack of common definitions, terms, and consistent counting procedures

(Clements, 1990). Notwithstanding the differences in definitions and calculations, "the Nation's dropout rate has become a lightning rod for a good deal of criticism and concern about the education system" (U.S. Department of Education, 1992, p. 79).

For students with mild disabilities it is an even greater tragedy. It was perhaps assumed that the special education programs provided during a student's elementary and middle school years would ameliorate whatever risk of dropping out these students might experience. Unfortunately, this was often not the case.

Interest in the dropout problem among special education students gained momentum with the publication of the 1988 *Annual Report to Congress on the Implementation of the Education for All Handicapped Children Act* (U.S. Department of Education, 1988). This report suggested that almost 214,000 students with disabilities exited school during the 1985–86 school year; 56,000 exited in the form of dropping out. Studies (e.g., Edgar, 1987; deBettencourt et al., 1989; Zigmond & Thornton, 1985) conducted in the mid-1980s suggested that the dropout rate among students with disabilities was higher than that of their nondisabled peers.

The U.S. government's concern about the high dropout rate led to the **National Longitudinal Transition Study (NLTS)** of Special Education Students, which was funded by the Office of Special Education Programs (OSEP) of the Department of Education to provide information to practitioners, policy makers, researchers, and others regarding the transition of youth with disabilities from secondary school to early adulthood. Their study included a nationally representative sample of more than 8,000 young people who were secondary special education students between ages 13 and 21 in the 1985–86 school year (Wagner, 1991). Their data were reported in the 1992 Annual Report to Congress.

The 1992 Annual Report to Congress on the Implementation of the Individuals with Disabilities Act suggested that the numbers had increased and a sizable percentage of students with disabilities had dropped out of school (approximately 1,016) and that the dropout rate for students with disabilities was significantly higher than that of students in the general population (U.S. Department of Education, 1992).

"The findings from the NLTS suggest four key points regarding school completion for students with disabilities:

- A sizable percentage of students with disabilities drop out of school—a significantly higher percentage than among typical students. The dropout problem is particularly acute for students with certain disabilities—those classified as having serious emotional disturbance, learning disabilities, speech impairments, or mental retardation (representing 90% of students in secondary special education).

- Dropping out of school is the culmination of a cluster of school performance problems, including high absenteeism and poor grade performance.

- A variety of student characteristics and behaviors are associated with poor school performance and a higher likelihood that students will drop out. Understanding these risk factors can help schools target dropout prevention programs to students most prone to early school leaving.

- Dropping out is not a function solely of student and family factors. There are significant relationships between aspects of students' school programs and student outcomes. Schools can make a difference in their students' performance. Schools can increase the likelihood that students will finish school" (U.S. Department of Education, 1992, p. 81).

Espin and Deno (1993b) suggested two paramount reasons for the lack of success for students with mild disabilities at the high school level. First, the "shift in curricular priorities is dramatic" (p. 47), and second, "we lack clarity in the focus of our remedial and special programs at this level" (p. 48). Secondary teachers are often reluctant to assume responsibility for development of literacy skills, and special programs may emphasize vocational outcomes rather than reading and writing literacy (see Zigmond, 1990).

Sitlington and Frank (1990) suggest dropouts with learning disabilities were not successfully crossing the bridge into adulthood. Only 38% of their sample of dropouts met the following criteria: (a) employed or "otherwise meaningfully engaged"; (b) living independently or with a parent or relative; (c) paying at least a portion of their living expenses; and (d) involved in more than one leisure activity. The majority of dropouts surveyed appear to have crossed the bridge to adulthood alone without the benefit of services from adult providers.

The NLTS research team, in their search for school factors that relate to better school performance and a lower probability of dropping out, provide the following guidelines:

Students who attended schools with fewer than 500 students were significantly less likely to drop out than those in schools with between 500 and 1,000.

Students who attended schools that reported routinely providing teachers with in-service training on mainstreaming were significantly more likely to have failed a course. (One potential explanation is that in-service training was being provided in schools with regular education teachers who were reluctant to receive mainstreamed students or who needed help in adapting their instructional approaches to accommodate the needs of those students. In such an environment, students in special education programs may have been doing less well than in schools in which regular education teachers accommodated mainstreamed students more readily or more effectively, making in-service training on the issue unnecessary.)

Students who took occupational training in their most recent school year were significantly less likely to have dropped out of school. Students with no time in regular education were significantly less likely to fail courses than other students; this relationship of time spent in regular education and the likelihood of receiving a failing grade was confirmed through further analysis.

A lower dropout rate was found for students who received help from a tutor, reader, or interpreter compared with those who did not. (Wagner, 1990, pp. 26–27)

Thus we see that differences in school policies and school programs can affect the chances for adolescent students with disabilities to succeed in school. The magnitude of the dropout phenomenon among students with disabilities, the highest for any subgroup of secondary-age youth, cannot be ignored (Gajar et al., 1993).

Adolescent Dilemmas and Their Effect on Schooling

Adolescence is the stage of development that falls between childhood and adulthood. The term *adolescence* comes from the Latin verb *adolescere,* which means "to grow up." Although this complex period is marked by dramatic physical, psychological, and social changes, most individuals successfully adapt. (See Chapter 2 on Adolescence.)

Students with disabilities are not immune to problems that are widespread among adolescents, such as drug abuse and delinquency (Gajar et al., 1993). Special and general educators must work together to provide effective instruction to students who are often confused and searching for personal survival and accomplishments (Masters et al., 1993).

Summary

As the NLTS data suggest, the seeds of successful postschool transitions for young people with disabilities are sown in secondary school—if schools give students powerful reasons to come to school and help them achieve in their courses, many students will persist in school. At the secondary level, educators are faced with a serious dilemma: students have limited time left in their school careers, and teachers must decide the most efficient and effective way to use that time (Espin & Deno, 1993). We believe that educators can influence their students' probabilities of school completion by effectively performing their primary educational mission. The following chapters of this book will assist with this mission.

Key Terms

learning disability

emotional disturbance

mental retardation

traumatic brain injury

Section 504 of the Rehabilitation Act

Individuals with Disabilities Education Act

Americans with Disabilities Act

National Longitudinal Transition Study

References

Alley, G., & Deshler, D. (1979). *Teaching the learning disabled adolescent: Strategies and methods.* Denver: Love.

Aponich, D. A., & Dembo, M. H. (1983). LD and normal adolescents' causal attributions of success and failure at different levels of task difficulty. *Learning Disability Quarterly, 6,* 31–39.

Baker, J. M., & Zigmond, N. (1990). Are regular education classes equipped to accommodate students with learning disabilities? *Exceptional Children, 56,* 515–526.

Bulgren, J., & Lenz, K. (1996). Strategic instruction in the content areas. In D. D. Deshler, E. S. Ellis, & B. K. Lenz (Eds.), *Teaching adolescents with learning disabilities: Strategies and methods* (pp. 409–473)(2nd ed.). Denver: Love.

Clark, F., Deshler, D., Schumaker, J., Alley, G., & Warner, M. (1984). Visual imagery and self-questioning: Strategies to improve comprehension of written material. *Journal of Learning Disabilities, 17,* 145–149.

Clements, B. (1990, February). *Recommendations for improving the reporting of graduation statistics.* Paper presented at the Office of Special Education Programs Conference on the Management of Federal/State Data Systems, Crystal City, VA.

Cline, B., & Billingsley, B. (1991). Teachers' and supervisors' perceptions of secondary learning disabilities programs: A multi-state survey. *Learning Disabilities Research and Practice, 6,* 158–165.

Davila, R. R., Williams, M. L., & MacDonald, J. T. (1991, September 16). *Clarification of policy to address the needs of children with attention deficit disorders within general and/or special education.* Washington, DC: Office of Special Education and Rehabilitation Services, U.S. Department of Education.

deBettencourt, L. U., Zigmond, N., & Thornton, H. (1989). Follow-up of postsecondary-age rural learning disabled graduates and dropouts. *Exceptional Children, 56,* 40–49.

Deshler, D. D., Ellis, E. S., & Lenz, B. K. (1996). *Teaching adolescents with learning disabilities: Strategies and methods* (2nd ed.). Denver: Love.

Deshler, D. D., Lowrey, N., & Alley, G. R. (1979). Programming alternatives for LD adolescents: A nationwide survey. *Academic Therapy, 14,* 389–397.

Deshler, D. D., & Putnam, M. L. (1996). Learning disabilities in adolescents: A perspective. In D. D. Deshler, E. S. Ellis, & B. K. Lenz (Eds.), *Teaching adolescents with learning disabilities: Strategies and methods* (pp. 1–7) (2nd ed.). Denver: Love.

Deshler, D. D., & Schumaker, J. B. (1986). Learning strategies: An instructional alternative for low-achieving adolescents. *Exceptional Children, 52,* 583–590.

Deshler, D. D., Warner, M. M., Schumaker, J. B., & Alley, G. R. (1983). The learning strategies intervention model: Key components and current status. In J. D. McKinney & L. Feagans (Eds.), *Current topics in learning disabilities* (pp. 245–283). Norwood, NJ: Ablex.

Donahoe, K., & Zigmond, N. (1990). Academic grades of ninth-grade urban learning-disabled students and low-achieving peers. *Exceptionality, 1,* 17–27.

Edgar, E. (1987). Secondary programs in special education: Are many of them justifiable? *Exceptional Children, 53,* 555–561.

Ellett, L. (1993). Instructional practices in mainstreamed secondary classrooms. *Journal of Learning Disabilities, 26,* 57–64.

Espin, C. A., & Deno, S. L. (1993a). Content-specific and general reading disabilities of secondary-level students: Identification and educational relevance. *Journal of Special Education, 27,* 321–337.

Espin, C. A., & Deno, S. L. (1993b). Performance in reading from content area text as an indicator of achievement. *Remedial and Special Education, 14*(6), 47–59.

Gajar, A., Goodman, L., & McAfee, J. (1993). *Secondary schools and beyond: Transition of individuals with mild disabilities.* Upper Saddle River, NJ: Prentice Hall.

Gresham, F. (1981). Social skills training with handicapped children: A review. *Review of Educational Research, 51,* 139–176.

Grossman, H. (1983). *Manual on terminology and classification in mental retardation.* Washington, DC: American Association on Mental Deficiency.

Hallahan, D. P., & Kauffman, J. M. (1994). *Introduction to exceptional individuals* (6th ed.). Boston: Allyn & Bacon.

Hardman, M. L., Drew, C. J., & Egan, M. W. (1996). *Human exceptionality: Society, school, and family* (5th ed.). Boston: Allyn & Bacon.

Heward, W. L. (1996). *Exceptional children: An introduction to special education* (5th ed.). Upper Saddle River, NJ: Prentice Hall.

Kauffman, J. (1989). *Characteristics of children's behavior disorders* (4th ed.). Upper Saddle River, NJ: Prentice Hall.

Laurie, T. E., Buchwach, L., Silverman, R., & Zigmond, N. (1978). Teaching secondary learning disabled students in the mainstream. *Learning Disability Quarterly, 1*(4), 62–72.

Luckasson, R., Coulter, D. L., Polloway, E. A., Reiss, S., Schalock, R. L., Snell, M. E., Spitalnik, D. M., & Stark, J. A. (1992). *Mental retardation: Definition, classification, and systems of supports.* Washington, DC: American Association on Mental Retardation.

Masters, L. F., Mori, B. A., & Mori, A. A. (1993). *Teaching students with mild learning and behavior problems: Methods, materials, strategies.* Austin, TX: PRO-ED.

Mercer, C. D. (1993). *Students with learning disabilities* (4th ed.). Upper Saddle River, NJ: Merrill/Prentice Hall.

Mercer, C. D., & Mercer, A. R. (1989). *Teaching students with learning problems* (3rd ed.). Upper Saddle River, NJ: Merrill/Prentice Hall.

National Commission on Excellence in Education. (1983). *A nation at risk.* Washington, DC: U.S. Government Printing Office.

Nolet, V., & Tindal, G. (1993). Special education in content area classes: Development of a model and practical procedures. *Remedial and Special Education, 14,* 36–48.

Owings, J., & Stockling, C. (1985). Characteristics of high school students who identify themselves as handicapped. *High school and beyond: A national longitudinal study for the 1980s.* Washington, DC: National Center for Education Statistics.

Sabatino, D. A., & Mann, L. (1982). *A handbook of diagnostic and prescriptive teaching.* Rockville, MD: Aspen.

Sabornie, E., Kauffman, J., & Cullinan, D. (1990). Extended sociometric status of adolescents with mild handicaps: A cross-categorical perspective. *Exceptionality, 1,* 197–209.

Savage, R. C. (1987). Educational issues for head-injured adolescents and young adults. *Journal of Head Trauma Rehabilitation, 2,* 1–10.

Schumaker, J. B., Sheldon-Wildgen, J., & Sherman, J. A. (1980). *An epidemiological study of learning disabled adolescents in secondary schools: Details of the methodology.* (Research Report No. 12). Lawrence: University of Kansas Institute for Research in Learning Disabilities.

Shriner, J. G., Ysseldyke, J. E., & Thurlow, M. L. (1994). Standards for all American students. *Focus on Exceptional Children, 26*(5), 1–19.

Sitlington, P. L. (1981). Vocational and special education in career programming for the mildly handicapped adolescent. *Exceptional Children, 47,* 592–598.

Sitlington, P. L., & Frank, A. R. (1990). Are adolescents with learning disabilities successfully crossing the bridge into adult life? *Learning Disability Quarterly, 13,* 97–111.

Smith, J. D. (1994). The revised AAMR definition of mental retardation: The MRDD position. *Education and Training in Mental Retardation, 29,* 179–183.

Torgesen, J. K. (1977). Memorization processes in reading disabled children. *Journal of Educational Psychology, 69,* 571–578.

Torgesen, J. K. (1982). The learning disabled child as an inactive learner: Educational implications. *Topics in Learning and Learning Disabilities, 2*(1), 45–52.

U.S. Department of Education. (1988). *Tenth annual report to Congress on the implementation of the Individuals with Disabilities Act.* Washington, DC: Author.

U.S. Department of Education (1990). *Twelfth annual report to Congress on the implementation of the Individuals with Disabilities Act.* Washington, DC: Author.

U.S. Department of Education (1992). *Fourteenth annual report to Congress on the implementation of the Individuals with Disabilities Act.* Washington, DC: Author.

U.S. Department of Education (1994). *Sixteenth annual report to Congress on the implementation of the Individuals with Disabilities Act.* Washington, DC: Author.

U.S. Office of Education. (1977). Education of handicapped children: Implementation of Part B of the Education of the Handicapped Act, *Federal Register.* Washington, DC: Author.

U.S. Senate. (1993). *Goals 2000: Educate America Act,* S. 1150, 103rd Congress, 1st Session.

Vitello, S. J. (1988). Handicapped students and competency testing. *Remedial and Special Education, 9*(5), 22–28.

Wagner, M. (1990). *The school programs and school performance of secondary students classified as learning disabled: Findings from the national longitudinal transition study of special education students.* Menlo Park, CA: SRI International.

Wagner, M. (1991). *Dropouts with disabilities: What do we know? What can we do?* Menlo Park, CA: SRI International.

Wagner, M., & Shaver, D. M. (1989). *Educational programs and achievements of secondary special education students: Findings from the national longitudinal transition study.* Menlo Park, CA: SRI International.

Ysseldyke, J., Algozzine, B., & Thurlow, M. L. (1992). *Critical issues in special education* (2nd ed.). Boston: Houghton Mifflin.

Zigmond, N. (1990). Rethinking secondary school programs for students with learning disabilities. *Focus on Exceptional Children, 23*(1), 1–24.

Zigmond, N., & Baker, J. M. (1995). Concluding comments: Current and future practices in inclusive schooling. *Journal of Special Education, 29,* 245–250.

Zigmond, N., & Sansone, J. (1986). Designing a program for the learning disabled adolescent. *Remedial and Special Education, 7*(5), 13–17.

Zigmond, N., & Thornton, H. (1985). Follow-up of postsecondary-age learning disabled graduates and dropouts. *Learning Disabilities Research, 1,* 50–55.

2

Adolescence and Its Characteristics

Objectives

After reading this chapter, the reader should be able to:

1. discuss the theories of adolescence from the perspective of many experts in child and adolescent development;

2. discuss in detail the physical and cognitive growth and changes that occur in adolescents;

3. discuss in detail some of the problems in behavior and development that affect adolescents;

4. discuss how theories of adolescence apply to adolescents with disabilities;

5. provide ways in which adolescents with disabilities are similar and dissimilar to nondisabled adolescents in terms of development.

This chapter concerns the notion of adolescence. Of all the developmental-maturational levels that one passes through in life, adolescence is usually remembered as a time of joy, but also as a period of great confusion. Adolescence is perceived by many as joyful because of the awakening of a personal identity that, finally, does not require parental supervision. The ages of 12 or 13 through the early 20s (these ages are chosen arbitrarily; little agreement exists on what specific chronological ages comprise adolescence) are cheerful for some because once a person reaches the onset of pubescence (usually around 12 or 13), he or she realizes that being a child is a thing of the past. Adolescents do not savor being treated like children, and they will be the first to tell you so.

The physical, psychological, cognitive, social, and other changes that occur during adolescence also entail new personal responsibilities, and many youths react by asking "Why me?" Adolescents want to be treated as adults, but they may be unready for the responsibility of such status. Adolescence is not a smooth sail on a waveless sea for many; some experiences during certain moments of adolescence would be comparable to a feather in a hurricane. Adolescents trying to find their identity and way in a world that looks very different from the one they knew as children struggle, stumble, and often fail. Consider the statistics on 8th- and 10th-grade students reported in Gans (1990): approximately 60% feel sad and hopeless; over 30% state that they have nothing to look forward to; about 30% seriously have thought about committing suicide; and about 10% have attempted suicide.

Our intent in this chapter is not to overemphasize the period of adolescence as one that is beyond the control of those experiencing it. Instead, we will attempt to present it in an objective manner. Theories of experts in child development and adolescence will be provided so that the reader understands the many ways in which adolescence is framed. Adolescent development will be examined from physical and cognitive foci. Problems of adolescence will be reviewed. Finally, we will draw implications from the general study of adolescence to how it interacts with the lives and characteristics of adolescents with mild disabilities. To comprehend how they respond to their environment it is necessary to understand adolescence as a singular concept.

Rationale

This chapter is presented here, before the subsequent discussion concerning the specific characteristics of adolescents with mild disabilities, because such youths are adolescents first, and disabled second. Although sometimes schools and professionals view students with disabilities between the ages of 13 and 18 as disabled only, issues that are often more robust than the effect of being disabled contribute heavily to reactions to an environment. The physical and other changes that take place in youth, particularly during puberty, are colossal. Disability by itself does not override their influence. Hence, we feel that examining the totality of adolescence is equally as important as awareness of mild disability.

Regarding terminology, differences and similarities between adolescence and pubescence need to be clear to the reader. Adolescence is the life stage of rapid growth—both psychosocial and biological—after childhood and immediately before adulthood (Atwater, 1983). The term *adolescence* is derived from Latin origins, and a literal translation would be analogous to "growing up." Pubescence also originates from Latin but translates as a combination of reaching adulthood and growing hair. At the onset of puberty, usually near the age of 12 or 13, reproductive bodily functions are awakened. Ausubel (1954) described pubescence as the short period of time when sexual maturation occurs. Pubescence, a subset of adolescence, includes the early years of adolescence and ends when reproductive organs reach maturity. Adolescence, however, may continue into a person's early 20s. Over the last century, evidence shows that the onset of puberty is occurring earlier in youth, growth spurts associated with adolescence are occurring sooner, and adolescents are reaching their adult height earlier than youth of preceding eras (Muuss, 1996; Sprinthall & Collins, 1995). Sprinthall and Collins (1995) and Atwater (1983) refer to these early growth and physical changes in today's youth as a *secular trend*. Table 2.1 presents the sequence of bodily changes, according to Muuss (1982), that are consistent with the period of pubescence, even for those with mild disabilities.

Adolescence is also an arbitrary construction in that it includes a person's behavioral, social, psychological, and cognitive changes. The social construction of adolescence is important because some non-Western societies see childhood leading directly to adulthood. Moreover, examining adolescence as a developmental period separate from childhood and adulthood has occurred only during the 20th century. In the 19th century individuals over the age of 12 were often employed and treated as adults, and one of the many justifications for the creation of high schools and mandatory school attendance laws in the U.S. was to keep teenagers from laboring in mines and factories.

While adolescence begins with the physiological changes associated with puberty, there is little agreement among experts regarding when it ends. G. Stanley Hall (1904), for example, stated that adolescence lasts up to age 25! Some have said that the end of adolescence is concurrent with the ability to support oneself; others have stated that adolescence ends when one reaches the legal age for voting, serving in the military, or ability to execute legal matters (Muuss, 1996).

Adolescence also deserves special scrutiny in light of the many problems and unresolved conflicts that affect adolescents. Confused behavior, hesitation in decision making, increased peer competition, and a desire for autonomy while being a member of a preferable peer clique are all characteristics that may overwhelm some adolescents.

Table 2.1
Physiological sequence of pubescence in males and females

Males	Females
Skeletal growth	Skeletal growth
Enlargement of testes	Breast development
Straight pigmented pubic hair	Straight pigmented pubic hair
Early voice changes	Maximum annual growth increment
Ejaculation	Kinky pigmented pubic hair
Kinky pigmented pubic hair	Menstruation
Maximum annual growth increment	Appearance of auxiliary hair
Appearance of downy facial hair	
Appearance of auxiliary hair	
Late voice change	
Coarse pigmented facial hair	
Chest hair	

Source: From *Theories of Adolescence* (4th ed.) (pp. 4–5) by R. E. Muuss, 1982, New York: McGraw-Hill.

Similarly, although many adults would give their life's savings to be younger again, being a teenager seems to be somewhat denigrated by society (except, perhaps, in commercial advertising). Morbidity and mortality statistics among adolescents also tell a story that is easy to comprehend. From 1960 to the present, in comparison to all other age groups (a) adolescents are the only group to demonstrate an increase in mortality rate; (b) accidents, suicide, and homicide are the most common causes of morbidity and mortality of adolescents; (c) mortality rates tend to increase across years of adolescence, with the rate of 18- and 19-year-olds higher than that of 12- to 14-year-olds; and (d) male adolescents have twice the injury and death rates of females (Millstein & Litt, 1990; Sprinthall & Collins, 1995; Wetzel, 1989). Reports of drive-by shootings and other serious, random acts of violence committed by adolescents are now, however sad and frightening, common in newspapers and on television news. Thirty percent of high school students know someone who has brought a weapon to school (Educational Communications, 1995). Knowledge of general adolescent traits and behavior, therefore, is important for any preservice or in-service educator contemplating interaction with middle schoolers or high schoolers.

Theories of Adolescence

The major theorists of adolescence originate in the 20th century. Notable philosophers, religious leaders, and scientists throughout the ages commented on aspects typical of adolescent behavior, but such commentary was concerned with general human development rather than a concern for adolescence alone. Aristotle, for example, divided human

Aristotle

0 - 7

7 - puberty (14)

14 - 21

Summary - a brief statement of the main points

development into three phases, each seven years in length: Infancy included the period of birth to age 7, boyhood lasted from age 7 to puberty, and young manhood spanned the years from the onset of puberty to age 21. Aristotle discussed the bodily desires, intense impulses and passion, and lack of self-control that typify the behavior of young men, and it is not difficult to see how Aristotle's version of behavior common to young manhood is still true of contemporary adolescents.

During the Renaissance, Comenius viewed human development in a way similar to Aristotle's view, but he suggested differential educational treatment based on a person's age. He believed that human development was divided into four stages, each six years in length; adolescence as we know it today would have been his third stage, from age 12 to 18. Comenius suggested that education during any of the four stages of human development should be matched to the cognitive capabilities of learners during each phase—a practice that still holds true today.

G. Stanley Hall's Views

The "father" of adolescent study as we know it today was G. Stanley Hall, the first recipient of a Ph.D. in psychology in the U.S. Credited to Hall are many of the ways in which contemporary society views adolescence, and his phrase *sturm und drang* (storm and stress) is still widely used to describe the lives of adolescents.

Hall (1904) constructed human development into four distinct phases. Infancy spanned the period of birth to age 4, childhood ranged from age 4 to 8, youth included the years between 8 and 12, and adolescence lasted from the onset of puberty (around age 12 or 13) through the mid-20s. Hall believed that adolescence was a rebirth and that adolescents experience the earlier phases of development one more time during adolescence. The theory that adolescents must endure the other developmental phases once again is also known as **recapitulation,** and according to Hall such an experience roughly follows the history of the human race from barbarism (infancy and childhood) to civilized existence (the end of adolescence, or adulthood).

Hall's writings of the early 20th century are full of colorful descriptions of the complexities of adolescence. He discussed the range of emotions of adolescent life by contrasting the heightened levels of energy, exuberance, and preoccupation with an ideal versus indifference, apathy, and disregard for beliefs other than one's own. Vanity and narcissism common to adolescents' behavior coexist with the opposites of shyness and a deep concern for others. Hall described how the significant others in a person's life change in adolescence from immediate family members to the peer group. Adolescents struggle to establish a separate identity that is autonomous, but still have strong desires to belong to a peer group. Education, from Hall's perspective, is also a very important independent variable in the lives of teenagers. Adolescents were to be educated very carefully because they are so easily influenced.

Some of Hall's theories fell on deaf ears because of his extreme position on some issues. His views on education, for example, are not in the mainstream of contemporary thought. Hall believed that only teenage males should be selected for an elitist form of educational training in leadership; other males would perform the manual labor needed by society, and females would develop the skills needed for marriage and child-rearing (Sprinthall & Collins, 1995). Despite these unpopular views Hall is generally regarded as the first to move the study of adolescence into scientific inquiry. Storm and stress certainly characterize adolescence, but perhaps not always at the level of penetrance that Hall conceived.

Sigmund Freud's Theories

Anyone remotely familiar with psychology recognizes the name of Freud, but few know that he had much to say about adolescent development. He, like Hall, saw adolescence as a time of great struggle and turmoil, and he too believed that it was a time of recapitulation, but he held that an adolescent relives only the first three psychosexual stages of development: oral (the first year of life), anal (age 2 to 3), and phallic (age 3 to 6). Between the phallic stage and adolescence is the latency period, which ends with the onset of puberty. The beginning of puberty until age 18 is Freud's *genital* phase, which he describes as an increase in sexual tension that needs gratification. Freud believed that the integration of sexual drive must occur in the personality of youth during the genital stage, or an adolescent will face sexual and psychological problems (i.e., neurosis). He recommended that, through a process called *sublimation,* the overwhelming sexual desires of adolescence should be channeled into other socially appropriate and productive outlets (such as sports, the arts, dancing, etc.).

Freud's preoccupation with the unconscious and sexual impulses that guide certain behaviors has led to much criticism by those concerned with adolescence. Conventional wisdom views the effects of the environment as contributing to sexual behavior more so than subconscious struggles with one's sexual desire (Atwater, 1983). Freud's theories have contributed heavily to shaping psychiatry, but his views on adolescent development are not so widely acclaimed.

Erickson's Theory of Identity Development

Erik Erickson is probably best known for his "Stages of Man" theory, which adapted and modified Freud's stance into one embracing psychosocial—rather than psychosexual—development. A simple characterization of Erickson's theory of development boils down to a search for an identity. In this search, humans face many crises while proceeding through different developmental phases. The fifth of Erickson's eight Stages of Man, *Identity versus Identity Confusion* (age 13 to 18), corresponds with adolescence and is discussed below.

Erickson (1950) stated that an adolescent is in constant struggle to assemble a personal identity and to avoid role diffusion. This involves personal introspection and thinking of the past and present and attempting to gaze into one's future. Much effort is expended by an adolescent in searching for an identity and in arduous attempts to belong to a peer group. Adolescents often use the peer group as an audience to answer identity questions. Peers willingly provide feedback to a member in coterie. Spending long hours of primping before a mirror is another way that an adolescent tries to establish an identity. Erickson observed that adolescents seem consumed with trying to see themselves in the eyes of others they encounter, particularly peers.

A true story from the high school teaching experience of the senior author illuminates Erickson's beliefs and the effect of the peer group on a person's identity.

> One winter morning during the first homeroom period that began every school day, Ralph, a 9th grader, walked into the classroom wearing very bright yellow-and-black-checkered trousers. Prior to this Ralph had usually worn blue jeans and casual shirts to school, comparable to most of the other male 9th graders at this large suburban high school. Immediately upon Ralph's entry into the classroom every one of his male peers (and some females, too) began laughing at him, poking fun at his pants, and generally chastising him because of his attire. Ralph was visibly shaken and embarrassed and, instead of sitting with his usual peer clique during homeroom, he sat in the front of the room near the teacher's desk. The homeroom teacher commented to Ralph that his peers were somewhat rough on him, but Ralph said nothing in response. The experience was so injurious to Ralph's identity that from that day forward he never wore anything else to school except his usual "uniform"—jeans and sport shirts or t-shirts.

Perhaps Ralph tried to change his identity with the brightly colored pants, but he was rebuffed in the attempt and returned to a more conformist identity, at least in the eyes of his peers.

Erickson also believed puberty, with its rapid physical and sexual changes, provides a crisis for the early adolescent seeking a personal identity. The rapid physiological changes in puberty may not fit with the person's view of his or her personal identity, and role diffusion may result. Early adolescents use expressions of sexuality in a trial-and-error fashion and as a way of reliability-checking their identity. After pubescence adolescents must reestablish the boundaries of their identity based on the physical changes that affected their appearance. At the end of adolescence Erickson believed that a healthy establishment of one's identity leads to *fidelity,* or trust in oneself and others and caring for all worthy humans. A robust identity in adolescence transforms into an egalitarian disposition as an adult.

Erik Erickson died in 1994 at the age of 94. In his view an adolescent who is unsuccessful in establishing a firm foundation to his or her identity will experience serious problems. Self-destructive behavior, poor self-concept, delinquency, and overdependence on the opinions of others (or the opposite, indifference) may all result for someone whose role in life is confused. Suicide is also a possible outcome for someone with identity befuddlement. Teachers concerned with adolescents whose role in life is in chaos should reinforce such students' attempts at proper role identification and be generally supportive of behavior that will win friends and influence peers in a positive direction. While not a member of an adolescent's peer group, a teacher can set a powerful stage that allows others to appreciate the appropriate behavior of an outsider.

Peter Blos's Views

The theories of adolescence of Blos (1941) are very similar to those of Freud. Blos, however, proposed a departure from Freud's beliefs of development stages. Whereas Freud had one stage to describe adolescence (genital), Blos conceived of five:

1. Preadolescence
2. Early adolescence
3. Adolescence proper
4. Late adolescence
5. Postadolescence

Blos also perceived personality development differently from Freud, who believed that personality was formed early in life, during the oral, anal, and phallic stages. Blos concluded (like Erickson) that adolescence contributed greatly to the formation of personality. Blos also saw male and female differences in psychological development that were contrary to the theories of Freud.

Blos, too, was an advocate of the theory of recapitulation. He concluded that not all, but only significant, childhood experiences were relived by adolescents. Perhaps his most significant contribution to understanding adolescent development is his *second individuation process,* which involves the adolescent shedding his or her dependencies on parents and objects associated with childhood in order to become an adult. Individuation allows a person to establish an identity in social and personal domains. The peer group plays an important role in Blos's individuation process of adolescence. Peers (a) guide adolescents in times of stress and anxiety, (b) validate the emerging identity of an adolescent, (c) provide security and support, and (d) evaluate and provide feedback regarding personal, social, and sexual behavior.

The second individuation process portrays an adolescent moving ahead in certain spheres of development and regressing at times in other areas. This back-and-forth (*regression* and *progression)* in development during adolescence leads to inner strife and unpredictability of behavior. Blos, surprisingly, viewed the anxiety and emotional crises of adolescence as healthy and necessary for normal adult emergence. If a therapeutic second individuation process does not occur, Blos predicted a host of personal difficulties: learning disorders, apathy, moodiness, and dependence on others rather than autonomy as an adult. Perhaps Blos's greatest legacy lies in his attempts to explain psychopathology, juvenile delinquency, and other psychological and developmental problems that he believed were caused by a problematic second individuation process in adolescence (Blos, 1941, 1970, 1971).

Lewin's Theory

Kurt Lewin's quasi-behavioral hypothesis of adolescence, his *field theory,* is noticeably different from those of Blos, Freud, Erickson, and others. Lewin attempted to explain adolescent behavior as a function of the interaction of the person and his or her environment, and stated that inappropriate behavior in adolescence is the result of an unstable environment. He called all the factors associated with an adolescent interacting with the environment the *life space,* which includes the goals and needs of the adolescent, as well as the physical, psychological, and social aspects of the environment. The mix of all these variables in the life space affects behavior.

(Lewin believed that the character of a life space is affected by positive and negative valence issues. When environmental variables block the needs or goals of an adolescent, they are said to have negative valence. If the environment assists a person in achieving his or her goals it has a positive valence. An adolescent will experience conflict when positive and negative valence are equal; when the environment has more positive than negative valence the person moves further toward the achievement of a goal. The adolescent will move away from a need or goal if the negative valence outweighs the positive in any environment.)

Similar to other theorists, Lewin believed that adolescence is a transition period between childhood and adulthood. In his writings (1939), the adolescent is a "marginal man," possessing characteristics of both children and adults. During adolescence a person must change his or her group of reference from the family to peers; in the process the life space changes from that experienced previously to the one the person will encounter as an adult.

Lewin viewed adolescence as a period of great disequilibrium and conflict. Field theory considers each person's development during adolescence as unique because of the individuality of the life space. Lewin believed that each person reacts differently to environmental variables, so adolescence is not universal across persons within an age span. Field theory is not completely behavioral in scope, but it does possess some of the ingredients of behaviorism—particularly in how the environment shapes a person's behavior.

Havinghurst's Developmental Tasks of Adolescence

Another theorist of adolescence who borrowed perspectives from those discussed above is Robert Havinghurst. The essence of Havinghurst's (1951) theory of adolescence rests not on a person attaining a certain stage of development, but on the behavior a person acquires at a certain point in life. Effort, maturation, and societal expectations contribute to a person exhibiting appropriate developmental tasks, and many tasks are prerequisite to others that follow. When age-appropriate developmental tasks and skills are not mastered at the proper time, social disapproval, adjustment difficulty, and anxiety result, and difficulty learning the skill at a later time may occur.)

Havinghurst (1951) described the developmental tasks necessary for adolescents (age 12 to 18) to acquire for appropriate adjustment. Sometimes viewed by contemporary society as provincial, these tasks include (a) cognizance of one's physical appearance and gender role; (b) fostering relationships with peers of both genders; (c) breaking free of dependence on family members; (d) developing skills for employment and achieving financial independence; (e) exhibiting behaviors indicative of civic competence and social responsibility; and (f) preparing for future marriage and life with one's own family.

Havinghurst's theory contributes to educational treatment of adolescents in that one would not teach a skill to youth until it was expected of them by society. Experts in special education have long believed that age-appropriate skills should be the foundation of any curriculum delivered to students with disabilities.

Piaget's Cognitive Theory of Adolescence

Most of what is known regarding Piaget's theory of cognitive development as it relates to adolescence is found in *The Growth of Logical Thinking* (Inhelder & Piaget, 1958). Piaget's cognitive developmental stage of formal operations corresponds roughly to the ages of preadolescence, early adolescence, and late adolescence. In the formal operations stage a person is capable of hypothetical and abstract thinking.

At or near the age of 11 or 12, until age 14 or 15, Piaget believed that youth entered substage III-A of formal operations. Early adolescents in III-A are first showing the capability of abstract thinking, albeit rather clumsily. Piaget's formal operational thought stage differs from the earlier phase of concrete operations in the ability to engage in verbal reasoning. Adolescents capable of exhibiting formal operational cognitions are capable of imagining their world beyond the present and are also capable of thinking about their own thought processes.

Adolescents in Piaget's III-B phase (age 14 to 15+) have reached full formal thought patterns that will carry them into adulthood. Creating an abstract personal, social, and philosophical world is now possible by adolescents in level III-B, and they are not hesitant to express such thoughts. Idealism in religious and political beliefs emerge in stage III-B, as well as the ability to see how the world can be improved, if only from a personal perspective. The mental creation of numerous logical possibilities emanate in problem solving among adolescents at stage III-B.

There is some argument regarding (a) how widespread the acquisition of formal thinking is in adolescents and (b) whether reliable and valid methods exist to measure the presence or absence of abstract thought. Muuss (1996) reviewed research showing that as few as 20% to 35% of older adolescents reached stage III-B of formal thought and that some abstract thinking ability does not generalize across content areas. Sprinthall and Collins (1995) also noted that formal thinking ability is acquired *gradually* in early adolescents. Despite the results of some research to the contrary, formal thinking is most often associated with adolescence. As the reader will see below, some adolescents with mild disabilities, unfortunately, never reach formal operational thought. Teachers of adolescents with mild disabilities need to be mindful of this void during instruction.

Kohlberg's Views on Adolescent Morality

Lawrence Kohlberg is best known for his theories of moral development in humans. The highest stage of his moral development that an adolescent can attain, although it occurs in only one out of 10 adults, is *moral autonomy.* Among other factors, attainment of moral autonomy depends on the adolescent's ability to engage in formal operations. Adolescents who reach the abstract thinking level can engage in ethical and responsible thought based on the simple premise of what is right or wrong. Kohlberg, unlike other theorists of human development, did not view adolescence as having its own level of moral attainment simply on the basis of maturation or chronological age. His *conventional level* of moral development does begin around the nascency of early adolescence (i.e., age 11 or 12), but many adults still function at this level of moral development.

teens will behave the way they think society wants them to

Kohlberg subdivided conventional moral development into two substages: (a) *interpersonal concordance orientation* and (b) *orientation toward authority, law, and duty.* During interpersonal concordance orientation, the adolescent can differentiate between need and morality. Adolescents at this stage will behave in appropriate ways not so much because of morality or the situation, but because appropriate behavior is reinforced by social approval. Teens in interpersonal concordance will be drawn to behave in ways that the peer group will reinforce rather than exhibiting a higher moral behavior that peers will ignore.

The orientation toward authority stage of conventional moral development, on the other hand, presents an adolescent with an entirely different view of moral behavior. Law and order become important guides for behavior at this stage, and morality is demonstrated to avoid the penalty of being caught by those in authority. Guilt is the result when caught by authorities, and adolescents will engage in willful moral behavior out of fear of "getting caught."

Kohlberg also believed that some late adolescents can reach the two substages of *postconventional* moral development: (a) *social contract orientation* (stage five) and (b) *universal ethical principles orientation* (stage six). Persons who reach stage five (also known as the *principled stage)* see individual rights as primary in any society, and the well-being of society at large must supercede that of the individual. Laws are meant to protect the human rights of all members of society. In Kohlberg's view, about one out of three adults reach stage five of postconventional moral development.

Stage six—*universal ethical principles orientation*—is the highest level of Kohlberg's postconventional moral development. Moral behavior in this stage is based on personal choices that place a premium on human life and egalitarianism. Rectitude is not the result of any laws or codes of society, but is based on a personal moral commitment for what is right. Laws do not govern a person in stage six of moral development; they are ruled by personal and ethical principles based on the rights of an individual. Approximately one in 10 adults reach the universal ethical principles stage of moral development (Kohlberg, 1963).

Kohlberg believed that his stages of moral development are not universal to all societies and that morality can be taught to students in school. In contemporary society of the U.S., with its ubiquitous violence and lawlessness, perhaps moral education should reach the level of importance that the "three Rs" have attained.

Selman's Theory of Social Cognition

Social cognition is the process by which a person obtains knowledge about the social domain and interrelationships and the thinking process that pertains to social matters (Muuss, 1996). It is the cognitive process that a person applies to interpersonal behavior and social problem-solving situations, or how a person perceives himself or herself and others in the environment. Social cognition has also been referred to as *social intelligence* and *interpersonal understanding.*

Selman (1980) viewed social cognition from a developmental perspective. Specifically, his concept of developmental social cognition, or social perspective-taking skills, is divided into five stages that begin at age 3 (egocentric undifferentiated stage) and continue into adulthood (in-depth and societal perspective-taking stages). Selman's adolescent stages of social cognition are divided into the *third person* or *mutual perspective-taking skills* (age 10 to 15), and the *societal perspective-taking skills* (age 12+). The two stages of Selman's social cognition during adolescence are discussed below.

During Selman's third-person perspective-taking stage an adolescent is capable of seeing social exchanges with others from the viewpoint of an impartial outsider (or third person). Prior to this stage, Selman concluded that a person could only take the perspective of another child with whom he or she is interacting. Adolescents can see their social interaction and those of another person in an abstract, objective way, as an unbiased judge would view them. Moreover, adolescents at this stage of social cognition can move beyond their own perspective (and that of a partner in an interaction) and assume the view of how a typical, or average, person would interpret a situation.

From adolescence through adulthood the last of Selman's social cognition stages, in-depth and societal perspective-taking, is possible. At this point in the development of social intelligence a person can remove himself or herself from an interpersonal interaction and see the situation from the perspective of society. An 18-year-old Democrat, for example, is having a political discussion regarding reform of the federal welfare system with a Republican of the same age. Both adolescents can see and understand the perspective of the other, and both can remove themselves from the discussion to view it from the angle of an independent third party. The adolescent who has reached societal perspective-taking can also see the myriad ways in which his or her political party views the issue and the historical way in which the party has acted on the dilemma. The party may not have acted in a uniform way toward the issue over the years, and the societal perspective-"taker" can also understand such nuances. The idealism found in adolescence fits well into Selman's (1980) theory of social cognition. His general beliefs regarding the developmental sequence of social cognition also mesh well with metacognitive methods that are used to teach social problem solving (Camp & Bash, 1981; Michenbaum & Goodman, 1971; Spivack & Shure, 1974). Selman's view of development, although narrow in scope, does add another dimension of understanding to the complex picture of the social storm and stress in the lives of adolescents.

Elkind's Theory of Adolescent Egocentrism

Egocentrism is the inability of a person to separate and differentiate himself or herself from the rest of the environment. It involves the application of an exceedingly subjective perspective of events, people, and objects that are present in a person's life. An egocentric person, from Selman's perspective-taking theory, cannot comprehend the viewpoint of another, let alone a third, person or society. The notion of egocentrism originated with Piaget's theory of cognitive development. Piaget found that egocentrism decreases as age and maturation increases. David Elkind (1967) concurred with the cognitive stages of development of Piaget, but he also believed that egocentrism changes as a person moves through different developmental stages. Elkind also concluded that people in each stage of development exhibit a different type of egocentrism. Elkind's beliefs of adolescent egocentrism, from age 11 to adulthood, are discussed in the following paragraphs.

As stated previously in the discussion of Piaget's formal operational thinking abilities, with the onset of abstract thinking comes the capacity to think of one's own thought processes. Elkind hypothesized that an adolescent will reflect greatly on his or her own thinking process and what everyone else (especially peers) thinks about him or her. Elkind's adolescent egocentrism is seen in the minds of youths who imagine that everyone, at all times, is thinking about them. The adolescent, in Elkind's (1967) opinion, has constructed an imaginary audience whose center of attention is the egocentric youth. He concluded that an egocentric adolescent has the capability of being so consumed by how everyone else views him or her that such cognitions cloud how the person actually sees himself or herself. Another example of adolescent egocentrism is when a youth spends an unreasonable amount of time in front of a mirror, consumed by a facial blemish. The peer group usually will not make an issue of such a minor problem in physical appearance (misery loves company, so to speak), but the individual adolescent believes that the thoughts directed by peers toward him or her cannot be complete without consideration of the blemish. In actuality, the adolescent peers are so concerned with their own appearance that the blemish may not be noticed.

Teachers of adolescents should not be alarmed by the egocentric tendencies of any youth, for Elkind believes such behavior is normal. One way to overcome excessive displays of egocentrism is to educate adolescents about the phenomenon. This is a form of *reactivity to measurement* and behavioral *self-control* (see Chapter 4). Perhaps if they understand that self-centered behavior is not the way to impress people, adolescents' egocentrism will be less time-consuming and distracting.

Sullivan's Theory of Adolescent Interpersonal Development

Sullivan (1953) was concerned with the biological and psychosocial drives of adolescents. The last three of his developmental epochs, preadolescence (age 8 to 14), early adolescence (age 12 to 18), and late adolescence (age 18 into adulthood) are characterized by the adolescent with different needs. In preadolescence, the youth must meet the needs of intimacy and having close peers of the same gender (*chumships,* as Sullivan referred to them). During early adolescence the needs of the person change to those related to sexual behavior and relationships with the opposite gender. Late adolescence brings with it the need for assimilation into adult society and the building of strong interpersonal relationships.

Sullivan believed negative personal consequences result when the biological and psychosocial needs of each stage of adolescent development are not met. During preadolescence, for example, a teen who cannot forge a close friendship with another of the same gender will face intimacy problems later in adolescence and adulthood with members of the opposite gender. Intimacy, honesty, and trust are important qualities for lasting relationships with others. The preadolescent who does not gain valuable experience (i.e., with honesty, trust, etc.) and security with a "chum relationship" will have problems with other alliances later in life.

During Sullivan's early adolescent period a person must overcome the anxiety and tension of dating and forming meaningful interrelationships with members of the opposite gender. The intimacy with a close friend of the same gender is replaced by a need for closeness with others of the opposite sex. The early adolescent may experiment with many different types of relationships with the opposite gender—from platonic to sexual. Some teens may have many dates with a multitude of partners, while others may find security and intimacy with only one companion. Youths who do not solve the problem of sexual intimacy and friendship with the opposite gender in early adolescence may, in Sullivan's opinion, seek lust with members of the same gender.

The late adolescent seeks long-term and satisfying relationships. Sullivan wrote of *chronic adolescent syndrome,* which is the inability to find the proper love entity. Indicative of this syndrome is the late adolescent who continually seeks strong relationships but is never satisfied with any partner. Others may be attracted to only those of the same gender, and still others may withdraw completely from attempting to form a strong relationship and become a loner. If strong interpersonal ties are made in late adolescence the typical person then seeks to become integrated into adult society.

Sullivan also believed that personality development is shaped by events during adolescence. Security and intimacy consume the adolescent in Sullivan's view, so parents and teachers should not block the many ways in which an adolescent can experience the necessities of this stage.

Adolescent Development

Our discussion now turns to the characteristics of adolescents regarding physical, cognitive, psychological, and other developmental spheres. We will examine what data actually indicate regarding such youth. Most of the data that we present are from group research. Readers should be careful, therefore, not to generalize from group averages to how an individual adolescent stacks up against the data. There are wide ranges of what is typical in most of these group findings. Our intent is simply to provide a glimpse of the attributes that have been said to affect the population of interest.

Physical Development

Without going into a formal treatise in biology, chemistry, and human anatomy, this section presents the physiological changes that occur throughout adolescence, beginning with puberty. Hormones, at the age of 10 or 11 in girls, and 12 or 13 in boys, are the largest contributors to the onset of puberty and the extensive physical changes that accompany it. The hormones found in the pineal gland begin the process. At some time in late childhood and prepuberty the level of the hormone *melatonin* decreases sharply in the pineal gland. Because melatonin's role is to prevent puberty, when the level drops sharply puberty is under way.

The drop in melatonin also serves as a catalyst to the endocrine system, which is controlled by the hypothalamus in the base of the brain. The hypothalamus activates the pituitary gland, which lies beside it and controls the level of hormones in the bloodstream. The pituitary gland begins to secrete hormones that interact with the thyroid, adrenal cortex, and the gonads (the testes in males and the ovaries in females). When the gonads and adrenal cortex are stimulated by hormones they begin to produce their own hormones. The hormones originating in the thyroid gland, pituitary gland, adrenal cortex, and gonads are responsible for the following:

1. Rapid growth in height and weight.
2. Development of the gonads.
3. Development of secondary sex characteristics, including changes in the genitals and breasts, growth of hair (pubic, facial, body), and continued development of sex organs.
4. Changes in quantity and distribution of muscle and fat.
5. Changes in respiratory and circulatory systems that result in greater physical endurance and strength. (Steinberg, 1985, p. 25)

Differences in male and female development during puberty are largely the result of dissimilar levels of the gonadal hormones androgen (in males) and estrogen (in females). Before and into puberty boys and girls possess both types of hormones. With the onset of puberty, however, the concentration of testosterone (the primary gonadal androgen in males) and estradiol (the primary gonadal estrogen in females) increases respective of gender. Estrogen and progesterone contribute to the appearance of secondary sex characteristics in females (i.e., growth of ovaries, development of breasts), as well as controlling the menstrual cycle. Testosterone allows for the voice change, growth of facial and bodily hair, and sperm production in males. Puberty involves such extraordinary somatic changes in humans that only at the time of birth are such transformations greater. What is puzzling regarding puberty, however, is the comparative lack of discourse on when it ends. The completion of puberty is simply when the level of sex hormones stabilizes at an adult level (Steinberg, 1985).

Finally, the secular trend of adolescents beginning puberty earlier than in the past is supported by data. Average age of voice change in males (occurring usually with the first changes in the genitals and the presence of pubic hair) is now between ages 12 and 13—far younger than it was during the last century (Atwater, 1983). Tanner (1978) and colleagues (Tanner, Whitehouse, & Takaishi, 1966) showed that **menarche,** the first menstrual period in females, appears at an average age of 12.8 years, nearly three years earlier than in the late 1800s. A very interesting research finding of Caspi and Moffitt (1991) points to problems with females who begin puberty at an early age relative to their peers. Caspi and Moffitt showed that girls (in New Zealand) who experienced menarche earlier than average engaged in more "problem behaviors" than did those who had on-time menarche and those who reached puberty later than the average.

Physical growth.   The hormones released in the endocrine system are also responsible for the growth spurt that occurs in early adolescence. Girls, on average, experience this growth spurt between ages 10 and 14. It peaks around age 11 or 12, and growth then sharply declines to pre-adolescent rates near the age of 14. Females usually reach their adult height and weight close to the age of 16 (Atwater, 1983; Tanner, 1978).

The growth spurt in adolescent boys typically occurs two years later than it does in girls. Prior to the growth spurt boys are usually taller than girls. Between the ages of 11 and 13, females are usually taller than males of the same age. After age 14, however, boys are on average taller than girls and the average height difference between the genders lasts into adulthood. Boys' growth spurt usually begins between 12 and 16 and reaches its zenith near the age of 14, and growth then slows to pre-adolescent rates at the age of 15 or 16. Boys usually reach their adult height and weight near age 18 (Tanner, 1978). An interesting growth phenomenon was reported by Malina (1990) regarding height changes in boys before and after the growth spurt. A pre-growth-spurt boy who is shorter than his peers of the same age will probably be shorter than those peers after he and they have experienced a growth spurt. The same situation applies for boys who were taller than average before the growth spurt.

Other physical changes accompany the growth spurt in early adolescents. Boys' shoulders usually broaden; girls retain narrow shoulders but obtain broader hips relative to the trunk. Boys' legs lengthen; girls' legs remain shorter relative to the trunk. Males lose sizable concentrations in body fat during the growth spurt; females retain more childhood fat than males (Malina, 1990; Sprinthall & Collins, 1995). Facial changes are also typical during the growth spurt; both girls and boys develop longer faces, more pronounced nose and jaw protrusions, and receding hairlines.

Strength and muscle growth during puberty and adolescence are also quite remarkable. Sprinthall and Collins (1995) reported that muscle growth in adolescent boys increases by a factor of 14 and by a factor of 10 in girls. The gross weight of the heart nearly doubles during the growth spurt, and the number of red corpuscles in the blood and blood volume also increase (Sprinthall & Collins, 1995). Lungs and breathing capacity grow dramatically during pubescence and adolescence. In general, increases in physical capacity during adolescence seem to favor boys more than girls, but there is considerable overlap across the sexes (Katchadourian, 1977).

Cognitive Development

Although the physical changes in adolescence are truly noteworthy, transformations in cognitive abilities are also easily observable. Be it from a Piagetian perspective, in which concrete operational thinking shifts to formal, or abstract, thinking ability, or from the impressions of Lewin's field theory, in which adolescent thought is shaped by the environment, cognitive development during adolescence is unique. The following section discusses the character of adolescent thought.

Perhaps the best way to frame the cognitive development of adolescents is to present the ways it is different from the thinking capabilities of children. Sprinthall and Collins (1995) have made such a comparison, which is presented in Table 2.2. As the reader will note in Table 2.2, one of the most striking attributes of adolescent cognition is the ability to engage in logical speculation. Children fixate on obvious concrete images of their environment, while adolescents ponder the range of possibilities and interactions that might exist in their surroundings. Adolescents—but not most children—can form hypotheses, anticipate many possibilities in thinking ahead, understand and dissect the perspectives of others, and spend much time contemplating their own thinking processes. Adolescent thought processes, therefore, are qualitatively more sim-

Table 2.2
Characteristics of adolescent versus childhood thought

Adolescent	Childhood
Thought extended to possibilities	Thought limited to here and now
Problem solving governed by planned hypothesis testing	Problem solving dictated by details of the problem
Thought expanded to ideas as well as concrete reality	Thought limited to concrete objects and situations
Thought enlarged to perspective of others	Thought focused on one's own perspective

Source: From *Adolescent Psychology: A Developmental View* (p. 99) by N. A. Sprinthall and W. A. Collins, 1995, New York: McGraw-Hill.

ilar to the way adults think than the way in which children use their cognition (Weithorn & Campbell, 1982).

Intelligence is a by-product of the way we think. Does intelligence improve during adolescence? The answer to this question is no, on average. Intelligence scores, derived from IQ tests, show a remarkable pattern of stability across the adolescent years. Yes, adolescents become more qualitatively—but usually not quantitatively—intelligent through the teen years. Intelligence quotient scores during adolescence show more stability than is shown during the childhood years. Stable quantitative intelligence of adolescents can be characterized in the same manner as relative height before and after the growth spurt. If a person scored higher than his or her peers on an IQ test given before adolescence, then during adolescence and in adulthood the person, on average, will also score higher on an IQ test than his or her peers.

Adolescent cognition is also characterized by more deliberate and reflective decision making than during the childhood years. This style of thinking is apparent in light of adolescents' ability to see more possibilities as solutions to real or imagined problems and in their aptitude to have flexible thought processes. More reflective and elaborate thought patterns by adolescents may also be the result of the accumulation of more knowledge and personal experience than was previously available (Canfield & Ceci, 1992).

Lastly, research has also examined the information-processing skills of adolescents and has shown differences in how children and adolescents (a) store and recall knowledge, (b) learn to generalize knowledge, (c) form discriminations in stimuli, and (d) organize cognitive processes (Sprinthall & Collins, 1995; Steinberg, 1985; Sternberg, 1977; Sternberg & Nigro, 1980). Adolescents are consistently shown to have better control over their information-processing ability, better memory, and more sophisticated cognitive routines than children.

Psychological and Other Disorders of Adolescence

The period of adolescence, unfortunately, is also laden with a host of issues that affect youth in deleterious ways. Psychological disturbances, suicide, and delinquency, to name just a few, have been associated with far too many adolescents. In the areas of behavioral, psychiatric, and emotional problems, the storm and stress of adolescence imposes an extensive toll. The preeminent source of problem behavior during adolescence is presented in *The Troubled Adolescent* (White, 1989), and below we emphasize some of the serious dilemmas of adolescence as discussed by White and many others.

Depression. White (1989) defined depression as "gloom, low self-esteem, dejection, downcast feelings, foreboding, helplessness, lack of energy, and loss of interest in usual activities" (p. 111). Temporary depressed feelings are typical of as many as 50% of adolescents (Achenbach & Edelbrock, 1981), and the most problematic, *clinical depression,* also proliferates during adolescence. Females express depression in higher proportions than do males, and inheritance also plays a role in the presence of clinical depression (Lavorie, Keller, Beardslee, & Dorer, 1988). Symptoms of depression are more likely to occur in late—rather than early—adolescence (Weiner, 1982). Beck (1972, 1978) divided the symptoms of depression into four clusters, which are presented in Figure 2.1, and White (1989) stated that mood (Cluster I) and cognitive symptoms (Cluster II) are the key features in adolescent depression.

The *Diagnostic and Statistical Manual of Mental Disorders* (DSM-IV) (American Psychiatric Association, 1994) provides similar depressive symptoms to Beck's, but states that at least four of their eight symptoms need to be apparent (daily) for a period of two weeks.

A particularly troubling aspect of adolescent depression is the frequency of other problems that occur with it. Sprinthall and Collins (1995) stated that the most common additional dilemmas of adolescent depression are eating and weight problems and a distorted body image (particularly in females).

Actual and suspected causes of adolescent depression are many. Hormonal changes in puberty have been suggested as a potential cause, but at present a causal link between the two factors has not been found. Hill and Lynch (1983) offered social expectations as a possible cause. Teens may feel that they cannot live up to their newly acquired "no longer a child" status, and retreat into depression. Gjerde and Block (1991) stated that depression in adolescent females may be the result of internalizing despondent feelings. White (1989) provided his perspective on how depression develops in adolescents, and his comments are provided in Figure 2.2.

Adolescent depression must not be ignored by any professional concerned with mental health. When adolescents show signs of depression, teachers need to demonstrate patience, understanding, and support. They should be observant in order to identify depressive symptoms and refer affected students to qualified specialists who can offer strong treatment. Depression in adolescents should not be treated casually; if left untreated, it can lead to suicide, the next topic of discussion.

Adolescent suicide. A few facts on adolescent suicide are presented here for dramatic effect: (a) the rate of adolescent suicide has increased over 300% in the past 30 years; (b) adolescent suicide is now the third leading cause of death in adolescence; (c) suicide is the second leading cause of death among college students; (d) approximately 6,000 adolescents commit suicide each year in the U.S.; and (e) suicide accounts for approximately 6% of deaths among 10- to 14-year-olds, and about 12% of deaths among 15- to

Figure 2.1
Beck's clusters of depression

I. Mood-emotive-affective

1. Profound sadness, despondency, gloom, blue, low, heavy-hearted, downcast, somber, woe, sullen, dejected
2. Zest and joy go out of living

II. Cognitive patterns, thoughts, and beliefs

1. Poor self-concept, self-devaluation, self-criticism, self-deprecation, excessive guilt, and shame
2. Belief that others don't care or that one is not worth caring about
3. Sense of foreboding, doom, hopelessness, and futility about the future
4. Overgeneralization of negative events
5. Belief that one is not attractive or desirable

III. Motivational-behavioral

1. Low energy, can't get started, person feels stuck, can't fight back
2. Difficulty concentrating or engaging in activities that require sustained concentration, indecisiveness
3. Withdrawal from social activities
4. Loss of interest in fun activities, dating, partying, work, hobbies
5. Loss of interest in daily activities

IV. Physical-vegetative

1. Irregular eating, sleep disturbances, little interest in romance or lovemaking
2. Excessive fatigue, person tires easily, slowing down of psychomotor activity

---

Source: From *Depression: Causes and Treatment* by A. T. Beck, 1972, Philadelphia: University of Pennsylvania.

19-year-olds (Sprinthall & Collins, 1995; White, 1989). These statistics are convincing and should warn the reader that adolescent suicide is a serious problem.

Gender is a significant factor in adolescent suicide. Female adolescents are more likely than males to attempt suicide (by a factor of 3), but male adolescents (by a factor of 4) are more likely to "complete" suicide in comparison to females (Sprinthall & Collins, 1995). Adolescent males are more successful at suicide because they use methods that are not easily reversed. Several factors have been identified as related to suicide attempts among adolescents; depression, not surprisingly, is the most commonly associated collateral symptom. Greuling and DeBlassie (1980) estimated that as many as 40% of adolescents who attempt or consistently think of suicide are affected by depression. Other experts (Husain & Vandiver, 1984) state that some suicidal adolescents may be

Figure 2.2

White's views on how depression develops in adolescents

---

1. Real loss, characterized by death, separation, romance breakup, or major disappointments, results in lowered self-esteem, despondency, and feelings of emptiness.

2. Adolescence is a vulnerable time during which teenagers must give up the security and safety of childhood to confront the responsibilities and uncertainties of the future.

3. Unrealistic expectations of self, one's experiences, and the future.

4. Existential helplessness, learned helplessness, or deficiencies in coping responses caused by the lack of positive reinforcement.

5. Failure to resolve childhood developmental tasks leaves a residual of shame, guilt, inferiority, and self-deprecation that can be easily activated by the ups and downs of adolescent living.

Source: From *The Troubled Adolescent* (p. 126) by J. L. White, 1989, New York: Pergamon Press.

experiencing a loss of reality. Preoccupation with death, inability to recover from a serious loss, and consistent feelings of rejection are also related to suicide. Adolescents who have experienced suicide in the family are vulnerable. Family factors, such as excessive conflict and disorganization, contribute to attempts at suicide. Adolescents who attempt suicide appear very self-critical. McCoy (1983) provided many helpful early warning signs of suicide among adolescents, and these are presented in Figure 2.3.

No teacher ever wants to encounter suicide in one of his or her students. The senior author has had such a personal experience. One of his former female students who had mild mental retardation committed suicide, using a prescription drug overdose, two years after leaving high school. Many of McCoy's (1983) early warning signs were apparent while the young woman was in high school, such as consistent depression and rejection by peers and frequent expressions of hopelessness and despair. While a high school special education teacher, the senior author was too naive to realize the seriousness of the young woman's depression, and her suicide came as a great shock and disappointment. Take this advice from someone who knows: Never ignore any of the symptoms of depression and suicide discussed above. If you have any questions regarding behavior that appears to be depressive or filled with despair, do not hesitate to refer the student to a professional who can assist.

Juvenile delinquency. Juvenile delinquency, from a historical perspective, is one of the most widely commented upon problem behaviors of adolescence. *Juvenile delinquency is a legal term that means violation of law by a minor.* The majority of states define minors as those under the age of 18, but a few states classify them as persons under the age of 16 or 17. Law-breaking behaviors considered delinquent include the obvious ones such as destruction of property, illegal possession of weapons, rape, assault, arson, and burglary. Sprinthall and Collins (1995) also include other behaviors considered "status

Figure 2.3
McCoy's early warning signs of suicide

1. Preoccupation with themes of death expressed in talking or writings.
2. Expressing suicidal thoughts or threats.
3. Actual suicidal attempts or gestures.
4. Prolonged depression with attitudes of hopelessness and despair.
5. Physical symptoms of depression such as changes in sleeping patterns, too much or too little sleep, or sudden and extreme changes in weight and eating habits.
6. Withdrawal and isolation from family and friends.
7. Deteriorating school performance reflected in lower grades, cutting classes, and dropping out of school activities.
8. Persistent abuse of drugs or alcohol.
9. Major personality and behavioral changes indicated by excessive anxiety or nervousness, angry outbursts, apathy, or lack of interest in personal appearance or the opposite sex.
10. Recent loss of close relationships through death or suicide.
11. Making final arrangements, drawing up a will, or giving away prized possessions.
12. Previous suicidal attempts.
13. Sudden, unexplained euphoria or heightened activity after a long period of gloom and doom. Suicide sometimes occurs when despondency is lifting. The person feels relieved because he or she has made a final decision and now has more energy available.

Source: From *Coping with Teenage Depression: A Parent's Guide* by M. McCoy, 1983, New York: New American Library.

offenses," which range from drug use and under-age consumption of alcoholic beverages to school truancy. Status offenses are so-called because the age of the accused relegates him or her to the status of a minor. Regardless of definition, age, or behaviors, approximately 1.3 million minors are brought before legal authorities for alleged lawbreaking each year.

Over 50% of juveniles come in contact with legal authorities for misdemeanor offenses. White (1989) stated that most law-breaking adolescents are not repeat or serious offenders. Youths from urban low-income families, and those from minority cultures (particularly African-American males) are more likely to be arrested than white middle-class adolescents. Minority culture youths are more likely to be repeat offenders and accused of serious offenses such as burglary and assault. Males are more likely to be arrested than females. Males are more likely than females to be involved with violent offenses and destruction of property. Females, on the other hand, are more likely than males to be involved in status offenses such as running away from home, curfew violation, and truancy. Far more law-breaking behavior is reported by adolescents than is recorded by police. Self-reports of delinquency by adolescents indicate that nearly 90% of youths have engaged in some form of law-breaking behavior (Gibbons & Krohn, 1986). Many acts of delinquency are committed in groups, and approximately 92,000 adolescents spend time daily in lockups of local jails (Allen-Hagen, 1991).

The rapid increase of violent crime and gang warfare among urban youth in the U.S. has created an extremely hazardous lifestyle for many adolescents. Millstein and Litt (1990) found murder accounted for a third of all deaths among African-American males age 15 to 19. Sprinthall and Collins (1995) reported dizzying statistics related to violence among adolescents: (a) 25% of students were victims of violence in or near schools; (b) 23% of males between 13 and 16 reported carrying a knife to school at least once in the past year; and (c) over 20% of males in inner-city high schools own guns.

Suspected causes of delinquency and violent crime among adolescents are many, but true answers to the problem are few. Some have pointed fingers at the breakdown in traditional family structure, with disrupted parenting practices accounting for a sizable number of juvenile offenders. Others have cited the overworked juvenile court system in which offenders are often released on parole and rarely, if ever, punished for repeated crimes. Perhaps some of the contemporary judicial mentality and laws of "three strikes and you're out" (i.e., three felony arrests equals lifelong jail terms without parole) is a reaction to the nonpunitive legal practices experienced by juvenile offenders. Still others mention the plethora of violence on television as the origin of delinquency and increasing crime rates. "Gangsta rap" music has also been accused of encouraging and endorsing increased violence. Finally, easy access to illicit, inexpensive drugs, particularly crack cocaine, has led to increased noncompliance with the law in the minds of many.

Walker, Colvin, and Ramsey (1995) divided delinquency into early and late starters based on the age of onset of delinquent acts. Early starters are socialized to delinquency from a very early age by family and environmental stressors. Late starters become delinquent as a result of peer group pressures and not as a result of ineffective family influences. Early starters experience academic failure and social rejection; late starters do not. Depending on the age of onset of the initial delinquent behavior, Walker et al. (1995) suggest different intervention schemes for the extinction of such inappropriate acts against society. Whatever the reason of origin and course of treatment, delinquency among adolescents is a national problem that is lamentable, expensive, widespread, and in dire need of effective ways in which to eliminate it.

Applications to Adolescents with Disabilities

Adolescents with disabilities are equally—if not more—in need of understanding from a theoretical and problem behavior perspective. They experience the joy and sorrow of adolescence in addition to the social stigma of the label of disability. Another true story from the high school teaching career of the senior author illustrates how the presence of mild disability can affect the exhilaration of adolescence.

John (not the student's real name) was a handsome and popular (at least with his peers who were also mildly disabled) 16-year-old male identified as learning disabled. John's father was a dentist, and his mother was a nurse at a local hospital. He spent about half of the school day in cross-categorical resource room instruction with four special education teachers, and the other half of the school day in regular classroom instruction in sophomore English, "basic" mathematics, beginning Earth science, and health and physical education. John, at least outwardly, had a healthy opinion of himself. He boasted to his peers in the resource room that he had many dates with attractive female adolescents, drove a nice car, and wore "cool" clothes. If it were not for his learning disability, John would be no different from any other teen at the large (2,100+ students) suburban high school. John and one of his male teachers (the senior author) had a positive, fun, and friendly relationship. John frequently poked fun at the clothes worn by the male teacher and the car that he drove. John occasionally caddied for the teacher after school.

The time for the annual fall semiformal dance at the high school arrived, and John's date for the dance was a popular, attractive, junior-varsity cheerleader. Days before the dance he frequently bragged in the resource room about his forthcoming "dream" date. One day before the dance John walked into the resource room in a very dour mood, saying nothing to anyone for the entire class period. He just sat in the back of the room staring out the window. Repeated attempts by the teacher to engage John in the usual academic activity in the resource room were futile.

At the end of the class period the teacher walked out of the classroom with John to find out what was wrong. After repeated questioning, John finally confessed that his date for the fall dance was canceled by the girl. John said that she broke the date with him because someone told her that he was a special education student, and that she "wasn't going out with a dummy."

Granted, the story above relates to only one adolescent with a learning disability. One cannot generalize from the experiences of a single youth to the larger population of adolescents with the same diagnosis. This true story, however, shows some of the reality of adolescence with a mild disability.

Research has examined adolescents with disabilities from the perspective of some of the theorists discussed above. Schonert and Cantor (1991), for example, examined the moral development of adolescents with the primary disability of behavior disorders. Twenty-five 9th through 12th graders (20 males and 5 females) with behavior disorders were compared with 28 nondisabled adolescents on the *Defining Issues Test,* which is used to evaluate adolescents' level of moral reasoning based on Kohlberg's (1981) theories. Results indicated that the adolescents with behavior disorders displayed significantly lower (i.e., less mature) moral reasoning than did the nondisabled groups.

Research attempting to examine the developmental tasks of adolescence among youth with disabilities, from the perspective of Havinghurst (1972), has also been conducted. Arnold (1984) compared the personal value system of adolescents with five different types of disabilities (those with the three types of mild disability were included), versus those who were nondisabled. Adolescent participants were asked to rank order issues such as self-respect, freedom, happiness, and world peace in terms of how much value they placed on each issue. Results showed that the value patterns of adolescents with disabilities did not differ significantly from those expressed by the nondisabled. This is one piece of evidence that shows that in some ways adolescents with disabilities are just like those without disabling conditions.

Selman's views on social cognition and perspective-taking have been examined in adolescents with mild disabilities, particularly those with learning disabilities (see Bryan & Bryan, 1986, for a review). The research findings are fairly consistent in showing that students with learning disabilities (including adolescents), when compared to the nondisabled, show (a) less understanding of social situations, (b) difficulty in interpreting nonverbal social communications, and (c) less sophisticated role-taking abilities. Adolescents with mild mental retardation have also been shown in research to experience some of the same social cognition difficulties as those with learning disabilities (Drew, Logan, & Hardman, 1992).

Many studies have examined Piaget's cognitive stages of development applied to adolescents with mild disabilities, particularly those with mental retardation (see Drew et al., 1992, for a review). In general, research has shown that persons with mental retardation will progress through Piaget's stages of cognitive development at a slower rate than the nondisabled. Acquisition of formal operational thought is possible for some adults with mild mental retardation, but youth are likely to spend most of their adolescent years still in concrete operational thought.

Chapter 3 of this text will discuss in detail some of the problems (e.g., depression, suicide, delinquency, etc.) that are characteristic of adolescents with mild disabilities. As a preview, problem behaviors and symptoms of morbidity tend to be particularly apparent and detrimental in the lives of adolescents with disabilities.

Summary

Adolescence, in many ways, is hardly like the experiences of Holden Caulfield in *The Catcher in the Rye* or those of an adolescent girl in a Judy Blume novel. Adolescents grow, think, and behave in a way that is far removed from childhood and adulthood, but their world shares characteristics of both children and grownups. The physical changes of puberty and adolescence allow them to see themselves in a light that is difficult to remember as an adult and incomprehensible to a child. The cognitive changes that affect adolescents give them a chance to think like adults, but not be like adults in terms of autonomy. Many adolescents are still not fully capable of meeting all the responsibilities of adulthood, but they surely do not care to be encumbered with the trivialities of childhood. With emotions and hormones running rampant, and society, family, and educational systems simultaneously pulling them in different directions, it is no wonder that adolescence continues to be referred to as a period of storm and stress nearly a century after Hall (1904) first referred to it as such.

This chapter advised the reader of how adolescence can be viewed, how it develops in humans, and what can happen to those in its midst. Anyone teaching adolescents should be able to observe the theories of the experts in some of the behavior and mannerisms of adolescents, including those with disabilities. We also hope that the reader will be able to react more knowledgeably when problem behaviors surface in adolescents' lives. Our intent was to inform, but also to assist teachers in preventing some of the less-than-positive consequences that befall adolescents.

Key Terms

recapitulation   egocentrism
social cognition   menarche

References

Achenbach, T. M., & Edelbrock, C. S. (1981). Behavioral problems and competencies reported by parents of normal and disturbed children aged four through sixteen. *Monographs of the Society for Research in Child Development, 46* (Serial No. 188).

Allen-Hagen, B. (1991, January). Public juvenile facilities: Children in custody 1989. *OJJDP Update on Statistics,* pp. 1-10.

American Psychiatric Association. (1994). *Diagnostic and statistical manual of mental disorders* (4th ed.). Washington, DC: Author.

Arnold, J. (1984). Values of exceptional students during early adolescence. *Exceptional Children, 51,* 230–234.

Atwater, E. (1983). *Adolescence.* Upper Saddle River, NJ: Prentice Hall.

Ausubel, D. P. (1954). *Theory and problems of adolescent development.* New York: Grune & Stratton.

Beck, A. T. (1972). *Depression: Causes and treatment.* Philadelphia: University of Pennsylvania.

Beck, A. T. (1978). *Beck depression inventory.* Philadelphia: Center for Cognitive Therapy.

Blos, P. (1941). *The adolescent personality: A study of individual behavior.* New York: Appleton-Century.

Blos, P. (1970). *The young adolescent: Clinical studies.* New York: Free Press.

Blos, P. (1971). The child analyst looks at the young adolescent. *Daedalus, 100,* 961–978.

Bryan, T. H., & Bryan, J. H. (1986). *Understanding learning disabilities* (3rd ed.). Palo Alto, CA: Mayfield.

Camp, B. W., & Bash, M. A. (1981). *Think aloud.* Champaign, IL: Research Press.

Canfield, R. L., & Ceci, S. J. (1992). Integrating learning into a theory of intellectual development. In R. J. Sternberg & C. A. Berg (Eds.), *Intellectual development* (pp. 278–300). Cambridge, England: Cambridge University Press.

Caspi, A., & Moffitt, T. E. (1991). Individual differences are accentuated during periods of social change: The sample case of girls at puberty. *Journal of Personality and Social Psychology, 61,* 157–168.

Drew, C. J., Logan, D. R., & Hardman, M. L. (1992). *Mental retardation: A life cycle approach.* Upper Saddle River, NJ: Merrill/Prentice Hall.

Educational Communications, Inc. (1995). *Who's who among American high school students.* Lake Forest, IL: Author.

Elkind, D. (1967). Egocentrism in adolescence. *Child Development, 38,* 1025–1034.

Erickson, E. H. (1950). *Childhood and society.* New York: W. W. Norton & Co.

Gans, J. (1990). *America's adolescents: How healthy are they?* Chicago: American Medical Association.

Gibbons, P. C., & Krohn, M. D. (1986). *Delinquent behavior* (4th ed.). Upper Saddle River, NJ: Prentice Hall.

Gjerde, P. F., & Block, J. (1991). Preadolescent antecedents of depressive symptomatology at age 18: A prospective study. *Journal of Youth and Adolescence, 20,* 217–232.

Greuling, J. W., & DeBlassie, R. R. (1980). Adolescent suicide. *Adolescence, 15,* 589–601.

Hall, G. S. (1904). *Adolescence* (2 vols.). New York: Appleton.

Havinghurst, R. J. (1951). *Developmental tasks and education.* New York: Longmans, Green.

Havinghurst, R. J. (1972). *Developmental tasks and education.* New York: McKay.

Hill, J. P., & Lynch, M. E. (1983). The intensification of gender-related role expectations during early adolescence. In J. Brooks-Gunn & A. C. Petersen (Eds.), *Girls at puberty* (pp. 201–228). New York: Plenum.

Husain, S. A., & Vandiver, T. (1984). *Suicide in children and adolescents.* New York: Spectrum Books.

Inhelder, B., & Piaget, J. (1958). *The growth of logical thinking.* New York: Basic Books.

Katchadourian, H. (1977). *The biology of adolescence.* San Francisco: Freeman.

Kohlberg, L. (1963). The development of children's orientations toward a moral order. *Vita Humana, 6,* 11–33.

Kohlberg, L. (1981). *The philosophy of moral development: Moral stages and the idea of justice.* New York: Harper & Row.

Lavorie, P. W., Keller, M. B., Beardslee, W. R., & Dorer, D. J. (1988). Affective disorder in childhood: Separating the familial component of risk from individual characteristics of children. *Journal of Affective Disorders, 15,* 303–311.

Lewin, K. (1939). Field theory and experiment in social psychology: Concepts and methods. *American Journal of Sociology, 44,* 868–896.

Malina, R. M. (1990). Physical growth and performance during the transitional years (9–16). In R. Montemayor, G. R. Adams, & A. P. Gullotta (Eds.), *From childhood to adolescence: A transitional period?* (pp. 41–62). Newbury Park, CA: Sage.

McCoy, M. (1983). *Coping with teenage depression: A parent's guide.* New York: New American Library.

Michenbaum, D., & Goodman, A. P. (1971). Training impulsive children to talk to themselves: A means of developing self-control. *Journal of Abnormal Psychology, 77,* 115–126.

Millstein, S. G., & Litt, I. F. (1990). Adolescent health. In S. S. Feldman & G. R. Elliott (Eds.), *At the threshold: The developing adolescent* (pp. 431–456). Cambridge, MA: Harvard University Press.

Muuss, R. E. (1982). *Theories of adolescence* (4th ed.). New York: Random House.

Muuss, R. E. (1996). *Theories of adolescence* (6th ed.). New York: McGraw-Hill.

Schonert, K. A., & Cantor, G. N. (1991). Moral reasoning in behaviorally disordered adolescents from alternative and traditional high schools. *Behavioral Disorders, 17,* 23–35.

Selman, R. L. (1980). *The growth of interpersonal understanding: Developmental and clinical analyses.* New York: Academic Press.

Spivack, G., & Shure, M. B. (1974). *Social adjustment of young children: A cognitive approach to solving real-life problems.* San Francisco: Jossey-Bass.

Sprinthall, N. A., & Collins, W. A. (1995). *Adolescent psychology: A developmental view.* New York: McGraw-Hill.

Steinberg, L. (1985). *Adolescence.* New York: Knopf.

Sternberg, R. (1977). *Intelligence, information processing, and analogical reasoning: The componential analysis of human abilities.* Hillsdale, NJ: Erlbaum.

Sternberg, R., & Nigro, G. (1980). Developmental patterns in the solution of verbal analogies. *Child Development, 51,* 27–38.

Sullivan, H. S. (1953). *The interpersonal theory of psychiatry.* New York: Norton.

Tanner, J. M. (1978). *Fetus into man: Physical growth from conception to maturity.* Cambridge, MA: Harvard University Press.

Tanner, J. M., Whitehouse, R., & Takaishi, M. (1966). Standards from birth to maturity for height, weight-height velocity and weight velocity; British children, 1965. *Archives of the Diseases of Childhood, 41,* 455–471.

Walker, H. M., Colvin, G., & Ramsey, E. (1995). *Antisocial behavior in school: Strategies and best practices.* Pacific Grove, CA: Brooks/Cole.

Weiner, I. B. (1982). *Child and adolescent psychopathology.* New York: John Wiley & Sons.

Weithorn, L. A., & Campbell, S. (1982). The competency of children and adolescents to make informed treatment decisions. *Child Development, 53,* 1589–1598.

Wetzel, J. R. (1989). *American youth: A statistical snapshot.* Washington, DC: William T. Grant Foundation.

White, J. L. (1989). *The troubled adolescent.* New York: Pergamon.

3

Characteristics of Secondary-Level Students with Mild Disabilities

Objectives

After reading this chapter, the reader should be able to:

1. discuss in detail the personal characteristics that are typical in adolescents with mild disabilities;

2. discuss the academic and intellectual characteristics that make adolescents with mild disabilities unique;

3. discuss the behavioral traits that are common in adolescents with mild disabilities;

4. compare and contrast some of the problem behaviors found in adolescents with and without mild disabilities;

5. compare and contrast characteristics that are typical of one category of adolescent with mild disability versus another student with a different label of disability.

This chapter presents the global characteristics of secondary (and post-secondary) level students with mild disabilities. Before a teacher can be effective with such students in classroom instruction he or she needs to know specific traits that make them unique. One of the myths is that students with mild disabilities look different from others their age. This could not be further from the truth; with few exceptions early and late adolescents with learning disabilities, mild mental retardation, and school-identified behavior disorders appear no different from nondisabled peers. There are a few adolescents with mild mental retardation who will appear to be different in physical appearance than other, ordinary teens; they may have other concomitant conditions that affect their gait (e.g., cerebral palsy) or facial aspects (e.g., Down syndrome). On the surface, however, most adolescents with mild disabilities are remarkably similar to the nondisabled.

Adolescents with mild disabilities are also very similar to other youth in additional ways. Just as nondisabled adolescents strive for their needs and desires to be fulfilled, so too do students with mild disabilities. They love, hate, laugh, and cry just like anyone else their age. They want to be members of popular peer groups, cruise the streets and highways, party, listen to rap and rock music, and hang out and be cool just like any contemporary teen.

No matter the number of similarities that are shared, adolescents with and without mild disabilities are different from each other in one very important area; the labels that schools place on students who demonstrate learning and behavior problems. Disability labels allow schools to educate students with mild disabilities separated from nondisabled peers. Specific laws protect the individualization of instruction for students with disabilities, but not for the nondisabled. Adolescents with learning disabilities are allowed to take college placement tests (e.g., SAT) and college and university examinations in nonstandardized fashion (e.g., with extra time, having questions read to them), but nondisabled youth are not allowed such privileges. Litigation has prevented students with disabilities from being expelled from school, but similar laws do not prohibit expulsion of students without disabilities. In spite of these apparent advantages, we have not seen an abundance of nondisabled students craving to be labeled and "included" in special education.

Adolescents with learning disabilities, mild mental retardation, and behavior disorders also share traits, but are very different with regard to other attributes. MacMillan, Siperstein, and Gresham (1996) concluded

51

that students with mild mental retardation are more similar to students with learning disabilities than other youth with more severe mental retardation. MacMillan et al. even go so far as to suggest the term *generalized learning disability* for persons currently identified as mildly mentally retarded.

The intent of this chapter is to compare and contrast adolescents with mild disabilities in terms of personal, academic, intellectual, and behavioral traits. We hope the reader is able to understand and appreciate the diversities and similarities that are demonstrated across different types of mild disability, and between the nondisabled and youth with mild disabilities.

Background

In the history of special education in the U.S., at both the classroom level in public schools and in the teacher training institutions of higher education, elementary-level students with disabilities attracted more concern than those attending secondary-level programs (Edgar, 1987; Zigmond, 1993). Cullinan and Epstein (1979) mentioned this phenomenon in the preface of their seminal text, *Special Education for Adolescents,* and we believe it is still true today. Many states still provide special education certification from K through 12. An abundance of special education methods and materials courses in colleges and universities do not differentiate elementary-level techniques from those that should be used with adolescents. Many generic methods texts pay little attention (i.e., usually one chapter out of many others) to the special adaptations in instruction needed to be effective at the secondary level. And so the tradition continues in the belief that if special education at the elementary level does its job, secondary-level special education will not be necessary.

We do not question the importance of education of students with mild disabilities at the elementary level. Learning and behavior problems at that level are serious and worthy of great attention. Short-term interventions (i.e., those applied only in the elementary grades), however, have a history of inadequacy (Kazdin, 1987). Problems in academic achievement and behavior of students with mild disabilities do indeed persist into the secondary level (Deshler, Schumaker, Alley, Warner, & Clark, 1982; Deshler, Warner, Schumaker, & Alley, 1983; Warner, Schumaker, Alley, & Deshler, 1980).

In our opinion, in order to educate adolescents with mild disabilities effectively, a teacher must first know what such students are like before learning how and what to teach them. It should be mentioned here that there is no such person as an "average" student with mild disability. We know much about the characteristics of students with mild disabilities, but each person so labeled is unique and will have distinctive needs and abilities. The labels that are used for mild disability separate students in each category by definition (see Chapter 1) and in many other ways. Although we agree with the first major work in this area (Hallahan & Kauffman, 1977) that students with mild disabilities are more similar than different, many features are endemic to only one category of exceptionality.

The majority of discourse in this chapter is meant to prepare the reader for what to expect in terms of general characteristics of adolescents with mild disabilities. Statistics and data are presented here to illuminate the traits that we feel are important for the reader to comprehend. After understanding the content of this chapter the reader should be able to tackle the specifics of how to teach adolescents with mild disabilities found in Parts II and III of this text.

Personal Characteristics

Much of what we know regarding the personal characteristics of adolescents and young adults with disabilities originates with Mary Wagner and her associates at the Stanford Research Institute (SRI) (Valdes, Williamson, & Wagner, 1990; Wagner, 1991a; 1991b; 1992; Wagner et al., 1991; Wagner, D'Amico, Marder, Newman, & Blackorby, 1992; Wagner, Blackorby, & Hebbeler, 1993; Wagner, Blackorby, Cameto, & Newman, 1994). Since 1985 SRI International has been under contract with the U.S. Office of Special Education Programs to study aspects of adolescents with disabilities through the National Longitudinal Transition Study (NLTS) of students in special education.

A second large source of information on adolescents with disabilities has been the U.S. Department of Education annual reports to Congress. Since school year 1976–77 the U.S. Department of Education has reported the number and various other traits of students with all disabilities served in special education in this country. The statistical sources for much of our discussion below originate with the work of Wagner and her colleagues and the U.S. Department of Education (1994, 1995).

General Demographics

The following statistics originate from the *Seventeenth Annual Report to Congress on the Implementation of The Individuals with Disabilities Education Act* (U.S. Department of Education, 1995). In the 50 states, the District of Columbia, and Puerto Rico, as of October 1, 1994, there were nearly 1.3 million adolescents aged 12 through 17 identified as learning disabled, 268,273 labeled mentally retarded of the same age (this would include others in addition to those in the mild range), and 250,389 between 12 and 17 recognized as seriously emotionally disturbed. These numbers reflect individuals receiving special educational services under Part B of IDEA and Chapter 1 of the Elementary and Secondary Education Act. Youth with learning disabilities account for approximately 63% of all adolescents aged 12 through 17 with disabilities, those with mental retardation comprise 12.9% of the same group, and students aged 12 through 17 with serious emotional disturbance amount to 12% of all those with disabilities of the same age. Adolescents with learning disabilities aged 12 through 17 comprise approximately 27% of all those with disabilities aged 6 to 21 under IDEA and Chapter 1. Youth with mental retardation aged 12 through 17 account for approximately 5.6% of all those receiving services under IDEA and Chapter 1 aged 6 to 21. Adolescents with serious emotional disturbance aged 12 through 17 total approximately 5.2% of all those counted under IDEA and Chapter 1 aged 6 to 21.

Adolescents with disabilities aged 18 to 21 (under IDEA and Chapter 1) in the 50 states, the District of Columbia, and Puerto Rico total 241,645. Of this number, 50% are learning disabled, 26.5% are designated as mentally retarded (again, other persons not in the mild range are counted here), and 9% are identified as seriously emotionally disturbed. The largest single age group of adolescents (i.e., aged 12 to 21) with learning disabilities is those aged 12; for those with mental retardation, 13, and for youths with behavior disorders, 14.

Gender. Males have historically comprised more than 50% of the populations referred to as learning disabled, mentally retarded, and behaviorally disordered. Valdes et al. (1990) examined gender in adolescents aged 15 through 21+ (average age = 17.5) and found that among adolescents with learning disabilities, 73.4% were male. In the population of adolescents identified as mentally retarded (not all were in the mild range) Valdes et al. found that 58% were male; of youth described as emotionally disturbed, 76.4% were male; and 68.5% of adolescents with all types of disabilities were male.

Race. In terms of race of adolescents with disabilities, Valdes et al. (1990) showed the following. Among youth with learning disabilities (n = 962) 21.6% were African-American, 67.2% were white, and 8.4% were Hispanic. In terms of adolescents with mental retardation (n = 924; all levels of severity) 31% were African-American, 61% were white, and 5.6% were Hispanic. Of those youth labeled emotionally disturbed in the sample (n = 632), 25.1% were African-American, 67.1% were white, and 6% were Hispanic. The above race proportions across mild disabilities are reasonably similar to the entire sample—24.2% African-American, 65% white, and 8.1% Hispanic.

Family characteristics. Valdes et al. (1990) found that 34% of adolescents with learning disabilities were from single-parent homes, and 5% lived with neither natural parent. Approximately 39% of homes were single-parent, and 6% had neither natural parent in the sample of those with mental retardation. In domiciles of adolescents with behavior disorders, 44.3% originated from single-parent homes, and 6% had neither natural parent present. Valdes et al. reported that in all adolescents with disabilities, 36.8% were from single-parent homes and 5.5% were from homes with neither natural parent.

Socioeconomic status. The Valdes et al. (1990) study of the socioeconomic status of adolescents with mild disabilities also tells an interesting story. The largest percentage (34.3%) of adolescents with learning disabilities lived in families where income ranged between $12,000 and $24,999; approximately 31% were from households in which the income was less than $12,000 a year. The largest proportion (42.1%) of adolescents with all levels of mental retardation came from families that earned less than $12,000 a year. Similarly, the largest proportion (38.2%) of youth with serious emotional disturbance also originated in households earning less than $12,000 a year. Roughly two thirds (or greater) of families of an adolescent with a mild disability earned less than $24,999 a year. As has been known for some time, mild disability interacts with low family income to a great extent. Table 3.1 presents a summary of the demographic characteristics reported above related to adolescents with mild disability.

Other disability-related characteristics. Some adolescents with mild disabilities experience more than one difficulty in addition to the learning or behavior problem that made referral and eligibility for special education possible. In this section we review how many

Table 3.1

Demographic characteristics of adolescents with learning disabilities, mental retardation*, and serious emotional disturbance

Characteristic	Ranking of those with LD, MR*, and SED (highest middle lowest)
Number of adolescents identified	LD
	MR
	SED
Gender (male-female ratio)	SED
	LD
	MR
Racial makeup (white-black ratio)	LD
	SED
	MR
Home background (percentage from single-parent homes and from families with neither natural parent present)	SED
	MR
	LD
Family income (percentage who come from families who earn <$24,999/year)	MR
	SED
	LD

LD = Learning Disabled

MR = Mentally Retarded (*not all in the mild range)

SED = Seriously Emotionally Disturbed

Source: Adapted from *Sixteenth Annual Report to Congress on the Implementation of The Individuals with Disabilities Education Act* by U.S. Department of Education, 1994, Washington, DC: Author; and *The National Longitudinal Transition Study of Special Education Students. Statistical Almanac* (Vol. 1, Overview), by K. A. Valdes, C. L. Williamson, and M. M. Wagner, 1990, Menlo Park, CA: SRI International.

youth with mild disability also receive assistance or related services for other conditions besides their primary disability. By "assistance or related service" we mean speech-language therapy, occupational therapy, physical therapy, and the use of tutors, readers, or interpreters. All of these data originate with Valdes et al. (1990).

In the three groups of mild disability (keeping in mind that of those identified with mental retardation in Valdes et al., 73.8% had IQs of 51 or more, which would place them roughly in the mild range based solely on IQ), 31% of adolescents identified as learning disabled, 51% of those described as mentally retarded, and 24% of those with serious emotional disturbance were also receiving speech-language therapy. Approximately 26% of adolescents with learning disabilities, 52% of youth with mental retardation, and 27% of those with behavior disorders received occupational therapy. In terms of receiving physical therapy, the adolescents with the largest percentage were those identified as mentally retarded (19.4%), followed by youth defined as learning disabled (3.5%) and those defined as behavior disordered (3.4%). Regarding the use of a tutor, reader, or interpreter, the group labeled learning disabled had the largest proportion of adolescents using such services (35%), followed by youth with emotional disturbance (32.8%) and juveniles with mental retardation (25.8%).

Interesting findings were reported in Valdes et al. (1990) regarding the length of time that adolescents with disabilities received special services for their primary label. The largest proportions of students identified as either learning disabled, mentally retarded (not all of whom were in the mild range), or behavior disordered first received special services between the ages of 6 and 12 (learning disabled = 73.3%, mentally retarded = 53.4%, and behavior disordered = 61.1%). Over twice the proportion of youth with mental retardation (24.4%) first received special services between the ages of 3 and 5 than those with learning disabilities (8.9%) and behavior disorders (9.2%) combined. Table 3.2 presents a summary of disability-related characteristics found across the three categories of mild disability.

Table 3.2

Disability-related characteristics of adolescents identified as learning disabled, mentally retarded, and seriously emotionally disturbed

Characteristic	Ranking of those with LD, MR*, and SED (highest middle lowest)
Proportion receiving speech-language therapy	MR LD SED
Proportion receiving occupational therapy	MR SED LD
Proportion receiving physical therapy	MR LD SED
Proportion receiving a tutor, reader, or interpreter	LD SED MR
Proportion first receiving special services between ages 6–12:	LD SED MR
Ages 3–5:	MR SED LD

LD = Learning Disabled
MR = Mentally Retarded (*not all in the mild range)
SED = Seriously Emotionally Disturbed

Source: Adapted from *The National Longitudinal Transition Study of Special Education Students. Statistical Almanac* (Vol. 1, Overview), by K. A. Valdes, C. L. Williamson, and M. M. Wagner, 1990, Menlo Park, CA: SRI International.

Intellectual and Academic Traits

Before we present the various intelligence and achievement comparisons across adolescents with the three types of mild disability, a few general statements about these constructs are in order. By definition, students with mental retardation consistently have lower intelligence than those with either learning disabilities or behavior disorders. It is very common, however, for students with learning disabilities and those with behavior disorders to also have lower than average IQs (Hallahan & Kauffman, 1977). Regarding academic achievement, similitude exists across categories of mild disability in that underachievement or low achievement is also typical of those with learning disabilities, mild mental retardation, and serious emotional disturbance. Without low achievement or underachievement, many youths with mild disability would never be identified as needing special education services (see Epstein, Kinder, & Bursuck, 1989, and Kauffman, Cullinan, & Epstein, 1987, for reviews).

Interesting findings related to intelligence of only those with either mild mental retardation or learning disability were reported by Gottlieb, Alter, Gottlieb, and Wishner (1994). A limitation of the Gottlieb et al. work related to the present discussion is that only elementary-school and middle-school youth were used for examination. Nevertheless, Gottlieb et al. showed that the average IQ of students with mild mental retardation varied very little across urban and suburban school districts (54 and 55, respectively). The researchers also discovered that the "IQ band" of students with mild mental retardation in the 1960s and 1970s was probably between 55 and 85, depending on the specific study. Students who were eligible (based on IQ) to be labeled educable mentally retarded 25 years ago are no longer being called mentally retarded. Polloway and Smith (1983) mentioned this fact more than a decade before Gottlieb et al., but the issue still remains—those identified as mildly mentally retarded in the 1990s are strikingly different in intelligence from students described as such a generation ago (see also MacMillan et al., 1996).

Compare the similarity of IQ in students with mild mental retardation (i.e., urban vs. suburban) with that demonstrated by students with learning disability in urban and suburban school districts and the picture changes dramatically (urban mean IQ = 81.4, suburban mean IQ = 102.8). Gottlieb et al. (1994) concluded that poverty in urban areas, but not in suburban districts, contributed greatly to the disparity of average IQ among students with learning disabilities from differing geographic locales. Culture and race were also discussed as factors in the incongruous average IQs across urban and suburban students with learning disabilities. Roughly 95% of the students with learning disabilities in the urban school sample of Gottlieb et al. originated from a minority culture.

One of the many arguments that Gottlieb et al. were attempting to raise is that many students formerly considered as having "borderline mental retardation" (i.e., IQ between 70 and 85) are now being called learning disabled in urban areas. Only 26% of the urban students with learning disabilities in the Gottlieb et al. report had IQs of at least 90, while roughly 17% had IQs lower than 70! Intelligence assumed to be in the "normal" range of those with learning disabilities—at least in the Gottlieb et al. work—is difficult to show in urban special education programs. Less than average intelligence among adolescents with learning disabilities has also been shown frequently in other reports examining a host of factors (Bryan & Bryan, 1986, Peiper & Deshler, 1981; Sabornie, Kauffman, & Cullinan, 1990; Schumaker, Warner, Deshler, Alley, & Clark, 1981).

Those identified as seriously emotionally disturbed have also demonstrated that less than average intelligence is common to them as a group. Kauffman (1993) reviewed the literature on IQ among students with serious emotional disturbance and concluded that such students, of all ages, demonstrate intelligence in the low-average range. He also said that it is easier to find students with behavior disorders in the lower ranges of intelligence than at levels reaching above average.

The following cross-categorical comparisons of intelligence originate with Valdes et al. (1990). The highest average IQ demonstrated by adolescents with mild disabilities was shown by youths with learning disability (mean = 87.1), followed by participants with serious emotional disturbance (mean = 86.4) and those with mental retardation (mean = 60.2). Similar to what Gottlieb et al. (1994) reported, 5.6% and 10.9% of adolescents with learning disabilities and behavior disorders, respectively, had IQs in the 51 to 70 range. Roughly 45% (the largest percentage of this group) of adolescents with mild mental disability had IQs between 51 and 70. The largest percentage of adolescents with learning disabilities (59.7%) and emotional disturbance (48.7%) demonstrated IQs in the 71 to 90 range. Surprisingly, 29% of adolescents with mild mental retardation also had IQs between 71 and 90. Approximately 29% and 34% of adolescents with learning disabilities and behavior disorders, respectively, demonstrated IQs between 91 and 110, and roughly 5% of each of the two groups showed IQs above 110. The average IQ of the entire Valdes et al. (1990) population ($\underline{N}$ = 4,383) of adolescents with all types of disabilities was 79.3. As the data show and as was mentioned above, many adolescents with mild disabilities do not perform in the average range (i.e., 85–115) of intelligence.

Academically-Related Characteristics

Again, the NLTS is the preeminent source of information regarding the school experiences of adolescents with all disabilities. Beginning with the work of Valdes et al. (1990), and continued in Wagner et al. (1993; cited in U.S. Department of Education, 1994), the picture of adolescents with disabilities in secondary schools has become unequivocal. In the following paragraphs, we provide statistics and discourse on the academic profiles of adolescents with mild disabilities as reported in the NLTS.

Wagner et al. (1993) showed very interesting findings related to grade-point average (GPA) of adolescents in secondary schools. A summary of these data, presented in Table 3.3, represents NLTS findings of adolescents with disabilities who attended regular schools, and not all students received grades in some courses. From the 9th to the 12th grades, all three groups of adolescents with mild disabilities improved in GPA, but the high school academic performance of such youth is far from stellar.

The percentages of adolescents with mild disabilities who failed at least one course from the 9th through the 12 grade were also reported by Wagner et al. (1993; cited in U.S. Department of Education, 1994). More adolescents with behavior disorders consistently failed at least one course in the 9th through the 12th grades than did youth with learning disabilities. More high schoolers with learning disabilities consistently failed at least one course than did teens with mental retardation. Tenth grade was the hardest for all three types of adolescents with mild disabilities in that the highest percentage of failing at least one course occurred at that grade level. It is interesting to note that the group with the

Table 3.3

Grade-point average (GPA) of adolescents with mild disabilities

[handwritten notes:]
males
blacks
single parents
low income

[handwritten sideways notes:]
higher % of disab.
SED - most absents
MR - less absents than LD

Category	Grade Level	GPA
LD	9th	1.9
LD	10th	1.9
LD	11th	2.0
LD	12th	2.3
LD	Cumulative	2.3
MR*	9th	2.0
MR	10th	2.1
MR	11th	2.2
MR	12th	2.4
MR	Cumulative	2.4
SED	9th	1.7
SED	10th	1.7
SED	11th	1.9
SED	12th	2.1
SED	Cumulative	2.2

LD = Learning Disabled

MR = Mentally Retarded (*not all in the mild range)

SED = Seriously Emotionally Disturbed

Source: Adapted from *Sixteenth Annual Report to Congress on the Implementation of The Individuals with Disabilities Education Act* by U.S. Department of Education, 1994, Washington, DC: Author; and *Beyond the Report Card: The Multiple Dimensions of Secondary School Performance for Students with Disabilities* by M. Wagner, J. Blackorby, and K. Hebbeler, 1993, Menlo Park, CA: SRI International.

lowest intelligence of the three types of mild disability—those with mental retardation—failed at least one course at a much lower percentage than either adolescents with learning disabilities or those with behavior disorders. Perhaps teachers hold adolescents with mental retardation to a different standard in comparison to the other two types of students with mild disability. Across all types of disability, female adolescents consistently outperformed males in GPA, and fewer females than males failed at least one course from 9th to 12th grade. Identical results were also demonstrated in comparisons of white versus black adolescents with disability; whites consistently outperformed blacks.

Absenteeism from school was also compared across adolescent disability categories in Wagner et al. (1993; cited in U.S. Department of Education, 1994). The NLTS chose absenteeism from school as a measure of "engagement in the educational process" (U.S. Department of Education, 1994). The average number of days absent from 9th through 12th grade were as follows: adolescents with learning disabilities, 13.4; those with mental retardation, 11.7; and youth with serious emotional disturbance, 15.3. Perhaps there is some interaction effect of absenteeism with GPA and failing courses. Adolescents with mental retardation, not all of whom were in the mild range, failed courses at lower percentage rates, had higher GPAs, and had lower absenteeism than both the adolescents with learning disabilities and those with serious emotional disturbance. Additional findings on the absenteeism found in adolescents with behavior disorders are in Hagborg (1989).

The three categories of adolescents with mild disability were remarkably similar in the average number of academic credits earned across the four grades of high school. "Academic" course credit here means courses in English, mathematics, social science, science, and foreign language (Wagner et al., 1993, cited in U.S. Department of Education, 1994). Adolescents with learning disability earned an average of 11.9 credits, and those with behavior disorders were almost identical with 11.8 credits. Youth with mental retardation averaged 11.2 credits. The three types of adolescents with mild disability (including those who were not in the mild range of mental retardation), in comparison to all other types of disability, were three of the four lowest groups in average number of academic credits earned in high school (adolescents with multiple disabilities averaged 11.3 academic credits and were the second lowest).

The percentage of time spent in regular education academic classes shows that adolescents with learning disabilities and those with emotional disturbance spend much more time in such arrangements in high school than do youth with mental retardation. Roughly 85% of adolescents with mental retardation spend 35% or less of the high school day in regular academic courses. Among those with learning disabilities, roughly 46% spend less than 35% of their school day in academic courses, but over one half spend from 36% to more than 50% of class time in academic courses. Only 26% of adolescents with behavior disorders spend 35% or less of the high school day in academic courses, while 63.4% spend at least 36% or more of the day in academic classes.

In contrast to enrolling in academic courses in high school is the opportunity to take courses in vocational education and work experience. Regarding vocational education course-taking, Wagner et al. (1993; cited in U.S. Department of Education, 1994) found that 40% of adolescents with learning disabilities enrolled in vocational courses through the 12th grade. On the other hand, 26% percent of youth with emotional disturbance and 21% of those with mental retardation enrolled in vocational courses through 12th grade. Approximately 45% of adolescents with mental retardation enrolled in work experience while in high school; roughly 39% of students with learning disabilities and 30% with behavior disorders did the same. Table 3.4 presents a summary of some of the academic characteristics of adolescents with mild disabilities.

Postsecondary school experiences.   Valdes et al. (1990) examined issues related to postsecondary school attendance of adolescents and young adults with disabilities and showed the following: (a) of those taking any postsecondary education credits during the last year of the study, 15.6% of adolescents with learning disabilities responded affirmatively (vs. 14.8% of those with behavior disorders and 8.4% of those with mental retardation); (b) of those taking postsecondary *vocational* courses in the last year of the study, 13% of youth with emotional disturbance said yes (vs. 11% of those identified as learning disabled and 8% of those referred to as mentally retarded); (c) 15% of youth with learning disabilities had a postsecondary GPA between 3.25 and 4.0 (vs. 14% of students with behavior disorders and 12% of those with mental retardation); (d) 30% of adolescents with serious emotional disturbance had postsecondary GPAs of 1.74 or lower (vs. 29% of those with mental retardation and 21% of adolescents and young adults with learning disabilities; and (e) 64% of postsecondary students with learning disabilities had GPAs between 3.24 and 1.75 (vs. 59% of those with mental retardation and 56% of youth with behavior disorders). It appears

Table 3.4

Academic characteristics of adolescents with mild disabilities

Characteristic	Ranking of those with LD, MR*, and SED (highest middle lowest)
Percentage of students failing at least one course in high school	SED LD MR
Absenteeism (average number of days absent in high school)	SED LD MR
Academic course credit earned while in high school	LD SED MR
Percentage of time spent in academic courses in high school	SED LD MR
Percentage enrolling in vocational classes through 12th grade	LD SED MR
Percentage enrolling in work experience while in high school	MR LD SED

LD = Learning Disabled
MR = Mentally Retarded (*not all in the mild range)
SED = Seriously Emotionally Disturbed

Source: Adapted from *Sixteenth Annual Report to Congress on the Implementation of The Individuals with Disabilities Education Act* by U.S. Department of Education, 1994, Washington, DC: Author; and *Beyond the Report Card: The Multiple Dimensions of Secondary School Performance for Students with Disabilities* by M. Wagner, J. Blackorby, and K. Hebbeler, 1993, Menlo Park, CA: SRI International.

that postsecondary-level students with learning disabilities are making the transition from high school to additional educational environments more frequently and with better success than those with either mental retardation or serious emotional disturbance.

Behavioral Characteristics

Chapter 2 presented some of the negative outcomes of adolescence in terms of depression, suicide, and juvenile delinquency. In this section we discuss how these same consequences and others relate to adolescents with mild disabilities. As the reader will see, the occurrence of these problems in adolescents with mild disabilities is serious, and teachers need to be prepared to deal with such disturbances in behavior.

Depression

The literature on depression in adolescents with mild disabilities is not as voluminous as the writing and research related to depression in nondisabled populations (Maag & Behrens, 1989). The studies that exist, however, relate more to those with learning disabilities and behavior disorders than to adolescents with mild mental retardation. One would expect to find ample depression in the population of students with behavior disorders because "a general pervasive mood of unhappiness or depression" is one way in which serious emotional disturbance is defined. The following studies examined depression among students with mild disabilities.

Cullinan, Schloss, and Epstein (1987) showed that regardless of age (both preadolescents and adolescents were examined) and gender, students identified as emotionally disturbed displayed significantly more depression than did the nondisabled. Depression among the children and youth with behavior disorders in Cullinan et al. existed independently of hyperactivity, academic problems, and intellectual ability, but it was related to lack of acceptance by peers. In other words, depression was widespread in the sample of students with emotional disturbance.

An interesting comparison of depression in adolescents with behavior disorders and in those with learning disabilities was performed by Maag and Behrens (1989). In this study, age (younger vs. older adolescents) and label (learning disabled vs. emotionally disturbed) did not predict the presence of depression. Both categories and all ages of adolescents were equally affected. Gender did predict the presence of severe depression in that females with mild disabilities were up to three times more likely to demonstrate high levels of depression than males. The fact that female adolescents were more likely than males to be depressed does lend more credence to the notion that females demonstrate an *internalizing* effect to many of their conflicts with the environment.

Maag, Behrens, and DiGangi (1992) examined depression in adolescents who were nondisabled, emotionally disturbed, and learning disabled in various school placements. Again, they did not find significant differences in depression when comparing the two groups with mild disabilities. Females with both types of mild disability showed (a) more depression than did their nondisabled, same-sex counterparts, and (b) more depression than male adolescents with mild disability. Males with mild disability, however, did not show more depression than nondisabled males. Lastly, incarcerated adolescents with mild disability showed more depression than did the participants with mild disability in the public schools.

Gregg, Hoy, King, Moreland, and Jagota (1992) examined depression in college-age adolescents identified as learning disabled. Participants (n = 42) originated from an undergraduate college placement or rehabilitation setting. Gregg et al. compared anxiety and depression scores of adolescents with learning disabilities to the norm group of the *Minnesota Multiphasic Inventory-2*. Results indicated that the majority of participants in the rehabilitation center displayed more depression than would be expected in the standardization population of the instrument.

In summary, depressive tendencies are not difficult to uncover in adolescents (particularly females) with either learning disabilities or behavior disorders. The present importance of the findings regarding depression relates to ways to assist youth with such problems. In light of the relationship between depression and suicide (see Chapter

2), teachers of adolescents with mild disabilities need to intervene before depression can no longer be reversed. Interventions exist to assist adolescents with depression (Maag, 1988; Reynolds & Stark, 1987), and it seems that it is never too soon to begin to implement—rather than ignore—such treatment.

Suicide (not a lot of research)

The research regarding suicide among adolescents with mild disabilities is very scant. Our review of the available reports revealed one discussion of risk factors among those with learning disabilities (Huntington & Bender, 1993) and two studies in which adolescents with learning disabilities were mentioned. Miller (1994) is the only study that examined suicidal behavior among adolescents with and without emotional disturbance in public schools. Huntington and Bender (1993), like other authorities, attempted to draw the connection between depression and suicide in adolescence. One would expect a similar relationship to exist between depression and suicide in youth with learning disabilities who exhibit poor self-concept and achievement problems.

Research (e.g., Hayes & Sloat, 1988; Peck, 1985) examining suicide records in a post hoc manner found that adolescents with learning disabilities are represented in those who commit suicide. The magnitude of suicidal penetrance in adolescents with learning disabilities, however, is not known, and research is needed to identify how common this serious problem is in those with all types of disabilities.

Miller (1994) compared suicidal ideation and attempts of adolescents with behavior disorders ($\underline{n}$ = 71) versus 13- to 18-year-olds who were nondisabled. Participants were asked six questions dealing with suicide-related thoughts and actions from a survey of 75 items. Sample questions included "Have you ever attempted suicide?" "How often have you thought about attempting or committing suicide?" and "Why have you attempted suicide?" Miller's results indicated that 66% of the group with behavior disorders (vs. 54% of the nondisabled) thought about committing suicide at least once. Fifty-five percent of the adolescents with emotional disturbance (vs. 18% of the nondisabled) reported attempting suicide, and females in both comparison groups reported higher suicidal ideation and attempts than males. The most common reason mentioned for suicide-related behavior in both groups was hopelessness; less frequently cited rationales were feelings of anger, self-hate, parental dislike, and drug abuse.

Juvenile Delinquency

The problem of juvenile delinquency has been extensively examined among those with mild disabilities (see Keilitz & Dunivant, 1986; Morgan, 1979; and Murphy, 1986, for reviews). Research examining the prevalence rate of delinquency among youth with emotional disturbance, as one would expect, shows that delinquency is higher in those identified as such than it is among the nondisabled (Kardash & Rutherford, 1983; Prout, 1981). One problem that exists in examinations of juvenile delinquency in adolescents with behavior disorders relates to definition. Juvenile delinquency is one form of socially maladjusted behavior, and the federal definition of serious emotional disturbance in IDEA excludes those with social maladjustment. Clearly identifiable distinctions in behavior between social maladjustment and emotional disturbance have yet to be shown, but delinquent-like behavior is a well-known and long-lived characteristic of adolescents with behavior disorders.

Like those with emotional disturbance, adolescents with learning disabilities are disproportionally represented in populations identified as juvenile delinquents (Broder, Dunivant, Smith, & Sutton, 1981; Bullock & Reilly, 1979; Lenz, Warner, Alley, & Deshler, 1980; Pasternack & Lyon, 1982). Murphy (1986) reported that prevalence rates of learning disabilities in delinquent populations range from 12% to as high as 70%. Keilitz and Dunivant (1986) showed that 26% of a sample of 973 adjudicated youth were learning disabled. These authors also provided many theories linking learning disabilities to juvenile delinquency. The following are a few of the suspected reasons for the co-occurrence of learning disability and delinquency: (a) school failure (learning disability produces achievement problems that then result in delinquency); (b) susceptibility (the personalities and cognitions of those with learning disability create opportunities for them to engage in delinquency); and (c) sociodemographic characteristics (poverty and poor motivation in academic areas are strong traits in both learning disability and juvenile delinquency).

Mild mental retardation among juvenile delinquents has been reported in research, and the general findings show that sizable proportions of delinquents also function in the mild range of mental retardation (Day & Joyce, 1982; Mesinger, 1976; Prescott & Van Houten, 1982; Sylvester, 1982). Mild mental retardation in the research cited above was considered only in terms of IQ and not adaptive skills. Juvenile delinquency on its own, however, would be sufficient to document maladaptive behavior or lack of appropriate adaptive skill. It is also interesting to note that adolescents with mental retardation below the mild range (i.e., at the moderate or trainable level) are seen as not cognitively capable enough to commit crime.

Arrest status.   A very interesting and seminal study of the arrest rates of adolescents with disabilities (i.e., learning disabled, behavior disordered, mentally retarded, speech-language disabled, hearing disabled, visually disabled, orthopedic disabled, and other health disabled) is reported in Doren, Bullis, and Benz (1996). The researchers used demographic and other characteristics to predict the arrest status of adolescents with disabilities while in school and one year after leaving school in Oregon and Nevada. Doren et al. found that (a) males with disabilities were 2.37 times more likely than females to be arrested while in school, (b) adolescents with behavior disorders were 13.3 times more likely to be arrested during their school years than peers with other disabilities, and (c) adolescents with learning disabilities were 3.87 times more likely to be arrested while in school than were youths with other disabilities. While in school, students with disabilities who later dropped out were 5.86 times more likely to be arrested than were those who never dropped out, and participants who scored low on social-personal skills were 2.31 times more likely to be arrested during their school years than those who were more skilled socially.

Doren et al. (1996) also found that one year after leaving school, youth with disabilities who were arrested while in school were 4.72 times more likely to be arrested again than were those who were never arrested. Youth with behavior disorders (vs. those with other disabilities) were 16.88 times more likely to be arrested one year after leaving school. Males with disabilities were once again more likely to be arrested after leaving school than females (by a factor of 2.92), and scoring low on social-personal indices also predicted arrest status in the postschool years. Individuals who were learning disabled and completed school were 3.65 times more likely to be arrested one year after leaving school than were those with other disabilities, while dropouts with learning disabilities were 49.48 times more likely to be arrested one year postschool than nondropouts with other disabilities. The stunning results of Doren et al. point directly to the need for preventing adolescents with disabilities from dropping out of school (Zigmond, 1993), for teaching social skills (Walker, Colvin, & Ramsey, 1995; Chapter 9 of this text), and for comprehensive, long-term interventions well into secondary school for youth with learning and behavior problems (Kazdin, 1987).

Other Problem Behaviors During Adolescence

The problems of adolescents with mild disabilities are not confined to those reported above. Other inappropriate behaviors have been found among such youth, and these also deserve special mention for teachers. Chemical dependency and drug use, for example, have been examined by various researchers. Karacostas and Fisher (1993) compared chemical dependency in samples of adolescents with and without learning disabilities and found that a significantly higher proportion of youth with learning disabilities were chemically dependent. The label of learning disabled was a stronger predictor of chemical dependency than were the demographics of gender, race, family composition, and socioeconomic status. Drug use among adolescents with and without serious emotional disturbance was examined by Devlin and Elliott (1992). As expected, drug use among adolescents identified as emotionally disturbed was significantly higher than the comparison group of nondisabled youth. Heavy use of marijuana, cocaine, and hallucinogens was reported among those with behavior disorders versus youth who were nondisabled. Teachers seeking ways in which to intervene with drug users among adolescents with mild disabilities should consult Kress and Elias (1993).

Epstein, Bursuck, and Cullinan (1985), using teacher-completed *Behavior Problem Checklists,* examined the behavior problems exhibited by adolescent males and females with learning disabilities. Both groups demonstrated psychopathology related to environmental conflict and personal disturbance, and conduct problems were a significant factor that characterized both genders.

Bryan, Pearl, and Herzog (1989) assessed whether adolescents with and without learning disabilities differed on crime victimization and perpetration and other inappropriate behaviors such as taking drugs and alcohol consumption. Results indicated that male adolescents with learning disabilities were more likely than nondisabled males to steal, sell drugs, and join a gang. Male youth with learning disabilities were also more frequently involved in shoplifting, destruction of property, and using alcohol and illegal drugs.

Sabornie, Cullinan, and Epstein (1993) examined the learning, social, and personal problems among a national sample of adolescents with and without behavior disorders. Results indicated that (a) youth with emotional disturbance had more social, personal, and learning problems than nondisabled peers, and (b) males with behavior disorders had more social conflict problems than females with the same condition.

Schonert-Reichl (1993) examined empathy and other factors among adolescents with and without behavior disorders. Results indicated that youth with emotional disturbance were significantly lower in empathy (emotional responsiveness to the emotional experiences of another) and had lower-quality relationships than nondisabled peers.

In summary, many more problem behaviors are typical of adolescents with mild disabilities than are common among nondisabled teens. The key question that relates to these less-than-positive findings is the singular influence of mild disability in the presence of maladaptive behavior. Does the stigma of mild disability coerce youth into behaviors that are not likely to be reinforced by society, or is engaging in problem behavior more reinforcing than not engaging in such conduct? Perhaps research will answer this question in the not too distant future, but until then teachers should be prepared to encounter several types of problem behavior in adolescents with mild disabilities.

Summary

This chapter examined the influence of adolescence in the lives of youth with mild disabilities. In general, we showed that adolescents in the categories of learning disabled, mildly mentally retarded, and seriously emotionally disturbed are somewhat different from each other in personal, intellectual, academic, and behavioral domains, but that they also share many traits. Our discussion also highlighted the numerous problem behaviors that are more typical of those with mild disabilities than nondisabled adolescents. The reader should now have a much better understanding of why adolescence is a crucial time in the development of students with mild disabilities. Storm and stress is perhaps far too common in the lives of youth with mild disabilities.

Adolescents with mild disabilities are not impossible to teach and shape into productive adults. Yes, they have many problems in comparison to peers and on average perhaps find less enjoyment in school-related matters than nondisabled students. Teaching youth with mild disabilities, however, is in many ways more satisfying than instructing students who do not demonstrate serious developmental and cognitive obstacles. Observing teenagers with mild disabilities when they finally understand an algebra equation or unlock the mysteries of auto mechanics is a picture that is hard to match in teaching at any level. Helping students acquire the skills that will assist them well into adulthood (see Chapter 11) is also very gratifying for teachers in light of the long-term benefit that students will gain. The problems of adolescence exhibited by students with mild disabilities must not obstruct the effort that all educators should attempt in teaching such youth. Interacting with adolescents with mild disabilities will bring more than sufficient reward to the teacher who engages in wise and effective pedagogy.

References

Broder, P. K., Dunivant, N., Smith, E. C., & Sutton, L. P. (1981). Further observations on the link between learning disabilities and juvenile delinquency. *Journal of Educational Psychology, 73,* 838–850.

Bryan, T. H., & Bryan, J. H. (1986). *Understanding learning disabilities* (3rd ed.). Palo Alto, CA: Mayfield.

Bryan, T., Pearl, R., & Herzog, A. (1989). Learning disabled adolescents' vulnerability to crime: Attitudes, anxieties, experiences. *Learning Disabilities Research, 5*(1), 51–60.

Bullock, L. M., & Reilly, T. F. (1979). A descriptive profile of the adjudicated adolescent: A status report. In R. B. Rutherford & A. G. Prieto (Eds.), *Monograph in behavior disorders* (Vol. 2) (pp. 153–161). Reston, VA: Council for Children with Behavior Disorders.

Cullinan, D., & Epstein, M. H. (Eds.). (1979). *Special education for adolescents.* Upper Saddle River, NJ: Merrill/Prentice Hall.

Cullinan, D., Schloss, P. J., & Epstein, M. H. (1987). Relative prevalence and correlates of depressive characteristics among seriously emotionally disturbed and nonhandicapped students. *Behavioral Disorders, 12,* 90–98.

Day, E., & Joyce, K. (1982). Mentally retarded youth in Cuyahoga County Juvenile Court: Juvenile court work research group. In M. B. Santamour & P. S. Watson (Eds.), *The retarded offender* (pp. 141–165). New York: Praeger.

Deshler, D. D., Schumaker, J. B., Alley, G. R., Warner, M. M., & Clark, F. L. (1982). Learning disabilities in adolescent and young adult populations: Research implications. *Focus on Exceptional Children, 15*(1), 1–12.

Deshler, D. D., Warner, M. M., Schumaker, J. B., & Alley, G. R. (1983). Learning strategies intervention model: Key components and current status. In J. McKinney & L. Feagans (Eds.), *Current topics in learning disabilities* (Vol. 1) (pp. 245–283). Norwood, NJ: Ablex.

Devlin, S. D., & Elliott, R. N., Jr. (1992). Drug use patterns of adolescents with behavior disorders. *Behavioral Disorders, 17,* 264–272.

Doren, B., Bullis, M., & Benz, M. R. (1996). Predicting the arrest status of adolescents with disabilities in transition. *The Journal of Special Education, 29,* 363–380.

Edgar, E. (1987). Secondary programs in special education: Are many of them justifiable? *Exceptional Children, 53,* 555–561.

Epstein, M. H., Bursuck, W., & Cullinan, D. (1985). Patterns of behavior problems among the learning disabled: Boys aged 12–18, girls aged 6–11, and girls aged 12–18. *Learning Disability Quarterly, 8,* 123–129.

Epstein, M. H., Kinder, D., & Bursuck, B. (1989). The academic status of adolescents with behavior disorders. *Behavioral Disorders, 14,* 157–165.

Gottlieb, J., Alter, M., Gottlieb, B. W., & Wishner, J. (1994). Special education in urban America: It's not justifiable for many. *The Journal of Special Education, 27,* 453–465.

Gregg, N., Hoy, C., King, M., Moreland, C., & Jagota, M. (1992). The MMPI-2 profile of adults with learning disabilities in university and rehabilitation settings. *Journal of Learning Disabilities, 25,* 386–395.

Hagborg, W. J. (1989). A study of persistent absenteeism and severely emotionally disturbed adolescents. *Behavioral Disorders, 15,* 50–56.

Hallahan, D. P., & Kauffman, J. M. (1977). Categories, labels, behavioral characteristics: ED, LD, and EMR reconsidered. *Journal of Special Education, 11,* 139–149.

Hayes, M. L., & Sloat, R. S. (1988). Preventing suicide in learning disabled children and adolescents. *Academic Therapy, 24,* 221–230.

Huntington, D. D., & Bender, W. N. (1993). Adolescents with learning disabilities at risk? Emotional well-being, depression, suicide. *Journal of Learning Disabilities, 26,* 159–166.

Karacostas, D. D., & Fisher, G. L. (1993). Chemical dependency in students with and without learning disabilities. *Journal of Learning Disabilities, 26,* 491–495.

Kardash, C. A., & Rutherford, R. B. (1983). Meeting the special education needs of adolescents in the Arizona Department of Corrections. *Journal of Correctional Education, 34*(3), 97–98.

Kauffman, J. M. (1993). *Characteristics of children's behavior disorders* (5th ed.). Upper Saddle River, NJ: Merrill/Prentice Hall.

Kauffman, J. M., Cullinan, D., & Epstein, M. H. (1987). Characteristics of students placed in special programs for the seriously emotionally disturbed. *Behavioral Disorders, 12,* 175–184.

Kazdin, A. (1987). *Conduct disorders in childhood and adolescence.* London: Sage.

Keilitz, I., & Dunivant, N. (1986). The relationship between learning disability and juvenile delinquency: Current state of knowledge. *Remedial and Special Education, 7*(3), 18–26.

Kress, J. S., & Elias, M. J. (1993). Substance abuse prevention in special education populations: Review and recommendations. *The Journal of Special Education, 27,* 35–51.

Lenz, B. K., Warner, M. M., Alley, G. R., & Deshler, D. D. (1980). *A comparison of youths who have committed delinquent acts with learning disabled, low-achieving, and normally-achieving adolescents.* (Research Report No. 29). Lawrence: University of Kansas Institute for Research in Learning Disabilities.

Maag, J. W. (1988). Treatment of childhood and adolescent depression: Review and recommendations. In R. B. Rutherford, Jr., & J. W. Maag (Eds.), *Severe behavior disorders of children and youth* (Vol. 11) (pp. 49-63). Reston, VA: The Council for Children with Behavior Disorders.

Maag, J. W., & Behrens, J. T. (1989). Epidemiologic data on seriously emotionally disturbed and learning disabled adolescents: Reporting extreme depressive symptomatology. *Behavioral Disorders, 15,* 21–27.

Maag, J. W., Behrens, J. T., & DiGangi, S. A. (1992). Dysfunctional cognitions associated with adolescent depression: Findings across special populations. *Exceptionality, 3,* 31–47.

MacMillan, D. L., Siperstein, G. N., & Gresham, F. M. (1996). A challenge to the viability of mild mental retardation as a diagnostic category. *Exceptional Children, 62,* 356–371.

Mesinger, J. R. (1976). Juvenile delinquents: A relatively untapped population for special education professionals. *Behavioral Disorders, 2,* 22–28.

Miller, D. (1994). Suicidal behavior of adolescents with behavior disorders and their peers without disabilities. *Behavioral Disorders, 20,* 61–68.

Morgan, D. J. (1979). Prevalence and types of handicapping conditions found in juvenile corrections: A national survey. *Journal of Special Education, 13,* 283–295.

Murphy, D. (1986). The prevalence of handicapping conditions among juvenile delinquents. *Remedial and Special Education, 7*(3), 7–17.

Pasternack, R., & Lyon, R. (1982). Clinical and empirical identification of learning disabled juvenile delinquents. *Journal of Correctional Education, 33*(2), 7–13.

Peck, M. L. (1985). Crisis intervention treatment with chronically and acutely suicidal adolescents. In M. Peck, N. Farbelow, & R. Litman (Eds.), *Youth suicide* (pp. 1–33). New York: Springer-Verlag.

Peiper, E. L., & Deshler, D. D. (1981). *Analysis of cognitive abilities of learning disabled adolescents specifically in arithmetic computation.* Unpublished manuscript, University of Kansas.

Polloway, E. A., & Smith, J. D. (1983). Changes in mild mental retardation: Population, programs, and perspectives. *Exceptional Children, 50,* 149–159.

Prescott, M., & Van Houten, E. (1982). The retarded juvenile offender in New Jersey: A report on research in correctional facilities and mental retardation facilities. In M. B. Santamour & P. S. Watson (Eds.), *The retarded offender* (pp. 166–175). New York: Praeger.

Prout, H. T. (1981). The incidence of suspected exceptional education needs among youth in juvenile facilities. *Journal of Correctional Education, 32*(4), 22–24.

Reynolds, W. M., & Stark, K. D. (1987). School-based intervention strategies for the treatment of depression in children and adolescents. In S. G. Forman (Ed.), *School-based affective and social interventions* (pp. 69–88). New York: Haworth.

Sabornie, E. J., Cullinan, D., & Epstein, M. H. (1993). Patterns and correlates of learning, behavior, and emotional problems of adolescents with and without serious emotional disturbance. *Journal of Child and Family Studies, 2,* 159–175.

Sabornie, E. J., Kauffman, J. M., & Cullinan, D. A. (1990). Extended sociometric status of adolescents with mild disabilities: A cross-categorical perspective. *Exceptionality, 1,* 197–209.

Schonert-Reichl, K. A. (1993). Empathy and social relationships in adolescents with behavior disorders. *Behavioral Disorders, 18,* 189–204.

Schumaker, J. B., Warner, M. M., Deshler, D. D., Alley, G. R., & Clark, F. (1981). *An epidemiological study of LD adolescents in secondary schools.* Unpublished manuscript, University of Kansas.

Sylvester, B. T. (1982). Opportunities and barriers in interagency collaboration: Perspectives of a juvenile justice board member. In M. B. Santamour & P. S. Watson (Eds.), *The retarded offender* (pp. 491–495). New York: Praeger.

U.S. Department of Education. (1994). *Sixteenth Annual Report to Congress on the Implementation of The Individuals with Disabilities Education Act.* Washington, DC: Author.

U.S. Department of Education. (1995). *Seventeenth Annual Report to Congress on the Implementation of The Individuals with Disabilities Education Act.* Washington, DC: Author.

Valdes, K. A., Williamson, C. L., & Wagner, M. M. (1990). *The National Longitudinal Transition Study of special education students. Statistical Almanac.* (Vol. 1, Overview). Menlo Park, CA: SRI International.

Wagner, M. (1991a). *Dropouts with disabilities. What do we know? What can we do?* Menlo Park, CA: SRI International.

Wagner, M. (1991b, April). *The benefits of secondary vocational education for young people with disabilities.* Paper presented at the annual meeting of the American Educational Research Association, Chicago, IL.

Wagner, M. (1992, April). *Being female—A secondary disability? Gender differences in the transition experiences of young people with disabilities.* Paper presented at the annual meeting of the American Educational Research Association (Special Education Interest Group), San Francisco.

Wagner, M., Newman, L., D'Amico, R., Jay, E. D., Butler-Nalin, P., Marder, C., & Cox, R. (1991). *Youth with disabilities: How are they doing? The first comprehensive report from the National Longitudinal Transition Study of special education students.* Menlo Park, CA: SRI International.

Wagner, M., D'Amico, R., Marder, C., Newman, L., & Blackorby, J. (1992). *What happens next? Trends in postschool outcomes of youth with disabilities. The second comprehensive report from the National Longitudinal Transition Study of special education students.* Menlo Park, CA: SRI International.

Wagner, M., Blackorby, J., & Hebbeler, K. (1993). *Beyond the report card: The multiple dimensions of secondary school performance for students with disabilities.* Menlo Park, CA: SRI International.

Wagner, M., Blackorby, J., Cameto, R., & Newman, L. (1994). *What makes a difference? Influences on postschool outcomes of youth with disabilities.* Menlo Park, CA: SRI International.

Walker, H. M., Colvin, G., & Ramsey, E. (1995). *Antisocial behavior in school: Strategies and best practices.* Pacific Grove, CA: Brooks/Cole.

Warner, M. M., Schumaker, J. B., Alley, G. R., & Deshler, D. D. (1980). Learning disabled adolescents in the public schools: Are they different from other low-achievers? *Exceptional Education Quarterly, 1*(2), 27–56.

Zigmond, N. (1993). Rethinking secondary school programs for students with learning disabilities. In E. L. Meyen, G. A. Vergason, & R. J. Whelan (Eds.), *Challenges facing special education* (pp. 105–140). Denver, CO: Love.

4

Effective Instruction and Behavior Management Techniques

Objectives

After reading this chapter, the reader should be able to:

1. describe the many teaching behaviors known as direct instruction;
2. define behavior in observable and measurable terms;
3. describe the learning stages of acquisition, proficiency, maintenance, and generalization;
4. describe how to increase and decrease behavior in various ways;
5. assess and record student behavior in various ways;
6. describe various ways to teach self-management behavior to adolescents;
7. describe ways to teach for generalization of behavior.

The purpose of this chapter is to discuss effective instruction and classroom management procedures to be used at the secondary level with adolescents identified as mildly disabled. We believe that effective instruction at the secondary level is more science than art; that is, educators need to define behaviors in specific ways and engage in specific behaviors while teaching in order for students to acquire, maintain, and generalize the knowledge presented in instruction. Effective instruction at the secondary level for students with mild disabilities should not include a great deal of teacher lecturing, copying from the chalkboard or overhead projector, or the completion of numerous worksheets at students' desks. Moreover, secondary-level teachers should not continue to use instructional materials that were successful when the students were at the elementary level. As we have learned through many years of classroom teaching at the secondary level, adolescents are not reluctant to tell teachers that certain tasks are "baby work" or "below them." Effective teachers of adolescents with mild disabilities—in both special and regular education environments—need to be very mindful of instructional delivery that is functional, motivating, and effective all at the same time. Providing effective, motivating, and functional instruction is often easier said than done, but this chapter explains how it can be accomplished. Specifics covered in this chapter under effective instruction include direct instruction of new skills, time management, teacher feedback, and many related topics.

Teachers working with secondary-level students with mild disabilities also need to know how to structure their classrooms so that effective instruction is fostered in all lessons. The second half of the chapter discusses how teachers should arrange and manipulate instructional environments. We emphasize the need for application of behavioral techniques in classrooms so that (a) adolescents know what is expected of them while in class; (b) teachers can analyze the antecedents and consequences of behavior in the classroom; and (c) a fair, age-appropriate, and consistent approach to classroom management is evident. Topics in this chapter that pertain to classroom management are ways in which to assess and record behaviors, techniques to increase and decrease behaviors, and methods to enhance maintenance and generalization of behavior. Without knowledge and application of secondary-level effective teaching and classroom management techniques, regular and special education teachers would be left with nothing more than whimsy to assist adolescents with mild disabilities.

Effective Instruction

Effective secondary-level instruction of adolescents with mild disabilities is, we believe, more difficult than teaching such students at the elementary level. One reason for this belief is the fact that as students with mild disabilities grow older, the gap between what is expected of them and what they actually achieve becomes greater through middle school and high school. It is not uncommon, therefore, for secondary-level teachers to encounter students with mild disabilities whose academic achievement capabilities are far below what is expected in higher grade levels (Algozzine, O'Shea, Crews, & Stoddard, 1987; Gregory, Shanahan, & Walberg, 1986; Smith, Finn, & Dowdy, 1993). In light of the discrepancy between what secondary-level students with mild disabilities should achieve and what they do achieve, instruction at the secondary level must be efficient so that students can catch up. However, they will have little chance of catching up if teachers do not deliver effective instruction.

Effective instruction is defined as providing teacher direction that will allow a student to acquire, display with proficiency, maintain, and generalize the learning as quickly as possible. Effective instruction can also be viewed from John Locke's *tabula rasa* (blank slate) perspective. Students enter secondary schools with blank slates in terms of meaningful skills, and teachers fill the slates quickly and comprehensively with valuable behaviors that are important for school as well as out-of-school functioning. In other words, effective teachers at the secondary level are able to increase achievement and performance levels of students faster than other, less effective teachers.

Other characteristics typify the process of delivering effective instruction as well. Stevens and Rosenshine (1981) stated that effective instruction takes place in groups, is teacher directed and academically focused, and is individualized. They did not imply that "individualization" meant that one student works independently on tasks of his or her choice. Rather, the authors wanted individualization to mean that *each and every student* in a class succeeds, demonstrates high levels of correct responding, and gains competence and confidence in the skills taught directly by a teacher. The reader will see in the following sections all of the many teaching behaviors that are required to become an effective teacher.

Defining Behaviors

Using observable and measurable language to define behaviors is the first step in the process of becoming an effective teacher. While this step requires no actual instruction, incorrect application of defining behaviors will result in less effective, ambiguous instruction. If a teacher cannot properly define the behavior she or he is trying to have students demonstrate, how can claims of students "knowing" and "doing" what is required be made? Defining behaviors forms the foundation of effective teaching; it is required in writing behavioral objectives for lesson plans and in Individual Education Plans (IEPs), and it leads to clear communication and accountability in instruction. Another benefit accrues from defining behaviors properly: Instructional materials can be chosen correctly when there is little doubt regarding what is expected in student performance.

The essence of defining behaviors properly rests in using unambiguous terms to describe what students are to demonstrate. Terms such as *learn, know,* or *understand* do not clearly describe what a student will perform in observable and measurable terms, but countless teachers continue to use such inappropriate descriptors in lesson plans and IEPs. Appropriate terms to use in defining behaviors are those that clearly describe exactly what is expected in terms of student action. Such descriptive terms include *state or read orally, write or fill in,* and *point to with a finger.* Four essentials to an appropriate definition of behavior include statements that (a) identify the learner, (b) describe the actual behavior, (c) specify the conditions under which the behavior is to be exhibited, and (d) identify the level of satisfactory performance (Alberto & Troutman, 1995). Examples of well-written definitions of behavior follow.

[handwritten margin note: 3 things in a goal → learner (name) / the conditions / behavior / level of performance]

In Math: Ralph [the learner], after 10 minutes of instruction [the conditions], will state orally and will pour correctly [the behaviors] the proper liquid detergent amount to use to wash his white fabric clothes with 100% accuracy [the level of performance].

In Reading: Elizabeth [the learner], after 4 days of instruction of 30 minutes per day [the conditions], will read orally [the behavior] with 90% decoding accuracy [the level of performance] directions for use from various over-the-counter medicines.

In Social Skills: Jamie [the learner] will overtly display with proper body movements [the behavior], the correct way to shake someone's hand in 4 out of 5 trials [the level of performance] after 30 minutes of classroom instruction [the conditions].

All teachers, no matter the level or competence of students, should always define behaviors for instruction in the manner described above. Using such exact instructional terms while communicating to others shows that the teacher (a) believes that effective teaching is a science, (b) has a professional approach and concern for students' behavior, (c) knows precisely what is expected in terms of student responses, and (d) is accountable for instructional outcomes in the classroom. On the other hand, just because a teacher knows how to define behaviors in observable and measurable terms does not mean that what is done in the classroom is necessarily efficacious and in the long-term interests of all students. Teachers still have to deliver instruction at the students' present level of performance, choose behaviors that lead to greater independence and that are functional in various environments, and structure the learning through teaching behaviors known to positively affect student achievement. The next sections describe how to become an effective instructional change agent through the demonstration of specific behaviors while teaching.

[handwritten right margin note: point → something new or a new behavior → when students learn something new or a new behavior]

[handwritten note: You want students to: / ① Acquire knowledge / ② be good at it / ③ / ④ maintain it]

Effective Teaching Behaviors

The intent of an effectively designed and delivered instructional sequence is to have students acquire, become proficient at, generalize, and maintain the learning. **Acquisition learning** is the point at which students first learn a previously unknown behavior or piece of knowledge. This phase of learning is analogous to when a person says "A-ha!" when first being able to understand or comprehend a concept or do something correctly for the first time. **Proficiency learning,** on the other hand, is the point at which the

[handwritten note: point at which can be done without hesitation]

Can do it over + over without any additional teaching

learner demonstrates the newly learned skill without hesitation. He or she has learned the behavior and now is able to exhibit it in a fluent, nearly errorless fashion. **Maintenance** is the ability to correctly perform newly acquired tasks over long periods of time, without contingencies and without any additional teaching. Maintenance is 100% accuracy in performance, which takes place long after learning has been acquired and has become fluent. Lastly, **generalization** is the stage when a student displays a behavior without the presence of the original stimuli that were used in the acquisition phase. Many students with mild disabilities, of all ages, demonstrate a problem in the generalization of learning. Ways exist to enhance generalization of learning among adolescents (Baer, Wolf, & Risley, 1968; Bourbeau, Sowers, & Close, 1986; Dehaven, Corley, Hofeling, & Garcia, 1982; Ellis, Lenz, & Sabornie, 1987a, 1987b; Emshoff, Redd, & Davidson, 1976; Horner, Eberhard, & Sheehan, 1986; Mastropieri & Scruggs, 1984; Stokes & Baer, 1977), and teachers must be especially aware of students' ability to generalize when teaching skills that require out-of-classroom application.

Direct Instruction

Students will have little chance of developing acquisition, proficiency, generalization, and maintenance of learning with an instructor who does not know how to deliver instruction effectively. Delivering instruction is also referred to as the *process* of teaching, and it should include the teacher behaviors highlighted in the following paragraphs . The effective teaching behaviors, collectively, have been referred to as **direct instruction** (Rosenshine, 1976). Direct instruction is the presentation of a lesson with specific teaching behaviors known to positively affect student achievement—the *product* of pedagogy. As the reader will notice, many specific behaviors are required for the teaching process to be effective.

What structuring does

Structuring the lesson. Performed immediately after the teacher has gained the attention of the students, this involves telling them what will be covered during instruction, what performance goals have been set, how today's lesson relates to previous learning (if possible) and, especially with adolescents, *why* the teacher is spending time with such instruction. Lesson structuring (a) allows students to focus their attention on the specific activities, (b) prepares them for what is to follow in class, and (c) encourages them to get involved (Kindsvatter, Wilen, & Ishler, 1988). Structuring the lesson has also been referred to as *previewing* and *providing an advance organizer.*

open-ended
direct

Asking many task-related questions. In this instance, the teacher restricts questions presented to students to matters that directly relate to what is being learned. These could be open-ended queries in which a student is asked to elaborate (e.g., "Tell me why it is important to balance your checkbook regularly"), or direct questions that simply require a yes or no response. Asking teacher-directed questions serves as a check to determine whether students have indeed acquired certain types of knowledge. Moreover, Brophy and Good (1986) reported that effective teachers demonstrate an appropriate "wait time" for a response depending on the type of question asked; not surprisingly, effective teachers are also good listeners to students and their responses.

Frequent review with reteaching. Effective teachers are skilled at infusing review into daily lessons. This can take place at the beginning of an instructional sequence and become part of lesson structuring, or it can occur in the middle of the teaching sequence or at the end of the lesson. Whenever it occurs, however, it takes place daily. Effective teachers never seem to forget that material covered six months ago needs to be reviewed to ensure skill maintenance. When review shows student performance below acceptable levels, effective instructors reteach the content. Reteaching may involve the same instruction presented previously or may include different examples or stimuli to assist the students. In order to be effective, teachers need to be flexible in lesson delivery so that review and reteaching can take place as necessary. Exposing students to previously taught material is appropriate in special and regular education classes serving adolescents with mild disabilities.

Modeling, guided rehearsal, and independent practice. Effective teachers actively show or model the new behavior that students are to acquire. Modeling involves more than simply telling students how to complete a task; teachers need to demonstrate for all to see exactly how something is done correctly. This may involve showing how to complete a task at the chalkboard, on an overhead projector, at a job site, or in the community. Thinking aloud while completing a task also helps students make a cognitive connection to the behavior. The teacher should provide many examples of ways to perform a skill (if possible); nonexamples, or ways in which *not* to exhibit a behavior, should also be modeled.

Guided practice, or *leading,* involves student rehearsal while the teacher performs the same behavior along with a student or the entire class. This could be in the form of spelling a word together, solving math problems aloud, or any other functional behavior in which more than one person is performing the same task. Guided practice also involves the teacher closely supervising students' work while they perform the new behavior.

Independent practice, also known as *testing,* involves the student performing a new task without assistance. At this point in an instructional sequence the teacher closely supervises how a student can complete the behavior and at what level of accuracy. Reteaching will be necessary if supervised, independent performance is less than desired.

An instructional period of 45 minutes should have an effective teacher modeling many behaviors, leading and observing students' rehearsal, and close supervision of students' independent practice. An effective teacher, however, would spend most of the class period in modeling and leading, with a much shorter length of time spent in student independent work (Rosenshine & Stevens, 1986). Finally, effective secondary-level teachers always actively monitor students' independent practice rather than sitting at their desks. Sitting at the desk, in essence, is inappropriate behavior for a teacher seeking an effective, teacher-directed lesson.

Performance feedback with correction. When students engage in rehearsal and independent practice, an effective teacher gives much immediate feedback related to their performance. This could entail verbal praise or other types of reinforcement for correct task completion or saying "no, that's not quite right" when students err. When performance is incorrect it is imperative that teachers not hesitate to tell the pupil; this pre-

[handwritten margin note: don't give correct answer right away...]

vents the errors from becoming firmly established in the student's skill repertoire. When errors occur, instead of immediately telling the student the correct answer or overtly showing him or her how to do a task, the effective teacher gives additional hints, clues, or prompts to foster correct performance and continued task engagement. The effective teacher will reteach with additional modeling if, after additional examples are shown, student performance is still inadequate. Performance feedback should be swift and direct, but it should not break the momentum of the student's overt task performance (e.g., saying "Yes! I like the way you answered that" after each step in a multistep problem).

Lesson pace and style. Effective teachers demonstrate a specific rhythm in their instruction so that lessons proceed at a brisk pace. They are able to cover more material in less time than ineffective teachers because their lessons have a specific academic focus, little time is wasted, and they are organized and prepared to conduct the lesson as expeditiously as possible. Related to the pace of lessons is the *style* of the instruction in the classrooms of effective teachers. Large amounts of content are dissected into short lessons so that most students are able to succeed, every student has a chance to participate, few students answer questions incorrectly (which requires additional time in reteaching), and transitions between different activities in the lesson are brief and smooth. In terms of teaching adolescents with mild disabilities who have documented and severe problems in learning, one might think that teachers, in order to be effective, need to proceed very deliberately through any type of lesson. This is a myth because if teachers instruct adolescents with mild disabilities at their present levels of performance, with age-appropriate content that is functional, learning can move briskly if delivered through short lessons by effective instructors.

[handwritten margin note: "withitness" a teacher who seems to attend to everyone & everything in the class at all times]

Another aspect that typifies the style and general tone of instruction of effective teachers is something called teacher "withitness." Experts have commented on and examined this trait of effective teachers in regular and special education (Englert, 1984a, 1984b; Englert & Thomas, 1982; Kounin, 1970); it means that effective teachers seem to be able to monitor all the action in a classroom even while working with a small group of students away from the center of the classroom. Successful teachers seem to be able to attend to everyone and everything in the classroom at all times. Beyond doubt, withitness contributes to effective classroom management, low levels of disruption, and keeping students on task and achieving.

[handwritten margin note: What students learn is related to the opportunity to learn]

Ensuring high levels of student-engaged time. We feel that providing a high degree of academic engaged time (AET) while students are in classrooms is the most important effective teaching procedure. The amount that students learn in classrooms is directly related to the opportunity to learn, so if teachers spend a great deal of time teaching meaningful skills in effective ways, students will learn efficiently. Instead of having students work independently at their desks with no previous direct instruction or supervision, effective teachers spend most of a class period modeling new skills to acquire and having students practice the new behavior under supervision; they also allow time for independent performance to be checked. Another part of ensuring high levels of AET is to plan for numerous questions and response opportunities for students. Effective teachers have a businesslike attitude regarding AET in that students quickly become aware

Academic engaged Time

that time spent in the classroom will be devoted to the teaching and acquisition of new and important skills—and nothing else. To provide optimal levels of AET, effective teachers adhere to lesson schedules, do not allow students to diverge in directions unrelated to the task at hand, and prepare materials and equipment to be used in the instruction before a lesson begins.

Walker, Colvin, and Ramsey (1995) defined AET as time when each student is "appropriately engaged in working on assigned academic material that is geared to his or her ability and skill level" (p. 162). Examples of AET include (a) attending to assigned material and tasks, (b) making desired motoric responses (e.g., raising one's hand to answer a question), (c) appropriately requesting assistance from the teacher or a peer, (d) appropriately interacting with others in the learning environment about matters to be learned, and (e) listening to the teacher's directions and instructions (Walker et al., 1995).

Establishing a positive climate. Effective teachers are able to arrange their classrooms and learning activities so that a healthy, positive effect is noticeable, and students enjoy spending time with such teachers. With regard to establishing a classroom climate that is pleasant and comfortable for all students, an effective teacher engages in several specific behaviors. Kindsvatter et al. (1988) suggested the following for teachers attempting to foster a positive climate in their classrooms.

1. Help students understand that success can be reached through their efforts.
2. The teacher (and school in general) must show that they are supportive of student success.
3. Adapt learning activities and materials to fit students' abilities.
4. Provide opportunities for all students to be successful.
5. Show an interest in all students.
6. Frequently check to ensure that all students understand directions and task requirements.
7. Give effective performance feedback to all.

Good (1981) also provided teacher behaviors that do not encourage a positive climate in the classroom. Teachers wanting to be more effective in creating a positive classroom atmosphere with adolescents should not (a) seat all the "good" students in certain places in the room; (b) make eye contact only with good students; (c) call on good students more frequently than slower students; (d) punish inappropriate behavior in slower students while ignoring it in good students; (e) wait less time for a response in slower students than one would wait for good students; and (f) display only the work of good students.

We would like to add that effective teachers use frequent reinforcement of desirable student behavior (Emmer, 1988; Lloyd & Keller, 1989). Instructors who are calm, consistent, and forgiving and those with self-deprecating humor are also strong contributors to enhanced student motivation and healthy classroom conditions (Spaulding, 1992). Teachers seeking a positive classroom climate do not overemphasize, exaggerate, or make examples of students who may engage in inappropriate behavior or academic

Things an Effective Tchr should no do

underachievement in a classroom. Such teachers also do not make performance comparisons across students for the sake of showing that one pupil is better than another. In short, effective teachers convey favorable expectations of students and have a positive disposition toward all in their classrooms. Such traits go far in establishing a therapeutic psychological environment.

Summary.   The effective teaching behaviors are presented here so that secondary-level teachers will use them frequently during classroom instruction. If it is true that teachers are predisposed toward interest for students rather than toward concern for content (McNair, 1978–1979), relating to students through the use of effective teaching behaviors should be little problem for most.

One will notice that the list of effective teaching behaviors made no reference to whether the classroom teacher is special or regular education in orientation or whether the students are mildly disabled or nondisabled. The effective teaching behaviors, therefore, are equally robust regardless of classroom or teacher type. Interested readers should consult the texts of Wittrock (1986), Mastropieri and Scruggs (1987), Kameenui and Simmons (1990), and Meyen, Vergason, and Whelan (1988) for additional information related to effective teaching.

Classroom Management at the Secondary Level

Effective teachers are also very capable student-behavior managers. The literature indicates that teachers who (a) keep students engaged, (b) conduct lessons in an organized, systematic manner, (c) spend most of class time actively instructing and monitoring students' work, (d) set clear classroom rules and consistently adhere to them, and (e) create a positive climate typically experience fewer student discipline problems in classrooms (Emmer, Evertson, Clements, & Worsham, 1994; Kindsvatter et al., 1988; Walker et al., 1995; Walker & Walker, 1991). Moreover, effective classroom management can be assisted by strong leadership by the principal and by discipline practices in force in all classrooms and school environments. Figure 4.1 presents the Walker et al. (1995) suggestions for establishing schoolwide discipline procedures that can have a dramatic effect on managing all students' behavior.

The intent of the remainder of this chapter, however, is to inform the secondary-level teacher—in regular and special education classes—how to manage and manipulate the classroom environment so that appropriate and functional behavior is fostered in students. This requires the teacher to first be a good assessor and recorder of behavior and also to be able to increase and decrease certain conduct in students.

In terms of measuring and recording behavior, good teachers take good data; to be effective in classroom management of adolescents with mild disabilities, a teacher needs to know how to measure and record socially valid, acceptable, and inappropriate behaviors in students. Teachers should constantly strive to increase good behavior and decrease poor behavior in students—the essence of good teaching at any level.

As the reader will note in the following paragraphs, there are user-friendly methods of recording behavior and also some that are burdensome. Furthermore, certain

Figure 4.1
Walker et al. recommendations to establish a schoolwide discipline program

1. Use discipline as an instrument to ensure effective instruction.
2. Use positive, proactive discipline approaches in problem solving and preventing inappropriate behavior (vs. using only punitive, reactive consequences).
3. Allow for visible, teacher-supportive leadership of the principal in terms of discipline.
4. Form collegial commitments by all teachers in the school to ensure consistent, comprehensive discipline practices.
5. Make staff development and effective teacher-training practices available to all school staff.
6. All school staff should set high expectations for students' learning and social behavior.
7. Ensure clear communication between administration and staff regarding which student behaviors warrant management in the classroom—or administrative referral.
8. Establish a strong, positive school climate.
9. Foster interdisciplinary cooperation and collaboration in establishing and overseeing the schoolwide discipline program.
10. Have clear, functional rules and expectations that all students and teachers understand.
11. Be accountable in using the schoolwide discipline plan by constant data-based measurement and evaluation of its effectiveness.

Source: From *Antisocial Behavior in School: Strategies and Best Practices* by H. M. Walker, G. Colvin, and E. Ramsey. Copyright © 1995 Brooks/Cole Publishing Company, Pacific Grove, CA 93950, a division of International Thomson Publishing Inc. By permission of the publisher.

certain

behaviors lend themselves to specific ways to measure them that are better than other assessment methods. Effective teachers should strive for classroom measurement of behavior that is accurate, but as simple as possible. Having a paraprofessional in the classroom can greatly assist in the collection of behavioral data. Secondary-level teachers should consider using the following types of measurement of behavior in classroom environments.

Measuring Behavior: Direct Observation

Direct observation is the most often used method of measuring behavior. It is simple in that all a teacher has to do is observe a student or a group of students and record what is taking place. In order to observe and record accurately, however, the behavior of interest must be defined in observable and measurable terms, as discussed earlier. There are many different ways to record behavior while using direct observation in the classroom, and these are offered next.

for accuracy
clear exact
behavior that
can be
measured &
observed

Anecdotal recording. Anecdotal recording is one of the more cumbersome ways to record behavior. It requires that the teacher closely observe a target student, keep an eye on time, and be able to write (record) quickly. Anecdotal behavior recording frequently is the first method used by teachers in attempting to screen behavior before an easier, less burdensome recording technique is directed toward a specific behavior discovered through anecdotal measuring. The anecdotal record requires the teacher (recorder) to write down everything that a student does, at what time, and in what context (e.g., responding to another person's overtures), but it does not require behavior to be written in strict, observable, and measurable terms. It also helps the recorder if understandable abbreviations of students and actions can be formulated before the actual recording occurs, and a recording sheet has already been drawn for use. Figure 4.2 includes a sample anecdotal recording of a 10th grader in a basic mathematics class.

Event recording. A frequently used method of direct observation of behavior is event recording, which allows for counting how many times a target behavior occurs; it is also known as *frequency recording.* When event recording is used in reference to time, it is known as *rate recording* (e.g., 10 times per minute, 5 times per hour, etc.). Event recording is best used when a target behavior has a definite beginning and end or is a discrete behavior (Alberto & Troutman, 1995).

Teachers at all levels engage in event recording, perhaps unwittingly. When counting the number of words spelled correctly and orally, the number of correct punctuation marks in a written passage, or the number of times an adolescent talks aloud without teacher permission in a 50-minute class, teachers are using frequency recording. Event recording allows for ease of use and data collection; methods can include slash marks written on a sheet of paper in one's pocket, inexpensive hand counters also concealed in a pocket, and moving rubber bands from one finger to the next at each display of a target behavior. Event recording, however, is not suitable for measuring all types of discrete behaviors. Counting the number of words spoken by a very fast talker or the number of times a student looks out the window when the length of glance is very long (e.g., over one minute), do not lend themselves to accurate or fully explanatory behavior measurement. Recording methods that are better suited for such examples are discussed below.

Duration recording. This type of behavior measurement is used when the teacher's intent is to determine how long a behavior lasts. In the above example, if a behavior lasts for some length of time (e.g., glancing out a window), the length of time it lasts may be more telling than the number of times it occurs. The number of times a high school student frequents a school's smoking area (three times per day) is somewhat insignificant if he or she stays in the smoking area about 45 minutes each visit. Duration recording is also well suited for behaviors that have a clear beginning and end, depending on how the target behavior is defined. Because time is a factor of this type of measurement, however, the recorder needs to use a clock or a watch, which makes duration recording more tedious than event recording.

Duration recording of behavior can be presented in two forms—average or total. Average duration requires the teacher to measure the length of time of the target behav-

Figure 4.2

Sample anecdotal record

Time: Date: 1/5	Actions, Activities, Behaviors Observed Target Student: Ralph
10 AM	R is looking out []; T tells ss to get bks out.
10:01	R looks under dsk & gets bk & ntbk; T begins w/ rev of hmwrk; R looks out [] while T talks.
10:02	T calls R for hmwrk answ #2; R asks T, "what prblm?" T says, "pay attention, R"; R says, "I am"; T tells R prblm #2; R says, "I didn't do #2"; T asks R, "did you do any prblms, R?"
10:03	R doesn't respond, looks out []; T repeats qu; R says (loudly), "no"; T calls E for #2 answ; R looks out [].
10:04–10:10	T calls on ss for hmwrk answs to all prblms; R looks out [] & taps pen on dsk.
10:11	R talks to J; J laughs; R laughs; T says, "pay attention, R & J"; R keeps talking to J.
10:12–10:20	T explains p. 213 to ss @ chlkbrd, doing many examples, asking many qus of many ss; R looks @ bk while T explains; glances briefly @ T @ chlkbrd 4X.
10:21–10:25	R writes in ntbk while other ss watch T @ chlkbrd.
10:26–10:35	T says to ss to do prbls 10–15 while T walks around rm & monitors ss wrk; R keeps writing in ntbk; T ignores R; R stops writing & taps on leg w/ pen while looking out [].
10:36	T tells R to go to main offc & wait til end of prd (10:50); R leaves rm.

Legend:

R = Ralph	rev = review	@ = at
[] = window	hmwrk = homework	chlkbrd = chalkboard
T = teacher	answ = answer	4X = 4 times
ss = students	# = number	rm = room
bk = book	prblm = problem	wrk = work
dsk = desk	qu = question	til = until
ntbk = notebook	E = Ellen	prd = period
w/ = with	J = Jim	offc = office

ior several times, and then average the time over the observation sessions (e.g., average per week, with five sessions per week). Total duration is easy to understand—all one does is add the duration each time the behavior occurs to get a sum for a given time period. Engaging in task-related independent seatwork in a 50-minute period, for example, would require the teacher to record the length of time of each occurrence of the target behavior (e.g., 5 min., 7 min., 3 min., and 12 min.) and then add those segments to obtain total time for the period (i.e., in this example 27 min.).

Time is an issue too.

doesn't give exact # of times behaviors occur

Latency recording. Latency recording is much like duration recording in that time is also an issue. In latency recording, however, the teacher assesses how long a student delays before actually engaging in a requested behavior. Latency recording would be appropriate in a classroom when a teacher asks a student to begin a written test. The teacher would begin timing at the end of the verbal request and complete timing when the student actually begins to work on the test. Another common classroom example in which a teacher would use latency recording is timing how long it takes a student or a class to be ready to work after a class period bell has rung. Latency recording, as the reader will note, requires some diligence on the part of the teacher timing a target student who is unresponsive. Like duration recording, latency recording can be calculated into average or total latency, depending on the needs of the teacher.

Interval recording. Another type of direct examination of overt behavior that requires some diligence on the part of the teacher is interval recording. In this method, the teacher selects a segment of time for observation (e.g., 15 min.), but the session is divided into smaller, but equal, time intervals. In *partial interval* recording, the teacher records the presence or absence of a target behavior if the student displays it at any time during an interval (e.g., 10 sec.), even if it does not last for the entire 10-second time span (e.g., 1 sec.). Even if the target behavior occurs more than once during the 10 seconds, only one notation is recorded for the interval. For this reason, partial interval recording does not give an exact number of times a behavior occurs during a set observation period; it provides only an estimate. A special recording sheet, on which each interval is separated from others, needs to be prepared by the teacher before observation is to begin. Teachers usually record a + (plus sign) or an *x* if the target behavior was evident during the interval, and a – (minus sign) or a zero if the target behavior was not observed during the interval.

When using *whole interval* recording, the teacher records the presence of a target behavior if, and only if, it lasts for an entire interval. For example, if an observation interval is 10 seconds long, and the target behavior (e.g., talking to peers without teacher permission) lasts for only 8 seconds of the 10-second period, the teacher does not record that the target behavior was evident during that specific interval. Whole interval, therefore, also provides only an estimate of the number of times a target behavior occurs. What is often reported in the literature when whole or partial interval recording is used is a percentage of total intervals (e.g., over a 15-min. session) that the target behavior was observed. Because of the very close attention required by the teacher when using partial or whole interval recording, these techniques may not be the first ones chosen for observation. Interval recording methods work well if the target behavior is continuous (e.g., out-of-seat behavior that lasts for more than a few seconds) or if a behavior occurs with such frequency (e.g., rapidly tapping a pencil on a desk) that obtaining an exact number would be almost impossible.

A third method of interval recording that teachers may want to consider in direct observation is *time sampling* (also known as *momentary* time sampling). In this technique an observation period of 30 minutes would be split into 15 equal 2-minute intervals. The teacher teaches and conducts the class as usual, but at the end of each 2-minute segment, he or she looks at a student to determine whether the target behavior was occurring only at that time. He or she would then mark the recording sheet to indicate whether the behavior was demonstrated. The teacher could be cued to the end of a 2-minute interval by some external device such as beeps on a previously prepared audiotape. As with the other types of interval recording, time sampling provides an estimate of the number of times a target behavior occurs; it is, however, much more teacher-friendly than partial or whole interval recording, and it works well with continuous—rather than discrete—behaviors. Interested readers should consult Powell, Martindale, Kulp, Martindale, and Bauman (1977) for an in-depth discussion of the nuances of time sampling measurement.

Permanent product recording. Permanent products are probably the most often used method of behavioral recording by teachers at any level. Whenever a teacher checks a written English test, an algebra worksheet, or the result of a physics experiment, he or she is engaged in the recording of permanent products. Videotaping or audiotaping behavior also provides a permanent product of students' action. Permanent products involve the inspection of the *results* or residual effects of an action, rather than the here-and-now presence or absence of a target behavior. Using permanent products furnishes a convenient, tangible, and very accurate record of behavior for teachers.

Reliability of observation. An important question that teachers need to contemplate in observing and recording behavior is "How accurate are my observations of a student's behavior?" Answering this question involves considerations of *reliability,* or *interobserver agreement.* Reliability is a measurement of how two or more people simultaneously recording the same behavior agree or disagree. Sometimes teachers make mistakes, and checking for reliability allows them to draw cogent conclusions from the data they have collected. The easiest way to check for reliability is to occasionally have another person observe and record behavior of a target student simultaneously with the teacher, using the exact same recording system as the teacher. This can be readily seen in applied behavior analysis research, where high interobserver agreement is a *sine qua non* of any published study.

Second observers who observe, record, and check the accuracy of a teacher's recording of behavior need to be aware of specific factors in order for the reliability check to be satisfactory. They need to know the observable and measurable definition of the target behavior to measure, they need to be familiar with the recording system in use, and they need to be objective and trustworthy in their assessment. Teachers, therefore, may need to train second observers before reliability is calculated for an observation session. While in the process of collecting observational data the teacher and second observer should not be in close physical proximity; this prevents each observer from seeing what the other person is marking on a recording sheet. The more complex the recording system, the more likely it is for reliability to be less than desirable.

A few ways exist to calculate interobserver agreement of a behavioral recording system (Birkimer & Brown, 1979; Harris & Lahey, 1978; Hartmann, 1977; Kazdin, 1977). For duration and latency recording, the usual method is to divide the shorter interval of time (i.e., collected by either recorder) by the longer length of time of the target behavior (also collected by either observer), and multiply this quotient by 100 to obtain the percentage of agreement for a session. In terms of calculating reliability for interval recording or permanent product methods, a *point-by-point* procedure is recommended. This involves checking each interval (or example or written response) for agreement or disagreement (of the presence or absence of the target behavior) between the two observers. The number of agreements found is then divided by the number of agreements plus the number of disagreements, and the quotient is multiplied by 100 to produce a percentage agreement datum. Any percentage of agreement above 80% is satisfactory for classroom situations but, plainly, the closer to 100% the interobserver agreement, the more one can conclude from the data.

A teacher may need additional guidance in terms of selecting the correct measurement system for a given target behavior. Alberto and Troutman (1995) provided the following questions to use when attempting to decide on a system to record classroom behavior:

1. Is the target behavior numerical or temporal?
2. If it is numerical,
   a. Is the behavior discrete or continuous?
   b. Is the behavior expected to occur at a high, moderate, or low frequency?
   c. Will I be able to collect data during intervention/instruction, or will I need a third party to collect the data so as not to interrupt instruction?
3. If it is temporal, do I want to measure the time before initiation of the response or time elapsed during performance of the response? (p. 133)

Increasing Behaviors in the Classroom

A teacher at the secondary level serving adolescents with mild disabilities wants his or her pupils to regularly display appropriate and correct responses in many different environments—in and out of school. Sometimes this is easier said than done, particularly in light of the many troublesome characteristics that are typical of pupils with mild disabilities, who may not respond appropriately to stimuli in their environment because they have not learned that pleasing consequences will follow if a specific response is demonstrated. This is the essence of increasing behavior in people; once someone learns that something good will result if a particular behavior is exhibited, he or she is likely to display the same behavior again. *Reinforcement,* in general, is a pleasant result given as a reward to someone who has displayed appropriate behavior. Behavior, in this instance, could be academic in constitution or an overt response of any nonacademic nature. The contingent presentation of a stimulus following a response that increases the future demonstration of the response is known as *positive reinforcement.* We believe that using positive reinforcement is the best way to increase the rate or degree of execution of a worthwhile behavior in any environment, and the following discussion provides teachers at the secondary level with advice on how to use it with any number of students.

Primary and secondary reinforcement.   Primary reinforcers satisfy a person's biological or physical needs. Examples include edibles that bring pleasure to a person and stimuli that appeal to the senses (e.g., the smell of fresh roses). The most famous primary reinforcer that is cited by those who oppose positive reinforcement is M & M candy.

Secondary reinforcers have no physical or biological attraction to the person who receives them, but they can be exchanged for other reinforcement. Tokens that can be exchanged for desirable objects and money (the most obvious) are examples of secondary reinforcers. The tokens and colored paper money are, fundamentally, not reinforcing. They become reinforcing, however, once a person learns that they can be exchanged for many things that are very reinforcing. When someone learns that stimuli can be exchanged for other valuables, he or she has been conditioned to the worth of the otherwise neutral objects. Hence, secondary reinforcers are frequently referred to as *conditioned reinforcers*.

We do not espouse the use of primary reinforcers for secondary-level students with mild disabilities, although many of them find soft drinks, pizza, and fast-food hamburgers much to their liking. Having the financial resources to buy many of such items on a regular basis for students, however, may be beyond the grasp of many teachers. Furthermore, use of primary reinforcers is often associated with students at the elementary level and may seem age-inappropriate for adolescents. If a teacher wishes to use primary reinforcers with adolescents with mild disabilities, we recommend that he or she pair edibles with social praise (see the following paragraph), and then gradually fade the edibles until only praise is used to maintain the behavior. Teachers should always move toward the use of natural reinforcers that are commonly used in an environment and not rely solely on contrived, artificial means long after they are necessary.

Social reinforcement. Social reinforcers are by far the easiest for secondary-level teachers to administer to students following appropriate behavior. Smiles, verbal praise, a pat on the back, and giving a thumbs-up gesture to a student after a correct response are all examples of social reinforcement. A consistent application of this type of reinforcement is typical of effective teachers. Teachers should also be aware that the presentation of any type of reinforcement—social or otherwise—should immediately follow the appropriate response and should be specifically directed toward the response (e.g., "I really like the way you corrected your algebra answer here, Ralph"). Nonspecific, generic praise serves only to confuse the student and to make him or her wonder why the teacher is being nice at that moment. Moreover, particularly with adolescents, teachers need to be sincere and not patronizing toward the student receiving the praise. Adolescents can readily uncover a phony, so try to be very convincing when delivering social reinforcement.

Activity reinforcement. Another type of positive reinforcement that is recommended for use by secondary-level teachers serving adolescents with mild disabilities is activity reinforcement. Free time, time at a classroom computer, going to the school library to read contemporary magazines, or having time to listen to music with headphones in the class are all examples of activity reinforcers. To determine which activity reinforcers students are likely to find desirable, teachers should provide a "menu" of possible activities and allow the students to choose for themselves. Teachers should remember that things that are attractive to them as adults are not necessarily reinforcing to adolescents.

Negative reinforcement. Negative reinforcement is a confusing concept to teachers first exposed to behavioral techniques in the classroom. Negative reinforcement is not punishment; when used properly, it increases the likelihood of future occurrences of a behavior. It is the contingent removal of an aversive stimulus following a response that results in an increase in performing that response. Use of the word *reinforcement* in the title should signal that even though negative reinforcement *is* negative, a behavior will increase when negative reinforcement is used immediately following or concurrent with a certain, desired response. A common, everyday example of negative reinforcement in application is when a person turns the ignition key of a car and hears a beeping, buzzing, or ringing sound, which is meant to be aversive to the driver. Once he or she buckles the seatbelt and shoulder harness, the aversive sound is extinguished, and buckling up is reinforced. Often a driver will buckle up before engaging the ignition and thus escape the possibility of hearing the annoying noise.

is not punishment

A classroom example of negative reinforcement follows:

> Elizabeth, a very capable 8th-grade student, does not complete her independent seatwork in 4th-period world history class when Ralph, her archenemy, sits directly behind her. The close physical proximity of Ralph is sufficient reason to give Elizabeth a case of the "uncooperatives." The teacher has tried many types of positive reinforcement for even the smallest portion of independent seatwork completed by Elizabeth (while Ralph is behind her), with little success. After asking Elizabeth about the source of her incomplete seatwork, the teacher learned that she and Ralph were not the best of friends. The teacher removed the aversive stimulus to Elizabeth by moving her desk as far away from Ralph as possible the next day at the beginning of 4th period. Elizabeth completed all her independent seatwork with very high accuracy for the remainder of the year after the new seating arrangement was implemented. By removing Ralph from the proximal environment of Elizabeth, the target behavior (complete and reasonably accurate independent seatwork) was negatively reinforced.

Negative reinforcement often produces escape or avoidance behavior in a target student. In the above example, Elizabeth surely wanted to escape from sitting in front of Ralph. We feel teachers should limit the amount of aversive stimuli that are present in a classroom (i.e., try to create a very positive climate) and therefore have limited opportunities to use negative reinforcement.

Schedules of reinforcement. Knowing the nuances of using different types of positive reinforcement is insufficient because teachers also need to be aware of a schedule on which reinforcement is delivered. *Continuous reinforcement* should be the schedule of choice during instruction of a new behavior or skill (i.e., while in acquisition learning). A teacher uses continuous reinforcement when a reinforcer is delivered to a student each time he or she exhibits the single desired response or engages in the new behavior for the desired length of time. Reinforcement should also be given to a student learning a new behavior when he or she displays some, but not all, of the steps required to fully perform the new behavior. Reinforcing incomplete exhibitions of all the steps in a task is called reinforcing *successive approximations,* or *shaping* a behavior.

Intermittent schedules of reinforcement should be applied after a student acquires a new skill and the teacher is interested in proficiency and maintenance learning. During intermittent reinforcement the teacher does not deliver reinforcement to a student after each display of the new skill, but after a certain number of times the behavior is shown or after a certain length of time. The beauty of intermittent reinforcement lies in its strength to prevent the extinction of the newly learned skill. ✳

Ratio schedules of reinforcement involve the presentation of positive reinforcement after a certain number of times a behavior is displayed by the target student. A fixed-ratio (FR) schedule requires the reinforcer to be given after a predetermined number of exhibitions of the behavior (e.g., after every five correct math problems on a worksheet, abbreviated FR5). A variable-ratio (VR) schedule of reinforcement is characterized by the delivery of reinforcement after a predetermined average number of desired responses (e.g., after an average of every 10 correct assembly completions, abbreviated VR10). In a VR schedule, reinforcement is given after a variable number of responses that always average to a specified count. Fixed- and variable-ratio schedules of reinforcement are effective in achieving fluency and maintaining a behavior because the student does not know exactly when the reinforcement will be delivered, so he or she continues to engage in the desired response.

Interval schedules of reinforcement require a time period to elapse before a positive consequence is delivered. In a fixed-interval (FI) schedule a student is reinforced the first time the desired behavior is exhibited after a predetermined length of time (e.g., a student is reinforced the first time the desired behavior is demonstrated after a 3-minute interval, abbreviated FI3). In a variable-interval (VI) schedule the time periods after which reinforcement of a behavior is delivered vary, but average to an a priori term (e.g., after an average of 7 minutes, abbreviated VI7). Again, the number of minutes after which reinforcement of a response is delivered changes in a VI system, but averages to a set period. Student demonstration of the target response in variable- and fixed-interval schedules is maintained at high levels due to the unpredictability of the time when positive consequences will be received.

Contingency contracting. Contingency contracting is used when a teacher and a student make a written agreement that reinforcement will be provided contingent on some desired behavior. In other words, the teacher and the adolescent sign a contract that specifies the conditions under which the pupil will be reinforced, at what criterion level, for how long, and in what environments. Contracts also typically include aversive consequences that will result if the student breaks the agreement. The contract should also specify what the teacher will do if certain student behaviors are in evidence. The common vernacular used in contingency contracts is "The teacher will . . . if the student does . . . . " Interested readers who wish to learn more about the specifics of contingency contracts should consult the now-classic text on this matter by Homme, Csanyi, Gonzales, and Rechs (1969), who recommend the following in constructing contingency contracting in classrooms.

1. Contracts should allow for reinforcement to be delivered for successive approximations toward overall target behaviors.

2. To enhance the strength of the contract, reinforcement should be delivered in frequent, small amounts rather than large rewards given infrequently.

3. Do not use noncontingent reinforcement; reward the student only after desired behaviors are demonstrated.

4. The contract should be fair, brief, and written in clear, positive terms. The student should be able to paraphrase in his or her own words the terms of the contract.

5. Be consistent in applying the terms of the contract.

A few general, closing comments are needed here regarding the use of reinforcement in secondary-level classrooms serving adolescents with mild disabilities. Teachers should always plan to fade the use of reinforcement, called *thinning,* as soon as possible. Thinning of reinforcement requires that at some later time the students' behavior will be maintained with naturally occurring reinforcers that are delivered without a schedule. Students should never become so dependent on reinforcement that they will do nothing unless a reinforcer is attached to every functional behavior. Unlike what is said in criticism of behaviorism in the classroom, behaviorist teachers see no reason to continue to use any kind of reinforcement if it is no longer necessary. Teachers espousing behaviorism use reinforcement to change behavior in the desired direction as quickly as possible. No teacher wants a student to be overly dependent on reinforcement. At the secondary level, a student who is too dependent on reinforcement will, perhaps, have some difficulty becoming independent as an adult. Secondary-level education of adolescents with mild disabilities should do everything in its power to ensure that such pupils are as independent as possible while in school and beyond.

Decreasing Behaviors in the Classroom

There would no doubt be far less burnout if teachers did not have to deal with the inappropriate behaviors that students demonstrate in school. Student behavior has become so extreme and violent that is not uncommon to find (a) police officers assigned full-time to middle schools and high schools, (b) metal detectors at school doors for all students to pass through at the beginning of each school day, and (c) student-to-student and student-to-teacher combat with guns and knives on school grounds. The scope of this chapter does not allow for extensive discussion of the prevention of school atrocities such as those involving weapons (see Walker et al., 1995), but we discuss how secondary-level teachers can effectively decrease inappropriate behavior that is classroom-based and essentially nonviolent. Effective teachers know how to efficiently increase *and decrease* behavior in students. Reinforcement, for example, can also be used to decrease inappropriate behavior when used in very specific ways. The sections below provide teachers with ways to eliminate those pesky, classroom-based inappropriate behaviors in adolescents with mild disabilities.

Differential reinforcement techniques.   The first strategies that secondary-level teachers should apply to decrease students' inappropriate behavior fall under the rubric of differential reinforcement. **Differential reinforcement of other behavior (DRO)** is reinforcement delivered to a student for a certain length of time in which a target inappropriate behavior was not exhibited. Take Ralph, for example, who constantly talks out without teacher permission. If DRO were used, the teacher would reinforce Ralph for not talking out for some length of time. The length of time would be short to begin this intervention and gradually lengthen until Ralph's talking out is eliminated or at least at a level that is not so annoying and distracting to others in the classroom. In this example, the "other" behavior that is reinforced is silence.

Differential reinforcement of incompatible behavior (DRI) occurs when a teacher reinforces a student for engaging in a behavior that is physically impossible (or incompatible) to perform while exhibiting the inappropriate behavior that the teacher wants to eliminate. A teacher wants Elizabeth not to yell her oral responses to questions. Whenever Elizabeth speaks softly or at a normal decibel level to answer a teacher-directed question the teacher provides positive reinforcement. Speaking normally is physically incompatible with yelling an answer.

Differential reinforcement of alternative behavior (DRA) is similar to DRI. With DRA, however, the teacher reinforces other behaviors than the inappropriate response, but the other behaviors need not be incompatible with the conduct to be eliminated. If a teacher wants to eliminate Elizabeth's incessant pencil-tapping on her desk, he or she would use DRA, reinforcing her for doing anything else appropriate besides pencil-tapping—regardless of whether the alternative behavior is incompatible with tapping a pencil.

Differential reinforcement of low rates of behavior (DRL) is the delivery of reinforcement whenever a student's rate or duration of responding is below a level determined to be appropriate by the teacher. The intent of DRL is not to completely eliminate the behavior but to have the student demonstrate it at a much lower level than ordinarily. Ralph has a problem with his desire to sharpen his pencil constantly during science class (i.e., average number of times per period = 8). While completely eliminating the opportunity to sharpen a pencil is not desirable, the teacher believes that Ralph could function well enough with only one or two opportunities per period. The teacher would first reinforce Ralph if he sharpened his pencil fewer than six times per period (for one week), then fewer than five times per period, and so on, until Ralph does it only once per class session. The same technique would apply if a student engages in a behavior far too long (e.g., time spent in the bathroom) and the teacher wants to shorten, but not eliminate, the duration.

Vicarious reinforcement. Although not a differential reinforcement technique, **vicarious reinforcement,** applied correctly, can also decrease inappropriate behavior. Vicarious reinforcement involves the ignoring of a student's inappropriate behavior while reinforcing other students not engaging in poor behavior in close proximity to the misbehaver. For example, in first-period English class Ralph is laughing at and teasing Elizabeth. Instead of scolding Ralph, the teacher ignores him and says to Bill, seated next to Ralph, "Bill, I really appreciate that you're paying attention right now, and that you're not ridiculing Elizabeth. You can have five minutes of free time to listen to music at the end of the period." Ralph should get the message and stop bothering Elizabeth if he, too, would like similar reinforcement. Vicarious reinforcement is a powerful tool in the hands of a skilled teacher who applies it correctly. It eliminates the need to scold a misbehaving student and contributes to maintaining a positive classroom environment.

Extinction.   Behavior can also be eliminated with other means. **Extinction,** which is the systematic removal of reinforcement that maintains an inappropriate behavior, can also decrease behavior. Extinction should be the next intervention to use if differential or vicarious reinforcement is not successful. One of the most powerful reinforcers in the classroom is teacher attention. Some adolescents will misbehave for the sole purpose of attracting comments by the teacher. When the teacher eliminates attention and ignores inappropriate behaviors that are not physically dangerous to anyone in the class, he or she is using extinction. A teacher attempting to implement extinction by ignoring should use it consistently and have patience. Students are likely to increase their rate or duration of inappropriate behavior just to test the teacher's resolve with the new approach. We recommend that teachers pair extinction procedures with reinforcement of appropriate classroom behavior for best results.

Presentation of aversive consequences.   After systematically attempting differential and vicarious reinforcement and then extinction procedures with little success in decreasing inappropriate behavior, the teacher is left with aversive consequences to use very carefully. We cannot overemphasize the need to exhaust all positive means to eliminate inappropriate behavior *before* turning to punishment techniques. **Punishment** is the contingent presentation of an undesirable (aversive) stimulus immediately following a behavior that decreases the future occurrence of the behavior. Aversives applied to students with disabilities to eliminate inappropriate behavior have been debated (McGinnis, Scott-Miller, Neel, & Smith, 1985) and will continue to be controversial. Punishment techniques are powerful tools in decreasing or eliminating inappropriate behavior when used as a last resort and with informed parental consent. Teachers also need to be reminded that punishment will have a robust effect when positive reinforcement continues to be available to students who deserve it. Just because a teacher applies aversive consequences to inappropriate behavior of one student does not mean that the use of positive reinforcement must be stopped with others in the classroom. Reinforcement and punishment should always be used together.

Removing desirables and privileges.   One of the least intrusive means of applying unwanted consequences to consistent inappropriate behavior is through **response cost,** the contingent removal of already gained reinforcement following inappropriate behavior. Teachers use response cost when they remove tokens from students or when they withhold computer time from someone who seriously misbehaves after earning the right to the computer. Teachers should make it clear to students when response cost will be used subsequent to specific rule-breaking behavior; it is wise to do this when first establishing rules in the beginning of the school year and later with periodic reminders.

   Overcorrection is another technique used to eliminate misbehavior. There are two types of overcorrection. *Positive practice overcorrection* requires the student to publicly perform the correct form of the misbehavior numerous times. The intent is to shame the student into never wanting to engage in similar misbehavior in the future. Ralph, for example, has a tendency to enter the morning homeroom period late and to slam the door loudly behind him. After a warning, the next time Ralph slams the door the teacher tells him he must open and close the door appropriately 10 times or face stiffer and more aversive consequences (e.g., a stay in in-school suspension). Ralph then rehearses entering the classroom by opening and closing the door correctly 10 times and never shuts the door loudly again.

Restitutional overcorrection involves a student restoring an environment that he or she has disrupted or soiled. The misbehaving student must restore the environment to the state it was before he or she disturbed it and correct the disruptions of others too. An example would be when Elizabeth throws a crumpled piece of paper across the room toward a wastebasket and misses her target. After a warning from the teacher, the next time Elizabeth throws and misses her mark she must pick up not only her piece of paper, but all the other pieces of paper lying on the floor in the classroom. The intent of restitutional overcorrection in this example is to prevent Elizabeth from attempting to throw her paper long distances in the future.

Time-out. One of the most controversial and dangerous punishment contingencies ever used in classrooms is time-out. *Time-out from positive reinforcement* denies a student the opportunity to receive desirable consequences for appropriate behavior. Using time-out is dangerous because of the possibility of excluding students from needed instruction; in addition, it may become reinforcing to a teacher (i.e., an "aversive"—the misbehaving student—is removed, thereby making the teacher feel better).

Three general types of time-out exist (Harris, 1985). A teacher contemplating the use of time-out should follow the doctrine of least intrusiveness and first try **nonexclusionary time-out.** This involves keeping the adolescent in the classroom, ignoring him or her, and denying access to reinforcers for a short period of time. The student is able to observe what is taking place in the class, but is unable to participate and receive desirables.

The next more intrusive method is **exclusionary time-out,** which requires that the offending student be removed from the classroom environment by, for example, standing outside the door in the hallway. Teachers have sent students to the hall for decades, perhaps not realizing that they were using exclusionary time-out.

The most intrusive form of time-out is **seclusionary time-out,** in which the student is removed from the classroom and placed in a special room devoted solely to isolating misbehaving students. (The senior author was once a hearing officer for a Public Law 94-142 due process hearing involving a disagreement over placement between a mother and a school district. Testimony in the case uncovered that a 13-year-old boy identified as behaviorally-emotionally disabled was often kept in seclusionary time-out for periods of up to three hours. The regular classroom teacher using the procedure did not refer to it as seclusionary time-out. She called it the BMA—behavior modification area.)

Any teacher using time-out of any type must be aware of important aspects. First, it is wise to obtain informed parental consent for its use. Some parents may object to having their child in such an arrangement, and a teacher may risk aversive consequences in implementing time-out against parents' will. Second, time-out is doomed to failure if the normal routine of the classroom is not reinforcing to the student. Removing a student from a nonreinforcing classroom environment may actually be desirable, particularly if the student standing in the hall can socialize with other adolescents walking by. A third issue concerns the amount of time spent in time-out. There are no set rules for the length of time removed from reinforcement, but it certainly should not last very long.

We suggest a *maximum* time period that is equal to one minute of time-out for each year of age of the student. Fourth, a seclusionary time-out room should be (a) of adequate size, (b) well ventilated, (c) void of objects that may prove dangerous to an aggressive student, and (d) within easy access of the teacher or someone else to monitor the student. Finally, the student should not be able to argue with the teacher over being placed in time-out. The teacher should implement it in a swift and professional way without making personal or derogatory comments. If the student resists, the teacher should remove additional highly desirable privileges.

Teachers should also take note of the efficacy of time-out for a student. If, after some short length of time-out, a misbehaving student continues with the same inappropriate behavior, the time-out punishment was not effective and other aversive consequences should be pursued. Because of the danger of misuse, we recommend that secondary-level teachers be extremely careful when using any type of time-out.

Self-Management of Behavior and Generalization Techniques with Adolescents

A successful secondary-level teacher should be able to master most, if not all, of the teaching and classroom management suggestions presented in this chapter. Other issues and concerns endemic to secondary-level students with mild disabilities, however, must be kept in mind to be effective. The two most important additional instructional and behavioral issues that teachers need to consider are (a) how a student can manage his or her own behavior without external supervision, and (b) how instruction can enhance generalization of needed skills. We will discuss ways to instruct for self-management of behavior and generalization in the following sections.

Self-management techniques. Kazdin (1975) defined **self-management** as behaviors that an individual selects to achieve personal goals and outcomes. In other words, someone engaging in self-management has a personal objective to be achieved and he or she engages in self-discipline in order to reach the desired outcome. This may involve self-assessment and recording of behavior, determinations of whether intermediate objectives have been met, and self-administration of reinforcement when the goal is reached. Dieting and exercising to reduce weight are common examples of people engaging in self-management. In schools, when students write what homework assignments are to be completed that night they are engaging in a form of self-management. The goal of self-management is to remove the need for and influence of an external stimulus (e.g., the teacher, a parent, or some other overseer) so that the person performs appropriate behavior independently and without supervision. Wouldn't it be great if adolescents could manage all aspects of their behavior?

There is ample evidence to suggest that students with mild disabilities are very capable of learning how to self-regulate their behavior (Lloyd, Landrum, & Hallahan, 1991). Self-control interventions have been used to increase math productivity, attention to task, accuracy of work, social skills, and appropriate classroom behavior, and to decrease disruptive behavior in school (Lloyd et al., 1991). The robust power of self-recording and self-management of behavior lies in *reactivity to measurement,* which is when the person becomes very aware of his or her behavior simply by measuring it. A person who becomes aware of the problematic dimensions of his or her own behavior is more likely to change it. Schloss and Smith (1994) provided many advantages of self-management of behavior, including that it is (a) inexpensive and ethical, (b) ideally suited to promote generalization, and (c) effective in increasing independence in students.

Numerous strategies exist for teachers to use in implementing self-management of behavior. Wolery, Bailey, and Sugai (1988) provided research-based guidelines to consider when teaching self-management (see Figure 4.3). Teaching students to self-manage their own behavior may not make the job of teaching easier, but, if successful, it will make the students more independent to face the challenges of the world outside school.

Enhancing generalization. Generalization is the demonstration of behavior in situations other than those used to initially teach the behavior. An example of generalization is when Elizabeth learns how to do her laundry in a classroom situation and then does it successfully at three different laundromats in the community. Secondary-level education

Figure 4.3
Guidelines to consider in teaching self-management

1. Students should be trained to administer self-managed consequences in a contingent fashion.
2. Teachers should check periodically to ensure fidelity of the self-management treatment (i.e., make sure it is proceeding as planned).
3. Self-management should be applied early in the student's response chain (i.e., start teaching self-management as soon as the student begins changing behavior through external means).
4. Outcomes of self-management should be arranged so that success is likely.
5. Goals of self-managed behavior should be age and culturally appropriate.
6. Cooperation from all parties involved in the program (e.g., the person, parents, teachers, anyone else involved) should be obtained prior to beginning.
7. Self-management techniques should be directed at behavior that has a long history and has proven difficult to change.
8. Determine whether the person has the prerequisite skills to engage in self-management.
9. Reinforce the student for keeping to the plan and for meeting intermediate goals.
10. Clearly define the behavior that is to be self-managed, and provide sufficient rationale for the program.
11. Teachers need to model the desired behavior, and the student needs to practice the steps in the self-management of behavior until firm.

Source: Adapted from *Effective Teaching: Principles and Procedures of Applied Behavior Analysis with Exceptional Students* by M. Wolery, D. B. Bailey, Jr., and G. M. Sugai, 1988, Boston: Allyn & Bacon.

[handwritten margin note: should be concerned with generalization (getting ready to deal in the community)]

has been charged with preparing students with mild disabilities for life as an adult. Any teacher serving adolescents with mild disabilities in a middle school or high school who is not concerned with generalization of student behavior to the community is not being effective. Many ways exist to teach generalization, and these are presented below.

One of the easiest ways to enhance generalization of behavior to the community is to engage in community-based instruction (also see Chapter 11) in addition to classroom-based intervention. Wolery et al. (1988) refer to this type of instruction as manipulation of a *setting variable,* and Stokes and Baer (1977) would call this training in multiple settings. A similar form of this type of generalization training common to schools is *transenviron-mental programming* (Alberto & Troutman, 1995), which involves a teacher determining the expectations of a target environment (e.g., a regular geometry class) and then inject-ing as many of those expectations as possible into a different training setting (e.g., the resource room) in order to prepare a student for inclusion into the geometry class. It also involves assessing how well the student functions after being placed in the target class and reinforcing him or her for displaying appropriate behaviors in the inclusive setting.

Manipulation of *antecedent variables,* or examples used in instruction, can also facilitate generalization (Wolery et al., 1988). Stokes and Baer (1977) refer to this as training sufficient exemplars. When a teacher examines an environment to extract its relevant characteristics and then presents those characteristics to students as examples in a lesson, he or she is enhancing generalization through using meaningful antecedent variables. An example of how to do this in instruction would be when a teacher attempts to instruct students to use a washing machine. It would be necessary for the teacher to (a) examine several commercially available machines, (b) determine what must be done correctly to operate the machines, (c) write down the various knobs, dials, and switches to engage with each machine (e.g., water level knob, water temperature knob, cycle type dial [knits, permanent press, etc.]), and (d) determine how to shut off the system. Once these salient characteristics are task analyzed and taught in a few lessons, any student who has mastered the objectives should be able to successfully operate any washing machine in any home, apartment, or laundromat. In other words, training sufficient exemplars requires instruction to pinpoint what is important, what the important stim-uli look like, and what you do with the important, relevant stimuli. A student learns to perform a skill using a few examples from a class of stimuli and, by doing so, learns to display the skill with all members of a class of stimuli (Alberto & Troutman, 1995).

Another technique to consider to enhance generalization involves choosing behav-iors that have great range of applicability in many different settings. Behaviors that are specific to one environment will have very little utility to students who rarely frequent that particular setting. The behavior of being on time has great applicability in numer-ous settings: in school, using public transportation, on the job, picking up a date for a movie, and so on. If being on time in various settings is reinforced, the student is likely to see its value and exhibit it thoroughly in many environments. Likewise, teachers should also reinforce student behavior that shows generalization just as they would for initial acquisition of any new skill. When teachers *plan* for generalization and put it into students' objectives on IEPs, its role grows to the significance level that it deserves. One last suggestion on how to deal with generalization in instruction is provided by Schloss and Smith (1994) (Figure 4.4).

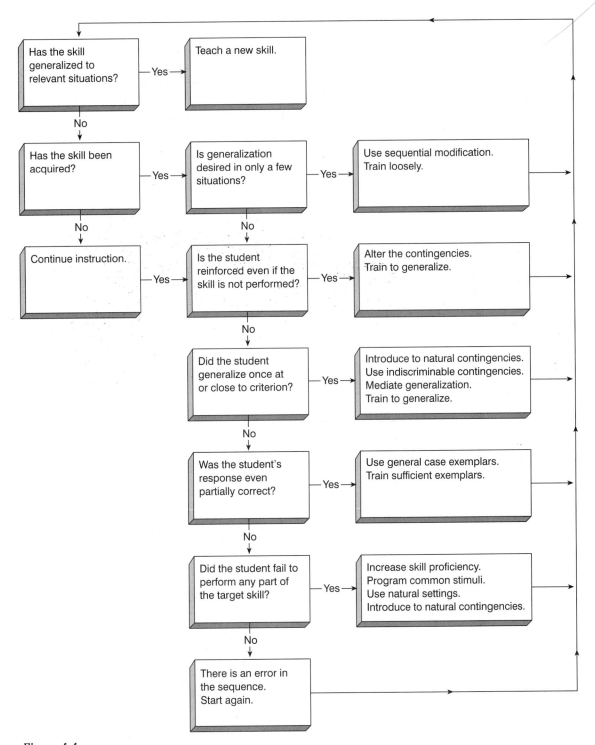

Figure 4.4
A flowchart to help teachers identify appropriate generalization techniques
Source: From *Applied Behavior Analysis in the Classroom* by P. J. Schloss and M. A. Smith, 1994, Boston: Allyn & Bacon.

Summary

Effective teaching and classroom management are learned behaviors. If a teacher does not currently exhibit the teaching behaviors known to greatly assist achievement and decorum, it would be in his or her best interest to begin to display them as soon as possible.

This chapter attempted to clarify the specifics that define the teaching role of those responsible for delivering secondary-level instruction to students with mild disabilities. Other aspects of this teaching role should also be kept in mind. Adolescents view their world in a way that we as teachers, at times, cannot comprehend. Table 4.1 presents data that some might find surprising as it pertains to the perspectives of adolescents in the United States.

As can be seen in Table 4.1, violence and hatred are now as common in secondary schools as are chalkboards and pep rallies. Teachers need not be intimidated by the perspectives of adolescents, but they should be conscious of them and not exacerbate any that lead to extreme inappropriate interactions with others. Teachers should also not dismiss adolescents' inappropriate behavior in school as a result of a poor home environment or membership in a gang that reinforces and condones such behavior. To combat

Table 4.1
Recent perspectives of high school students in the United States

	Students who think race relations in the United States are getting worse	Students who have felt racial or ethnic discrimination	Students who admit to using a derogatory word to refer to a member of a different racial or ethnic group
All students	53%	40%	48%
African American	58%	71%	51%
Asian American	58%	79%	38%
White	52%	33%	49%
Latino	50%	60%	57%

Students who report gangs at their school (I)				Students who report gangs at their school (II)		
All Students	Suburban	Urban	Rural	Public	Parochial	Private
17%	24%	23%	9%	20%	13%	6%

Of students who report gangs at their school, those who report a violent incident:

Frequent fights between students	Students attacking a teacher	Knife fights between students	Rape or sexual assault	Shooting on school grounds	Teacher hitting a student	Mugging
79%	31%	19%	18%	16%	13%	11%

Source: From *Who's Who Among American High School Students,* 1993, Los Angeles: Educational Communications, Inc.

some of the negative aspects of the adolescent's world, teachers should strive to make each classroom a safe haven where all students are respected, treated fairly, held accountable, and expected to contribute to the process of learning. When a teacher is successful at creating a positive environment, perhaps the troubles that adolescents face in other aspects of their world will be temporarily suspended.

Any middle school or high school teacher who can demonstrate that his or her students (a) gain important academic and functional skills when in the classroom, (b) are well prepared for independent, postsecondary school life, and (c) display appropriate behavior in most settings is truly remarkable. Such a teacher is astonishing but not impossible to become.

Key Terms

effective instruction
acquisition learning
proficiency learning
maintenance
generalization
direct instruction
differential reinforcement of other
    behavior
differential reinforcement of incompatible
    behavior
differential reinforcement of alternative
    behavior

differential reinforcement of low rates of
    behavior
vicarious reinforcement
extinction
punishment
response cost
overcorrection
nonexclusionary time-out
exclusionary time-out
seclusionary time-out
self-management

References

Alberto, P. A., & Troutman, A. C. (1995). *Applied behavior analysis for teachers* (3rd. ed.). Upper Saddle River, NJ: Merrill/Prentice Hall.

Algozzine, B., O'Shea, D. J., Crews, W. B., & Stoddard, K. (1987). Analysis of mathematics competence of learning disabled adolescents. *The Journal of Special Education, 21,* 97–107.

Baer, D. M., Wolf, M. M., & Risley, T. R. (1968). Some current dimensions of applied behavior analysis. *Journal of Applied Behavior Analysis, 1,* 91–97.

Birkimer, J. C., & Brown, J. H. (1979). Back to basics: Percentage agreement measures are adequate, but there are easier ways. *Journal of Applied Behavior Analysis, 12,* 535–543.

Bourbeau, P. E., Sowers, J., & Close, D. E. (1986). An experimental analysis of generalization of banking skills from classroom to bank settings in the community. *Education and Training of the Mentally Retarded, 21,* 98–107.

Brophy, J., & Good, T. L. (1986). Teacher behavior and student achievement. In M. C. Wittrock (Ed.), *Handbook of research on teaching* (3rd ed.) (pp. 328–375). New York: Macmillan.

Dehaven, E. D., Corley, M. J., Hofeling, D. V., & Garcia, E. (1982). Developing generative vocational behaviors in a business setting. *Analysis and Intervention in Developmental Disabilities, 2,* 345–356.

Ellis, E., Lenz, K., & Sabornie, E. J. (1987a). Generalization and adaptation of learning strategies to natural environments. Part I: Critical agents. *Remedial and Special Education, 8*(1), 6–20.

Ellis, E., Lenz, K., & Sabornie, E. J. (1987b). Generalization and adaptation of learning strategies to natural environments. Part II: Research into practice. *Remedial and Special Education, 8*(2), 6–23.

Emmer, E. T. (1988). Praise and the instructional process. *Journal of Classroom Interaction, 23,* 32–39.

Emmer, E. T., Evertson, C. M., Clements, B. S., & Worsham, M. E. (1994). *Classroom management for secondary teachers* (3rd ed.). Boston: Allyn & Bacon.

Emshoff, J. G., Redd, W. H., & Davidson, W. S. (1976). Generalization training and the transfer of treatment effects with delinquent adolescents. *Journal of Behavior Therapy and Experimental Psychiatry, 7,* 141–144.

Englert, C. S. (1984a). Effective direct instruction practices in special education settings. *Remedial and Special Education, 5*(2), 38–47.

Englert, C. S. (1984b). Measuring teacher effectiveness from the teacher's point of view. *Focus on Exceptional Children, 17*(2), 1–15.

Englert, C. S., & Thomas, C. C. (1982). Management of task involvement in special education classrooms. *Teacher Education and Special Education, 5,* 3–10.

Good, T. (1981). Teacher expectations and student perceptions: A decade of research. *Educational Leadership, 38,* 415–422.

Gregory, J. F., Shanahan, T., & Walberg, H. (1986). A profile of learning disabled twelfth-graders in regular classes. *Learning Disability Quarterly, 9,* 33–42.

Harris, F. C., & Lahey, B. B. (1978). A method for combining occurrence and nonoccurrence interobserver agreement scores. *Journal of Applied Behavior Analysis, 11,* 523–527.

Harris, K. R. (1985). Definitional, parametric, and procedural considerations in timeout interventions and research. *Exceptional Children, 51,* 279–288.

Hartmann, D. P. (1977). Considerations in the choice of interobserver reliability estimates. *Journal of Applied Behavior Analysis, 10,* 103–116.

Homme, L. E., Csanyi, A. P., Gonzales, M. A., & Rechs, J. R. (1969). *How to use contingency contracting in the classroom.* Champaign, IL: Research Press.

Horner, R. H., Eberhard, J. M., & Sheehan, M. R. (1986). Teaching generalized table bussing: The importance of negative teaching examples. *Behavior Modification, 10,* 457–471.

Kameenui, E. J., & Simmons, D. C. (1990). *Designing instructional strategies: The prevention of academic learning problems.* Upper Saddle River, NJ: Merrill/Prentice Hall.

Kazdin, A. E. (1975). *Behavior modification in applied settings.* Homewood, IL: Dorsey Press.

Kazdin, A. E. (1977). Artifact, bias, and complexity of assessment: The ABCs of reliability. *Journal of Applied Behavior Analysis, 10,* 103–116.

Kindsvatter, R., Wilen, W., & Ishler, M. (1988). *Dynamics of effective teaching.* New York: Longman.

Kounin, J. (1970). *Discipline and group management in classrooms.* New York: Holt, Rinehart, & Winston.

Lloyd, J. W., & Keller, C. E. (1989). Effective mathematics instruction: Development, instruction, and programs. *Focus on Exceptional Children, 21*(7), 1–10.

Lloyd, J. W., Landrum, T. J., & Hallahan, D. P. (1991). Self-monitoring applications for classroom intervention. In G. Stoner, M. R. Shinn, & H. M. Walker (Eds.), *Interventions for achievement and behavior problems* (pp. 201–213). Silver Spring, MD: National Association of School Psychologists.

Mastropieri, M. A., & Scruggs, T. E. (1984). Generalization: Five effective strategies. *Academic Therapy, 19,* 427–431.

Mastropieri, M. A., & Scruggs, T. E. (1987). *Effective instruction for special education.* Boston: College-Hill.

McGinnis, E., Scott-Miller, D., Neel, R., & Smith, C. (1985). Aversives in special education programs for behaviorally disordered students: A debate. *Behavioral Disorders, 10,* 295–304.

McNair, K. (1978–1979). Capturing in-flight decisions: Thoughts while teaching. *Education Research Quarterly, 3*(4), 66–77.

Meyen, E. L., Vergason, G. A., & Whelan, R. J. (Eds.). (1988). *Effective instructional strategies for exceptional children.* Denver, CO: Love.

Powell, J., Martindale, B., Kulp, S., Martindale, A., & Bauman, R. (1977). Taking a closer look: Time sampling and measurement error. *Journal of Applied Behavior Analysis, 10,* 325–332.

Rosenshine, B. (1976). Recent research on teaching behaviors and student achievement. *Journal of Teacher Education, 27,* 61–64.

Rosenshine, B., & Stevens, R. (1986). Teaching functions. In M. C. Wittrock (Ed.), *Handbook of research on teaching* (3rd ed.) (pp. 376–391). New York: Macmillan.

Schloss, P. J., & Smith, M. A. (1994). *Applied behavior analysis in the classroom.* Boston: Allyn & Bacon.

Smith, T. E. C., Finn, D. M., & Dowdy, C. A. (1993). *Teaching students with mild disabilities.* Fort Worth, TX: Harcourt Brace Jovanovich.

Spaulding, C. L. (1992). *Motivation in the classroom.* New York: McGraw-Hill.

Stevens, R., & Rosenshine, B. (1981). Advances in research on teaching. *Exceptional Education Quarterly, 2*(1), 1–9.

Stokes, T. E., & Baer, D. M. (1977). An implicit technology of generalization. *Journal of Applied Behavior Analysis, 10,* 349–367.

Walker, H. M., Colvin, G., & Ramsey, E. (1995). *Antisocial behavior in school: Strategies and best practices.* Pacific Grove, CA: Brooks/Cole.

Walker, H. M., & Walker, J. E. (1991). *Coping with noncompliance in the classroom.* Austin, TX: PRO-ED.

Wittrock, M. C. (Ed.). (1986). *Handbook of research on teaching* (3rd ed.). New York: Macmillan.

Wolery, M., Bailey, D. B., Jr., & Sugai, G. M. (1988). *Effective teaching: Principles and procedures of applied behavior analysis with exceptional students.* Boston: Allyn & Bacon.

5

Reading Instruction for Adolescents with Mild Disabilities

Objectives

After reading this chapter, the reader should be able to:

1. discuss potential problems of secondary students with mild disabilities in the curriculum area of reading;

2. delineate several types of formal and informal reading assessment procedures;

3. discuss various instructional strategies that may be appropriate for secondary students with mild disabilities;

4. summarize the issues surrounding the teaching of reading at the secondary level to students with mild disabilities;

5. discuss special considerations in reading instruction for adolescents with mild disabilities in mainstream classrooms.

Our society values reading ability highly; excellence in high school and beyond is unattainable without the ability to read (Chall, 1983). The purpose of this chapter is to discuss reading instruction at the secondary level for students who have mild disabilities. Ways in which an educator can assess secondary-level students in the content area of reading are also discussed, and specific assessment devices are summarized. Several instructional techniques that have been supported by research are clarified, along with appropriate commercial curricula and computer software.

Students with Mild Disabilities and Reading Problems

Secondary students with mild disabilities are indeed a heterogeneous group. Most teachers would agree, however, that a large majority of youth with mild disabilities exhibit reading difficulties. *Reading Report Card,* a publication of the U.S. Department of Education (1986), documents that many students are unable to read enough to understand and complete grade-appropriate reading assignments. The report states that 40% of 13-year-olds and 16% of 17-year-olds attending high school are unable to read intermediate-level reading materials. These students are also unable to search for specific information or to make generalizations from information in their social studies, science, or literature textbooks.

Many students with mild disabilities perform poorly in their content-area classes because they possess limited knowledge about effective reading strategies (Baker & Brown, 1984; Wong, 1987), and they do not possess sufficient prerequisite subject-matter knowledge to learn readily from association (Wong, 1985). When they graduate, if they do, they score below 8th-grade proficiency on basic skills assessments in reading (deBettencourt, Zigmond, & Thornton, 1989; Thornton & Zigmond, 1987; Zigmond & Thornton, 1985). It appears that most secondary students with mild disabilities are often deficient in their reading skills and are unable to effectively gain information from a wide variety of reading materials.

These students are incapable of meeting the increasingly high demands for literacy that are present in today's mainstream high schools (Donahoe & Zigmond, 1990). Also, unfortunately, students with mild disabilities who cannot read often drop out of school (deBettencourt et al., 1989; Zigmond & Thornton, 1985), thus removing themselves from an opportunity to improve their reading skills. Students with mild disabilities who leave high school unable to read join the increasing masses of adult illiterates (Kozol, 1985). Unfortunately for these students, we have entered an era in which high school reading ability is necessary for a minimal level of proficiency in coping with the increasingly complex reading tasks of our technical age (Chall, 1983). In order for secondary students with mild disabilities to meet the demands of the adult world they will require specific instruction in reading.

Teaching Reading as a Complex Process

Most educators agree that the most critical element in reading is the reader's ability to fit the new information in a reading selection to his or her prior knowledge (Alvermann, Moore, & Conley, 1987; Wixson & Peters, 1987). In the secondary grades, students are expected to use their reading skills to gain information in subject areas such as English, history, and the sciences and assimilate this information with their prior knowledge. The secondary student who has not mastered word recognition skills faces the insurmountable task of memorizing every word; the secondary student who has not mastered comprehension monitoring techniques will have much difficulty acquiring information from content area classes. Many students with mild disabilities have difficulties in both the word recognition and the comprehension facets of the reading process. This heterogeneous nature of the adolescent with learning problems underscores the need to offer a variety of instructional services (Mercer & Mercer, 1991). Selecting the correct teaching approach is a debated issue in the reading field; few agree that there is any single method or technique that is most effective with all students with mild disabilities.

Importance of Functional Reading Skills for Adolescents with Mild Disabilities

The need for academic remediation for adolescents with mild disabilities in the content area of reading is readily agreed upon, yet what curriculum should be included in that academic remediation is not as easily decided. Some educators (Deshler, Schumaker, Lenz, & Ellis, 1984) have noted that most secondary-level remedial reading materials are developed for elementary-age students and are clearly not appropriate for adolescents. Deshler and colleagues (1984) and Ellis (1996), among others, feel that time is growing short for many of these students and that academic remediation should be provided in conjunction with other services that address the functional nature of reading and survival skills (Zigmond, 1990).

A **functional curriculum** or essential-living reading skills program should be designed for students whose reading skills are very low (Mercer & Mercer, 1991). Typically, career-related (e.g., vocational education) instructional programs are provided by regular educators in conjunction with special education faculty. But it is often unclear what emphasis should be put on the functional curriculum and also what exactly a functional reading curriculum encompasses. Kokaska and Brolin (1985) list nine important areas in planning a functional-living curriculum (Figure 5.1). Many of these skills can be taught within the regular curriculum, and many require reading skills.

The decision to teach functional reading skills versus remedial reading skills continues to be a dilemma for teachers of adolescent students with disabilities. Polloway, Patton, Payne, and Payne (1989) suggest that choosing the most appropriate approach for each student depends on such factors as:

1. the student's attitude, energy, and motivation for learning to read,
2. the teacher's assessment of the previously used instructional approaches,
3. diagnostic information related to causes of an inability to read,
4. the teacher's knowledge of strategies essential to reading progress for the student, and
5. identifying the type of program that will provide a successful experience for the student. (p. 223)

The ultimate decision should be made in conjunction with the student and, if necessary, the parents. It may be best to provide a functional reading curriculum in conjunction with remedial skills.

Figure 5.1
Functional-living curriculum areas

1. Managing family finances
     identifying money and making correct change
     making wise purchases
     using bank and credit facilities
     keeping financial records
     paying taxes and buying insurance

2. Selecting, managing, and maintaining a home
     selecting housing
     maintaining a home
     using appliances and tools

3. Caring for personal needs
     appropriate dress
     proper hygiene and grooming
     physical fitness and nutrition
     illness prevention and treatments

4. Raising children—family living
     responsibilities of marriage
     child raising (personal care)
     child raising (psychological)
     family safety

5. Buying and preparing food
     proper eating skills
     planning meals
     purchasing and storing food
     preparing meals

Assessment of Reading Skills at the Secondary Level

Reading ability is probably the most studied academic area in special education assessment at the elementary and secondary levels. Reading problems typically have been the most common reason for students' initial referrals for special education evaluations (Carnine, Silbert, & Kameenui, 1990; Kaluger & Kolson, 1978), but because reading ability is such a complex phenomenon no single test can encompass all of its aspects. Educators have many tools available for assessing students' reading abilities—standardized norm-referenced tests, tests that accompany many reading programs, informal teacher-made tests, classroom observations, samples of students' work, and so on (McLoughlin & Lewis, 1990; Valencia & Pearson, 1988). Each procedure has its own set of unique strengths and weaknesses.

Before choosing an assessment procedure educators should be aware of the many questions about assessment of reading at the secondary level. Why would one assess reading at the secondary level? How would one assess reading at the secondary level?

6. Buying and caring for clothes
    washing clothing
    storing clothing
    simple mending
    buying clothes

7. Engaging in civic activities
    basic local government and laws
    basic American government
    citizenship rights and responsibilities
    voting procedures
    Selective Service information
    communications with law officers

8. Utilizing recreation and leisure time
    group and individual sports activities
    role of art and music in daily living
    understanding recreational values
    using recreational resources
    choosing activities wisely

9. Getting around the community
    knowledge of safety rules
    competence in use of public transportation
    driving a car

Source: From *Teaching Students with Learning Problems* (4th ed.) (p. 640) by C. D. Mercer and A. R. Mercer, 1991, Upper Saddle River, NJ: Merrill/Prentice Hall.

Why Assess Reading?

The skills of secondary students with mild disabilities are assessed for several reasons. Eligibility or reevaluation testing for special programs may need to be determined; because reading is a critical component of school achievement, it is often part of such testing. Reading proficiency is also one of the minimum competencies assessed for graduation from many high schools. Many states require students with mild disabilities to pass minimum competency examinations (McLoughlin & Lewis, 1990). Reading skills should also be assessed for planning instruction, determining a student's current level of reading performance, evaluating a student's strengths and weaknesses, and evaluating a reading program's effectiveness.

How Does One Assess Reading?

There is an abundance of formal tests, often called standardized norm-referenced tests, available for secondary learners with mild disabilities. The major characteristic of these tests is that one can interpret the quality of a given score by comparing it with scores acquired by others. The numerous tests available vary somewhat in the range of skills they assess. Some are designed for comprehensive assessment of the reading process and include measures of several of the important reading skills; an example is the **Woodcock Reading Mastery Test—Revised** (Woodcock, 1987). Other tests assess only one part of reading (e.g., comprehension or vocabulary); an example of such a test is the *Test of Reading Comprehension—R* (Brown, Hammill, & Wiederholt, 1986). Others measure oral reading; still others measure silent reading. Reading tests that are administered individually allow the examiner to observe the student's behavior more closely.

Among the advantages of using formal testing at the secondary level are first, that students' performances can be contrasted to the performance of a norm group. The resulting data can help professionals plan instruction by identifying areas in the reading curriculum where students fail to perform as well as their peers and document changes in performance relative to grade- and age-level expectations. A second advantage is that the testing materials are readily available with little effort on the part of the teacher. Third, many standardized test packages include computer software programs that score the tests and often pinpoint areas of strengths and weaknesses. For many teachers standardized tests provide a beginning point in the investigation of their students' reading problems.

There are several disadvantages of using formal testing in reading for secondary-level students with mild disabilities. First, the norms may be inappropriate, that is, they may be based on students with whom your students should not be compared (e.g., younger, not mildly disabled). Second, standardized tests often require timed testing and the slow but thorough reader may fail to complete the comprehension section of a test and get a low score compared to the established norm when in reality the student's comprehension could be excellent. Third, since comprehension occurs when students are able to associate the unknown with the known, prior knowledge may be a factor in test performance. Depending on the degree to which this is true on particular test questions, the resulting scores can yield an unfair comparison between individuals. Finally, a fifth disadvantage to using norm-referenced reading tests is that standardized tests of reading comprehension, in many cases, emphasize factual recall of relatively insignificant facts.

Using Standardized, Criterion-Referenced, and Diagnostic Tests: Selected Instruments

Table 5.1 provides a list of commercially prepared reading tests commonly used with secondary students with mild disabilities. In the following section we discuss several selected instruments.

Botel Reading Inventory (Botel, 1978) is a group-administered reading inventory to be used with students in grades 1 through 12. Its purposes include assessing student skills in decoding, word recognition, word opposites, and spelling.

Diagnostic Reading Scales (Spache, 1981) is an individually administered diagnostic reading test to be used with students in grades 1 through 7 and with high school students who are reading below normal. Three word lists and 22 passages of increasing dif-

Table 5.1

List of commonly used commercially prepared reading tests appropriate for use with secondary students with mild disabilities

Name (Authors)	Ages or Grades	Skill Areas Assessed	
		Decoding	Comprehension
Brigance Diagnostic Comprehensive Inventory (Brigance, 1983)	Gr. K–9	*	*
Brigance Diagnostic Inventory of Basic Skills (Brigance, 1977)	Gr. K–6	*	*
Brigance Diagnostic Inventory of Essential Skills (Brigance, 1981)	Gr. 4–12	*	*
Classroom Reading Inventory (5th ed.) (Silvaroli, 1986)	Preprimer–Gr. 8	*	*
Diagnostic Reading Scales (Spache, 1981)	Gr. 1–8	*	*
Ekwall Reading Inventory (2nd ed.) (Ekwall, 1986)	Preprimer–Gr. 9	*	*
Formal Reading Inventory (Wiederholt, 1986)	Ages 7–18	*	*
Gilmore Oral Reading Test (Gilmore & Gilmore, 1968)	Gr. 1–8	*	*
Gray Oral Reading Tests – 3rd ed. (Wiederholt & Bryant, 1992)	Ages 7–18	*	*
Iowa Silent Reading Tests (Farr, 1973)	Gr 6–college	*	*
Standford Diagnostic Reading Test (3rd ed.) (Karlsen, Madden, & Gardner, 1984)	Gr. 1–12, college	*	*
Test of Reading Comprehension (Rev. ed.) (Brown, Hammill, & Wiederholt, 1986)	Ages 7–18		*
Wechsler Individual Achievement Test (Psychological Corporation, 1992)	Ages 5–19	*	*
Woodcock Reading Mastery Tests – Revised (Woodcock, 1987)	Ages 5–75+	*	*

ficulty are used to assess student skills in phonics, word recognition, listening, oral reading, silent reading, and comprehension.

Formal Reading Inventory (Wiederholt, 1986) is an individually administered norm-referenced test intended for students in grades 1 through 12. Its purposes include assessing skill development in oral and silent reading.

Gates-MacGinitie Reading Tests (MacGinitie, 1978) is a group-administered reading survey intended for students in grades 7 through 12. It is composed of two levels with each level consisting of a vocabulary subtest and a comprehension subtest.

Gilmore Oral Reading Test (Gilmore & Gilmore, 1968) is an individually adminis-tered diagnostic reading test intended for students in grades 1 through 8. Ten para-graphs of increasing difficulty are used to assess oral reading rate and comprehension.

Gray Oral Reading Test—Revised (GORT—R) (Wiederholt & Bryant, 1986) is a norm-referenced, individually administered, diagnostic reading test intended for stu-dents ages 6.6 to 17.11. It comprises two alternate, equivalent forms, each of which con-tains 13 developmentally sequenced passages with five comprehension questions. It assesses oral reading rate and accuracy and comprehension. The manual provides a sys-tem for performing miscue analysis, and a software scoring system is available.

Test of Reading Comprehension—Revised (TORC—R) (Brown, Hammill, & Wieder-holt, 1986) is a small-group or individually administered reading comprehension test for students in grades 2 through 12. The test measures both general reading comprehension and specific knowledge needed to read in three content areas (i.e., mathematics, science, and social studies). It is not necessary to administer the entire battery.

Stanford Diagnostic Reading Test (3rd ed.) (Karlsen, Madden, & Gardner, 1984) is a group-administered reading test designed for students in grades 1 through 12. The test measures vocabulary, decoding, comprehension, and rate.

Wechsler Individual Achievement Test (WIAT) (Psychological Corporation, 1992) is an individually administered diagnostic achievement test intended for students ages 5.0 to 19.11. The WIAT is composed of eight subtests, one of which is the basic reading sub-test that assesses a student's ability to decode and read words.

Woodcock Reading Mastery Test—Revised (Woodcock, 1987) is a norm-referenced individually administered diagnostic reading test intended for students in kindergarten through college. Five subtests include letter identification, word identification, word attack, word comprehension, and passage comprehension. The *WRMT—R* is a broad-based read-ing test used to identify students' strengths and weaknesses in reading skill development.

Using Informal Reading Assessment Procedures

Secondary special education teachers are most concerned with assessment that can be used to provide direct services to students; most informal assessment tools do just that. Informal assessment tools differ from standardized tests primarily in that they do not use norms as standards for comparison, employing instead a relative standard or criterion, which implies adequate achievement in a given task or assignment. Secondary teachers use informal reading procedures to identify students' specific reading strengths and weak-nesses, monitor their students' progress, and evaluate their instructional program.

There are several advantages of informal tests. They are frequently quick and easy to administer, and they are designed for the reading level of your students. As informal instruments are designed to describe current conditions, not predict future performance, the data obtained provide relevant instructional recommendations.

The disadvantages include some informal assessment devices that are time-consuming for teachers to prepare. Informal assessment measures are not standardized; therefore, technical adequacy is often not present. Most informal assessments represent a smaller range of items within the curriculum than is possible with standardized tests.

In the curriculum area of reading there are several informal assessment procedures. Two of the more common ones that classroom teachers use at the secondary level are the

informal reading inventory and the **cloze procedure.** A third, less-common procedure, but one that assists educators in planning instruction, is the content reading inventory. A fourth newly designed procedure, curriculum-based assessment, is rapidly gaining support in the literature. The following sections discuss each of these procedures and a few selected others.

Informal reading inventories. Informal reading inventories (IRIs) are made up of graded word lists and graded reading selections. Students begin by reading material at a lower grade level and continue reading until the material becomes too difficult to decode and/or comprehend. A student's independent, instructional, frustration, and listening levels are determined on the basis of the number of words recognized and the percentage of correct answers to comprehension questions. Kirk, Kliebhan, and Lerner (1978) suggest the following criteria to determine three reading levels:

- 98% to 100% word recognition accuracy and 90% to 100% accuracy in comprehension for the **Independent Level,**
- 95% word recognition accuracy and 75% accuracy in comprehension for the **Instructional Level,** and
- 90% or less word recognition accuracy and 50% or less accuracy in comprehension for the **Frustration Level.**

Box 5.1 details procedures to use to construct your own IRI; however, there are several commercially prepared informal reading inventories available. A few of the more commonly used include *The Advanced Reading Inventory: Grades Seven Through College* (Johns, 1981); *The Burns/Roe Informal Reading Inventory* (Roe, 1985); *The Classroom Reading Inventory* (Silvaroli, 1986); *The Ekwall Reading Inventory* (2nd ed.) (Ekwall, 1986); and *The Sucher-Allred Reading Placement Inventory* (Sucher & Allred, 1981). Many informal reading inventories are designed for the elementary-age student. Be sure to preview the commercially prepared inventory you choose to ensure that it addresses the content and interest level of your secondary students.

The cloze procedure. The cloze procedure (e.g., Bormuth, 1968; Jongsma, 1971; Rye, 1982) provides the teacher with a simple, economical method of determining the reading level of students. Originally designed as a measure of readability, the cloze procedure

---

BOX 5.1

• •

Constructing Your Own Informal Reading Inventory

1. Construct a graded word list by randomly picking 20 to 25 words from each grade level from glossaries of a graded basal reader series.
2. Select passages from the graded basal series that consist of 50 words at the preprimer level and increasing to 200 words maximum at the secondary level.
3. Construct five questions for each passage. The questions should require students to recall facts, make inferences, and define vocabulary.

involves the systematic deletion of words from a text selection. Students are then asked to supply the deleted words. Their ability to correctly supply the missing words is an indicator of how well they can read and construct meaning from print.

Readence, Bean, and Baldwin (1989) suggest the following classifications based on a student's performance on the cloze procedure:

Using Cloze with Text Material:

Reading Level	Cloze %	Difficulty Level	Solution
Independent	61+	Too Easy	Supplementary materials
Instructional	40–60	Adequate	Structured reading with guidance
Frustration	< 39	Too Difficult	Structured listening/easier text

Box 5.2 describes how to design your own cloze procedure assessment materials.

Content reading inventory.   A third informal technique that may be useful for secondary teachers in assessing students' ability to gain understanding from their content textbooks is the content reading inventory (Readence et al., 1989), which provides a way to obtain additional information about a student's ability to process text material successfully. It is an informal, group, silent, diagnostic test and consists of three major sections. The first section concerns knowledge of and ability to use the various aids within content text-books, such as the table of contents, index, and pictorial aids. The student's ability to use resource aids that supplement the textbook, such as an encyclopedia, are examined also. The rationale behind the content reading inventory is that a student's ability to use the internal and external aids of a content-area text effectively is critical to learning from it.

In the last two sections of such an inventory, students are asked to read a short (three to four pages) selection from the text. Section two then determines ability to deal with technical and specialized vocabulary encountered in the reading. Both vocabulary through recall and in context are examined. Section three examines the ability to comprehend text information as well as to understand the author's text structure. See Figure 5.2 for an example of a content reading inventory.

BOX 5.2

Procedures to Follow to Design Your Own Cloze Procedure Materials

Choose a passage (approximately 250 words) from the beginning of the text. Use complete paragraphs. Before deleting any words leave a lead-in of at least 25 words. This will allow the student to grasp the author's language structure, vocabulary, and meaning. Delete every fifth word and replace with a blank. All blanks replacing words should be of uniform length. Fifteen typed spaces are often recommended. Provide some guided group exercises utilizing a cloze format. Do not impose a time limit and offer some alternative activity for those who finish early.

Curriculum-based assessment in reading. **Curriculum-based assessment,** a recently studied method of evaluating student performance using the school curriculum as the standard of comparison, was developed by Deno and his colleagues (Deno, 1985, 1986; Deno & Fuchs, 1987). It differs from formal assessment in that the essential measure of success is the student's progress in the curriculum of the local school system (Tucker, 1985).

In the area of reading, a teacher may decide that by the year's end he or she wants a student to be proficient on grade 11 material and that proficiency is reading at least 90 words per minute correctly with no more than five errors. Using curriculum-based measures, the teacher could evaluate the student's skills by having the student read aloud from content area textbooks for one minute twice weekly. The teacher would then count the number of words read correctly and the number of errors made (Deno & Fuchs, 1987). These scores would be charted on traditional graph paper with the performance criterion of 90 words per minute for the year's end placed on the graph. A goal line

Figure 5.2
Example of a content reading inventory

Section I: Textual Reading/Study Aids

Directions: Using your textbook or your previous knowledge, answer each of the following questions on a separate sheet of paper.

A. Internal Aids

1. On what page does Chapter Three begin? What is the title of the section of which it is a part?
2. On what page(s) would you find information regarding the Guided Listening Procedure?
3. Where would you look in the text to find the definition of "slicing?"
4. Of what use is the section entitled "Rationale" at the beginning of Chapter Eight?
5. Using the checklist on page 193, what recommendations would you make concerning the student's writing?
6. Where would you look to find out how this text is organized?

B. External Aids

7. What library guide would aid you in locating a book on attitudes and attitude development?
8. If you were to give an oral report in class about content area reading and you knew that much of the information you needed would be in current periodicals, what guide would you use to help you find the information?
9. Name one set of encyclopedias. How are the topics in it arranged?

Directions: Read the sections in your text entitled "Words" and "Vocabularies" on pp. 83–85. Based upon what you have read, answer the questions in sections II and III on a separate sheet of paper.

Figure 5.2, continued

Section II: Vocabulary Knowledge

10. Define the concept of "word" as used in this text.

11. Compare and contrast denotations and connotations. Provide an example.

12. Define the italicized word as it is used in this sentence: "A vocabulary is a *corpus* of many thousands of words and their associated meanings."

13. What term refers to the process by which new information is incorporated into existing schemata?

14. Define the italicized word as used in this sentence:

    "Technical vocabulary presents labels for unfamiliar concepts which must be accommodated by modifying *extant* schemata."

Section III: Comprehension

15. Why do adult language users have little difficulty agreeing whether or not a particular sequence of sounds or symbols is a word?

16. Learning new words (concepts) requires more than a simple explanation by the teacher. Why?

17. What are the largest vocabularies for literate adults?

18. Describe the differences between the words (concepts), "Cold War" and "crass."

19. Describe the process involved with regard to the schemata of students when the word "secant" is presented to them.

20. Explain the role of the school with regard to the development of the expressive and receptive vocabularies of students.

21. How is the section entitled "Vocabularies" organized?

Source: From *Content Area Reading: An Integrated Approach* (3rd ed.) (pp. 252–253) by J. E. Readence, T. W. Bean, and R. S. Baldwin, 1989, Dubuque, IA: Kendall/Hunt Publishing Co.

would be drawn between the baseline data and the goal criterion. The teacher would analyze the data after collecting seven to ten data points by first drawing a line of best fit through the student's data and then comparing the steepness of this line to the goal line. If the actual progress was less steep than the goal line, the teacher should modify the instructional program (Fuchs, Deno, & Mirkin, 1984).

Curriculum-based assessment data can be used to make instructional and eligibility decisions. The curriculum-based procedures also can be facilitated by the use of computers (Fuchs, Fuchs, Hamlett, & Hasselbring, 1987). Computer programs are available that simplify the procedures for teachers (Fuchs, Hamlett, Fuchs, Stecker, & Ferguson, 1988).

Checklists and observation.   Teachers can use a variety of checklists developed from a summary of reading competencies to informally assess students' reading skills; some checklists are designed to identify difficulties in reading. The teacher selects a particular area in reading to assess and during a classroom lesson observes and records a student's skills on the checklist.

Error analysis is a frequently used observation technique to study students' oral reading mistakes. A student's incorrect responses provide data about how he or she is processing the content-area text. Two copies of the reading material are needed; one is for the student to read and the other is for the teacher to use in recording the student's miscues. Error analysis can be used to study comprehension as well as decoding skills (McLoughlin & Lewis, 1990). Figure 5.3 presents an error analysis chart for recording oral reading errors suggested by Morsink and Gable (1990).

Figure 5.3
Error analysis chart used for recording oral reading errors

	Error Type/Number	Prioritized Instruction	
Ignore Punctuation			Proficiency
Hesitation			
Repetition			
Insertion			Transition
Self-Correct			
Substitution			Acquisition
Teacher Aid			
Mispronounce			

Student _____ Dates _____

Material/Level _____

Number of readings _____
Average number of words _____
Average time of readings _____
Correct rate _____ Error rate _____

Source: From "Errors in Reading" by C. V. Morsink and R. A. Gable, 1990, in R. A. Gable and J. M. Henderson (Eds.), *Assessing Students with Special Needs* (p. 53), White Plains, NY: Longman.

Reading Instruction at the Secondary Level

Reading instruction is considered by most educators as the cornerstone of a student's education and is a factor in the extent to which the student will be able to benefit from instruction in specific content areas (McGill-Franzen, 1987). However, as Leinhardt, Zigmond, and Cooley (1981) suggested, despite explicit emphasis on reading achievement, students spend a very small percentage of the school day in oral and/or silent reading instructional activities. High school students with mild disabilities, in particular, may not be making progress in reading because they are receiving so little reading instruction (Zigmond, 1990). In addition, expectations regarding reading in secondary schools vary widely across different classrooms. In some, extensive reading is required; in others little or none is necessary (Ellis, 1996).

"Instruction in reading at the secondary school level needs to be interesting and imaginative" (Zigmond, 1990, p. 7). As Zigmond suggested, the objectives of reading instruction at the secondary level should be "to make students independent, fluent readers, confident enough in decoding skills to be willing to attack unfamiliar text in a popular magazine, a novel, a technical manual or a mainstream textbook" (p. 7). Merely providing verbal direction instructions (e.g., advanced organizers) does not work because they are not sufficient to activate the use of an effective strategy (Lenz, Alley, & Schumaker, 1987). Students need to be taught specifically to attend to and use the advance organizers presented by their teachers. In essence, effective reading instruction needs to encourage and train students to participate actively and strategically in the reading process (Baker & Brown, 1984; Bulgren, Schumaker, & Deshler, 1988; Ellis, 1996).

There are several approaches to reading instruction; most at the secondary level are organized around a two-part curriculum: vocabulary and comprehension. Yet at this level it is important that careful attention be paid, not only to teaching such critically needed curricula, but also to the student's self-confidence in reading. Many students with mild disabilities are not motivated to read and often remain passive during the reading activity. There are others who do not know where to invest their energy and devote too much time to word pronunciations or repeated readings (Paris & Oka, 1989). Many students with reading difficulties require instruction that (a) motivates them to expend effort to learn to use the appropriate strategies and (b) builds their self-confidence at the same time. The following sections discuss selected instructional strategies that have fostered effective reading processes among students with mild disabilities.

Vocabulary Development

Most current reading research theory supports reading as an interactive process (Bos & Anders, 1990). The reader is characterized as an active participant who interacts with the text to construct meaning. One of the most important aspects of this prior knowledge is the student's labels for events and experiences, or vocabulary knowledge (Johnson & Pearson, 1984).

Vocabulary used at the elementary level is usually controlled; in the middle and high school levels the vocabulary used in content passages is not as carefully controlled. Many students with reading disabilities consequently have great difficulty with the vocabulary. The ability to identify unknown words is an increasingly important text-reading skill during adolescence (e.g., reading application forms, reading instructions, etc.). Because many students fear being embarrassed by revealing their failure to read important words, teachers need to spend additional time on vocabulary instruction.

Bos and Anders (1990) found that rich, elaborated vocabulary instruction can facilitate reading comprehension for students with mild disabilities. They recommend teaching definitions within the content area context. Beck and her associates (Beck, Perfetti, & McKeown, 1982) suggest that vocabulary instruction can facilitate reading comprehension only if words are learned thoroughly—to the point at which the word's meaning can be assessed quickly and automatically.

Opportunities to develop vocabulary can also be assisted by the use of semantic mapping or webbing, which assists students in seeing the relationships between word meanings and concepts (McKeown & Beck, 1988). Bulgren et al. (1988) refer to a semantic mapping technique as making "concept diagrams." A concept diagram includes the word's definition, characteristics of the concept, and examples and non-examples of the concept. See Figure 5.4 for an example of a concept diagram.

Carnine, Silbert, and Kameenui (1990) recommend teaching vocabulary through the use of (a) synonyms, (b) modeling, (c) definitions, (d) contextual analysis, (e) dictionary usage, and (f) morphemic analysis. Synonym teaching supplements students' vocabulary by building on their previous knowledge. Modeling examples can be used when there are no words available to define the concept adequately. Definition teaching is especially helpful at the secondary level as terms become more involved. Contextual analysis helps the student learn the meaning of unknown words by using the words in the sentence that surround the unknown. Teaching dictionary usage is vital at the secondary level. Teachers should encourage students to use the dictionary during independent reading. Morphemic analysis is a vocabulary aid that teaches the student to break a word into its parts and use the meaning of the parts to understand the whole.

Ellis (1996) suggests that specific strategies for problem solving unknown words be taught to students. For example, the **DISSECT** word identification strategy (Lenz, Schumaker, Deshler, & Beals, 1984) has been demonstrated to improve word-attack skills (see Lenz & Hughes, 1990): **D: D**iscover the context; **I: I**solate the prefix; **S: S**eparate the suffix; **S: S**ay the stem; **E: E**xamine the stem; **C: C**heck with someone; and **T: T**ry the dictionary. The authors recommend that students use this strategy with words that seem particularly important.

Students must be taught to establish ownership of words and their meanings (Johnson & Pearson, 1984), which requires that they develop an understanding of what they already know about a topic and compare it with what they are going to read (Idol, 1988).

Given the increasing difficulty of words found in content-area textbooks, the teacher needs to ensure that the students can decode and pronounce the words and understand their meanings. The above-mentioned strategies will enable a student to build his or her vocabulary, but the strategies will not work without consistent direct instruction, substantial practice, and occasional review by the teacher. Vocabulary instruction is a critical component of prereading activities at all levels.

Figure 5.4

Example of a concept diagram

Concept Name:	democracy

Definitions:	A democracy is a form of government in which the people hold the ruling power, citizens are equal, the individual is valued, and compromise is necessary.

Characteristics Present in the Concept:

Always	Sometimes	Never
form of government	direct representation	king rules
people hold power	indirect representation	dictator rules
individual is valued		
citizen equal		
compromise necessary		

Example:	Nonexample:
United States	Russia
Mexico	Cuba
West Germany today	Germany under Hitler
Athens (about 500 B.C.)	Macedonia (under Alexander)

Source: From "Effectiveness of a Concept Teaching Routine in Enhancing the Performance of LD Students in Secondary-Level Mainstream Classes" by J. A. Bulgren, J. B. Schumaker, and D. D. Deshler, 1988, *Learning Disability Quarterly, 11,* pp. 3–17.

Comprehension Instruction

Palincsar and Brown (1984), among others, define reading comprehension as "the product of three main factors: (1) considerate texts, (2) the compatibility of the reader's knowledge and text content, and (3) the active strategies the reader employs to enhance understanding and retention, and to circumvent comprehension failures" (p. 118). This interactive view of reading comprehension emphasizes more than practice on isolated skills and fluent decoding (Paris & Oka, 1989). Therefore, new instructional techniques have been suggested that attempt to make secondary students motivated and active participants in the process of strategic reading. Several approaches that may be easily implemented in classrooms are discussed here.

Reciprocal teaching is an instructional technique that embodies four comprehension-fostering activities: self-directed summarizing, questioning, clarifying, and predicting (Palincsar & Brown, 1984). The procedure involves the teacher and the students taking turns leading a dialogue concerning sections of a text. Initially, the teacher explains and models the key activities of self-questioning (related to the main idea), summarizing, clarifying, and predicting (identifying and clarifying difficult sections of the text). Box 5.3 provides suggestions for each of the four strategies.

A comprehensive review of the reading instruction research revealed that these activities were inherent in successful comprehension (Brown, Palincsar, & Armbruster, 1984). Reciprocal teaching makes these behaviors both observable and accessible.

Students participate at whatever level they can. The teacher provides guidance and feedback. The students take turns playing teacher and leading their peers through the set of structuring activities, with guidance from the adult teacher and helpful criticism from the other students. See Figure 5.5 for an example of such a dialogue.

BOX 5.3

• •

Discussion of Four Strategies Incorporated in Reciprocal Teaching

Summarizing important information: Students are trained to use five main condensing rules: (1) deletion of trivia, (2) deletion of redundancy, (3) superordination, (4) selection of a topic sentence, and (5) invention of a topic sentence for a paragraph where one was not explicitly stated. (Brown & Day, 1983)

Questioning: Students are trained to generate four or five questions a classroom teacher might ask to test the students' knowledge of the paragraph.

Clarifying: Students are trained to point out what does not make sense—can it be clarified?

Predicting: Students are trained to predict what the next topic might be.

Figure 5.5
Example of dialogue in reciprocal teaching

READING:
There are many different creatures in the sea. Many of the fish you see will be swimming in schools. They are looking for food. Most of them are friendly. But you might see some unusual fish. You might see a big, flat fish. It looks as if it has wings. You might see a sea horse. It swims with its head up and its tail down. It carries baby sea horses in a pocket on its front.

1. T: I need someone to ask a question about the new information I just shared with you.

2. S2: How does the sea horses...carry their babies in their pouch?

3. T: Okay. Does someone remember the answer?

4. S5: Um, that's the only way they can carry them. They don't have any hands or anything.

5. T: Now, was he doing a little bit of predicting or figuring out how that sea horse is able to do that? Did the story really tell why they carry them in their pouches?

6. S5: Or they might drowned. They might not be able to swim and they might drowned.

7. T: You are right in all of your answers and thinking. Your question was a good question in that it got us all thinking about why they did have pouches and why they carry their babies there, but, you were going a bit further than the written word. You were pretty smart to figure that out. Can anyone think of a question that they did give us the answer to in the story?

8. S4: Um, what kind of animals are they?

9. S6: Um...sea horses.

10. T: What else did they see besides the sea horses?

11. S6: Um...crawfish.

12. T: See, what you might have wanted to ask, and C_____ might have wanted to ask "Why were they called unusual fish or animals?"

         Why do they call a sea horse unusual?...Because they carry babies in a pouch. Most fish don't do that, right? That you could have asked using information here.

One of the reasons for the success of this approach is that throughout the reading lesson, the teacher explicitly tells the students that these key activities (i.e., strategies) will help them better understand what they read. Reciprocal teaching (Palincsar & Brown, 1984; Palincsar, Brown, & Martin, 1987) appears to be a promising approach for engaging students directly in the use of reading strategies. It has met with great success in both listening and reading comprehension (Brown, Campione, Reeve, Ferrara, & Palincsar, 1991).

Direct instruction is one form of instruction that encompasses use of a systematic lesson structure as well as a set of key instructional behaviors (Becker, Engelmann, Carnine, & Maggs, 1982; Carnine & Silbert, 1979; Carnine, Silbert, & Kameenui, 1990). Direct instruction uses a variety of techniques, including questioning, cueing, and rewarding students. The primary function of the content teacher is to structure the learning climate and to mediate students' use of learning strategies for efficient learning (Ellis & Lenz, 1990).

13. S3: Why do fish go to school?

14. T: Great question. I did say that. Who could answer his question?

15. S2: Um…(pause) Maybe to keep safe, away…

16. S1: I know another way. A big pile, a school, a big pile of fish is called a school of fish.

17. T: Do you think that maybe R_____ wasn't quite sure what school meant in this story?
Is it the kind of school that we are in? We come to school to learn, don't we? But in this story it does mean a big gathering of fish. But, I bet that they do learn how to get food, and it's also for…

18. S1: To protect them.

19. T: Very good. Okay, can someone summarize what we've learned in this part? What was the most important information that we've learned from this story already, M_____?

20. S4: Them going to school.

21. T: Who's them?

22. S4: The fish.

23. T: Do they go to school or are they living in schools? Do you think they have rooms like we do?

24. S2: Yeah.

25. T: They just gather together and that's how they make a school. And, that might seem a little unusual. Now, let's see what other unusual creatures there might be. Do you know what I mean by creatures?

Source: From "The Role of Dialogue in Providing Scaffolded Instruction" by A. S. Palincsar, 1986, *Educational Psychologist, 21,* 87–89.

Three frequently used strategies in direct instruction techniques are questioning, paraphrasing, and visual imagery. Evidence suggests that adolescents who are mildly disabled can benefit from instruction in the use of these strategies (Pressley, 1977; Wong, 1991). See the section on commercially prepared materials for a description of the *Corrective Reading Program,* which uses the direct instruction approach.

The use of *learning strategies* has become an increasingly common form of intervention in secondary programs for students with mild disabilities. Learning strategies (Deshler & Schumaker, 1986) focus on how to perform specific routine tasks commonly found in content area classrooms (e.g., preparing for tests, reading texts, writing notes, preparing reports). Schumaker, Denton, and Deshler (1984) suggest the use of a paraphrasing strategy for facilitating reading comprehension. RAP (Schumaker et al., 1984) includes the following three steps: (a) **R**ead the paragraph, (b) **A**sk yourself what the paragraph is about, and (c) **P**ut the main idea and two details in your own words. Students can be taught these strategies (see Chapter 8 on Cognitive Strategy Training and Study Skills Instruction) in special education settings, and the mainstream content-area teacher can cue students when to use them. This can be accomplished via verbal cues, for example, "This is a good time to use the RAP strategy."

Learning strategies can also be incorporated into the mainstream curriculum for all students' benefit. Several studies have demonstrated that when secondary students with mild disabilities are taught learning strategies in a special education setting, they do generalize the use of the strategy in the mainstream if provided with cues (Ellis, Lenz, & Sabornie, 1987a, 1987b).

Critical Features of Reading Instruction

Paris and Oka (1989) suggested the following list of key features of effective reading instructional approaches:

1. Effective reading instruction focuses on process as well as content.
2. Strategies need to be explained sensibly and explicitly.
3. Students need to attribute successful comprehension to appropriate strategies.
4. Dialogues about thinking promote self-regulated learning.
5. Effective instruction maximizes task involvement, intrinsic motivation, and cooperation.
6. Effective instruction promotes transfer of strategies to content areas. (p. 39)

Secondary students with mild disabilities who receive this type of innovative instruction will become active and willing participants in the reading process.

Selected Commercial Reading Curricula for Adolescents with Reading Difficulties

A large number of commercial reading materials are available for adolescents with reading difficulties. These materials may be used to supplement content instruction.

Reading for Understanding, published by Science Reading Associates, is an individualized multilevel comprehension-building kit that may be used to help students develop and use the following skills: critical thinking, inferential logic, and drawing conclusions. Students read a selection, then choose a logically appropriate ending from four suggested conclusions. Level two is suggested for students in grades 1 through 3; level three is suggested for students in grades 7 through 12.

Advanced Reading Skill Builders, published by Reader's Digest Services, is a series of books using a magazine format with short reading selections followed by comprehension, vocabulary, and discussion questions. The emphasis is on building critical thinking skills, study skills, and literary skills. Designed for students in grades 7 through 9.

Specific Skill Builders, published by Barnell Loft, is composed of booklets that are designed to provide practice in several reading comprehension skills. At each grade level there are booklets for each of the following skills: using the context, getting the main idea, following directions, getting the facts, determining the sequence, drawing the conclusion, locating the answer, and working with sounds. Booklets G through L are appropriate for students reading at grade levels 7 through 12.

Stars Paperbacks, published by Opportunities for Learning, are examples of sets of reproducible books that feature some of today's most popular celebrities from the worlds of sports, film, music, and more (e.g., Bruce Springsteen, Magic Johnson, Michael Jordan, Madonna, and others). High-interest stories and pictures hold students' attention; questions and activities reinforce comprehension. Each book features 17 stars in 30 pages. Vocabulary levels range from 2.0 to 4.0. There are eight books.

Corrective Reading Program (Engelmann, Becker, Hanner, & Johnson, 1980), published by Science Research Associates, is a remedial program designed for students in grades 4 through 12. It may also be used with adults. The program is based on direct instruction techniques and is divided into two strands, decoding and comprehension. A teacher's presentation book is available to direct the teacher through the 340 lessons.

Selected Computer Software for Reading Instruction at the Secondary Level

Microcomputers are becoming part of the regular curriculum in all schools. There are several programs that can be used effectively to develop basic skills in reading as well as to reinforce comprehension and inferential skills. The following software programs focus on reading skills that may be appropriate for adolescents with mild disabilities.

Cloze-Plus, published by Milliken, is designed to develop reading comprehension skills and vocabulary through the use of structured cloze and context analysis activities. Reading selections are presented with one word omitted. The student is given five possible choices for the answer and may request context clues in which pertinent information is highlighted. Six levels are available for students with vocabulary ranging from 3rd-through 8th-grade reading levels.

The Gapper Reading Lab, published by Opportunities for Learning, is a reading comprehension program for use at any grade level from 4th to 12th. Paragraphs of reading material are displayed, using the cloze technique; students use their knowledge of word structure, spelling, grammar, and meaning in context to fill in the blanks. Other features include a built-in readability analysis program, comprehensive record-keeping facilities, adjustable difficulty levels, a teacher authoring system, and a print option.

Comprehension Power, published by Milliken, is designed to develop reading comprehension skills and reading rate. Stories are presented on a wide range of high-interest topics at either a preassigned rate (e.g., 60 words per minute) or page by page, with the student advancing the page manually. After each story the student answers comprehension questions that are followed by immediate feedback. The programs are designed for students reading at grade levels 4th through 12th. There are also three programs for junior and senior high school students who are reading at extremely low levels.

Hint and Hunt I and *II,* published by Developmental Learning Materials, are designed to teach vocabulary skills by focusing on vowel and vowel groups. The instructional phase, Hint, features realistic voice stimuli and animated graphics. The practice phase, Hunt, is designed in a fast-action game format. The programs require the addition of Supertalker, a plug-in board available from DLM to allow the student to hear selected words pronounced.

Word Man and *Word Radar,* published by Developmental Learning Materials, are included in the series Academic Skill Builders in Language Arts, published by DLM. Word Man uses a game format that consists of a maze of rectangular tracks with groups of letters placed along the rows. The student must decide when a word is formed as he or she watches a consonant move past the letter combinations. Word Radar provides practice in matching basic sight words by having the student portray a control tower who scans words that increase in length. Speed, length, content, and difficulty level can be adjusted.

Special Considerations in Reading Instruction of Adolescents with Mild Disabilities in Mainstream Classrooms

Importance of Motivation for Learning

Many secondary students with reading problems have serious motivational problems (Deshler, Schumaker, & Lenz, 1984). These students' negative reading experiences have been repetitive and cumulative. These reading deficiencies may have caused such adolescents to withhold effort from any task that requires reading. It becomes essential for educators at this level to foster motivation in order for instruction to be effective. As Adelman and Taylor (1983) suggest, "if a student is motivated to learn something [he or she] can do much more than anyone would have predicted was possible" (p. 384).

A critical recommendation that appears frequently in the motivation literature is to involve the student in the planning stages. If students take part in selecting and ordering their academic reading goals they have a more personal involvement and often are motivated to achieve more. Paris and Oka (1989) suggest that these students acquire *motivational empowerment* to regulate their own reading. As students realize that comprehension depends on a combination of personal effort, ability, and strategy use, they become more active readers. Successful approaches foster better understanding of cognitive active strategies while increasing students' motivation for reading.

Deshler, Schumaker, and Lenz (1984) suggest two motivational categories: extrinsic and intrinsic. Several extrinsic control techniques that have been successful are token economies, contingency contracting, and verbal feedback. Zigmond, Sansone, Miller, Donahoe, and Kohnke (1986) listed extrinsic reinforcers that appear effective with adolescents who have learning difficulties. Several of their suggestions are presented in Figure 5.6.

Techniques that focus on building intrinsic motivation such as self-control or self-monitoring, goal setting, and self-reinforcement have also been shown to improve motivation for secondary students with mild disabilities (Deshler et al., 1984; Seabaugh & Schumaker, 1981).

Figure 5.6
List of suggestions for reinforcers
for secondary students

1. Tokens for achievement
2. Self-recording or chart of academic progress
3. Grades in school tied to allowances at home
4. Time to spend in a game center or recreational activity
5. Time to play tapes or records
6. Opportunity to schedule when academic lessons take place
7. Use of "bank account" to buy privileges or free time
8. Tangible reinforcers, such as fast-food coupons, magazines, and movie tickets
9. Exemption from an additional assignment or homework
10. Extra time for lunch or for a break

Source: From *Teaching Learning Disabled Students at the Secondary Level* (pp. 17–18) by N. Zigmond, J. Sansone, S. E. Miller, K. A. Donahoe, and R. Kohnke, 1986, Reston, VA: Council for Exceptional Children.

Importance of Teaching Reading Skills for Generalization

If a reading instructional procedure is to be successful, it must promote the use of the newly learned skills outside the setting in which the skills were taught. It is critical that secondary students with mild disabilities be taught reading skills that will generalize to situations on the job and in the community, and to independent adult life.

Ellis, Lenz, and Sabornie (1987b) present the following sequence of instructional steps for promoting generalization:

1. Describe the major components of the new skills, emphasizing the different contexts in which they can be used.
2. Model the skills in different contexts.
3. Have students verbally rehearse the components of the skills to an automatic level.
4. Control the students' practice of the skills so that gradual application in other (easy reading level) context materials is possible. Keep materials at this step at the students' easy reading level.
5. Have students practice the skill in situations that vary greatly from the trained situation.
6. Provide corrective feedback and encourage students to request feedback from content teachers.
7. Have students demonstrate mastery by performing skills in real-world materials.

Adaptations to Mainstream Classrooms

Ellis and Lenz (1990) discuss five instructional options that many mainstream teachers use to promote content-area learning among students with mild disabilities and students who are low achievers. They suggest that most mainstream teachers employ one or more of the following options in their content-area classes. The teachers may "(a) adjust the curriculum so students do not have to learn as much, (b) select textbooks that are conducive to learning, (c) enhance content through the use of study guides, (d) use audio-recordings of text material, and/or (e) promote the use of appropriate and metacognitive strategies during direct instruction of content-area subject matter" (pp. 2–3).

The first two options, although commonly chosen by mainstream teachers, may negatively affect the potential for future learning. If the curriculum content is reduced or controlled, the amount or kind of learning is limited even before learning can take place. The student's potential for learning is often not maximized. Ellis (1996) suggests that teachers consider readability and attractiveness when they are making adaptive textbook decisions. Because textbooks play a major role in delivering content-area information, selection of texts should be made carefully.

The use of study guides, graphic organizers, and other technological devices (e.g., tape recordings, microcomputers) facilitates the learning process by providing organizational cues and encouraging students to become active participants in the reading process (see Chapter 10). Many students with mild disabilities use learning strategies effectively when cued by others (i.e., teachers or machines) (Ellis & Lenz, 1990). "The positive benefits of tape-recording texts are likely to accrue only when the texts and the recordings have been adapted to students so students are cued specifically to think strategically about the material (e.g., stop and summarize a paragraph just read to them on tape)" (Ellis, 1996, p. 117). Research also has supported the prompting of students to employ various cognitive processes (e.g., summarizing, paraphrasing, predicting) or other learning strategies when teaching content-area information (Deshler, Ellis, & Lenz, 1996).

For students with and without mild disabilities to be active and successful participants in mainstream classrooms, regular teachers can and should be trained to provide cues for the use of appropriate strategies (e.g., "now might be a good time to use the RAP strategy") and to provide feedback on the use of an appropriate strategy (e.g., "that was a good time to use the paraphrasing strategy we learned yesterday"). Teachers need to use strategic teaching, which is "a form of instruction in which the teacher compensates for students' lack of strategies and models and guides students in learning how to learn" (Bulgren & Lenz, 1996, p. 441). It may also be good to pair students—one good reader with one in need of assistance. Many secondary teachers are providing more opportunities for peer-assisted learning to cope with the increased academic diversity in their classrooms (Lenz, Schumaker, & Deshler, 1991). Learning from a partner can facilitate the learning process.

In summary, to make the mainstream class successful for many students who have difficulty with reading, much cooperation and coordination are needed between special and regular educators. The appropriate strategy instruction can be provided in the special or the general education classroom. Regular teachers and peers can be recruited to cue the students to apply the strategies in the mainstream. The student's motivation and self-confidence should be addressed in both situations.

Summary

Success in school ultimately depends on one's ability to read. This is magnified at the secondary level because so much of what is learned is acquired through reading of text. Reading instruction at the secondary level for many students with mild disabilities is their last chance to become independent—it must be interesting, intensive, engaging, and explicit.

Key Terms

functional curriculum
Woodcock Reading Mastery Test—Revised
informal reading inventory

cloze procedure
curriculum-based assessment
reciprocal teaching

References

Adelman, H. S., & Taylor, L. (1983). Enhancing motivation for overcoming learning and behavior problems. *Journal of Learning Disabilities, 16,* 384–392.

Alverman, D. E., Moore, D. W., & Conley, M. W. (Eds.). (1987). *Research within reach: Secondary school reading.* Newark, DE: International Reading Association.

Baker, L., & Brown, A. L. (1984). Metacognitive skills and reading. In P. D. Pearson, M. Kamil, R. Barr, & P. Mosenthal (Eds.), *Handbook of reading research* (pp. 353–394). New York: Longman.

Beck, I. L., Perfetti, C., & McKeown, M. (1982). The effects of long-term vocabulary instruction on lexical access and reading comprehension. *Journal of Educational Psychology, 74,* 506–521.

Becker, W. C., Engelmann, S., Carnine, D. W., & Maggs, A. (1982). Direct instruction technology: Making learning happen. In P. Karoly & J. J. Steffen (Eds.), *Improving children's competence: Advances in child behavioral analysis and therapy* (Vol. 1) (pp. 151–204). Lexington, MA: Heath.

Bormuth, J. R. (1968). The cloze readability procedure. *Elementary English, 45,* 429–436.

Bos, C. S., & Anders, P. L. (1990). Effects of interactive vocabulary instruction on the vocabulary learning and reading comprehension of junior-high learning disabled students. *Learning Disability Quarterly, 13,* 31–42.

Botel, M. (1978). *Botel Reading Inventory.* Chicago: Follett.

Brown, A. L., & Day, J. D. (1983). Macrorules for summarizing texts: The development of expertise. *Journal of Verbal Learning and Verbal Behavior, 22,* 1–14.

Brown, A. L., Campione, J. C., Reeve, R. A., Ferrara, R. A., & Palincsar, A. S. (1991). Interactive learning and individual understanding: The case of reading and mathematics. In L. T. Landsmann (Ed.), *Culture, schooling and psychological development.* Hillsdale, NJ: Erlbaum.

Brown, V. L., Hammill, D. D., & Wiederholt, J. L. (1986). *Test of reading comprehension* (rev. ed.). Austin, TX: PRO-ED.

Brown, A. L., Palincsar, A. S., & Armbruster, B. B. (1984). Instructing comprehension-fostering activities in interactive learning situations. In H. Mandl, N. L. Stein, & T. Trabasso (Eds.), *Learning and comprehension of text* (pp. 255–286). Hillsdale, NJ: Erlbaum.

Bulgren, J. A., Schumaker, J. B., & Deshler, D. D. (1988). Effectiveness of a concept teaching routine in enhancing the performance of LD students in secondary-level mainstream classes. *Learning Disability Quarterly, 11,* 3–17.

Bulgren, J., & Lenz, K. (1996). Strategic instruction in the content areas. In D. D. Deshler, E. S. Ellis, & B. K. Lenz (Eds.), *Teaching adolescents with learning disabilities: Strategies and methods* (2nd ed.) (pp. 409–473). Denver: Love.

Carnine, D., & Silbert, J. (1979). *Direct instruction reading.* Upper Saddle River, NJ: Merrill/Prentice Hall.

Carnine, D., Silbert, J., & Kameenui, E. J. (1990). *Direct instruction reading* (2nd ed.). Upper Saddle River, NJ: Merrill/Prentice Hall.

Chall, J. S. (1983). *Stages of reading development.* New York: McGraw-Hill.

deBettencourt, L. U., Zigmond, N., & Thornton, H. S. (1989). Follow-up of postsecondary age rural learning disabled graduates and dropouts. *Exceptional Children, 56,* 40–49.

Deno, S. L. (1985). Curriculum-based measurement: The emerging alternative. *Exceptional Children, 52,* 219–232.

Deno, S. L. (1986). Formative evaluation of individual student programs: A new role for school psychologists. *School Psychology Review, 15,* 358–374.

Deno, S. L. (1987). Curriculum-based measurement. *Teaching Exceptional Children, 20,* 41–42.

Deno, S. L., & Fuchs, L. S. (1987). Developing curriculum-based measurement for special education problem-solving. *Focus on Exceptional Children, 19,* 1–16.

Deshler, D. D., Ellis, E. E., & Lenz, B. K. (1996). *Teaching adolescents with learning disabilities: Strategies and methods* (2nd ed.). Denver: Love Publishing.

Deshler, D. D., & Schumaker, J. B. (1986). Learning strategies: An instructional alternative for low-achieving adolescents. *Exceptional Children, 52,* 219–232.

Deshler, D. D., Schumaker, J. B., & Lenz, B. K. (1984). Academic and cognitive interventions for LD adolescents: Part I. *Journal of Learning Disabilities, 17,* 108–117.

Deshler, D. D., Schumaker, J. B., Lenz, B. K., & Ellis, E. S. (1984). Academic and cognitive interventions for LD adolescents: Part II. *Journal of Learning Disabilities, 17,* 170–187.

Donahoe, K., & Zigmond, N. (1990). Academic grades of ninth-grade urban learning disabled students and low-achieving peers. *Exceptionality, 1*(1), 17–27.

Ekwall, E. E. (1986). *Ekwall Reading Inventory* (2nd ed.). Boston: Allyn & Bacon.

Ellis, E. S. (1996). Reading strategy instruction. In D. D. Deshler, E. S. Ellis, & B. K. Lenz (Eds.), *Teaching adolescents with learning disabilities: Strategies and methods* (2nd ed.). (pp. 61–125). Denver: Love Publishing.

Ellis, E. S., & Lenz, B. K. (1990). Techniques for mediating content-area learning: Issues and research. *Focus on Exceptional Children, 22*(9), 1–16.

Ellis, E. S., Lenz, B. K., & Sabornie, E. J. (1987a). Generalization and adaptation of learning strategies to natural environments: Part 1—Critical agents. *Remedial and Special Education, 8*(1) 6–20.

Ellis, E. S., Lenz, B. K., & Sabornie, E. J. (1987b). Generalization and adaptation of learning strategies to natural environments: Part 2—Research into practice. *Remedial and Special Education, 8*(2), 6–23.

Engelmann, S., Becker, W., Hanner, S., & Johnson, G. (1980). *Corrective reading program.* Chicago: Science Research Associates.

Fuchs, L. S., Deno, S. L., & Mirkin, P. (1984). The effects of frequent curriculum-based measurement and evaluation on pedagogy, student achievement, and student awareness of learning. *American Educational Research Journal, 21,* 449–460.

Fuchs, L. S., Fuchs, D., Hamlett, C. L., & Hasselbring, T. S. (1987). Using computers with curriculum-based monitoring: Effects on teacher efficiency and satisfaction. *Journal of Special Education Technology, 8,* 14–27.

Fuchs, L. S., Hamlett, C. L., Fuchs, D., Stecker, P. M., & Ferguson, C. (1988). Conducting curriculum-based measurement with computerized data collection: Effects of efficiency and teacher satisfaction. *Journal of Special Education Technology, 9*(2), 73–86.

Gilmore, J. V., & Gilmore, E. C. (1968). *Gilmore Oral Reading Test.* San Antonio, TX: Psychological Corporation.

Idol, L. (1988). Johnny can't read: Does the fault lie with the book, the teacher, or Johnny? *Remedial and Special Education, 9,* 8–25.

Jongsma, E. (1971). *The cloze procedure as teaching technique.* Newark, DE: International Reading Association.

Johns, J. L. (1981). *Advanced Reading Inventory: Grades seven through college.* Dubuque, IA: William C. Brown.

Johnson, D., & Pearson, P. D. (1984). *Teaching reading vocabulary* (2nd ed.). New York: Holt, Rinehart & Winston.

Kaluger, G., & Kolson, C. J. (1978). *Reading and learning disabilities* (2nd ed.). Upper Saddle River, NJ: Merrill/Prentice Hall.

Karlsen, B., Madden, R., & Gardner, E. F. (1984). *Stanford Diagnostic Reading Test* (3rd ed.). San Antonio, TX: Psychological Corporation.

Kirk, S. A., Kliebhan, J. M., & Lerner, J. W. (1978). *Teaching reading to slow and disabled readers.* Boston: Houghton Mifflin.

Kokaska, C. J., & Brolin, D. E. (1985). *Career education for handicapped individuals* (2nd ed.). Upper Saddle River, NJ: Merrill/Prentice Hall.

Kozol, J. (1985). *Illiterate America.* New York: Plume Publishers.

Leinhardt, G., Zigmond, N., & Cooley, W. (1981). Reading instruction and its effects. *American Educational Research Journal, 6,* 343–361.

Lenz, B. K., Alley, G. R., & Schumaker, J. B. (1987). Activating the inactive learner: Advance organizers in the secondary content classroom. *Learning Disability Quarterly, 10,* 53–67.

Lenz, B. K., & Hughes, C. A. (1990). A word identification strategy for adolescents with learning disabilities. *Journal of Learning Disabilities, 23,* 149–158, 163.

Lenz, B. K., Schumaker, J. B., & Deshler, D. D. (1991). *Planning in the face of academic diversity: Whose questions should we be answering?* Paper presented at American Educational Research Association Conference, Chicago.

Lenz, B. K., Schumaker, J. B., Deshler, D. D., & Beals, V. L. (1984). *Learning strategies curriculum: The word identification strategy.* Lawrence, KS: University of Kansas.

MacGinitie, W. H. (1978). *Gates-MacGinitie Reading Tests.* Boston: Houghton Mifflin.

McGill-Franzen, A. (1987). Failure to learn to read: Formulating a policy problem. *Reading Research Quarterly, 22,* 475–490.

McKeown, M. G., & Beck, I. L. (1988). Learning vocabulary: Different ways for different goals. *Remedial and Special Education, 9,* 42–52.

McLoughlin, J. A., & Lewis, R. B. (1990). *Assessing special students* (3rd ed.). Upper Saddle River, NJ: Merrill/Prentice Hall.

Mercer, C. D. (1987). *Students with learning disabilities* (3rd ed.). Upper Saddle River, NJ: Merrill/Prentice Hall.

Mercer, C. D., & Mercer, A. R. (1991). *Teaching students with learning problems* (4th ed.). Upper Saddle River, NJ: Merrill/Prentice Hall.

Morsink, C. V., & Gable, R. A. (1990). Errors in reading. In R. A. Gable & J. M. Hendrickson (Eds.), *Assessing students with special needs* (pp. 46–62). White Plains, NY: Longman.

Palincsar, A. S., & Brown, A. L. (1984). Reciprocal teaching of comprehension-fostering and comprehension-monitoring activities. *Cognition and Instruction, 1,* 117–175.

Palincsar, A. S., Brown, A. L., & Martin, S. M. (1987). Peer interaction in reading comprehension instruction. *Educational Psychologist, 22,* 231–254.

Paris, S. G., & Oka, E. R. (1989). Strategies for comprehending text and coping with reading difficulties. *Learning Disability Quarterly, 12,* 32–42.

Polloway, E. A., Patton, J. R., Payne, J. S., & Payne, R. A. (1989). *Strategies for teaching learners with special needs* (4th ed.). Upper Saddle River, NJ: Merrill/Prentice Hall.

Pressley, M. (1977). Imagery and children's learning: Putting the picture in developmental perspective. *Review of Educational Research, 47,* 586–622.

Psychological Corporation. (1992). *Wechsler Individual Achievement Test.* San Antonio, TX: Author.

Readence, J. E., Bean, T. W., & Baldwin, R. S. (1989). *Content area reading: An integrated approach* (3rd ed.). Dubuque, IA: Kendall/Hunt Publishing Co.

Roe, B. D. (1985). *Burns/Roe Informal Reading Inventory.* Boston: Houghton Mifflin.

Rye, J. (1982). *Cloze procedure and the teaching of reading.* London: Heinemann Educational Books.

Schumaker, J. B., Denton, P. H., & Deshler, D. D. (1984). *Learning strategies curriculum: The paraphrasing strategy.* Lawrence, KS: University of Kansas.

Seabaugh, G. O., & Schumaker, J. B. (1981). *The effects of self-regulation training on the academic productivity of LD and NLD adolescents* (Research Report No. 37). Lawrence, KS: The University of Kansas Institute for Research in Learning Disabilities.

Silvaroli, N. J. (1986). *Classroom Reading Inventory* (5th ed.). Dubuque, IA: William C. Brown.

Spache, G. D. (1981). *Diagnostic Reading Scales.* Monterey, CA: CTB/McGraw-Hill.

Sucher, F., & Allred, R. A. (1981). *The New Sucher-Allred Reading Placement Inventory.* Oklahoma City, OK: Economy.

Thornton, H. S., & Zigmond, N. (1987, April). *Post-secondary follow-up of learning disabled and non-handicapped completers of mainstream vocational education programs.* Paper presented at Annual Meeting of American Educational Research Association, Washington, DC.

Tucker, J. A. (1985). Curriculum-based assessment: An introduction. *Exceptional Children, 48,* 529–530.

U.S. Department of Education. (1986). *Reading report card.* Washington, DC: Author.

Valencia, S. W., & Pearson, P. D. (1988). Principles for classroom comprehension assessment. *Remedial and Special Education, 9,* 26–35.

Wiederholt, J. L. (1986). *Formal Reading Inventory.* Austin, TX: PRO-ED.

Wiederholt, J. L., & Bryant, B. R. (1986). *Gray Oral Reading Test—Revised.* Austin, TX: PRO-ED.

Wixson, K. K., & Peters, C. W. (1987). Comprehension assessment: Implementing an interactive view of reading. *Educational Psychologist, 22,* 333–356.

Wong, B. Y. L. (1991). The relevance of metacognition to learning disabilities. In B. Y. L. Wong, (Ed.), *Learning about learning disabilities* (pp. 231–258). New York: Academic Press.

Wong, B. Y. L. (1987). How do the results of metacognitive research impact the learning disabled individual? *Learning Disability Quarterly, 10,* 189–195.

Woodcock, R. W. (1987). *Woodcock Reading Mastery Test—Revised.* Circle Pines, NM: American Guidance Service.

Zigmond, N. (1990). Rethinking secondary school programs for students with learning disabilities. *Focus on Exceptional Children, 23,* 1–12.

Zigmond, N., & Thornton, H. S. (1985). Follow-up of post secondary age LD graduates and dropouts. *Learning Disabilities Research, 1*(1), 50–55.

Zigmond, N., Sansone, J., Miller, S. E., Donahoe, K. A., & Kohnke, R. (1986). *Teaching learning disabled students at the secondary level: What research and experience says to the teacher of exceptional children.* Reston, VA: Council for Exceptional Children.

6

Written Language Instruction for Adolescents with Mild Disabilities

Objectives

After reading this chapter, the reader should be able to:

1. discuss potential problems of secondary students with mild disabilities in the curriculum area of written language;

2. delineate several types of formal and informal written language assessment procedures;

3. discuss various instructional strategies that may be appropriate for secondary students with mild disabilities;

4. summarize issues surrounding the teaching of written language at the secondary level to students with mild disabilities;

5. discuss special considerations in written language instruction of adolescents with mild disabilities in mainstream classrooms.

" . . . writing is something you can never do as well as it can be done. It is perpetual challenge and it is more difficult than anything else that I have ever done—so I do it. And it makes me happy when I do it well."

"Written language is a mediator for other academic learning and serves as the main method for demonstrating a student's learning; thus, facility in written language is essential for school success" (Christenson, Thurlow, Ysseldyke, & McVicar, 1989, p. 219). The purpose of this chapter is to discuss written language instruction at the secondary level for students who have mild disabilities. Ways in which an educator can assess secondary-level students in the area of written language are also discussed and specific assessment devices summarized. Several techniques that have been supported by research are clarified along with appropriate commercial curricula and computer software.

Students with Mild Disabilities and Written Language Problems

Written language skills are essential for school success at the secondary level. Writing is a challenging skill for all students to master and it is particularly difficult for students with mild disabilities (Graham, 1982; Graham, 1992; Graham & MacArthur, 1987; Thomas, Englert, & Gregg, 1987). Adolescents with mild disabilities score lower in nearly every area of written language as measured by norm-referenced tests (Poplin, Gray, Larsen, Banikowski, & Mehring, 1980).

There are many reasons that secondary students with mild disabilities have difficulty with written language. They may notice problems, but not know how to fix them (Graham & Harris, 1993; Graham, Harris, MacArthur, & Schwartz, 1991). They may lack knowledge of criteria for evaluation of their writing (Graham, Schwartz, & MacArthur, 1991). They may lack executive control skills required to monitor their writing and coordinate their revision process (Englert & Raphael, 1988; Englert, Raphael, Anderson, Gregg, & Anthony, 1989). They also may not develop a sense of audience or purpose for writing (Englert, Raphael, Fear, & Anderson, 1988; Graves, 1983). Adolescents with mild disabilities do not know effective writing strategies nor do they necessarily employ the strategies they do know (Ellis & Colvert, 1996). Figure 6.1 lists several factors many researchers feel may result in a student's difficulties in written language.

Research has also shown that in comparison to their peers' work, the compositions written by students with mild disabilities are shorter (Deno, Marston, & Mirkin, 1982),

Figure 6.1
Several factors contributing to students' difficulties in written language

1. Students may not be sufficiently knowledgeable regarding the topics they are asked to write about, or they may not effectively access knowledge they do possess.

2. They may not be adequately knowledgeable about the characteristics of different types of writing genres, or they are ineffective in retrieving the genre-specific knowledge they do have.

3. The mechanical demands of text production may interfere with more substantive writing processes such as planning, framing, or revising text.

4. Students may use ineffective (or no) strategies when engaging in writing processes such as generating, framing, or revising text.

5. Students' writing problems may result from difficulties with executive control; processes and strategies must be brought into play at the right time and in proper relationship to each other.

Source: From "Composition Instruction with Learning Disabled Students: Self-Instructional Strategy Training" by S. Graham, K. R. Harris, and R. Sawyer, 1987, *Focus on Exceptional Children, 20*(4), 1–11.

are less cohesive (Nodine, Barenbaum, & Newcomer, 1985), contain more mechanical errors, and are poorer in quality (Poplin et al., 1980).

Because most secondary students with mild disabilities spend all or a large part of their school day in the regular class environment and are asked to write clearly and coherently, it is imperative that their written language deficits be addressed. The advent of minimum competency testing at the secondary level has resulted in an increase in the number of states that demand that students demonstrate the ability to write before they can be awarded a high school diploma (Graham & Harris, 1988). Such demands make it especially important that regular and special educators work collaboratively to design an effective written language program for these students.

Teaching Written Language as a Complex Process

Composing is no longer perceived as a simple linear activity but as a complex recursive activity involving problem solving and integration of many cognitive processes (Bereiter & Scardamalia, 1987; Hayes & Flower, 1986; Scardamalia & Bereiter, 1987). Proficient writing necessitates the ability to monitor and direct the composing process while simultaneously dealing with mechanics, organization, purpose, clarity, and so forth (Graham, 1982). This requires the coordination of a vast array of skills (Englert et al., 1989). Skilled writers must also remain sensitive to the needs of their intended audience in deciding what information to include, in monitoring and revising text, and in producing reader-friendly text. As Englert and Raphael (1988) state, "the composing difficulties of exceptional students are manifested in three areas of writing: idea generation, text organization, and metacognitive knowledge" (p. 514).

Studies have shown the composition process as coordinating three major operations: planning, translating or sentence generation, and reviewing or revising (Hayes & Flower, 1986). The purpose of the planning phase is to generate ideas from background information, organize relevant information, and develop a plan. Research suggests that students with mild disabilities do not appropriate time for planning in advance of writing (e.g., MacArthur & Graham, 1987). The translating phase transforms the relevant information into acceptable written English. Writers consider all ideas listed, as well as their own purpose for writing and the needs of their audience. Research suggests that students with mild disabilities do not consider the needs of their audience (e.g., Graves, 1983). The function of the third phase, reviewing or revising, is to improve the quality of the written material. Students with mild disabilities may correct their mechanical errors, but many do not go beyond the mechanics (e.g., Graham and MacArthur, 1987).

Importance of Functional Writing Skills for Adolescents with Mild Disabilities

To be successful at the secondary level, students need to possess writing skills such as taking notes, answering chapter questions, and writing reports or essays. Class assignments in various content-related subject areas increasingly require students to compose materials of an expository nature (Thomas, Englert, & Gregg, 1987).

What employers ranked highest in writing

Why skills are important at this level

Writing skills are also important at this level for success in future occupations. Job-related writing tasks include writing business letters, writing résumés, and completing college and/or job applications; responses on job applications often influence the decision to proceed with an interview. Algozzine, O'Shea, Stoddard, and Crews (1988) found employers ranked writing accurate messages and requests, noting work assignments, and completing forms as the most important writing tasks needed by their employees.

Assessment of Written Language Skills at the Secondary Level

Traditionally, written language skills have been measured by standardized tests with questionable content validity (Isaacson, 1984). During the past 15 years, both formal measures and informal measures have improved. Several such measures of written language are currently available to assist an assessment team in identifying written language skill deficiencies.

Because written language requires the writer to focus on the objective (e.g., story, plot, etc.) while also focusing on the techniques of writing, such as handwriting, spelling, punctuation, and the correct use of grammar and style, this section will discuss assessment, with both formal and informal measures, of many of these component skills.

Regardless of the purpose of assessment, Tindal and Parker (1991) suggest that the method chosen should meet the following criteria:

1. be consistently administered and scored reliably;
2. discriminate among students from different skill levels;
3. bear at least low-moderate relation to other accepted assessment methods; and
4. show score improvement by students over the course of the year. (p. 211)

Using Standardized Criterion-Referenced and Diagnostic Tests: Selected Instruments

some measure only 1 thing

Writing measures can be used to distinguish between successful and unsuccessful writers and to identify students in need of remedial assistance. Formal instruments, such as norm-referenced tests, often have been used for this purpose. Many such instruments measure only one specific skill area, such as spelling; other instruments measure only mechanical aspects of writing, such as grammar; and a few others do include a measure of composition.

The number of written language measures has increased dramatically in the past few years. Table 6.1 provides a list of commonly used commercially prepared written language tests appropriate for use with secondary students with mild disabilities. In the following section we discuss several selected instruments.

Peabody Individual Achievement Test—Revised (Markwardt, 1989). This broad-range achievement test consists of a battery of subtests that are appropriate for students

Table 6.1

List of commonly used commercially prepared written language tests appropriate for use with secondary students with mild disabilities

Name (Authors)	Ages or Grades	Skill Area(s) Assessed		
		Spelling	Handwriting	Composition
BRIGANCE Diagnostic Comprehensive Inventory of Basic Skills (Brigance, 1983)	Gr. K–9	*	*	*
BRIGANCE Diagnostic Inventory of Basic Skills (Brigance, 1977)	Gr. K–6	*	*	
BRIGANCE Diagnostic Inventory of Essential Skills (Brigance, 1981)	Gr. 4–12	*	*	*
Spellmaster Assessment and Teaching System (Greenbaum, 1987)	Gr. K–10	*		
Test of Adolescent Language–3 (Hammill, Brown, Larsen, & Wiederholt, 1994)	Ages 12–18.5	*		*
Test of Written Language–3 (Hammill & Larsen, 1994)	Ages 7–17	*		*
Test of Written Spelling–3 (Larsen & Hammill, 1994)	Ages 6–18.5	*		
Woodcock Johnson Psycho-Educational Battery–Revised (Woodcock & Johnson, 1989)	Ages 2–90	*	*	*

aged 5 through 18. It includes a spelling section in which the student must identify the correctly spelled word. The written expression subtest consists of rating the student's composition on content, mechanics, and organization.

Woodcock-Johnson Psycho-Educational Battery—Revised (Woodcock & Johnson, 1989). This broad-range achievement test includes two measures of spelling: a dictation subtest and a proofing subtest. It also measures spelling, punctuation, and capitalization. Students are required to write sentences that are evaluated on quality of expression.

Test of Adolescent Language—3 (TOAL—3) (Hammill, Brown, Larsen, & Wiederholt, 1994) is a norm-referenced measure developed for students in grades 6 through adults aged 24. It assesses a wide range of language skills (i.e., listening, reading, writing). There are two subtests that assess written language. The writing/grammar subtest requires the student to read two sentences and then write one sentence that combines the meaning of the original sentences. The writing/vocabulary subtest requires the student to read a word and write a sentence including that word. The raw scores can be converted into scaled scores. The subtest scores can be combined to form a writing composite score.

Test of Written Spelling—3 (TWS—3) (Larsen & Hammill, 1994) is a norm-referenced measure designed for students aged 6 to 18. There are two standard dictation subtests that measure a student's ability to spell both phonetically regular and irregular words, which are drawn from ten basal spelling programs and popular graded word lists. The TWS—3 can be administered to groups or individuals and yields standard scores and percentile ranks.

Test of Written Language—3 (TOWL—3) (Hammill & Larsen, 1996) was developed to assess the adequacy of abilities in handwriting, spelling, and the various other components of written expression of students in grades 2 through 12. The TOWL—3 uses both essay analysis (spontaneous) formats and traditional test (contrived) formats to assess various aspects of written language. The student looks at three pictures and writes a story based on the pictures. Subtests included are: (a) thematic maturity, (b) contextual vocabulary, (c) syntactic maturity, (d) contextual spelling, (e) contextual style, (f) vocabulary, (g) style, (h) spelling, (i) logical sentences, and (j) sentence combining. The test can be given to individuals or small groups. Two alternate, equivalent forms are available, and percentiles and standard scores are provided.

The Spellmaster Assessment and Teaching System (Greenbaum, 1987) is composed of a series of criterion-referenced tests for students in all grade levels. The system includes eight diagnostic tests for measuring spelling of phonetically regular words, eight homonym tests, and eight entry-level tests to pinpoint students' strengths and weaknesses.

Wechsler Individual Achievement Test (WIAT) (Psychological Corporation, 1992) is composed of a required written piece that is scored on organization, development, coherence, vocabulary, sentence structure, ideas, and variety. The writing score is a composite of spelling and writing.

Using Informal Written Language Assessment Procedures

Informal assessment of written language is often necessary for planning individually appropriate instruction. Unlike standardized tests, informal measures enable the teacher to identify problems unique to individual students. Informal assessments are also more sensitive to small increments of skill growth across short to medium periods of time (Tindal & Parker, 1989). Informal assessment procedures enable a teacher to use assessment results to formulate goals on students' individualized educational programs (IEPs). Work sample analysis, informal inventories, criterion-referenced tests, and observation are all informal means used to evaluate a student's written language ability.

Writing portfolio analysis.   Informal measures usually involve scoring a student's writing sample on several measures. Teachers should collect samples of the student's writing with varying intents (e.g, creative writing, letters, theme paper). A writing portfolio is a purposeful collection of a student's writing (Graves & Sunstein, 1992) that contains products that the student selects to represent his or her best work.

Wesson, Otis-Wilborn, Hasbrouck, and Tindal (1989) described another structured method for collecting a brief written language sample; it involves 10 minutes of class time. See Box 6.1 for directions given to students.

After collecting several samples of a student's written products, analysis of individual strengths and weaknesses can be made by counting the number of words used

---

BOX 6.1
• •

Directions to Students for the Purpose of Collecting a Brief Written Language Sample

"I want you to write a story. I will read the beginning of a story to you first. Then I want you to write a story about what happens next. You will have 30 seconds to plan what you will write. Use that time to decide what will happen in your story. You will have 3 minutes to write. At the end of 3 minutes, I will say 'time' and you will mark a star on your paper after the last word you wrote. (Demonstrate on the board.) If you like, you will then be able to finish your story and give it a title. Start your story with your own words. You should not write the words I read to you. You won't write a title for this story until you are finished. Are there any questions? . . . Listen carefully. For the next 30 seconds I want you to think about a story that starts like this: (Example) 'I went up to the old deserted house. The door was open, so I walked in. Suddenly, . . . '"

Source: From "Linking Assessment, Curriculum, and Instruction of Oral and Written Language" by C. Wesson, A. Otis-Wilborn, J. Hasbrouck, and G. Tindal, 1989, *Focus on Exceptional Children, 22*(4), 1–12.

---

appropriately, the number of words spelled correctly, the number of sentences, the types of sentences (e.g., simple, compound, complex), the length of sentences, and so forth. Rousseau (1990) suggests dividing **error analysis** of a student's writing into two activities: (a) assessment of errors based on examination of the written product, and (b) use of an **oral edit** to gain understanding of the student's intent. The information can be charted or graphed and used to assist the teacher in preparing appropriate instruction. Figure 6.2 contains the definitions of terms one might use in an error analysis and a form that allows one to chart the types of errors made (Rousseau, 1990). The oral edit involves having the student read his or her story into a tape recorder, then having the teacher (while listening to the tape) count the number of oral edits the student makes.

Informal inventories. A teacher may also want to use informal inventories, such as checklists or rating scales, to monitor students' written language improvement, especially in the area of spelling. Checklists and rating scales assess skill development by breaking down the broad skill of composition into more specific subskill areas. A teacher can determine which areas may need further assessment.

Criterion-referenced tests. Teachers can prepare their own criterion-referenced tests to measure progress toward their curriculum goals. There are also several published criterion-referenced tests, such as the measures by Brigance (1977, 1981, 1983). For example, the

Error Analysis Form

Student __Tony__ Age __11-3__ Grade __6__ Date __9/20/89__

Writing time (min.) __30__ Picture __#4__ Topic __#3__

Total words __83__ No. T-units __8__

Garbled words __16__ Average words/T-units __8.38__

Readable words __67__ Scorer _____

Error Category	Error Type	Number per T-unit	Prior
Careless	Omitted words	0/8 = 0	
	Substituted words	3/8 = 0.38	
Excessive Usage (and/so/but/or)	Beginning of T-unit	7/8 = 0.88	
	Within T-unit	1/8 = 0.13	
Verbs	Inflections	1/8 = 0.13	
	Subject-verb	0/8 = 0	
	Verb tense changes	3/8 = 0.38	
Nouns	Number	0/8 = 0	
	Possession	0/8 = 0	
Pronouns	Possession	0/8 = 0	
	Agreement/antecedent	0/8 = 0	
Punctuation	End	8/8 = 1.00	
	Within T-unit	0/8 = 0	
Capitalization	Beginning	6/8 = 0.75	
	Proper nouns	6/8 = 0.75	
	Inapprop. capital.	4/8 = 0.50	
Paragraphs	Extraneous T-units	# = 0	
	New line/ea. T-unit	Yes No	

Figure 6.2

Error analysis form for recording errors in written language

Source: From "Errors in Written Language" by M. K. Rousseau, in *Assessing Students with Special Needs* (pp. 89–101), by R. A. Gable and J. M. Hendrickson (Eds.), 1990, New York: Longman.

Brigance Diagnostic Inventory of Essential Skills (1981) measures skills such as completing applications, income tax forms, social security forms, and so forth.

Observations. Aspects of the writing process can be evaluated through observations; in the context of the three phases of the writing process, observations of a student's actions may prove helpful. Some students do not engage in any planning, but begin writing immediately after an assignment is given. Or a student may spend most of the class period planning but very little time actually writing. Observing students during the writing process may allow the teacher further understanding of each student's individual strengths and weaknesses.

Written Language Instruction at the Secondary Level

The neglect of writing instruction in the public schools has been well documented (Bridge & Hiebert, 1985; Christenson et al., 1989; Graham, 1982; Graham & Harris, 1988; Roit & McKenzie, 1985). Although writing may be perceived as a valued skill, this perception has not been translated into actual classroom practice (Graves, 1983; Isaacson, 1987, 1988). The amount of time allocated to instruction in written language varies from as little as 6.5% of the school day (Bridge & Hiebert, 1985) to 24.6% (Thurlow, Ysseldyke, Graden, & Algozzine, 1984). The actual amount of time students with mild disabilities spend writing averages about 10 minutes per day (Bridge & Hiebert, 1985; Leinhardt, Zigmond, & Cooley, 1981). The small number of objectives for writing on individual educational programs of students with mild disabilities (Schenck, 1981) also points to the neglect of written language instruction.

In the past, what little written language instruction there was tended to emphasize only the mechanical aspects, such as handwriting, spelling, and usage; however, new directions suggest that teachers should avoid excessive correction of the mechanical aspects of writing. The first step toward implementing a successful writing program is to allocate time for writing as an ongoing part of your curriculum. Vallecorsa, Ledford, and Parnell (1991) suggest 40 minutes for group settings per day and 30 minutes for individual students. Whenever possible, writing should be integrated with other academic subjects; this will increase instructional time.

The second step in written language instruction is to create a positive attitude about writing. A student at the secondary level who has had difficulty writing for many years needs to be motivated and needs to feel comfortable expressing himself or herself. Students need to learn that writing can be useful and meaningful.

There are several opportunities for meaningful writing in secondary classrooms. Students can write narratives about their personal experiences; they can keep journals with their teachers; they can write letters to gather more information; and they can set up pen-pal relationships with people their same age in other countries. They also can record notes on an experiment or write reports about themes they are studying in social studies or history classes. Development of writing circles or writers' conferences may also foster positive social responses to writing at the secondary level. The teacher needs to develop a supportive classroom environment that encourages students to write for a wide variety of purposes (MacArthur, Schwartz, & Graham, 1991).

The third step is to expose students to a broad range of writing tasks. They should be shown how to use writing to meet their social, academic, occupational, and recreational goals (Graham & Harris, 1988). Instruction should be such that their writing tasks are aimed at authentic audiences.

The fourth step toward implementing a successful writing program is to provide more specific instruction in writing strategies and less emphasis on the mechanics of the writing process. Because writing is so multifaceted and requires mastery of a variety of skills, several distinct methods for encouraging and developing writing ability have been advocated. We will discuss several models of instruction that have proved to be successful with adolescent students with mild disabilities.

Instruction Using Cognitive Models

One method used to help secondary students with writing disabilities to overcome the difficulties inherent in the composing process is the use of metacognitive strategy instruction (Graham, Harris, & Sawyer, 1987). The two assumptions underlying strategy instruction are: (1) students need to become active participants in the learning process, and (2) cognitive activity mediates behavior. With this method, students are taught powerful strategies for planning, writing, and revising their written products.

Features of a cognitive model of instruction that are essential for success are (Graham et al., 1987):

1. modeling of the strategy;
2. an instructional sequence that encourages the teacher and the student to interact in the cognitive process;
3. development of inner language or metacognitive skills,
4. emphasis on what the strategy is and when and how and why to use it (Brown & Palincsar, 1982; Thomas et al., 1987);
5. emphasis within the context of writing papers on the writing subprocesses and steps of writing text (Englert et al., 1988).

Self-instructional strategy training is one example of a cognitive model of instruction that has been used to improve students' written language skills. Seven basic steps provide the framework of self-instructional strategy training (Harris & Graham, 1985; Graham & Harris, 1987). See Box 6.2 for a more detailed description of each step.

Step 1.   pretraining
Step 2.   review of current performance
Step 3.   description of the strategy
Step 4.   modeling of the strategy and self-instructions
Step 5.   mastery of the composition strategy
Step 6.   controlled practice of the strategy and self-instructions
Step 7.   independent performance/ data collection

BOX 6.2

• •

Self-Instructional Strategy Development: Basic Stages

Stage 1: Preskill development. Develop to mastery any preskills necessary for understanding, learning, and executing the targeted strategy that are not already in the learner's repertoire.

Stage 2: Review current performance level. Teacher and student examine and discuss baseline data and any strategies the student currently uses; negative or ineffective self-statements or strategies can also be discussed. The significance and potential benefits of the proposed instruction are discussed; commitment to participate as a partner and to attempt the strategies is established; and goals are established in a positive, collaborative manner.

Stage 3: Describe the executive strategy. The teacher describes the executive strategy (e.g., recursive steps in prewriting or revision); teacher and student discuss the advantages of the strategy, as well as how and when to use it.

Stage 4: Model the strategy and self-instructions. The teacher (or peer) models the strategies to be learned, in context. Teacher and student then discuss the model's performance, and the student generates and records her/his *own* self-instructions in each category modeled. Teacher and student may also collaborate on any changes that make the strategy more efficient or effective.

Stage 5: Mastery of the strategy. The student is required to memorize the self-instructions and steps in the strategy. Paraphrasing is then allowed as long as meaning remains intact.

Stage 6: Collaborative practice of strategy steps and self-instructions. The student practices the strategy and self-instructions *while performing the task. Self-regulation* procedures (i.e., goal setting, self-monitoring, self-recording, self-assessment, and self-reinforcement) are discussed, decided upon, and used throughout this step. Prompts, interaction, and guidance are faded over practice sessions until independent performance is achieved. Challenging, proximal goals are determined cooperatively; criterion levels are gradually increased until the final goal is met. Teacher and student plan for transfer and maintenance of the strategy.

Stage 7: Independent performance. Transition to covert self-instructions is encouraged as the student is instructed to use the strategy independently. Self-regulation procedures are continued. Plans for transfer and maintenance are implemented; strategy effectiveness and performance are evaluated collaboratively.

Note: Stages are flexible, recursive, and individualized as necessary; instruction is criterion-based rather than time-based.

Source: From "The Nature of Cognitive Strategy Instruction: Interactive Strategy Construction" by K. R. Harris and M. Pressley, 1991, *Exceptional Children, 57,* 397.

Four self-instructional strategies that have proved effective with students with mild disabilities are: (a) increasing vocabulary, (b) generating content, (c) planning composition, and (d) revising and editing texts (Graham et al., 1987). Self-instructional statements were also taught to the students (e.g., What is it I have to do? Have I included all the word types?). Stories written by students who were trained to use the strategy and the self-instructional statements evidenced substantial increases in the number and diversity of verbs, adverbs, and adjectives.

Graham and Harris (1987) taught 6th-grade students with mild disabilities to generate content for a written story. Their strategy had the following steps:

1. look at the picture;
2. let your mind be free;
3. write down the story parts: remember

   WHO is the main character

   WHEN does the story take place

   WHERE does the story take place

   WHAT does the main character do

   WHAT happens when he or she tries to do it

   HOW does the story end

   HOW does the main character feel
4. write down story part ideas for each part
5. write your story

The stories written by the students after training were rated higher in terms of quality by both students and teachers.

Harris and Graham (cited in Graham, Harris, & Sawyer, 1987) taught students to generate notes during the advanced planning stage of the writing process by teaching them the following strategy:

1. Think who will read this and why I am writing this;
2. Plan what to say using **TREE** (**T**opic sentence, note **R**easons, **E**xamine reasons, and note **E**nding);
3. Write and say more.

Schumaker & Sheldon (1985) designed a sentence-writing strategy that taught students a set of steps and formulas that allowed them to recognize and write different kinds of sentences. "The purpose is not for the student to make the writing complex by writing longer sentences but, rather, to make it readable and to communicate ideas more effectively" (Ellis & Colvert, 1996, p. 167). The acronym **PENS** assisted students in remembering the steps of the strategy:

Schumaker & Sheldon (handwritten margin note)

P—**P**ick a formula

E—**E**xplore words to fit the formula

N—**N**ote the words

S—**S**ubject and verb identification comes next.

revision process (handwritten margin note)

Schumaker and Sheldon (1985) demonstrated that teaching students the PENS strategy improved both the technical points and the sophistication of the students' sentences. Harris and Graham (1985) taught students to increase the number of verbs, adverbs, and adjectives in a creative story. The strategy was as follows: (1) look at the picture and write down good describing words; (2) think of good story ideas to use these words in; (3) write the story; (4) read back the story; and (5) fix the story. The revision process is viewed as a goal-directed problem-solving process in which writers identify problems in their texts, diagnose the problems, and try alternatives to improve their texts (Flower, Hayes, Carey, Schriver, & Stratman, 1986; Scardamalia & Bereiter, 1987).

Most students do not enjoy having to rewrite something they considered finished. Current research suggests several ways to avoid a negative response when students are asked to revise. Have them write their sentences on separate slips of paper (Crealock, Sitko, Hutchinson, Sitko, & Martlett, 1985) and tape the sentences on a larger sheet of paper with room for adding or changing details. Students may also be instructed to write their first draft on different-colored paper (Raphael, Kirschner, & Englert, 1986). Teachers might also suggest that the first draft be written on paper and the final draft on a word processor (Graham & MacArthur, 1988).

Error Monitoring (handwritten margin note)
Schumaker, Nolan, & Deshler (handwritten margin note)

Revising and editing stories is often difficult for many students who are mildly disabled. Several strategies have been developed to facilitate this part of the writing process. Schumaker, Nolan, and Deshler (1985) designed an error-monitoring strategy that offers students specific questions that will cue them to detect four kinds of common errors. The acronym **COPS** assists the students in remembering the steps of the error-monitoring strategy:

C—Have I **C**apitalized the first word and proper names?

O—How is the **O**verall appearance? Have I made any handwriting, margin, messy, or spacing errors?

P—Have I used **P**unctuation, commas, and semicolons correctly?

S—Do the words look as if they are **S**pelled right? Can I sound them out, or should I use a dictionary?

Vallecorsa et al. (1991) suggest a more extensive evaluation guide to help students direct their self-questioning during their revisions (Figure 6.3). They suggest that teachers model the use of this guide by "thinking aloud" so that students can develop a sense of what thought processes are used during such an evaluation.

Graham and MacArthur (1987) taught students to revise and edit their essays on a microcomputer, using the following strategy:

Figure 6.3
Evaluation guide

I. Organization of ideas

_____	A.	Topic sentences
_____	B.	Supporting details
_____	C.	Order of ideas
_____	D.	Use of transition words

II. Style

_____	A.	Vocabulary
_____	B.	Sentence structure
_____	C.	Grammar

III. Spelling

_____	A.	Spelling demons
_____	B.	Personal trouble words

IV. Handwriting

_____	A.	Clarity
_____	B.	Spacing
_____	C.	Neatness

V. Conventions of print

_____	A.	Format
_____	B.	Capitalization
_____	C.	Punctuation

Source: From "Strategies for Teaching Composition Skills to Students with Learning Disabilities" by A. L. Vallecorsa, R. R. Ledford, and G. G. Parnell, 1991, *Teaching Exceptional Children, 25*(2), 55.

1. Read your essay.
2. Find the sentence that tells what you believe. Is it clear?
3. Add two reasons why you believe it.
4. Scan each sentence. Does it make sense? Is it connected?
5. Make changes.
6. Reread the essay and make final changes.

Essays written by the students after such training were much longer and had dramatic improvements in overall quality.

Deshler and his colleagues have suggested the **TOWER** strategy for teaching students to write themes or reports:

T—**T**hink about the content

O—**O**rder ideas, topics, details

W—**W**rite the rough draft

E—**E**dit: look for errors, use **COPS**

R—**R**ewrite, revise

Ellis and Friend (1991) present **DEFENDS,** a metacognitive strategy similar to **TOWER** for developing written language skills used for defending a position.

D—**D**ecide on your exact position

E—**E**xamine the reasons for your position

F—**F**orm a list of points that explain each reason

E—**E**xpose your position in the first sentence

N—**N**ote each reason and supporting points

D—**D**rive home the position in the last sentence

S—**S**earch for errors and correct.

Using **TOWER** or **DEFENDS** encourages students to become active participants, requiring them to think and organize their thoughts prior to the motoric act of writing and to edit their written material.

The models of self-instructional strategy training discussed in this section have been shown to be successful in teaching a variety of different writing strategies to adolescent students with mild disabilities. Such models have been recommended as a particularly promising means for achieving maintenance and generalization (Harris, 1982). They also have been shown to improve students' self-confidence concerning written assignments (Graham & Harris, 1989).

[handwritten margin note: 1. Success 2. improves self-confidence in writing.]

Instruction Using Reciprocal Peer Editing

Another successful teaching strategy for improving students' written language skills is reciprocal peer editing (MacArthur, Schwartz, & Graham, 1991; Stoddard & MacArthur, 1993). Students work in pairs to help each other improve their compositions. This reciprocal peer revision strategy is designed to help students in both the cognitive and the social aspects of response and revision of their writing. Students with mild disabilities tend to do little revision beyond correction of mechanical errors (MacArthur et al., 1991). A **process approach** to writing instruction is used and has been shown to work in the natural classroom setting (MacArthur et al., 1991).

The strategy involves two meetings between the students. The first meeting focuses on substantive revision, the second on correction of mechanical errors. The peer editor is trained to: (1) listen and read along as the author reads aloud; (2) tell the author what the paper is about and what he or she likes best; (3) reread the paper to himself or herself, making notes about revision suggestions; and (4) discuss his or her suggestions with the author (MacArthur et al., 1991, p. 203). The procedure is reciprocal. The second meeting's discussion centers on the revisions that were made, then the students edit each other's papers for mechanical errors.

4 Types of problem to look for in peer asses.

2 more than

Two questions are employed by the students during the revision phase: (a) Is there anything that is not clear? and (b) Where could more details and information be added? Each student is given a checklist for mechanical errors that addresses four types of problems: complete sentences, capitalization, punctuation, and spelling.

Such collaboration can involve more than two students. A teacher could divide the class into teams. Establishing such a social context for writing (e.g., peer conferences, writing conferences, author's chairs, debates, etc.) has many benefits. Students become more aware of their audience when they are required to read in front of their peer group. Their motivation toward writing and their revising process also can be enhanced through such use of peer groups. As in all peer instruction, peers should be trained to focus on positive reactions first; negative reactions should be stated as questions.

Concluding Comments on Instruction

In summary, as Graham and Harris (1988) suggest, the following recommendations may help teachers design and develop writing programs for students with disabilities.

1st goal increase productively

1. Allocate time for writing instruction;
2. Expose students to a broad range of writing tasks;
3. Create a social climate conducive to writing development;
4. Integrate writing with other academic subjects;
5. Aid students in developing the processes central to effective writing;
6. Automate getting language onto paper;
7. Help students develop explicit knowledge about characteristics of good writing;
8. Help students develop the skills and abilities to carry out more sophisticated composing processes;
9. Assist students in the development of goals for improving their written products;
10. Avoid instructional practices that do not improve students' writing performance.

Tape rec. computer free writing

For students who are hesitant to express their ideas in writing or have slow motoric output, the first goal should be to increase productivity. Adolescents with slow output should be encouraged to develop their ideas and not be concerned initially with the mechanical aspects of their writing (Ellis & Colvert, 1996). Elbow (1973) suggested that students engage in "free writing" exercises, which encourage students to write quickly for 10 to 15 minutes without worrying about mechanics.

Students who have difficulty with written output may also be encouraged to translate their thoughts into printed words via tape recorders or computers with specialized software. Students can record their ideas into a tape recorder; later the tape can be transcribed for them. Computer software is available that allows a student to input spoken words; then the computer will translate their speech into written text. Word processing programs also provide assistance to students with mild disabilities.

Written language can no longer be a forgotten component of academic instruction, but needs to be an integral part of students' curriculum at all levels—including the secondary level.

Selected Commercial Written Language Curricula for Adolescents with Written Language Difficulties

Commercial written language materials are available for adolescents with written language difficulties and may be used to supplement content instruction. Many publishing companies include such materials in their catalogs. A selected few are described below:

> *Lessons for Better Writing* (published by Curriculum Associates) is designed for students in 6th through 12th grades. It provides practice in editing sentences and developing vocabulary. Spirit master books are provided.

> *Writing Skills for the Adolescent* (published by Educators Publishing Service, Inc.) is designed particularly for adolescents with writing difficulties. Cursive handwriting, keyboarding, and composition are included, as well as a chapter focused on spelling skills, sample compositions, and an annotated bibliography.

> *Writing with a Point* (published by Educators Publishing Service, Inc.) is a program for adolescents that teaches the writing process through brainstorming and observing. It provides exercises and models for teaching students to write their points of view.

> *Teaching Competence in Written Language* (published by PRO-ED, Inc.) is a systematic, individualized, and highly structured written language program. Practice in writing is combined with practice in different uses and kinds of writing to develop competence in written language expression. A teacher's guide, student lesson book, and student tablet are provided.

> *Life Skills Writing Skillbooks* (published by Opportunities for Learning, Inc.) are 96-page skillbooks for adolescents that focus on writing skills needed in everyday life. Vocabulary is structured for grade levels 3 and 4. Example exercises include applying for a job, taking messages, and writing letters.

Selected Computer Software for Written Language Instruction at the Secondary Level

Microcomputers are becoming part of the regular curriculum in all schools. There are several programs that can be used effectively to develop written language skills. The following selected software programs focus on written language skills that may be appropriate for adolescents with mild disabilities.

> *Bank Street Writer Plus* (published by Broderbund Software and available through Opportunities for Learning) is appropriate for upper elementary and high school levels. Students create and edit stories, reports, or other written material quickly and easily. The program includes a spell check and a thesaurus.

> *Spelling Wiz* (published by Educational Activities) uses the letter cloze technique to reinforce correct spelling. The program teaches 240 words and allows the teacher to

add more. Correct answers are rewarded and the student can advance from simple to more complex patterns.

Verb Viper, Word Invasion, Word Master (published by DLM Teaching Resources) are three programs that use a friendly creature to help students with learning grammar rules and building vocabulary.

The Writing Adventure (published by DLM Teaching Resources) uses a main character that the student directs through an adventure. The student designs the story, taking notes as the adventure continues. Editing aids are provided.

Spelling Blizzard and *Spelling Jungle* (published by Sierra) are two programs that use a wisecracking parrot who entertains while teaching children how to spell hundreds of the most commonly misspelled words. The parrot will entice a child to navigate through mazes to help rescue letters while surviving in the Arctic or the jungle.

Storybook Weaver (published by MECC) is a writing program that allows students to create their own stories, journals, or books, using words, pictures, and sounds; they can also create their own graphics. Students can have their books read aloud in English or Spanish.

Special Considerations in Written Language Instruction of Adolescents with Mild Disabilities in Mainstream Classrooms

Use of the computer with instruction. Computers are said to have motivational appeal, especially with students who have had difficulty writing for many years. Although word processors may have some advantages with some students, research has not yet confirmed that those advantages are true for all students (MacArthur, 1988). MacArthur & Graham (1987) suggested that simply providing students with mild disabilities with practice and exposure in using a word processor as a writing stylus will not necessarily ensure improved or significantly altered revising behavior or written products. In order for word processors to contribute to improvement of a student's writing skills, teachers must teach the necessary preskills (e.g., keyboarding).

Computers and the use of word processing programs may be beneficial for students who have difficulty with motoric output. Students who can compose quickly but have difficulty writing by hand may produce better written language products by using word processing writing programs.

The need to focus on career development. As students move from the elementary to the secondary level of schooling, curricular emphases become important to their futures (Polloway, Patton, Payne, & Payne, 1989). In relation to the curriculum area of written language, several functional skills need to be included in the students' curriculum, such as filling in income tax forms, completing job applications, writing letters, etc. Too often the content material selected for adolescent students with mild disabilities is appropriate for younger students, and the written language skills needed for postsecondary careers are not taught. Teachers need to focus on the written language skills students need to make a successful transition from high school to the world of work.

Summary

Secondary students with mild disabilities should be given plenty of opportunities to write and should experience a variety of practical, imaginative, and creative assignments. Teachers at all levels must allocate instructional time for writing, reviewing, and editing of written products. An undue preoccupation with drill, mechanics, and worksheets in special education classrooms, especially at the secondary level, will not enhance the development of mature writing strategies necessary to sustain the thinking processes associated with planning and drafting expository discourse (Roit & McKenzie, 1985).

Key Terms

error analysis	TOWER
oral edit	process approach
COPS	

References

Algozzine, B., O'Shea, D. J., Stoddard, K., & Crews, W. B. (1988). Reading and writing competencies of adolescents with learning disabilities. *Journal of Learning Disabilities, 21,* 154–161.

Bereiter, C., & Scardamalia, M. (1987). *The psychology of written expression.* Hillsdale, NJ: Erlbaum.

Brigance, A. H. (1977). *BRIGANCE Diagnostic Inventory of Basic Skills.* N. Billerica, MA: Curriculum Associates.

Brigance, A. H. (1981). *BRIGANCE Diagnostic Inventory of Essential Skills.* N. Billerica, MA: Curriculum Associates.

Brigance, A. H. (1983). *BRIGANCE Diagnostic Comprehensive Inventory of Basic Skills.* N. Billerica, MA: Curriculum Associates.

Bridge, C., & Hiebert, E. (1985). A comparison of classroom writing practices, teachers' perceptions of their writing instruction, and textbook recommendations on writing practices. *Elementary School Journal, 86,* 155–172.

Brown, A., & Palincsar, A. (1982). Inducing strategic learning from texts by means of informed, self-control training. *Topics in Learning and Learning Disabilities, 2,* 1–17.

Christenson, S. L., Thurlow, M. L., Ysseldyke J. E., & McVicar, R. (1989). Written language instruction for students with mild handicaps: Is there enough quantity to ensure quality? *Learning Disability Quarterly, 12,* 219–229.

Crealock, C. M., Sitko, M. C., Hutchinson, A., Sitko, C., & Martlett, L. (1985, April). *Creative writing competency: A comparison of paper and pencil and computer technologies to improve the writing skills of mildly handicapped adolescents.* Paper presented at the Annual Meeting of the American Educational Research Association (ERIC Document Reproduction Service No. ED 259 531).

Deno, S. L., Marston, D., & Mirkin, P. K. (1982). Valid measurement procedures for continuous evaluation of written expression. *Exceptional Children, 48,* 368–371.

Elbow, P. (1973). *Writing without teachers.* New York: Oxford University Press.

Ellis, E. S., & Colvert, G. (1996). Writing strategy instruction. In D. D. Deshler, E. S. Ellis, & B. K. Lenz (Eds.), *Teaching adolescents with learning disabilities: Strategies and methods* (2nd ed.) (pp. 127–207). Denver: Love Publishing.

Ellis, E. S., & Friend, P. (1991). The adolescent with learning disabilities. In B. Y. K. Wong (Ed.), *Learning about learning disabilities* (pp. 506-561). Orlando, FL: Academic Press.

Englert, C. S., & Raphael, T. E. (1988). Constructing well-formed prose: process, structure, and metacognitive knowledge. *Exceptional Children, 54,* 513–520.

Englert, C. S., Raphael, T. E., Anderson, L. M., Gregg, S. L., & Anthony, H. M. (1989). Exposition: Reading, writing, and the metacognitive knowledge of learning disabled students. *Learning Disabilities Research, 5,* 5–24.

Englert, C. S., Raphael, T. E., Fear, K. L., & Anderson, L. M. (1988). Students' metacognitive knowledge about how to write informational texts. *Learning Disability Quarterly, 11,* 18–46.

Flower, L., Hayes, J. R., Carey, L., Schriver, J., & Stratman, J. (1986). Detection, diagnosis, and the strategies of revision. *College Composition and Communication, 37,* 16–55.

Graham, S. (1982). Composition research and practice: A unified approach. *Focus on Exceptional Children, 14,* 1–16.

Graham, S. (1992). Helping students with LD progress as writers. *Intervention in School and Clinic, 27,* 134–149.

Graham, S., & Harris, K. R. (1987). Improving composition skills of inefficient learners with self-instructional strategy training. *Topics in Language Disorders, 7,* 66–77.

Graham, S., & Harris, K. R. (1988). Instructional recommendations for teaching writing to exceptional students. *Exceptional Children, 54,* 506–512.

Graham, S., & Harris, K. R. (1989). Improving learning disabled students' skills at composing essays: Self-instructional strategy training. *Exceptional Children, 56,* 201–214.

Graham, S., & Harris, K. R. (1993). Teaching writing strategies to students with learning disabilities: Issues and recommendations. In L. Meltzer (Ed.), *Strategy assessment and instruction for students with learning disabilities* (pp. 271–292). Austin: PRO-ED.

Graham, S., Harris, K., MacArthur, C., & Schwartz, S. (1991). Writing instruction. In B. Y. L. Wong (Ed.), *Learning about learning disabilities* (pp. 309–341). San Diego: Academic Press.

Graham, S., Harris, K. R., & Sawyer, R. (1987). Composition instruction with learning disabled students: Self-instructional strategy training. *Focus on Exceptional Children, 20*(4), 1–11.

Graham, S., & MacArthur, C. (1987). Written language of the handicapped. In C. Reynolds & L. Mann (Eds.), *Encyclopedia of special education* (pp. 1678–1681). New York: Wiley.

Graham, S., & MacArthur, C. (1988). Improving learning disabled students' skills at revising essays produced on a word processor: Self-instructional strategy training. *Journal of Special Education, 22,* 133–152.

Graham, S., Schwartz, S.S., & MacArthur, C.A. (1993). Knowledge of writing and the composing process, attitude toward writing, and self-efficacy for students with and without learning disabilities. *Journal of Learning Disabilities, 26,* 237–249.

Graves, D. (1983). *Writing: Teachers and children at work.* Portsmouth, NH: Heinemann.

Graves, D. H., & Sunstein, B. S. (1992). *Portfolio portraits.* Portsmouth, NH: Heinemann.

Greenbaum, C. R. (1987). *Spellmaster: The Spellmaster Assessment and Teaching System.* Austin, TX: PRO-ED.

Hammill, D. D., Brown, V. L., Larsen, S. C., & Wiederholt, J. L. (1994). *Test of Adolescent Language—3.* Austin, TX: PRO-ED.

Hammill, D. D., & Larsen, S. C. (1988). *Test of Written Language—2.* Austin, TX: PRO-ED.

Harris, K. R. (1982). Cognitive behavior modification: Application with exceptional students. *Focus on Exceptional Children, 15,* 1–16.

Harris, K. R., & Graham, S. (1985). Improving learning disabled students' composition skills: Self-control strategy training. *Learning Disability Quarterly, 8,* 27–36.

Harris, K. R., & Pressley, M. (1991). The nature of cognitive strategy instruction: Interactive strategy construction. *Exceptional Children, 57,* 392–404.

Hayes J., & Flower, L. (1986). Writing research and the writer. *American Psychologist, 41,* 1106–1113.

Isaacson, S. (1984). Evaluating written expression: Issues of reliability, validity, and instructional utility. *Diagnostique, 9,* 96–116.

Isaacson, S. (1987). Effective instruction in written language. *Focus on Exceptional Children, 19*(6), 1–12.

Isaacson, S. (1988). Assessing the writing product: Qualitative and quantitative measures. *Exceptional Children, 54,* 528–534.

Larsen, S. C., & Hammill, D. D. (1994). *Test of Written Spelling—3.* Austin, TX: PRO-ED.

Leinhardt, G., Zigmond, N., & Cooley, W. (1981). Reading instruction and its effects. *American Educational Research Journal, 18,* 343–361.

MacArthur, C. A. (1988). The impact of computers on the writing process. *Exceptional Children, 54,* 536–542.

MacArthur, C. A., & Graham, S. (1987). Learning disabled students' composing under three methods of text production: Handwriting, word processing, and dictation. *The Journal of Special Education, 21,* 22–42.

MacArthur, C. A., Schwartz, S. S., & Graham, S. (1991). A model for writing instruction: Integrating word processing and strategy instruction into a process approach to writing. *Learning Disabilities Research and Practice, 6,* 230–236.

Markwardt, F. C. (1989). *Peabody Individual Achievement Test—Revised.* Circle Pines, MN: American Guidance Service.

Nodine, B. F., Barenbaum, E., & Newcomer, P. (1985). Story composition for learning disabled, reading disabled, and normal children. *Learning Disability Quarterly, 8,* 167–179.

Polloway, E. A., Patton, J. R., Payne, J. S., & Payne, R. (1989). *Strategies for teaching learners with special needs* (4th ed.). Upper Saddle River, NJ: Merrill/Prentice Hall.

Poplin, M., Gray, R., Larson, S., Banikowski, A., & Mehring, T. (1980). A comparison of components of written expression abilities in learning and non-learning disabled children at three grade levels. *Learning Disability Quarterly, 3*(4), 46–53.

Psychological Corporation. (1992). *Wechsler Individual Achievement Test.* San Antonio, TX: Author.

Raphael, T. E., Kirschner, B. W., & Englert, C. S. (1986). *Text structure instruction within process-writing classrooms: A manual for instruction* (No. 104). East Lansing: Michigan State University, Institute for Research on Teaching.

Roit, M. L., & McKenzie, R. G. (1985). Disorders of written communication: An instructional priority for LD students. *Journal of Learning Disabilities, 18,* 258–260.

Rousseau, M. K. (1990). Errors in written language. In R. A. Gable & J. M. Hendrickson (Eds.), *Assessing students with special needs* (pp. 89–101). New York: Longman.

Scardamalia, M., & Bereiter, C. (1987). *The psychology of written composition.* Hillsdale, NJ: Erlbaum.

Schenck, S. J. (1981). The diagnostic/instructional link in individualized educational programs. *Journal of Special Education, 14,* 337–345.

Schumaker, J. B., Nolan, S. M., & Deshler, D. D. (1985). *Learning strategies curriculum: The error monitoring strategy.* Lawrence, KS: University of Kansas.

Schumaker, J. B., & Sheldon, J. (1985). *Learning strategies curriculum: The sentence writing strategy.* Lawrence, KS: University of Kansas.

Stoddard, B., & MacArthur, C. A. (1993). A peer editor strategy: Guiding learning disabled students in response and revision. *Research in the Teaching of English, 27,* 76–103.

Thomas, C. C., Englert, C. S., & Gregg, S. (1987). An analysis of errors and strategies in the expository writing of learning disabled students. *Remedial and Special Education, 8*(1), 21–46.

Tindal, G., & Parker, R. (1989). Assessment of written expression for students in compensatory and special education programs. *Journal of Special Education, 23,* 169–183.

Tindal, G., & Parker, R. (1991). Identifying measures for evaluating written expression. *Learning Disabilities Research and Practice, 6,* 211–218.

Thurlow, M. L., Ysseldyke, J. E., Graden, J. L., & Algozzine, B. (1984). Opportunity to learn for LD students receiving different levels of special education service. *Learning Disability Quarterly, 6,* 172–182.

Vallecorsa, A. L., Ledford, R. R., & Parnell, G. G. (1991). Strategies for teaching composition skills to students with learning disabilities. *Teaching Exceptional Children, 23*(2), 52–55.

Wesson, C., Otis-Wilborn, A., Hasbrouck, J., & Tindal, G. (1989). Linking assessment, curriculum, and instruction of oral and written language. *Focus on Exceptional Children, 22*(4), 1–12.

Woodcock, R. W., & Johnson, M. B. (1989). *Woodcock-Johnson Psycho-Educational Battery—Revised.* Allen, TX: DLM Teaching Resources.

Teaching Mathematics to Adolescents with Mild Disabilities

Objectives

After reading this chapter, the reader should be able to:

1. provide a rationale for the teaching of functional math skills to adolescents with mild disabilities;

2. discuss the many ways informal and standardized tests can be used to assess mathematics ability;

3. cite research that shows effective ways in which math skills can be taught to students with mild disabilities;

4. discuss the many specifics of functional math instruction with adolescents with mild disabilities;

5. choose and adapt curricula to be used in math instruction of students with mild disabilities;

6. discuss ways to enhance motivation and generalization of math skills in students with mild disabilities.

Educators of adolescents with mild learning and behavior problems should not be surprised to learn that such students have numerous achievement problems in mathematics. In contrast to the number of studies that examined reading problems of students with mild disabilities, however, the research literature dealing with math underachievement is less abundant (Kirby & Becker, 1988; Rizzo & Zabel, 1988). Still, research has identified a plethora of math-related problems of adolescents with disabilities. Cawley and Miller (1989), for example, found that students with mild disabilities average one grade level gain in math for every two years they spend in instruction. Cawley, Kahn, and Tedesco (1989) found that the majority of students with mild disabilities exit formal schooling at between the 5th- and 6th-grade levels of achievement. Montague, Bos, and Doucette (1991) showed that 8th-grade students with learning disabilities, when compared to nondisabled students, demonstrate (a) a poor attitude toward mathematics and (b) low self-perception of math ability and achievement. McLeod and Armstrong (1982) found the following math skills deficient among adolescents with learning disabilities, as perceived by their teachers: (a) division of whole numbers; (b) basic operations including fractions, decimals, and percentages; (c) fraction terminology and multiplication of whole numbers; (d) place value; (e) measurement skills; and (f) language of mathematics. Moreover, secondary-level teachers of students with learning disabilities in the McLeod and Armstrong survey reported that roughly two thirds of their students needed intensive math instruction. Light and DeFries (1996) found some youth with learning disabilities who were reading disabled *and* math disabled were so because of genetic influences.

Adolescents with serious emotional disturbance also experience problems in math achievement. Luebke, Epstein, and Cullinan (1989) showed that teachers rated the arithmetic achievement of junior high and senior high pupils with behavior disorders significantly lower than they rated the math achievement of nondisabled youth. Kauffman, Cullinan, and Epstein (1987) also showed that math achievement problems were more serious than word recognition and reading comprehension difficulties among youth (aged 12 to 18) identified as emotionally disturbed. Math-related problems among students with behavior disorders also include spatial and size relationships, left-right confusion, distractibility, perseveration, understanding math symbols, and abstract thinking ability (Rizzo & Zabel, 1988).

Many pupils with mild mental retardation also leave school in late adolescence and early adulthood with persistent math problems. English and Browning (1974) concluded that arithmetic is the most important academic skill for adult workers with mental retardation. In light of the severe math underachievement exhibited by students with mental retardation of all ages, it is no wonder that some professionals (e.g., Cawley, Baker-Kroczynski, & Urban, 1992; Cawley, Miller, & Carr, 1989; Mastropieri, Bakken, & Scruggs, 1991; Patton & Polloway, 1988; Polloway & Patton, 1993) recommend a change in the focus of traditional math instruction so that adult, transition-related math needs are met.

Teachers need to be aware of the difference between **arithmetic** and **mathematics** instruction delivered to adolescents with disabilities. *Arithmetic* is used here to refer to manipulations with numbers and computation; *mathematics* is concerned with thinking about quantities and relationships among them (Polloway & Patton, 1993). Arithmetic is simply a branch of mathematics. Mathematics education at the secondary level must go beyond simple arithmetic instruction, for computation has little long-term value for certain adults with disabilities (Levine & Langress, 1985). Instruction should have a strong focus on mathematical problem solving for daily living, and we support the use of calculators for use in computation instruction. Most adults without disabilities use calculators for various tasks such as balancing checkbooks, calculating loan interest rates and balances, completing tax forms, and keeping a household budget; secondary-level students with mild disabilities, therefore, should be able to do the same in order to exhibit behaviors that are typical of adults.

One way of thinking about math instruction for adolescents with mild disabilities is from a functional perspective, which means that students should be exposed to instruction that has a good chance of helping them in meaningful ways outside the confines of classrooms. In other words, **functional mathematics** instruction is concerned with practical skills that have a strong relationship to success in everyday community living. Teachers of students with mild disabilities need to ask themselves, "If some (perhaps most) of my students are not going to college or a postsecondary education setting, what mathematical abilities will they need to enhance independence as adults?"

This chapter will address answers to the above question. Assessment of math skills will be discussed, mathematics instruction research across categories of mild disability will be examined, general and functional math educational techniques will be presented in terms of problem-solving and mathematical process instruction, commercial math curricula will be reviewed, and special considerations for adolescents with mild disabilities receiving math instruction in special and regular classrooms will be highlighted.

Assessing Math Skills

Measuring the mathematical capabilities of secondary-level students with mild disabilities involves the application of many techniques. Informal measures, curriculum-based measurement techniques, and standardized tests, for example, should be used frequently to determine the rate of progress these adolescents exhibit over time. Below is a discussion of the various methods for assessing adolescents' mathematical abilities.

Standardized, Criterion-Referenced, and Diagnostic Tests

The *Brigance Diagnostic Inventory of Essential Skills* (BDIES) (Brigance, 1981) is one of the most popular criterion-referenced tests used for continuous tracking of students' mathematical abilities. The goal of criterion-referenced testing is to determine a student's ability in comparison to some behavioral standard (e.g., accuracy percentages on instructional objectives), and experts (e.g., Taylor, 1984) have said that tests such as the BDIES are the most valuable of classroom-based assessment procedures. The BDIES is appropriate for use with students in grades 4 through 12 and provides a measure of mathematical abilities in the following areas:

Schedules and Graphs (e.g., reading television schedules)

Math Grade Placement (e.g., assessment of computational and math comprehension abilities)

Numbers (e.g., rounding off numbers)

Number Facts (e.g., knowledge of number facts using the four operations)

Computation of Whole Numbers (e.g., computing averages)

Fractions (e.g., computation of fractions)

Decimals (e.g., understanding the principles of decimals)

Percentages (e.g., converting decimals and fractions into percentages)

Measurement (e.g., use and understanding of time, calendars, rulers, and converting measurements)

Metrics (e.g., using the metric system of measurement)

Math Vocabulary (e.g., word usage and knowledge of basic geometric shapes and concepts)

Travel and Transportation (e.g., use of mileage tables), and

Money and Finance (e.g., computing interest on loans).

Because the BDIES does include some focus on functional mathematical abilities, it is recommended for assessment of secondary-level skills with students experiencing mild disabilities.

KeyMath—Revised (KM—R) (Connolly, 1988) is a diagnostic arithmetic test designed for use with students from kindergarten through grade 9. The 13 subtests of the KM—R measure student arithmetic skill in three domains: (a) Basic concepts (e.g., rational numbers, geometry, and numeration); (b) Operations (e.g., adding, subtracting, multiplying, dividing, and mental computation); and (c) Applications (e.g., knowledge and application of skill in time and money, interpreting data, problem solving, measurement, and estimating). *KeyMath—Revised* items are presented orally to individual respondents who view visual stimuli. Test results are available for total test score, domain, area, and subtests, and scores are intended to demonstrate a student's strengths and weaknesses. Grade and age equivalent scores are provided through conversion tables, and computer software is available for scoring. The test does not require the examinee to read or write, and research using the original *KeyMath* was able to discriminate adolescents with learning disabilities from those without such conditions (Greenstein & Strain, 1977). It is recommended that the KM—R be used as either a screening test or a diagnostic test of the arithmetic abilities of early adolescents with mild disabilities in middle schools.

The *Test of Mathematical Abilities* (TOMA) (Brown & McEntire, 1984) is a norm-referenced instrument that assesses story problems, math-related vocabulary, general information in mathematics, computation, and attitude toward math of students in grades 3 through 12. Four of the five sections of the test can be used in group situations, but the general information subtest must be administered individually. Test administration time ranges from 45 minutes to one hour and 45 minutes. The TOMA provides percentiles and standard scores on all subtests. The administration manual is particularly helpful to teachers; it includes, along with the necessities for interpretation and use, resources for additional mathematics testing and classroom instruction. Students with disabilities were included in the standardization sample, but using the TOMA with non-readers is not recommended. The TOMA, therefore, may have limited utility with very low-functioning adolescents with mild disabilities.

The *Stanford Diagnostic Mathematics Test* (SDMT) (Beatty, Madden, Gardner, & Karlsen, 1984), claimed by its publisher to be "the most popular diagnostic mathematics test in the country," measures math skills and concepts vital to daily living. The Brown level is used with pupils in grades 6 and 7 and low-achieving 8th graders through high schoolers; the Blue level is used with students in grades 8 through 12. The main objective of the SDMT is to identify math skills with which pupils have difficulty by using a multiple-choice testing format. Both Brown and Blue levels contain three subtests that assess computation, applications, and numeration, and the test can be administered either to a group or to individuals. Items include foci on whole numbers and decimal place value, computation using the four operations, problem solving, interpreting graphs, geometry, and measurement. Scores can be transformed as percentiles and grade equivalents, and machine scoring is available. A unique feature of scoring in the SDMT is the *Pi* cutoff score, used to pinpoint students who have reached minimum competency necessary for success at a particular instructional level. The SDMT has sufficient technical adequacy, and secondary-level teachers should be able to use it easily in determining students' strengths and weaknesses in math application, computation, and number concepts.

The *Enright Inventory of Basic Arithmetic Skills* (IBAS) (Enright, 1983) assesses arithmetic skills typical at the elementary and middle or junior high levels. The test is subdivided into 13 sections and includes measurement of computation with whole numbers as well as fractions and decimals. Items are arranged in task analytic fashion for administration in either individual or group format. Testing results allow for concentration on what skills a student has mastered and global grade-level functioning. Guidelines are also provided for teachers to perform error analyses. Enright identified 233 different errors that are possible in students' computation; these error types are further subdivided into seven clusters (e.g., omissions, lack of attention to operation signs). Teachers can learn much about students' arithmetic computation mistakes by using the error analysis guidelines found in the IBAS manual. Moreover, IBAS testing results using error analysis allow for computational goals to be easily written into students' IEPs. The IBAS is therefore recommended for use by teachers of students with mild disabilities in middle or junior high schools.

Informal Assessment Procedures

Informal math assessment procedures are used by teachers on a routine basis to determine whether students are mastering the everyday math curriculum. No matter what curriculum is used in math instruction of adolescents with mild disabilities, informal assessment procedures should be administered on a regular basis so that a teacher can receive quick feedback on his or her teaching effectiveness. Without ongoing use of informal math assessment techniques, a teacher would not know how well students are meeting with success on math IEP objectives. It is therefore incumbent upon special education teachers to know what procedures to use and how to use informal math assessment to determine student progress in math.

Curriculum-based measurement (CBM) of math skills. The goal of CBM is to assess a student's success rate in the actual curriculum used by a teacher in the classroom. In contrast to task-analyzed measurement, in which behaviors are categorized into a hierarchy and teachers instruct and assess student performance on each subskill of the hierarchy, teachers using CBM pinpoint skills to be instructed over some period of time (e.g., an entire unit or semester) and routinely assess students' performance toward mastering all of the requirements of the curriculum. Fuchs, Fuchs, Hamlett, and Stecker (1991) claim that CBM offers (a) an efficient determination of when student achievement is less than adequate and (b) an objective method for determining when an adjustment of instructional strategy is necessary. Fuchs et al. (1991) also showed that in comparison to teachers not using CBM, teachers who used this assessment technique made more adjustments in instruction, and that students' gains in math achievement were greater in CBM versus non-CBM classrooms.

A teacher using CBM in math would organize all of the skills he or she is going to teach students over a period of time (e.g., adding 25 fractions and mixed numbers correctly in a 10-minute period). Next, the teacher would set on a graph the behavioral goal at the end of instruction involving adding the fractions and whole numbers (e.g., to be able to add 25 fractions and mixed numbers with 100% accuracy in a 10-minute period). Assessment at the beginning of instruction would set the baseline for individual student performance with such skills. A straight line is then drawn from the baseline functioning level to the end, or instruction goal. The teacher conducts regular assessment of students' accuracy level involving the target behavior, using parallel forms of the same test throughout the duration of instruction. If student performance consistently falls below the line indicating steady progress toward the goal, the teacher decides whether a change of instructional approach is necessary. By charting student performance through ongoing assessment of the goal, teachers are made immediately aware of student achievement or lack thereof. Figure 7.1 is an example of a graph that could be used when using CBM in math instruction. Curriculum-based measurement has a large body of literature showing its effectiveness in special education settings (Deno, 1985; Deno & Fuchs, 1987; Fuchs & Deno, 1991; Fuchs, Deno, & Mirkin, 1984; Fuchs, Fuchs, & Hamlett, 1989; Fuchs, Fuchs, Hamlett, & Allinder, 1989; Germann & Tindal, 1985; King-Sears, 1994; Shinn, 1989; Tucker, 1985), and effective teachers will use it often in math instruction of adolescents with mild disabilities.

Informal inventories and teacher-made math tests.   Assessment devices created by teachers for use in everyday math instruction are called informal inventories and teacher-made tests. Most educators are familiar with such devices, and they are frequently used to determine the extent to which students have mastered specific math skills. Such tests consist of worksheets or similar presentations that include specific math skills the teacher wants students to learn. Teachers usually collect a sample of problems that they wish students to master after instruction takes place and use the same types of problems in pre- and posttesting (i.e., before and after instruction takes place). Simple computation examples, word problems, and math application items are typically found on informal inventories and teacher-made tests. The intent of this type of assessment is to determine (a) present levels of math performance in various areas (e.g., measurement, multiplication, changing decimals to fractions, etc.); (b) what the focus of instruction should be (e.g., strengthening skills shown deficient through assessment); and (c) how effective instruction has been. Figure 7.2 presents an example of an informal test involving fractions.

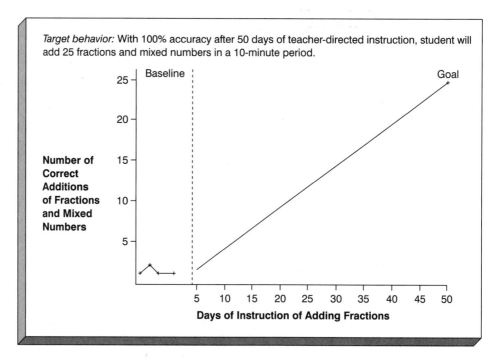

Figure 7.1
An example of curriculum-based measurement in secondary-level math instruction

A. Write the fraction that tells how much of the figure is shaded.

1.   **2.**   **3.**

Write the fraction that tells how much of the set is shaded.

4.   **5.**   **6.**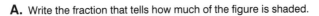

Write the fraction for the division expression.

7. $3 \div 5$ **8.** $1 \div 6$ **9.** $8 \div 7$

B. Write the mixed numeral that tells how many circles are shaded.

1.   **2.**   **3.**

Write the mixed numeral for the sum.

4. $3 + \frac{2}{3}$ **5.** $7 + \frac{5}{6}$ **6.** $2 + \frac{5}{8}$

C. Write the missing number.

1. $\frac{2}{3} = \frac{\blacksquare}{6}$ **2** $\frac{6}{8} = \frac{\blacksquare}{4}$ **3.** $\frac{4}{12} = \frac{2}{\blacksquare}$

4. $\frac{1}{4} = \frac{\blacksquare}{8}$ **5.** $\frac{5}{15} = \frac{1}{\blacksquare}$ **6.** $\frac{\blacksquare}{18} = \frac{5}{6}$

7. $\frac{4}{6} = \frac{16}{\blacksquare}$ **8.** $\frac{8}{16} = \frac{\blacksquare}{4}$ **9.** $\frac{2}{\blacksquare} = \frac{12}{18}$

Write the whole number equivalent to the fraction.

10. $\frac{20}{5}$ **11.** $\frac{16}{2}$ **12.** $\frac{21}{7}$

Figure 7.2
Informal test involving fractions

Source: From *Diagnosis: An Instructional Aid; Mathematics Level B, Lab B2,* 1980, Chicago: Science Research Associates, Inc.

Mathematics diagnostic interview.   In a **diagnostic math interview,** the teacher simply models (with several examples) how he or she solves a math problem by "thinking aloud," and then asks the student to do the same with problems solved incorrectly. In doing so, the teacher uncovers any deficient or incorrect cognitive routines used to solve problems by individual students. If a student states that he or she multiplied 7 × 8 for a product of 58 in the example 247 × 608, the teacher can easily detect the error and provide corrective instruction and reteaching as necessary. The interview method can be used with any type of math problem; a noteworthy shortcoming, however, is that it can become rather time consuming when a student makes several types of errors.

Error analysis.   Another widely used assessment technique in mathematics is error analysis. In this method, the teacher searches for a pattern to the errors made by a student in math problem solving. Many frameworks for detecting errors among math computation problems exist, and a sample of one is found in Figure 7.3.

Research-Validated Math Instruction: Adolescents with Mental Retardation

Given the plethora of curricula available to teach math to adolescents with mild disabilities, teachers should also be aware of specific teaching strategies and noncommercial approaches that have been shown to be effective in research. Studies that examined various approaches to teaching math skills to adolescents span a number of years and espouse numerous techniques. Table 7.1 presents a brief synopsis of studies that examined teaching various math skills to adolescents with mild mental retardation. Subsequently, we review studies that demonstrated acquisition of math skills through intervention among adolescents with mild mental retardation.

Miller (1976), in research with early adolescents identified as mildly mentally retarded, used music paired with token reinforcement contingencies to increase accuracy in addition and subtraction problem solving. Students' performance in addition and subtraction computation improved over 26 sessions with music used as a reinforcer. Generalization and maintenance of skills, however, were not examined with the students.

Broome and Wambold (1977) used a "package" of treatments (e.g., contingency contracting, peer teaming, small-group and one-on-one instruction, learning center activities) to teach basic arithmetic facts to early adolescents with mild mental retardation. Over a 7-month period the researchers demonstrated that the package of instructional methods was effective in the adolescents' acquisition of basic math facts. Maintenance and generalization of skills were not examined in the study.

Smeets, Lancioni, Striefel, and Willemsen (1984) used colors as a discrimination tool in teaching early adolescents with mild mental retardation. Computation of missing digits in simple addition and subtraction problems was the dependent measure. The researchers showed that colors used as a discrimination aid were effective in increasing the students' calculation skills over a period of 25 days, and the acquired skills generalized to similar problems. Maintenance of learned skills (over several weeks to months, depending on the student) was also demonstrated among the pupils.

Figure 7.3

Example of a math error analysis

Source: From *Educational Assessment of Learning Problems: Testing for Teaching* (2nd ed.) (p. 397) by G. Wallace, S. C. Larsen, and L. K. Elksnin, 1992, Boston: Allyn & Bacon. Reprinted by permission.

Analysis	Example
Does not rename hundreds digit after regrouping.	532 −181 ─── 451
Does not rename hundreds or tens when renaming units.	906 −238 ─── 778
Does not rename tens when zero is in tens place, although hundreds are renamed.	803 −478 ─── 335
When there are two zeros in minuend, renames hundreds twice but does not rename tens.	5 6 700 −326 ─── 284
Decreases hundreds digit by one when unnecessary.	3 7 1 −1 3 4 ─── 1 3 7
Uses units place factor as addend.	32 × 4 ─── 126
Adds regrouped number to tens but does not multiply.	35 × 7 ─── 65*

*   7 × 5 = 35;
    30 + 30 = 60

| Multiplies digits within one factor. | 31
× 4
───
34* |

*   4 × 1 = 4;
    1 × 30 = 30

| Multiplies by only one number. | 457
× 12
───
914 |

Table 7.1
Math instructional research with students with mild mental retardation

Author(s)	Sample Studied	Intervention Used	Results
Borakove & Cuvo (1976)	MR	Training in coin counting using fingers or using fingers plus displacement (removal) procedure	Increase in coin counting in both groups with displacement group increasing the most
Broome & Wambold (1977)	MR	Drill and practice activities on math facts	Procedures effective in teaching basic facts
Horton (1985)	MR	Training in addition, subtraction, multiplication, and division computations on paper with pencil, and with calculator	Calculators increase performance
Miller (1976)	MR	Reinforcement (preferred music vs. nonpreferred music) for addition and subtraction computations	Increase in arithmetic performance; no differences between preferred vs. nonpreferred music
Smeenge, Page, Iwata, & Ivanic (1980)	MR	Training in measurement skills including preskills and ruler usage	Increase in measurement skills
Smeets, Lancioni, Striefel, & Willemsen (1984)	MR	Training in missing minuends using discrimination training involving colors	Training effect for missing minuend problems
Thurlow & Turnure (1977)	MR	Training in time and money units	Increase in time and money responses

Horton (1985) taught adolescents with mild retardation how to use calculators to solve problems in the basic operations of addition, subtraction, multiplication, and division. The study also examined accuracy of problem solving in paper-and-pencil fashion versus using a calculator. After 12 days Horton demonstrated that students using calculators were more accurate and faster than when they solved the problems with paper and pencil. Generalization and maintenance probes were not implemented in Horton's investigation.

Borakove and Cuvo (1976) used teacher modeling, guided practice, and independent student performance to teach adolescents with mental retardation how to combine and accurately count pennies, nickels, dimes, quarters, and half-dollars. Immediate feedback (i.e., praise for correct responses, and "no" for incorrect answers) were also used after student overt responding. Students learned how to count a coin in isolation before another coin was added and counted. Accurate coin counting was demonstrated by the adolescents after 4 weeks of intervention, but generalization and maintenance of skills were not measured. Other research results using similar procedures applied to coin-counting skills of adolescents or adults with mental retardation can be found in Cuvo, Veitch, Trace, and Konke (1978), Lowe and Cuvo (1976), McDonagh, McIlvane, and Stoddard (1984), and Trace, Cuvo, and Criswell (1977).

Smeenge, Page, Iwata, and Ivanic (1980) attempted to teach estimating and measuring skills to three adolescents and young adults with mild mental retardation. Task analysis and direct instruction (i.e., feedback, detailed instructions) were used over 15 sessions, and all subjects demonstrated higher functioning in measurement skills through a follow-up phase. Generalization of learned skills was also shown by two of the three students.

In a very comprehensive study involving many adolescents with mild mental retardation ($\underline{n}$ = 133), Thurlow and Turnure (1977) attempted to teach time and money concepts through the use of learning units with instructional books. Coin equivalence and new vocabulary terms with meanings were emphasized; the time unit lasted for 8 weeks, and instruction in money skills equaled 20 weeks. Adolescents with mild mental retardation were able to dramatically increase their skills, as measured by unit tests, in both money and time concepts. Thurlow and Turnure did not consider maintenance and generalization of learned behavior.

Research-Validated Math Instruction: Adolescents with Learning Disabilities

Rivera and Smith (1988) showed the efficacy of using teacher modeling and demonstration to produce positive change in computational skills among young adolescents with learning disabilities. After the teacher showed how to complete computational problems, students with learning disabilities were instructed to complete problems of a similar nature; they were able to learn, maintain, and generalize their computational skills. Table 7.2 is a brief presentation of Rivera and Smith's (1988) and other studies that examined math instructional research with adolescents identified as learning disabled. Other studies are reviewed in greater detail in the following paragraphs.

In an interesting study that examined more than simple math skills of early adolescents with learning disabilities, Schunk (1985) showed how self-determination can be effective in the teaching of math. Schunk compared three randomly assigned groups of students on performance in subtraction with borrowing problems: (a) students who decided themselves how many subtraction worksheet pages to complete in one day (i.e., between 4 and 10 pages); (b) students who were assigned a set number of pages to complete; and (c) students who set no goals for rate of completion of worksheets. Schunk's results showed that the group who self-set the number of pages performed higher in subtraction than the two other comparison groups. Both goal-setting groups, however, completed more problems and had higher subtraction accuracy levels in comparison to the no-goals group.

In a similar study, Fuchs, Bahr, and Reith (1989) examined goal setting in math performance among high school students with learning disabilities. Computer-assisted mathematics instruction was used to compare number of digits computed per minute for groups with self-selected or assigned goals. The results were comparable to Schunk's in that the self-selected goal group significantly outperformed the assigned-goals group.

Schunk and Cox (1986), in a comprehensive study examining subtraction with regrouping performance among middle school students with learning disabilities, showed the efficacy of students' verbalizations while problem solving and teacher feed-

Table 7.2
Math instructional research with secondary-level students with learning disabilities

Author(s)	Sample Studied	Intervention Used	Results
Bennett (1980)	LD & SLD	Preorganizers and postorganizers on word problems	Improvement on problems with lower and higher levels of syntactic complexity for LD; only improvement on 1-step problems with lower syntactic complexity for SLD
Fuchs, Bahr, & Reith (1989)	LD	1. Self-selected computational goals vs. worksheet page completion goals 2. Contingent vs. noncontingent game play	1. Self-directed goals: more digits per minute 2. No effects for contingent vs. noncontingent
Maheady, Sacca, & Harper (1987)	Mainstreamed: n = 91 with 28 students with mild disabilities	Peer mediated instruction with classwide student tutoring teams	Class-wide performance raised 20.53 % pts. for 9th grade, 23 % pts. for 10th grade. Comparable improvement for students with mild disabilities
Montague & Bos (1986)	LD	8-step cognitive strategy on verbal math problems	May provide general approach for solving word problems; does not ensure correct computation
Nuzum (1983)	LD	6-phase instruction model on word problems	Increase in performance with phase progression; high performance on posttest
Rivera & Smith (1987)	LD	Modeling (DPPM) on acquisition and generalization of computation skills	Significant improvement during DPPM intervention phase
Schunk (1985)	LD	Participation in goal setting	Higher performance for self-set goals group on measures of self-efficacy, subtraction skills and expectancy of goal attainment
Schunk & Cox (1986)	LD	Verbalization and effort feedback on subtraction with regrouping, self-efficacy, and attributions	Significant main effects for verbalization and effort feedback on self-efficacy and subtraction skills. Higher effort attributions for effort feedback and in first half of training sessions

back regarding student effort. Early adolescents who verbalized problem-solving strategies while completing subtraction with regrouping items performed higher than students who did not verbalize. Moreover, adolescents who received effort feedback from their teachers while solving subtraction problems showed higher performance than students who did not receive effort feedback.

Nuzum (1987) attempted to increase the math word-problem-solving ability (i.e., involving addition, subtraction, and two-step problems requiring both) of four adolescents with learning disabilities. Cards describing steps to use while solving word problems were presented to the students, and corrective feedback was given related to performance. Modeling, verbalization, and guided and independent practice were also important components in the training. Posttesting of the four students indicated that accuracy of word problem solving increased as well as number of word problems solved correctly.

Montague and Bos (1986) used a cognitive strategy to foster the word problem solving of adolescents with learning disabilities. The strategy was taught to students through the use of modeling, rehearsal, and feedback, and cards describing the steps of the strategy were also used in training phases. The experimenters taught six students how to solve two-step word problems with the intent of fostering generalization to three-step problems. The results indicated that four of the six students generalized the strategy to three-step problems, but computation and operation-choice errors remained persistent in the subjects.

Bennett (1980) used a four-step advance organizer (i.e., read problem, underline numbers, reread problem, make a decision on operation and type of problem), and a five-step postwork strategy (i.e., read problem, check operation, check math statement, check calculations, write labels) to assist secondary-level students with learning disabilities in math word problem solving. The use of the strategies was gradually faded over time with the intent of analyzing the students' ability to solve word problems with varying syntactical level and computational complexity. The results showed that strategy use was effective in improving the students' ability to solve word problems with higher levels of syntactic difficulty.

Maheady, Sacca, and Harper (1987) used cooperative grouping with 9th- and 10th-grade students with mild disabilities to improve their overall grades in regular math classes. Students were divided into small groups with three to five members; teachers taught new math skills for two days, and small-group members practiced the new skills in coterie for two days or more. Each small-group team member rotated as either tutor or tutee during practice sessions. Reinforcement was provided to the groups for high math performance. The results indicated that the cooperative grouping system was remarkably effective in increasing the students' math grades.

Summary.　　The above-mentioned studies indicate that there is a multitude of research-proven strategies to enhance various aspects of math performance among secondary-level students with mild disabilities. Teachers should be able to adapt most of the instructional methods offered here for individual classroom and student situations. It should also be noted that many of the studies cited included the use of reinforcement, direct instruction teaching behaviors, cognitive strategies, and combinations of these approaches. In essence, instruction delivered consistently, efficiently, and systematically should have the desired effect on math achievement of adolescents with mild disabilities.

Functional Math Instruction

A **functional mathematics** curriculum concentrates on typical everyday-life experiences, using mathematics concepts, problem solving, and application of such skills in the community. Its focus is not so much to ensure classroom-based competency in mathematics skills, although this is important for some adolescents with mild disabilities with plans for college, but to provide students with enough experience and learning so that they achieve independence in the adult world. With increased focus on functional skills in math and the body of literature indicating lack of success among adolescents and young adults with disabilities in the "real world" (Edgar, 1987; Frank, Sitlington, & Carson, 1991; Hasazi, Gordon, & Roe, 1985; Sitlington & Frank, 1990), functional academic instruction in mathematics should become a priority among special and regular education teachers at the secondary level.

Some experts in the area of math instruction in special education (Cawley et al., 1992; Cawley & Parmar, 1992; Cawley & Miller, 1989; Mastropieri, Scruggs, & Shiah, 1991) question the need for a continuation of rote learning and memorization when students are learning math skills. While rote memorization and math routines stressing basic computational facts may be necessary for primary-level students to acquire basic math skills, at the secondary level there needs to be a change of attack in order for adolescents to make a smooth transition into independent community living and working.

Consumer mathematics skills.   **Consumer math skills** include effectively planning, choosing, and purchasing necessities in community settings. Consumer math instruction emphasizes the need for comparison shopping in making purchases of essentials and in participating in recreation and leisure activities. The following is a partial list of skills that should be stressed in consumer math instruction.

- Ordering items from a catalog (including costs of shipping)
- Comparison shopping, using newspaper advertisements (e.g., comparing rents of apartments or houses)
- Using credit for purchases (including use of credit cards)
- Comparing costs of similar items at different types of stores (e.g., grocery, clothing, department, hardware, etc.)
- Buying in bulk to save money on groceries
- Computing sales tax
- Obtaining consumer loans
- Budgeting for and estimating expenses for food, rent, recreation, heating, phone, transportation, clothing, etc.
- Paying bills using cash, check, bank debits, etc.
- Checking sales slips and exchanging items at stores
- Installment buying and buying on sale

Teachers should remember that the best way to teach such consumer-related math skills is to make the learning situations as authentic as possible, using age-appropriate examples. An attempt should be made to take the students into the surrounding community for actual guided practice and testing of skills stressed in the classroom—to build learning around real-life experiences, not artificial or extraneous ones. Students should be observed performing the tasks in the community and assessed for accuracy of completion, and teachers should not only plan for present-day needs of students as consumers, but project for future needs as well. An example problem for one of the necessary consumer skills follows:

Find the Better Buy:

Item	Store A	Store B
Margarine	2 lbs. in tub	2 lbs. in sticks
	$1.09 per lb.	$1.12 per lb.
Oranges	$.79 per lb.	5 lb. bag $2.39

Homemaking and home care math skills. This area of math instruction deals with how to use one's income to purchase necessities of daily living in an apartment, house, or other type of community residence. Homemaking math instruction emphasizes the need for awareness of all the expenses one must plan for when living away from parents or guardians. While this area of instruction may seem obvious to teachers of secondary-level students with mild disabilities, research indicates that many young adults with mild disabilities face adjustment problems in independent community living (see Peraino, 1992, and Chapter 11 of this text for reviews). The following is a sample of the skills that teachers should emphasize in home care math.

- Deciding whether to rent or buy a house
- Deciding on a furnished or unfurnished place of residence
- Understanding closing costs and mortgage lending
- Calculating property and real estate taxes
- Considering cost of electricity, water, cable television, etc.
- Understanding the cost of telephone service
- Computing average monthly expenses
- Leasing or purchasing furniture and appliances
- Purchasing homeowner's or renter's insurance
- Planning for house maintenance and home improvement costs
- Buying appliances and tools (e.g., vacuum cleaner, refrigerator, lawn mower, hammers, etc.) for home upkeep

Example word problem:

Elizabeth is renting an unfurnished apartment for $400 a month. Her net pay is $675 a month. Her monthly apartment expenses include $35 for electricity, $12 for water, and $20 for natural gas. What is left of her net pay after paying rent and expenses?

One way for teachers to make this area of math instruction particularly meaningful is to take students on field trips to local apartment complexes or homes for rent and allow them to see firsthand what a certain amount of money will allow for a particular style of living quarters. If students with mild disabilities are to live independently in the community, they should be exposed, as early as possible, to the realities, responsibilities, and expenses required for any domicile.

Health-care math skills.   Acquiring health-care math skills will prepare the student for the sophisticated network we call personal health maintenance. In light of the ever-rising and often prohibitive costs of personal health maintenance in the U.S., students with mild disabilities need careful instruction and many specific skills to be able to successfully access this very important domain. Without very specific knowledge and skills, the adult with a mild disability may face costs that place him or her in a position of undue hardship. The following areas of instruction in health care should become part of any secondary program that aims for serving students with mild disabilities in a realistic, contemporary, and effective fashion.

- Knowledge of health insurance: its cost and nuances
- Comparing the costs and benefits of different health-care plans
- Obtaining and buying prescription drugs
- Insurance deductibles and co-payments
- Using a thermometer
- Measuring and dispensing correct dosage levels of prescriptions
- Counting calories, cholesterol, fat, etc.
- Understanding blood pressure and pulse rate

Example problem:

Calculate how much this person must pay:

Cost of Medical Expense	Deductible	% Paid by Insurance	Amount Paid by Insured
$440	$250	80%	_____

Health-care math skills are important for students with mild disabilities living independently in the community, and they are vital for all young adults faced with financing their personal health care. This type of math instruction is very functional for all adolescents and young adults, considering the present-day expense of health care.

Auto care and transportation math skills.   Although not all adolescents need a car to be independent in the community, most teenagers dream of the day they can afford their own form of personal transportation, and students with disabilities are no different in this dream. Moreover, given the high reinforcement value of owning one's own car, math instruction that is based on auto care and transportation should prove highly motivating to adolescents. The following car-care and related math areas should be highlighted by teachers serving adolescents with mild disabilities.

- Buying, leasing, down payments, and financing
- Calculating miles per gallon of gasoline
- Calculating monthly gasoline expenses
- Understanding costs of car insurance
- Estimating and calculating operating and car maintenance costs
- Comparing costs of used cars
- Computing parts and labor costs from a repair bill
- Calculating distances in miles between two points
- Using local, state, and national maps
- Understanding bus schedules
- Computing taxi fares
- Using and purchasing bus passes
- Knowledge of bus, train, and air fares

Example word problem:

Ralph has purchased a used (1990) Chevrolet Camaro for $6,000. He gave the dealer a $1,500 down payment and agreed to finance the balance over 36 months at a 10% annual percentage rate (APR). What is the total cost of the car to Ralph after paying off the balance over 3 years?

Teachers can easily make this type of math instruction meaningful by having students peruse the used car classifieds in daily newspapers, visiting car lots for *in situ* instruction, and having insurance representatives visit their classrooms for discussions related to collision and liability insurance. Similarly, having students choose the right bus route and then traveling from one point to another in the community should assist in skill maintenance in this important curricular domain.

Home care mathematics skills.   Whether one rents an apartment or owns a home, from time to time it is necessary to repair appliances, change the decor, or replace worn or broken items. Maintaining or making improvements in a place of residence involves many areas of mathematics, particularly using money. Adolescents with mild disabilities should be prepared to deal with such life experiences by exposing them to common expenses in home care and by making them aware of possibilities they may face in this area. The following aspects should be covered by teachers attempting to prepare secondary-level students with mild disabilities for home care exigencies.

- Reading utility meters to estimate costs
- Buying lumber, paint, carpeting, etc. for home repairs

- Calculating perimeters and areas for lawn care, fertilizing, fence construction or repair, etc.
- Calculating wall areas for wallpapering
- Pricing incidentals such as furnace air filters, lightbulbs, batteries for appliances, etc.
- Comparing cost of replacing floors with carpeting vs. tile vs. hardwood
- Buying furniture, appliances, cable TV service, etc.
- Buying and replacing broken windows, door locks, plumbing fixtures, etc.

Example word problem:

> *Elizabeth wants to wallpaper her bathroom. The three walls she wants to wall-paper are 9 ft. high and 8 ft. wide. What is the total area of wall space of the bathroom? If a double roll of wallpaper covers 50 sq. ft., how many rolls of wallpaper are needed to cover the whole room? If a double roll of wallpaper sells for $17.00, what will it cost to wallpaper the whole bathroom?*

Having students participate in wallpapering an actual wall would also assist in exposing them to the difficulties of one type of home improvement. Teachers, whenever possible, should plan to have students engaged in practicing some of the actual home improvement tasks. Students who have difficulty in performing some of these tasks should be given a dose of reality by factoring in the costs of having a trained professional install or repair common household items. Hands-on practice with manipulatives should also enhance motivation of secondary-level students unaware of how math is used in home upkeep.

Vocational math skills. **Vocational math** concerns the mathematical skills needed in various forms of employment. The scope of this specific area of functional math skills could be very large or small, depending on student interest and how a secondary-level teacher responds to such interest (we recommend that teachers respond with a curriculum that fits individual student needs). Depending upon the particular area of vocational or occupational interest, different mathematics-related skills would be emphasized. The math skills and knowledge of a nurse assistant, for example, would be very different from those of a carpenter, salesclerk, or auto mechanic. Nevertheless, the following *generic* vocational math skills should be emphasized by teachers of students with mild disabilities at the secondary level.

- Calculating wages based on hourly pay or piecework
- Calculating salary based on commission
- Calculating federal, state, local, and property taxes
- Calculating social security taxes
- Filing federal and state income taxes
- Calculating cost-of-living raises
- Calculating overtime wages
- Understanding gross pay and net pay
- Comparing employer benefits vs. out-of-pocket expenses for benefits

Example word problem:

> *Which of the following is paid more for a one-year period—a salesclerk earning $5.50 per hour, based on a 40-hour work week and 50 weeks per year, or a plumber's helper earning $10.00 per hour, based on a 40-hour work week and only working 25 weeks of the year?*

The intent of vocationally oriented math is to prepare workers for what is in store for them when they begin to earn money on their own. Many occupations have some very specific math skills that must be mastered for success (e.g., measuring by a carpenter), while others do not (e.g., a lifeguard). Understanding what happens to earnings because of payroll deductions, however, should be a math skill that all students with mild disabilities should have. Filing state and federal income taxes accurately is a very challenging and worthwhile math activity for youth preparing for the world of work, and teachers should ensure that their students have had at least some exposure to and practice with this activity. Teachers should allow students who already hold jobs to bring to class their payroll receipts so that other students can see firsthand what happens to all their hard-earned pay. Because of the nature of vocational math skills, this curricular area should be highly motivating to students and extremely functional.

Mathematical Process Instruction

Cawley and Parmar (1992) cautioned against using rote memorization for the teaching of computation; they also stated that computation instruction for students with disabilities has progressed very little over the last 50 years and that a heavy emphasis on memorization for acquisition of computation still exists. They suggest that cognitive psychology could be used more frequently in teaching math to students in special education. Specifically, they recommend that in teaching computation skills to students with disabilities it would be helpful to use problems that (a) may have several solutions or several ways to arrive at a correct response, (b) are drawn from real-life circumstances, and (c) activate prior knowledge of students. These authors also concluded that special education programs can no longer justify the teaching of multiplication tables to 16-year-olds when the majority of instructional routines still overemphasize memory with little attention directed toward understanding computation and the requirements of the world outside the walls of the school. We could not agree more, and the following sections discuss the teaching of computation, problem solving, and application from the view that all should be taught by examining how instruction in the classroom can be made more relevant and useful to adolescents' lives in the community.

Computation and problem solving.   In learning or relearning the basics of computation in solving math word problems, adolescents with mild disabilities should be provided with examples and situations taken from their everyday lives. Instead of expecting students to complete reams of worksheets involving the operations of addition, subtraction, multiplication, and division, Cawley and Parmar (1992) recommend using manipulatives so that students are allowed to *reason* correct responses to computation and word problems. One example of using manipulatives to solve a computation word problem would be the following:

> *You have $420 (the students are presented with four $100 bills and four $5 bills). How would you divide this amount equally among your four children?*

This problem encourages students to pursue alternative ways to solve the problem (i.e., reason), it uses manipulatives, and highlights the need for communication between and among teacher and students. Stress is placed on the *meaning* of functional computation and problem solving, rather than on the process of computation and rote memorization of difficult-to-remember math facts (Cawley & Parmar, 1992).

As in the above example, manipulatives and reasoning can also be used to teach computation and word problems involving ratios, fractions, and any number of secondary-level math skills. The following example includes an explanation of how ratios in employment can be used in classroom instruction.

> *You are making bathroom cabinets with boards and nails. If you used 10 boards of equal length to make three cabinets, how many more boards of the same length will you need to make two additional cabinets? (The teacher provides the boards, models the use of 10 boards to make three cabinets, and allows students to manipulate the remaining boards to determine how many are needed for two more cabinets.)*

The following example includes elaboration of how computation of fractions in word problems can be made more meaningful in classroom instruction.

> *A nurse's assistant must mix a saline and sterile water solution to irrigate a patient's wound. She must mix ⅛ of a 32-mL container of saline solution with ⅘ of a 100-mL container of sterile water. What is the total amount of the completed mixture in mL? (The teacher provides the model of mixing two solutions together and calculating the sum, and then allows the students to do the same to solve the specific problem.)*

To further stimulate interest in solving computational problems, teachers should allow students to provide additional examples of math problems taken from their own jobs, hobbies, and daily lives. The important feature of this type of computational or problem-solving instruction is the need to create situations in which students can handle actual materials, manipulate or change them, and reason and see the results in actual situations. This manipulation-and-reasoning math instruction involving student-provided examples challenges students, relates the instruction to out-of-school situations, and can assist in keeping students motivated to acquire new skills that impact their personal contexts.

Application of math in employment.   It is in the area of employment-related math skills that secondary-level teachers can truly enhance students' motivation for success in math. This area is filled with any number of skills that can be emphasized, from measurement to manipulations of fractions, decimals, and percentages to reading charts and graphs. For the instruction to be functional, however, teachers will need to comb the local community employment sites for examples of math on the job and bring such illustrations into the classroom, or take students to the actual job sites to see math on the job in reality. Figures 7.4 and 7.5 present examples of math used in various jobs suitable for adolescents with mild disabilities. Teachers should examine them and think of other employment sites in their community where similar math skills are needed.

Figure 7.4
Example of math on the job from the U.S. Postal Service

Form 3602-R—Third-Class Regular Rate—Permit Imprint		
Postage Computation—Bulk Rates		

Entry Discount (If Any)	Presort/ Automation Discounts	Net Rate	Count (Pcs/Lbs)	Charge	Entry Discount (If Any)	Presort/ Automation Discounts	Net Rate	Count (Pcs/Lbs)	Charge
Automation-Compatible Letter (DMM 520)					**Non-Automation-Compatible Letter** .2067 lb. (3.3067 oz.) or less				
None	Saturation W/S	.124 x	____ pcs. = $ ____		**None**	Saturation W/S	.124 x	____ pcs. = $ ____	
	Carrier Route	.131 x	____ pcs. = $ ____			Carrier Route	.131 x	____ pcs. = $ ____	
	5-Digit Barcoded	.146 x	____ pcs. = $ ____			3/5-Digit Presort	.165 x	____ pcs. = $ ____	
	3-Digit Barcoded	.154 x	____ pcs. = $ ____			Basic	.198 x	____ pcs. = $ ____	
	3/5-Digit ZIP + 4	.161 x	____ pcs. = $ ____						
	3/5-Digit Presort	.165 x	____ pcs. = $ ____						
	Basic Barcoded	.179 x	____ pcs. = $ ____						
	Basic ZIP + 4	.189 x	____ pcs. = $ ____						
	Basic	.198 x	____ pcs. = $ ____						
BMC Entry	Saturation W/S	.112 x	____ pcs. = $ ____		**BMC Entry**	Saturation W/S	.112 x	____ pcs. = $ ____	
	Carrier Route	.119 x	____ pcs. = $ ____			Carrier Route	.119 x	____ pcs. = $ ____	
	5-Digit Barcoded	.134 x	____ pcs. = $ ____			3/5-Digit Presort	.153 x	____ pcs. = $ ____	
	3-Digit Barcoded	.142 x	____ pcs. = $ ____			Basic	.186 x	____ pcs. = $ ____	
	3/5-Digit ZIP + 4	.149 x	____ pcs. = $ ____						
	3/5-Digit Presort	.153 x	____ pcs. = $ ____						
	Basic Barcoded	.167 x	____ pcs. = $ ____						
	Basic ZIP + 4	.177 x	____ pcs. = $ ____						
	Basic	.186 x	____ pcs. = $ ____						
SCF Entry	Saturation W/S	.107 x	____ pcs. = $ ____		**SCF Entry**	Saturation W/S	.107 x	____ pcs. = $ ____	
	Carrier Route	.114 x	____ pcs. = $ ____			Carrier Route	.114 x	____ pcs. = $ ____	
	5-Digit barcoded	.129 x	____ pcs. = $ ____			3/5-Digit Presort	.148 x	____ pcs. = $ ____	
	3-Digit Barcoded	.137 x	____ pcs. = $ ____			Basic	.181 x	____ pcs. = $ ____	
	3/5-Digit ZIP + 4	.144 x	____ pcs. = $ ____						
	3/5-Digit Presort	.148 x	____ pcs. = $ ____						
	Basic Barcoded	.162 x	____ pcs. = $ ____						
	Basic ZIP + 4	.172 x	____ pcs. = $ ____						
	Basic	.181 x	____ pcs. = $ ____						
DDU Entry	Saturation W/S	.102 x	____ pcs. = $ ____		**DDU Entry**	Saturation W/S	.102 x	____ pcs. = $ ____	
	Carrier Route	.109 x	____ pcs. = $ ____			Carrier Route	.109 x	____ pcs. = $ ____	
Total—Part A (Carry to front of form)		$ ____			**Total—Part B (Carry to front of form)**		$ ____		

Figure 7.4, continued

Nonletter—.2067 lb. (3.3067 oz.) or Less			All Mail—More than .2067 lb. (3.3067 oz.) But less than 1.0 lb. (16.0 oz.)		
None	Saturation W/S	.127 x _____ pcs. = $ _____	**None**	Saturation W/S	.003 x _____ pcs. = $ _____
	Carrier Route	.142 x _____ pcs. = $ _____		plus	.600 x _____ lbs. = $ _____
	3/5-Digit Presort	.187 x _____ pcs. = $ _____		Carrier Route	.018 x _____ pcs. = $ _____
	Basic	.233 x _____ pcs. = $ _____		plus	.600 x _____ lbs. = $ _____
				3/5-Digit Presort	.063 x _____ pcs. = $ _____
				plus	.600 x _____ lbs. = $ _____
				Basic	.109 x _____ pcs. = $ _____
				plus	.600 x _____ lbs. = $ _____
BMC	Saturation W/S	.115 x _____ pcs. = $ _____	**BMC**	Saturation W/S	.003 x _____ pcs. = $ _____
Entry	Carrier Route	.130 x _____ pcs. = $ _____	**Entry**	plus	.542 x _____ lbs. = $ _____
	3/5-Digit Presort	.175 x _____ pcs. = $ _____		Carrier Route	.018 x _____ pcs. = $ _____
	Basic	.221 x _____ pcs. = $ _____		plus	.542 x _____ lbs. = $ _____
				3/5-Digit Presort	.063 x _____ pcs. = $ _____
				plus	.542 x _____ lbs. = $ _____
				Basic	.109 x _____ pcs. = $ _____
				plus	.542 x _____ lbs. = $ _____
SCF	Saturation W/S	.110 x _____ pcs. = $ _____	**SCF**	Saturation W/S	.003 x _____ pcs. = $ _____
Entry	Carrier Route	.125 x _____ pcs. = $ _____	**Entry**	plus	.519 x _____ lbs. = $ _____
	3/5-Digit Presort	.170 x _____ pcs. = $ _____		Carrier Route	.018 x _____ pcs. = $ _____
	Basic	.216 x _____ pcs. = $ _____		plus	.519 x _____ lbs. = $ _____
				3/5-Digit Presort	.063 x _____ pcs. = $ _____
				plus	.519 x _____ lbs.= $ _____
				Basic	.109 x _____ pcs. = $ _____
				plus	.519 x _____ lbs. = $ _____
DDU	Saturation W/S	.105 x _____ pcs. = $ _____	**DDU**	Saturation W/S	.003 x _____ pcs. = $ _____
Entry	Carrier Route	.120 x _____ pcs. = $ _____	**Entry**	plus	.496 x _____ lbs. = $ _____
				Carrier Route	.018 x _____ pcs. = $ _____
				plus	.496 x _____ lbs. = $ _____
Total—Part C (Carry to front of form) $ _____			**Total—Part D (Carry to front of form) $ _____**		

Math Instruction via Cognitive Strategies

Research has shown that another effective way of teaching math (particularly problem solving) to secondary-level students with mild disabilities is through the use of cognitive strategies. Montague (1992) and Montague, Applegate, and Marquard (1993) showed that students' performance on math word problems can be improved through the use of a combination cognitive-metacognitive strategy (COG-MET). Montague and colleagues demonstrated that not only did problem-solving performance improve after adolescents with learning disabilities received specific strategy training, but that also, their enhanced problem-solving skill was maintained over a 5-week period. Figures 7.6 and 7.7 depict the procedures involved in the delivery of the COG-MET strategy and a sample of a scripted lesson to use when introducing the strategy.

Case, Harris, and Graham (1992) taught 5th- and 6th-grade students with learning disabilities a strategy to improve their solving of addition and subtraction word problems. They first instructed students to recognize key words that denote certain opera-

THIRD-CLASS REGULAR RATE
BULK MAIL
MINIMUM PER PIECE RATE MAIL

	Cents
A. LETTERS	
Basic	19.8
3/5 Digit	16.5
Carrier Route	13.1
Saturation	12.4

Letter-size mail which meets all Postal regulations and which bears correct ZIP+4 and/or ZIP+4 barcodes is eligible for automation rates as follows:

Basic	
ZIP+4	18.9
ZIP+4 Barcode	17.9
3/5 Digit	
ZIP+4	16.1
Barcode—3-Digit Sort	15.4
Barcode—5-Digit Sort	14.6

B. NON-LETTERS (flats, parcels, etc.)	
Basic	23.3
3/5 Presort	18.7
Carrier Route	14.2
Saturation Walk Sequence	12.7

TRANSPORTATION DISCOUNTS

Minimum per piece rate mail is eligible for destination entry discounts. The following discounts are deducted from the above rates.

All Minimum Per Piece Rate Mail	
BMC	1.2
SCF	1.7
Carrier Route and Saturation Walk-Sequence Only	
Delivery Unit	2.2

Source: From U.S. Postal Service

tions in math word problems (e.g., "how many left," "have all together," "how much more"). The next steps in learning the problem-solving strategy involved teaching the students to (a) read the problem out loud, (b) look for important words and circle them, (c) draw pictures to help tell what is occurring, (d) write down the math sentence, and (e) write down the answer. Thinking aloud was also modeled by the instructor so that students could do the same when faced with solving a math word problem (e.g., "What is it that I have to do?" "How can I solve this problem?" "How am I doing?" "Does this make sense?" etc.). Case et al. demonstrated that teaching the students the five-step problem-solving strategy resulted in improved word problem performance and fewer

Breading Facts

EQUIVALENTS

3 Teaspoons	=	1 Tablespoon
2 Tablespoons	=	1 Ounce
8 Ounces	=	1 Cup
2 Cups	=	1 Pint
2 Pints	=	1 Quart
32 Ounces	=	1 Quart
16 Ounces	=	1 Pound

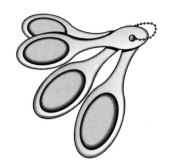

SCOOPS (# = the number of scoops to fill 1 Quart (32 ounces)

#70	=	$\frac{1}{2}$ Ounce
#24	=	$1\frac{1}{2}$ Ounces
#12	=	3 Ounces
#8	=	4 Ounces

BREADINGS YOU USE

- Seafood Breading — *shrimp, scallops, crab cakes, pollock, flounder, popcorn shrimp, fresh fish*

- Lemon Pepper Breading — *shrimp, fish*

- Catfish Breading — *catfish*

Promotional Breading

- Cajun Breading — *shrimp, popcorn shrimp*

- Oriental Breading — *shrimp*

PRODUCTS YOU USE
(Ask your manager about counts used in your store)

- Shrimp

Large	_____ count	$\frac{3}{8}$ – $\frac{1}{2}$" cut
Round	_____ count	$\frac{1}{8}$ - $\frac{3}{16}$" cut
Popcorn	_____ count	

- Scallops _____ count — no larger than $\frac{3}{4}$ ounces

- Frozen fish
  Pollock — $\frac{1}{2}$ inch thick or less for frying
  Flounder/Sole

- Crab Cake Mix (D.C. Mix)

- Zucchini — $\frac{1}{4}$" cut

Figure 7.5
Example of math on the job from Red Lobster restaurants

Broil Station Set-Up & Cooking Times for Pizza Oven

Each day when you arrive for work, check your station for meal readiness.

Check:

____ Tongs (Chicken items, Grill)	____ Spatula
____ Seafood seasoning	____ Sanitizer Bucket/Towel
____ Water source working	____ Blackened fish pans
____ Plates/Platters/lg. platter	____ Blackened Seasoning
____ Buttersauce	____ Pre-soak bucket for pie tins
____ Waste tub	____ Tested Sanitizer

ITEM	APPROXIMATE MINUTES	MINIMUM TEMPERATURE	SIGNS TO LOOK FOR
SHRIMP			
Shrimp Scampi 7	5	150°	Shrimp meat turning
Shrimp Scampi 11	6	150°	white and tail turning a
Key West Shrimp 11	7	150°	pinkish color.
FISH			
Broiled Flounder	5–6	150°	Turns white and flaky
Lunch Stuffed Flounder	7	165°	Fish becomes white and flaky and stuffing is lightly browned
Pollock/Casserole	6	150°	Moisture showing
Broiled Pollock	6	150°	throughout fish
Blackened Pollock	8	150°	
Broiled Fish 5 oz.	8–10	150°	
Broiled Fish 10 oz.	8–10	150°	
Blackened Fish 5 oz.	8–10	150°	
Blackened Fish 10 oz.	8–10	150°	
MAINE LOBSTER			
Whole Stuffed 1¼ lb.	9	165°	
Whole Stuffed 2 lb.	15	165°	
LOBSTER			
Petite Deep Sea	5	150°	Turns white underneath meat
Langostino 4 oz.	5	150°	
Rock 6 oz. Fluffed	9	150°	
9 oz. Fluffed	10	150°	
12-14 oz. Fluffed	13	150°	
CASSEROLE			
Seafood Broil	8	165°	Scallops to turn white, shrimp to pink

* Time may vary a little because of volume and number of times oven door is opened.

Figure 7.6
COG-MET math strategy instruction

Read (for understanding)
    Say: Read the problem. If I don't understand, read it again.
    Ask: Have I read and understood the problem?
    Check: For understanding as I solve the problem.

Paraphrase (your own words)
    Say: Put the problem in my own words.
                 Underline the important information.
    Ask: Have I underlined the important information?
                 What is the question? What am I looking for?
    Check: That the information goes with the question.

Visualize (a picture or a diagram)
    Say: Make a drawing or diagram.
    Ask: Does the picture fit the problem?
    Check: The picture against the problem information.

Hypothesize (a plan to solve the problem)
    Say: Decide how many steps and operations are needed.
                 Write the operation symbols $(+, -, \times, \div)$.
    Ask: If I do... , what will I get?
                 If I do... , then what do I need to do next?
                 How many steps are needed?
    Check: That the plan makes sense.

Estimate (predict the answer)
    Say: Round the numbers, do the problem in my head, and write
                 the estimate.
    Ask: Did I round up and down?
                 Did I write the estimate?
    Check: That I used the important information.

Compute (do the arithmetic)
    Say: Do the operations in the right order.
    Ask: How does my answer compare with my estimate?
                 Does my answer make sense?
                 Are the decimals or money signs in the right places?
    Check: That all the operations were done in the right order.

Check (make sure that everything is right)
    Say: Check the computation.
    Ask: Have I checked every step?
                 Have I checked the computation?
                 Is my answer right?
    Check: That everything is right. If not, go back.
                 Then ask for help if I need it.

Source: From "Cognitive Strategy Instruction and Mathematical Problem Solving Performance of Students with Learning Disabilities" by M. Montague, B. Applegate, and K. Marquard, 1993, *Learning Disabilities Research & Practice, 8,* 223–232.

Figure 7.7
Scripted lesson in teaching the COG-MET math strategy

COG–MET Teacher Routine for Day 9

When we started instruction, we talked about what good problem solvers do when they solve problems. Raise your hand if you remember what good problem solvers do. [Call on students to recite the seven cognitive processes.]

Yes, you have just verbalized the seven processes of the strategy for math problem solving. However, just memorizing this strategy is not really enough to improve your problem solving. You have all learned the strategy very well and have improved your problem solving. It is important that you continue to improve and do even better. It is also important that you continue to use the strategy every time you need to solve problems in school and outside of school. When might you need to solve a problem outside of school? [Elicit responses—at the store, measuring, etc.]

Today I am going to add another part to the strategy. I am going to teach you several things to do when you use each process in the strategy.

People who are good math problem solvers do several things in their head when they solve problems. First, they say different things to tell themselves what to do. Second, they ask themselves questions. Third, they check to see that they have done what they needed to do to solve the math problems. I have these activities written in these little booklets for you to use and study. I will give them to you at the end of class today for you to take home and study. I also wrote the activities on this big chart for you while you are learning the activities as you solve word problems.

[Show the booklet and charts to the students. Point to each activity and verbalization as you read and explain it.]

Now I have put each say, ask, and check activity with the right process on these charts. Your booklets look exactly like these charts. [Read through the charts.] Questions?

All right, now I would like you to read through the charts. I will help you with words if you need help. [Have students read the chart two or three times as a group.]

Now I would like you to read the process and the words *say, ask* and *check,* and I will read the activities.

Now I will read the process and the words *say, ask,* and *check,* and you will read the activities.

Now I want you to read everything. [Call on each student to read the entire strategy one time.]

Now I want you to watch me as I solve this problem using the entire strategy. [Show the problem on the overhead projector.]

In the Orange Bowl parade, there were 50 marching bands. Twenty-eight bands had 660 members, and the remainder of the bands had 45 members each. How many band members were in all the marching bands?

Use the following routine. During modeling, use the expressions "now I will say to myself… ," "now I will ask myself… ," "now I will check myself…. " Use this routine when first modeling the strategy out loud. Later, students will verbalize the words say *and so on, or the teacher will verbalize the cue words for the students. The goal is to eventually fade these cue words and have students automatically self-instruct, question, and check themselves. Self-cueing will consist of remembering the processes, although students will appear to fade on certain processes as well.*

[Teacher modeling] Read the problem for understanding. Now I will say to myself—"Read the problem" [Read the problem.] "If I do not understand it, read it again." [Read the problem again.] Now I will ask myself, "Have I read and understood the problem?" I will read it one more time. [Read the problem again.] Now I will check myself by checking for understanding as I solve the problem.

Paraphrase the problem. Now I will say to myself, "Put the problem into my own words." Fifty bands altogether. Twenty-eight had 660 members altogether. The rest had 45 members each. How many kids altogether? "Underline the important information." [Underline 50 marching bands, 28 bands had 660, remainder of the bands had 45 members.] Now I will ask myself, "Have I underlined the important information?" Yes. "What is the question?" How many band members were in all the marching bands? "What am I looking for?" The total number of people in all the bands. Now I will check myself by checking that the information goes with the question—28 with 660, the rest with 45 each—50 bands in all. Yes, the information goes with the question.

Visualize the problem. Now I will say to myself "Make a drawing or a diagram." [Draw a suitable picture or diagram for the problem.]

Now I will ask myself "Does the picture fit the problem?" Yes, it does.

Now I will check myself by checking the picture against the problem information.

Hypothesize. Set up a plan to solve the problem. Now I will say to myself, "Decide how many steps and operations are needed." First I will subtract 28 from 50. Then I will multiply the answer by 45 and add that to 660… subtract, multiply, add. Write the operation symbols. [Write –, x, +] There are three steps in this problem.

Now I will ask myself, "If I subtract 28 bands from 50, I will get the remainder of bands, then what do I do next?" Then I will multiply that answer by 45 to get the number of people in the remainder of bands, then what do I do next? Then I add that number to 660 and get the total number of band members. Then what do I do next? Nothing, I am finished. Now I will ask myself: "How many steps are needed?" Three. Now I will check myself by checking that the plan makes sense. If not, I will ask for help.

Estimate. Predict the answer. Now I will say to myself, "Round the numbers, do the problem in my head, and write the estimate." I will round down 28 to 25 and subtract 25 from 50 = 25 times 40 [do the arithmetic] = 1000 and 660 = about 1,600 members.

Now I will ask myself, "Did I round up and down?" Yes. "Did I write the estimate?" Yes.

Now I will check myself by checking that I used the important information.

Compute. Do the arithmetic. Now I will say to myself, "Do the operation in the right order." [Do the arithmetic.]

Now I will ask myself, "How does my answer compare with my estimate?" Is it very close? Does my answer make sense? Yes. Are the decimals or money signs in the right order? None are needed. I just need a comma to separate the thousands from the hundreds.

Now I will check myself by checking that all the operations were done in the right order.

Check. Make sure everything is right. Now I will say to myself, "Check the computation," Now I will ask myself, "Have I checked every step?" Yes. "Have I used the right numbers? Have I checked the computation?" Yes. "Is my answer right?" Yes.

Now I will check myself by checking that everything is right. If not, I will go back. Then I will ask for help if I need it.

This is the model that will be used throughout the second level of this routine.

You have memorized the strategy. I want you to continue to practice the strategy but now add the say, ask, check procedure so that you know the activities that go with each process. Study these activities.

Provide group and individual review of the strategy until the class ends.

Source: From "Cognitive Strategy Instruction and Mathematical Problem Solving Performance of Students with Learning Disabilities" by M. Montague, B. Applegate, and K. Marquard, 1993, *Learning Disabilities Research & Practice, 8,* 223–232.

errors from executing the wrong operation. Not only did students' problem-solving performance improve, but also, their strategy use generalized to another setting.

Commercial Mathematics Curricula for Adolescents

Teachers of secondary-level students with mild disabilities often use "packaged" curricula in instruction. Commercial math series used in special and regular education settings have the advantage of ease of use and sequenced skill instruction, and most can be easily adapted for learners whose skills are behind those of their same-age peers. In this section we review some commercial math curricula that can be used with secondary-level youth with mild disabilities.

Corrective Mathematics (Engelmann & Carnine, 1982) appears to be the most efficacious program in terms of providing research-proven math instruction (see Engelmann, Carnine, & Steely, 1991, for a review) to secondary-level students with mild disabilities. The intent of this program is to teach the basic mathematics skills of addition, subtraction, multiplication, and division to students from grade 3 through postsecondary levels. Additional *Mathematics Modules* (Engelmann & Steely, 1981), which are companion programs to *Corrective Mathematics,* cover basic fractions, ratios and equations, fractions, decimals, and percentages. The partner programs are designed to teach advanced math skills. The division scope and sequence chart of *Corrective Mathematics* is presented in Figure 7.8.

The series has a strong emphasis on the learning of number facts, operations, place value, and story problems. A particular strength of the program is the emphasis on applying strategies to select the correct operation in solving math word problems. In the subtraction module, for example, the following discrimination strategy is taught: "If the problem gives the big number, it's a subtraction problem; if the problem does not give the big number, it's an addition problem" (Engelmann & Carnine, 1982, p. 10). The "big number" referred to is the minuend in a subtraction problem and the sum in an addition problem. The following word problem illustrates how the use of this strategy applies to subtraction:

> *Mr. Yamada had 36 books. Last week he bought some more books at the used book shop. Now he has 58 books. How many books did he buy last week?*

Instructional lessons in *Corrective Mathematics* involve teacher-directed activities such as modeling, leading, testing, and following scripted lesson presentations. Many effective teaching behaviors (see Chapter 4) are also scripted for teachers implementing daily lessons. Students are actively involved in answering teachers' questions orally or completing written tasks in workbooks. Student independent work, as well as a "Fact Game," are scheduled into most daily lessons, which last between 25 and 45 minutes, depending on the size of the group. Because *Corrective Mathematics* includes many of the teaching routines known to affect student achievement in a positive manner, and because voluminous research does show its effectiveness (see Tarver, 1996), we strongly recommend its use in both regular and special education settings serving adolescents

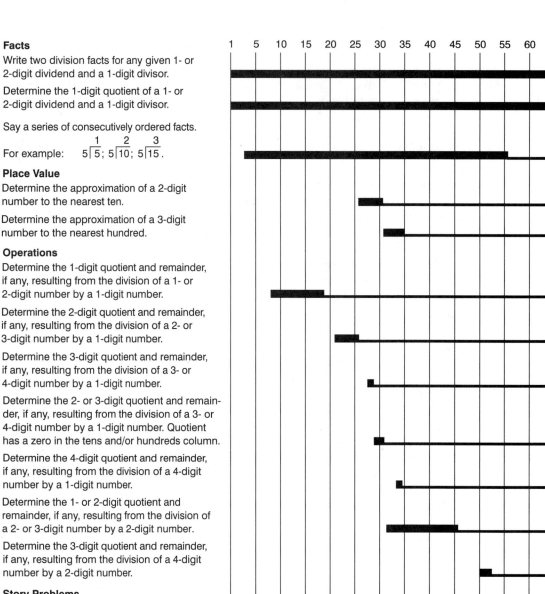

Facts

Write two division facts for any given 1- or 2-digit dividend and a 1-digit divisor.

Determine the 1-digit quotient of a 1- or 2-digit dividend and a 1-digit divisor.

Say a series of consecutively ordered facts.

For example: $5\overline{\smash{)}5}^{\,1}$; $5\overline{\smash{)}10}^{\,2}$; $5\overline{\smash{)}15}^{\,3}$.

Place Value

Determine the approximation of a 2-digit number to the nearest ten.

Determine the approximation of a 3-digit number to the nearest hundred.

Operations

Determine the 1-digit quotient and remainder, if any, resulting from the division of a 1- or 2-digit number by a 1-digit number.

Determine the 2-digit quotient and remainder, if any, resulting from the division of a 2- or 3-digit number by a 1-digit number.

Determine the 3-digit quotient and remainder, if any, resulting from the division of a 3- or 4-digit number by a 1-digit number.

Determine the 2- or 3-digit quotient and remainder, if any, resulting from the division of a 3- or 4-digit number by a 1-digit number. Quotient has a zero in the tens and/or hundreds column.

Determine the 4-digit quotient and remainder, if any, resulting from the division of a 4-digit number by a 1-digit number.

Determine the 1- or 2-digit quotient and remainder, if any, resulting from the division of a 2- or 3-digit number by a 2-digit number.

Determine the 3-digit quotient and remainder, if any, resulting from the division of a 4-digit number by a 2-digit number.

Story Problems

Determine the quotient or product of 2 numbers in a story problem.

Determine the sum or difference of 2 numbers in a story problem.

Determine the quotient, product, sum or difference of 2 numbers in a story problem.

KEY: ■ Teaching   — Review

Figure 7.8

Chart of scope and sequence of the *Corrective Mathematics* curriculum (division)

Source: From *Corrective Mathematics* by S. Englemann and D. Carnine, 1982, Chicago: SRA.

with mild disabilities. The only drawback to the program is that it does not have a specific focus on math skills needed in community environments.

Essentials of Mathematics: Consumer/Career Skills Applications (Gerardi, Jones, & Foster, 1987), a commercial math series developed with attention to math skills needed in adulthood, is aimed at non-college-bound high school students who have completed at least one course in general mathematics. Major math skill areas are covered in detail in separate chapters (e.g., decimals, fractions, ratios and percentages, income tax, banking, travel, housing, budgeting, algebra). What makes this curriculum unique, however, is that many chapters also include calculator skills applications, and all chapters include a focus on using math in various careers. Calculator skills, for example, are stressed in using a calculator for estimation, finding a percentage of a number, and checking addition, subtraction, multiplication, and division calculations. Given that we support the use of calculators in math instruction of adolescents with mild disabilities, *Essentials of Mathematics* provides a systematic and organized way of providing such emphasis in the classroom. Math applications in careers are emphasized in each chapter by providing activities and examples of how math is used in the work of stock clerks, bus drivers, electricians, nurses, salesclerks, and many other occupations. If secondary-level teachers of students with mild disabilities cannot regularly take students into the community for instruction in math, at least *Essentials of Mathematics: Consumer/Career Skills Applications* provides a classroom-based alternative with a career-oriented, functional math skills approach.

Transition Mathematics (Usiskin, Flanders, Hynes, Polonsky, Porter, & Viktora, 1987). Although secondary-level teachers of students with mild disabilities should be attracted to the title of this commercial math material, they need not spend too much time considering it for adoption in the classroom. The intent of this curriculum is to prepare students for studying algebra; it has little, if any, focus on functional math skills. Some students with mild disabilities, however, will enroll in high school algebra and they may benefit from math instruction using *Transition Mathematics.* The scope and sequence is similar to that of other published secondary-level basic math curricula; the four operations, decimals, percentages, measurement, problem solving, and using formulas are all covered in great detail in daily lessons. Chapter mastery tests are also included for teachers to use in judging students' progress and their own instructional effectiveness. The **SPUR** approach (**S** = skills needed in math; **P** = properties of numbers and operations; **U** = uses of numbers and math concepts; and **R** = representations of numbers, algorithms, and problem solving), which is emphasized throughout the curriculum, is designed to help students acquire both math skills and understanding of concepts. Given the somewhat traditional math instructional format used in *Transition Mathematics,* perhaps it would be better for teachers of adolescents with mild disabilities to consider other curricula for teaching functional math.

Mathematics Skills for Daily Living (Shulte, Haynes, & Bell, 1986) is another commercial mathematics curriculum purporting to be "a motivating text that helps students apply math" in their everyday lives. Teachers of adolescents with mild disabilities, however, will need to look closely at this package to determine whether it fits the functional needs of students soon to exit school. The content includes instruction in problem-solving strategies, math puzzles, practice in applying skills, building consumer skills, using calculators,

[handwritten note in left margin:] Not good √ one for L.D. Students

use as a supplement

and exposure to how math is used in both professional and nonprofessional careers (e.g., chefs, machinists, registered nurses, carpenters, bricklayers, meteorologists, bookkeepers). Performance objectives in all chapters are provided for teacher reference, time allotments for instruction (in days) are included, and related projects for students to explore independently are suggested to ensure high motivation. While *Mathematics Skills for Daily Living* does include some focus on functional skills needed in employment, the total amount of emphasis on career-oriented math skills is slight. Teachers of adolescents with mild disabilities, therefore, may wish to use *Mathematics Skills for Daily Living* as a supplementary text in daily and functional math instruction.

Practical Mathematics: Consumer Applications (Fredrick, Postman, Leinwand, & Wantuck, 1989) is a commercial math program that may appeal to students with mild disabilities and to their teachers. What is unique about this program is its consistent presentation of learning math skills and concepts in real-life situations. The authors stress that teenagers need knowledge, experience, and the ability to make good consumer decisions in a society that is complicated. Available to teachers using this program are the traditional teaching aids such as chapter objectives, instructional pacing charts, and a multitude of suggestions to present daily lessons. For the student, the program presents the learning of mathematics through chapters concerned with using calculators, part-time and summer jobs, recreation and sports, basic purchases, automobile expenses, housing, and several other real-life conditions. *Practical Mathematics: Consumer Applications* is very different from most of the commercial math programs reviewed previously. Adolescents with mild disabilities who will not attend college need as much instruction as possible in math for daily living, and this program offers much promise in meeting this need. At the same time, research will be needed to determine whether secondary-level students with mild disabilities will benefit from its use. Because of its concentration on community-based math skills, we believe that *Practical Mathematics: Consumer Applications* deserves at least some adoption consideration by teachers serving adolescents with mild disabilities.

Adapting commercial math materials used in regular education classes. Many adolescents with mild disabilities will spend some of their school day in regular education math courses. In order for them to obtain benefit from such courses and still receive instruction that addresses their IEP goals and objectives and their need for math skills that will help them in everyday life, curricular and material adaptations may be necessary. Conventional materials used in regular education math classes may be beneficial to the masses, but are they equally helpful for adolescents with mild disabilities who are deficient in math skills? The following section describes the issues involved in adapting regular education materials to fit the needs of students with mild disabilities in secondary schools. Keep in mind, however, that little is known about the kinds of changes regular classroom educators are likely to make to accommodate students with mild disabilities (Ysseldyke, Thurlow, Wotruba, & Nania, 1990).

Cawley and Parmar (1990) provided an interesting perspective on adapting regular education math materials. They cited four problems relevant to students with mild disabilities who use regular education math materials and are asked to perform in regular math classes: (a) publishers rarely consider students with mild disabilities when developing math curricula to be used in regular classes; (b) math performance standards set by school districts do not consider students with mild disabilities who may not be able to meet such standards; (c) regular class math teachers are faced with strict time lines in terms of what the school district expects to be covered in a textbook or commercial math program; and (d) math teachers' instructional effectiveness and performance are scrutinized annually by how much gain their students demonstrate. Given these issues it should not surprise any prospective or in-service secondary-level teacher that curricular modifications in mathematics are easier said than done.

Cawley and Parmar (1990) suggested that one way to determine whether a student needs a change or adaptation in curriculum or instruction is to closely examine daily math performance. Homework assignments, daily or weekly tests, and everyday classroom assignments should be reviewed frequently by the teacher to determine whether a pattern of low scores is evident. If low scores on math assignments occur over two or three days in succession, Cawley and Parmar recommend an immediate curricular adjustment. In cases in which math curricular adaptations are necessary, Cawley and Parmar suggest that teachers consult instructor's manuals to find additional instructional recommendations that pertain to presentation of the math concept or process. We also recommend that regular education math teachers consult special educators to receive additional advice on different ways to present learning tasks, particularly from a task analysis perspective.

Cawley and Parmar's major theme, however, was not so much the need to adapt math curricula to fit the needs of students with mild disabilities in regular classes, but rather to make math instruction more meaningful. Specifically, they strongly recommended that math teachers in all settings decrease their reliance on computation, drill and practice, and rote learning of math, and instead concentrate on math problem solving needed in everyday contexts. Cawley and Parmar also posited that the time spent on math problem solving (not very much) and computation (lengthy periods) be reversed for students with disabilities. Lastly, they suggested that teachers should consider the *Interactive Unit* (Cawley, Fitzmaurice-Hayes, & Shaw, 1988) as the ideal way to adapt math materials to fit the needs of students with mild disabilities. The *Interactive Unit* allows teachers to examine single pages in math textbooks and, by using specific methods of manipulation, to find several different ways to present the same material. Interested readers should consult *Mathematics for the Mildly Handicapped: A Guide to Curriculum and Instruction* (Cawley et al., 1988), the definitive text on this topic.

A very different perspective on adapting textbooks to fit the needs of adolescents with mild disabilities is provided by Lovitt and Horton (1991), who cite three main reasons that textbooks need to be adapted to address the needs of adolescents with mild disabilities: (a) many students with mild disabilities cannot read assigned textbooks to the extent that allows for full comprehension of the material (this is particularly true of math word problems); (b) most secondary-level texts are poorly organized and not very user-friendly; and (c) many teachers (in content-area classes) are neither well prepared nor trained sufficiently in their instructional areas. The authors also note that the last dilemma is compounded when secondary-level special-education teachers are asked to deliver instruction in history, biology, and so forth; special-education teachers know applied behavior analysis and how to individualize instruction, but academic content-area instruction is typically not their strength.

Lovitt and Horton (1991) support specific ways in which to adapt textbooks at the secondary level that easily apply to the teaching of mathematics. They do *not* recommend two common methods of adapting texts to assist adolescents with mild disabilities: (a) rewriting texts to reduce reading difficulty and (b) tape-recording selected passages from textbooks. Lovitt and Horton cite research that has shown that these commonplace accommodation methods for adolescents with mild disabilities do not deliver what they promise: better comprehension and performance on the part of students exposed to such techniques. Figure 7.9 is a presentation of Lovitt and Horton's recommendations for adapting texts for adolescents with mild disabilities.

Verbal Format: Advance Organizers (AOs) are the bridge between what students already know and what they are expected to learn. Teachers should cue students with what has been taught previously (e.g., balancing a checkbook) to what will be learned today (e.g., computing interest on a checking account or savings account).

Figure 7.9
Lovitt and Horton's recommended and nonrecommended methods for adapting textbooks

Source: From "Adapting Textbooks for Mildly Handicapped Adolescents" by T. C. Lovitt and S. V. Horton. In G. Stoner, M. R. Shinn, and H. M. Walker (Eds.), *Interventions for Achievement and Behavior Problems* (pp. 439–471), 1991, Silver Spring, MD: National Association of School Psychologists. Reprinted by permission.

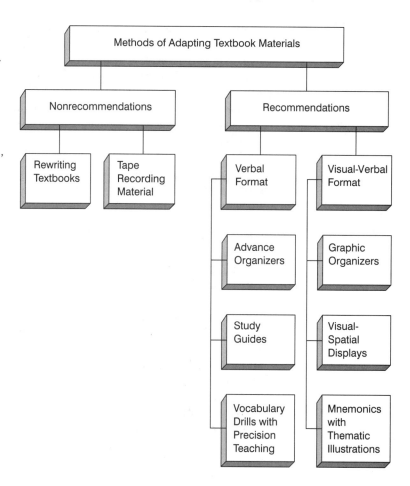

In a related note, Lenz, Alley, and Schumaker (1987) suggested the following 12 components of an effective AO to be used with adolescents experiencing learning disabilities:

1. Inform the learner of the purpose of the AO.
2. Clarify the task's physical parameters in terms of actions to be taken by the teacher.
3. Clarify the task's physical features in terms of actions to be taken by the student.
4. Identify the topic of the learning task.
5. Identify subtopics related to the task.
6. Provide background information.
7. State the concepts to be learned.
8. Clarify the concepts to be learned.
9. Motivate students through rationales for completing the task.
10. Introduce or repeat new terms or words.
11. Provide an organizational framework for the learning task.
12. State the desired outcomes from the learning activity.

Luiten, Ames, and Ackerman (1980) also demonstrated that AOs were instrumental in assisting students in learning and retaining information and that the experimental effects of using AOs (vs. no AOs) were greater for students with mild disabilities than for nondisabled students.

Verbal Format: Study Guides are questions or comments that appear on permanent products (e.g., worksheets) to assist students in learning during or after first exposure to a topic. A study guide example in functional math instruction would be listing or depicting the steps necessary to complete an automatic teller machine withdrawal on an index card. Lovitt and Horton (1991) recommend the following for teachers developing study guides:

1. Analyze the material to be understood by the student from both comprehension and performance perspectives.
2. Select the information to be emphasized during instruction.
3. Decide on the routines that students must demonstrate in acquiring the skill.
4. Consider the ability level of the students in comparison to what skill is to be acquired and vary the style of the study guides to enhance generalization.
5. Do not present too much written information in the study guide; try to keep students from becoming frustrated or overwhelmed with something intended to assist them.
6. Prepare the study guides in a manner that will be interesting and motivating to students.
7. Ensure that the study guide includes important information required for skill acquisition and demonstration.

Verbal Format: Vocabulary Drills are a series of timed drills (e.g., one minute) in which students match terms and definitions from a math textbook. In math, a teacher could create a one-minute drill of terms and definitions found on a monthly bank statement of a checking account (e.g., deposit, withdrawal, credit, debit, interest, etc.). This also allows for an easy application of curriculum-based measurement. Teachers should not use too many terms and definitions so as to limit confusion and frustration during the one-minute daily assessment.

Visual-Verbal Format: Graphic Organizers are verbal and visual representations of key terms and information found in textbooks and presented as a tree diagram with categories and subcategories. Again, using a money theme, teachers could diagram important terms that are necessary in completing tax form 1040EZ (e.g., total wages, salaries, tips, adjusted gross income, net income, etc.) that go beyond what is typically presented in a math textbook.

Visual-Verbal Format: Visual-Spatial Displays are diagrams that combine terms in one column and realistic pictures of the terms in another column. In teaching banking skills, a teacher could write *deposit slip, check, monthly statement,* and *canceled check* in one column of a poster and position the actual banking forms in the second column.

Visual-Verbal Format: Mnemonic Keywords evolve from the joining of important terms and line drawings to facilitate recall. Teachers use keywords presented with illustrations so that students can make a novel connection and remember the concept. *Gross income* for tax form 1040EZ, for example, could be represented by a line drawing of a garage where a person accumulates things (gross income is the accumulation of all earned income). Secondary-level teachers interested in learning more about textbook adaptations using the mnemonic keyword method should consult Mastropieri, Scruggs, McLoone, and Levin (1985).

In closing the discussion on math curricular adaptations, all teachers—in special or regular education—should consider the following in any decision regarding curriculum or instructional changes to meet the needs of adolescents with mild disabilities. Any changes should:

> (a) be responsive to the needs of an individual student at the current time, (b) balance maximum interaction with nondisabled peers against critical curricular needs, (c) be derived from a realistic appraisal of potential adult outcomes of individual students, (d) be consistent with an individual's transitional needs across the lifespan, and (e) be sensitive to graduation goals and specific diploma track requirements.(Edgar & Polloway, 1994, p. 445)

Mathematics Instruction of Adolescents with Mild Disabilities in Regular Classes

Many adolescents with mild disabilities will likely spend some of their secondary-school careers in regular education math courses such as basic algebra and geometry. Regular classroom teachers, in order to be effective, need to be aware of some of the problems that students are likely to encounter in such environments. Mercer (1992) and Smith (1994) provided the following in terms of what regular education math teachers are likely to view in students' poor math performance:

Visual perception problems. Students may have difficulty in differentiating visual stimuli such as numbers and shapes.

Memory difficulties. Students may have difficulty in recalling math algorithms and theorems, especially in algebra and geometry.

Motor functions. Students may have difficulty in writing math-related terms and manipulating objects used in math problems.

Language problems. Adolescents with mild disabilities may encounter difficulty in comprehending math-related terms and using uncommon terms in verbal responses (e.g., *hypotenuse, trapezoid,* etc.).

Abstract reasoning. Many adolescents with mild disabilities may not acquire abstract thinking ability until long after they reach early adolescence, so solving sophisticated word problems and drawing hypothetical conclusions may be very difficult for them (see Chapter 2).

Adaptation problems. Students learn to solve one type of math problem and incorrectly apply the same strategy to solve other problems that require a different approach.

In order for adolescents with mild disabilities to be successful in regular secondary-level math classes, teachers will need to make accommodations to foster student success. Chalmers (1991) provided numerous recommendations to make regular classes more responsive to the needs of students with mild disabilities, and next, we discuss how these accommodations apply to secondary-level math instruction.

Vocabulary and major concepts.   Regular math teachers must ensure that adolescents with mild disabilities understand the often-difficult terms used in algebra and geometry. Failure to understand the vocabulary often leads to failure of an entire assignment. Teachers may need to engage in more repetition than usual, keep important terms on the chalkboard longer, and prompt students to remember important terms and concepts during assignment completion.

State the purpose of the lesson.   Effective teachers tell students *why* they have to do classroom tasks (see Chapter 4). If teachers can provide a convincing rationale for learning very abstract terms and concepts in math, motivation (see the following section) is likely to improve.

Redundant instruction.   Regular math teachers of adolescents with mild disabilities should not assume that one presentation of a concept or task is sufficient for student understanding. Numerous opportunities for review and reteaching should be part of the lesson plans of teachers serving students with mild disabilities in regular math. Very clear directions with easily understood examples may decrease the amount of review and reteaching necessary. Allowing students to audiotape math lectures provides another opportunity for them to review. Another suggestion: Try not to get too frustrated or lose patience when students with disabilities do not understand something that nondisabled youth easily comprehend.

Adjust assignment time.   Part of the responsibility in teaching adolescents with mild disabilities in regular math classes is to ensure that all students succeed. In order for this to take place, some may need adjustments in the amount of time required for assignment completion. Even in testing situations, the key issue for teachers to remember is that completing an assignment correctly is more important than the length of time a student needs to finish the assignment.

Immediate assignment feedback.   Adolescents with mild disabilities need quick feedback so that error routines do not become their usual task completion pattern. Positive feedback is also very important for students with a history of less-than-adequate achievement in math.

Assignment folders.   Many students with mild disabilities are very unorganized with their school assignments and responsibilities. Requiring them to keep a math assignment notebook is one way to assure that at least homework and other materials will not be misplaced.

Alternative assignments.   Students with mild disabilities should be allowed the opportunity to complete assignments in nontraditional fashion. Math tests could be completed orally or audiotaped, one student could read the test to another, or the vocabulary used could be reworded so that students with language difficulties understand better.

Many of these suggestions require regular-class math teachers to go beyond what is typical in their instructional routines. These accommodations, however, should not be viewed as allowing adolescents with mild disabilities an unfair advantage over the nondisabled. Effective math teachers want all students to succeed, so Chalmers's (1991) recommendations are simply additional ways to ensure that it happens.

Additional Considerations in Math Instruction

Motivation issues.   Any secondary-level teacher involved in mathematics instruction for adolescents with mild disabilities needs to keep in mind the past history of his or her students. What that means for teachers is that certain math instructional procedures need to be relied upon in daily instruction, and other methods that may have a long but unproven tradition need to be discarded as inappropriate for contemporary adolescents with mild disabilities. The first math instructional procedure to eliminate is giving adolescents with mild disabilities stacks of worksheets to practice their paper-and-pencil computational skills. A similar math instructional procedure to ignore is the rote memorization of math facts without an emphasis on understanding. These activities serve no functional purpose, do not relate math to students' everyday lives, and are likely to detract from motivation to do mathematics.

One addition to consider and one we highly recommend is allowing students to use calculators. Horton, Lovitt, and White (1992) demonstrated the efficacy of teaching calculator skills and allowing adolescents with mild mental retardation to use calculators in math computation, and we recommend that they be made available to all students with a history of weakness in computation.

② A second practice that should be included in math education of adolescents with mild disabilities is community-based application of math skills taught in classrooms. Much has been said about the efficacy of community-based instruction (Rusch, Destefano, Chadsey-Rusch, Phelps, & Szymanski, 1992; Wehman, 1992). Mathematics instruction affords a teacher a wealth of opportunities to take the learning to the natural environment (e.g., banks, grocery stores, shopping malls, etc.), which is an easy way to enhance motivation of students with a history of failure in academics. For a complete discussion on motivation in the secondary-level classroom, see Ames and Ames (1989) and Mehring and Colson (1993).

Generalization issues.   What is very important in the learning of new math skills is for students to exhibit the skill in situations that are different from those under which initial learning occurred. The community-based instruction discussed previously (i.e., training in various settings) (Stokes & Baer, 1977) is one of many methods to enhance generalization of math skills; another way is to have different trainers involved in the instruction and maintenance of the newly learned skills (e.g., special education teacher, regular education teacher, brother or sister, parents, job coaches, etc.).

Generalization of math skills can also be improved by teaching adolescents to identify conditions under which certain math skills or behaviors should occur. An example of this would be when a person is asked to measure lengths of wooden boards. An instructor should teach the different ways boards can be measured (e.g., by using a tape measure, a folding ruler, a yardstick, a 12-inch ruler, etc.). If a tape measure is not available (the easiest way of measuring boards), the person still knows that he or she can also measure accurately with one of the other types of rulers. While generalization of any newly learned skill is often the most difficult task to demonstrate to adolescents with mild disabilities, effective teachers applying proven instructional methods in mathematics can make it happen.

Secondary-level math instruction should also be viewed from a slightly different perspective from what has been the case in the past. We should teach students to be successful in math courses so that they can pass from one grade level to the next, but we also need to consider the math skills an adolescent will need to function as an independent adult. Few, if any, standardized tests assess math ability from the latter perspective, but those skills are needed by adolescents with mild disabilities and must be taught. If students with mild disabilities will not be attending college or receiving any formal postsecondary training, we believe that teaching math skills that allow for independent adult functioning is equally compelling as passing from grade to grade.

Summary

In 1989, the National Council of Teachers of Mathematics (NCTM) called for reform in the way mathematics is taught in public schools. *Curriculum Evaluation Standards for School Mathematics* (National Council of Teachers of Mathematics, 1989) attempts to set the stage for math curricula and instruction for the next decade. This undertaking of the NCTM is laudable and worthwhile, for the NCTM standards call for, among other things, the teaching of math reasoning and problem solving to replace the teaching of computation and rote memorization of math facts. Figure 7.10 specifies NCTM standards for grades K through 12.

Figure 7.10
NCTM curriculum standards by grade level K through 12

Grades K–4

Standard	1:	Mathematics as Problem Solving
Standard	2:	Mathematics as Communication
Standard	3:	Mathematics as Reasoning
Standard	4:	Mathematical Connections
Standard	5:	Estimation
Standard	6:	Number Sense and Numeration
Standard	7:	Concepts of Whole Number Operations
Standard	8:	Whole Number Computation
Standard	9:	Geometry and Spatial Sense
Standard	10:	Measurement
Standard	11:	Statistics and Probability
Standard	12:	Fractions and Decimals
Standard	13:	Patterns and Relationships

Grades 5–8

Standard	1:	Mathematics as Problem Solving
Standard	2:	Mathematics as Communication
Standard	3:	Mathematics as Reasoning
Standard	4:	Mathematical Connections
Standard	5:	Number and Number Relationships
Standard	6:	Number Systems and Number Theory
Standard	7:	Computation and Estimation
Standard	8:	Patterns and Functions
Standard	9:	Algebra
Standard	10:	Statistics
Standard	11:	Probability
Standard	12:	Geometry
Standard	13:	Measurement

Grades 9–12

Standard	1:	Mathematics as Problem Solving
Standard	2:	Mathematics as Communication
Standard	3:	Mathematics as Reasoning
Standard	4:	Mathematical Connections
Standard	5:	Algebra
Standard	6:	Functions
Standard	7:	Geometry from a Synthetic Perspective
Standard	8:	Geometry from an Algebraic Perspective
Standard	9:	Trigonometry
Standard	10:	Statistics
Standard	11:	Probability
Standard	12:	Discrete Mathematics
Standard	13:	Conceptual Underpinnings of Calculus
Standard	14:	Mathematical Structure

Source: From *Curriculum and Evaluation Standards for School Mathematics,* 1989, by the National Council of Teachers of Mathematics, Reston, VA: Author.

The NCTM standards, however, were not written *specifically* with adolescents with mild disabilities in mind. Secondary-level teachers of students with mild disabilities should not get caught up in the groundswell of reform just for the singular sake of doing something different (and perhaps not grounded in research) in math instruction. Even some experts in special education (e.g., Hofmeister, 1993a, 1993b; Mercer, Harris, & Miller, 1993) question the efficacy of the NCTM standards with students with disabilities.

We believe that reform in the teaching of math to adolescents with mild disabilities is needed. Continuing to rely on elementary-level teaching techniques and procedures and teaching math skills without a functional perspective are no longer acceptable. By using the suggested math teaching methods in this chapter, teachers should know that they are indeed involved in the reform-of-mathematics-instruction movement—but reform with the right outcomes in mind.

Key Terms

arithmetic

mathematics

functional mathematics

diagnostic math interview

consumer math skills

vocational math

References

Ames, C., & Ames, R. (Eds.) (1989). *Research on motivation in education: Volume 3—Goals and cognitions.* San Diego, CA: Academic Press.

Beatty, L., Madden, R., Gardner, E., & Karlsen, B. (1984). *Stanford Diagnostic Mathematics Test.* New York: Harcourt Brace Jovanovich.

Bennett, K. (1980). *The effects of syntax and verbal mediation on learning disabled students' verbal mathematical problem scores.* Unpublished doctoral dissertation, Northern Arizona State University, Flagstaff.

Borakove, L. S., & Cuvo, A. J. (1976). Facilitative effects of coin displacement on teaching coin summation to mentally retarded adolescents. *American Journal of Mental Deficiency, 81,* 350–356.

Brigance, A. H. (1981). *Brigance Diagnostic Inventory of Essential Skills.* North Billerica, MA: Curriculum Associates.

Broome, K., & Wambold, C. L. (1977). Teaching basic math facts to EMR children through individual and small group instruction, pupil teaming, contingency contracting, and learning center activities. *Education and Training of the Mentally Retarded, 12,* 120–124.

Brown, V., & McEntire, E. (1984). *Test of Mathematical Abilities.* Austin, TX: PRO-ED.

Case, L., Harris, K., & Graham, S. (1992). Improving the mathematical problem solving skills of students with learning disabilities: Self-instructional strategy development. *The Journal of Special Education, 21,* 1–19.

Cawley, J. F., Baker-Kroczynski, S., & Urban, A. (1992). Seeking excellence in mathematics education for students with mild disabilities. *Teaching Exceptional Children, 24*(2), 40–43.

Cawley, J., Fitzmaurice-Hayes, A. M., & Shaw, R. (1988). *Mathematics for the mildly handicapped: A guide to curriculum and instruction.* Newton, MA: Allyn & Bacon.

Cawley, J. F., Kahn, H., & Tedesco, A. (1989). Vocational education and students with learning disabilities. *Journal of Learning Disabilities, 22,* 630–634.

Cawley, J. F., & Miller, J. (1989). Cross-sectional comparisons of the mathematics performance of children with learning disabilities: Are we on the right track toward comprehensive programming? *Journal of Learning Disabilities, 22,* 250–254, 259.

Cawley, J., Miller, J., & Carr, S. (1989). Arithmetic. In G. A. Robinson, J. R. Patton, E. A. Polloway, and L. R. Sargent (Eds.), *Best practices in mild mental retardation* (pp. 67–86). Reston, VA: Division on Mental Retardation, The Council for Exceptional Children.

Cawley, J. F., & Parmar, R. S. (1990). Issues in mathematics curriculum for handicapped students. *Academic Therapy, 25,* 507–521.

Cawley, J. F., & Parmar, R. S. (1992). Arithmetic programming for students with disabilities: An alternative. *Remedial and Special Education, 13*(3), 6–18.

Chalmers, L. (1991). Classroom modifications for the mainstreamed student with mild handicaps. *Intervention in School and Clinic, 27,* 40–42.

Connolly, A. J. (1988). *KeyMath Revised: A diagnostic inventory of essential mathematics.* Circle Pines, MN: American Guidance Service.

Cuvo, A. J., Veitch, V. D., Trace, M. W., & Konke, J. L. (1978). Teaching change computation to the mentally retarded. *Behavior Modification, 2,* 531–548.

Deno, S. L. (1985). Curriculum-based measurement. The emerging alternative. *Exceptional Children, 52,* 219–232.

Deno, S. L., & Fuchs, L. S. (1987). Developing curriculum-based measurement systems for data-based special education problem solving. *Focus on Exceptional Children, 19*(6), 1–16.

Edgar, E. (1987). Secondary programs in special education: Are many of them justifiable? *Exceptional Children, 53,* 555–561.

Edgar, E., & Polloway, E. A. (1994). Education for adolescents with disabilities: Curriculum and placement issues. *The Journal of Special Education, 27*(4), 438–452.

Englemann, S., & Carnine, D. (1982). *Corrective Mathematics.* Chicago: SRA.

Englemann, S., & Steely, D. (1981). *Mathematics Modules.* Chicago: SRA.

Englemann, S., Carnine, D., & Steely, D. G. (1991). Making connections in mathematics. *Journal of Learning Disabilities, 24,* 292–303.

English, R. W., & Browning, P. L. (1974). Prevocational considerations in rehabilitating the mentally retarded. In P. L. Browning (Ed.), *Mental retardation rehabilitation and counseling* (pp. 100–119). Springfield, IL: Charles C Thomas.

Enright, B. (1983). *The Enright Diagnostic Inventory of Basic Arithmetic Skills.* North Billerica, MA: Curriculum Associates.

Frank, A. R., Sitlington, P. L., & Carson, R. (1991). Transition of adolescents with behavioral disorders: Is it successful? *Behavioral Disorders, 16,* 180–191.

Fredrick, M. M., Postman, R. D., Leinwand, S. J., & Wantuck, L. R. (1989). *Practical Mathematics: Consumer Applications.* Austin, TX: Holt, Rinehart, & Winston.

Fuchs, L. S., Bahr, C. M., & Reith, H. J. (1989). Effects of goal structures and performance contingencies on math performance of adolescents with learning disabilities. *Journal of Learning Disabilities, 22,* 554–560.

Fuchs, L. S., & Deno, S. L. (1991). Paradigmatic distinctions between instructionally relevant measurement systems. *Exceptional Children, 57,* 488–501.

Fuchs, L. S., Deno, S. L., & Mirkin, P. K. (1984). Effects of frequent curriculum-based measurement and evaluation on pedagogy, student achievement, and student awareness of learning. *American Educational Research Journal, 21,* 449–460.

Fuchs, L. S., Fuchs, D., & Hamlett, C. L. (1989). Effects of alternative goal structures within curriculum-based measurement. *Exceptional Children, 55,* 429–438.

Fuchs, L. S., Fuchs, D., Hamlett, C. L., & Allinder, R. M. (1989). Reliability and validity of skills analysis within curriculum-based measurement. *Diagnostique, 14,* 203–221.

Fuchs, L. S., Fuchs, D., Hamlett, C. L., & Stecker, P. M. (1991). Effects of curriculum-based measurement and consultation on teacher planning and student achievement in mathematics operations. *American Educational Research Journal, 28,* 617–641.

Gerardi, W. J., Jones, W. L., & Foster, T. R. (1987). *Essentials of mathematics: Consumer/career skills applications* (Revised ed.). Orlando, FL: Harcourt Brace Jovanovich.

Germann, G., & Tindal, G. (1985). An application of curriculum- based measurement: The use of direct and repeated measurement. *Exceptional Children, 52,* 244–265.

Greenstein, J., & Strain, P. S. (1977). The utility of the KeyMath Diagnostic Arithmetic Test for adolescent learning disabled students. *Psychology in the Schools, 14,* 275–282.

Hasazi, S. B., Gordon, L. R., & Roe, C. A. (1985). Factors associated with the employment status of handicapped youth exiting high school from 1979–1983. *Exceptional Children, 51,* 455–469.

Hofmeister, A. M. (1993a). Elitism and reform in school mathematics. *Remedial and Special Education, 14*(6), 8–13.

Hofmeister, A. M. (1993b). Invited rejoinder: Innovativeness is not a synonym for effectiveness. *Remedial and Special Education, 14*(6), 33–34.

Horton, S. (1985). Computation rates of educable mentally retarded adolescents with and without calculators in comparison to normals. *Education and Training of the Mentally Retarded, 20,* 14–24.

Horton, S. V., Lovitt, T. C., & White, O. R. (1992). Teaching mathematics to adolescents classified as educable mentally handicapped: Using calculators to remove the computational onus. *Remedial and Special Education, 13*(3), 36–60.

Kauffman, J. M., Cullinan, D., & Epstein, M. H. (1987). Characteristics of students placed in special programs for the seriously emotionally disturbed. *Behavioral Disorders, 12,* 175–184.

King-Sears, M. E. (1994). *Curriculum-based assessment in special education.* San Diego, CA: Singular.

Kirby, J. R., & Becker, L. D. (1988). Cognitive components of learning problems in arithmetic. *Remedial and Special Education, 9*(5), 7–16.

Lenz, B. K., Alley, G. R., & Schumaker, J. B. (1987). Activating the inactive learner: Advance organizers in the secondary content classroom. *Learning Disability Quarterly, 10,* 53–67.

Levine, H., & Langress, L. (1985). Everyday cognition among mildly retarded adults: An ethnographic approach. *American Journal of Mental Deficiency, 90,* 18–26.

Light, J. G., & DeFries, J. C. (1996). Comorbidity of reading and mathematics disabilities: Genetic and environmental etiologies. *Journal of Learning Disabilities, 28,* 96–106.

Lovitt, T. C., & Horton, S. V. (1991). Adapting textbooks for mildly handicapped adolescents. In G. Stoner, M. R. Shinn, & H. M. Walker (Eds.), *Interventions for achievement and behavior problems* (pp. 439–471). Silver Spring, MD: National Association of School Psychologists.

Lowe, M. L., & Cuvo, A. J. (1976). Teaching coin summation to the mentally retarded. *Journal of Applied Behavior Analysis, 9,* 483–489.

Luebke, J., Epstein, M. H., & Cullinan, D. (1989). Comparison of teacher-rated achievement levels of behaviorally disordered, learning disabled, and nonhandicapped adolescents. *Behavioral Disorders, 15,* 1–8.

Luiten, T. C., Ames, W., & Ackerman, G. (1980). A meta-analysis of the effects of advance organizers on learning and retention. *American Educational Research Journal, 17,* 211–218.

Maheady, L., Sacca, M. K., & Harper, G. F. (1987). Classwide student tutoring teams: The effects of peer mediated instruction on the academic performance of secondary mainstreamed students. *The Journal of Special Education, 21,* 107–121.

Mastropieri, M. A., Bakken, J. P., & Scruggs, T. E. (1991). Mathematics instruction for individuals with mental retardation: A perspective and research synthesis. *Education and Training in Mental Retardation, 26,* 115–129.

Mastropieri, M. A., Scruggs, T. E., McLoone, B., & Levin, J. R. (1985). Facilitating learning disabled students' acquisition of science classifications. *Learning Disability Quarterly, 8,* 299–309.

Mastropieri, M. A., Scruggs, T. E., & Shiah, S. (1991). Mathematics instruction for learning disabled students: A review of research. *Learning Disabilities Research & Practice, 6,* 89–98.

McDonagh, E. C., McIlvane, W. J., & Stoddard, L. T. (1984). Teaching coin equivalences via matching to sample. *Applied Research in Mental Retardation, 5,* 177–197.

McLeod, T., & Armstrong, S. (1982). Learning disabilities in mathematics—skill deficits and remedial approaches at the intermediate and secondary level. *Learning Disability Quarterly, 5,* 305–311.

Mehring, T. A., & Colson, S. E. (1993). Motivation and mildly handicapped learners. In E. L. Meyen, G. A. Vergason, & R. J. Whelan (Eds.), *Educating students with mild disabilities* (pp. 29–48). Denver, CO: Love.

Mercer, C. D. (1992). *Students with learning disabilities* (4th ed.). Upper Saddle River, NJ: Merrill/Prentice Hall.

Mercer, C. D., Harris, C. A., & Miller, S. P. (1993). Reforming reforms in mathematics. *Remedial and Special Education, 14*(6), 14–19.

Miller, D. M. (1976). Effects of music-listening contingencies on arithmetic performance and music preference of EMR children. *American Journal of Mental Deficiency, 81,* 371–378.

Montague, M. (1992). The effects of cognitive and metacognitive strategy instruction on mathematical problem solving of middle school students with learning disabilities. *Journal of Learning Disabilities, 25,* 230–248.

Montague, M., Applegate, B., & Marquard, K. (1993). Cognitive strategy instruction and mathematical problem solving performance of students with learning disabilities. *Learning Disabilities Research & Practice, 8,* 223–232.

Montague, M., & Bos, C. S. (1986). The effect of cognitive strategy training on verbal math problem solving performance of learning disabled adolescents. *Journal of Learning Disabilities, 19,* 26–33.

Montague, M., Bos, C., & Doucette, M. (1991). Affective, cognitive, and metacognitive attributes of eighth-grade mathematical problem solvers. *Learning Disabilities Research & Practice, 6,* 145–151.

National Council of Teachers of Mathematics. (1989). *Curriculum and evaluation standards for school mathematics.* Reston, VA: Author.

Nuzum, M. (1987). Teaching the arithmetic story problem process. *Journal of Reading, Writing, and Learning Disabilities International, 3*(1), 53–61.

Patton, J. R., & Polloway, E. A. (1988). Curricular orientations for students with mental disabilities. In G. Robinson, J. R. Patton, E. A. Polloway, & L. R. Sargent (Eds.), *Best practices in mental disabilities* (Vol. 2) (pp. 27–38). Des Moines, IA: Bureau of Special Education, Department of Education, State of Iowa.

Peraino, J. M. (1992). Post-21 follow-up studies: How do special education graduates fare? In P. Wehman (Ed.), *Life beyond the classroom: Transition strategies for young people with disabilities* (pp. 21–70). Baltimore: Paul H. Brookes.

Polloway, E. A., & Patton, J. R. (1993). *Strategies for teaching learners with special needs* (5th ed.). Upper Saddle River, NJ: Merrill/Prentice Hall.

Rivera, D. H., & Smith, D. D. (1988). Using a demonstration strategy to teach middle school students with learning disabilities. *Journal of Learning Disabilities, 21,* 77–81.

Rizzo, J. V., & Zabel, R. H. (1988). *Educating children and adolescents with behavioral disorders: An integrative approach.* Boston: Allyn & Bacon.

Rusch, F. R., Destefano, L., Chadsey-Rusch, J., Phelps, L. A., & Szymanski, E. (Eds.) (1992). *Transition from school to adult life: Models, linkages, and policy.* Pacific Grove, CA: Brooks/Cole.

Schunk, D. H. (1985). Participation in goal setting: Effects on the self-efficacy and skills of learning disabled children. *The Journal of Special Education, 19,* 307–317.

Schunk, D. H., & Cox, P. D. (1986). Strategy training and attribution feedback with learning disabled students. *Journal of Educational Psychology, 78,* 201–209.

Shinn, M. R. (Ed.). (1989). *Curriculum-based measurement: Assessing special children.* New York: Guilford.

Shulte, A. P., Haynes, H., & Bell, E. D. (1986). *Mathematics skills for daily living.* River Forest, IL: Laidlaw Brothers.

Sitlington, P., & Frank, A. (1990). Are adolescents with learning disabilities successfully crossing the bridge into adult life? *Learning Disability Quarterly, 13,* 97–111.

Smeenge, M. E., Page, T. J., Iwata, B. A., & Ivanic, M. T. (1980). Teaching measurement skills to mentally retarded students: Training, generalization, and follow-up. *Education and Training of the Mentally Retarded, 15,* 224–230.

Smeets, P. M., Lancioni, G. E., Striefel, S., & Willemsen, R. J. (1984). Training EMR children to solve missing minuend problems errorlessly: Acquisition, generalization, and maintenance. *Analysis and Intervention in Developmental Disabilities, 4,* 379–402.

Smith, C. R. (1994). *Learning disabilities: The interaction of learner, task, and setting.* Boston: Allyn & Bacon.

Stokes, T., & Baer, D. (1977). An implicit technology of generalization. *Journal of Applied Behavior Analysis, 10,* 349–367.

Tarver, S. G. (1996). Direct instruction. In W. Stainback & S. Stainback (Eds.), *Controversial issues confronting special education* (2nd ed.). Boston: Allyn & Bacon.

Taylor, R. (1984). *Assessment of exceptional students.* Upper Saddle River, NJ: Prentice Hall.

Thurlow, M. L., & Turnure, J. E. (1977). Children's knowledge of time and money: Effective instruction for the mentally retarded. *Education and Training of the Mentally Retarded, 12,* 203–212.

Trace, M. W., Cuvo, A. J., & Criswell, J. L. (1977). Teaching coin equivalence to the mentally retarded. *Journal of Applied Behavior Analysis, 10,* 85–92.

Tucker, J. A. (1985). Curriculum-based assessment: An introduction. *Exceptional Children, 52,* 199–204.

Usiskin, Z., Flanders, J., Hynes, C., Polonsky, L., Porter, S., & Viktora, S. (1987). *Transition mathematics.* Chicago: University of Chicago.

Wallace, G., Larsen, S. C., & Elksnin, L. K. (1992). *Educational assessment of learning problems: Testing for teaching* (2nd ed.). Boston: Allyn & Bacon.

Wehman, P. (1992). *Life beyond the classroom: Transition strategies for young people with disabilities.* Baltimore: Paul H. Brookes.

Ysseldyke, J. E., Thurlow, M. L., Wotruba, J. W., & Nania, P. A. (1990). Instructional arrangements: Perceptions from general education. *Teaching Exceptional Children, 22,* 4–8.

8

Cognitive Strategy Training and Study Skills Instruction

Objectives

After reading this chapter, the reader should be able to:

1. define the term *cognitive strategy training;*

2. distinguish between the terms *cognitive strategy training* and *study skills instruction;*

3. discuss the impetus for developing cognitive strategy training procedures;

4. list several formal and informal procedures used to assess cognitive strategies;

5. identify several examples of cognitive strategies associated with standard curriculum areas.

Are cognitive strategies similar to study skills? What do we mean by cognitive learning strategies? Why teach cognitive strategies at the secondary level? How can one design instructional programs to teach such strategies? How should cognitive strategies be taught? Can such strategies be taught so they generalize across academic settings and into the world of work? These questions and others embody issues that are being addressed by educators in schools today.

The purpose of this chapter is to define **cognitive strategy training** in relation to secondary students with mild disabilities, distinguish it from **study skills,** illustrate ways to assess cognitive strategies, and provide several strategy training procedures currently shown to be successful with students at the secondary level.

There is no doubt that cognitive strategy training has become a hot topic in both regular and special education (Deshler, Ellis, & Lenz, 1996; Pressley, Symons, Snyder, & Cariglia-Bull, 1989). Research examining the extent to which adolescents with mild disabilities can be trained to use cognitive strategies to improve their performances has increased dramatically in the last 10 years (Swanson, 1989). Several lines of research concerning cognitive behaviors (i.e., metacognition, memory, and selective attention) have provided the impetus for cognitive strategy training.

Each perspective describes and defines cognitive strategy training in unique ways, causing much confusion as to what constitutes strategy intervention. It appears that strategy training programs suffer from many of the same problems that have continued to plague the field of learning disabilities—problems of definition of terms, methodological issues, and issues of generalization (deBettencourt, 1987). However, it is generally agreed that strategy usage is a critical component of independent learning (Pressley et al., 1989). The independent use of cognitive strategies is particularly essential for students with mild disabilities at the secondary level.

Teaching Cognitive Strategy Training at the Secondary Level

The secondary school is a complex environment that many students with mild disabilities find difficult. Deshler and Lenz (1989) summarize the demands placed on secondary students:

1. academically, students must gain information from books, manuals, lectures, and presentations and demonstrate this information in task completion, in writing, and on tests;

2. socially, students must follow rules and interact appropriately with peers, adults, and authority figures;

3. motivationally, students are expected to set, plan for, and carry out short- and long-term goals; and

4. executively, students must independently solve problems and generalize learning across situations. (p. 8)

Researchers have suggested that students with mild disabilities do not function well in secondary-school settings because demands such as those described above are placed upon them and that most students with mild disabilities appear to reach a learning plateau in high school that is equivalent to about a 4th- or 5th-grade achievement level (Deshler, Schumaker, Alley, Warner, & Clark, 1982; deBettencourt, Zigmond, & Thornton, 1989). This achievement level is the point at which basic skills instruction generally stops and students move on to apply those skills to inferential reading comprehension, math applications, expository writing, and extensive use of content textbooks for learning science and social studies (Deshler, Warner, Schumaker, Alley, & Clark, 1984). Academic learning at the secondary level requires that students know *how* to learn rather than just *what* to learn. Such strategic learning is essential for successful functioning in the mainstream (Sheinker, Sheinker, & Stevens, 1984).

However, in the past the most common approaches to remediating students' learning difficulties has been basic skills remediation and tutorial instruction (Deshler, Schumaker, Lenz, & Ellis, 1984). Although these techniques directly address students' problems, the students make minimal gains. Donahoe and Zigmond (1990) found that many students with disabilities from a large northeastern urban school system who participated in a resource-room program that was remedial in nature did not make enough gains to perform successfully in general education. Zigmond (1990) suggests that many students with disabilities enter 9th grade barely literate and leave high school after one, two, three, or four years with their literacy skills unchanged. Alternative service delivery models that include direct instruction in cognitive learning strategies may increase the likelihood that students with disabilities improve their academic performance (Donahoe & Zigmond, 1990).

There is yet other evidence that the present secondary-level classes for pupils who are mildly disabled are not meeting students' needs. Current research has illustrated that many of these students are opting to leave school early (Cobb & Crump, 1984;

deBettencourt et al., 1989; Fardig, Algozzine, Schwartz, Hensel, & Westling, 1985; Hasazi, Gordon, & Roe, 1985; White, Schumaker, Warner, Alley, & Deshler, 1980; Zigmond & Thornton, 1985). Strategy training instruction may keep these students in school and help them learn at a rate that will allow them to graduate, enter postsecondary institutions, and/or seek employment.

The advantages of strategy training approaches for improving the performance of secondary-age students with mild disabilities are numerous. Primarily, they focus on instructional principles rather than internal processing deficiencies. Second, cognitive strategy instruction is based on effective instructional procedures (Bickel & Bickel, 1986; Rosenshine, 1983). Third, strategy training approaches encourage the student to become more actively involved in his or her learning activities. Fourth, strategy training approaches, because they include metacognitive training, have provided students with disabilities with a motivational aspect to learning (Paris, Lipson, & Wixson, 1983; Paris & Oka, 1989). Fifth, cognitive strategy training might encourage students with mild disabilities to remain in secondary school until graduation (Zigmond, 1990). Finally, cognitive strategies may hold the greatest promise for spanning the distance between settings (Deshler, Schumaker, & Lenz, 1984; Deshler & Lenz, 1989).

6 approaches for improving performance (handwritten margin note)

Impetus for Developing Cognitive Strategy Training Procedures

During the past 10 years, research in cognition provided the impetus for development of cognitive strategy training procedures for instruction of students with mild disabilities. The following section does not provide a comprehensive review of the research but instead highlights research in metacognition, memory, and selective attention that is particularly pertinent to the development of strategy training (Figure 8.1).

Figure 8.1
Impetus for developing cognitive
strategy training procedures

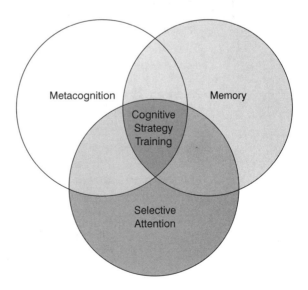

skills
- self-monitoring
- predicting
- reality testing
- coordinating the processes of studying + learning

Metacognition.   **Metacognition** refers to individuals' awareness of their own cognitive performance and their use of this awareness in altering their own behavior (Flavell, 1970, 1979); it involves knowing about and controlling one's own thinking and learning. Metacognitive skills include self-monitoring, predicting, reality testing, and coordinating the processes of studying and learning. Problems that students with mild disabilities experience in applying strategies may be caused by their lack of awareness of when and how to use effective and efficient strategies (deBettencourt, 1987). As Loper (1982) suggested, the critical metacognitive variable may not be students' cognitive abilities, but their application of such information. Palincsar and Brown (1989) suggested that the metacognitive knowledge of some students with disabilities can be enhanced by their learning of executive control skills that monitor strategies across various tasks.

Memory.   Torgesen and his colleagues have conducted several investigations in the area of memory that suggest that poor performance may, in part, be due to inefficient use of cognitive strategies (e.g., Torgesen & Goldman, 1977; Torgesen & Houck, 1980; Torgesen, Murphy, & Ivey, 1979). Results of these investigations support hypotheses that many of the performance problems of students with disabilities may not stem from limited memory or learning capacity, but rather from failure to apply efficient task strategies. When students with disabilities are instructed to use a strategy such as a verbal rehearsal, they do approach tasks in an active manner (e.g., Torgesen et al., 1979).

Selective attention.   Inattention or selectively attending to tasks is a characteristic frequently associated with students with mild disabilities. Hallahan and his colleagues at the University of Virginia studied attention processes in students with learning disabilities. The results of their investigations suggest that many students with mild disabilities exhibit a developmental lag in their selective attention abilities relative to their normal peers. Although students with mild disabilities, especially learning disabilities, do not routinely apply a cognitive strategy, they perform similarly to normal children (Dawson, Hallahan, Reeve, & Ball, 1980; Hallahan, Tarver, Kauffman & Graybeal, 1978; Tarver, Hallahan, & Kauffman, 1976). Thus, as with metacognitive and memory research, the investigations in the area of selective attention suggest that poor performance on the part of students with mild disabilities may be due in part to inefficient use of cognitive strategies.

Distinction Between Cognitive Strategy Training and Study Skills Training

Many researchers have examined the importance of cognitive and metacognitive strategy training for increasing secondary-age students' academic learning potential.

However, a precise understanding of what cognitive strategy training involves is rarely defined clearly. Each researcher or author defines his or her strategy training approach uniquely.

Cognitive learning strategies is the generic term most often used to describe a series of task-specific strategies that incorporate features of cognitive and metacognitive training (Ellis, Lenz, & Sabornie, 1987a). Alley and Deshler (1979) define *learning strategies* as "techniques, principles or rules that will facilitate the acquisition, manipulation, integration, storage and retrieval of information across situations and settings" (p. 13). Often a learning strategy is composed of a set of self-instructional steps the student proceeds through to solve a problem. The steps cue the student to use specific cognitive strategies (e.g., paraphrasing) or to employ metacognitive strategies (e.g., self-monitoring) (Ellis et al., 1987a). A mnemonic device is often employed to help the student remember the steps.

Many learning strategies are designed to improve a student's academic performance by teaching him or her how to acquire, manipulate, store, or retrieve knowledge. Some cognitive strategies overlap these areas. For example, a strategy may instruct a student to identify the relevant information from the text and then to organize it some way to facilitate memory. Although students with mild disabilities have been shown to have difficulty with such executive functions, research has shown that these students can learn to use strategies in controlled situations (Clark, Deshler, Schumaker, & Alley, 1984).

Thus, cognitive learning strategy training procedures are viewed as specific approaches for facilitating the independent use of planning, executing, and evaluating performance on a task and its outcomes. The similarities between such strategy training procedures and study skills training methods have often been confusing to teachers. Basically, cognitive strategy training encompasses study skills instruction. However, it is more comprehensive than a study skills program in that, in addition to learning how to perform particular skills, students also learn *why and when to use these skills and how to monitor their implementation.* The focus of strategy training approaches is on the appropriate selection and use of skills as well as on what students think in the process of assessing the requirements of a given task. Strategy training programs include critical guidelines and rules for selecting the best procedure and how to make decisions about its use (Deshler & Lenz, 1989). Such procedures assist students to connect what content they need to know with what efficient skills will assist them in obtaining this knowledge.

Essentially, learning strategy instruction encompasses study skills instruction. Study skills instructional areas usually include note taking, test taking, and time management. Figure 8.2 presents an example of a schedule a teacher would introduce to assist a student who has difficulty managing his or her time. In contrast, cognitive learning strategies also include procedures for self-monitoring the use of such skills.

NAME __Marie__

WEEK OF _____11/12–11/18_____

	MONDAY	TUESDAY	WEDNESDAY	THURSDAY	FRIDAY	SATURDAY	SUNDAY
9:00	Math Midterm				Awards Assembly†	Clean Room	Family Visit to Aunt Martha
10:00			Science Midterm			Laundry	
11:00							
12:00							
1:00	History Midterm						
2:00						Science Project with Paul and Sally at my House‡	
3:00							
4:00		Tryout for Xmas Play	Photog. Club*	Interview for job at Jones' Store**			

Figure 8.2
Time management schedule

5:00						
6:00	Homework		Homework			
7:00	Study for Science Test with Jane at her House	Homework	Work on Science Project with Paul and Sally at Sally's House	Homework			Homework
8:00		Study for Science Test			Community Center Dance	Date with Bob	Complete Weekly Planning for 11/19–11/25
9:00						
10:00						

Notes: *Have camera checked for spot on lens.
     **Fill out application and drop off before Thursday.
     †Get congratulations card for Roberta.
     ‡Get snacks and soda.

Source: From *Teaching Study Strategies to Students with Learning Disabilities* (pp. 337–338) by S. S. Strichart and C. T. Mangrum III, 1993, Boston: Allyn & Bacon.

Assessment of Cognitive Learning Strategies

Although much progress has been made in the development of instructional models, the assessment of cognitive learning strategies has received less attention (McLoughlin & Lewis, 1990). Specific formal tests that measure skills in isolation do not provide sufficient information because they do not test the skills in the context of actual learning situations. Success in the middle and secondary grades is often dependent upon the student's ability to demonstrate mastery of basic study skills applications and the metacognitive knowledge of when to use a strategy and which strategy is the most efficient.

However, we will include a section here on the formal instruments that do test study skills for two reasons. First, study skills, although more closely tied to specific school tasks, are often part of students' use of specific learning strategies; second, assessment of study skills may be a beginning and give the assessment team further direction.

Using Standardized, Criterion-Referenced and Diagnostic Tests: Selected Instruments

Study skills are included as a subtest in several general achievement batteries (Wallace & Kauffman, 1986). A few norm-referenced multiple-battery achievement tests include study skill subtests (e.g., *California Achievement Test, SRA Achievement Series*). Additionally, there are a few norm-referenced tests that specifically assess study skills (see Table 8.1).

Table 8.1
Standardized study skills tests

Name of Test	Grade Level	Study Skills Evaluated
Study Attitudes and Methods Survey (Michael, Michael, & Zimmerman, 1972)	HS & College	Academic interest, academic drive, study methods, study anxiety
Study Skills Checklist (Estes & Vaughan, 1985)	11–14	Test taking, use of graphic aids, note taking, outlining
Study Skills Test: McGraw-Hill Basic Skills System (Raynor, 1970)	11–14	Problem solving, underlining, library information, study skills information and inventory of study habits and attitudes
Survey of Study Habits and Attitudes (Brown & Holtzman, 1967)	7–12, 12–14	Study habits and attitudes
The Cornell Learning & Study Skills Inventory (Pauk & Cassell, 1970)	7–13, 13–16	Goal orientation, activity structure, scholarly skills, lecture mastery, textbook mastery, examination mastery, and self-mastery
Wisconsin Tests of Reading Skill Development Study Skills (Stewart, Kamm, Allen, & Sols, 1972)	K–7	Skills necessary for locating, interpreting, using reference materials

Source: From *Teaching Students with Learning and Behavior Problems* (3rd ed.) (p. 293) by G. Wallace and J. M. Kauffman, 1986, Upper Saddle River, NJ: Merrill/Prentice Hall.

Using Informal Study Skills and Cognitive Strategy Assessment Procedures

Designing informal instruments to determine the types of secondary curriculum demands that the student is failing to meet (e.g., taking notes, writing well-organized paragraphs) is an integral part of cognitive learning strategy instruction. Pertinent data on a student's knowledge and use of cognitive learning strategies can be produced by informal assessment procedures such as observations, work sample analysis, and teacher interviews.

Cohen and deBettencourt (1984) discuss five aspects of independent studying activities: following directions, approaching tasks, obtaining assistance, gaining feedback, and gaining reinforcement. These five components could form the basis for designing an observation of students' independent behavior. Brown (1978) discusses study skills behaviors and provides a set of descriptions for teachers to use in student interviews (see Figure 8.3). Deshler and his colleagues include an informal task-

Figure 8.3
Independent study behaviors

A.	Finished assigned work
B.	Do as well as I can
C.	Usually understand assignments
D.	Don't understand purpose of most assignments
E.	Collect all materials needed
F.	Budget time for study
G.	Can explain what "studying" means
H.	Can't stand studying
I.	Check over completed assignments
J.	Concentrate well
K.	See little real value in studying
L.	Use textbooks well
M.	Study with tests in mind
N.	Learn a lot from assignments
O.	Take notes well
P.	Begin assigned work
Q.	Prefer to study alone
R.	Study as well as my friends do
S.	Take notes well
T.	Keep study records
U.	Easily distracted from study
V.	Ask for help with studying
W.	Organize study time well
X.	(your own idea)_____
Y.	Can outline Study materials
Z.	Study only subjects I like

Source: From "Independent Study Behaviors: A Framework for Curriculum Development" by V. Brown, 1978, *Learning Disability Quarterly 1*(2), 80.

Figure 8.4
Study skills inventory

Completed by: _____ Student: _____ Date: _____

Place the appropriate number (1, 2, or 3) in the box next to each study skill subskill (1 = Mastered—regular, appropriate use of skill: 2 = Partially Mastered—needs some improvement: 3 = Not Mastered—infrequent use of skill).

Reading Rate
☐ Skimming
☐ Scanning
☐ Rapid reading
☐ Normal rate
☐ Study or careful reading
☐ Understands importance of reading rates

Listening
☐ Attends to listening activities
☐ Applies meaning to verbal messages
☐ Filters out auditory distractions
☐ Comprehends verbal messages
☐ Understands importance of listening skills

Notetaking/Outlining
☐ Uses headings/subheadings appropriately
☐ Takes brief and clear notes
☐ Records essential information
☐ Applies skill during writing activities
☐ Uses skill during lectures
☐ Develops organized outlines
☐ Follows consistent notetaking format

☐ Understands importance of notetaking
☐ Understands importance of outlining

Report Writing
☐ Organizes thoughts in writing
☐ Completes written reports from outline
☐ Includes only necessary information
☐ Uses proper sentence structure
☐ Uses proper punctuation
☐ Uses proper grammar and spelling
☐ Proofreads written assignments
☐ States clear introductory statement
☐ Includes clear concluding statements
☐ Understands importance of writing reports

Oral Presentations
☐ Freely participates in oral presentations
☐ Oral presentations are well organized
☐ Uses gestures appropriately
☐ Speaks clearly
☐ Uses proper language when reporting orally
☐ Understands importance of oral reporting

---

informal task-

related pretest when beginning instruction in any one of their learning strategies. The informal pretest stage in the strategies instructional approach is designed to motivate students to learn a new strategy by (a) illustrating how the strategy will assist them in classes in which they may be having difficulty; (b) informing them of other students' success with the particular strategy; and (c) establishing a baseline of how they are currently performing in meeting the targeted demand (Ellis & Lenz, 1996).

The information obtained by such informal assessments will enable the teacher to understand the demands in the environment that the students are not meeting in order

Graphic Aids

☐ Attends to relevant elements in visual material

☐ Uses visuals appropriately in presentations

☐ Develops own graphic material

☐ Is not confused or distracted by visual material in presentations

☐ Understands importance of visual material

Test Taking

☐ Studies for tests in an organized way

☐ Spends appropriate amount of time studying different topics covered on a test

☐ Avoids cramming for tests

☐ Organizes narrative responses appropriately

☐ Reads and understands directions before answering questions

☐ Proofreads responses and checks for errors

☐ Identifies and uses clue words in questions

☐ Properly records answers

☐ Saves difficult items until last

☐ Eliminates obvious wrong answers

☐ Systematically reviews completed tests to determine test-taking or test-studying errors

☐ Corrects previous test-taking errors

☐ Understands importance of test-taking skills

Library Usage

☐ Uses cataloging system (card or computerized) effectively

☐ Able to locate library materials

☐ Understands organizational layout of library

☐ Understands and uses services of media specialist

☐ Understands overall functions and purposes of a library

☐ Understands importance of library usage skills

Reference Materials

☐ Able to identify components of different reference materials

☐ Uses guide words appropriately

☐ Consults reference materials when necessary

☐ Uses materials appropriately to complete assignments

☐ Able to identify different types of reference materials and sources

☐ Understands importance of reference materials

Time Management

☐ Completes tasks on time

☐ Plans and organizes daily activities and responsibilities effectively

to develop instruction to help them cope with those demands. Hoover & Patton (1995) developed a study skill inventory that will assist in gaining a general overview of a student's study skill abilities and usage (see Figure 8.4). As Polloway and Smith (1992) suggest, such informal observations or checklists provide for direct conversion of results into remedial activities.

Assessment of cognitive learning strategies is a new adventure in special education (McLoughlin & Lewis, 1990). At present, assessment teams must rely primarily on informal instruments to evaluate students' cognitive learning strategies at the secondary level.

Figure 8.4, continued

☐ Plans and organizes weekly and monthly schedules

☐ Reorganizes priorities when necessary

☐ Meets scheduled deadlines

☐ Accurately perceives the amount of time required to complete tasks

☐ Adjusts time allotment to complete tasks

☐ Accepts responsibility for managing own time

☐ Understands importance of effective time management

Self-Management

☐ Monitors own behavior

☐ Changes own behavior as necessary

☐ Thinks before acting

☐ Responsible for own behavior

☐ Identifies behaviors that interfere with own learning

☐ Understands importance of self-management

Summary of Study Skill Proficiency

Summarize in the chart below the number of Mastered (1), Partially Mastered (2), and Not Mastered (3) study skill subskills. The number next to each study skill represents the total number of subskills for each area.

Study Skill	M	PM	NM	Study Skill	M	PM	NM
Reading Rate—6				Test Taking—13			
Listening—5				Library Usage—6			
Notetaking/Outlining—9				Reference Materials—6			
Report Writing—10				Time Management—9			
Oral Presentations—6				Self-Management—6			
Graphic Aids—5							

Summary Comments:

Source: From *Teaching Students with Learning Problems to Use Study Skills: A Teacher's Guide* (pp. 14–16) by J. J. Hoover and J. R. Patton, 1995, Austin, TX: PRO-ED.

Development of a Cognitive Learning Strategies Curriculum

A cognitive strategy includes how a student thinks and acts when planning, executing, and evaluating his or her performance on a task (Lenz, Clark, Deshler, & Schumaker, 1988). Deshler and Lenz (1989) discuss a set of common features of a cognitive strategies intervention model, which relate to: (a) selection of the content, (b) design of the content, and (c) usefulness of the strategy to the student. These features are important to consider when developing a cognitive strategy training program in your own classroom.

Selection of Strategy Content

As you develop your strategy you should review the following ten guidelines and evaluate whether it has successfully met these conditions. If not, modifications should be made in the content.

1. The strategy should contain a set of steps that lead to a specific and successful outcome (e.g., Did the strategy help the student complete the assignment?).

2. The steps of the strategy should be sequenced in a manner that results in the best and most efficient approach to the task.

3. The steps of the strategy should cue the student to use specific cognitive strategies.

4. The steps of the strategy should cue the student to use metacognition (e.g., self-questioning, self-checking).

5. The steps of the strategy should cue the student to select and use appropriate procedures, skills, or rules. That is, a guide is provided for the student to proceed through the skill sequence.

6. The steps of the strategy should cue the student to take some type of overt/physical action. The student takes active steps.

7. Overt/physical actions should be supported by a clear explanation of the associated mental actions that need to take place.

8. The steps of the strategy should be able to be performed by an individual in a limited amount of time.

9. Unnecessary steps or explanations should be eliminated.

10. Information related to why to use the strategy, when to use the strategy, and where to use the strategy should be included. (Deshler & Lenz, 1989, pp. 10–14)

Design of Strategy Content

The content of the strategy should be organized to promote success and optimal learning. Deshler and Lenz (1989) suggest the following seven guidelines for designing the strategy.

1. Entry level skills should be clearly specified or taken into consideration as part of the steps of the strategy.

2. A remembering system should be incorporated into the intervention to facilitate memorization of the strategy steps and explanations.

3. Each step of the remembering system should be short.

4. Each step of the remembering system should begin with a verb or key word directly related to the mental or physical action that the step is designed to cue.

5. There should be seven or fewer key steps in the remembering system for the strategy.

6. The remembering system should relate to the overall process that the strategy is designed to address.

7. The vocabulary used to convey the strategy steps and explanations should be familiar. (pp. 15–17)

Usefulness of Learning Strategies

The relevance of a cognitive strategy to the student is of utmost importance, especially at the secondary level. The strategy must be designed for a particular present or future need of your students. The rationale for learning the strategy must be given to the students. For example, "Use of this strategy will assist you in learning the vocabulary words in biology." Deshler and Lenz (1989) suggest the following four guidelines for making the strategy relevant to students with mild disabilities:

1. The strategy should address a key problem that is found in settings that the student must face.
2. The strategy should relate to a demand that is frequently required across settings.
3. The strategy must generalize across a variety of settings, situations, and contexts.
4. The strategy should relate to future demands that the student will encounter that are similar to those for which the strategy was originally taught. (p. 17)

For example, a 15-year-old high school sophomore who is reading at a 4th-grade level and is unable to demonstrate test-taking skills such as prioritizing, allocating time, and methodically proposing and/or eliminating alternatives would find a test-taking strategy most helpful. Such a strategy would assist the student in meeting the demands at the sophomore level and also help him or her relate to future demands.

Instruction of Learning Strategies

Once the teacher has developed the content, design, and usefulness of the specific cognitive strategy, the strategy can then be taught to the student. Studies conducted by the Kansas Institute for Research in LD have shown that an effective instructional program for adolescents with learning disabilities consists of a 10-step program (Figure 8.5) (Alley

Figure 8.5
Learning strategies 10-step procedure

1. Testing the student's current level of functioning
2. Describing the steps of the strategy and providing rationale for each step
3. Modeling the strategy so that the student could observe all the processes involved in the strategy
4. Verbal rehearsal of the steps of the strategy 100% criterion
5. Practice in controlled materials written at the student's reading ability level
6. Positive and corrective feedback
7. Testing in materials written at the student's reading ability level
8. Practice in content materials from the student's grade placement level
9. Positive and corrective feedback
10. Posttest

Source: Adapted from "Learning Strategies: An Instructional Alternative for Low-Achieving Adolescents" by D. D. Deshler and J. B. Schumaker, 1986, *Exceptional Children, 52,* 583–590.

& Deshler, 1979; Deshler et al., 1982) that is designed to give students the knowledge, motivation, and practice necessary to apply the learning strategy successfully. You may want to adapt this procedure to fit your students' needs.

Specific Examples of Cognitive Learning Strategies

Cognitive learning strategy procedures can be grouped into several categories, using a variety of methods. As secondary curricula are often content driven, we have presented a section of examples of cognitive strategies for three major content areas along with a study skills section on taking notes, organizing one's time, and taking tests. (See also other content chapters.)

Reading

The ability to read independently is essential for success in today's society. Methods to teach reading are abundant and the decision as to which is the most effective remains an issue. We have presented below a select group of cognitive learning strategies that have been proven effective in increasing the ability of adolescents with mild disabilities to comprehend written material.

At the secondary level many content-area textbooks contain vocabulary words that are unknown to students with mild disabilities. A word identification strategy suggested by Lenz, Schumaker, Deshler, and Beals (1984) provides an active and organized strategy for pronouncing and learning new vocabulary. The strategy is remembered by the acronym **DISSECT**.

> **D**—**D**iscover the context,
> **I**—**I**solate the prefix,
> **S**—**S**eparate the suffix,
> **S**—**S**ay the stem,
> **E**—**E**xamine the stem,
> **C**—**C**heck with someone,
> **T**—**T**ry the dictionary.

Paraphrasing or restating in one's own words information gained from printed material is also a valuable reading comprehension tool. A paraphrasing strategy introduced by Schumaker, Denton, and Deshler (1984) teaches students to read a paragraph and ask themselves a few questions, thus becoming active readers. Teachers may incorporate this strategy into their daily lesson plans, for example, asking the students to use the **RAP** strategy with a friend to study for a test.

> **R**—**R**ead a paragraph.
> **A**—**A**sk yourself "What are the main ideas and details in this paragraph?"
> **P**—**P**ut the main idea and details into your own words.

both writing & reading

like SQ3R

Semantic mapping, another cognitive strategy that is frequently taught to students when writing, may also assist them in reading comprehension. Students can be taught to use a semantic mapping or webbing procedure to organize main ideas and details of a passage or chapter they read (see Figure 8.6 for an example of semantic mapping).

A reading comprehension strategy that is an adaptation of the SQ3R method, the multipass strategy (Schumaker, Deshler, Alley, & Denton, 1982), is designed to enable students to gain information from textbook chapters. In this procedure, students pass through a content chapter three times to familiarize themselves with the main ideas and organization of the passage, to gain specific information, and to test themselves on the chapter material.

Reading comprehension is the essence of the reading act. The strategies just described will assist secondary students with mild disabilities to become more active, and thus more effective, readers.

Written Language

Written language is an area of the curriculum that presents many problems for students with mild disabilities. Much of the difficulty stems from the fact that writing is a complex process and that teachers are often unfamiliar with instructional strategies that will assist students. The strategies described in this section encourage students to become active participants in the writing process and also give them a structure to follow when composing.

A sentence-writing strategy designed by Schumaker & Sheldon (1985) can be used to assist students with the basic principles of sentence construction and expression. The strategy includes learning the formulas for recognizing and writing different sentences. The acronym **PENS** helps the student remember the steps.

Figure 8.6
Semantic mapping, or webbing

Semantic Mapping or Webbing

👉 Use semantic mapping or webbing to organize main ideas and details; to show parts of a whole; and to organize steps to complete for an activity.

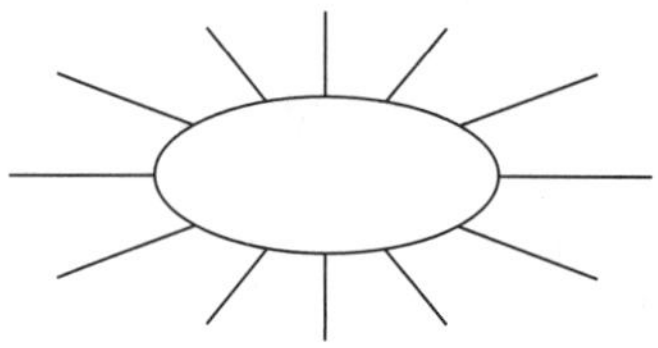

Write your topic or main idea in the center of the bubble.

Add details or subtopics at the end of each line.

To use as a time manager, list activities or steps to be completed. Then, number the steps in order.

P—**P**ick a formula,

E—**E**xplore words to fit the formula,

N—**N**ote the words,

S—**S**ubject and verb identification come next.

However, at the secondary level students often are required to write not only sentences and paragraphs but also theme papers and reports. Deshler and his colleagues have suggested **TOWER,** a cognitive strategy that provides a structured approach to writing theme papers.

T—**T**hink,

O—**O**rder ideas,

W—**W**rite,

E—**E**dit,

R—**R**ewrite.

A related strategy for writing theme papers suggested by Ellis and Lenz (1987) is remembered by the acronym **DEFENDS.**

D—**D**ecide on your exact position.

E—**E**xamine the reasons for your position.

F—**F**orm a list of points that explain each reason.

E—**E**xpose your position in the first sentence.

N—**N**ote each reason and supporting points.

D—**D**rive home the position in the last sentence.

S—**S**earch for errors and correct.

Yet another strategy for writing papers may be remembered by the acronym **PLEASE.**

P—**P**ick your topic and writing format.

L—**L**ist the information and ideas to be used in writing.

E—**E**valuate—is the list correct?

A—**A**ctivate the paragraph with a topic sentence.

S—**S**upply a supporting sentence.

E—**E**nd with a concluding sentence; evaluate your writing.

As students become proficient in written expression, they must also learn to proofread and edit their work. An error-monitoring strategy developed by Schumaker et al. (1981) called **COPS** is used to detect and correct errors in written products.

C—Have I **c**apitalized the first word and proper names?

O—How is the **o**verall appearance?

P—Have I used end **p**unctuation, commas, and semicolons correctly?

S—Do the words look as if they are **s**pelled correctly?

A writing strategy that incorporates the COPS strategy uses the acronym **WRITER** to help students remember.

W—**W**rite on every other line.

R—**R**ead the paper for meaning.

I—**I**nterrogate yourself, using COPS.

T—**T**ake the paper to someone to proofread.

E—**E**xecute a final copy.

R—**R**eread your paper a final time.

And yet another strategy that encourages students to review their final product in an organized fashion is remembered by the acronym **HOW.**

H—**H**ow is my heading, which should include name, date, subject, and page number?

O—Am I **o**rganized? Did I start on the front of the page, are my margins okay, and is the paper well spaced?

W—Is the paper **w**ritten neatly? Are words or numbers on the line and are they neatly formed? Are errors neatly erased or crossed out?

When adolescents with mild disabilities are asked to review their written work, many do so quickly and unsuccessfully, mainly because they do not know what the teacher means by "review your work." The written language strategies presented above provide clues to help them understand and remember what to do.

Mathematics

Some students with mild disabilities are referred for special education because they have academic problems in the mathematics curriculum area. They demonstrate poor performance "due to an inability to memorize basic facts and/or an inability to remember how to complete a variety of mathematical problems" (Miller & Mercer, 1993, p. 78). These students may have trouble with such math activities as basic operations, decimals, percentages, and problem solving. Several cognitive strategies can be taught to encourage them to become more active participants and to learn to monitor their performance during mathematics problem solving.

SQRQCQ, a strategy suggested by Forgan & Mandrum (1989), has six steps that students follow to solve math word problems.

Survey—read the entire problem,

Question—state the problem in the form of a question,

Read—identify critical information,

Question—ask what computation is needed,

Compute—do the computation,

Question—does my answer make sense?

The use of acronyms and mnemonics can assist students in answering math problems correctly. The **SOLVE** and **DRAW** (Miller & Mercer, 1993) strategies were designed to cue students to answer a math fact from memory. **SOLVE** stands for the following steps:

S—**S**ee the sign.

O—**O**bserve and answer (if unable to answer, keep going).

L—**L**ook and draw.

V—**V**erify your answer.

E—**E**nter your answer.

DRAW, another cognitive strategy that assists students with solving word problems, has only four steps (Miller & Mercer, 1993).

D—**D**iscover the sign,

R—**R**ead the problem,

A—**A**nswer or draw a picture,

W—**W**rite the answer.

Study Skills

Research has shown that secondary students spend a great deal of the school day listening to oral presentations by teachers (Bos & Vaughn, 1988; Mastropieri & Scruggs, 1987). However, students with mild disabilities do not take class notes nor do they know how to study in a systematic manner. Many of them fail in content-area classes due to lack of skills needed for processing and using information. Direct instruction in note-taking and other study skills is imperative at this level (see Strichart & Mangrum, 1993, for further information and reproducibles to be used when teaching study skills).

Incorporation of study strategies can result in improved achievement. Such study skills instruction may assist students in attributing their success to the systematic selection and application of strategies rather than luck or assistance from others. Teaching students to use study strategies may encourage the use of more proactive approaches to academic tasks.

Research generally indicates that note-taking is one of the most frequently used study skills and one of the most valuable in facilitating recall. As Vogel (1987) pointed out, the task of note-taking is relatively complex, involving simultaneous listening, understanding, recognizing, and synthesizing information long enough to coherently write it down. Many students do not take notes effectively or efficiently. Students with mild disabilities may need to be convinced of the importance of taking notes. Research supports the benefits of note-taking (Suritsky & Hughes, 1996).

A variety of formats should be presented so that students can choose the one that is most effective for them. An outline format that stresses the identification of a main idea and supporting subordinate ideas and a columnar format are two of the more common. In general, an outline format is more difficult to learn than a columnar format, and a two-column format is easier than a three-column format. (A two-column format is shown in Figure 8.7.)

2 Most common Note taking tasks

Figure 8.7
Note-taking strategy

Class _____ Period _____ Date _____ Page _____

Rough Notes   Don't Understand

Vocabulary

Source: From *Teaching Study Strategies to Students with Learning Disabilities* (p. 94) by S. S. Strichart and C. T. Mangum, 1993, Boston: Allyn & Bacon.

In a two-column format the main ideas are placed in the left column and the details in the right. But any strategy that enables students to identify organizational cues in lectures, to note key words, and to organize key words into a structured and organized format should be taught to students with mild disabilities.

For some students who have difficulty taking notes, it may be helpful to begin with guided notes. The teacher provides a structured outline of a class lecture (e.g., Shields & Heron, 1989). As he or she lectures, the students fill in the missing items.

Whichever method the students choose to learn, the teacher should model effective use of the note-taking strategy. For example, while the class watches a videotape of a lecture, the teacher could take notes on an overhead projector.

Another study skill area that presents problems for students with mild disabilities is taking tests. Even though students with mild disabilities spend their elementary school years taking quizzes and tests, they are not necessarily accomplished test takers (Scruggs & Mastropieri, 1988). Many students attend to the wrong part of test directions, are misled by irrelevant and distracting information, and are not persistent in searching for information (Hughes, 1996).

Tests are given to evaluate whether students have grasped the concepts and learned the material. However, many students with mild disabilities who have learned the material have difficulty doing well on tests (Scruggs & Mastropieri, 1988). It is important that tests measure students' knowledge of information and concepts, rather than their lack of test-taking skills (Hoover, 1988). Preparation for a test and test-taking strategies should be taught to secondary students with mild disabilities. Just as you would prepare students for a comprehension activity or a research activity, you must also prepare students to take tests.

"Before describing the 'what' and the 'how' of test-taking instruction, two points should be stressed. First, test-taking skills do not replace adequate studying, and second, guessing strategies should only be used when they have attempted to answer and have no idea what the correct answer is" (Hughes, 1996, p. 249).

The use of the **SCORER** test-taking strategy, suggested by Carman & Adams (1972) and validated with students with mild disabilities by Idol-Maestas and Ritter (1986), is illustrated in Figure 8.8.

Another test-taking strategy, called **PIRATES,** was suggested by Hughes, Ruhl, Deshler, and Schumaker (1993). The letters refer to the following steps:

P—**P**repare for the test, **p**repare to succeed;

I — **I**nspect the instructions;

R—**R**ead each question;

A—**A**nswer or abandon each question;

T—**T**urn back;

E—**E**stimate answers for the remaining questions;

S—**S**urvey your test.

Figure 8.8

Test-taking strategy—SCORER

Source: Adapted from *Study Skills: A Student's Guide for Survival* (p. 225) by R. A. Carman and W. R. Adams, 1972, New York: Wiley.

Test Taking Strategy – SCORER

S – **Schedule your time.** (Review the entire test and plan to use your time according to the number of items, the point value of each item, and the level of difficulty of the items.)

C – **Look for clue words.** (For example, words such as *always* and *never* usually indicate a statement is false, whereas *usually* and *sometimes* frequently indicate a statement is true.)

O - **Omit difficult items.** (Answer questions you are sure of first, to allow more time for difficult items. Mark all items that you skip, so you won't forget to answer them later.)

R - **Read carefully.** (Careful reading of the directions, as well as each question, can significantly improve your score. Underline specific directions on the test. Don't let misreading cause you to confuse your facts or make careless errors which cost you points.)

E - **Estimate your answers.** (On test items requiring calculations or problem solving you should roughly estimate the answer. This helps to catch careless errors. If you are unsure of an answer, then guess. It is important to answer all questions. You don't have a chance to get it right if you don't put down something.)

R - **Review your work.** (If you have extra time when you have completed the test, reread all of your answers. Don't be too eager to change your answers. Change them only if you have a good reason. Make sure your name is on every page of the test.)

Both **SCORER** and **PIRATES** strategies have been taught to students and helped them be more successful (deBettencourt, 1995).

Taking standardized tests is difficult for many students with mild disabilities. Scruggs and Mastropieri (1992) suggest that students be taught the following strategies:

- to fold the test booklet and answer sheets so only one page shows at a time;
- to check page numbers whenever they go to the next page;
- to check the item number with the matching answer sheet number;
- to mark the bubble correctly and to review the answer sheet; and
- to check whether the answer sheet has two pages.

Becoming familiar with test formats can build the self-confidence of students with mild disabilities.

Considering the demands placed on high school students to complete tasks at specific times and to participate in a host of competing activities, it is especially important that their time management skills be effective.

Studying for a test includes a complex set of activities requiring planning, organization, implementation, and monitoring. Many adolescents with mild disabilities do not use efficient study routines; they do not organize their time efficiently. They need instruction in managing their time.

Hoover and Kabideau (1995) illustrated the use of semantic webs as a tool for teaching students to study more efficiently. Hildreth, Macke, and Carter (1995) suggested the use of a comprehensive calendar for an organizational tool. Rooney (1988) suggested the use of wheels and ovals to help students organize their time. A wheel can be used to organize tasks or activities in a visual format. "Put whatever is being organized inside the wheel and attach the tasks or activities as spokes around the wheel. Number all the items around the wheel. Next, figure out how much time is available to complete the numbered items. Then break the amount of available time down into manageable units. Distribute the tasks over the units of time and set a timer so that the end of each unit serves as a point to monitor progress" (Rooney, 1988, p. 6). For many students, instruction in how to organize their time at the beginning of each term can promote success for much of the year.

Executive strategies can assist students in taking advantage of mainstream opportunities by increasing their class participation. Ellis (1989) suggested starter strategies that enable students to combine nonverbal, cognitive, and verbal behaviors to activate their participation in class. (See Figure 8.9 for some examples.) These strategies, also called **survival skills**, include such skills as getting to class on time, responding to teacher requests, keeping track of assignments, and so on (Schaeffer, Zigmond, Kerr, & Heidi, 1990). Zigmond and her colleagues designed a school survival skills curriculum, which is outlined in Figure 8.10.

The examples provided in the previous sections represent only a few of the many cognitive strategy training procedures currently discussed in the literature. Although we are advocates of students becoming active learners through the use of cognitive strategy training, teachers should adopt only procedures that have been empirically validated. The following section discusses several other cautions in using cognitive strategy training procedures.

SLANT – An Executive Strategy for Increasing Attention

Sit up.

Lean forward.

Ask and Answer questions.

Nod to show you understand.

Track the teacher, chalkboard, overhead, and important visuals with your eyes.

Think Back with WISE

Were goals met?
Did you learn what you wanted to learn?
Did you meet your participation goals?

Itemize important information.
Review study guide, notes, and/or textbook.   Mark key information.

See how information can be remembered.
Draw graphic displays.   Create mnemonic devices.   Create study cards.

Explain what you learned to someone.
Use your notes to teach someone about the topic.

Think Ahead with PREP

Prepare materials
Mark notes, study guides, and textbook.
Get notebook, study guide, pencil, and textbook ready for class.

Review what you know.
Read notes, study guide, and textbook cues.
Relate cues to what you already know about the topic.

Establish positive mind-set
Tell yourself to learn.   Suppress "put-downs."   Make a positive self-statement.

Pinpoint goals.
Decide what you want to find out.   Note participation goals.

Figure 8.9
SLANT, PREP, and WISE

Source: Adapted from "A Metacognitive Intervention for Increasing Class Participation" by E. S. Ellis, 1989, *Learning Disabilities Focus, 5,* 36–37.

Figure 8.10
School survival skills curriculum

ATTENDANCE
- Coming to school
- Coming to class
- Coming on time
- Coming prepared

ASSIGNMENT COMPLETION
- Keeping track of assignments
- Turning in classwork/homework

IN CLASS BEHAVIOR
- Being more "on-task"
- Responding to teacher request
- Asking questions/Making comments

BEHAVIOR
- Reducing disruptive behavior
- Talking more "appropriately"

Source: From "Rethinking Secondary School Programs for Students with Learning Disabilities" by N. Zigmond, 1990, *Focus on Exceptional Children, 23*(1), 1–22.

Generalization of Strategy Training

A critical aspect of cognitive strategy training is the degree to which the strategies generalize across settings and are maintained over time (Ellis & Lenz, 1996). This is especially important at the secondary level, where the intention is to promote active learning among students who are at risk for dropout and later limited employment and/or students who are preparing for postsecondary training. Cognitive strategy training procedures are successful if such students use the strategies taught under controlled conditions in other settings within and outside the world of school. To assure promotion of **generalization**, Ellis, Lenz, and Sabornie (1987b) suggest the following tips for packaging of strategies:

1. the learning strategy should contain a set of steps that lead to a specific outcome;
2. the learning strategy should be designed to cue use of cognitive strategies and metacognitive processes;
3. the strategy should contain no more than seven steps;
4. each step should begin with a verb or other word that directly relates to the action being cued;
5. a remembering system should be attached to the strategy to facilitate recall;
6. the learning strategy should be task specific rather than situation specific or content specific. (p. 8)

In essence, at this level it is critical to give students training in cognitive strategies that will promote their independent active participation in their learning experiences in and out of the classroom.

Adaptations to Mainstream Classrooms

Many of the strategies suggested in this chapter can be easily adapted to content-area classroom instruction. A teacher must be able to identify the range of general strategies that can be applied to his or her specific discipline (e.g., strategies for learning biology or social studies content) (Deshler & Putnam, 1996). Content-area teachers "must know the strategies that are most related to success, must understand their critical features, and must be able to articulate them in a meaningful way to students" (Ellis & Lenz, 1996, p. 23).

Initial instruction in a learning strategy may require the content-area teacher to reduce the demands of learning the content so as to direct students' attention to mastery of the strategy (e.g., practice note-taking on class lectures). Once students understand the dimensions of the strategy, the instructional demands can increase. For strategies to be effective, they must be integrated in the students' repertoire at the automatic level (Pressley, Johnson, & Symons, 1987).

Bulgren and Lenz (1996) suggest that "the most effective teaching methods and materials are those that promote the student's active learning through learning cues. The more limited a student's ability to mediate learning internally through appropriate cognitive strategies, the greater is the need for teaching agents to promote mediation externally through learning cues or to support a student's use of internal mediators" (p. 424). The most successful mainstreamed situations for students with disabilities are those in which the teacher understands each student's level of cognitive strategy usage.

Summary

The goals associated with cognitive learning strategy instruction are such that students with mild disabilities are taught to use their existing skills in a strategically optimal fashion so that content information can be acquired, manipulated, stored, retrieved, expressed, and generalized (Deshler, Schumaker, Lenz, & Ellis, 1984). The abundance of investigations studying strategy training illustrates that educators/researchers are pursuing the best strategies for teaching students with mild disabilities.

Key Terms

cognitive strategy training

study skills

metacognition

COPS

SCORER

executive strategies

survival skills

generalization

References

Alley, G., & Deshler, D. (1979). *Teaching the learning disabled adolescents: Strategies and methods.* Denver: Love Publishing Co.

Bickel, W. E., & Bickel, D. D. (1986). Effective schools, classrooms, and instruction: Implications for special education. *Exceptional Children, 52,* 489–500.

Bos, C. S., & Vaughn, S. (1988). *Strategies for teaching students with learning and behavior problems*. Needham Heights, MA: Allyn & Bacon.

Brown, V. L. (1978). Independent study behaviors: A framework for curriculum development. *Learning Disability Quarterly, 1*(2), 78–84.

Brown, W. F., & Holtzman, W. H. (1967). *Survey of study habits and attitudes*. New York: Psychological Corporation.

Bulgren, J., & Lenz, K. (1996). Strategic instruction in the content areas. In D. D. Deshler, E. S. Ellis, & B. K. Lenz (Eds.), *Teaching adolescents with learning disabilities: Strategies and methods* (2nd ed.) (pp. 409–473). Denver: Love Publishing.

Carman, R. A., & Adams, W. R. (1972). *Study skills: A student's guide for survival*. New York: Wiley.

Clark, F. L., Deshler, D. D., Schumaker, J. B., & Alley, G. R. (1984). Visual imagery and self-questioning: Strategies to improve comprehension of written material. *Journal of Learning Disabilities, 17,* 145–149.

Cobb, R., & Crump, W. (1984). *Post-school status of young adults identified as learning disabled while enrolled in learning disabilities programs*. Final report U.S.D.E. Grant No. G008302185. Tuscaloosa: University of Alabama.

Cohen, S., & deBettencourt, L. (1984). Teaching children to be independent learners: A step-by-step strategy. In E. L. Meyen, G. A. Vergason, & R. J. Whelan (Eds.) *Effective instructional strategies for exceptional children* (pp. 319–334). Denver: Love Publishing Co.

Dawson, M. M., Hallahan, D. P., Reeve, R. E., & Ball, D. W. (1980). The effect of reinforcement and verbal rehearsal on selective attention in learning disabled children. *Journal of Abnormal Child Psychology, 8,* 133–144.

deBettencourt, L. U. (1987). Strategy training: A need for clarification. *Exceptional Children, 54,* 24–30.

deBettencourt, L. U. (1995, November). *Preparing for middle and high school students with learning disabilities: A study skills approach*. Paper presented at the TED conference, Honolulu, Hawaii

deBettencourt, L. U., Zigmond, N., & Thornton, H. S. (1989). Follow-up of post-secondary age rural learning disabled graduates and dropouts. *Exceptional Children, 56,* 40–49.

Deshler, D. D., Ellis, E. S., & Lenz, B. K. (1996). *Teaching adolescents with learning disabilities: Strategies and methods* (2nd ed.). Denver: Love Publishing Co.

Deshler, D. D., & Lenz, B. K. (1989). *The strategies instructional approach*. Unpublished manuscript.

Deshler, D. D., & Putnam, M. L. (1996). Learning disabilities in adolescents: A perspective. In D. D. Deshler, E. S. Ellis, & B. K. Lenz (Eds.), *Teaching adolescents with learning disabilities: Strategies and methods* (2nd ed.) (pp. 1–7). Denver: Love Publishing Co.

Deshler, D. D., Schumaker, J. B., Alley, G. R., Warner, M. M., & Clark, F. L. (1982). Learning disabilities in adolescents and young adult populations: Research implications. *Focus on Exceptional Children, 15*(1), 1–12.

Deshler, D. D., Schumaker, J. B., & Lenz, B. K. (1984). Academic and cognitive interventions for LD adolescents: Part II. *Journal of Learning Disabilities, 19,* 66–70.

Deshler, D. D., Schumaker, J. B., Lenz, B. K., & Ellis, E. (1984). Academic and cognitive interventions for LD adolescents: Part I. *Journal of Learning Disabilities, 17,* 108–117.

Deshler, D. D., Warner, M. M., Schumaker, J. B., Alley, G. R., & Clark, F. L. (1984). The learning strategies intervention model: Key components and current status. In J. D. McKinney & L. Feagans (Eds.), *Current topics in learning disabilities* (pp. 245–284). Norwood, NJ: Ablex.

Donahoe, K., & Zigmond, N. (1990). Academic grades of ninth grade urban learning-disabled students and low-achieving peers. *Exceptionality, 1,* 17–27.

Ellis, E. S. (1989). A metacognitive intervention for increasing class participation. *Learning Disabilities Focus, 5*(1), 36–46.

Ellis, E. S., & Lenz, B. K. (1987). A component analysis of effective learning strategies for LD students. *Learning Disabilities Focus, 2*(2), 94–107.

Ellis, E. S., & Lenz, B. K. (1996). Learning disabilities in adolescents: A perspective. In D. D. Deshler, E. S. Ellis, & B. K. Lenz (Eds.), *Teaching adolescents with learning disabilities: Strategies and methods* (2nd ed.) (pp. 9–60). Denver: Love Publishing Co.

Ellis, E. S., Lenz, B. K., & Sabornie, E. J. (1987a). Generalization and adaptation of learning strategies to natural environments: Part 1: Critical agents. *Remedial and Special Education, 8*(1), 6–20.

Ellis, E. S., Lenz, B. K., & Sabornie, E. J. (1987b). Generalization and adaptation of learning strategies to natural environments: Part 2: Research into practice. *Remedial and Special Education, 8*(2), 6–23.

Estes, T. H., & Vaughan, J. L., Jr. (1985). *Reading and learning in the content classroom: Diagnostic and instructional strategies.* Boston: Allyn & Bacon.

Fardig, D., Algozzine, R., Schwartz, S., Hensel, J., & Westling, D. (1985). Post-secondary vocational adjustment of rural, mildly handicapped students. *Exceptional Children, 52,* 115–121.

Flavell, J. (1970). Developmental studies of mediated memory. In H. Reese & L. Lipsitt (Eds.), *Advances in child development and behavior* (Vol. 5, pp. 181–211). New York: Academic Press.

Flavell, J. (1979). Metacognition and cognitive monitoring: A new area of cognitive-developmental inquiry. *American Psychologist, 34,* 906–911.

Forgan, H. W., & Mangrum, C. T. (1989). *Teaching content area reading skills* (4th ed.). Upper Saddle River, NJ: Merrill/Prentice Hall.

Hallahan, D. P., Tarver, S. G., Kauffman, J. M., & Graybeal, N. L. (1978). A comparison of the effects of reinforcement and response cost in the selective attention of learning disabled children. *Journal of Learning Disabilities, 11,* 430–438.

Hasazi, S., Gordon, L., & Roe, C. (1985). Factors associated with the employment status of handicapped youth exiting from high school from 1979–1983. *Exceptional Children, 51,* 455–469.

Hildreth, B. L., Macke, R. A., & Carter, M. L. (1995). The comprehensive calendar: An organizational tool for college students with learning disabilities. *Intervention in School and Clinic, 30,* 306–308.

Hoover, J. J. (1988). *Teaching handicapped students study skills.* (2nd ed.). Lindale, TX: Hamilton Publications.

Hoover, J. J., & Patton, J. R (1995). *Teaching students with learning problems to use study skills: A teacher's guide.* Austin, TX: PRO-ED.

Hoover, J. J., & Kabideau, D. K. (1995). Semantic webs and study skills. *Intervention in School and Clinic, 30,* 292–296.

Hughes, C. A. (1996). Memory and test-taking strategies. In D. D. Deshler, E. S. Ellis, & B. K. Lenz (1996). *Teaching adolescents with learning disabilities: Strategies and methods* (2nd ed.) (pp. 209–266). Denver: Love Publishing Co.

Hughes, C. A., Ruhl, K. L., Deshler, D. D., & Schumaker, J. B. (1993). Test-taking strategy instruction for adolescents with emotional and behavioral disorders. *Journal of Emotional and Behavioral Disorders, 1,* 189–198.

Hughes, C. A., Schumaker, J. B., Deshler, D. D., & Mercer, C. D. (1988). *The test taking strategy.* Lawrence, KS: Edge Enterprises.

Idol-Maestas, L., & Ritter, S. (1986). Teaching middle school students to use a test-taking strategy. *Journal of Educational Research, 79,* 350–357.

Lenz, B. K., Clark, F. C., Deshler, D. D., & Schumaker, J. B. (1988). *The strategies instructional approach.* (Preservice Training Package). Lawrence: University of Kansas Institute for Research in Learning Disabilities.

Lenz, B. K., Schumaker, J. B., Deshler, D. D., & Beals, V. L. (1984). *Learning strategies curriculum: The word identification strategy.* Lawrence: The University of Kansas.

Loper, A. B. (1982). Metacognitive training to correct academic deficiency. *Topics in Learning and Learning Disabilities, 2*(1), 61–68.

Mastropieri, M. A., & Scruggs, T. E. (1987). *Effective instruction for special education.* Boston: College-Hill Press.

McLoughlin, J. A., & Lewis, R. B. (1990). *Assessing special students* (3rd ed.). Upper Saddle River, NJ: Merrill/Prentice Hall.

Michael, W. B., Michael, J. J., & Zimmerman, W. S. (1972). *Study attitudes and methods survey.* San Diego, CA: Educational and Industrial Testing Service.

Miller, S. P., & Mercer, C. D. (1993). Mnemonics: Enhancing the math performance of students with learning difficulties. *Intervention in School and Clinic, 29,* 7–82.

Palincsar, A. S., & Brown, A. L. (1989). Teaching and practicing thinking skills to promote comprehension in the context of group problem solving. *Remedial and Special Education, 9,* 53–59.

Paris, S. G., Lipson, M. Y., & Wixson, K. K. (1983). Becoming a strategic reader. *Contemporary Educational Psychology, 8,* 293–316.

Paris, S. G., & Oka, E. R. (1989). Strategies for comprehending text and coping with reading difficulties. *Learning Disability Quarterly, 12,* 32–42.

Pauk, W., & Cassell, R. (1970). *The Cornell Learning and Study Skills Inventory.* Jacksonville, IL: Psychologists and Educators.

Polloway, E. A., & Smith, T. E. C. (1992). *Language instruction for students with disabilities* (2nd ed.). Denver: Love Publishing Co.

Pressley, M., Johnson, C. J., & Symons, J. (1987). Elaborating to learn and learning to elaborate. *Journal of Learning Disabilities, 20,* 76–91.

Pressley, M., Symons, S., Snyder, B. L., & Cariglia-Bull, T. (1989). Strategy instruction research comes of age. *Learning Disability Quarterly, 12,* 16–30.

Raygor, A. L. (1970). *Study skills test: McGraw-Hill Basic Skills System.* New York: McGraw-Hill.

Rooney, K. (1988). *Independent strategies for efficient study.* Richmond, VA: J. R. Enterprises.

Rosenshine, B. V. (1983). Teaching functions in instructional programs. *Elementary School Journal, 83,* 330–338.

Schaeffer, A. L., Zigmond, N., Kerr, M. M., & Heidi, E. F. (1990). Helping teenagers develop school survival skills. *Teaching Exceptional Children, 23,* 35–38.

Schumaker, J. B., Denton, P. H., & Deshler, D. D. (1984). *The paraphrasing strategy: A learning strategies curriculum.* Lawrence: University of Kansas Institute for Research in Learning Disabilities.

Schumaker, J. B., Deshler, D. D., Alley, G. R., & Denton, P. (1982). Multipass: A learning strategy for improving reading comprehension. *Learning Disability Quarterly, 5,* 295–304.

Schumaker, J. B., Deshler, D. D., Nolan, S., Clark, F. L., Alley, G. R., & Warner, M. M. (1981). *Error monitoring: A learning strategy for improving academic performance of LD adolescents* (Research Report No. 32). Lawrence: University of Kansas Institute on Learning Disabilities.

Schumaker, J. B., & Sheldon, J. (1985). *The sentence writing strategy.* Lawrence: The University of Kansas.

Scruggs, T. E., & Mastropieri, M. A. (1988). Are learning disabled students "test-wise?" A review of recent research. *Learning Disabilities Focus, 3,* 87–97.

Scruggs, T. E., & Mastropieri, M. A. (1992). *Teaching test taking skills: Helping students show what they know.* Cambridge, MA: Brookline.

Sheinker, A., Sheinker, J. M., & Stevens, L. J. (1984). Cognitive strategies for teaching the mildly handicapped. In E. L. Meyen, G. A. Vergason, & R. J. Whelan (Eds.), *Effective instructional strategies for exceptional children* (pp. 194–215). Denver: Love Publishing Co.

Shields, J., & Heron, T. E. (1989). Teaching organizational skills to students with learning disabilities. *Teaching Exceptional Children, 21*(2), 8–13.

Stewart, D. M., Kamm, K., Allen, J., & Sols, D. K. (1972). *Wisconsin Tests of Reading Skill Development: Study Skills.* Minneapolis: NCS Interpretive Scoring Systems.

Strichart, S. S., & Mangrum, C. T. (1993). *Teaching study strategies to students with learning disabilities.* Boston: Allyn & Bacon.

Suritsky, S. K., & Hughes, C. A. (1996). Notetaking strategy instruction. In D. D. Deshler, E. S. Ellis, & B. K. Lenz (Eds.), *Teaching adolescents with learning disabilities: Strategies and methods* (2nd ed.) (pp. 267–312). Denver: Love Publishing Co.

Swanson, H. L. (1989). Strategy instruction: Overview of principles and procedures for effective use. *Learning Disabilities Quarterly, 12,* 3–14.

Tarver, S. G., Hallahan, D. P., & Kauffman, J. M. (1976). Verbal rehearsal and selective attention in children with learning disabilities: A developmental lag. *Journal of Experimental Child Psychology, 22,* 375–385.

Torgesen, J., & Goldman, T. (1977). Verbal rehearsal and short-term memory in reading-disabled children. *Child Development, 48,* 56–60.

Torgesen, J. K., & Houck, D. G. (1980). Processing deficiencies of learning disabled children who perform poorly on the digit span test. *Journal of Educational Psychology, 72,* 141–160.

Torgesen, J. K., Murphy, H. A., & Ivey, C. (1979). The influence of an orienting task on the memory performance of children with reading problems. *Journal of Learning Disabilities, 12,* 396–401.

Vogel, S. A. (1987). Issues and concerns in LD college programming. In D. J. Johnson & J. W. Blalock (Eds.), *Adults with learning disabilities: Clinical studies* (pp. 67–80). New York: Plenum.

Wallace, G., & Kauffman, J. M. (1986). *Teaching students with learning and behavior problems* (3rd ed.). Upper Saddle River, NJ: Merrill/Prentice Hall.

White, W. J., Schumaker, J. B., Warner, M. M., Alley, G. R., & Deshler, D. D. (1980). *The current status of young adults identified as learning disabled during their school career* (Research Report No. 21). Lawrence: University of Kansas Institute for Research in Learning Disabilities.

Zigmond, N. (1990). Rethinking secondary school programs for students with learning disabilities. *Focus on Exceptional Children, 23*(1), 1–22.

Zigmond, N., & Thornton, H. (1985). Follow-up of postsecondary age LD graduates and dropouts. *Learning Disability Research, 1,* 50–55.

9

Social Skills Instruction

Objectives

After reading this chapter, the reader should be able to:

1. provide definitions of social skills;
2. differentiate social skills from social competence;
3. list methods of observational assessment of social skills;
4. discuss different ways in which to measure social status;
5. discuss teacher ratings of adolescents' social skills;
6. provide different ways in which social skills can be taught to adolescents with mild disabilities;
7. list ways in which social skills can be generalized to noninstructional settings.

Is social skills training as important as instruction in reading, math, language arts, and cognitive strategies? Are all adolescents with mild disabilities equally in need of instruction in social skills? Can teachers train adolescents in social skills without using a specific curriculum? How does a teacher measure social skills? How does a teacher of adolescents with mild disabilities assist in generalization of learned prosocial behaviors so that youth perform such skills in key environments?

These questions and others deal with a growing field of influence in special education, that is, teaching appropriate social-behavioral responses to students found lacking in such skills. Research has identified social skills of students with disabilities as an area worthy of instructional focus, but until the 1980s, little attention was directed at assisting students who are truly in need of such instruction.

Social integration into society is a worthwhile outcome of schooling, and there is little argument that prosocial behaviors are important for students with disabilities to acquire and maintain throughout their lives. Youth identified as mildly disabled who are without appropriate social skills are often more difficult to manage in classroom environments, lack an adequate number of chronologically age-appropriate friends, and historically have been judged to be unpopular when placed in inclusive classrooms with nondisabled classmates. While adolescents with mild disabilities have well-known academic problems, many, if not most, of these same students also exhibit deficits in social competence. If special and regular educators wish to comprehensively address the problems that adolescents with mild disabilities evince, social skills instruction must become part of the educational regimen.

This chapter presents ways that teachers can assess and teach skills related to social functioning of adolescents with mild disabilities. Specifically discussed are (a) definitional issues related to social skills, (b) direct observational methods used for measuring specific social target behaviors, (c) sociometric measurement techniques for determining social relationships of students, and (d) teacher rating scales of social skills and social competence. Also presented are the many ways that social skills can be taught to adolescents with disabilities. Emphasis is placed on methods that are efficacious from an empirical standpoint, as well as on techniques that have been shown to be easily applied in classroom situations. The key in instructing students with social skill deficits is to consider their social problems equal in importance to academic difficulties. A longitudinal focus is also important. Just as an educa-

233

tor would not stop teaching and emphasizing reading skills after a 12-week unit on "Reading Skills Needed in the Workplace," so too should teachers consider social skill instruction as a long-term necessity over the middle school and high school careers of students with mild disabilities.

Rationale for Social Skills Instruction

The social skills of students with mild disabilities are important to educators for a number of reasons. Adolescents with disabilities have been shown to experience problems in social acceptance when placed in inclusive classrooms (see Gresham, 1982; Sabornie, 1985; Schloss, Schloss, Wood, & Kiehl, 1986; Schumaker & Hazel, 1984a, for reviews), and some not only are rejected *by* their peers, but they also direct reciprocal social rejection *at* their nondisabled classmates (Sabornie & Kauffman, 1987). High school students with mild disabilities attract fewer and have less stable friendships than comparison youth without disabilities (Zetlin & Murtaugh, 1988). Low participation levels in school-related and out-of-school activities are common among adolescents with disabilities (Deshler & Schumaker, 1983; Sabornie, Thomas, & Coffman, 1989), and these same youth express dissatisfaction with their social lives (White, Schumaker, Warner, Alley, & Deshler, 1980). Loneliness is often expressed by adolescents with mild disabilities as well as feelings of being noninte-grated into the social activities in middle schools (Luftig, 1988; Sabornie & Thomas, 1989). Young adolescents with disabilities are also victimized (e.g., having possessions stolen from them and being threatened with bodily harm) more often than nondisabled students in middle schools (Sabornie & Thomas, 1989). The social problems of adolescents with disabilities are serious, multifaceted, and worthy of the attention of concerned educators attempting to improve their social functioning ability (Walker, Colvin, & Ramsey, 1995).

Many factors, including social cognition deficiencies (e.g., inability to comprehend nonverbal behaviors and emotions of others), have been blamed for the social difficulties of adolescents with mild learning and behavioral disabilities (Bryan, 1977). Kronick (1978) stated that some students simply lack the necessary social behaviors considered appropriate for an age group; others have mentioned that certain students with disabilities have the requisite social skills but lack the motivation and knowledge to display such behaviors in an appropriate manner (Perlmutter, 1986). Schumaker and Hazel (1984a) and Gresham (1986) discussed the origins of social skill difficulties among students with disabilities in terms of three domains: (a) **performance deficits** (i.e., having the appropriate skill, but not applying it when it would be appropriate), (b) **social skill deficits** (i.e., simply lacking the social skill required for a situation), and (c) **behavioral excesses** (i.e., exhibiting an inappropriate behavior too frequently). Gresham (1988) has also provided a list of "interfering responses" that lead to dilemmas for socially unskilled persons. These social problem behaviors are listed in Table 9.1.

Perhaps the suspected causes of students' social problems are not so surprising when one considers the heterogeneity of characteristics that are common among youth with disabilities. Whatever the causes for the social difficulties, educators should not use them as excuses for failing to improve the social skills of those in need of such training.

Table 9.1
Social "interfering" problem
behaviors

[handwritten: interfering responses]

Behavioral Type	Characteristics
Cognitive-verbal	Depressive thoughts
	Poor problem-solving ability
	Inadequate role-taking skills
	Low self-efficacy
Overt-motoric	Disruptive behavior
	Aggressive behavior
	Excessive motor movement
	Impulsive behavior
Physiological-emotional	Anxiety
	Anger
	Depression
	Fear

Source: Adapted from "Social Skills: Conceptual and Applied Aspects of Assessment, Training, and Social Validation" by F. M. Gresham, 1988. In J. C. Witt, S. N. Elliott, and F. M. Gresham (Eds.), *Handbook of Behavior Therapy in Education* (pp. 523–546), New York: Plenum.

Definitions

Although social skills can be defined in many ways, choosing a definition is important because it affects the manner in which actual measurement takes place. Moreover, it is a commonly accepted, efficacious procedure to define what is to be measured; this holds true in terms of assessment for identification purposes as well as for measuring change in behavior after a specific intervention (Sabornie, 1991).

The term *social skills* is not the same as *social competence;* social competence does not require performance of a task to be exemplary, but merely adequate (McFall, 1982). Social skills are the specific behaviors that an individual evinces to perform interpersonal behaviors competently. Social competence, on the other hand, requires evaluation and judgments of others that indicate that a person has performed a social behavior appropriately. The evaluation opinions necessary to determine social competence include the judgments of teachers or parents, the number of social tasks completed satisfactorily in relation to some criteria, or comparisons to some normative sample (Gresham, 1986).

Some formal definitions of social skills can also be found in the general psychological literature. One widely cited conceptualization of social skills is that of Combs and Slaby (1977), which reads:

> the ability to interact with others in a given social context in specific ways that are societally acceptable or valued and as they sometimes are personally beneficial, mutually beneficial or beneficial primarily to others. (p. 162)

Libet and Lewinsohn (1973) state that social skill is

> the complex ability both to emit behaviors that are positively or negatively reinforced and not to emit behaviors that are punished or extinguished by others. (p. 304)

[handwritten left margin: Social competence • adequate performance • requires evaluation • judgments of others on performance]

Social skills as defined by Foster and Ritchey (1979) include

those responses, which within a given situation, prove effective, or in other words, maximize the probability of producing, maintaining, or enhancing positive effects for the interaction. (p. 626)

Another definition of social skills that is particularly comprehensive is that of Walker et al. (1983), who defined social skills as

a set of competencies that (a) allow an individual to initiate and maintain positive social relationships with others, (b) contribute to peer acceptance and to a satisfactory school adjustment, and (c) allow one to cope effectively and adaptively with the larger social environment. (p. 1)

Walker et al. (1995) stated that this last definition is different from the others because it includes foci on three essential components of social competence: (a) recruiting social support networks and friendships; (b) meeting the demands of teachers who control the environment of classrooms and peers who control other settings such as playgrounds; and (c) adapting to changing and difficult conditions in a person's environment. Walker et al. provided another model of school-related social skills and social-behavioral competence, which is presented in Figure 9.1. This unique model depicts social-behavioral competence and adjustment as they pertain to a student's interactions with both teachers and peers. One can see that different behaviors are necessary for a person to be viewed positively from the perspective of a teacher versus through the eyes of a peer. Moreover, the Walker et al. (1995) paradigm also demonstrates some of the potential outcomes of adjustment given certain behavioral antecedents in place over time.

A **peer acceptance definition of social skills** (Gresham & Elliott, 1984) exists because of the plethora of studies that examined the social status of students with mild disabilities in inclusive classrooms (see Gresham, 1982; Sabornie, 1985; Schloss et al., 1986; Schumaker & Hazel, 1984a, for reviews). This definition holds that students who are accepted by their peers are also considered socially skilled. While this definition of social skills is relatively easy to comprehend and technically adequate methods exist to uncover social acceptance and rejection in classrooms, it falls short because assessment data of this type do not identify specific behaviors that result in acceptance or rejection by peers. Because teachers need specific behaviors to target through instruction, the peer acceptance definition of social skills may not be in an educator's best interest for treatment purposes.

A **behavioral definition of social skills** (Gresham & Elliott, 1984) is also found in the literature. This method of defining social skills considers behaviors in specific situations. By examining responses to social interactions, one can determine whether a behavior will be continued through reinforcement or discontinued because of punishment or extinction that follows. Naturalistic observation is required with this definition to judge the outcomes that emerge from interpersonal interaction. While this definition has strengths in comparison to the peer acceptance version, assessment espousing this approach to social skill cannot determine whether specific behaviors are socially important. If a student walks away from another who made some type of invitation to play a

Figure 9.1
Model of interpersonal social-behavioral competence within school settings

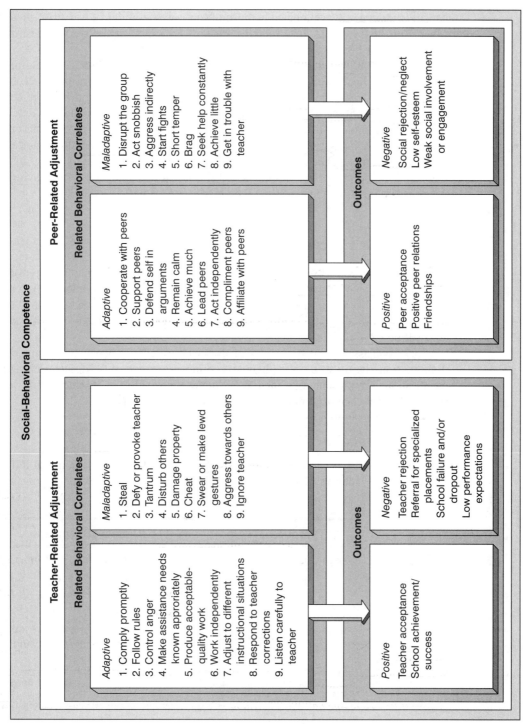

Source: From *Antisocial Behavior in School: Strategies for Practitioners* by H. M. Walker, G. Colvin, and E. Ramsey. Copyright © 1995 Brooks/Cole Publishing Company, Pacific Grove, CA 93950, a division of International Thomson Publishing, Inc. By permission of the publisher.

237

game, for example, it may not be because of the way the initiative was performed, but rather prior history (e.g., inappropriate previous attempts) of the student desiring to interact with the person receiving the invitation.

The social validity definition of social skills (Gresham & Elliott, 1984) claims that social skills are those behaviors that predict desirable outcomes such as peer acceptance, others' positive judgments of behavior, and social manifestations known to be consistently associated with acceptance or others' favorable opinions. This definition requires a multifaceted approach to measuring social skills where observations, sociometry, and significant others' (e.g., teachers) judgments are all considered equally important in assessment strategies. The social validity definition requires educators to engage in comprehensive measurement of students' social skills, and this approach serves as the basis of the discussion regarding assessment strategies that follows.

Assessment Procedures

Three general techniques exist for teachers to use in measuring the many different facets of a student's social capabilities. These methods are (a) direct observation, (b) sociometry, and (c) teacher rating scales. Advances in these techniques have led to a great number of technically adequate devices with demonstrated effectiveness for use with adolescents with mild disabilities.

Social skill assessment strategies can also be classified into two general domains: (a) identification-classification and (b) intervention-programming. These measurement classifications are presented in Table 9.2. Note that sociometrics, teacher rating scales, and direct observation fall under different classification areas.

Direct Observation

Assessing students' social interaction in natural settings (e.g., in classrooms, at lunch in the cafeteria, in hallways between classes, etc.) through direct observation is one of the

Table 9.2
Social skills assessment classifications

Purpose	Assessment Type
Classification-diagnosis	Peer nomination
	Sociometric rating scales
	Other ratings by teachers, parents, and peers
Intervention-therapy	Direct observations in classrooms, on playgrounds at recess, and in lunchrooms

Source: Adapted from "Social Skills: Conceptual and Applied Aspects of Assessment, Training, and Social Validation" by F. M. Gresham, 1988. In J. C. Witt, S. N. Elliott, and F. M. Gresham (Eds.), *Handbook of Behavior Therapy in Education* (pp. 523–546), New York: Plenum.

allows teacher to establish functional relationships & specific things as

most valid ways to measure social skills for intervention purposes. This method allows a teacher to establish functional relationships between specific antecedents and consequences and actual social behaviors. Users of this assessment technique first must operationally define what social behaviors are to be measured (e.g., responses to peers' questions answered in a pleasant tone of voice; verbally abusive language directed at another in the room) and record the overt motor or verbal responses performed by target students. The power of this assessment method is evident in that it is not limited by environment; it can be used in any setting where appropriate social functioning is important.

What is to be measured

In deciding which social behaviors are to be targeted for direct observation, the following questions should be asked in an effort to determine which skills or behaviors are most important for a particular adolescent:

These ?'s need to be asked to determine skills & behaviors needed

- Are there any behavioral excesses that contribute to a student's lack of social competence (e.g., verbally abusive language, physical aggression displayed too often)?

- Do inappropriate social behaviors seem to be dependent on specific environments (i.e., in one classroom but not in another) or on others (i.e., with Ralph but not with Elizabeth) in the same setting?

- What events serve as catalysts to inappropriate social behaviors (e.g., when given independent seat work versus direct instruction by a teacher)?

- What specific skills does the student lack for social success in an environment (e.g., can he or she share with others, does he or she use "please" and "thank you" when appropriate, can he or she take turns in a game or in conversation)?

- What specific social behaviors are expected in certain settings (e.g., standing in line appropriately in the cafeteria, being respectful to a teacher who expects such courtesy)?

Answers to the above questions should serve as the initial phase to guide direct observation of social skills. Of particular importance in this type of assessment is to view students' social exchanges in relation to antecedents, behavior, and consequences; by doing so, a teacher views individual behaviors with respect to the total reciprocal exchange of interpersonal interaction, or interaction between a student and his or her environment (Strain, Odom, & McConnell, 1984).

Direct Observation Recording Procedures

Because social interactions often occur at unexpected times, choosing the most appropriate observational recording method is important for validity. The recording procedures presented here are ideally suited for the purpose of observing the social skills of adolescents with mild disabilities.

Frequency recording. In light of the nature of social skills, frequency recording is often the easiest way to measure them in school environments. This recording method requires the teacher to simply tally the number of times a social behavior occurs during a specific time interval. To use event recording for instructional purposes, teachers record behaviors of interest before intervention, apply a social skill training procedure, and record again to determine whether change in a positive direction occurs. Examples of prosocial behaviors (Stephens, 1978) that best fit event recording include:

- following classroom rules and directions
- responding to teasing appropriately
- saying "please" and "thank you" when necessary
- looking into a person's eyes while talking
- gaining attention of others in appropriate ways
- smiling when meeting a friend or acquaintance
- greeting others by name
- introducing oneself to others
- helping someone when asked
- giving directions when asked
- talking in a tone of voice that is acceptable
- initiating informal conversation
- making relevant remarks in conversation
- waiting for one's turn in a game
- complimenting others
- sharing possessions with others
- making apologies when necessary
- avoiding doing something wrong when asked to participate
- keeping one's possessions in order
- accepting correction without anger

Event, or frequency, recording of individual social skills often involves the measurement of infrequently displayed behaviors. Teachers may find this recording procedure easy in terms of application (especially when using wrist counters, pocket click counters, or slash marks on an index card), but for reliability purposes, educators of adolescents with mild disabilities should not attempt to count too many behaviors at one time. The more complex the recording scheme is to apply, the greater the chance of measurement error. Another way to simplify this recording procedure is to create preformatted recording sheets to be used for specific periods of time divided into short intervals, such as that shown in Figure 9.2.

Duration recording.   When a teacher wishes to know how long a specific social behavior lasts, duration recording is the most appropriate assessment method. Duration recording of social behaviors is necessary when the goal of instruction is to increase or decrease the amount of time that a behavior is in evidence. Using duration recording of

Figure 9.2
Preformatted recording sheet for event recording

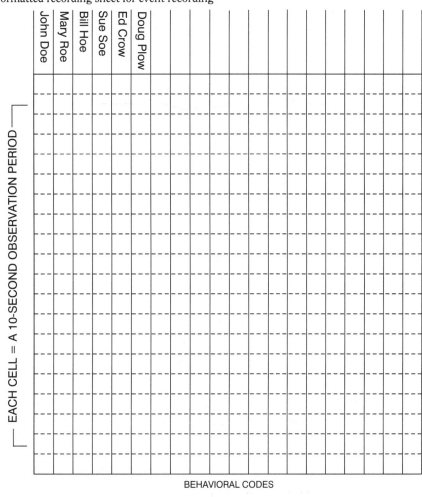

EACH CELL = A 10-SECOND OBSERVATION PERIOD

Column headers: John Doe, Mary Roe, Bill Hoe, Sue Soe, Ed Crow, Doug Plow

BEHAVIORAL CODES

1 =verbal aggression
2 =physical aggression
3 =not saying please
4 =not saying thank you
5 =getting angry with peers
6 =getting angry with teacher
7 =interrupting others in conversation
8 =not waiting for turn
9 =making irrelevant remarks in conversation
10 =not sharing with others

A =answering questions appropriately
B =making eye contact while speaking
C =smiling at others when appropriate
D =giving directions appropriately
E =voice tone appropriate for situation
F =helping others needing assistance
G =apologizing when necessary
H =initiating conversation appropriately
I =inviting others to participate
J =listening to speaker appropriately

PLACE NUMBER (FOR INAPPROPRIATE BEHAVIOR) OR LETTER (FOR APPROPRIATE SOCIAL
BEHAVIOR) IN BOX FOR EACH BEHAVIOR OBSERVED DURING EACH 10 SECOND INTERVAL.

Classroom: _____

Date: _____

Time: from _____ to _____

social skills for instructional purposes is similar to frequency recording: (a) record (i.e., during a baseline period), (b) direct some type of treatment toward the social behavior (i.e., intervention), and (c) record subsequently to determine whether behavioral change occurred. The following list of social skills (Stephens, 1978) is adequately suited for duration recording.

- length of conversation
- complying with requests during an acceptable time frame
- following classroom rules for extended periods of time
- playing a game with others for acceptable periods of time
- waiting one's turn for an appropriate amount of time
- responding to others' questions in a reasonable time frame
- assisting others for appropriate lengths of time
- paying attention in conversation
- length of time that sharing is displayed
- listening to speaker while conversation is in progress
- displaying a willingness to try without giving up easily
- continuing to work on a task until it is complete
- working cooperatively with others on the same task
- finding acceptable uses of free time in a classroom
- ignoring distractions by others

Duration recording is somewhat cumbersome for use in educational environments. A teacher would need access to a wall clock, wristwatch, or other timing device (e.g., stopwatch) in order to engage in this type of recording. A well-organized teacher, however (especially one with a teacher's aide), should be able to use duration observational recording with few problems if social behaviors are (a) defined in advance, (b) few in number with regard to recording, and (c) easily identifiable in an instructional or other setting.

Time sampling procedures. By far the easiest way for teachers to record social skills in adolescents is to note the presence or absence of a specific behavior *at the end* of a specified time interval (e.g., every 60 seconds). This method can be used when it is impractical to observe youth for extended periods of time, when high-rate social behaviors are typical of performance (e.g., behavioral excesses), and with behaviors that do not have an easily identifiable beginning and end (Cartledge & Milburn, 1986). Although easier to apply than event or duration recording, time sampling requires a teacher to be completely aware of time, particularly the termination of specified intervals. The power of time sampling lies in its simplicity (although training and practice may be necessary), and it provides an adequate *estimate* of the presence or absence of target behaviors.

Considerations in the use of observation. Direct observation of adolescents' social behaviors has strengths and weaknesses that teachers should be aware of before applying any of the methods described. Naturalistic observations are particularly sensitive to changes in students' behaviors over time, and they allow for examination of antecedents and consequences of target behaviors. Repeated measures of social skills through observation are also seen as a robust means of monitoring students' variability of performance while in classrooms and other school-related settings. Moreover, direct observation allows teachers to concentrate on individual social skills rather than focusing on global constructs such as social withdrawal or immaturity.

While the strengths of naturalistic observation are noteworthy, so too are its shortcomings. One weakness to consider in observation is related to the person conducting the actual behavioral recording. Observer bias, drift (i.e., not paying attention), and prior history with target students may lead to less than desirable reliability of measurement. Second, simply examining the rate of social behavior and increasing the rate of social interaction among students through intervention is not widely recognized as a desirable outcome of social skill instruction (Gresham, 1981; Schumaker & Hazel, 1984a). Quality of interaction, therefore, is also seen as a necessary component in any observation system involving the social skills of adolescents with disabilities and their interaction with nondisabled peers. Lastly, because of the vast array of behaviors required of students in order to be called "socially competent," concentration on individual skills (or lack thereof) through observation appears to be a rather narrow focus. When direct observation is combined with sociometrics and teacher ratings of social competence, however, a more dynamic view of a student's true social competence is obtained.

Sociometry

Sociometric assessment is an example of measurement used for identification of adolescents with peer relationship problems. **Sociometry** is measurement concerned with (a) identifying an individual's social position in a group, (b) documenting change in group social position following intervention, and (c) highlighting behavioral characteristics related to differential social standing (McConnell & Odom, 1986). What follows is a description of the different types of sociometric assessment used for the purposes offered by McConnell and Odom.

Peer nomination.   Peer nomination is the sociometric assessment method having the longest history of use in classroom situations. Administration of this type of sociometry is relatively uncomplicated; examiners simply ask respondents to list a specific number of classmates (usually 3 to 5, but it can be unrestricted) whom they wish to work with, play with, sit next to, and so on. In addition, participants can be asked to list the classmates they like best or those who are their best friends in the same room. The specific style of question asked and its wording should be chosen with caution; nominations can change when adolescents are asked to name workmates versus best friends. The relative number of positive nominations determines the level of popularity or friendship among group members.

Negative nominations also can be used to determine a different category of sociometric status (i.e., dislike or rejection). Nominations of this type ask youth to name peers whom they like least, those with whom they do not like to work, and so on.

negative is used less often

Although sociometric choices described with negative statements have been used less frequently in comparison to using only positive criteria, negative nominations are necessary for comprehensive screening of adolescents who may need social skill intervention. Ethical concerns often have prevented sociometric practitioners from including negative nominations in their efforts to determine social standing of target students. Some have assumed, for example, that having pupils name others they do not like may serve as a catalyst for additional negative perceptions and rejection in social interactions. Some experts (e.g., Havyren & Hymel, 1983; Hops & Lewin, 1984), however, have questioned the notion that use of negative criteria in peer nomination is unethical. Havyren and Hymel (1983) showed that among nondisabled preschool children, use of negative nominations did not affect quality of child-to-child interactions subsequent to their use in classrooms. Additional research is necessary to verify or reject the belief that negatively oriented sociometric choices among adolescents with mild disabilities lead to questionable assessment activities.

Combining information from both positive and negative classroom nominations leads to identification of students who may be candidates for interventions aimed at improving their social standing among peers. Comprehensive data treatment methods for peer nominations were first proposed by Peery (1979) and later refined by Coie, Dodge, and Coppotelli (1982) and require a systematic approach to tabulation of nominations. Summing a student's number of positive and negative nominations yields what is called *social impact*, which is viewed as the overall social profile of a target pupil. *Social preference* is derived when the number of negative nominations is subtracted from a student's total of positive sociometric choices. Social preference is viewed as the relative extent to which a person is either liked or rejected in coterie. A positive social preference score indicates that more students are accepting rather than rejecting a peer; a negative social preference score indicates the opposite. At the classroom level, five distinct subgroups of social status are identified when social impact and social preference indices are combined:

- Popular—students very high in social preference, above average in acceptance, and below average in rejection
- Rejected—those very low in social preference, above average in rejection, and below average in acceptance
- Neglected—pupils with very low social impact scores and zero positive nominations
- Controversial—youth with very high social impact scores and above average negative and positive nominations
- Average—those near the mean in social preference

Sociometrically rejected students have been described as at risk and worthy of attention with regard to social skill treatment. Coie (1985) and Putallaz and Gottman (1983) characterized rejected students as aggressive, unhappy, easily provoked to anger, frequently off-task and disruptive in the classroom, lacking in socially facilitative behavior, uncooperative, seeking help often, and engaging in high levels of inappropriate play such as initiating activities that exclude classmates, hitting peers, aversive verbal and physical behavior, and aggressive reactions to aversive behaviors. Thus, rejected youth should be a focal group of teachers who are concerned with the social adjustment and competence of students in classrooms. While peer nomination techniques have found students with mild disabilities to be sociometrically rejected in inclusive classrooms (e.g., Bryan, 1974, 1976; Bryan & Bryan, 1978; Gresham & Reschly, 1986; Hutton & Polo, 1976; Iano, Ayers, Heller, McGettigan, & Walker, 1974; Johnson, 1950; Lapp, 1957; Prillaman, 1981; Scranton & Ryckman, 1979; Siperstein, Bopp, & Bak, 1978), the Coie et al. (1982) nomination procedures have been applied infrequently (not with adolescents, however), as specified here, with these pupils in inclusive settings (Kistner & Gatlin, 1989; Stone & La Greca, 1990). There is a clear need for additional application of these sociometric data treatment methods in light of the concerns about the behavior of rejected adolescents in general.

Sociometric rating scales. An alternative method of sociometric assessment involves the use of rating scales. These instruments also have been applied extensively with students with mild disabilities in regular classrooms (Baldwin, 1958; Bruininks, 1978; Bruininks, Rynders, & Gross, 1974; Coben & Zigmond, 1986; Gottlieb & Budoff, 1973; Monroe & Howe, 1971; Rucker, Howe, & Snider, 1969; Sabornie, 1987; Sabornie & Kauffman, 1985, 1986, 1987; Sabornie, Kauffman, Ellis, Marshall, & Elksnin, 1987–1988; Sabornie, Marshall, & Ellis, 1988, 1990).

Rating scales ask student respondents to judge classmates listed on a class roster, and a numerical or pictorial (i.e., faces, stick figures) classification is usually associated with each type of rating. Such instruments typically include ratings that are positive (e.g., best friends, other friends), neutral (e.g., not friends but OK), related to familiarity (e.g., do not know the person), and negative (e.g., do not care for him or her, dislike him or her). Participants simply read classmates' names prepared on a class roster and rate each peer with one of the choices. Descriptive paragraphs, which usually include situations such as working with, interacting with, and sitting next to a peer, are used to explain and highlight the numerical or other code associated with each rating type.

The *Ohio Social Acceptance Scale* (OSAS) (Fordyce, Yauck, & Raths, 1946) is a multiple-category rating scale intended for use with secondary-level respondents. Ratings are numbered 1 through 6 (found after roster names) and denote the following: 1 = "my very, very best friends"; 2 = "my other friends"; 3 = "not friends, but OK"; 4 = "don't know them"; 5 = "don't care for them"; and 6 = "dislike them." Research using the OSAS with youth with mild disabilities in inclusive educational settings consistently has shown such pupils to be low in acceptance and high in rejection. Sabornie, Kauffman, and Cullinan (1990), for example, used OSAS rating scale data to determine the mainstream social standing of high school adolescents with mild disabilities (i.e., learning disabled, mildly mentally retarded, behavior disordered). In this study, the researchers applied the Coie et al. (1982) peer nomination data treatment technique to rating scale scores and found more students identified as mildly mentally retarded and behaviorally disordered, in comparison to the number of adolescents with learning disabilities and no known disabilities, in the rejected sociometric category. Replication of this study will determine whether such results consistently indicate that students with behavior disorders and mild mental retardation are more socially incompetent among peers than those identified as learning disabled.

Sociometric assessment considerations.   Several issues should be kept in mind when considering which sociometric measurement type to employ with students identified as mildly disabled. Hops and Lewin (1984), for example, stated that peer nomination questions such as "play with" and "work with" are assessing two distinct types of social acceptance. In other words, a playmate may not necessarily be chosen as a workmate. Students have been known to positively nominate a peer but spend very little time interacting with him or her in a group (Greenwood, Walker, Todd, & Hops, 1979). There is also some agreement that rating scales measure acceptance or likability, and peer nomination methods tap friendship (Asher, 1985; Asher & Taylor, 1981; Gresham, 1981; Gresham & Elliott, 1989). Acceptance and friendship, therefore, are not necessarily the same. Enhancing acceptance is a more easily attained outcome in comparison to fostering friendships (Sabornie & Ellis, 1987).

The sociometric literature also supports the technical adequacy of peer nomination and rating scales. Rating scales tend to have higher test-retest reliability in comparison to peer nomination techniques (Asher & Taylor, 1981; Hops & Lewin, 1984). Moreover, because of the multiple shades of sociometric status that are used (e.g., acceptance, tolerance, familiarity, rejection), rating scales are more sensitive to change in status over time. The exact role that sociometric tolerance plays in correlations with overt behaviors and adjustment, however, awaits further testing. Validity of sociometric assessment techniques has also been documented in research, although it is important to note here that adolescents with mild disabilities in inclusive settings were not featured in the samples studied. Criterion-related validity is shown in the close association between teacher ratings of peer popularity and acceptance status (Connolly & Doyle, 1981; Greenwood et al., 1979). Sociometrically rejected adolescents simultaneously demonstrate increased aggression and inability to make friends (Dodge, Coie, & Brakke, 1982; Gottman, Gonso, & Rasmussen, 1975), which indicates concurrent validity strength.

Another consideration involved in sociometry with adolescents with mild disabilities is the relationship between acceptance and rejection. One study (Hartup, Glazer, & Charlesworth, 1967) showed that peer nomination acceptance and rejection were correlated only moderately. This finding leads to the conclusion that acceptance and rejection are not opposites of the same continuum, but rather two distinct phenomena on separate continua. Sabornie et al. (1988), however, showed that rating scale acceptance was significantly—and strongly—negatively correlated with rejection across groups of students identified as mildly disabled.

Finally, Parker and Asher (1987) raised another issue that teachers should keep in mind when using sociometry with adolescents with mild disabilities. They concluded that sociometrically rejected adolescents may experience such status in only one classroom, but not in other environments outside school. In Parker and Asher's words, such adolescents would become "six-hour unpopular children." The need exists, therefore, to consider the global (i.e., outside school) peer relationships of classroom-based, rejected adolescents.

Teacher Rating Scales

The use of teacher ratings to identify adolescents lacking in specific social skills is one of the easiest ways for educators to engage in assessment for screening, identification, and intervention. In conjunction with naturalistic observations and sociometrics, teacher ratings of social competence provide an accurate depiction of those who may need comprehensive educational treatment that includes instruction in appropriate social behavior. Two instruments that have been developed for use in various educational settings with adolescents with mild disabilities are reviewed in the following paragraphs.

The Walker-McConnell Scale of Social Competence and School Adjustment (WMC). A social skill teacher rating scale with superb technical adequacy, the Walker-McConnell instrument (Walker & McConnell, 1992) represents one of the best instruments for teacher assessment of the social competence of adolescents with mild disabilities.

The WMC measures school-oriented interpersonal competence and adaptive behavior of secondary-level students (i.e., grades 7 through 12). The test consists of 53 items divided into four subscales: Self-Control (Subscale 1; 12 items), Peer Relations (Subscale 2; 20 items), School Adjustment (Subscale 3; 12 items), and Empathy (Subscale 4; 3 items). Respondents (i.e., regular and special education teachers) reply to the items, using a 5-point Likert scale ranging from *never* to *frequently,* and the items are written so that they can be included as objectives on target students' Individual Education Plans (IEPs).

The test administration manual presents more than adequate technical adequacy data with regard to internal consistency reliability, test-retest reliability, and total score interrater reliability. The manual also offers impressive data with regard to item, factorial, discriminant, criterion-related, and construct validity. Sabornie et al. (1989) showed that the WMC, administered to regular classroom teachers serving young adolescents with behavior disorders, could separate youth with behavior disorders from nondisabled peers with 89% accuracy. Sabornie and Thomas (1989) found the discriminant accuracy of the WMC to be 75% with adolescents identified as learning disabled, behaviorally disordered, and nondisabled when rated by regular educators in inclusive settings. Special education teachers of students with learning disabilities, however, in comparison to regular teachers of the same students, rated the social competence of their students in resource rooms significantly higher. The WMC is strongly supported for assessment of social competence of adolescents. Its relative ease of completion (i.e., usually less than 15 minutes) is another positive benefit of its use, especially with teachers who are already overburdened with the paperwork aspects of their jobs.

Social Skills Rating System (SSRS) (Gresham & Elliott, 1990). The secondary-level teacher rating scale of the SSRS comprises 51 items divided into the domains of self-control, externalizing problems (e.g., aggression), internalizing problems (e.g., sadness), assertion, and cooperation. This instrument is intended for use with youth in grades 7 through 12. Teachers rate students' social behaviors on a 3-point frequency metric ranging from *never* to *often true.* The system includes for teacher respondents additional rating criteria concerned with perceived importance of the individual behaviors being rated (e.g., not important, important, critical). The authors state that the additional criteria used for teacher ratings contribute to enhanced social validity and identification of social skills for intervention (see also Gresham & Elliott, 1989). In field testing, teachers completing the SSRS on students' behavior perceived certain social skills as being more important than others. The specific social skills deemed important and not so important are found in Table 9.3.

The SSRS demonstrates more than adequate discriminant ability among students with and without disabilities in mainstream classrooms (Gresham, Elliott, & Black, 1987). The internal consistency coefficients of the SSRS are quite robust, as are those for test-retest and interrater reliability. Content, concurrent, and predictive validity data are all more than sufficient. The SSRS was standardized on 4,700 children of representative national and racial groups, including pupils identified as exceptional and nondisabled. The SSRS package also offers parent and self-rating scales—features not found in other rating scale test batteries. The scope of the SSRS, therefore, is very comprehensive. It is highly recommended for use by teachers concerned with assessing the social skills of adolescents with mild disabilities.

highly recommended

Not found in other test

Table 9.3
Most and least important social skills as rated by teachers

10 Most Important Skills	10 Least Important Skills
1. Completes classroom assignments in required time	1. Invites peers to play
2. Looks at teacher when instructed	2. Introduces self to other children
3. Follows teacher's verbal instructions	3. Praises peers
4. Requests assistance, explanations, or instructions from teacher	4. Makes positive statements to other children
5. Uses time productively while waiting for teacher assistance	5. Presents academic work before class
6. Asks questions of teacher when unsure of what to do in school work at appropriate times and in an appropriate manner	6. Cooperates with peers without being told
7. Produces correct academic work	7. Appropriately expresses opinions or beliefs on some issue by giving reasons for expressed opinion or belief
8. Controls temper in conflict situations	8. Appropriately expresses anger or annoyance when a classmate takes a belonging without asking
9. Attends to class speakers	9. Attempts classroom tasks before asking for teacher assistance
10. Ignores peer distractions when doing classwork	10. Tolerates peers whose characteristics are different from one's own (e.g., ethnic group, disability, etc.)

Source: Adapted from "Social Skills: Conceptual and Applied Aspects of Assessment, Training, and Social Validation" by F. M. Gresham, 1988. In J. C. Witt, S. N. Elliott, and F. M. Gresham (Eds.), *Handbook of Behavior Therapy in Education* (pp. 523–546), New York: Plenum.

General measurement considerations.　Although sociometry and teacher ratings of social behaviors are highly recommended for implementation by teachers, several notes of caution must be added to fully understand how each contributes to functional treatment schemes. Sociometric assessment does not involve the measurement of specific student behaviors—only the consequences (i.e., acceptance, rejection) of such overt manifestations in classrooms. For this reason, sociometry should be viewed as an initial screening device in spite of its correlation to specific student behaviors. Sociometrics should also be used to determine whether target students are in need of additional assessment that focuses on distinct social behaviors and to judge efficacy of intervention in pretesting and posttesting fashion. If social skill training is effective, there should be minimal correlation between target students' sociometric status before and after treatment. Direct observation of social behavior in natural settings (not contrived ones) does not measure the same constructs as do sociometrics, but rather specific behaviors that may hinder or enhance acceptance and rejection. Teacher ratings, on the other hand, enable teachers to express student social skill with regard to proximity of normative samples. In terms of intervention, teacher rating scales show to what level of severity a particular student may need social skill training. Often overlooked is that teachers deserve much credit for being excellent judges of student social functioning in all educational environments (Walker et al., 1995). Teachers who use the assessment procedures reviewed here, with their limitations and foci in mind, will find subsequent results of social skill training easier to interpret.

Intervention Methods

The global objective of any social skill training procedure is to enhance the social competence of individuals receiving treatment. Those responsible for instruction in this area should choose target skills that (a) are acquired in an expeditious manner, (b) can be used readily when encountering others within and outside the instructional setting, and (c) will be powerful enough to elicit positive reciprocal responses from others. This last point, concerning social reciprocity, is one that is often neglected in training regimens that target increased social competence of students (Strain et al., 1984; Walker, Greenwood, Hops, & Todd, 1979). Instructional programs aimed at enhanced social relationships of youth with mild disabilities in inclusive settings, therefore, must consider procedures that shape the behavior of both the adolescent with mild disability and his or her peers. Schumaker, Pederson, Hazel, and Meyen (1983) recommended that effective social skill training curricula for adolescents with mild disabilities should address the following:

- Does the curriculum promote social competence (i.e., ability to perform social tasks at an acceptable level)?
- Does the curriculum accommodate the learning characteristics of individuals with mild disabilities?
- Does the curriculum target the social skills deficits of those with mild disabilities?
- Does the curriculum provide training in situations as well as skills?
- Does the curriculum incorporate instructional methodologies found to be effective with students with mild disabilities?

The following section discusses empirically valid social skill training packages that are targeted for adolescents with mild disabilities who spend time in inclusive classrooms.

Social Skill Training Curricula

The ACCESS program.   The *ACCESS* program (Walker, Todis, Holmes, & Horton, 1988) is designed for use with middle and high school level students in special and regular classroom environments. The program emphasizes the learning of peer-to-peer social skills (e.g., having conversations), self-management skills (e.g., being organized), and relating-to-adults skills (e.g., getting an adult's attention). The program also emphasizes reinforcement and performance feedback, contracting for generalization, role-play practice activities, and suggestions for grouping students. The program manual provides keys to behavior management and enhancing students' motivation—a particularly important component in working with adolescents. The comprehensiveness of *ACCESS* is impressive; based on its scope, low cost, appropriateness for use in inclusive classrooms, and focus on generalization, teachers should consider use of this program for youth in middle and high school settings.

The Skillstreaming program.   *Skillstreaming the Adolescent* (Goldstein, Sprafkin, Gershaw, & Klein, 1980), a social skills training package designed for teaching prosocial behavior alternatives to antisocial outbursts, was developed for adolescents who are mildly disabled or those who are withdrawn, immature, or aggressive, The program is built around the components of "structured learning," a psychoeducational and behavioral approach to instruction.

Skillstreaming consists of teaching prosocial behaviors through (a) modeling, (b) role-playing, (c) performance feedback, and (d) transfer of training. Each individual social skill is task analyzed, and subcomponent skill parts are taught to mastery levels. Students observe models performing the exact skill to be learned, rehearse individual behaviors, and receive feedback from other students and trainers. Procedures are selected that increase the likelihood of demonstrating the social skill in real-life situations. The manual describes trainer behavioral steps, problem behavior management techniques, procedures that facilitate skill training (e.g., making instructions clear), and content of modeling activities. Methods of teaching a specific social skill and a transcript of an actual lesson are given in the manual, but instructional scripts are not provided.

The 50 prosocial skills included in the *Skillstreaming* package are divided into six domains: (a) beginning social skills (e.g., asking a question), (b) advanced social skills (e.g., giving instructions), (c) skills for dealing with feelings (e.g., understanding the feelings of others), (d) skill alternatives to aggression (e.g., sportsmanship after a game), (e) skills for dealing with stress (e.g., being a good sport after a game), and (f) planning skills (e.g., deciding on something to do). The program can be used in either regular or special education environments, but ideally it should be used in both settings for maximum effectiveness.

The Social Skills in the Classroom program.   *Social Skills in the Classroom* (Stephens, 1978) has been used with students of all ages who are identified as mildly disabled.

Although the program is recommended for use with populations with disabilities (see Cartledge & Milburn, 1986), it has little research validation to demonstrate its efficacy. For this reason, teachers should use caution when determining whether to choose this approach. The program was developed with the "directive teaching" instructional model as its foundation. Social skill instructors using the Stephens curriculum first define the behavior to be acquired in observable terms (i.e., with modeling), specify the exact movements that are needed for task completion, and stress the conditions under which the specific target behavior is to occur. Social skill performance levels are subsequently assessed and, based on this measurement (using Stephens's 1981 formal assessment instrument is recommended), corrective teaching strategies are developed. Guidelines for writing social skill instructional strategies are presented in the manual. The last step in the instructional sequence is evaluation of the effectiveness of the instructional strategy. Stephens recommends the use of reinforcement strategies and contingency contracting in order to motivate students to perform the newly learned prosocial behaviors.

A noteworthy aspect of the Stephens curriculum is the sheer number (136) of social skills that can be taught when using this program. Another feature of the package that is particularly useful to teachers is the inclusion of suggestions for a consultant's use of the program (pp. 12–22). Specific weaknesses of the Stephens program include scant research validation, lack of attention to skill generalization, and nonscripted lesson presentations. The effectiveness of this program, therefore, is unknown and likely to be limited if social skills are taught to target students in only one environment (i.e., in special education classes but not in inclusive settings). Figure 9.3 presents the entire list of 136 social skills that can be taught using the Stephens (1978) program.

The ASSET program. ASSET (Hazel, Schumaker, Sherman, & Sheldon-Wildgen, 1981a) is one of the most widely used programs for teaching social skills to adolescents at risk. One drawback of this package is its cost ($1,400), but that has not prevented *ASSET* from attaining acclaim and acceptance that surpass nearly all other social skill training regimens (e.g., at one time it was being used in middle schools across the entire state of South Carolina). This program features videocassettes that are used to teach the following social skills: giving positive and negative feedback, accepting negative feedback, resisting peer pressure, problem solving, negotiation, following instructions, and conversation. The leader's guide includes more than 150 pages of scripted lessons, instructional procedures, and objectives for each filmed lesson. The films, which keep participant reading to a minimum, show adolescents modeling appropriate and inappropriate social skills in interactions with peers, teachers, parents, and adults.

ASSET is a skills approach to the teaching of prosocial behaviors. Specific behaviors to be learned are practiced by participants in structured role-plays with instructor feedback, until criterion performance levels are attained. Lessons are introduced by providing the rationale for learning the specific skill. Program evaluation includes parents, who judge their adolescent's newly acquired prosocial behavior. Research has established the efficacy of *ASSET* (see Hazel, Schumaker, Sherman, & Sheldon-Wildgen, 1981b, 1982, for research validation), and this program is also very appropriate in educators' work with adolescents with mild disabilities who have social behavior problems.

[handwritten margin note: most widely used / drawback— costly]

Figure 9.3
Social skills list

ENVIRONMENTAL BEHAVIORS (EB)

Care for the Environment (CE)
> To dispose of trash in the proper container.
> To drink properly from water fountain.
> To clean up after breaking or spilling something.
> To use classroom equipment and materials correctly.
> To use playground equipment safely.

Dealing with Emergency (DE)
> To follow rules for emergencies.
> To identify accident or emergency situations that should be reported to the teacher.
> To report accident or other emergency to the teacher.

Lunchroom Behavior (LR)
> To use eating utensils properly.
> To handle and eat only one's own food.
> To dispose of unwanted food properly.

Movement Around Environment (MO)
> To walk through the hall quietly at a reasonable pace.
> To enter classroom and take seat without disturbing objects and other people.
> To form and walk in a line.
> To follow safety rules in crossing streets.

INTERPERSONAL BEHAVIORS (IP)

Accepting Authority (AA)
> To comply with request of adult in position of authority.
> To comply with request of peer in position of authority.
> To know and follow classroom rules.
> To follow classroom rules in the absence of the teacher.
> To question rules that may be unjust.

Coping with Conflict (CC)
> To respond to teasing or name-calling by ignoring, changing the subject, or using some other constructive means.
> To respond to physical assault by leaving the situation, calling for help, or using some other constructive means.
> To walk away from peer when angry to avoid hitting.
> To refuse the request of another politely.
> To express anger with nonaggressive words rather than physical action or aggressive words.
> To handle constructively criticism or punishment perceived as undeserved.

Gaining Attention (GA)
> To gain teacher's attention in class by raising hand.
> To wait quietly for recognition before speaking out in class.
> To use please and thank-you when making requests of others.
> To approach teacher and ask appropriately for help, explanation, instructions, etc.
> To gain attention from peers in appropriate ways.
> To ask a peer for help.

Greeting Others (GR)

- To look others in the eye when greeting them.
- To state one's name when asked.
- To smile when encountering a friend or acquaintance.
- To greet adults and peers by name.
- To respond to an introduction by shaking hands and saying how-do-you-do.
- To introduce oneself to another person.
- To introduce two people to each other.

Help Others (HP)

- To help teacher when asked.
- To help peer when asked.
- To give simple directions to a peer.
- To offer help to teacher.
- To offer help to a classmate.
- To come to defense of peer in trouble.
- To express sympathy to peer about problems or difficulties.

Making Conversation (MC)

- To pay attention in a conversation to the person speaking.
- To talk to others in a tone of voice appropriate to the situation.
- To wait for pauses in a conversation before speaking.
- To make relevant remarks in a conversation with peers.
- To make relevant remarks in a conversation with adults.
- To ignore interruptions of others in a conversation.
- To initiate conversation with peers in an informal situation.
- To initiate conversation with adults in an informal situation.

Organized Play (OP)

- To follow rules when playing a game.
- To wait for one's turn when playing a game.
- To display effort to the best of one's ability in a competitive game.
- To accept defeat and congratulate the winner in a competitive game.

Positive Attitude toward Others (PA)

- To make positive statements about qualities and accomplishments of others.
- To compliment another person.
- To display tolerance for persons with characteristics different from one's own.

Playing Informally (PL)

- To ask another student to play on the playground.
- To ask to be included in a playground activity in progress.
- To share toys and equipment in a play situation.
- To give in to reasonable wishes of the group in a play situation.
- To suggest an activity for the group on the playground.

Property: Own and Others' (PR)

- To distinguish one's own property from the property of others.
- To lend possessions to others when asked.
- To use and return others' property without damaging it.
- To ask permission to use another's property.

SELF-RELATED BEHAVIORS (SR)

Accepting Consequences (AC)

To report to the teacher when one has spilled or broken something.

To make apology when actions have injured or infringed on another.

To accept deserved consequences of wrongdoing.

Ethical Behavior (EB)

To distinguish truth from untruth.

To answer truthfully when asked about possible wrongdoing.

To identify consequences of behavior involving wrongdoing.

To avoid doing something wrong when encouraged by a peer.

Expressing Feelings (EF)

To describe one's own feelings or moods verbally.

To recognize and label moods of others.

Positive Attitude toward Self (PA)

To say thank you when complimented or praised.

To be willing to have one's work displayed.

To make positive statements when asked about oneself.

To undertake a new task with a positive attitude.

Responsible Behavior (RB)

To be regular in school attendance.

To arrive at school on time.

To hang up one's clothes in required place.

To keep one's desk in order.

To take care of one's own possessions.

To carry messages for the teacher.

To bring required materials to school.

Self-Care (SC)

To use toilet facilities properly.

To put on clothing without assistance.

To keep face and hands clean.

TASK-RELATED BEHAVIOR (TR)

Asking and Answering Questions (AQ)

To answer or attempt to answer a question when called on by teacher.

To acknowledge when one does not know the answer to a question.

To volunteer an answer to teacher's question.

To ask a question appropriate to the information needed.

Attending Behavior (AT)

To look at the teacher when a lesson is being presented.

To watch an audio-visual presentation quietly.

To listen to someone speaking to the class.

Classroom Discussion (CD)

    To use tone of voice in classroom discussion appropriate to the situation.

    To make relevant remarks in a classroom discussion.

    To participate in a classroom discussion initiated by teacher.

    To bring things to class that are relevant to classroom discussion.

    To express opinion in classroom discussion even when contrary to opinions of others.

    To provide reasons for opinions expressed in group discussion.

Completing Tasks (CT)

    To complete assigned academic work.

    To complete assigned academic work within the required time.

    To continue working on a difficult task until it is completed.

    To complete and return homework assignments.

Following Directions (FD)

    To follow teacher's verbal directions.

    To follow written directions.

    To follow directions in taking a test.

Group Activities (GA)

    To share materials with others in a work situation.

    To work cooperatively on a task with a partner.

    To carry out plans or decisions formulated by the group.

    To accept ideas presented in a group task situation that are different from one's own.

    To initiate and help carry out a group activity.

Independent Work (IW)

    To attempt to solve a problem with school work before asking for help.

    To find productive use of time while waiting for teacher assistance.

    To find acceptable ways of using free time when work is completed.

On-Task Behavior (OT)

    To sit straight at desk when required by teacher.

    To do a seatwork assignment quietly.

    To work steadily for the required length of time.

    To ignore distractions from peers when doing a seatwork assignment.

    To discuss academic material with peers when appropriate.

    To change from one activity to another when required by the teacher.

Performing before Other (PF)

    To participate in a role playing activity.

    To read aloud in a small group.

    To read aloud before a large group of the entire class.

    To make a report before a small group.

    To make a report before a large group or the entire class.

Quality of Work (QW)

    To turn in neat papers.

    To accept correction of school work.

    To make use of teacher's corrections to improve work.

    To go back over work to check for errors.

Source: From *Social Skills in the Classroom* by T. M. Stephens, 1978, Columbus, OH: Cedars Press.

The Social Skills for Daily Living program.   *Social Skills for Daily Living* (Schumaker, Hazel, & Pederson, 1988) is designed for youth identified as mildly disabled aged 12 to 21. Its goal is for students to acquire 30 social skills in four domains: (a) program basics (e.g., facing a person, making eye contact), (b) conversation and friendship skills (e.g., active listening, answering questions), (c) skills for getting along with others (e.g., accepting thanks, apologizing), and (d) problem-solving skills (e.g., following instructions, joining group activities).

The authors claim that the materials available for purchase (total cost $330) have been designed specifically for the interests and capabilities of secondary-level students with mild disabilities. All student materials (e.g., students' skill books and workbooks, tests, books written in comic book format, role-play practice cards) require minimal reading at the 4th-grade level. The instructor's manual contains scripted lessons for teachers to apply so that students understand each skill, memorize the skill steps, practice the skill in role-play situations, and apply the skill in real-life situations. Frequent review and performance reinforcement are important features of the program, and it can be used in inclusive classrooms as well as special education settings. The efficacy of this program regarding appropriate outcomes after students are exposed to its methodology, however, is still to be demonstrated.

The Social Skills on the Job program.   A social skills training program with a very specific focus, *Social Skills on the Job* (Macro Systems, 1989), is designed for use with adolescents identified as learning disabled, mildly mentally disabled, and behaviorally disordered. The program emphasizes social skills that are critical for social success in the workplace; it provides a videotape that features 14 different social skills presented via 28 vignettes of social situations at actual job sites (e.g., in restaurants, hotels, shops, offices). Some of the workplace-oriented social skills emphasized in the program include wearing appropriate clothes on the job, using good personal hygiene, calling in when sick, admitting mistakes, dealing with teasing from a coworker, and dealing with criticism from an employer.

The instructor's manual includes specific instructions so that students obtain and generalize their newly acquired social skills. Discussions and role-play activities are used with each videotaped vignette, and scripted lessons are included for teachers to apply. New vocabulary terms are introduced before students complete skill-related worksheets, and computer software that includes additional practice activities is also available. The program was developed for use with high school students aged 15 and over in special education classes with enrollments ranging from 4 to 12 students. Because the program includes only special education settings for implementation, generalization to actual work sites may be a problem if students are not exposed to such environments at other times during the day. Moreover, the efficacy of this program still awaits research that examines work-related outcomes with adolescents and young adults applying its procedures.

Noncommercial Social Skills Training Procedures

Although many packaged approaches exist to teach prosocial behaviors to adolescents with mild disabilities, other teaching procedures have also been tested outside the boundaries of a formal social skill training curriculum. The research from which these additional instructional methodologies originate will not be reviewed here, but individual techniques that have been shown to be effective will be discussed. Interested readers should peruse the following for excellent reviews of research related to the "nonpackaged" social skill training procedures: Ager and Cole, 1991; Gresham, 1981; Hollinger, 1987; Schumaker and Hazel, 1984b; Schumaker et al., 1983; Zaragoza, Vaughn, and McIntosh, 1991.

Individual social skill teaching techniques proven effective with adolescents having mild disabilities can be classified into those related to (a) manipulation of antecedents and consequences, (b) modeling or coaching, (c) descriptive procedures, and (d) rehearsal and performance feedback.

Concerning manipulation of antecedents and consequences, a teacher can change environmental events in an attempt to ensure the future occurrence of prosocial behaviors. This can be accomplished through reinforcement after an appropriate social interaction of two or more students, using "confederates" to initiate social contacts with target students, withholding reinforcement or privileges when appropriate social behaviors are not exhibited, and applying group contingencies to change the social interactions of one student or an entire group.

Modeling or coaching involves the simple demonstration of the desired social behavior, which can be accomplished through physical and verbal displays on a videotape or through actual teacher actions. The goal of this procedure is to provide the student with a sequence of the appropriate prosocial behavior.

Descriptive procedures involve verbal explanations or descriptions of performance related to desired social behaviors. For adolescents with mild disabilities, descriptive procedures usually involve (a) defining the behavior, (b) providing a rationale for use of the behavior (e.g., "You smile at other people so that they know you are interested in or amused at what they are saying or doing"), (c) stating (or asking the students to state) the situations in which the behavior is to be used, and (d) describing in sequence the steps to be applied when performing the behavior (Schumaker & Hazel, 1984a). A good example of descriptive procedures used to teach transition-related social skills is found in *The Self-Advocacy Strategy for Educational and Transition Planning* (Van Reusen, Bos, Schumaker, & Deshler, 1994). The social and family-living skills list of Van Reusen et al. is presented in Figure 9.4.

Two different types of rehearsal have typically been used in social skills training—verbal and actual practice. Verbal rehearsal requires the adolescent to memorize the steps in the sequence of performing the behavior and instruct himself or herself in what occurs next. Actual practice involves a teacher arranging a role-play in which students demonstrate their mastery through performance. Both verbal and videotaped feedback are used to tell the adolescent how well the behavior was rehearsed or demonstrated in a role-play and whether they met the performance criteria levels. Most of these teaching techniques have been used in various combinations in research to determine the effectiveness of this type of social skill training (Cartledge & Milburn, 1986).

Social Skills for School and Community (Sargent, 1991) is a particularly valuable source of information in using a nonpackaged approach to teaching social skills to students with disabilities. This text provides an extensive discussion of (a) the rationale for

Figure 9.4
Social and family-living skills list

CAN YOU:
1. *Actively listen* to others?
2. *Introduce yourself* to strangers?
3. *Start* and *hold a conversation* with someone?
4. *Correctly interrupt* someone while they are doing something else?
5. *Make friends*?
6. *Accept* and *give compliments*?
7. *Accept* and *give criticism*?
8. *Apologize* to someone when you've made a mistake?
9. *Resist peer pressure*?
10. *Ask others for help* and *provide help* when needed?
11. *Respect others' beliefs and points of view*?
12. Effectively *work with others to solve a problem*?
13. *Negotiate* with someone so both parties win?
14. *Dress appropriately* and *use good manners*?
15. *Join an on-going* group *activity*?
16. *Plan a social activity* or *date*?
17. *Respect another person's rights and feelings* in a relationship?
18. *Describe adjustments in lifestyle* that are necessary *for* a successful *marriage*?
19. *Describe potential problems* that can occur *in a marriage*?
20. *Practice precautions* related to *sexual relationships*?
21. *Describe the major responsibilities* in running a home and marriage?
22. *Take responsibility for* raising *children*?
23. Create a *supportive home and family* environment for children (e.g., emotion-ally, physically, and financially)?
24. *Locate* and *select appropriate child care*?
25. *Practice* effective *parenting skills*?

This *Skills List* can be modified based on your students' grade
or developmental level.

Source: From *The Self-Advocacy Strategy for Educational and Transition Planning* (p. 167) by A. K. Van Reusen, C. S. Bos, J. B. Schumaker, and D. D. Deshler, Lawrence, KS: Edge Enterprises.

social skill instruction, (b) direct instruction of social skills, and (c) social skill instructional lessons for students from the primary level through high school. All lessons in Sargent's program ($\underline{n} = 100$) are based on direct instruction of a social skills paradigm and include the following six steps:

- *Establishing the need*   The teacher states why the specific social skill is important and what consequences may follow if the behavior is not displayed. To establish the need for dealing appropriately with a failure experience (one of the high school level skills that are taught), the teacher discusses with students (a) if they ever failed at anything, (b) if they ever lost their temper when they failed, and (c) if getting angry was an appropriate behavioral alternative to exhibit. In most lessons specific short stories and vignettes are read to the class that also establish the need for a specific social skill.

- *Identifying skill components*   Quite simply, this step involves the presentation and verbal rehearsal of actions that comprise the specific social skill. In dealing with failure, the teacher presents and rehearses the following: (a) deciding that you failed, (b) thinking about why you failed, (c) holding anger or frustration to yourself, (d) thinking about how to avoid failure next time, and (e) deciding to try again or take a different approach to the same situation.

- *Modeling the skill*   The teacher overtly displays the behavior that is required for correct student performance, thinking aloud as each step occurs. In dealing with failure, the teacher creates a contrived situation in which failure has occurred and displays and thinks aloud the above skill components.

- *Role-playing the skill*   The students overtly practice the skill and the teacher provides feedback on their performance. Again, using the dealing-with-failure lesson, students select a failure situation that may occur in their lives, and they think aloud and demonstrate the skill components. The teacher and fellow students then give feedback to the role-players, and students evaluate their own performance.

- *Practice*   For students who may have had difficulty in role-playing, the practice step allows for additional opportunities to exhibit the skill and receive feedback from the teacher. Teacher feedback at this point in the lesson allows for skill refinement and maintenance. In the practice step for dealing with failure the teacher sets up fictitious failure situations and observes student performance and gives additional feedback.

- *Generalization and transfer*   This step involves the discussion of performance of the newly learned social skill outside the classroom environment, with different people, and at different times. In terms of generalization for dealing with failure, the social skills teacher would ask other teachers to provide feedback to a student who dealt with a failure experience in an appropriate manner in another classroom. As review, teachers should also ask students how they dealt with failure in other situations subsequent to instruction.

The *Social Skills for School and Community* text also includes a social skills rating checklist that teachers will find helpful, and 32 homework forms that follow certain of the skills emphasized in the program. Teachers without access to Sargent's text can and should use the same six steps to teach any social skill. For skills that are particularly important to social functioning outside school (e.g., asking for directions to a specific place or street in a community, initiating a conversation), the teacher should conduct social skills training lessons in the community. Sargent's program materials are relatively inexpensive (approximately $18, available from the Council for Exceptional Children) and lessons include the effective teaching behaviors known to affect positive change in students. Secondary-level teachers should consider this approach appropriate for systematic instruction in social skills. Research, however, has yet to demonstrate its efficacy when applied to adolescents with mild disabilities. Table 9.4 presents the middle school/junior high and senior high school skills that are included in Sargent's *Social Skills for School and Community* text.

Social Skills Training for Employment

The comprehensive teaching of social skills to adolescents with mild disabilities is not complete without a focus on behaviors necessary for achieving success in employment. Some teachers may wonder why social skills are needed in employment settings. The rationale for social skills training for employment is very clear: Studies have shown that job termination and difficulties in employment settings among young adults with mild disabilities stem from problems of a personal or social nature (Campbell, Hensel, Hudson, Schwartz, & Sealander, 1987; Hoffman et al., 1987; Neubert, Tilson, & Ianacone, 1989; Rusch, Destefano, Chadsey-Rusch, Phelps, & Szymanski, 1992; Salzberg, Lignugaris/Kraft, & McCuller, 1988; Test, Farebrother, & Spooner, 1988; Wehman, 1992). With increased emphasis on preparing adolescents with mild disabilities for a successful transition from school to independent adult life (see Chapter 11), social skill training for employment should command great importance on IEPs for youth who need such treatment.

Much of the research that has attempted to teach social skills for employment to youth with mild disabilities has concentrated on cognitive-behavioral interventions. The following techniques have been effective in teaching job-related social skills to such youth (Warger, 1990). Teachers are encouraged to apply such techniques in their own teaching of social skills for employment at the secondary level.

Modeling. Similar to the discussion regarding Sargent's (1991) social skills program, *modeling* here refers to demonstration of the skill to be learned, usually by a teacher. Student observers are asked to reproduce the behavior that the model displayed. When combined with the other cognitive-behavioral techniques discussed in this section, modeling is an important part of any treatment regimen attempting to teach social skills for employment. Studies that successfully used modeling in conjunction with other cognitive-behavioral techniques include Montague (1988) and Foss, Auty, and Irvin (1989).

Coaching. Teachers using this technique instruct students in the actual environment (i.e., job setting) where the social skill is to be exhibited. Social skill trainers guide the students in task performance and provide feedback. The trainer also uses modeling, prompting, and rehearsal to assist the person learning the social skill on the job.

Sargent's Social Skills

Table 9.4

Middle school/junior high school and high school social skills training lessons included in *Social Skills for School and Community*

Middle School/Jr. High School	High School
Classroom-Related Skills	**School-Building-Related Skills**
Completing homework on time	Using free time productively (class time)
	Dealing with an accusation in school
School-Building-Related Skills	
Responding to school authorities	**Personal Skills**
	Dealing with failure
Personal Skills	Dealing with being left out
Accepting praise	
Staying out of fights	**Interactive Initiative Skills**
Dealing with embarrassment	Expressing feelings
Choosing appropriate clothing for social events	Expressing affection
	Standing up for a friend
Interaction Initiative Skills	Asking for a date
Introducing self	Giving a compliment
Making introductions	Making a complaint
Initiating a conversation	
Joining activities with peers	**Interaction Response Skills**
Congratulating peers and adults	Responding to constructive criticism
Apologizing	Recognizing feelings of others
Excusing self	Respecting space of others
	Responding to peer pressure
Interaction Response Skills	Dealing with an angry person
Maintaining a conversation	Making refusals
Responding to teasing and name calling	Answering a complaint
Community-Related Skills	**Community-Related Skills**
Asking for directions or information to a public place	Dealing with public officials over the phone
Giving directions	
Sportsmanship as a participant in games	**Work-Related Skills**
Polite behavior and sportsmanship as a spectator	Setting goals for work
Disposing of waste materials and debris in	Negotiating on the job
public places	Responding to unwanted criticism
Respecting the rights of others in public places	Asking for feedback on the job
Respecting public property	Minding one's own business on the job
Audience behavior	Choosing a time for small talk
Responding to public authority	Knowing the consequences of and refraining from
Asserting self to gain service in place of business	excessive complaining

Source: Adapted from *Social Skills for School and Community* by L. R. Sargent, 1991, Reston, VA: The Division on Mental Retardation of the Council for Exceptional Children.

Behavior rehearsal.   Similar to Sargent's (1991) rehearsal methods, *behavior rehearsal* here refers to practicing the actual social skill in an employment setting. Instruction and feedback in the work setting are also necessary components of behavioral rehearsal in the workplace. Foss et al. (1989) and Whang, Fawcett, and Mathews (1984) used extensive behavior rehearsal to successfully increase the employment social skills of adolescents with mild disabilities.

Problem solving.   Adolescents discuss a specific problem that they may be having in the workplace, and the instructor teaches them how to distinguish between effective and ineffective behavioral responses to the dilemma. Foss et al. (1989), Park and Gaylord-Ross (1989), and Roessler and Johnson (1987) used problem solving and other cognitive-behavioral instructional methods to help adolescents with mild disabilities solve social problems in employment situations. Problem solving in the Park and Gaylord-Ross (1989) study also assisted youth in generalization of the appropriate behavioral responses to difficult social situations on the job.

Self-control and self-monitoring training.   These procedures help the learner understand the antecedents and consequences of his or her behavior and teach him or her how to self-assess behavior. In the behavioral literature the combined effects of self-control and self-monitoring procedures attempt to have the learner react appropriately to the self-measurement of behavior. The student counts or measures his or her behavioral responses, is therefore more aware of such behaviors, and thus reduces the frequency or intensity of inappropriate social interactions or increases the frequency of prosocial actions. Self-monitoring, along with other cognitive-behavioral techniques, was used successfully to teach adolescents with behavior disorders how to respond correctly to critical feedback in the Warrenfeltz et al. study (1981).

In addition to the cognitive-behavioral procedures in the teaching of social skills for success in employment, other approaches can be found in Stowitschek and Salzberg (1987). In light of research that has demonstrated the job-related social problems of adolescents with mild disabilities, secondary-level teachers can no longer ignore such an important area of instruction. To overlook the social domain of students with mild disabilities is, in the minds of some (e.g., Sabornie et al., 1990), analogous to educational neglect. No conscientious teacher would ever want to be accused of being neglectful of his or her students' needs.

Teaching Social Skills in Regular Classrooms

Special and regular education teachers collaborating in separate classrooms or in the same classroom can do much to enhance the social skills acquisition of adolescents with mild disabilities. They need to communicate effectively with each other so that social skills instruction can be reviewed, reinforced, and retaught (if necessary) in both placement options. Maintenance and generalization of important social skills will also be enhanced if more than one teacher is involved in providing instruction in more than one setting. Given the content coverage responsibilities of regular education teachers at the secondary level, we feel the reality of the situation is that *most* social skill instruction will occur in special education placements. Regular education teach-ers, however, can and should infuse social skill demonstration opportunities into con-tent area instruction (Friend & Bursuck, 1996). Special education teachers need to make regular education teachers aware of the social skills needs of students with mild disabilities, and regular educators should plan for opportunities when students can demonstrate prosocial behavior while they observe, give feedback and correction, and, of course, reinforcement.

Walker et al. (1995) provided additional instructional steps that regular educators should consider for adoption when social skill instruction is needed by adolescents with mild disabilities. These suggestions include:

- *Specify expected behaviors.*   If regular class instructors want adolescents to engage in specific prosocial behaviors while in class, they need to make their expecta-tions known to all present. At the secondary level, the social behaviors expected by teachers are typically those that support academic instruction such as following direc-tions, cooperating with peers and the teacher, and being prepared for class activities.

- *Prompt expected behavior.*   Opportunities to prompt target students' appropri-ate social behaviors should occur often if regular class teachers expect positive growth to occur. Students acquiring new interpersonal skills should be reminded of when and where new behaviors are to be shown (e.g., "This would be a good time to ask if you could borrow Elizabeth's science notes"). Walker et al. (1995) also recommend that reg-ular class teachers remind students of expected behaviors when providing advance orga-nizers for lesson activities.

- *Provide skill practice times and procedures.*   Regular class teachers, as men-tioned previously, need to provide regularly scheduled opportunities for social skill demonstration so that mastery and generalization can occur. Role-plays and simulated social interactions at regular intervals serve this purpose, but students also need to be aware of the timing and rationale of such activities.

- *Identify and provide contingencies.*   Effective teachers "catch" students behaving appropriately and provide positive reinforcement for doing so. This is especially important in the social domain, because positive social interchanges are often taken for granted by teachers. Teachers should inform target students that when a specific social skill is demonstrated, a specific reinforcement will follow. Verbal praise and access to desired privileges are typical reinforcers in secondary-level classrooms, and teachers should not hesitate to use them when target students have displayed desired social responses. Vicarious reinforcement (i.e., reinforcing students behaving appropriately while ignoring a student who is near and engaged in inappropriate social behavior) is also an effective correction procedure when shaping the behavior of a student in need of additional social skills.

Finally, students' social skill demonstration in inclusive classrooms should be moni-tored and measured so that progress toward goals and objectives can be judged. This need not entail a cumbersome evaluation system but simply some type of counting procedure whereby the number of times a certain behavior occurs, in what context, and with whom can be documented. Skilled teachers could also use the evaluation system to inform target students of progress made toward expected behavioral standards.

Important Considerations in the Teaching of Social Skills

It is necessary to understand some of the issues that surround social skill instruction and how the teaching of social skills fits into a comprehensive secondary-school curriculum for adolescents with mild disabilities. From a school administrative standpoint, it is likely that few principals will be completely supportive of the teaching of social skills to adolescents with mild disabilities (Wells, 1987). Unless a school principal has an extensive background in special education, he or she will not be aware of the social problems that adolescents with mild disabilities face in many different environments. A teacher, therefore, may have to "sell" the need for social skills training to administrators in charge of instruction at the local school level. Ideally, much of the secondary-level social skill (and other) training should take place in community environments, so teachers will be pressured to convince administrators of the need to leave the school grounds for instruction. In addition, travel and logistical issues need to be addressed from insurance and liability perspectives (see Chapter 11).

Another group that may need to understand the rationale for teaching social skills to secondary-level students with mild disabilities are the parents and guardians of the adolescents. Because the teaching of social skills does not fit into the traditional Three Rs that students should receive in school, some parents may balk at the time spent in the teaching of prosocial behaviors. The authors have interacted with parents who did not want anything on their adolescents' IEP except traditional courses offered in secondary schools, preferably in an inclusive classroom. A teacher of adolescents with mild disabilities is faced with quite a dilemma when he or she knows that a student could benefit from learning additional social skills, but the student's parents see no need for such intervention. Parents have the final authority in such matters, so secondary-level teachers must respect their wishes—even though it may not be in the student's best educational and long-term interest.

Methodological issues involved in social skill instruction also need to be mentioned here. Social behavior rarely, if ever, stands alone; it melds into the behaviors required for language, school, work, and play (Stowitschek & Salzberg, 1987). A teacher then has to decide which related area should take precedence—social skills for language or some other domain? Moreover, much academic content instruction can be presented in a logical and task analyzed sequence, but no such analogous order exists with social skill training. The secondary-level teacher is thus faced with selecting which social skills should be taught first, second, and so on, without knowing a preferred sequence.

Another decision teachers have to make in instruction of social skills at the secondary level is related to the curriculum. Should a teacher choose a packaged curriculum, with a set number of social skills to teach, even though some students may not need instruction in all the skills included in the program? Or is it better to choose certain skills for students to learn and teach them, using Sargent's (1991) recommended six instructional steps? Both instructional choices have their respective strengths and weaknesses. A skilled teacher's best judgment should lead to the correct answer while keeping in mind the suggestions of Walker et al. (1995), presented in Figure 9.5.

Teachers involved in social skill training must also be concerned with students' generalization of learned prosocial behaviors. Without a specific plan for promoting adolescents' social skills generalization, especially in inclusive classes and outside the school environment where they are perhaps needed most, teaching efforts may not be very reinforcing for educators involved in such instruction. Walker et al. (1995) provide some excellent tips for teachers who seek generalization and maintenance of students' social skills. These suggestions include (a) trying to teach social skills that will be supported in a variety of settings; (b) involving the student in determining the skills in which he or she seems weak, then setting goals with the adolescent for those skills to be displayed when necessary; (c) being careful to observe teachable moments when students interact

Figure 9.5
Cardinal rules for conducting social skills training

- Social skills should be taught as *academic* subject matter content using instructional procedures identical to those for teaching basic academic skills (e.g., reading, language, mathematics).
- Whenever possible, social skills should be directly taught along with possible variations in their appropriate application.
- The critical test of the efficacy of social skills training is the functional integration of newly taught skills into one's behavioral repertoire and their demonstration/application within *natural* settings.
- The social context and situational factors both mediate the use of social skills and must be taken into account systematically in facilitating students' use of them.
- Social skills training procedures are not an effective intervention for complex behavior disorders or problems. They represent only a partial solution and should not be used by themselves to remediate aggressive or disruptive behavior patterns.
- Social skills training can be an important complement to the use of behavioral reduction techniques in that it teaches adaptive alternatives to maladaptive or problematic behavior.
- The instructional acquisition of social skills does not guarantee either their application or topographic proficiency within applied settings.
- There is considerable inertia operating against the behavioral integration of newly taught social skills into one's ongoing behavioral repertoire, as is the case with any newly acquired skill.
- To be effective, social skills instruction must be accompanied by the provision of response opportunities, feedback, and incentive systems within natural settings to provide for their actual demonstration and mastery.
- Social validation of social skills by target consumer groups is a critical step in both the selection and training of social skills.
- There are two types of deficits in social-behavioral adjustment: skill deficits (can't do) and performance deficits (won't do). These deficits should be assessed and treated differently as they require different forms of intervention for effective remediation.

Source: From *Antisocial Behavior in School: Strategies for Practitioners* by H. M. Walker, J. Colvin, and E. Ramsey. Copyright © 1995 Brooks/Cole Publishing Company, Pacific Grove, CA 93950, a division of International Thomson Publishing Inc. By permission of the publisher.

and should or should not be engaged in specific social responses; (d) teaching a variety of universal responses that are appropriate in many settings; (e) teaching social skills in different settings (particularly in the community) with many people involved in the training; (f) fading consequences so that students begin to internalize the motivation for performing the specific skills; and (g) attempting to teach adolescents self-regulatory and self-management techniques and reinforcing them for doing so. Stokes and Osnes (1986) also provided suggestions for enhancing the generalization of learned social skills; they are presented in Figure 9.6. Teachers of secondary students with mild disabilities are encouraged to consider these suggestions and apply them whenever possible. Finally, another good resource for social skills instructional pointers related to generalization is Alberg, Petry, and Eller (1994).

Figure 9.6
Planning for generalization of social skills

I.   Take advantage of natural environment for reinforcement

   A. Teach relevant behaviors (i.e., those that are functional in a variety of settings).

   B. Modify environments supporting maladaptive behaviors.

   C. Recruit "natural communities" of reinforcement (i.e., teach child to ask for reinforcement when deserved).

II.   Train diversely

   A. Use sufficient examples (i.e., vary ways of teaching the same response or behavior).

   B. Use sufficient response examples (i.e., teach various appropriate ways of responding to the same situation).

   C. Train loosely (using antecedents that are similar to real-life situations).

   D. Use undiscriminable contingencies that are hard to separate from the naturally occurring state.

   E. Reinforce *unprompted* generalization.

III. Incorporate functional mediators

   A. Use common physical stimuli that are not contrived.

   B. Use common social stimuli (i.e., teach students to discriminate certain people with specific social behaviors).

   C. Use self-mediated stimuli (use language to train students to remind themselves of appropriate social responses).

Source: Adapted from "Programming the Generalization of Children's Social Behavior" by T. Stokes and P. Osnes (1986). In P. Strain, M. Guralnick, and H. M. Walker (Eds.), *Children's Social behavior: Development, Assessment, and Modification* (pp. 407–443), New York: Plenum.

Summary

Social skills assessment and training are interrelated in that intervention should not exist without systematic assessment to determine instructional effectiveness. Sociometric measurement, teacher ratings, and behavioral observation should serve as the basis for judging specific outcomes of social skill training regimens. With consistent assessment of changes (or lack thereof) in target students' prosocial behaviors, teachers can use such data to decide which skills need more emphasis, reteaching, or no therapeutic concentration. Furthermore, sociometric research has documented that not all students with mild disabilities are equally deficient in social standing in mainstream classes (Sabornie & Kauffman, 1986; Sabornie et al., 1990). Concentrating on only those students who are truly in need of social skills training, determined through assessment, is likely to make a teacher's job somewhat easier.

Ideally, social skills intervention should include many qualified trainers in different educational settings (i.e., special and regular classes) to help ensure program success. Moreover, without attention to generalization of learned prosocial skills, much of the effort to change adolescents' behavior will be lost. The teaching of appropriate social response repertoires should not be considered a short-term endeavor; follow-up checks and programming for skill maintenance are also necessary components. Improving the social skills of youth who are lacking in this area should become part of a systematic daily instructional regimen, rather than an informal or unstructured activity. Teachers must view social skills training as a basic necessity—not as a burden—in working with many adolescents with mild disabilities.

Key Terms

performance deficits

social skill deficits

behavioral excesses

social competence

social skills

peer acceptance definition of social skills

behavioral definition of social skills

social validity definition of social skills

sociometry

References

Ager, C., & Cole, C. (1991). A review of cognitive-behavioral interventions for children and adolescents with behavioral disorders. *Behavioral Disorders, 16,* 276–287.

Alberg, J., Petry, C., & Eller, A. (1994). *A resource guide for social skills instruction.* Longmont, CO: Sporis West.

Asher, S. R. (1985). An evolving paradigm in social skill training research with children. In B. H. Schneider, K. H. Rubin, & J. E. Ledingham (Eds.), *Children's peer relations: Issues in assessment and intervention* (pp. 157–171). New York: Springer-Verlag.

Asher, S. R., & Taylor, A. R. (1981). Social outcomes of mainstreaming: Sociometric assessment and beyond. *Exceptional Education Quarterly, 1*(4), 13–30.

Baldwin, W. K. (1958). The educable mentally retarded child in the regular grades. *Exceptional Children, 25,* 106–108.

Bruininks, V. L. (1978). Peer status and personality characteristics of learning disabled students. *Journal of Learning Disabilities, 11,* 484–489.

Bruininks, R. H., Rynders, J. E., & Gross, J. C. (1974). Social acceptance of mildly retarded pupils in resource rooms and regular classes. *American Journal of Mental Deficiency, 78,* 377–383.

Bryan, T. (1974). Peer popularity of learning disabled children. *Journal of Learning Disabilities, 7,* 621–625.

Bryan, T. (1976). Peer popularity of learning disabled children: A replication. *Journal of Learning Disabilities, 9,* 307–311.

Bryan, T. (1977). Learning disabled children's comprehension of nonverbal communication. *Journal of Learning Disabilities, 10,* 501–506.

Bryan, T., & Bryan, J. H. (1978). Social interactions of learning disabled children. *Learning Disability Quarterly, 1,* 35–38.

Campbell, P., Hensel, J. W., Hudson, P., Schwartz, S. E., & Sealander, K. (1987). The successfully employed worker with a handicap: Employee/employer perceptions of job performance. *Career Development for Exceptional Individuals, 10,* 85–93.

Cartledge, G., & Milburn, J. F. (1986). *Teaching social skills to children* (2nd ed.). New York: Pergamon.

Coben, S. C., & Zigmond, N. (1986). The social integration of learning disabled students from self-contained to mainstream elementary school settings. *Journal of Learning Disabilities, 19,* 614–618.

Coie, J. D. (1985). Fitting social skills intervention to the target group. In B. H. Schneider, K. H. Rubin, & J. E. Ledingham (Eds.), *Children's peer relations: Issues in assessment and intervention* (pp. 141–156). New York: Springer-Verlag.

Coie, J. D., Dodge, K. A., & Coppotelli, H. (1982). Dimensions and types of social status: A cross-age perspective. *Developmental Psychology, 18,* 557–570.

Combs, M. S., & Slaby, D. A. (1977). Social skills training with children. In B. B. Lahey & A. E. Kazdin (Eds.), *Advances in child clinical psychology* (Vol. 1, pp. 111–203). New York: Plenum.

Connolly, J., & Doyle, A. (1981). Assessment of social competence in preschoolers: Teachers versus peers. *Developmental Psychology, 17,* 454–462.

Deshler, D. D., & Schumaker, J. B. (1983). Social skills of learning disabled adolescents: Characteristics and intervention. *Topics in Learning and Learning Disabilities, 3*(2), 15–23.

Dodge, K. A., Coie, J. D., & Brakke, N. P. (1982). Behavior patterns of socially rejected and neglected preadolescents: The roles of social approach and aggression. *Journal of Abnormal Child Psychology, 10,* 389–410.

Fordyce, W. G., Yauck, W. A., & Raths, L. (1946). *A manual for the Ohio guidance tests for the elementary grades.* Columbus: Ohio State Department of Education.

Foss, G., Auty, W. P., & Irvin, L. K. (1989). A comparative evaluation of modeling, problem-solving, and behavioral rehearsal for teaching employment-related interpersonal skills to secondary students with mental retardation. *Education and Training in Mental Retardation, 24,* 17–27.

Foster, S. L., & Ritchey, W. L. (1979). Issues in the assessment of social competence in children. *Journal of Applied Behavior Analysis, 12,* 625–638.

Friend, M., & Bursuck, W. (1996). *Including students with special needs: A practical guide for classroom teachers.* Boston: Allyn & Bacon.

Goldstein, A. P., Sprafkin, R. P., Gershaw, N. J., & Klein, P. (1980). *Skillstreaming the adolescent.* Champaign, IL: Research Press.

Gottlieb, J., & Budoff, M. (1973). Social acceptability of retarded children in nongraded schools differing in architecture. *American Journal of Mental Deficiency, 78,* 15–19.

Gottman, J. M., Gonso, J., & Rasmussen, B. (1975). Social interaction, social competence, and friendship in children. *Child Development, 46,* 709–718.

Greenwood, C. R., Walker, H. M., Todd, N. M., & Hops, H. (1979). Selecting a cost-effective screening device for the assessment of preschool social withdrawal. *Journal of Applied Behavior Analysis, 12,* 639–652.

Gresham, F. M. (1981). Social skills training with handicapped children: A review. *Review of Educational Research, 51,* 139–176.

Gresham, F. M. (1982). Misguided mainstreaming: The case for social skills training with handicapped children. *Exceptional Children, 48,* 422–433.

Gresham, F. M. (1986). Conceptual and definitional issues in the assessment of children's social skills: Implication for classification and training. *Journal of Clinical Child Psychology, 15,* 3–15.

Gresham, F. M. (1988). Social skills: Conceptual and applied aspects of assessment, training, and social validation. In J. C. Witt, S. N. Elliott, & F. M. Gresham (Eds.), *Handbook of behavioral therapy in education* (pp. 523–546). New York: Plenum.

Gresham, F. M., & Elliott, S. N. (1984). Advances in the assessment of children's social skills. *School Psychology Review, 13,* 292–301.

Gresham, F. M., & Elliott, S. N. (1989). Social skills assessment technology for LD students. *Learning Disability Quarterly, 12,* 141–152.

Gresham, F. M., & Elliott, S. N. (1990). *Social skills rating system.* Circle Pines, MN: American Guidance Service.

Gresham, F. M., Elliott, S. N., & Black, F. L. (1987). Teacher-rated social skill of mainstreamed mildly disabled and nondisabled children. *School Psychology Review, 16,* 78–88.

Gresham, F. M., & Reschly, D. J. (1986). Social skill and low peer acceptance of mainstreamed learning disabled children. *Learning Disability Quarterly, 9,* 23–32.

Hartup, W. W., Glazer, J. A., & Charlesworth, R. (1967). Peer reinforcement and sociometric status. *Child Development, 38,* 1017–1024.

Havyren, M., & Hymel, S. (1983). Ethical issues in sociometric testing: The impact of sociometric measures on interactive behavior. *Developmental Psychology, 20,* 844–849.

Hazel, J. S., Schumaker, J. B., Sherman, J. A., & Sheldon-Wildgen, J. (1981a). *ASSET: A social skills program for adolescents.* Champaign, IL: Research Press.

Hazel, J. S., Schumaker, J. B., Sherman, J. A., & Sheldon-Wildgen, J. (1981b). The development and evaluation of a group skills training program for court-adjudicated youth. In D. Upper & S. Ross (Eds.), *Behavioral group therapy: An annual review* (pp. 113–152). Champaign, IL: Research Press.

Hazel, J. S., Schumaker, J. B., Sherman, J. A., & Sheldon-Wildgen, J. (1982). Application of a group training program in social skills and problem solving to learning disabled and non-learning disabled youth. *Learning Disability Quarterly, 5,* 398–408.

Hoffman, F. J., Sheldon, K. L., Minskoff, E. H., Sautter, S. W., Steidle, E. F., Baker, D. P., Bailey, M. B., & Echols, L. D. (1987). Needs of learning disabled adults. *Journal of Learning Disabilities, 20,* 43–53.

Hollinger, J. (1987). Social skills for behaviorally disordered children as preparation for mainstreaming: Theory, practice, and new directions. *Remedial and Special Education, 8*(4), 17–27.

Hops, H., & Lewin, L. (1984). Peer sociometric forms. In T. H. Ollendick & M. Hersen (Eds.), *Child behavioral assessment: Principles and procedures* (pp. 124–147). New York: Pergamon.

Hutton, J. B., & Polo, L. (1976). A sociometric study of learning disability children and type of teaching strategy. *Group Psychology and Psychodrama, 29,* 113–120.

Iano, R. P., Ayers, D., Heller, H. B., McGettigan, J. F., & Walker, V. S. (1974). Sociometric status of retarded children in an integrative program. *Exceptional Children, 40,* 267–271.

Johnson, G. O. (1950). A study of the social position of mentally disabled children in the regular grades. *American Journal of Mental Deficiency, 55,* 60–89.

Kistner, J. A., & Gatlin, D. (1989). Correlates of peer rejection among children with learning disabilities. *Learning Disability Quarterly, 12,* 133–140.

Kronick, D. (1978). An examination of psychosocial aspects of learning disabled adolescents. *Learning Disability Quarterly, 1,* 86–93.

Lapp, E. R. (1957). A study of the social adjustment of slow learning children who were assigned part-time to regular classes. *American Journal of Mental Deficiency, 62,* 254–262.

Libet, J. M., & Lewinsohn, P. M. (1973). Concept of social skills with special reference to the behavior of depressed persons. *Journal of Consulting and Clinical Psychology, 40,* 304–312.

Luftig, R. L. (1988). Assessment of the perceived school loneliness and isolation of mentally retarded and nonretarded students. *American Journal of Mental Retardation, 92,* 472–475.

Macro Systems. (1989). *Social skills on the job.* Circle Pines, MN: American Guidance Service.

McConnell, S., & Odom, S. L. (1986). Sociometrics: Peer referenced measures and the assessment of social competence. In P. Strain, M. Guralnick, & H. M. Walker (Eds.), *Children's social behavior: Development, assessment, and modification* (pp. 215–284). Orlando, FL: Academic Press.

McFall, R. M. (1982). A review and reformulation of the concept of social skills. *Behavioral Assessment, 4,* 1–33.

Monroe, J. D., & Howe, C. E. (1971). The effects of integration and social class on the acceptance of retarded adolescents. *Education and Training of the Mentally Retarded, 6,* 20–24.

Montague, M. (1988). Job-related social skills training for adolescents with handicaps. *Career Development for Exceptional Individuals, 11,* 26–41.

Neubert, D. A., Tilson, G. P., & Ianacone, R. N. (1989). Postsecondary transition needs and employment patterns of individuals with mild disabilities. *Exceptional Children, 55,* 494–500.

Park, H. S., & Gaylord-Ross, R. (1989). A problem solving approach to social skills training in employment settings with mentally retarded youth. *Journal of Applied Behavior Analysis, 22,* 373–380.

Parker, J. G., & Asher, S. R. (1987). Peer relations and later personal adjustment: Are low-accepted children at risk? *Psychological Bulletin, 102,* 357–389.

Peery, J. C. (1979). Popular, amiable, isolated, rejected: A reconceptualization of sociometric status in preschool children. *Child Development, 50,* 1231–1234.

Perlmutter, B. (1986). Personality variables and peer relations of children and adolescents with learning disabilities. In S. J. Ceci (Ed.), *Handbook of cognitive, social and neuropsychological aspects of learning disabilities* (Vol. 1, pp. 339–359). Hillsdale, NJ: Erlbaum.

Prillaman, D. (1981). Acceptance of learning disabled students in a mainstream environment: A failure to replicate. *Journal of Learning Disabilities, 14,* 344–352.

Puttalaz, M., & Gottman, J. M. (1983). Social relationship problems in children: An approach to intervention. In B. B. Lahey & A. E. Kazdin (Eds), *Advances in clinical child psychology* (Vol. 6, pp. 1–39). New York: Plenum.

Roessler, R. T., & Johnson, V. A. (1987). Developing job maintenance skills in learning disabled youth. *Journal of Learning Disabilities, 20,* 428–432.

Rucker, C. N., Howe, C. E., & Snider, B. (1969). Participation of retarded children in junior high academic and nonacademic regular classes. *Exceptional Children, 35,* 679–680.

Rusch, F. R., Destefano, L., Chadsey-Rusch, J., Phelps, L. A., & Szymanski, E. (Eds.). (1992). *Transition from school to adult life: Models, linkages, and policy.* Pacific Grove, CA: Brooks/Cole.

Sabornie, E. J. (1985). Social mainstreaming of handicapped students: Facing an unpleasant reality. *Remedial and Special Education, 6*(2), 12–16.

Sabornie, E. J. (1987). Bi-directional social status of behaviorally disordered and nonhandicapped elementary school pupils. *Behavioral Disorders, 13,* 47–57.

Sabornie, E. J. (1991). Measuring and teaching social skills in the mainstream. In G. Stoner, M. Shinn, & H. M. Walker (Eds.), *Interventions for academic and behavior problems* (pp. 161–177). Silver Spring, MD: National Association of School Psychologists.

Sabornie, E. J., & Ellis, E. S. (1987). Sociometry for teachers of behaviorally disordered students. In R. B. Rutherford, C. M. Nelson, & S. R. Forness (Eds.), *Severe behavior disorders of children and youth* (pp. 28–40). San Diego: College-Hill.

Sabornie, E. J., & Kauffman, J. M. (1985). Regular classroom sociometric status of behaviorally disordered students. *Behavioral Disorders, 10,* 268–274.

Sabornie, E. J., & Kauffman, J. M. (1986). Social acceptance of learning disabled adolescents. *Learning Disability Quarterly, 9,* 55–60.

Sabornie, E. J., & Kauffman, J. M. (1987). Assigned, received, and reciprocal social status of adolescents with and without mild mental retardation. *Education and Training in Mental Retardation, 22,* 139–149.

Sabornie, E. J., Kauffman, J. M., & Cullinan, D. A. (1990). Extended sociometric status of adolescents with mild disabilities: A cross-categorical perspective. *Exceptionality, 1,* 197–209.

Sabornie, E. J., Kauffman, J. M., Ellis, E. S., Marshall, K. J., & Elksnin, L. K. (1987–1988). Bi-directional and cross-categorical social status of LD, BD, and nondisabled adolescents. *The Journal of Special Education, 21*(4), 39–56.

Sabornie, E. J., Marshall, K. J., & Ellis, E. S. (1988). Behaviorally disordered, learning disabled, and nonhandicapped students' social status in mainstream classes. *Monograph in Severe Behavioral Disorders of Children and Youth, 11,* 32–45.

Sabornie, E. J., Marshall, K. J., & Ellis, E. S. (1990). Restructuring of mainstream sociometry with learning disabled and nondisabled students. *Exceptional Children, 56,* 314–323.

Sabornie, E. J., & Thomas, V. (1989). *Social/affective adjustment of mildly disabled and nondisabled early adolescents.* Paper presented at the annual meeting of the American Educational Research Association, San Francisco, CA.

Sabornie, E. J., Thomas, V., & Coffman, R. M. (1989). Assessment of social/affective measures to discriminate between BD and non-disabled early adolescents. *Monograph in Behavior Disorders: Severe Behavior Disorders of Children and Youth, 12,* 21–32.

Salzberg, C. L., Lignugaris/Kraft, B., & McCuller, G. L. (1988). Reasons for job loss: A review of employment termination studies of mentally retarded workers. *Research in Developmental Disabilities, 9,* 153–170.

Sargent, L. R. (1991). *Social skills for school and community.* Reston, VA: The Division on Mental Retardation of the Council for Exceptional Children.

Schloss, P. J., Schloss, C. N., Wood, C. E., & Kiehl, W. S. (1986). A critical review of social skills research with behaviorally disordered students. *Behavioral Disorders, 12,* 1–14.

Schumaker, J. B., & Hazel, J. S. (1984a). Social skills assessment and training for the learning disabled: Who's on first and what's on second? Part I. *Journal of Learning Disabilities, 17,* 422–431.

Schumaker, J. B., & Hazel, J. S. (1984b). Social skills assessment and training for the learning disabled: Who's on first and what's on second? Part II. *Journal of Learning Disabilities, 17,* 492–499.

Schumaker, J. B., Hazel, J. S., & Pederson, C. S. (1988). *Social skills for daily living.* Circle Pines, MN: American Guidance Service.

Schumaker, J. B., Pederson, C. S., Hazel, J. S., & Meyen, E. L. (1983). Social skills curricula for mildly handicapped adolescents: A review. *Focus on Exceptional Children, 16*(4), 1–16.

Scranton, T., & Ryckman, D. (1979). Sociometric status of learning disabled children in an integrative program. *Journal of Learning Disabilities, 12,* 49–54.

Siperstein, G. N., Bopp, M. J., & Bak, J. J. (1978). Social status of learning disabled children. *Journal of Learning Disabilities, 11,* 49–53.

Stephens, T. M. (1978). *Social skills in the classroom.* Columbus, OH: Cedars Press.

Stephens, T. M. (1981). *Social Behavior Assessment.* Columbus, OH: Cedars Press.

Stokes, T., & Osnes, P. (1986). Programming the generalization of children's social behavior. In P. Strain, M. Guralnick, & H. M. Walker (Eds.), *Children's social behavior: Development, assessment, and modification* (pp. 407–443). Orlando, FL: Academic Press.

Stone, W. L., & La Greca, A. M. (1990). The social status of children with learning disabilities: A reexamination. *Journal of Learning Disabilities, 23,* 32–37.

Stowitschek, J. J., & Salzberg, C. L. (1987). *Job success for handicapped youth: A social protocol curriculum.* Reston, VA: The Council for Exceptional Children.

Strain, P. S., Odom, S. L., & McConnell, S. (1984). Promoting social reciprocity of exceptional children: Identification, target behavior selection, and intervention. *Remedial and Special Education, 5*(1), 21–28.

Test, D. W., Farebrother, C., & Spooner, F. (1988). A comparison of the social interactions of workers with and without disabilities. *Journal of Employment Counseling, 25,* 122–131.

Van Reusen, A. K., Bos, C. S., Schumaker, J. B., & Deshler, D. D. (1994). *The self-advocacy strategy for educational and transition planning.* Lawrence, KS: Edge Enterprises.

Walker, H. M., Colvin, G., & Ramsey, E. (1995). *Antisocial behavior in school: Strategies for practitioners.* Belmont, CA: Brooks/Cole.

Walker, H. M., Greenwood, C. R., Hops, H., & Todd, N. M. (1979). Differential effects of reinforcing topographic components of social interaction. *Remedial and Special Education, 5*(1), 21–28.

Walker, H. M., Greenwood, C. R., Hops, H., & Todd, N. M. (1979). Differential effects of reinforcing topographic components of social interaction. *Behavior Modification, 3,* 291–321.

Walker, H. M., & McConnell, S. R. (1992). *The Walker-McConnell scale of social competence and school adjustment: A social skills rating scale for teachers* (secondary level ed.). Austin, TX: PRO-ED.

Walker, H. M., McConnell, S., Holmes, D., Todis, B., Walker, J., & Golden, N. (1983). *The Walker social skills curriculum: The ACCEPTS program.* Austin, TX: PRO-ED.

Walker, H. M., Todis, B., Holmes, D., & Horton, G. (1988). *The Walker social skills curriculum. The ACCESS program.* Austin, TX: PRO-ED.

Warger, C. L. (1990). *Can social skills for employment be taught?* (ERIC Clearinghouse on Handicapped and Gifted Children, Research and Resources on Special Education, Number 28, November). Reston, VA: Council for Exceptional Children.

Warrenfeltz, R. B., Kelly, W. J., Salzberg, C. L., Beegle, C. P., Levy, S. M., Adams, T. A., & Crouse, T. R. (1981). Social skills training of behaviorally disordered adolescents with self-monitoring to promote generalization to a vocational setting. *Behavioral Disorders, 7,* 18–27.

Wehman, P. (1992). *Life beyond the classroom: Transition strategies for young people with disabilities.* Baltimore, MD: Brookes.

Wells, R. L. (1987). Social validity of social skills for individuals with mild handicaps in transition from school to independent living. *Dissertation Abstracts International, 47,* 3399A.

Whang, P. L., Fawcett, S. B., & Mathews, R. M. (1984). Teaching job-related social skills to learning disabled adolescents. *Analysis and Intervention in Developmental Disabilities, 4,* 29–38.

White, W. J., Schumaker, J. B., Warner, M. M., Alley, G. R., & Deshler, D. D. (1980). *The current status of young adults identified as learning disabled during their school career* (Research Report No. 21). Lawrence: University of Kansas Institute for Research in Learning Disabilities.

Zaragoza, N., Vaughn, S., & McIntosh, R. (1991). Social skills interventions and children with behavior problems: A review. *Behavioral Disorders, 16,* 260–275.

Zetlin, A. G., & Murtaugh, M. (1988). Friendship patterns of mildly learning handicapped and non-handicapped high school students. *American Journal of Mental Retardation, 92,* 447–454.

10

Improving Adaptability of Adolescents with Mild Disabilities in Secondary Classrooms

Objectives

After reading this chapter, the reader should be able to:

1. discuss curricular issues surrounding the inclusion of students with mild disabilities in regular classrooms at the secondary level;

2. discuss minimum competency testing and secondary grading practices and their effect on students with mild disabilities at the secondary level;

3. describe several content enhancements appropriate for effective instruction at the secondary level;

4. identify several instructional strategies that help students with mild disabilities succeed with independent learning activities.

The purpose of this chapter is to discuss the recent trend of inclusion at the secondary level and its implications for students with mild disabilities. Ways to improve their general (i.e., not content-specific) coping strategies are discussed. Various issues and dilemmas (e.g., curriculum standards, grading practices, minimum competency testing procedures) concerning the teaching of adolescent students with mild disabilities in regular classrooms are also discussed. Several instructional strategies regular secondary teachers can implement in their classrooms are presented.

Issues and Dilemmas in Mainstream Secondary Classrooms

For more than a decade, the most prevalent service delivery model for secondary students with mild disabilities has been resource room pull-out (Ellett, 1993). The success of pull-out programs has always been dependent on the cooperation and interaction of regular educators and resource teachers (Lerner, 1993). More recently, the push has been to serve students with mild disabilities in the regular classroom with little or no pull-out services (e.g., a full-inclusion model). Current estimates are that approximately 70% to 75% of all special education students spend a substantial amount of school time in the general education setting (U.S. Department of Education, 1995; Ysseldyke & Algozzine, 1995). Thus, general education teachers have been given the responsibility to integrate into their regular classroom program effective instructional techniques for many mainstreamed students with disabilities.

In today's secondary programs, general education teachers are overwhelmed with their regular content-specific teaching responsibilities, which often leave them little time and little inclination to deal with the educational demands of students with disabilities. However, given the increased diversity of student achievement within regular classrooms, adapting instruction or modifying it has become imperative. For example, Jenkins, Jewell, Leceister, Jenkins, and Troutner (1990) reported that today's typical general education classroom includes students with skills at an average of 5.4 different grade equivalents. Thus, educating adolescent students with disabilities and those at risk in the regular classroom has become particularly difficult because of the discrepancy between students' performance levels and the curriculum demands in the content classes (Schumaker & Deshler, 1984).

There are also significant differences between elementary regular classroom instruction and secondary content-class instruction. The program organization, program content, and student characteristics increase the difficulties for content-area teachers, who frequently express a feeling of helplessness over their inability to identify alternative instructional strategies within their curriculum area to assist students with disabilities (Fuchs, Fuchs, & Bishop, 1992). It is often unclear to them what constitutes appropriate instructional practice for students with disabilities in their regular classrooms.

Curriculum Express Instruction

Adding to their frequent inability to identify alternative strategies, secondary content teachers feel compelled to teach at a rapid pace. Their lesson plans are frequently instruction-driven because of the quantity of content they are required to cover (Schumaker & Deshler, 1988). For teachers to provide successful experiences for students with mild disabilities (i.e., graduation from high school), many feel that they need, at the very least, more time to provide intensive instruction to these students at risk. Most states' year-end curriculum standards do not allow for more time or for a slow or remedial pace.

When all courses are viewed together, the prescribed number of core subjects and electives combined to establish minimum requirements for graduation in most states do not allow for creative instructional programming. Although policies for graduation vary from state to state and even from school to school, most, if not all, secondary teachers feel a great deal of pressure to meet the increased curricular standards of the school districts. To do so, they have increased the standards in their own classes, making it even more difficult for students with disabilities to experience success (Retish, Hitchings, Horvath, & Schmalle, 1991).

Standards for Graduation

The most recent call for excellence in education has caused many schools not only to increase the number of units required for graduation, but also to require that students pass **minimum competency tests** (Edgar, 1987). The minimum competency test (MCT) movement was initially a response to the public outcry for higher performance standards and teaching accountability (Haney & Madaus, 1978). Unfortunately, it appears that as a group, students with mild disabilities perform very poorly on MCTs (Gajar, Goodman, & McAfee, 1993). In fact, the MCT requirements present an insurmountable obstacle for many such students and may be contributing to the high rate of dropouts among them.

Recent and comprehensive figures indicate that approximately 40 states have enacted MCT programs (Education Commission of the States, 1985); however, there is much variability among the states. According to Vitello (1988), who organized state policies concerning MCT testing and students with disabilities, five different options may be offered:

1. students with disabilities can receive a high school diploma if they complete their individual educational program (IEP) requirements (21 states);

2. students with disabilities are required to pass an MCT in order to receive a high school diploma (8 states);

3. the decision as to the use of an MCT with students with disabilities is made at the local school level (5 states);

4. other tests are used with students with disabilities (1 state);

5. MCT policies are not yet finalized (5 states).

Students who do not receive a regular high school diploma are at a disadvantage after high school. If states require students to pass the minimum competency tests for promotion from one grade to the next or for graduation, students with disabilities are at a disadvantage. Many advocates for persons who are disabled have contended that modifications to the minimum competency tests be allowed to circumvent the impact of an individual's disability and to allow him or her to demonstrate a true level of skill (Gajar et al., 1993). A few examples of procedural modifications are modified testing procedures, environmental modifications, performance adjustments, and flexible pacing. See Figure 10.1 for other examples of test modifications. Grise, Beattie, and Algozzine (1982) and Scott (1983) demonstrated that simple modifications (e.g., different formats, additional examples) improved the performance of students with learning disabilities on minimum competency tests.

Figure 10.1
Examples of test modifications

> 1. Completion of subsections of the test that include 30–40 items at a time
>
> 2. Adding at least one example for each different set of items within any section of the test
>
> 3. Grouping items that measure similar skills together in progressive order of difficulty from easiest to hardest content
>
> 4. Placing answer options in a vertical format with flattened, horizontal elliptical oval for answer bubbles placed to the right
>
> 5. Using unjustified formats for reading comprehension passages and placing them in separate boxes set off from the sentences testing comprehension
>
> 6. Using continuation arrows and stop signs to organize the flow of items within the tests

Source: From "Assessment of Minimum Competency in Fifth Grade Learning Disabled Students" by P. Grise, S. Beattie, and B. Algozzine, 1982, *Journal of Educational Research, 76,* 40.

Grading Practices at the Secondary Level

Grades have been defined as arbitrary symbols that reflect a student's quality of work; the most basic use of grades is as a measure of performance. This concept and practice of grading students is an integral part of our educational system (Kiraly & Bedall, 1984). However, limited agreement exists within the educational community as to the most appropriate method of grading students (Rojewski, Pollard, & Meers, 1991), and grading practices for mainstreamed students with disabilities at the secondary level are especially controversial (Carpenter, Grantham, & Hardister, 1983). See Figure 10.2 for a list of common grading practices at the secondary level. "The grades received by students who are disabled can be seen as reflective of their limited ability, the standards maintained by classroom teachers, the types of grades given and their bases, the effectiveness of adaptations being used by general education teachers, or more likely, some combination of these factors" (Polloway et al., 1996, p. 138).

Warger (cited in Rojewski et al., 1991) found secondary teachers made relatively few *instructional* modifications; however, *grading* modifications were made frequently for students with mild disabilities. Many teachers used differential grading standards for students with mild disabilities; for example, teachers reported taking such students' effort, attitude, and attendance into greater consideration when issuing grades (Calhoun & Beattie, 1984; Carpenter & Grantham, 1985). Other studies have shown that despite mainstreamed students doing poorly on teacher-made tests in the regular classes and maybe failing to do homework, most passed their high school mainstream classes (e.g., Zigmond, Levine, & Laurie, 1985). Some consider such passing grades inflated.

Figure 10.2
Common grading practices at the secondary level for students with mild disabilities

Grades are based on a modified grading scale (e.g., from 93 to 100 = A, 90 to 100 = A)

Grades are based on meeting IEP objectives

Grades are based on meeting the requirements of academic or behavioral contracts

Grades are adjusted according to student ability

Separate grades are given for progress (e.g., effort) and product (e.g., tests)

Grades are based on amount of improvement an individual makes

Grading weights are adjusted (e.g., efforts on projects count more than tests)

Grades are based on less content than the rest of the class

Students are passed if they make an effort to pass

Students are passed no matter what

Source: From "Treatment Acceptability: Determining Appropriate Interventions Within Inclusive Classrooms" by E. A. Polloway, W. D. Bursuck, M. Jayanthi, M. H. Epstein, and J. S. Nelson, 1996, *Intervention in School and Clinic, 31,* 138. Copyright 1996 by PRO-ED, Inc. Reprinted by permission.

Some other researchers suggest that time spent in regular education corresponds to the likelihood of receiving a failing grade (Warger et al., 1991); that is, a student's chances of receiving a failing grade increase when more graded courses are taken, apart from the nature or placement of such courses (U.S. Department of Education, 1995). A national longitudinal study suggested that 11% of students with disabilities do not receive any grades in their secondary courses (Warger et al., 1991). The data suggested that receiving grades was strongly related to the nature and severity of students' disabilities. It may be that the students with disabilities who do receive grades are the cream of the crop of the total population of students with disabilities; that is, students with more severe disabilities or with lower functioning skills do not receive grades (U.S. Department of Education, 1995).

In many secondary schools, teachers do not have the option to employ other methods of reporting student progress. However, when possible, regular content-area teachers should determine ways to modify their measuring system for students with mild disabilities. In addition, if and when teachers choose such modifications they need to clearly indicate their procedures on students' reports.

Carpenter (1985) suggests using the following questions to guide grading decisions: (a) On what criteria are grades to be based? (b) How frequently are grades to be given? (c) What types of grades are to be used? (e.g., letter, pass-fail), and (d) Who will participate in the grading process? In addition, teachers may want to include written and oral supplemental information to reflect effort, attitude, or study skills habits. Schultz, Carpenter, and Turnbull (1991) suggest linking the grades to a criterion-referenced skill list so specific objectives can be checked as mastered or not. Henley, Ramsey, and Algozzine

(1996) suggest assigning grades with codes to indicate functioning level. For example, if a 7th-grade student earned an A in mathematics but his actual functioning level was 6th grade, A6 would appear on his report card.

Special and general educators should meet regularly to discuss students' progress, and whenever possible, they should engage in cooperative grading arrangements (Henley et al., 1996). Collaboration in terms of grading appears to be on the rise (Polloway et al., 1994).

Students with Mild Disabilities and the Curricular Demands of Secondary School

By definition, students with mild disabilities have academic deficits. Many enter high school with deficiencies in reading, written language, mathematics, and social and study skills (Deshler, Schumaker, Lenz, & Ellis, 1984). By the time they reach secondary school they not only lag behind their peers in basic skills, but also lack proficiency in higher-order skills (Schumaker & Deshler, 1988). Without the necessary prerequisite skills, they cannot master the rigorous high school curriculum.

Some schools have implemented a tracking system that allows students to choose the demanding academic track or a less demanding vocational track. Unfortunately, tracking allows for limited flexibility in course selection at the secondary level; some students with mild disabilities are not able to meet the postsecondary requirements for admission, even though they have the potential for college-level studies (McGuire, Norlander, & Shaw, 1990). By virtue of curricular decisions that are made early in a student's high school program, professionals and parents may unwittingly be limiting postsecondary options that could have far-reaching effects with respect to employability and quality of living.

An alternate approach to tracking a student into courses that do not meet graduation requirements or do not allow the student postsecondary options is to provide accommodations in the regular content-area instruction classes. These accommodations will likely increase academic success and allow the option of attending postsecondary institutions. The following sections discuss some modifications that have been shown to improve the adaptability and success in secondary school of students with mild disabilities.

Effective Content-Area Instruction

Secondary students are expected to read independently and to demonstrate competency in content areas such as science, history, and literature. These tasks may prove difficult for students with mild disabilities if they do not receive additional assistance from their content teachers (Hudson, Lignugaris-Kraft, & Miller, 1993). Deshler and Schumaker (1988) suggest that content-area teachers lessen the difficulty of the content-area tasks for students with mild disabilities by providing instruction that actively involves all students.

Hudson et al. (1993) suggest three components that comprise effective and efficient instruction in the content classroom: "the use of an instructional cycle, effective teaching practices, and content enhancement techniques" (p. 106). The instructional cycle refers to an effective sequence of planning, implementing, and evaluating instruction. Effective teaching, as Rosenshine and Stevens (1986) suggest, refers to a sequence of daily review and homework check, presentation of new material, guided practice, independent practice, and regular review of material learned. **Content enhancements** should also be used in conjunction with effective teaching practices during each phase of the instructional cycle. "Content enhancements are techniques used by the teacher to help students identify, organize, comprehend, and retain critical content information" (Lenz, Bulgren, & Hudson, 1990, p. 125).

One advantage of the use of content enhancements is that teachers can implement these strategies with a large, diverse group of students. Table 10.1 illustrates how such content enhancements can be utilized in an effective teaching instructional cycle. As is often the case in general content classrooms at the secondary level, the complexity and difficulty of individualized adaptations or modifications may be prohibitive to teachers, yet content enhancements can be utilized for all students. Hudson and colleagues (1993) suggested the following seven types of content enhancements (see also Figure 10.3):

1. advance organizers
2. visual displays
3. study guides
4. mnemonic devices
5. audio recordings
6. computer-assisted instruction
7. peer-mediated instruction

Table 10.1

Integration of content enhancements into an effective instructional cycle

		Instructional Cycle				
		Plan Instruction	Learning Set	Present New Material and Guided Practice	Independent Practice	Evaluate Student Progress
Content Enhancements	Advance Organizers		X			
	Visual Displays		X	X	X	X
	Study Guides		X	X	X	X
	Mnemonic Devices		X	X		
	Audio Recordings			X		
	Computer-assisted Instruction			X	X	X
	Peer-mediation				X	X

Source: From "Using Content Enhancements to Improve the Performance of Adolescents with Learning Disabilities in Content Classes" by P. Hudson, B. Lignugaris-Kraft, and T. Miller, 1993, *Learning Disabilities Research and Practice, 8,* 107.

Figure 10.3
List of content enhancements

- **advance organizers** that prepare students for the upcoming lesson
- **visual displays** that graphically depict the upcoming lesson
- **study guides** that are used to highlight critical content information
- **mnemonic devices** that help students remember content information
- **audio recordings** that help students acquire information
- **computer-assisted instruction** that provides students opportunities to practice new content independently
- **peer-mediated instruction** that provides opportunities for students to practice skills and build fluency with their peers

Source: From "Using Content Enhancements to Improve the Performance of Adolescents with Learning Disabilities in Content Classes" by P. Hudson, B. Lignugaris-Kraft, and T. Miller, 1993, *Learning Disabilities Research and Practice, 8,* 107.

Each of the noted content enhancements and one other technique, called survival skills training, are described in more detail in the following paragraphs.

Advance Organizers

Ausubel and Robinson (1969) introduced the concept of **advance organizers** as pre-instructional methods to enhance students' ability to gain information from lectures or textbooks. At the secondary level, advance organizers can be presented prior to the content-area lesson to assist all students in preparing for the upcoming lesson. As Lenz, Alley, and Schumaker (1987) suggested, advance organizers may be presented in many different forms (e.g., written, verbal, or question format) to elicit the information from the students. Darch and Gersten (1986) suggested that advance organizers be designed for specific instructional purposes. For some students with disabilities, the specificity may be more beneficial than less structured discussion-oriented advance organizers.

Teachers can orient students to new content by using advance organizers such as **anticipation guides** (Vaca, Vaca, & Grove, 1987), which might include a set of questions that the students answer and discuss prior to reading a chapter in the textbook. See Figure 10.4 for an example of an anticipation guide.

Examples of instructional advance organizers might be a list of vocabulary words written on the board, an oral discussion centered around specific questions and answers concerning the upcoming topic, or a set of preplanned verbal statements made by the teacher that elaborate background information needed to understand the upcoming topic. Advance organizers can generate students' motivation, enhance their previous background knowledge, and increase their performance on unit tests (Hudson et al., 1993).

Figure 10.4
Anticipation guide on energy resources

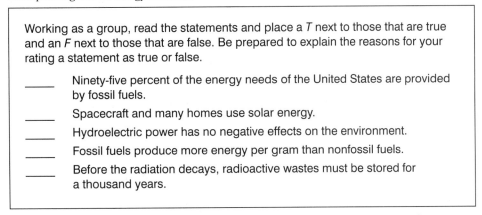

Working as a group, read the statements and place a *T* next to those that are true and an *F* next to those that are false. Be prepared to explain the reasons for your rating a statement as true or false.

_____ Ninety-five percent of the energy needs of the United States are provided by fossil fuels.

_____ Spacecraft and many homes use solar energy.

_____ Hydroelectric power has no negative effects on the environment.

_____ Fossil fuels produce more energy per gram than nonfossil fuels.

_____ Before the radiation decays, radioactive wastes must be stored for a thousand years.

Source: From *Effective Mainstreaming* (2nd ed.) (p. 406) by S. J. Salend, 1994, New York: Macmillan.

Visual Displays

Visual displays, which are "visual illustrations that portray the relationship between two or more pieces of information" (Hudson et al., 1993, p. 108), may be used in any part of the lesson, for example, in the presentation of new material, in guided practice, or in the independent practice phases of instruction (e.g., homework assignments). Visual displays, similar to advance organizers, assist students in organizing and highlighting critical information. Studies have shown that using visual displays in combination with effective teaching practices enhances content learning more than using visual displays in isolation of effective teaching routines (e.g., Horton, Lovitt, Givens, & Nelson, 1989).

A visual display may be a diagram or concrete model that requires labeling, a semantic mapping display that requires the depiction of relationships of ideas presented (e.g., Bulgren, Schumaker, & Deshler, 1988), or hierarchical boxes that require delineation of degrees of relationships of presented concepts. See Figure 10.5 for an example of a visual display.

Recently, visual displays have come to refer to the use of computer videos. The Cognition and Technology Group at Vanderbilt University (1990) conducted a series of studies that used visual displays on instructional computer videos to assist students' learning. "The 15–25 minute 'anchors' combined computer video and audio in a narrative format that posed a multi-step problem. The students must first identify pertinent information and then formulate strategies they expect will lead to its overall solution" (Bottge & Hasselbring, 1993, p. 557). Results of the studies using such an approach with adolescents with mild disabilities suggest that instruction using contextualized video anchors can help students notice critical features of a problem and then successfully find the solution (Bottge & Hasselbring, 1993).

Meaningful contexts combined with technological capabilities can be powerful motivational and instructional tools for enhancing the problem-solving skills of stu-

Figure 10.5
Visual display

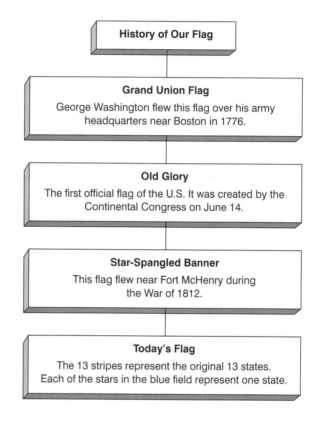

dents with disabilities. Video technology can free the teacher to perform other executive functions and provide high-quality instruction in the mode of curriculum presentation (Woodward & Gersten, 1992).

To assist students in gaining information from visual displays that are part of the textbook, Barry (cited in Ellis & Lenz, 1987) developed the **Reading Visual Aids Strategy (RVAS)**, which involves the following steps:

1. **R**—Read the written material until you are referred to a visual aid or until the material is not making sense.

2. **V**—View the visual aid, using **CLUE:**

   C—Clarify the stated facts in the written material

   L—Locate the main ideas and details

   U—Uncover the signal words

   E—Examine the logic

3. **A**—**A**sk yourself the relationship between the visual aid and the written material, using **FUR:**

    F—Ask how the visual aid and the written material **f**it together

    U—Ask how the visual aid can help you **u**nderstand the written material

    R—Ask how the visual aid can help you **r**emember the written material

4. **S**—**S**ummarize the most important material (Ellis & Lenz, 1987, p. 98).

Study Guides

A study guide is a set of statements or questions provided by the teacher that emphasizes important content information the student is required to understand. Study guides can be used to facilitate the presentation of new information or to review material during the guided practice phase of instruction. Initially, their use should be modeled and completed with teacher-directed practice. Study guides can highlight critical information for students; however, they will be of little use if students do not understand how to use them. Many students with disabilities may need teacher-guided instruction to enhance completion of their study guides.

Examples of study guides include outlines with incomplete sections, matching vocabulary words with definitions, questions that require written answers, or diagrams with missing parts. In comparison to self-study conditions, the use of study guides has been shown to improve performance of students with mild disabilities (Bergerud, Lovitt, & Horton, 1988).

Mnemonic Devices

Mnemonic devices are verbal or pictorial techniques used to facilitate students' recall of content-area information. Mnemonics can make unfamiliar or confusing material easier to remember (e.g., "*i* before *e* except after *c* or when sounded like *a* as in *neighbor* or *weigh*"). Nagel, Schumaker, and Deshler (1986) used the first letters of the five sensory organs to help the students remember their sense organs (**TEENS: T**ongue, **E**yes, **E**ars, **N**ose, **S**kin). Mnemonics can also help students remember a process to use in reviewing their written products (**COPS:** Have I **c**apitalized all proper nouns, etc.? Have I checked the **o**verall appearance of my paper? Have I used appropriate **p**unctuation? Have I checked my **s**pelling?) (Schumaker et al., 1981). The use of mnemonic devices provides students with a method to increase their ability to memorize the content-area information that often appears on tests. Mastropieri and Scruggs (1989) reported that, on the average, students who used mnemonic devices learned 75% of the information presented, compared to control students, who learned only 43.8% of the information. Scruggs and Mastropieri (1990) contended that "mnemonic instructional strategies have produced some of the largest, most consistently positive outcomes in special education intervention research" (p. 279).

Examples of mnemonic devices include key words (a picture of a familiar object that is phonetically similar to the unknown concept), pictures (picture of a globe to remind students of the continents), symbolic representations (a picture of Uncle Sam to represent the U.S.), first-letter mnemonics (COPS), or peg words (familiar words used to remind students of unknown words).

Audio Recordings

Listening to tape recordings can enhance students' learning at the secondary level; students who have difficulty reading independently can gather new content information through their use. Audio recordings can be used to present new information, to highlight key information, to serve as a study guide (e.g., use audio recordings together with a worksheet), to use as an advance organizer (e.g., present background information or provide instructions), or to assess students' knowledge.

Studies have shown that listening to audio recordings can improve students' test scores (e.g., Schumaker, Deshler, & Denton, 1984). Audio recordings are often used in the context of learning a second language, but not as frequently in other content-area instruction. Audiotapes may serve as yet another source of enhancement for students with disabilities.

Computer-Assisted Instruction

Computer-assisted instruction is instruction delivered to students with the use of computers. Computer literacy is becoming a must for all students, particularly at the secondary level. Computer-assisted instruction can be of several varieties: tutorial, simulations, or drill and practice. The difficulty for teachers is determining whether the instructions, the pace of the lessons, and the type of feedback provided by the computer program selected will be appropriate for students with mild disabilities. Many programs are available to teach students new content, but the directions may be too difficult to follow or the feedback provided may not be corrective. The program may not be designed to identify students' errors. Thus, many computer programs may be more effective when they are used during guided practice rather than as independent learning activities.

Peer-Mediated Instruction

Peer-mediated instructional strategies are procedures used in the classroom in which peers are used as instructional agents (Lloyd, Crowley, Kohler, & Strain, 1988). Peer tutoring may involve cross-age or same-age peer tutoring (i.e., classwide peer tutoring, or CWPT). Cross-age tutoring involves older students working with younger ones and classwide peer tutoring involves same-age students within the same class. Using CWPT (see Maheady, Harper, & Sacca, 1988), teachers randomly divide students into two groups and assign tutoring dyads within the groups. The members of the dyads take on one role (e.g., instructor or student) and after a set amount of time the roles are reversed.

Cooperative learning is another peer-mediated instructional strategy often used at the secondary level. In a cooperative learning situation, students work in small groups to solve an academic task (Lloyd et al., 1988). Teachers need to train the students to work in small groups and to take on different roles within the group. Cooperative learning techniques work well at the secondary level when the format provided is highly structured (Johnson & Johnson, 1986). Initially, teachers should use small groups of two or three students, increasing the size to no more than five when students become accustomed to cooperative learning (Johnson & Johnson, 1986).

Having students work together often increases the opportunities for more students to be actively engaged in instructional activities. The more actively involved students are in the learning process the more likely it is that they will retain the content provided. However, students may need to learn to work cooperatively. Cooperative learning strategies should be taught gradually, building on the students' experiences (Salend, 1994).

School Survival Skills

General survival skills can facilitate the success of students in the integrated mainstream class. Schaeffer, Zigmond, Kerr, and Heidi (1990) suggest that many students with mild disabilities fail in mainstream classes because of their lack of certain **survival skills,** which are often called "teacher-pleasing behaviors" because they result in positive interactions between students and teachers. Kerr, Nelson, and Lambert (1987) defined school survival skills as "those skills that enable students to meet the demands of the regular curriculum" (p. 86). Schaeffer et al. (1990) described six survival skills that many students with mild disabilities need to develop:

1. attending class;
2. arriving promptly;
3. going to class prepared;
4. meeting assignment deadlines;
5. talking to teachers appropriately;
6. reading and following directions.

Because many adolescents with mild disabilities may not be successful without these teacher-pleasing behaviors, teaching such skills should become a critical component of their secondary curriculum. Studies that compared the behavior and achievement of mainstreamed and regular high school students found that attendance and organizational skills related most strongly to achievement (Brown, Kerr, Zigmond, & Harris, 1984). See Figure 10.6 for an example of a class attendance lesson.

Having all the materials and equipment for class is another survival skill that presents problems to students with mild disabilities. Many secondary-school teachers inadvertently reinforce their students' poor habits by providing them with paper, pencils, and books instead of setting the expectation that students take the responsibility for their own preparedness. If necessary, teachers could "rent" materials to students.

Goal-setting and planning skills can be taught to adolescents with learning disabilities and can have a positive impact on task completion (Lenz, Ehren, & Smiley, 1991). Lenz et al. suggest that "goal attainment instruction applied to weekly, monthly, yearly,

Figure 10.6
Class attendance lesson

SCRIPT

Today I want to talk about *Attending Class Every Day* and *Getting to Class on Time.*

1. Q: Why do you think it's important to attend class every day?

    A: 1) so you don't miss assignments
        2) so you can learn what the teacher is teaching
        3) so you can have an easier time passing tests and getting good grades
        4) the teacher will view you as an interested student, as someone who tried to do well

    Q: Why do students miss classes?

    A: 1) they are sick
        2) they're not good in that subject so they skip that class
        3) they think it's not important to learn that subject
        4) they don't like the teacher

    Q: What can you do about these things?

    A: 1) If you are sick and miss a class, call a classmate to find out what you missed. Or next day, ask your teacher what you missed.
        2) If you're not good in a subject: GET HELP! Ask your teacher for help; work after school with a friend; ask your counselor to set up a tutor for you. Not coming to class won't change the fact that you need help in that class.
        3) Even if you think that the subject matter in a class isn't important, you know that it's much better to pass a class than to fail it. You can't pass if you don't attend.
        4) Nobody likes every single teacher. But if you don't go to class, and you fail, you are only hurting yourself.

---

or longer applications may be too abstract, whereas day-to-day goal-setting applications that students must face on classroom tasks may be a more appropriate forum for initial instruction" (p. 175). The concepts of homework and assignment completion have been found to be highly correlated with school success.

Students with mild disabilities are likely to experience difficulties with homework (Epstein, Polloway, Foley, & Patton, 1993), but there are many promising strategies secondary teachers can use to make homework more successful for them. Polloway et al. (1996) suggest the following instructional strategies to facilitate completion of homework:

1. *types of homework:* give assignments that practice skills already taught or allow for completion of unfinished classwork;

2. *teacher-directed activities:* get students started on assignments in class and establish clear expectations;

2. Q: Why is it important to get to class on time?

A:
1) so you won't miss things (announcements, assignments)
2) so you start off class "on the right foot"
3) so you won't disturb the class by coming in late
4) so the teacher won't have to repeat things
5) so you don't make the teacher angry
6) so you develop good habits
7) so your teacher will think you care about how you are doing in school

Q: Why are students late to class?

A:
1) they are talking to friends
2) they have to get things from their lockers
3) their next class is far away from the class they are leaving

Q: What can *you* do to make sure you get to your class on time?

A:
1) Don't have long conversations with friends between classes
2) Plan to take all materials you need for your classes with you so you don't have to stop at your locker. If you have a lot to carry, try to get a knapsack or canvas bag to carry them in.
3) If your classes are far apart, walk quickly. Don't make any stops.

Q: How much time do you have between classes?

A:
1) 5 minutes

That seems like very little time, but actually, it's a lot of time. Let me show you how long it is. (GET OUT STOPWATCH, GIVE TO 1 STUDENT, TELL OTHER STUDENTS TO SEE IF THEY CAN KEEP THEIR EYES CLOSED AND STAY PERFECTLY STILL FOR 1 MINUTE)

Source: From *Helping Adolescents with Learning and Behavior Problems* (p. 95) by M. M. Kerr, C. M. Nelson, and D. L. Lambert, 1987, Upper Saddle River, NJ: Merrill/Prentice Hall.

3. *consequences:* establish clear and specific guidelines for what happens when assignments are not completed;

4. *adaptations:* provide modifications such as adjusting the length of assignments, giving fewer assignments, or changing grade criteria when necessary; and

5. *communication with parents:* keep communication open by requiring parents' signatures or by calling parents when necessary.

Collaboration at the Secondary Level

Few special education teachers of adolescents with mild disabilities work alone (Knackendoffel, 1996). As Dettmer, Thurston, and Dyck (1993) suggest, education for such students is most effective when teachers pool their expertise and teach cooperatively. Cooperative teaching is integral at the secondary level (Knackendoffel, 1996).

Cooperative teaching (Bauwens, Hourcade, & Friend, 1989) is a process that involves problem solving, which teachers engage in when they identify students, place them in programs, and determine appropriate instructional interventions. In a cooperative teaching arrangement general and special educators teach students jointly in an educationally integrated setting. The educators have mutual ownership, joint accountability, and combined resources.

Knackendoffel (1996) describes three different cooperative teaching arrangements appropriate for the secondary level: (a) team teaching, (b) supplementary learning activities, and (c) complementary instruction. Determining which option is appropriate for your school situation will depend on the individual teachers' strengths and weaknesses and the composition of the students in the class.

Team teaching involves teachers both planning and teaching an academic subject to all students in the class. Each teacher may assume primary responsibility for specific types of instruction or portions of the curriculum. One may provide the advance organizer while the second provides the lecture. One can lecture while the other provides examples on the overhead to highlight key terms.

Using *supplemental learning activities* involves joint planning and teaching; however, the special education teacher may develop and implement supplemental activities. Such activities may include role-playing, simulations, partner readings, debates, and so forth. The general educator is responsible for the delivery of the content lecture.

Complementary instruction involves two teachers working together to deliver the content. The general educator is responsible for teaching the specific academic content; the special educator teaches critical cognitive strategies or study skills necessary for learning the content. For example, the general educator delivers a lecture on the Civil War and the special educator provides instruction on note-taking, outlining, or test-taking skills that will enable the students to benefit from the specific content instruction (see Chapter 8, on cognitive strategies and study skills). The special educator can provide his or her instruction in a separate setting or in the general education classroom.

Adolescents with mild disabilities are not taught by one educator. Successful programming at the secondary level involves several professionals working together. Teachers who have used a collaborative approach have reported inclusion of students with mild disabilities in the regular classroom to be successful (Nowacek, 1992).

Summary

Unfortunately, there is no single answer to what works best in improving the success of adolescent students with mild disabilities in regular content-area instruction classes because of the tremendous and growing diversity of students attending schools today. However, it is believed that early and effective interventions that assist students in actively identifying with school, both socially and academically, increase their success at the secondary level. It is also believed that students who are successful and graduate from high school have a distinct advantage as they enter the postschool phase of their lives (U.S. Department of Education, 1995).

This chapter provided an overview of many issues surrounding success for secondary students with mild disabilities. Several instructional modifications were discussed and described. Research suggests that it is not enough to provide teachers with effective instructional strategies to use with students with mild disabilities (Johnson & Pugach, 1990). Teachers' perceptions regarding the use of such strategies are also important; that is, teachers must accept such instructional modifications as the content enhancements in their content-area classes.

For the most part, such modifications are practical, easy to use, will not require significant changes in teachers' styles, and will benefit all their students. Teachers who have concern about developing enhancements should be encouraged to collaborate in the development of enhancements and to access current teaching guides for further suggestions (Hudson et al., 1993).

Key Terms

minimum competency tests
content enhancements
advance organizers

anticipation guides
Reading Visual Aids Strategy
survival skills

References

Ausubel, D. P., & Robinson, F. G. (1969). *School learning: An introduction to educational psychology*. New York: Holt, Rinehart & Winston.

Bauwens, J., Hourcade, J., & Friend, M. (1989). Cooperative teaching: A model for general and special education integration. *Remedial and Special Education, 10*(4), 19–24.

Bergerud, D., Lovitt, T. C., & Horton, S. (1988). The effectiveness of textbook adaptations in life science for high school students with learning disabilities. *Journal of Learning Disabilities, 21,* 70–76.

Bottge, B. A., & Hasselbring, T. S. (1993). A comparison of two approaches for teaching complex, authentic mathematics problems to adolescents in remedial math classes. *Exceptional Children, 59,* 556–566.

Brown, G., Kerr, M. M., Zigmond, N., & Harris, A. (1984). What's important for success in high school? Successful and unsuccessful students discuss school survival skills. *The High School Journal, 68,* 10–17.

Bulgren, J., Schumaker, J. B., & Deshler, D. D. (1988). Effectiveness of a concept teaching routine in enhancing the performance of LD students in secondary level mainstream classes. *Learning Disabilities Quarterly, 11,* 3–17.

Calhoun, M. L., & Beattie, J. (1984). Assigning grades in the high school mainstream: Perceptions of teachers and students. *Diagnostique, 9,* 218–225.

Carpenter, D. (1985). Grading handicapped pupils: Review and position statement. *Remedial and Special Education, 6*(4), 54–59.

Carpenter, D., & Grantham, L. B. (1985). A statewide investigation of grading practices and options concerning mainstreamed handicapped pupils. *Diagnostique, 11,* 31–39.

Carpenter, D., Grantham, L. B., & Hardister, M. P. (1983). Grading mainstreamed handicapped pupils: What are the issues? *The Journal of Special Education, 17,* 183–188.

Cognition and Technology Group at Vanderbilt. (1990). Anchored instruction and its relationship to situated cognition. *Educational Researcher, 19*(3), 2–10.

Darch, C., & Gersten. R. (1986). Direction-setting activities in reading comprehension: A comparison of two approaches. *Learning Disabilities Quarterly, 9,* 235–243.

Deshler, D. D., & Schumaker, J. B. (1988). An instructional model for teaching students how to learn. In J. L. Graden, J. E. Zins, & M. J. Curtis (Eds.), *Alternative educational delivery systems: Enhancing instructional options for all students* (pp. 391–411). Washington, DC: National Association of School Psychologists.

Deshler, D. D., Schumaker, J. B., Lenz, B. K., & Ellis, E. (1984). Academic and cognitive interventions for LD adolescents: Part II. *Journal of Learning Disabilities, 17,* 170–179.

Dettmer, P., Thurston, L. P., & Dyck, N. (1993). *Consultation, collaboration, and teamwork for students with special needs.* Boston: Allyn & Bacon.

Edgar, E. (1987). Secondary programs in special education: Are many of them justifiable? *Exceptional Children, 53,* 555–561.

Education Commission of the States. (1985). *Clearing house notes. State activity: Minimum competency testing as of November, 1985.* Washington, DC: Author.

Ellett, L. (1993). Instructional practices in mainstreamed secondary classrooms. *Journal of Learning Disabilities, 26,* 57–64.

Ellis, E. S., & Lenz, B. K. (1987). A component analysis of effective learning strategies for LD students. *Learning Disabilities Focus, 2,* 94–107.

Epstein, M. H., Polloway, E. A., Foley, R. M., & Patton, J. R. (1993). Homework: A comparison of teachers' and parents' perceptions of the problems experienced by students identified as having behavioral disorders, learning disabilities, or no disabilities. *Remedial and Special Education, 14*(5), 40–50.

Fuchs, L. S., Fuchs, D., & Bishop, N. (1992). Teacher planning for students with learning disabilities: Differences between general and special educators. *Learning Disabilities Research and Practice, 7,* 120–128.

Gajar, A., Goodman, L., & McAfee, J. (1993). *Secondary schools and beyond: Transition of individuals with mild disabilities.* Upper Saddle River, NJ: Merrill/Prentice Hall.

Grise, P., Beattie, S., & Algozzine, B. (1982). Assessment of minimum competency in fifth grade learning disabled students: Test modifications make a difference. *Journal of Educational Research, 76,* 35–40.

Haney, W., & Madaus, G. (1978). Making sense of the competency testing movement. *Harvard Educational Review, 48,* 462–484.

Henley, M., Ramsey, R. S., & Algozzine, R. F. (1996). *Characteristics and strategies for teaching students with mild disabilities* (2nd ed.). Boston: Allyn & Bacon.

Horton, S. V., Lovitt, T. C., Givens, A., & Nelson, R. (1989). Teaching social studies to high school students with academic handicaps in a mainstreamed setting: Effects of a computerized study guide. *Journal of Learning Disabilities, 22,* 102–107.

Hudson, P., Lignugaris-Kraft, B., & Miller, T. (1993). Using content enhancements to improve the performance of adolescents with learning disabilities in content classes. *Learning Disabilities Research and Practice, 8,* 106–126.

Jenkins, J. R., Jewell, M., Leceister, N., Jenkins, L., & Troutner, N. (1990, April). *Development of a school building model for educating handicapped and at risk students in general education classrooms.* Paper presented at the annual meeting of the American Educational Research Association, Boston.

Johnson, D. W., & Johnson, R. T. (1986). Mainstreaming and cooperative learning strategies. *Exceptional Children, 52,* 553–561.

Johnson, L. J., & Pugach, M. C. (1990). Classroom teachers' views of intervention strategies for learning and behavior problems: Which are reasonable and how frequently are they used? *The Journal of Special Education, 24,* 69–84.

Kerr, M. M., Nelson, C. M., & Lambert, D. L. (1987). *Helping adolescents with learning and behavior problems.* Upper Saddle River, NJ: Merrill/Prentice Hall.

Kiraly, J., Jr., & Bedall, J. J. (1984). Grading the mainstreamed handicapped student. *NASSP Bulletin, 68,* 111–115.

Knackendoffel, E. A. (1996). Collaborative teaming in the secondary school. In D. D. Deshler, E. S. Ellis, & B. K. Lenz (Eds.), *Teaching adolescents with learning disabilities: Strategies and methods* (2nd ed.) (pp. 579-616). Denver: Love Publishing Co..

Lenz, B. K., Alley, G. R., & Schumaker, J. B. (1987). Activating the inactive learner: Advance organizers in the secondary content classroom. *Learning Disability Quarterly, 10,* 53–67.

Lenz, B. K., Bulgren, J., & Hudson, P. J. (1990). Content enhancement: A model for promoting the acquisition of content by individuals with learning disabilities. In T. Scruggs & Y. L. B. Wong (Eds.), *Intervention research in learning disabilities* (pp. 122–165). New York: Springer-Verlag.

Lenz, B. K., Ehren. B. J., & Smiley, L. R. (1991). A goal attainment approach to improve completion of project-type assignments by adolescents with learning disabilities. *Learning Disabilities Research and Practice, 6,* 166–176.

Lerner, J. W. (1993). *Learning disabilities: Theories, diagnosis, and teaching strategies* (6th ed.). Boston: Houghton Mifflin.

Lloyd, J. W., Crowley, P. E., Kohler, F. W., & Strain, P. S. (1988). Redefining the applied research agenda: Cooperative learning, prereferral, teacher consultation, and peer-mediated interventions. *Journal of Learning Disabilities, 21,* 43–52.

Maheady, L., Harper, G. F., & Sacca, M. K. (1988). Peer-mediated instruction: A promising approach to meeting the diverse needs of LD adolescents. *Learning Disability Quarterly, 11,* 108–113.

Mastropieri, M. A., & Scruggs, T. E. (1989). Constructing more meaningful relationships: Mnemonic instruction for special education. *Educational Psychology Review, 1,* 83–111.

McGuire, J. M., Norlander, K. A., & Shaw, S. F. (1990). Postsecondary education for students with learning disabilities: Forecasting challenges for the future. *Learning Disabilities Focus, 5,* 69–74.

Nagel, D. R., Schumaker, J. B., & Deshler, D. D. (1986). *The first letter mnemonic strategy.* Lawrence: University of Kansas Institute for Research in Learning Disabilities.

Nowacek, E. J. (1992). Professionals talk about teaching together: Interviews with five collaborating teachers. *Intervention in School and Clinic, 27,* 262–276.

Polloway, E. A., Bursuck, W. D., Jayanthi, M., Epstein, M. H., & Nelson, J. S. (1996). Treatment acceptability: Determining appropriate interventions within inclusive classrooms. *Intervention in School and Clinic, 31,* 133–144.

Polloway, E. A., Epstein, M. H., Bursuck, W., Roderique, T. W., McConeky, J., & Jayanthi, M. (1994). Classroom grading: A national survey of policies. *Remedial and Special Education, 15,* 162–170.

Retish, P., Hitchings, W., Horvath, M., & Schmalle, B. (1991). *Students with mild disabilities in the secondary school.* New York: Longman.

Rojewski, J. W., Pollard, R. R., & Meers, G. D. (1991). Grading mainstreamed special needs students: Determining practices and attitudes of secondary vocational educators using a qualitative approach. *Remedial and Special Education, 12,* 7–15, 28.

Rosenshine, B., & Stevens, R. (1986). Teaching functions. In M. D. Wittrock (Ed.), *Handbook of research on teaching* (3rd ed.) (pp. 376–391). New York: Macmillan.

Salend, S. J. (1994). *Effective mainstreaming* (2nd ed.). New York: Macmillan.

Schaeffer, A. L., Zigmond, N., Kerr, M. M., & Heidi, E. F. (1990). Helping teenagers develop school survival skills. *Teaching Exceptional Children, 23,* 6–9.

Schultz, J. B., Carpenter, C. D., & Turnbull, A. P. (1991). *Mainstreaming exceptional students: A guide for classroom teachers.* Boston: Allyn & Bacon.

Schumaker, J. B., & Deshler, D. D. (1984). Setting demand variables: A major factor in program planning for LD adolescents. *Topics in Language Disorders, 4*(2), 22–44.

Schumaker, J. B., & Deshler, D. D. (1988). Implementing the Regular Education Initiative in secondary schools: A different ball game. *Journal of Learning Disabilities, 21,* 36–42.

Schumaker, J. B., Deshler, D. D., & Denton, P. H. (1984). An integrated system for providing content to learning disabled adolescents using an audio-taped format. In W. M. Cruickshank & J. M. Klebham (Eds.), *Early adolescence to early childhood* (Vol. 5, pp. 79–107). Syracuse, NY: Syracuse University Press.

Schumaker, J. B., Deshler, D. D., Nolan, S., Clark, F. L., Alley, G. R., & Warner, M. M. (1981). *Error monitoring: A learning strategy for improving academic performance of LD adolescents* (Research Report No. 32). Lawrence: University of Kansas Institute for Research in Learning Disabilities.

Scott, C. S. (1983). The effect of test format modifications on the minimum competency test performance of mildly handicapped students. *Dissertation Abstracts International, 44*(9), 2737-A.

Scruggs, T. E., & Mastropieri, M. A. (1990). Mnemonic instruction for students with learning disabilities: What it is and what it does. *Learning Disability Quarterly, 13,* 271–280.

U.S. Department of Education. (1995). *Seventeenth annual report to Congress on the implementation of the Education of the Handicapped Act.* Washington, DC: Author.

Vaca, J. L., Vaca, R. T., & Grove, M. K. (1987). *Reading and learning to read.* Boston: Little, Brown.

Vitello, S. J. (1988). Handicapped students and competency testing. *Remedial and Special Education, 9*(5), 22–28.

Warger, M., Newman, L., D'Amico, R., Jay, E. D., Butler-Nalin, P., Marder, C., & Cox, R. (1991). *Youth with disabilities: How are they doing? The first comprehensive report from the National Longitudinal Transition Study of Special Education Students.* Menlo Park, CA: SRI International.

Woodward, J., & Gersten, R. (1992). Innovative technology for secondary students with learning disabilities. *Exceptional Children, 58,* 407–421.

Ysseldyke, J., & Algozzine, B. (1995). *Special education: A practical approach for teachers* (3rd ed.). Boston: Houghton Mifflin.

Zigmond, N., Levine, E., & Laurie, T. E. (1985). Managing the mainstream: An analysis of teacher attitudes and student performance in mainstream high school programs. *Journal of Learning Disabilities, 18,* 535–541.

Transition-Related Instruction

Objectives

After reading this chapter, the reader should be able to:

1. provide a rationale for providing transition-related instruction to adolescents with mild disabilities;

2. discuss the many ways transition-related skills can be assessed;

3. cite research and its findings that have examined transition-related variables and outcomes with adolescents with mild disabilities;

4. provide ways to address the career education needs of students with mild disabilities;

5. provide a rationale and methods for conducting community-based instruction of adolescents with mild disabilities;

6. understand the concept and nuances of interagency collaboration for transition purposes.

The purpose of this chapter is to present information related to a very strong need for most adolescents with mild disabilities—transition programming. Although special and regular educators have been concerned with the postschool adjustment and the quality of adult life of persons with disabilities for quite some time, it was not until Will (1983) established transition-related issues as priorities of the U.S. Department of Education, Office of Special Education and Rehabilitative Services, that this area of secondary-level education became paramount. Transition-related instruction has been of concern mostly to special educators since Will's initiative began over a decade ago. Very few regular educators have played a dominant role in this area of instruction, but in these times of ever-increasing full-inclusion school placements for persons with disabilities, there is a need for regular educators to be involved as equal and contributing members of transition teams in public schools. Perhaps more in transition programming than in other areas of education, a team approach involving various professionals is the recommended means of assisting adolescents and young adults with disabilities.

Historically, transition-related instruction and services for students other than those with mental retardation or moderate to severe developmental disabilities have not been a major concern of secondary-level educational programs (Dunn, 1996; Reiff & deFur, 1992; Rojewski, 1992; Sitlington, 1996). Adolescents with mild disabilities—particularly those with learning disabilities—have been overlooked in programs that provide students with employment-related skills, community adaptation exposure, and additional assistance in independent adult living. Reiff and deFur (1992) uncovered myths that explain why youth with learning disabilities have been neglected in transition planning: (a) they do not encounter difficulty in employment; (b) they can achieve and succeed as adults commensurate with their nondisabled peers; and (c) because a learning disability is hidden, it is not serious. We, too, would like to dispel these myths by saying that although adolescents with *mild* disabilities may function at a higher level and be more capable than their cohorts with moderate to severe levels of disability, there is ample evidence (see Table 11.1) to suggest that their adjustment and their quality of life as adults are troublesome.

This chapter discusses the rationale for transition programming, career education, functional skills, the role of vocational education in the transition process, employment issues, assessment, the role of the educator, and many other important issues that surround transition-related instruction at the secondary level. Throughout this discussion the reader will find many ways to assist adolescents and young adults with disabilities. In order for a secondary-level teacher to be an effective change agent and affect positive growth in adolescents and young adults with disabilities—not only in classrooms but also in the community after they leave school—applying the information and following the recommendations found in this chapter are necessary.

Rationale and Introduction

Transition programming is important in the education of adolescents and young adults with mild disabilities for many different reasons. The first justification for this type of educational service delivery can be found in federal legislation that specifies that transition-related programming be provided to youth who need it.

IEP & Federal $ was made available

Early federal legislation concentrated on the need for vocational education to be made available to students with disabilities. The Vocational Education Act of 1976, Public Law 482, allowed for students with disabilities to receive vocational education and mandated that regular educators be involved in delivering such instruction. Individualized Education Plans (IEPs) pertaining to vocational education were also required under PL 482, and federal money was specifically directed toward assisting students with disabilities in vocational education classes.

The Carl D. Perkins Vocational and Applied Technology Education Acts of 1984 and 1990, which attempted to increase access of students with disabilities to "quality" vocational education services, required vocational evaluations for eligible students in order to formulate appropriate, individualized career choices. Postsecondary educational programs were also affected by the Perkins Acts in that such institutions were required to provide transition-oriented training and assist persons with disabilities in applying to community colleges and similar institutions.

In 1983, Section 626 of the Education Amendments found in Public Law 98-199 made funds available to study transition programs and service delivery. The specific focus of Section 626 was to improve secondary-level special education service delivery in order to enhance students' ability to gain competitive employment and to access postsecondary educational training opportunities. This law also set the stage for initiating transition-related instruction early in students' school years and for implementing interagency collaboration for various transition needs.

Transition programming received great impetus, however, in 1990 when the Individuals with Disabilities Education Act (IDEA, PL 101-476) mandated that the following be provided to eligible persons with disabilities:

> a coordinated set of activities for a student, designed within an outcome-oriented process, which promotes movement from school to post-school activities, including post-secondary education, vocational training, integrated employment (including supported employment), continuing and adult education, adult services, independent living, or community participation. The coordinated set of activities shall be based upon the

individual student's needs, taking into account the student's preferences and interests, and shall include instruction, community experiences, the development of employment and other post-school adult living objectives, and, when appropriate, acquisition of daily living skills and functional vocational evaluation. (PL 101-476, 20 U.S.C.1401 [a][19])

IDEA includes additional specifics related to the provision of transition services. With regard to IEPs and transition, the law states that IEPs must now include (a) the necessary services for each student no later than age 16 (or age 14 if appropriate) and (b) statements related to the interagency collaboration that will occur before the person exits school.

A second justification for transition-related instruction originates in research. A large body of research has shown that adolescents with mild disabilities, as a group, struggle when moving from being a student to being an independent adult. The majority of studies using follow-up and follow-along procedures (see Peraino, 1992, for a review) involving adolescents and young adults with mild disabilities have shown that (a) many more students with mild disabilities than nondisabled peers drop out of school; (b) unemployment rates of young adults with mild disabilities greatly exceed those of nondisabled workers; (c) fewer high school graduates with mild disabilities, versus nondisabled graduates, participate in postsecondary educational programs; and (d) young adults with mild disabilities, in comparison to similar-age peers without disabilities, express dissatisfaction with their social lives. Notwithstanding the methodological problems in the research (Halpern, 1990; Levine & Edgar, 1994), these studies and their findings provide more than sufficient rationale for a better approach to secondary-level special education service delivery than was the case in the past. Moreover, regarding only female adolescents and young adults with mild disabilities in the transition process, gender may be just as large a burden as is the presence of disability (Fulton & Sabornie, 1994; Wagner, 1992). Table 11.1 displays the follow-up and follow-along research that has examined numerous transition-related variables involving adolescents and young adults with mild disabilities.

Definitions

Various definitions of the transition process (outside of legislation) exist to provide additional clarity to this type of educational service. One of the first comprehensive definitions of what is meant by transition for adolescents with mild disabilities was provided by Will (1984):

> Transition from school to working life is an outcome-oriented process encompassing a broad array of services and experiences that lead to employment. Transition is a period that includes high school, the point of graduation, additional postsecondary education or adult services, and the initial years in employment. Transition is a bridge between the security and structure offered by the school and the opportunities and risks of adult life. (p. 3)

Wehman, Kregel, Barcus, and Schalock (1986) defined transition in the following manner:

Table 11.1
Follow-up and follow-along research examining adolescents and young adults with mild disabilities and transition-related variables

Author(s)	Sample(s) Studied	Variables Examined
Brolin (1972)	MR	Employment, Adult service agency involvement
Brolin, Durand, Kromer, & Muller (1989)	MR	Drop-out rate, Employment
Bucher, Brolin, & Kunce (1987)	LD, MR	Employment
Chaffin, Spellman, Regan, & Davison (1971)	MR	Employment
deBettencourt, Zigmond, & Thornton (1989)	LD (rural areas)	Drop-out rate, Employment
Edgar & Levine (1987)	LD, SED, MR	Drop-out rate, Employment, Postsecondary education, Residential status, Engagement in productive activities
Fafard & Haubrich (1981)	LD	Employment
Fairweather, Stearns, & Wagner (1989)	LD, SED, MR (and others)	School experiences, Adult service agency involvement
Fardig, Algozzine, Schwartz, Hensel, & Westling (1985)	LD, MR	Drop-out rate, Employment
Fass, D'Alonzo, & Stile (1990)	LD	Employment by personality type interaction, Self-satisfaction
Fourqurean, Meisgeier, Swank, & Williams (1991)	LD	Employment
Frank, Sitlington, & Carson (1991)	SED	Drop-out rate, Employment, School experiences
Frank, Sitlington, Cooper, & Cool (1990)	MR	Employment, Postsecondary education, Residential status, Social adjustment
Haring & Lovett (1990)	MR	Employment, Postsecondary education, Residential status, Social adjustment
Haring, Lovett, & Smith (1990)	LD	Employment, Postsecondary education, Engagement in productive activities, Residential status, Social adjustment
Hartzell & Compton (1984)	LD	Postsecondary education, Academic success, Social adjustment, Employment
Hasazi, Gordon, & Roe (1985)	LD, SED, MR	Drop-out rate, Employment, School experiences, Adult service agency involvement
Hasazi, Gordon, Roe, Finck, Hull, & Salembier (1985)	MR	Drop-out rate, Employment, Postsecondary education, Engagement in productive activities, Residential status

Reference	Disability	Outcomes
Hill, Hill, Wehman, Banks, Pendleton, & Britt (1985)	MR	Employment
Hoisch, Karen, & Franzini (1992)	LD, MR	Employment, Employment satisfaction, Employer satisfaction
Humes & Brammer (1985)	LD	Employment, Postsecondary education, Engagement in productive activities
Iowa Department of Education (1989a, 1989b, 1990)	LD, SED, MR	Drop-out rate, Employment, Postsecondary education, Residential status
Janes, Hesselbrock, Myers, & Penniman (1979)	SED	Drop-out rate, Employment, Postsecondary education, Social adjustment
Kranstover, Thurlow, & Bruininks (1989)	LD, SED, MR (and others)	Employment, Social adjustment
Kregel, Wehman, Seyfarth, & Marshall (1986)	MR	Social adjustment, Residential status, Self-satisfaction
Levin, Zigmond, & Birch (1985)	LD	Drop-out rate
Levine & Edgar (1994)	LD, SED, MR (and others)	Employment, Residential status, Social adjustment (marital status)
Lichtenstein (1993)	LD	Employment, School experiences, Adult service agency involvement, Residential status, Drop-out rate
Linden & Forness (1986)	MR	Engagement in productive activities, Residential status
Menz, Hansen, Smith, Brown, Ford, & McCrowley (1989)	Persons Registered for Vocational Rehabilitation	Employment, Adult service agency involvement
Mithaug, Horiuchi, & Fanning (1985)	LD (and others)	Employment
Miller, Rzonca, & Snider (1991)	LD	Postsecondary education, School experiences, Adult service agency involvement, Community adaptation
National Longitudinal Transition Study (1989)	LD, SED, MR	Drop-out rate, Employment, Postsecondary education, Social adjustment, Engagement in productive activities
Neel, Meadows, Levine, & Edgar (1988)	SED	Employment, Engagement in productive activities, Postsecondary education
Neubert, Tilson, & Ianacone (1989)	LD, MR	Employment

Table 11.1, continued

Author(s)	Sample(s) Studied	Variables Examined
Perotti (1985)	MR	Employment, Social adjustment, School experiences
Posthill & Roffman (1991)	LD	Employment, Residential status, School experiences
Roessler, Brolin, & Johnson (1990)	LD, MR	Employment, Adult service agency involvement, Residential status, Self-satisfaction
Sands & Kozleski (1994)	MR (and others)	Social adjustment, Adult service agency involvement, Participation in community and recreation activities
Roessler, Brolin, & Johnson (1990)	LD, MR	Employment, Adult service agency involvement, Residential status, Self-satisfaction
Schalock, Wolzen, Ross, Elliott, Werbel, & Peterson (1986)	LD, MR	Employment, Postsecondary education, Residential status
Scuccimarra & Speece (1990)	LD	Employment, Residential status, Social adjustment
Sitlington & Frank (1990)	LD	Employment, Residential status, School experiences, Social adjustment
Sitlington, Frank, & Carson (1992)	LD, SED, MR	Employment, Residential status, School experiences, Social adjustment
Spruill & Cohen (1990)	LD, MR (rural area)	Employment, Residential status, School experiences
Wagner (1992)	LD, SED, MR (and others)	Social adjustment, Employment, Residential status
White, Alley, Deshler, Schumaker, Warner, & Clark (1982)	LD	Social adjustment, Job satisfaction, School experiences
Zigmond & Thornton (1985)	LD	Drop-out rate

Legend: LD = Learning Disabled SED = Seriously Emotionally Disturbed MR = Mentally Retarded a carefully planned process, which may be initiated either by school personnel or adult service providers, to establish and implement a plan for either employment or additional vocational training of a handicapped student who will graduate or leave school in 3 to 5 years; such a process must involve special educators, vocational educators, parents and/or the student, an adult service system representative, and possibly an employer. (p. 114)

Gajar, Goodman, and McAfee (1993) provided their version of what is meant by transition for students with mild disabilities when they expressed the following:

Transition for the mildly disabled is the process or movement through secondary education into adulthood and encompasses a number of critical periods in an individual's life, including the sequence from secondary education, to postsecondary education or employment, and on to retirement. Transition includes all of the environments (social family, community, employment, leisure, etc.) that in combination influence and define a person who is mildly disabled as an individual. Transition is the movement from the protection and dependence of childhood to the risk and independence of a fully realized adulthood. (p. 19)

As can be seen, transition is the process by which adolescents with mild disabilities move through their secondary schooling years and early adulthood period. Appropriate outcomes of a successful transition include competitive employment, independent living, full community adaptation and participation, and general satisfaction with adult life. Effective transition programming involves many different people who should share responsibility for service delivery: the student, his or her parents or guardians, special and regular educators, vocational instructors, career education specialists, job coaches, employers, and mental health and developmental disabilities professionals. Three goals comprise the transition process of moving from dependent secondary-school life to independent adulthood: (a) the provision of opportunities that support appropriate adult living, (b) maintaining integration with the nondisabled in living and working environments, and (c) enhancing the productivity and independence of persons leaving school systems (McDonnell, Sheehan, & Wilcox, 1983).

There are many related fields under the transition "umbrella." Transition programming should include **vocational education,** which is defined as

organized educational programs which are directly related to the preparation of individuals for paid or unpaid employment or for additional preparation for a career requiring other than a baccalaureate or advanced degree. (PL 94-142, Section 121a. 14[b][3])

Vocational education should involve awareness of work roles in society, exploration of such work roles as they interest a person, appropriate vocational decision making, and preparation for specific jobs (Hoyt, Evans, Mackin, & Mangum, 1974). Effective vocational education has numerous benefits for adolescents with mild disabilities, and the connection between exposure to vocational training in school and positive adult outcomes is clear (Evers, 1996).

Effective transition programming should also include **career education,** which is the totality of experiences through which one learns to live a meaningful, satisfying work life. Career education provides the opportunity for children to learn, in the least restrictive environment possible, the academic, daily living, personal-social, and occupational knowledge and specific vocational work skills necessary for attaining their highest levels of economic, personal and social fulfillment. The individual can obtain this fulfillment through work (both paid and unpaid) and in a variety of other societal roles and personal life styles—as a student, citizen, volunteer, family member and participant in meaningful leisure-time activities. (Council for Exceptional Children, 1978, p. 1)

The inclusion of career education under transition programming is noteworthy in that the former views a person in totality. Employment success is a focus, but the person's *overall* functioning as a contributing citizen in society is career education's major concern. Additional key components of career education for students with *learning disabilities* were provided by Brolin, Elliott, and Corcoran (1984) when they said, among many other things, that it (a) begins in early childhood and reaches into retirement years, (b) should comprise the total school curriculum, and (c) should involve the community for training in life skills.

Vocational rehabilitation (VR) services include evaluation, counseling and guidance, physical and mental restoration, vocational training, job placement, and training or placement services, including supported employment (Szymanski, King, Parker, & Jenkins, 1989). Most of these services are key components of the transition process for adolescents and young adults with mild disabilities. Vocational rehabilitation support services such as providing interpreters, notetaking, rehabilitation engineering, and orientation and mobility training are also under the aegis of VR agencies. The essentials of the VR process can be seen in Figure 11.1; the interactions among VR, vocational education, and special education can be seen in Table 11.2.

Transition: Employment Issues

One of the most important goals of transition programming, to be discussed in detail later in this chapter, concerns successful employment. Secondary-level special education has been concerned with employability of its students and graduates for quite some time (Halpern, 1992) but, in many respects, this concern has not translated into successful intervention. Most adolescents with mild disabilities, with appropriate training, are capable enough to obtain and keep positions in **competitive employment,** which includes situations in which workers with and without disabilities work side-by-side for the same wages and benefits. **Supported employment** is work in integrated settings of at least 20 hours per week in which a **job coach** helps employees with disabilities learn the skills necessary for success on the job and provides continuing support while they are on the job. A job coach may be involved in one or all of the following tasks: (a) vocational counseling, (b) vocational training, (c) travel training, (d) job-client matching, (e) educating parents, and (f) daily instruction and supervision of workers with disabilities (Wehman & Melia, 1985). In the supported employment model the job coach gradually fades his or her presence on the job until the worker can maintain employment without further assistance or with assistance on an intermittent basis. Supported employment is usually reserved for persons

Figure 11.1
The basic vocational rehabilitation process

Application	People who apply or are referred to the state department of vocational rehabilitation must complete applications for service. Every state has such a department.
Eligibility determination	Each person is then evaluated to determine eligibility and potential for employment. Eligible persons: • Have a physical, mental, or emotional disability • Have a disability that is a substantial barrier to employment • Are reasonably expected to be employable after receiving rehabilitation services
Rehabilitation plan	Eligible individuals have been determined to work with counselors to pre-pare individualized written rehabilitation plans (IWRPs) that include: • A vocational goal with estimated start and completion dates • Counseling and guidance activities • Specific services and their providers • The individual's rehabilitation responsibilities • Intermediate objectives • Financial services (when necessary) • Job placement activities
Services provided	Rehabilitation counselors may provide any or all of the following 15 services to eligible individuals: • Guidance and counseling • Vocational evaluation • Physical health, mental health, and medical services • Vocational training • Financial maintenance • Transportation • Family services • Interpreter services • Telecommunication aids and devices • Recruitment services in public service employment • Job placement, including supported employment placement • Postemployment services • Occupational licenses needed to enter specific occupations or employment • Rehabilitation engineering services • Any other services that can reasonably be expected to benefit an individual with a disability in obtaining employment
Job placement	At the conclusion of rehabilitation, the counselors work with the clients to find and secure suitable employment. Cases are considered closed when clients have been employed at least 60 days in suitable jobs.

Source: From *Life Beyond the Classroom: Transition Strategies for Young People with Disabilities* by P. Wehman (Ed.), 1992, Baltimore: Paul H. Brookes.

Table 11.2
Service delivery system differences among vocational rehabilitation, special education, and vocational education

Category of Difference	Vocational Rehabilitation	Special Education	Vocational Education
Legislation	Rehabilitation Act as Amended (PL 99–506)	Individuals with Disabilities Education Act (PL 101–476)	Carl D. Perkins Vocational Education and Applied Technology Act (PL 101–392)
Administration	Office of Special Education and Rehabilitative Services, Rehabilitation Services Administration	Office of Special Education and Rehabilitative Services, Office of Special Education Programs	Office of Vocational and Adult Education
Funding	75% federal, 25% state; no local funds	Federal, state, and local; largest share local and state	Federal, state, and local; largest share local and state
Eligibility	Disability, vocational handicap, and potential to benefit employability	Disability, need for special education services	Attendance
Populations Served	Adults and adolescents with disabilities	Persons with disabilities from birth through age 21	Adolescents and adults
Scope of Services	Range of services for employment and independent living	Range of special education and related services	Vocational assessment, vocational instruction
Service Mechanism	District vocational rehabilitation offices/rehabilitation counselors	Local school districts/special education teachers and related service personnel	Local school districts, postsecondary programs/teachers, etc.
Evaluation	Numbers rehabilitated; percent with severe disabilities	Compliance with law; service in least restrictive environment	Number of students served
Personnel Qualifications	May lack relevant preservice education	Usually certified to teach	Usually certified to teach

Source: Adapted from "Systems Interface: Vocational Rehabilitation, Special Education, and Vocational Education" by Szymanski, E. M., Hanley-Maxwell, C., & Asselin, S. B., in F. R. Rusch, L. DeStefano, J. Chadsey-Rusch, A. Phelps, and E. Szymanski (Eds.) *Transition from School to Adult Life: Models, Linkages, and Policy.* Copyright © 1992 Sycamore Publishing Co. By permission of Brooks/Cole Publishing Company, Pacific Grove, CA 93950, a division of International Thomson Publishing Inc.

with more severe disabilities rather than adolescents and adults with mild disabilities. Revell, Wehman, Kregel, West, and Rayfield (1994) reported that as of 1991, a total of 74,960 persons participated in supported employment in the U.S., and that persons with mental retardation accounted for approximately 63% of the total involved in such employment conditions. Those with "mental illness" accounted for 22% of the population, while those with learning disability and other disabilities accounted for only 8% of those studied. Revell et al. also reported that the average hourly wage for those in supported employment was $4.45. Similar to supported employment, job coaches can also be used in competitive employment situations with the same gradual fading of their presence and support.

While a strong focus on employment issues in the transition process comprises the majority of concern for students with mild disabilities, a comprehensive program emphasizing transition-related instruction would not be complete without other areas of attention. These ancillary areas are presented briefly below, and each is discussed in detail later in this chapter. One should keep in mind, however, that some "best practices" in the transition literature, while advocated by many experts, lack substantiation in research (Kohler, 1993). Areas such as interagency collaboration and interdisciplinary transition teams, for example, have yet to be shown to be indispensable in empirical studies.

Transition: Collateral Areas

Additional support for adolescents with mild disabilities involved in the transition process should include the following areas of emphasis in instruction (Gajar et al., 1993): (a) personal management (e.g., consumer skills, budgeting, travel skills, banking, shopping, etc.); (b) personal health (e.g., preventive health measures, personal hygiene, etc.); (c) leisure skills (e.g., recreational activities, constructive use of free time, etc.); (d) citizenship (e.g., civic participation, resisting criminal activity, etc.); and (e) social skills. These other, non-employment-based, transition-related areas are necessary in instruction for adolescents and young adults with mild disabilities because of the numerous skill deficits and adjustment difficulties that research has shown to be prevalent among such persons (see Table 11.1).

On the other hand, current and prospective secondary-level teachers of adolescents with mild disabilities might be overwhelmed by the sheer number of areas in which transition-related instruction is needed. After all, there are only a limited number of hours available for instruction in the traditional school day. A well-organized, conscientious, comprehensive, and good-faith effort in instruction is needed to address these collateral areas, and we feel it can and should be done in secondary-level special and regular education. Special and regular educators must now realize that past secondary-level instructional efforts have been largely unsuccessful in ensuring adult independence and success for adolescents with mild disabilities. We also believe that for *effective* transition-related instruction to occur, classroom-based instruction related to employment and the ancillary areas should be minimal and opportunities for *community-based* instruction should be maximized. This does not mean that teachers simply take students on field trips to community settings. We recommend that community-based instruction related to transition occur on a regular basis, that students be given ample opportunities to practice community-related skills in the environments where they are necessary, and that community-based instructional activities be documented appropriately on students' IEPs. Secondary-level teachers of students with mild disabilities must agree that a certain level of extra effort is necessary to end the ineffective instructional practices of the past.

Assessment for Transition Programming

[handwritten: intent of assessment]

The intent of assessment for transition is to determine the level of preparedness and skills that students have for instruction related to employment, independent community living and access, recreation and leisure, and further education and training in junior or community colleges and traditional colleges and universities. The focus that teachers should have regarding assessment in the transition process is to determine what discrepancies exist (if any) between what an adolescent with a mild disability presently demonstrates in the community and what the behavioral expectations are in the various settings that the person will frequent as an independent adult. In other words, teachers should assess to determine what a student does in the settings that are important and what the student needs to do in such environments. In this type of assessment, direct observation will be used most often by the teacher seeking performance data (see Chapter 4).

[handwritten left margin: focus — determine what they know & what they need.]

Berkell and Brown (1989) and Phelps and McCarty (1984) outlined student-centered information that can be useful in planning and delivering transition-related instruction. This information is useful in developing a profile of the student so that teachers can make informed decisions regarding his or her needs related to transition. The following areas or sources are suggested for teachers to explore in searching for meaningful and important data on which to base transition-related instruction.

[handwritten left margin: information that can be important for transition]

Academic skills.   In this area, the general academic achievement levels in reading, mathematics, writing, and so on, are assessed, but in a different way. Rather than assessing how a student reads and comprehends a nondescript passage, the teacher would assess his or her ability to read such things as a fast-food restaurant menu, a laundry detergent label, a credit card application, a retail store sales slip, a bus schedule, a prescription drug label, or a federal tax form. The teacher should assess what and how an adolescent writes when completing a job application. The *functional nature* (i.e., skills needed in local, out-of-school environments) of academic ability, therefore, is paramount in assessment for transition. Reading, mathematics, and writing skills are important for school success, but applying these skills in a way that enhances a person's ability to function independently in the community is the scope of academic skill assessment for transition. Secondary-level teachers should obtain community-based documents to directly observe and record students' ability to perform the academic skills needed for success with the individual task.

Medical profiles.   This area is important in assessment for transition because a person's health may stand in the way of vocational and other types of success as an independent adult in the community. Medical history reports and results from medical examinations are important sources of data in designing transition goals for IEPs. The possible effects of prescription drugs on endurance and attentiveness, for example, should be noted by the teacher in planning appropriate instructional exercises in the community. Coordination and level of caution are also important if someone is to work in close proximity to dangerous machinery and materials. Most adolescents with mild disabilities will not need extensive adaptations in living or working conditions in order to succeed; for the few who need extra assistance because of existing medical conditions, assessing individual transition needs and adaptations is a must for the comprehensive transition educator.

Interest and aptitude measures. In terms of interest and aptitude, a teacher is interested in determining any student characteristics that can lead to efficient transition-related decision making. Information of a psychological nature (e.g., IQ level), usually found in confidential school folders or in portfolios, is important in describing psychological attributes, but is of limited utility to teachers planning transition programming for adolescents with mild disabilities. Additional quasi-psychological traits that are particularly important in the transition process include vocational interests and aptitudes and adaptive skills. Adolescents identified as mentally retarded or developmentally disabled will have had an adaptive behavior scale administered to them as part of the eligibility-assessment process. Results from these measures are helpful in determining what vocational and community-referenced skills are lacking and identifying maladaptive behaviors that may inhibit independent living in the community. Adolescents identified as behaviorally and emotionally disabled, in most cases, should have behavior rating scale testing results in their eligibility and identification folders; these testing results can also add meaningful information regarding overt behavior and how it may interfere with living as an independent adult.

Interest and aptitude inventories, however, can supplement other transition-related assessment information so that a better idea can be obtained by the teacher in planning individualized instruction. Tables 11.3 and 11.4 include lists of commonly used vocational interest and aptitude tests that teachers may peruse to determine whether such data may be useful in planning for the transition needs of adolescents with mild disabilities. Teachers should also be mindful of the limitations of such tests. Most of these scales were not constructed with adolescents with mild disabilities in mind and therefore may be somewhat limited in technical adequacy. Single aptitude tests, moreover, should never be used to make final judgments regarding a person's capacity to solve problems or ability to learn transition-related skills. An alternative to using such tests would be to list community-based occupations that are available in a specific local area and ask students which of the occupations would interest them. Similarly, teachers could ask the adolescents with mild disabilities which local jobs interest them (see Vocational skills and Interviewing on p. 310). In doing so, a teacher should also uncover the behavioral and task-related requirements of local job opportunities and assess whether a student can perform the specific occupational behaviors.

Generalizable skills. Generalizable skills such as communication, reasoning, interpersonal skills, and a wide variety of academic behaviors are basic to many occupational and vocational pursuits (Greenan, 1983a). Mithaug, Martin, and Agran (1987) referred to generalizable skills as *adaptability;* they included decision making, independent performance, self-evaluation, and adjustment. No matter the semantics used to describe this area in the transition process, teachers need to know what behaviors to concentrate on in assessment and certainly in instruction. Direct observation, self-reports, standardized tests, curriculum-based assessment, and teacher ratings are available for measurement of generalizable skills or adaptability.

Table 11.5 presents specific skills that teachers should assess in adolescents with mild disabilities. These assessment targets are a compilation of those suggested in

Table 11.3
Selected interest inventories

Instrument	Description	Time Required
Gordon Occupational Checklist (Gordon, 1981)	Requires 6th-grade reading level; Intended for non-college students	25 min.
Strong-Campbell Interest Inventory (Strong, Campbell, & Hansen, 1985)	Requires 6th-grade reading level; Computer scorable; Interest toward professional occupations	25 min.
The Self-Directed Search (Holland, 1985)	Requires 6th-grade reading level; Self-administered, scored, and interpreted	40 min.
Career Assessment Inventory (Johansson, 1986)	Requires 6th-grade reading level; Focus on jobs not requiring a 4-yr. college degree; Computer scorable	20-40 min.
Interest Checklist (U.S. Department of Labor, 1981)	Requires 6th-grade reading level; Serves as an aid in interviewing	20-30 min.
Geist Picture Interest Inventory (Geist, 1988)	Self-administered; Pictorial displays; Intended for non-college-bound students	15 min.

Source: From *Assessment: The Special Educator's Role* by C. Hoy and N. Gregg. Copyright © 1994 Brooks/Cole Publishing Company, Pacific Grove, CA 93950, a division of International Thomson Publishing Inc. By permission of the publisher.

Greenan (1983a), and Mithaug et al. (1987). Interested readers should also see the VITAL checklist and curriculum of Mithaug, Martin, and Burger (1986), which has been field tested and shown to be effective in assessment of adaptability in students with mild to severe disabilities. Also worthy of consideration in assessment of generalizable *academic* skills is the checklist created by Greenan (1983b), which includes 115 different skills that are cross-listed with relevant occupations requiring performance of such behaviors.

Vocational skills. This area of assessment in the transition process has had the longest history and the most emphasis as it pertains to students with disabilities. Vocational assessment is the process of collecting student performance data in areas related to work and work-related behavior. We believe that effective vocational assessment is the most important area in transition programming; it is multifaceted and should include many different types of data from different sources. Phelps and McCarty (1984) concluded that vocational assessment should be an integral part of any career/vocational program serving students with disabilities and recommended the use of four different types of vocational assessment: (a) interviewing, (b) work samples, (c) job simulations, and (d) on-the-job measurement. Each of these is discussed in detail.

Interviewing. In this type of assessment, the student provides his or her personal perspective regarding various facets of the world of work. Previous paid or unpaid work experiences, extent of awareness of and exposure to occupations available in the local community, and what the person does during leisure time that may be related to work are some pieces of information that may be obtained from directly interviewing the student. Other questions of a personal nature such as the student's desires regarding work

Table 11.4
Selected aptitude tests

Instrument	Description	Time Required
General Aptitude Test Battery (U.S. Department of Labor, 1970a)	Measures general learning ability, verbal aptitude, numerical aptitude, spatial aptitude, form perception, clerical perception, motor coordination, finger and manual dexterity; Intended for those who have yet to choose an occupation; Probably the most widely used of all tests of this type	2 hrs. 15 min.
Nonreading Aptitude Test Battery (U.S. Department of Labor, 1970b)	This test is a nonreading version of the General Aptitude Test Battery; Developed for assessing learners originating from at-risk and disadvantaged backgrounds	2 hrs. 10 min.
Differential Aptitude Test (Bennett, Seashore, & Wesman, 1982)	Measures verbal reasoning, numerical ability, abstract reasoning, clerical speed and accuracy, mechanical reasoning, space relations, spelling and language usage; Minimal reading required; Computer scorable; Two versions available: Level 1 for grades 7–9, Level 2 for grades 10–12	3 hrs.
Minnesota Clerical Test (Andrews, Paterson, & Longstaff, 1961)	Measures number checking and name scoring; Intended for grades 8–12	30 min. or less
Crawford Small Parts Dexterity Test (Crawford & Crawford, 1975)	Measures fine motor coordination; Intended for adults only	15 min. or less

Source: From *Assessment: The Special Educator's Role* by C. Hoy and N. Gregg. Copyright © 1994 Brooks/Cole Publishing Company, Pacific Grove, CA 93950, a division of International Thomson Publishing Inc. By permission of the publisher.

or additional, postsecondary vocational training are also appropriate in the interview process. Asking questions of parents or guardians about how well the adolescent completes jobs around the home and what level of prompting is necessary for accurate task completion also provides important information.

A slightly different application of interviewing assessment and how it can be used in the transition process was described by Gaylord-Ross (1986). He recommended that teachers should interview potential employers in the local community to determine:

- General job descriptions for positions that may be filled by workers with disabilities;
- Difficulty of new tasks to be learned on the job;
- Production rate demands for those employed in various positions;
- Tolerance for errors committed by employees;
- Duration of work (i.e., hours per day, length of time between breaks, length of time at one specific task, overall stamina required by employees);

Table 11.5
Generalizable skills to assess for transition success

Domain	Specific Skills
Mathematics	Employment math, taxes, savings and interest, checking, budgeting (see also Math Chapter)
Reading	Reading maps and charts, directions for assembling household objects, reading menus, want ads, prescription directions
Writing	Writing a want ad, writing letters of inquiry for employment, creating a resumé
Interpersonal Relations	Conversational skills, elimination of inappropriate behavioral excesses, personal hygiene, being courteous
Reasoning	Problem solving, finding solutions in different ways, planning for an activity, finding a destination, understanding consequences, avoiding problem areas if possible, knowing how and when to use free time
Independent Performance	Cooking, cleaning, and shopping for oneself, being on time, completing work without supervision
Self-Evaluation	Accepting consequences, realizing mistakes
Adjustment	Asking for directions when necessary, asking to change a situation when necessary, becoming more efficient in task completion, selecting tasks and activities appropriately

- Specific occupational tasks required to work successfully and get along with others in the workplace;
- General attitude of employer regarding employing persons with disabilities, and how current or previous persons with disabilities functioned on the job; and
- Accessibility of workplace via public transportation.

Knowing the answers to these issues will allow teachers to be better able to match students' abilities and interests to particular community-based job sites and to provide intensive instruction so that students can meet the employment rigors at those jobs.

Work samples. This type of assessment requires the adolescent to complete tasks with tools and materials that are reasonably similar or exactly like those in actual local work environments. A teacher would gather or borrow employment-related equipment from job sites in the local community and ask students to do certain tasks with the various tools while assessing their accuracy of completion, rate of production, and so on. This type of assessment has the advantage of observing a student engaged in realistic work; some of the generalization problems often demonstrated by students with mild disabilities are also overcome by having the person work and manipulate the actual or lifelike materials found on the job. Another positive aspect of work sample assessment is that involving the student with actual tools is likely to be more motivating than having him or her read about the requirements of a job.

To conduct work sample assessment a teacher would engage in direct observation of students' manipulations of the actual tools. Frequency, rate of behavior per a set time period, and duration of task-related behavior while using the tools are the most likely measurement indices used for work sample analysis. Topography of the behavior (e.g., the way a person holds or uses a tool that may be unconventional) would also be noted by the assessor.

Community-based, on-the-job assessment   In this situation a teacher, job coach, manager, or job supervisor observes the student (trainee) perform the actual requirements of a real job. The assessor is particularly interested in determining the strengths and weaknesses that a person demonstrates in terms of performance accuracy, level of attention, getting along with coworkers, customers, and supervisors, production rate capabilities, stamina, and acceptable work habits. The assessment data should provide, ideally, any discrepancies that exist between what the specific expectancies are on the job and the person's ability to respond to the rigors of employment. Another aspect of this type of assessment is to determine any environmental modifications that may be necessary for a person to achieve success in the specific place of employment. Hence, careful direct observation will be needed in conducting *in vivo* assessment of an adolescent with mild disabilities at an actual job site.

Assessment of program offerings.   In order to develop effective secondary programs that meet the transition needs of students with mild disabilities, teachers need to assess their current program offerings to determine whether maintaining the status quo is in the best interest of each adolescent. Teachers should provide—through student-centered transition-related instruction—a program that has a positive, outcome-oriented mentality that meets the independent adult needs of as many adolescents with mild disabilities as possible. In other words, teachers need to look at their current secondary-level program offerings to determine whether students will exit with skills that are meaningful and useful. Answering the following questions and taking action when necessary will assist in designing an appropriate secondary-level program for adolescents with mild disabilities.

- Do students have opportunities to be involved in work experiences before they exit school?
- Can parents and guardians of adolescents with mild disabilities guide their offspring in finding appropriate adult services?
- Are adult service providers in the local community presently involved in program delivery collaboration before students exit high school, and are written agreements in place with such personnel?
- Are students currently involved in community-based training on a regular basis, or does most instruction still occur inside the walls of the school?
- How many employers are currently providing training sites? Should there be more? (Berkell & Brown, 1989)

Standardized tests specifically developed for transition.   In addition to the tests we have already discussed, several standardized test batteries have been published with transition-related skills as the main focus. These instruments, presented in Table 11.6, give personnel involved in the transition process more options for comprehensive evaluation of the present level of adolescents' performance related to various facets of independent adult life (Clark, 1996).

Table 11.6
Summary of current examples of transition-referenced assessment instruments

Instrument/Procedure Name	Target Group	Features
Social and Prevocational Information Battery—Revised (Halpern et al., 1986)	Adolescents and adults with mild mental retardation or low functioning students with learning disabilities.	1. Subscales include Banking, Budgeting and Purchasing Skills, Job Skills and Job-Related Behavior, Home Management, Health Care, Hygiene and Grooming, and Ability to Read Functional Words. 2. Orally administered except for items on functional signs. 3. Designed especially for secondary school students. 4. True–false item format. 5. 277 items in the battery. 6. 20–30 minutes administration time.
Tests for Everyday Living (Halpern et al., 1979)	All junior high students and average to low functioning senior high school students in remedial programs, including those labeled as having learning disabilities.	1. Subtests include Purchasing Habits, Banking, Budgeting, Health Care, Home Management, Job Search Skills, and Job-Related Behavior. 2. Orally administered except where reading skills are critical to an item. 3. 245 items across seven subtests. 4. Diagnostic at the subtest level. 5. 20–30 minutes estimated administration time per subtest.
Transition Behavior Scale (McCarney, 1989)	Any disability group; mild to severe levels of severity.	1. Subscales include Work-Related Behaviors, Interpersonal Relations, Social/Community Expectations. 2. Ratings are completed by at least three persons. 3. Items are rated on a 3-point scale. 4. Estimated completion time is 15 minutes. 5. Scores in percentile ranks are based on national standardization sample.
LCCE Knowledge Battery (Brolin, 1992)	Mild cognitive disabilities; moderate to severe learning disabilities; mild to moderate behavioral disorders; Grades 7–12.	1. Curriculum-based assessment related to LCCE Curriculum. 2. 200 multiple-choice items covering 20 of 22 LCCE competency areas. 3. Standardized on a national sample.

Instrument	Population	Description
Quality of Life Questionnaire (Schalock & Keith, 1995)	Mild to severe cognitive disabilities; ages 18 and older.	1. Subscales include Satisfaction, Competence/ Productivity, Empowerment/Independence, and Social Belonging/Community Integration. 2. Administered in interview format for most persons; alternative format is possible by obtaining two independent ratings and averaging. 3. Items are rated on a 3-point scale. 4. Administration time is estimated at 20 minutes. 5. Scores in percentile ranks are based on standardization sample.
Quality of Student Life Questionnaire (Keith & Schalock, 1995)	All disability populations, ages 14–25; mild through severe levels of disability.	1. Subscales include Satisfaction, Well-Being, Social Belonging, and Empowerment/Control. 2. Administered in interview format for most persons; alternative formats include a written format or obtaining two independent ratings and averaging. 3. Items are rated on a 3-point scale. 4. Administration time is estimated at 15 minutes. 5. Scores in percentile ranks are based on secondary and post-secondary standardization samples.
Transition Planning Inventory (Clark & Patton, 1995)	All disability populations, ages 14–25; mild through severe levels of disability.	1. Areas covered in the inventory include Employment, Further Education/Training, Daily Living, Living Arrangements, Leisure Activities, Community Participation, Health, Self-Determination, Communication, and Personal Relationships. 2. 0–5 rating scale completed independently by student, parent/guardian, and a school representative. 3. Administration may be self-administration, guided administration, or oral administration. 4. 56 inventory items plus open-ended items on the student form (optional on parent form) related to preferences and interests. 5. A profile sheet permits visual comparisons of the respondents' responses to each item. 6. Planning notes form encourages transformation of relevant assessment data into IEP goals, objectives, and interagency linkages.

Table 11.6, continued

Instrument/Procedure Name	Target Group	Features
Enderle-Severson Transition Rating Scale (Enderle & Severson, 1991)	Any disability group; mild to severe levels of disability; ages 14–21.	1. The scale is an informal, criterion-referenced instrument. 2. Subscales include Jobs and Job Training, Recreation and Leisure, Home Living, and Post-Secondary Training and Learning Opportunities. 3. Scale is completed by the student's teacher and a parent or primary caregiver. Framework for transition planning.
LCCE Performance Battery (Brolin, 1992)	Mild cognitive disabilities; moderate to severe learning disabilities; mild to moderate behavioral disorders; Grades 7–12.	1. The battery is a nonstandardized, criterion-referenced instrument providing skill rather than knowledge assessment of critical life skills. 2. Items are based on skills related to LCCE Curriculum. 3. Estimated time for administration is 3–4 hours.
Life Skills Inventory (Brigance, 1995)	All disability populations, high school ages and adults; mild cognitive disabilities, with reading grade levels 2–8.	1. Subscales include Speaking and Listening, Functional Writing, Words on Common Signs and Warning Labels, Telephone Skills, Money and Finance, Food, Clothing, Health, Travel, and Transportation. 2. Administered individually or in groups; administration may be oral or written. 3. Criterion-referenced assessment, providing specific knowledge and skill assessments for life skill items paired with instructional objectives. 4. Learner Record Book provided to show color-coded record of performance and instructional objectives generated from the results. 5. Optional Program Record Book is available to track progress of a group or class; optional Rating Scales are available to evaluate behavior, attitudes, and other traits related to life skills and employability. 6. Companion assessment to Employability Skills Inventory (Brigance, 1995b).

Source: From "Transition Planning Assessment for Secondary Students with Learning Disabilities" by G. M. Clark, 1996, *Journal of Learning Disabilities, 29,* 79–92. Copyright 1996 by PRO-ED, Inc. Reprinted by permission.

Career Education in the Transition Process

Career education, or career development, has had a place in schooling of students with mild disabilities for quite some time, and there is little doubt that it has a rightful place in preparation of adolescents with mild disabilities for independent adulthood. Moreover, if it had been consistently provided to students with disabilities beginning at the elementary level (as it should have been), perhaps the transition problems that have been documented among adolescents and young adults with mild disabilities would not be as serious as they are. Career education has a very wide focus in instruction, and it should not be considered a treatment solely concerned with having students find and keep long-term employment. Rather than being narrow in scope, effective career education looks at the whole person in terms of independent living in the community, interpersonal skills, and behaviors that result in gainful employment. In the following paragraphs, we describe how career education should be delivered for students with mild disabilities.

The most comprehensive educational program for delivering career education originates with Brolin (1989) and his *Life-Centered Career Education* (LCCE) curriculum. Cummings and Maddux (1987) rated the LCCE as the most efficacious program available to deliver career education to students with disabilities, and we agree. The LCCE is truly unique in its scope and approach; its main areas of emphasis include (a) independent living in the community, (b) identifying and using resources of the school, home, and community to ensure adequate functioning and adjustment as an adult, and (c) support in any level of career development. Brolin's program provides instruction aimed at 22 major competencies, divided into 102 subcategories, covering three foci: daily living skills, personal-social skills, and occupational guidance and preparation. Figure 11.2 presents the areas of emphasis of Brolin's LCCE curriculum.

The *career awareness* phase of the LCCE, which is usually emphasized in the elementary school years, comprises activities to help students with all types of disabilities become aware of their feelings and potential, understand behaviors that members of society are likely to reinforce, and develop effective communication. In addition, positive attitudes toward work are stressed, awareness of different jobs and specific occupational responsibilities are addressed, and students are exposed to appropriate work habits and behaviors.

Of particular importance to secondary- and postsecondary-level teachers of students with mild disabilities are the career exploration, occupational preparation, placement, follow-up, and continuing education phases of the LCCE, which are to be part of the curricula of middle and high school students. During career exploration, teachers guide students in self-examination of their needs and abilities, concentrate on prerequisites of the local labor market, and allow students the opportunity to try unpaid work experiences through hands-on trials. Work samples and simulated job experiences are included in career exploration, as well as the beginning stages of assessment of interests and aptitudes. The "whole person" is also emphasized during the exploration phase with lessons concerning clothes to wear, things to cook, learning how to iron one's clothing, marriage roles, and building relationships.

The LCCE *preparation* phase requires teacher attention when students are near the end of middle school and beginning their high school experience. Preparation is emphasized during the elementary school years, but it is at the secondary level that this stage

Figure 11.2
Areas of emphasis in the LCCE curriculum

Curriculum Area	Competency	Subcompetency	
Daily Living Skills	1. Managing Family Finances	1. Identify money and make correct change	2. Make wise expenditures
	2. Selecting, Managing, and Maintaining a Home	6. Select adequate housing	7. Maintain a home
	3. Caring for Personal Needs	10. Dress appropriately	11. Exhibit proper grooming and hygiene
	4. Raising Children, Enriching Family Living	14. Prepare for adjustment to marriage	15. Prepare for raising children (physical care)
	5. Buying and Preparing Food	18. Demonstrate appropriate eating skills	19. Plan balanced meals
	6. Buying and Caring for Clothing	24. Wash clothing	25. Iron and store clothing
	7. Engaging in Civic Activities	28. Generally understand local laws and government	29. Generally understand Federal Government
	8. Utilizing Recreation and Leisure	34. Participate actively in group activities	35. Know activities and available community resources
	9. Getting around the Community (Mobility)	40. Demonstrate knowledge of traffic rules and safety practices	41. Demonstrate knowledge and use of various means of transportation
Personal-Social Skills	10. Achieving Self-Awareness	43. Attain a sense of body	44. Identify interests and abilities
	11. Acquiring Self-Confidence	48. Express feelings of worth	49. Tell how others see him/her
	12. Achieving Socially Responsible Behavior	53. Know character traits needed for acceptance	54. Know proper behavior in public places
	13. Maintaining Good Interpersonal Skills	58. Know how to listen and respond	59. Know how to make and maintain friendships
	14. Achieving Independence	62. Understand impact of behaviors upon others	63. Understand self-organization
	15. Achieving Problem-Solving Skills	66. Differentiate bipolar concepts	67. Understand the need for goals
	16. Communicating Adequately with Others	71. Recognize emergency situations	72. Read at level needed for future goals
Occupational Guidance & Preparation	17. Knowing and Exploring Occupational Possibilities	76. Identify the personal values met through work	77. Identify the societal values met through work
	18. Selecting and Planning Occupational Choices	82. Identify major occupational needs	83. Identify major occupational interests
	19. Exhibiting Appropriate Work Habits and Behaviors	87. Follow directions	88. Work with others
	20. Exhibiting Sufficient Physical-Manual Skills	94. Demonstrate satisfactory balance and coordination	95. Demonstrate satisfactory manual dexterity
	21. Obtaining a Specific Occupational Skill		
	22. Seeking, Securing, and Maintaining Employment	98. Search for a job	99. Apply for a job

318

3. Obtain and use bank and credit facilities	4. Keep basic financial records	5. Calculate and pay taxes		
8. Use basic appliances and tools	9. Maintain home exterior			
12. Demonstrate knowledge of physical fitness, nutrition and weight control	13. Demonstrate knowledge of common illness prevention and treatment			
16. Prepare for raising children (psychological care)	17. Practice family safety in the home			
20. Purchase food	21. Prepare meals	22. Clean food preparation areas	23. Store food	
26. Perform simple mending	27. Purchase clothing			
30. Understand citizenship rights and responsibilities	31. Understand registration and voting procedures	32. Understand Selective Service procedures	33. Understand civil rights and responsibilities when questioned by the law	
36. Understand recreational values	37. Use recreational facilities in the community	38. Plan and choose activities wisely	39. Plan vacations	
42. Drive a car				
45. Identify emotions	46. Identify needs	47. Understand the physical self		
50. Accept praise	51. Accept criticism	52. Develop confidence in self		
55. Develop respect for the rights and properties of others	56. Recognize authority and follow instructions	57. Recognize personal roles		
60. Establish appropriate heterosexual relationships	61. Know how to establish close relationships			
64. Develop goal seeking behavior	65. Strive toward self-actualization			
68. Look at alternatives	69. Anticipate consequences	70. Know where to find good advice		
73. Write at the level needed for future goals	74. Speak adequately for understanding	75. Understand the subtleties of communication		
78. Identify the remunerative aspects of work	79. Understand classification of jobs into different occupational systems	80. Identify occupational opportunities available locally	81. Identify sources of occupational information	
84. Identify occupational aptitudes	85. Identify requirements of appropriate and available jobs	86. Make realistic occupational choices		
89. Work at a satisfactory rate	90. Accept supervision	91. Recognize the importance of attendance and punctuality	92. Meet demands for quality work	93. Demonstrate occupational safety
96. Demonstrate satisfactory stamina and endurance	97. Demonstrate satisfactory sensory discrimination			
100. Interview for a job	101. Adjust to competitive standards	102. Maintain postschool occupational adjustment		

Source: From *Life-Centered Career Education: A Competency Based Approach* (3rd ed.) by D. Brolin, 1989, Reston, VA: The Council for Exceptional Children.

becomes increasingly important. Lifestyles, interests, and aptitudes are discussed in greater detail, and instruction is specifically designed to explore occupations and vocational skill during the last stage of the LCCE. Comprehensive vocational assessments should be completed at this time to determine how well a particular student fits into his or her chosen area of interest and demonstrated aptitude. Careful teacher guidance is necessary during this phase so that secondary-level courses are indeed meeting the desires of the student and his or her parents. Actual work experiences (the *placement* and *follow-up* stages) before the student leaves school are also an essential part of the LCCE curriculum, and teachers should ensure that all adolescents with mild disabilities have a wide variety of community-based employment options. Some examples of the instructional activities that comprise the latter phases include sex education, ordering and paying for meals in a restaurant, community recreation, and accepting praise and criticism. Figure 11.3 presents a sample lesson from Activity Book Two of the LCCE (Glascoe, Miller, & Kokaska, 1986).

The continuing education phase of Brolin's program includes the Lifelong Career Development (LCD) Model and has the community college as its base of operations. Transition centers have been established in community colleges so that individuals with mild disabilities who do not qualify for vocational rehabilitation and those who do not care to continue to be identified as disabled can receive assistance (Brolin, 1984). The LCD personnel team involved in assisting at the community college level include counselors, college staff, family members, adult service agency personnel, and local business leaders. The LCD teams involved in service provision stress that the community college (a) is a normalized setting and is ideal for persons with disabilities to resolve life problems, (b) is a liaison between service providers who should work together to continue assisting adolescents and young adults with mild disabilities, (c) focuses on career development in providing additional opportunities for students with mild disabilities to acquire skills needed as independent adults, and (d) provides assistance throughout adulthood (Kokaska & Brolin, 1985). Brolin and his associates have been evaluating the efficacy of the LCD centers at community colleges, and Gajar et al. (1993) stated that this program is one of the most promising for long-term intervention of adults with mild disabilities.

In essence, the LCCE and LCD provide intervention for a wide variety of skills needed by adolescents and adults with mild disabilities in the transition process. The LCCE curriculum materials do not include scripted lesson plans, but the instructions in the teacher's activity books are sufficiently specific regarding what teachers need to do and use in each lesson. Given the wide scope of what all teachers (both elementary and secondary level and in both regular and special education) need to teach, some may wonder whether there exists sufficient time to teach academic subjects *and* career education. Our answer to this concern is that effective instruction for transition *must* include domains that stretch far beyond traditional academic subjects.

We believe that Brolin's comprehensive approach to career education—beginning with instruction in the elementary grades—is the paradigm that other curriculum developers should emulate. Long-term emphasis on the skills that the majority of adolescents with mild disabilities need for adult independence and success should not be left to chance. Special and regular education teachers should share in the responsibility of implementing

Figure 11.3
Sample LCCE lesson

Domain: Occupational Skills
Competency: 19. Exhibiting Appropriate Work Habits and Behaviors
Subcompetency: 87. Following Directions

Academic Components
Reading
Language (Oral Expression)
(Behavior Management)

Types of Activity
Discussion
Chart/Bulletin Board
(Behavior Management)

Objectives

1. The student will understand and follow posted classroom rules and guidelines.

2. The student will identify ways in which following directions at school is similar to or different from following directions at work.

Activity

1. Post a chart in the classroom listing classroom rules in "job" terminology (see example).

2. At the beginning of the school year, explain to the students how the work habits they develop now will help them when they are older and get a job. Discuss all rules in relation to both the world of work and school. Review the chart several times during the first month of school; thereafter, refer to it as needed.

Follow-up; Evaluation

1. The student shows improvement in following classroom rules.

2. Given a classroom rule, the student tells how it is the same or different from rules at work.

> **Ten Ways to Keep Your Job (And Not Get Fired!)**
>
> 1. Go to work every day.
> 2. Be on time.
> 3. Be prepared.
> 4. Follow your supervisor's directions.
> 5. Do your very best work all the time.
> 6. Finish all your work.
> 7. Be kind and cooperative with other workers.
> 8. Respect the rights and property of others.
> 9. Keep your work area neat.
> 10. Remember that a friendly worker will always be more successful than an unpleasant worker!

Source: From *Life-Centered Career Education: Activity Book Two* by L. G. Glascoe, L. S. Miller, and C. J. Kokaska, 1986, Reston, VA: The Council for Exceptional Children.

such instruction and make specific plans to infuse it into the daily curriculum regimen. Developing work personalities needs to be emphasized, community-based employment should be made available to all who choose such a course, adaptability instruction should be provided in special, regular, and community college courses, and instructional time spent on personal-social behaviors needs to gain the level of importance that academic skill interventions command. Career education has an outcome-oriented focus that fits well into the mandate of PL 101-476, and it also mirrors the de-emphasis on regular academic tracks in which the large majority of adolescents with mild disabilities have failed over the years (Division on Mental Retardation and Developmental Disabilities, 1994). We recommend its use in secondary and postsecondary education programs as much as possible.

Community-Based Instruction at the Secondary Level

As noted, the goal of transition-related instruction at the secondary level is to enable students to live, work, recreate, and function as independent adults in the community. The community, therefore, should become the classroom for adolescents with mild disabilities who have demonstrated problems in appropriate functioning in such environments. Success in school-based activities is important, but for students with mild disabilities at the secondary level the outcome-oriented environment that needs to be considered for success is the world outside the school walls.

It is a known fact that community-based instruction is successful (Stodden & Browder, 1986) and that generalization has a better chance of occurring if intervention occurs in the setting where the generalized behavior is required (Gaylord-Ross, Forte, & Gaylord-Ross, 1986). Why is it, then, that only about 7% of teachers of students with mild disabilities use community-based instruction (Halpern & Benz, 1987)? This state of inefficient instructional affairs is one reason that Edgar (1987) concluded that many secondary-level education programs are not justifiable.

Community-based training, as its name implies, involves educators implementing instruction and requiring students to perform behaviors in work sites, recreational areas, restaurants, grocery stores, shopping malls, and other places in the local community that they are likely to frequent as adults. Relying exclusively on classroom-based instruction is no longer considered functional for adolescents involved in the transition process. Wehman (1992) recommends that teachers should identify local community sites in which 50% of instruction could occur. Community travel experiences, home living, recreational activities, and *in situ* vocational training are just a few of the community-based activities that should be used in assessment and actual instruction.

In terms of community-based *vocational* training, teachers need to be aware of and in compliance with regulations of the U.S. Department of Labor that govern such activities. Each of the following criteria, specified by the Fair Labor Standards Act of 1938, must be met before a student can be considered a "trainee."

1. The training, even if it includes the actual operation of the employer's facility, is similar to that given in vocational schools.

2. The training is for the benefit of the trainees and not the employer.

The trainees do not displace regular employees, but work under their supervision.

Employers providing training derive no immediate advantage from the activities of trainees, and the training may actually hinder typical operations at the job site.

Trainees are not entitled to full- or part-time employment when training is completed.

The parties involved are aware that trainees are not entitled to wages for training time. (Wehman, 1992)

Use of several community-based vocational sites should be a goal of any teacher providing transition and work-related intervention. Wehman (1992) suggests that one to three student trainees should be placed at a vocational training site. Teachers should plan to rotate students (trainees) through various employment sites, with sufficient training time at each site to learn the necessary job activities. Use of several vocational training sites also has an advantage for students: They are able to compare jobs and decide which type of job they like best or least.

Finding numerous training sites for students requires extra time on the part of secondary-level teachers. Potential training sites need to be visited, nuances and expectations of each environment need to be noted, and personnel at the sites need to be contacted before instruction takes place. When the teacher is cognizant of what each environment offers for instruction, specific instructional objectives can be formulated.

Other vocational training strategies provided by Wehman (1992) should also be kept in mind. For example, employers need to fully understand that all trainees may not be capable of producing exemplary work, and that a few trainees may be necessary to produce the amount of work of one nondisabled employee. Employers should not believe that the purpose of trainees on the job is for them to produce more work. Teachers, employers, site supervisors, nondisabled coworkers, and persons with disabilities need to be mindful of the notion of *training* in order to foster a successful placement.

Wehman (1992) also suggests that any site used for vocational training should allow trainees opportunities to (a) perform a variety of tasks, (b) be fully integrated into the workforce, and (c) interact with nondisabled coworkers. Figure 11.4 presents questions that should be considered when evaluating the overall quality of any placement.

Potential problems in community-based instruction. Teachers should be aware of some of the potential obstacles that they are likely to encounter in their efforts to implement community-based training at the secondary level. Wehman (1992) has identified the problems most often faced by teachers as staffing and scheduling, transportation, liability and safety, and costs. Each will be discussed briefly.

In terms of staffing, the issue lies with how to have a sufficient number of staff to oversee the instruction of the students. Paraprofessionals, parent volunteers, high school service club members, and even student teachers should be involved as much as possible, so long as they are aware of the goals of instruction and how to deliver it efficiently in the community. Peer tutoring should also be implemented whereby students fluent in a community-based skill can show how a skill should be performed. Staggering schedules so that some students remain with a teacher aide at the school while the teacher

Figure 11.4
Questions to consider in evaluating job quality and integration

1. Will the student work with nondisabled co-workers?
2. Will the student have regular contact with co-workers throughout the workday?
3. Will the student move around in the different areas of the company during work hours?
4. Will the student take full advantage of formal supports provided by the company, such as employee assistance programs and organized car pools?
5. Will the student take full advantage of the informal supports provided by the employer (e.g., transportation)?
6. Will the student regularly participate in company-sponsored social activities, such as picnics?
7. Will the student attend employee activities and have access to gathering places, such as break rooms and locker rooms?
8. Will the student socialize throughout the workday, such as at shift changes and when work is completed?
9. Will the student work in physical proximity to co-workers?
10. Will the student follow the same work schedules as co-workers?
11. Will the student work with other co-workers to complete job duties?
12. Will the company supervisor oversee the activities of the student?
13. Will the student participate in staff or other group meetings?
14. Will the student take lunch and breaks at the same times as the co-workers?
15. Will the student receive assistance from co-workers with work and work-related matters?
16. Will the student have regular contact with the public throughout the workday?
17. Will the student follow a similar routine to the other co-workers (e.g., schedule, uniform, etc.)?
18. Will the student interact with co-workers throughout the day?
19. Will the student be able to joke around and talk about non-work-related matters with co-workers during work hours?
20. Will the student interact with co-workers during lunch and breaks?
21. Will the student joke around and talk about non-work-related topics during lunch and breaks?
22. Will the student participate in social activities with co-workers during work hours (e.g., holiday parties)?
23. Will the student participate and recognize special occasions and personal events in the lives of employees (e.g., birthdays, illnesses, etc.)?
24. Will the student have the opportunity to participate in social activities with co-workers outside work hours?
25. Will the student receive fringe benefits from the company while in training (e.g., free meals)?

Source: From *The Vocational Integration Index: A Guide for Rehabilitation Professionals* by W. S. Parent, J. Kregel, and P. Wehman, 1992, Stoneham, MA: Andover Medical Publishers.

conducts lessons in the community is also recommended. A 1:4 (or less) instructor-to-student ratio is recommended for community-based instruction (Wehman, 1992).

With regard to transportation problems encountered when a teacher wants to move instruction to the community, a little creative thinking may be in order. School districts that have vans or special activity buses could be used for transporting students to community sites. We are familiar with teachers who use their own vehicles (with special insurance riders) to transport students to and from school and receive reimbursement for mileage. Teachers in urban areas where schools are located near public bus or mass transportation routes should use these forms of travel for community-based training.

Liability issues need a great deal of attention before community-based instruction is to occur, but little work is required after all the details are completed. All schools have liability insurance that covers instructional programs, but teachers need to check with the school district's legal authorities to make sure instructional liability is in force while students and instructors are outside the property lines of the school. Special riders on the district's insurance may be necessary so that instruction can extend to the community. Students and any volunteers may also need special addenda on existing insurance policies so that they are also covered while off school grounds. Liability issues, therefore, are important for anyone involved in community-based instruction.

From our experience, the cost of providing community-based instruction is *the* major problem, especially in these days of budget austerity by public schools. If possible and with appropriate planning, the cost of providing community-based instruction should be a specific budget line each year for each school involved. Wehman (1992) suggested that teachers' regular supply funds could also be used for community-based training as well as contributions from local community service groups (e.g., Lions Club, veterans groups, Kiwanis Club, Jaycees, etc.). School car washes and bake sales have also been used in the past to supplement funds for instruction in the community. Here again, the conscientious teacher who knows that community-based instruction is a necessity will be required to spend extra time and effort to ensure that everything necessary is in place. We believe that any time spent in making secondary-level instruction more responsive to students' needs in the community is time well spent.

Role of the Educator in the Transition Process

Much has been said regarding the rather nontraditional role of the teacher—in special or regular education—concerned with adolescents with mild disabilities in the transition process. Such a teacher will truly have to put forth a great deal more effort, in comparison to those at the elementary level, to (a) ensure that transition-related goals are placed on students' IEPs and that such objectives are met, (b) plan and conduct career education and community-based instruction, and (c) organize and direct vocational training in local employment sites. Unfortunately, the list of required teacher activities for students with mild disabilities at the secondary level does not stop there. School-based classroom instruction that fosters independence and a smooth transition process still must be delivered, and interagency service agreements must be put in place. In the following sections we discuss additional responsibilities of the secondary-level educator assisting adolescents with mild disabilities in the transition process.

additional responsibility for 2nd part

definition of functional Skills

Curriculum

The secondary-level special educator is responsible for *designing* most of the classroom instruction that will attempt to assist students with mild disabilities in their future years. For the majority of adolescents with mild disabilities (i.e., those not planning on postsecondary education), this means that the teacher should concentrate on developing and delivering a **functional skills curriculum**. Wimmer (1981) defined functional skills as "specific, observable, and measurable performance demonstrated by the student and essential in carrying out everyday social, personal, and on the job tasks" (p. 613). Wimmer also specified aspects that are typical of functional skills:

- They are student-centered rather than content-centered.
- They are built around real-life experiences rather than artificial, vicarious settings.
- They are community-based, with activities taking place in the community as well as the school.
- They involve cooperation between students and teachers in the planning of learning experiences.
- They emphasize process-oriented objectives, such as problem solving or provision of services or goods.
- Activities are centered around small groups and/or individuals rather than a large-group lecture format.
- The teacher functions as a guide to student learning as well as an information giver.
- They often involve teams of teachers from various disciplines.
- Students acquire skills through active participation rather than passive cooperation. (pp. 613–614)

Wehman (1992) also provided additional areas that a functional curriculum should include, and these skills pertain to (a) domestic living (e.g., cleaning one's room and workspace, cooking meals, maintaining clothing, etc.); (b) community orientation (e.g., having sufficient prosocial skills to interact appropriately with anyone in the community, using community restaurants, shopping at department stores, depositing checks in bank accounts, etc.); (c) leisure and recreational ability (e.g., going to the movies, playing video games, going to an athletic event or theater, jogging or exercising, etc.); and (d) vocational fulfillment (e.g., finding and maintaining gainful employment). If secondary-level teachers can meet the specifics of Wimmer's (1981) and Wehman's (1992) functional skills curriculum, there is no doubt that students with mild disabilities will benefit in their transition to independent adult life.

when student can't get out in community

If instruction cannot take place every day in the community, teachers can plan other activities while on the school grounds that assist adolescents with mild disabilities. School-based, work-related training has been implemented for years at the secondary level (Halpern, 1992) and includes tasks such as (a) typing, data entry, faxing, and photocopying in the main office; (b) microfilming, cataloging, or on-line searching in the school library; (c) cooking, packaging, and displaying food properly in the cafeteria; and (d) maintaining and repairing the physical plant and grounds of the school. Teachers also need to engage in classroom-based instruction pertaining to generalizable skills and social skills. Generalizable skills to emphasize in classroom instruction would cover (a) working steadily and accurately without supervision and interruption, (b) accepting a change in assignments without complaining, (c) recognizing one's own mistakes and correcting them, (d) initiating work on time and offering assistance to others who may be slower, and (e) responding to correction appropriately and maintaining improved performance after correction (also see Chapter 9).

Interagency Cooperation

Another important part of the transition process for adolescents with mild disabilities is for educators to arrange for adult service agency assistance before the student receiving transition assistance leaves high school (as IDEA now mandates). By default and because they are the logical choice for initiating such activities, special educators will be responsible for structuring the interaction among the various parties that should be involved in helping youth in the transition process. Interagency collaboration is the act of planning, coordinating, and delivering adult service of various types to adolescents and adults with disabilities for the sole purpose of ensuring a smooth transition from school to independent adulthood. Instead of fragmented service with gaps and duplication of services, interagency collaboration attempts to bring together all service parties so that comprehensive, meaningful, and continual adult service is available to those who need it. The interagency cooperative agreement among service providers that begins while the person is still in school should, ideally, remain in place as long as he or she needs it as an adult. The people who should be involved in forming an interagency transition team of transdisciplinary personnel usually include educators (both regular and special education and school-based guidance counselors), vocational rehabilitation personnel, developmental disabilities specialists, adult mental health agency staff, client advocates, job coaches, employers from the community, community group home or apartment living operators (both public and private), community college representatives, social workers, public transportation personnel, the person receiving the transition assistance, and his or her parents.

Wehman (1992) outlined five different tasks that a local transition interagency team should undertake when beginning the process of cooperation. These include:

- Establish a reason for existence (i.e., to improve and coordinate the provision of services for youth making the transition from school to community living);
- Delineate the goals of the planning team, which include completing a local needs assessment and writing a formal, interagency agreement;
- List and rank by priority the activities that will enable the team to accomplish its goals;
- Divide the list of activities and assign persons to be responsible for completion of activities; and
- Establish deadlines for completion of activities. (p. 123)

The local needs assessment uncovers information such as the number of graduates who will be leaving school in the near future, how many of these individuals are currently receiving services from the cooperating agencies, how many youth are waiting for services, what adult services are available in the community and the capacity of each, and what additional services are still needed in the community (Wehman, 1992).

One outcome that derives from proper interagency collaboration is the lifting of full transition responsibility from public-school educators. Educators must realize that there are many adult service providers who can lend great assistance to an adolescent with mild disabilities while the student is still in school, and, of course, when he or she exits public school. A potential problem on the part of educators in building an effective interagency agreement is that few, if any, educators are trained in the process of team building, interdisciplinary management of the process, and postschool follow-up of students (Johnson, Bruininks, & Thurlow, 1987). Johnson et al. emphasize using a common language to share accurate information about service consumers and understanding the policies, regulations, and eligibility requirements of each agency on the team. Systematic evaluation to provide needed data on costs, availability of services, and needed program modifications to improve transition success should also be part of team duties.

Finally, secondary-level teachers involved in organizing interagency cooperation should pay close attention to the information shown in Figures 11.5 and 11.6. Figure 11.5 provides a checklist that should be used when formulating interagency agreements among adult service providers. Figure 11.6 includes guidelines for enhancing parent participation on the transition team involved in interagency collaboration. We feel that this information, particularly as it pertains to parents, is important in assisting teachers to form effective transition service teams across disciplines.

Other Issues in Transition Programming

The complexity of effective transition programming will no doubt have an effect on the manner in which special educators perform their duties at the secondary level. The requirements of transition-related intervention may force them from a strict instructional role to those of manager, liaison between school services and adult service agencies, and valuable team player. These changes in job description and performance of an effective transition educator must be accompanied by a similar change in attitude toward such responsibilities. Transition-related training is still education—but with a different focus—and special education teachers need not become overwhelmed with the minimal amount of school-based, classroom instruction that they may be presenting. Okolo and Sitlington (1986), with regard to adolescents with learning disabilities, recommended that special education teachers need to provide classroom-based instruction in interpersonal skills and *job-related* academic skills. Okolo and Sitlington also suggested that special education teachers provide vocationally relevant services in cooperation with vocational educators at school. Vocational educators should be active members of the school-based transition team, and they must be given sufficient guidance in how to instruct with an outcome-oriented, successful transition perspective. We believe that such efforts by secondary-level special and vocational education teachers should also be provided to all students with mild disabilities (including those with mild mental retardation or developmental disability and those with emotional and behavioral disabilities).

Another aspect of providing an effective transition curriculum that regular educators must realize is that strict academic content instruction must be more responsive to the

Figure 11.5
Interagency agreement checklist

The agreement should include or address the following:
1. Mission statement or purpose of agreement
2. Number and names of agencies involved in the agreement
3. Measurable goals to be accomplished by core team as preliminary activities to the writing of the interagency agreement
4. Definitions of terms
5. Descriptions of roles and responsibilities of each agency in agreement implementation
6. Description of eligibility determination processes for each agency
7. Delineation of referral procedures for each agency's services
8. Description of staffing allocations from each agency for transition and interagency operations
9. Implementation procedures
10. Plan for dissemination of agreement
11. Plan for interagency inservice
12. Time overlapping/service coordination
13. List of service options available (direct or purchase)
14. Procedure for development of new services
15. Provisions for individuals with severe disabilities
16. Time-limited and ongoing service provision
17. Cost sharing
18. Data sharing (formative and evaluative)
19. Procedures for information release and confidentiality policy
20. Attendance of IEP/ITP meetings
21. Schedule for implementation
22. Schedule for renegotiation or modification of agreement terms
23. Policy on service delivery (e.g., duplication, repeating, initiation dates)
24. Identification of agency liaisons to participating agencies
25. Schedule of interaction between liaisons
26. Desired outcomes of agreement
27. Dissemination of services available to parents and candidates
28. Procedure and schedule for ongoing needs assessment

Source: From *Life Beyond the Classroom: Transition Strategies for Young People with Disabilities* by P. Wehman (Ed.), 1992, Baltimore: Paul H. Brookes.

Figure 11.6

Guidelines for enhancing parental and professional partnerships in transition programs

- Spend time discussing shared values and a mission statement.
- Assist parents in understanding services, terminology, regulations.
- Be sensitive to the use of professional jargon when speaking with parents; avoid being condescending.
- Ensure that all meetings are well-planned and organized.
- Schedule and structure meetings so that all members contribute and participate.
- Provide adequate notification of meetings.
- Establish communication mechanisms so that parents are included in the information loop.
- Include parents in organizing the agenda.
- Include parents in all aspects of the planning process.
- Encourage parents to assume leadership positions whenever possible.
- Make sure that all team members, including parents, leave the meeting with some assignment or responsibility for the next meeting.

Source: From "Interagency Teams: Building Local Transition Programs Through Parental and Professional Partnerships" by Everson, J. M. & McNulty, K., in F. R. Rusch, L. DeStefano, J. Chadsey-Rusch, A. Phelps, and E. Szymanski (Eds.) *Transition from School to Adult Life: Models, Linkages, and Policy.* Copyright © 1992 Sycamore Publishing Co. By permission of Brooks/Cole Publishing Company, Pacific Grove, CA 93950, a division of International Thomson Publishing Inc.

needs of adolescents with mild disabilities. With the ever-increasing implementation of the full inclusion movement, regular educators may not be well prepared to deliver functional lessons that address the transition needs of each student with a disability. This potential problem must be strongly considered by anyone suggesting that adolescents with mild disabilities should spend as much time as possible in regular content-area courses such as English literature, trigonometry, physics, or any other course that will not equip them with functional skills leading to independence as an adult. Special and regular educators, therefore, must fully collaborate in order for general education classes to become meaningful and truly related to the transition needs of adolescents with mild disabilities. Unfortunately, making middle and high school regular classes more functional in content is easier said than done and will take serious effort on the part of all parties concerned.

Summary

Secondary-level education of adolescents with mild disabilities in the late-20th and 21st centuries must no longer assume that such students will do fine as adults so long as they are provided with the "3 Rs" throughout their schooling. This chapter outlined several ways to go beyond the traditional in structuring secondary-level education for students with mild disabilities. These suggestions are intended for implementation; having such knowledge and not using it with students who need such assistance does little more than continue past mistakes.

When effective transition programs are put in place, positive results for students accrue. Wagner, D'Amico, Marder, Newman, and Blackorby (1992), for example, showed that since 1987 (a) the number of persons with disabilities living independently has tripled, (b) the number of students with disabilities in postsecondary education has nearly doubled, and (c) almost 40% of persons with disabilities now earn more than $6.00 an hour. Evers (1996) also showed that adolescents with mild disabilities exposed to vocational education and paid work experiences while still in school are more successful in later employment than those not involved in such experiences. These results are sizable improvements over the recent past and in comparison to many of the studies shown in Table 11.1. The key to these findings, however, lies not in their positive nature but in how we can improve the postschool fate of *all* adolescents and adults with mild disabilities. When transition programming as outlined in this chapter is implemented on a widespread basis, we will be better able to answer the question "Secondary programs in special education: Are many of them justifiable?" (Edgar, 1987) with a positive response.

Key Terms

vocational education

career education

vocational rehabilitation

competitive employment

supported employment

job coach

functional skills curriculum

interagency collaboration

References

Andrews, D. M., Paterson, D. G., & Longstaff, H. P. (1961). *Minnesota clerical tests.* New York: Psychological Corporation.

Bennett, G. K., Seashore, H. G., & Wesman, A. G. (1982). *Differential aptitude test* (5th ed.). New York: Psychological Corporation.

Berkell, D. E., & Brown, J. E. (1989). *Transition from school to work for persons with disabilities.* New York: Longman.

Brigance, A. H. (1995). *Life skills inventory.* North Billerica, MA: Curriculum Associates.

Brolin, D. (1972). Value of rehabilitation services and correlates of vocational success with the mentally retarded. *American Journal of Mental Deficiency, 76,* 644–651.

Brolin, D. (1984). *Preparing handicapped students to be productive adults.* Paper presented at the Western Regional Resource Center Topical Conference Serving Secondary Mildly Handicapped Students, Seattle.

Brolin, D. (1989). *Life-centered career education: A competency based approach* (3rd ed.). Reston, VA: The Council for Exceptional Children.

Brolin, D. (1992). *Life-centered career education (LCCE) knowledge and performance batteries.* Reston, VA: The Council for Exceptional Children.

Brolin, D., Durand, R., Kromer, K., & Muller, P. (1989). Post-school adjustment of educable retarded students. *Education and Training in Mental Retardation, 24,* 144–148.

Brolin, D. E., Elliott, T. R., & Corcoran, J. R. (1984). Career education for persons with learning disabilities. *Learning Disabilities, 3*(1), 1–14.

Bucher, D. E., Brolin, D. E., & Kunce, J. T. (1987). Importance of life-centered career education for special education students: The parent's perspective. *Journal of Career Development, 13*(4), 63–69.

Chaffin, J., Spellman, C., Regan, C., & Davison, R. (1971). Two follow-up studies of former educable mentally retarded students from the Kansas work-study project. *Exceptional Children, 37,* 733–738.

Clark, G. M. (1996). Transition planning assessment for secondary-level students with learning disabilities. *Journal of Learning Disabilities, 29,* 79–92.

Clark, G. M., & Patton, J. R. (1995). *Transition planning inventory.* Austin, TX: PRO-ED.

Council for Exceptional Children. (1978). *Position paper on career education.* Reston, VA: Author.

Crawford, J. E., & Crawford, D. M. (1975). *Crawford small parts dexterity test.* New York: Psychological Corporation.

Cummings, R. W., & Maddux, C. D. (1987). *Career and vocational education for the mildly handicapped.* Springfield, IL: Thomas.

deBettencourt, L., Zigmond, N., & Thornton, H. (1989). Follow-up of postsecondary-age rural learning disabled graduates and dropouts. *Exceptional Children, 56,* 40–49.

Division on Mental Retardation and Developmental Disabilities. (1994). Dealing with secondary curricula & policy issues for students with MR/DD. *MRDD Express, 4*(3), 3–4.

Dunn, C. (1996). A status report on transition planning for individuals with learning disabilities. *Journal of Learning Disabilities, 29,* 17–30.

Edgar, E. (1987). Secondary programs in special education: Are many of them justifiable? *Exceptional Children, 53,* 555–561.

Edgar, E., & Levine, P. (1987). *Special education students in transition: Washington state data 1976–1987.* Unpublished manuscript.

Enderle, J., & Severson, S. (1991). *Enderle-Severson transition rating scale.* Moorehead, MN: Practical Press.

Evers, R. B. (1996). The positive force of vocational education: Transition outcomes for youth with learning disabilities. *Journal of Learning Disabilities, 29,* 69–78.

Faas, L. A., D'Alonzo, B. J., & Stile, S. W. (1990). Personality patterns of successful and unsuccessful adults with learning disabilities. *Career Development for Exceptional Individuals, 13,* 1–12.

Fafard, M., & Haubrich, P. A. (1981). Vocational and social adjustment of learning disabled adults: A follow-up study. *Learning Disability Quarterly, 4,* 122–130.

Fairweather, J. S., Stearns, M. S., & Wagner, M. M. (1989). Resources available in school districts serving secondary special education students: Implications for transition. *The Journal of Special Education, 22,* 419–432.

Fardig, D., Algozzine, R., Schwartz, S., Hensel, J., & Westling, D. (1985). Postsecondary vocational adjustment of rural, mildly handicapped students. *Exceptional Children, 52,* 115–121.

Fourqurean, J. M., Meisgeier, C., Swank, P. R., & Williams, R. E. (1991). Correlates of postsecondary employment outcomes for young adults with learning disabilities. *Journal of Learning Disabilities, 24,* 400–405.

Frank, A., Sitlington, P., & Carson, R. (1991). Transition of adolescents with behavior disorders—Is it successful? *Behavioral Disorders, 16,* 180–191.

Frank, A., Sitlington, P., Cooper, L., & Cool, V. (1990). Adult adjustment of individuals enrolled in Iowa mental disabilities programs. *Education and Training in Mental Retardation, 25,* 62–75.

Fulton, S. A., & Sabornie, E. J. (1994). Evidence of employment inequality among females with disabilities. *The Journal of Special Education, 28*(2), 149–165.

Gajar, A., Goodman, L., & McAfee, J. (1993). *Secondary schools and beyond: Transition of individuals with mild disabilities.* Upper Saddle River, NJ: Merrill/Prentice Hall.

Gaylord-Ross, R. (1986). The role of assessment in transitional, supported employment. *Career Development for Exceptional Individuals, 11,* 129–134.

Gaylord-Ross, C., Forte, J., & Gaylord-Ross, R. (1986). The community classroom: Technological vocational training for students with severe handicaps. *Career Development for Exceptional Individuals, 9*(1), 24–33.

Geist, H. (1988). *GEIST picture interest inventory* (rev. ed.). Los Angeles: Western Psychological Services.

Glascoe, L. G., Miller, L. S., & Kokaska, C. J. (1986). *Life-centered career education: Activity book two.* Reston, VA: The Council for Exceptional Children.

Gordon, L. V. (1981). *Gordon occupational checklist.* New York: Psychological Corporation.

Greenan, J. P. (1983a). Identification and validation of generalizable skills in vocational programs. *Journal of Vocational Education Research, 8*(3), 46–71.

Greenan, J.P. (1983b). *Identification of generalizable skills in secondary vocational programs: Executive summary.* Springfield: Illinois State Board of Education, Department of Adult, Vocational, and Technical Education.

Halpern, A. S. (1990). A methodological review of follow-up and follow-along studies tracking school leavers from special education. *Career Development for Exceptional Individuals, 13,* 13–27.

Halpern, A. S. (1992). Transition: Old wine in new bottles. *Exceptional Children, 58,* 202–211.

Halpern, A. S., & Benz, M. R. (1987). A statewide examination of secondary special education for students with mild disabilities: Implications for the high school curriculum. *Exceptional Children, 54,* 122–129.

Halpern, A. S., Irvin, L., & Landman, J. J. (1979). *Tests of everyday living.* Monterey, CA: CTB/McGraw-Hill.

Halpern, A. S., Irvin, L., & Munkres, J. (1986). *Social and prevocational information battery— Revised.* Monterey, CA: CTB/McGraw-Hill.

Haring, K., & Lovett, D. (1990). A follow-up study of special education graduates. *The Journal of Special Education, 23,* 465–477.

Haring, K., Lovett, D., & Smith, D. (1990). A follow-up study of recent special education graduates of learning disabilities programs. *Journal of Learning Disabilities, 23,* 108–113.

Hartzell, H., & Compton, C. (1984). Learning disability: 10-year follow-up. *Pediatrics, 74,* 1058–1064.

Hasazi, S. B., Gordon, L. R., & Roe, C. A. (1985). Factors associated with the employment status of handicapped youth exiting high school from 1979–1983. *Exceptional Children, 51,* 455–469.

Hasazi, S. B., Gordon, L. R., Roe, C. A., Finck, K., Hull, M., & Salembier, G. (1985). A statewide follow-up on post high school employment and residential status of students labeled "mentally retarded." *Education and Training of the Mentally Retarded, 20,* 222–234.

Hill, J. W., Hill, M., Wehman, P., Banks, P. D., Pendleton, P., & Britt, C. (1985). Demographic analyses related to successful job retention for competitively employed persons who are mentally retarded. In P. Wehman & J. W. Hill (Eds.), *Competitive employment for persons with mental retardation: From research to practice* (Vol. 1, pp. 65–88). Richmond: Rehabilitation Research and Training Center, Virginia Commonwealth University.

Hoisch, S. A., Karen, R. L., & Franzini, L. R. (1992). Two-year follow-up of the competitive employment status of graduates with developmental disabilities. *Career Development of Exceptional Individuals, 15,* 149–155.

Holland, J. (1985). *The self-directed search.* New York: Psychological Corporation.

Hoy, C., & Gregg, N. (1994). *Assessment: The special educator's role.* Pacific Grove, CA: Brooks/Cole.

Hoyt, K. B., Evans, R. N., Mackin, E., & Mangum, G. L. (1974). *Career education: What it is and how to do it.* Salt Lake City, UT: Olympus.

Humes, C., & Brammer, G. (1985). LD career success after high school. *Academic Therapy, 21,* 171–176.

Iowa Department of Education. (1989a). *Iowa statewide follow-up study: Adult adjustment of individuals with learning disabilities one year after leaving school.* Unpublished manuscript.

Iowa Department of Education. (1989b). *Iowa statewide follow-up study: Adult adjustment of individuals with mental disabilities one year after leaving school.* Unpublished manuscript.

Iowa Department of Education. (1990). *Iowa statewide follow-up study: Adult adjustment of individuals with behavior disorders one year after leaving school.* Unpublished manuscript.

Janes, C., Hesselbrock, V., Myers, D., & Penniman, J. (1979). Problem boys in young adulthood: Teachers' ratings and 12-year follow-up. *Journal of Youth and Adolescence, 8,* 453–472.

Johansson, C. B. (1986). *Career assessment inventory enhanced version.* Minneapolis, MN: National Computer Systems.

Johnson, D. R., Bruininks, R. H., & Thurlow, M. L. (1987). Meeting the challenge of transition service planning through improved interagency cooperation. *Exceptional Children, 53,* 522–530.

Keith, K. D., & Schalock, R. L. (1995). *Quality of student life questionnaire.* Worthington, OH: IDS.

Kohler, P. D. (1993). Best practices in transition: Substantiated or implied? *Career Development for Exceptional Individuals, 16,* 107–121.

Kokaska, C. J., & Brolin, D. E. (1985). *Career education for handicapped individuals.* Upper Saddle River, NJ: Merrill/Prentice Hall.

Kranstover, L. L., Thurlow, M. L., & Bruininks, R. H. (1989). Special education graduates versus nongraduates: A longitudinal study of outcomes. *Career Development for Exceptional Individuals, 12,* 153–166.

Kregel, J., Wehman, P., Seyfarth, J., & Marshall, K. (1986). Community integration of young adults with mental retardation: Transition from school to adulthood. *Education and Training of the Mentally Retarded, 21,* 35–42.

Levin, E., Zigmond, N., & Birch, J. (1985). A follow-up study of 52 learning disabled adolescents. *Journal of Learning Disabilities, 18,* 2–7.

Levine, P., & Edgar, E. (1994). Respondent agreement in follow-up studies of graduates of special and regular education programs. *Exceptional Children, 60,* 334–343.

Lichtenstein, S. (1993). Transition from school to adulthood: Case studies of adults with learning disabilities who dropped out of school. *Exceptional Children, 59,* 336–347.

Linden, B., & Forness, S. (1986). Post-school adjustment of mentally retarded persons with psychiatric disorders: A ten-year follow-up. *Education and Training of the Mentally Retarded, 21,* 157–164.

McCarney, S. B. (1989). *Transition behavior scale.* Columbia, MO: Hawthorne Educational Service.

McDonnell, J., Sheehan, M., & Wilcox, B. (1983). *Effective transition from school to work and adult services: A procedural handbook for parents and teachers.* Lane County, OR: Lane County Education Service District.

Menz, F. E., Hansen, G., Smith, H., Brown, C., Ford, M., & McCrowley, G. (1989). Gender equity in access, services, and benefits from vocational rehabilitation. *Journal of Rehabilitation, 55,* 31–40.

Miller, R. J., Rzonca, C., & Snider, B. (1991). Variables related to the type of postsecondary education experience chosen by young adults with learning disabilities. *Journal of Learning Disabilities, 24,* 188–191.

Mithaug, D. E., Horiuchi, C., & Fanning, P. N. (1985). A report on the Colorado statewide follow-up survey of special education students. *Exceptional Children, 51,* 397–404.

Mithaug, D. E., Martin, J. E., & Agran, M. (1987). Adaptability instruction: The goal of transition programming. *Exceptional Children, 53,* 500–505.

Mithaug, D. E., Martin, J. E., & Burger, D. L. (1986). *VITAL checklist and curriculum guide.* Colorado Springs, CO: Ascent Publications.

National Longitudinal Transition Study. (1989, March). *The transition experiences of youth with disabilities: A report from the NLTS.* Paper presented at the annual meeting of the Council for Exceptional Children, San Francisco.

Neel, R., Meadows, N., Levine, P., & Edgar, E. (1988). What happens after special education: A statewide follow-up study of secondary students who have behavioral disorders. *Behavioral Disorders, 13,* 209–216.

Neubert, D. A., Tilson, G. P., & Ianacone, R. N. (1989). Postsecondary transition needs and employment patterns of individuals with mild disabilities. *Exceptional Children, 55,* 494–500.

Okolo, C. M., & Sitlington, P. (1986). The role of special education in LD adolescents' transition from school to work. *Learning Disability Quarterly, 9,* 141–155.

Parent, W. S., Kregel, J., & Wehman, P. (1992). *The vocational integration index: A guide for rehabilitation professionals.* Stoneham, MA: Andover Medical Publishers.

Peraino, J. M. (1992). Post-21 follow-up studies: How do special education graduates fare? In P. Wehman (Ed.), *Life beyond the classroom: Transition strategies for young people with disabilities* (pp. 21–70). Baltimore: Paul H. Brookes.

Perotti, F. (1985). A comparison of the vocational adjustment of educable mentally retarded adults after completion of work-study, vocational-technical and resource room high school programs. *Dissertation Abstracts International, 45,* 2487A.

Phelps, L. A., & McCarty, T. (1984). Students assessment practices. *Career Development for Exceptional Individuals, 7,* 30–38.

Posthill, S. M., & Roffman, A. J. (1991). The impact of a transitional training program for young adults with learning disabilities. *Journal of Learning Disabilities, 24,* 619–629.

Reiff, H. B., & deFur, S. (1992). Transition for youths with learning disabilities: A focus on developing independence. *Learning Disability Quarterly, 15,* 237–249.

Revell, W. G., Wehman, P., Kregel, J., West, M., & Rayfield, R. (1994). Supported employment for persons with severe disabilities: Positive trends in wages, models, and funding. *Education and Training in Mental Retardation and Developmental Disabilities, 29,* 256–264.

Roessler, R. T., Brolin, D. E., & Johnson, J. M. (1990). Factors affecting employment success and quality of life: A one year follow-up of students in special education. *Career Development of Exceptional Individuals, 13,* 95–107.

Rojewski, J. W. (1992). Key components of model transition services for students with learning disabilities. *Learning Disability Quarterly, 15,* 135–150.

Rusch, F. R., Destefano, L., Chadsey-Rusch, J., Phelps, L. A., & Szymanski, E. (Eds.). (1992). *Transition from school to adult life: Models, linkages, and policy.* Pacific Grove, CA: Brooks/Cole.

Sands, D. J., & Kozleski, E. B. (1994). Quality of life differences between adults with and without disabilities. *Education and Training in Mental Retardation and Developmental Disabilities, 29,* 90–101.

Schalock, R. L., & Keith, K. D. (1995). *Quality of life questionnaire.* Worthington, OH: IDS.

Schalock, R., Wolzen, B., Ross, I., Elliott, B., Werbel, G., & Peterson, K. (1986). Post-secondary community placement of handicapped students: A five-year follow-up. *Learning Disability Quarterly, 9,* 295–303.

Scuccimarra, D., & Speece, D. (1990). Employment outcomes and social integration of students with mild handicaps: The quality of life two years after high school. *Journal of Learning Disabilities, 23,* 213–219.

Sitlington, P. L. (1996). Transition to living: The neglected component of transition programming for individuals with learning disabilities. *Journal of Learning Disabilities, 29,* 31–39, 52.

Sitlington, P., & Frank, A. (1990). Are adolescents with learning disabilities successfully crossing the bridge into adult life? *Learning Disability Quarterly, 13,* 97–111.

Sitlington, P., Frank, A., & Carson, R. (1992). Adult adjustment among high school graduates with mild disabilities. *Exceptional Children, 59,* 221–233.

Spruill, J. A., & Cohen, L. G. (1990). An analysis of the transition process in Maine. *Rural Special Education Quarterly, 10*(2), 30–35.

Stodden, R. A., & Browder, P. M. (1986). Community based competitive employment preparation of developmentally disabled persons: A program description and evaluation. *Education and Training of the Mentally Retarded, 21,* 43–53.

Strong, E. K., Campbell, D. P., & Hansen, J. (1985). *The Strong-Campbell interest inventory.* Minneapolis, MN: National Computer Systems.

Szymanski, E. M., King, J., Parker, R. M., & Jenkins, W. M. (1989). The state-federal rehabilitation program: Interface with special education. *Exceptional Children, 56,* 70–77.

U.S. Department of Labor. (1970a). *General aptitude test battery.* Washington, DC: U.S. Government Printing Office.

U.S. Department of Labor. (1970b). *Nonreading aptitude test battery.* Washington, DC: U.S. Government Printing Office.

U. S. Department of Labor. (1981). *Interest checklist.* Washington, DC: U.S. Government Printing Office.

Wagner, M. (1992, April). *Being female—A secondary disability? Gender differences in the transition experiences of young people with disabilities.* Paper presented at the annual meeting of the American Educational Research Association (Special Education Special Interest Group), San Francisco.

Wagner, M., D'Amico, R., Marder, C., Newman, L., & Blackorby, J. (1992). *What happens next? Trends in postschool outcomes of youth with disabilities.* Menlo Park, CA: SRI International.

Wehman, P. (Ed.). (1992). *Life beyond the classroom: Transition strategies for young people with disabilities.* Baltimore: Paul H. Brookes.

Wehman, P. H., Kregel, J., Barcus, J. M., & Schalock, R. L. (1986). Vocational transition for students with developmental disabilities. In W. E. Kiernan & J. A. Stark (Eds.), *Pathways to employment for adults with developmental disabilities* (pp. 110–134). Baltimore: Paul H. Brookes.

Wehman, P., & Melia, R. (1985). The job coach: Function in transitional and supported employment. *American Rehabilitation, 11,* 4–7.

White, W., Alley, G., Deshler, D., Schumaker, J., Warner, M., & Clark, F. (1982). Are there learning disabilities after high school? *Exceptional Children, 48,* 273–274.

Will, M. (1983). *OSERS programming for the transition of youth with disabilities: Bridges from school to working life.* Washington, DC: U.S. Department of Education, Office of Special Education and Rehabilitative Services.

Will, M. (1984, June). Bridges from school to working life. *Interchange,* 2–6.

Wimmer, D. (1981). Functional learning curricula in the secondary schools. *Exceptional Children, 47,* 610–616.

Zigmond, N., & Thornton, H. (1985). Learning disabled graduates and dropouts. *Learning Disability Quarterly, 8,* 50–55.

12

Education of Students with Mild Disabilities in Postsecondary Programs

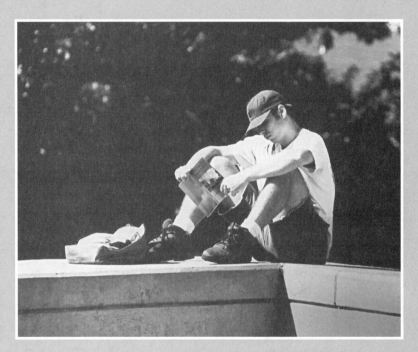

Objectives

After reading this chapter, the reader should be able to:

1. discuss several factors that have contributed to the increasing emergence of special programs at the postsecondary level;

2. discuss the recent litigation and legislation that affects service providers at the postsecondary level in their admission requirements for, delivery of services to, and assessment of students with disabilities;

3. delineate a continuum of service options available for adults with disabilities at postsecondary institutions;

4. identify the skills students with mild disabilities must have in their repertoire for successful completion of postsecondary training;

5. discuss the issues of training adults with learning disabilities at the postsecondary level;

6. identify recent technological advances appropriate to assist students with mild disabilities in postsecondary settings.

Postsecondary programs, which include vocational and technical programs as well as community colleges and four-year colleges and universities, offer many individuals with disabilities age-appropriate integrated environments in which they can expand their personal, social, and academic abilities. This chapter discusses the impetus for studying postsecondary training with persons with mild disabilities, the diversity and scope of programs for adults with mild disabilities at the postsecondary level, and guidelines for assessment and preparation of students for successful postsecondary training.

Impetus for Studying Postsecondary Training with Persons with Mild Disabilities

An increasing number of students with mild disabilities are entering colleges, vocational schools, and advanced technical schools (Mangrum & Strichart, 1988; McGuire, Norlander, & Shaw, 1990; Vogel, 1993). In the late 1980s, Matthews, Anderson, and Skolnick (1987) estimated that more than 130,000 students with learning disabilities were accessing college-level programs. According to the American Council on Education's freshman norms for 1988 (Astin, Green, Korn, Schalit, & Berz, 1988), 6% of all college freshman reported having at least one disability. These students represent the fastest-growing group of college students with disabilities (Norlander, Shaw, & McGuire, 1990; Shaw & Norlander, 1986)—more than twice the number of students with disabilities of a decade ago (Vogel & Adelman, 1992, 1993). According to Brinkerhoff, Shaw, and McGuire (1993), an estimated 35,000 students with identified learning disabilities attend four-year colleges in the United States.

In response to the influx of such students at the postsecondary level, numerous support programs have been developed. The pressure to expand programs for students with mild disabilities has come from various groups (see Figure 12.1). Such forces as the enactment and enforcement of Section 504 of the Rehabilitation Act of 1973 guaranteeing the right of equal access, lobbying efforts by parents and support groups (e.g., Learning Disabilities Association) persuading personnel to develop programs, enrollments of traditional college students declining, outgrowth of services at the elementary and high school levels, and legislation such as the Americans with Disabilities Act of 1990 have all played a part in

Figure 12.1
Factors contributing to pressure to expand postsecondary programs

PL 94-142, implemented in 1978, created mandated services that have contributed to students' success through high school.

Emphasis on full inclusion has assisted students in obtaining sufficient credits for postsecondary institutions.

Transition plans have caused personnel and families to begin to prepare for the future at an earlier point in time.

Recent technological developments have assisted students with disabilities in compensating for their differences in postsecondary settings.

Increasing public awareness of learning disabilities and advocacy groups have resulted in increased awareness of postsecondary options.

Section 504 of Rehabilitation Act of 1973 provided for equal access to public institutions and the Americans with Disabilities Act of 1990 expanded equal access into the private sector.

Instructional modifications are becoming more common in high schools along with effective instruction in learning strategies and metacognitive approaches.

the development of postsecondary programs for students with disabilities. Students themselves have also played a major role in the development of programs to suit their needs. They want to pursue their dreams, just as much as those students without disabilities.

Many students with disabilities choose to enter postsecondary institutions for the very same reasons as their peers. The transition from high school into postsecondary settings is a complex time for all students, with or without disabilities (Halpern, Yovanoff, Doren, & Benz, 1995). Some students with disabilities have been successful in postsecondary institutions and have achieved associate's, bachelor's and graduate degrees. They have developed friendships, participated in extracurricular activities, and sought employment.

Postsecondary-Level Educational Programs for Adults with Mild Disabilities

The expanding numbers of students with disabilities in higher education and their presence in university and college classrooms are realities that must be addressed by higher-education institutions. Persons with learning disabilities are not the only group of young adults with disabilities who are taking advantage of postsecondary programs (Gajar, Goodman, & McAfee, 1993); students with emotional-behavioral disorders and mild mental retardation have also recently accessed similar special programs (Gajar et al., 1993). As these students pursue their advanced studies, postsecondary institutions are being legally and ethically challenged to meet the needs of this emerging group of special students (Dalke, 1991).

Legal Foundations for Postsecondary Educational Programs

Since the beginning of the 1970s many of the rights and freedoms taken for granted by persons without disabilities have been made available to individuals with disabilities. Due to legislative changes, the rights of these students to receive nondiscriminatory education began to be recognized. Equal access was viewed from a lifelong perspective and was expanded to all postsecondary educational settings, including four-year colleges and universities, two-year community colleges, vocational technical schools, technical institutes, trade schools, and adult education programs.

In 1973, through the passage of **Section 504 of the Rehabilitation Act** of 1973 (PL 93-112), individuals with disabilities were guaranteed the right of equal access to any program receiving federal funding. This law, which changed the way individuals with disabilities are treated, reads as follows:

> No otherwise qualified handicapped individual in the United States shall solely by reasons of his handicap, be excluded from participation in, be denied the benefits of, or be subjected to discrimination under any program or activity receiving Federal financial assistance. (PL 93-112, 1973)

Since the inception of this law, there has been much controversy about the interpretation and implementation of the regulations of Section 504. The phrase "no otherwise qualified handicapped individual" has caused educators to be concerned that the standards of their programs would become jeopardized. Mangrum and Strichart (1988) attempted to clarify what is meant by "qualified individual":

> A qualified handicapped person is defined as one who meets the academic and technical standards requisite to admission or participation in an education program or activity . . . who with an auxiliary aid or reasonable program modification, can meet the academic requirements that an institution can demonstrate are essential to its educational programs. (p. 12)

Basically, an institution cannot disqualify an applicant with a disability who can meet the program's criteria for admission.

Program accessibility is another crucial term in Section 504, as it applies to all aspects of higher education. The term refers to (a) recruitment, (b) admissions, (c) academic programs, (d) treatment of students, and (e) nonacademic services. Students with disabilities cannot be denied accessibility to all aspects of higher education as a result of their disability. Some examples: if a student in a wheelchair needs a course that meets on the second floor of a building without an elevator, the class would have to be moved to the first floor; if a student with learning disabilities had difficulty taking timed tests, he or she should be allowed to take tests in the Disabled Student Services Offices with "untimed" accommodations.

Diversity and Scope of Programs

Available support services for students with disabilities are very diverse. The extent of services offered by particular institutions varies according to service goal priorities, size of the institution, and types of degrees offered. Ryan and Price (1992) list sample accommodations for adults with disabilities in four postsecondary settings (see Table 12.1). Taped texts, tutoring, course waivers, reduced course loads, and altered assessment and admission procedures are among the most common.

Shaw and Brinkerhoff (1990) suggested the following continuum of postsecondary support services most commonly available for students with learning disabilities:

1. No services available
2. Decentralized and limited
   no formal contact person
   limited service
3. Loosely coordinated
   contact person available, part-time staff
   students often referred to on-campus resources
4. Centrally coordinated
   often provided through Disabled Student Services
   part-time or full-time coordinator
   generic services (e.g., testing accommodations)
   student self-identification requires documentation

Table 12.1
Sample accommodations for adults with disabilities in four postsecondary settings

Adult Basic Education	Higher Education	Vocational Education	Pre-Employment Employment
Literacy/numeracy tutoring	Content area tutoring	Performance tutoring	Job shadowing
Individualized instruction	One-to-one/small group tutoring	One-to-one/small group tutoring	Job mentoring
			Time-limited job coaching
Peer tutoring	Peer tutoring	Peer tutoring	Prerequisite skill training
Developmental level courses	Developmental level courses	Developmental level courses	Task substitution
	Course waivers	Course waivers	Job sharing
Self-paced courseload	Reduced courseload	Reduced courseload	Manuals and directions on audiotape
Texts on audiotape	Texts on audiotape	Texts/manuals on audiotape	Performance demonstrations on videotape
		Performance demonstrations on videotape	Note takers
	Note takers	Note takers	
Special test site	Special test site	Special test site	On-site evaluation
Extra time on tests	Extra time on tests	Extra time on tests	Request for time extension
Performance-based assessment		Performance-based assessment	Performance-based assessment

Source: From "Adults with LD in the 1990s" by A. G. Ryan and L. Price, 1992, *Intervention in School and Clinic, 28,* 12. Copyright by PRO-ED, Inc. Reprinted by permission.

5. Data-based

    full-time coordinator

    IEP based on diagnostic testing

    tutoring and accommodations provided

    liaison with other campus resources

6. Specialized

    nonmainstreamed setting

    program specifically designed for LD students only

    may be vocationally or educationally oriented

    services provided by trained staff (p. 8)

Services for students with disabilities vary considerably from one institution to another; in addition, they vary across institutions within a category of service. For example, tutoring may include content-area tutoring and/or study-skills tutoring.

Specific Two-Year and Four-Year College Programs

Because there are many more two- and four-year colleges admitting students with disabilities than actually have well-developed programs, it is imperative that secondary-school personnel help each student select a program that fits the unique needs of that student (McGuire & Shaw, 1987).

    There are several academic and social considerations school personnel and perspective students should review prior to selecting a two- or four-year college institution. The following list of selected accommodations and services that are provided by some institutions should be reviewed by prospective entering freshman:

1. admission procedures
2. availability of precollege courses
3. availability of developmental and remedial classes
4. course waiver provisions
5. size of the institution
6. size of individual classes
7. specific support services
8. availability of transition services

There are several two- and four-year institutions that specifically accommodate incoming students with mild disabilities. The University of Wisconsin-Whitewater, for example, has a five-week noncredit summer transition program that enables students with learning disabilities to enter the fall semester with the confidence needed to experience success. The program, known as ASSIST (Adult Services Supporting Instruction Survival Tactics) was designed with the following goals (Dalke & Schmitt, 1987):

To provide an opportunity to explore and address the emotional factors involved in losing a family support system

To provide an educational experience similar to what is expected in college

To familiarize students with the layout of the campus and community

To identify and describe organizational agencies and related services available to students

To provide direct instruction in study skills, time management, note-taking skills, and library usage. (p. 177)

In the 1990s, the surge of interest in postsecondary education for students with disabilities has encouraged many more institutions to develop support service programs to attract such students (deBettencourt, Bonero, & Sabornie, 1995).

No two postsecondary programs are alike in the services available for students with disabilities. Kravets and Wax (1993) organized the available services into three categories: (a) structured programs, (b) coordinated services, and (c) services. Structured programs offer the most comprehensive services, coordinated services are not as comprehensive, and services are the least comprehensive. Teachers, parents, and students should identify which of the three levels is most appropriate.

Technical Education and Vocational Rehabilitation Programs

Many students with mild disabilities leave secondary schools to attend a vocational rehabilitation training program. The past decade has demonstrated that adults with disabilities have a wide variety of vocational options at the postsecondary level. The Carl Perkins Vocational and Technical Act of 1984 (PL 98-524) encouraged program administrators to provide vocational training for students with disabilities. (See Figure 12.2 for specific requirements of Public Law 98-524.)

Figure 12.2
Carl D. Perkins Vocational Education Act of 1984 (Public Law 98-524)

---

1. The student's individualized education program (IEP) must address vocational planning and programming.

2. The student's vocational interests, abilities, and special needs must be assessed.

3. Vocational instruction, curriculum, equipment, and facilities must be adapted to meet the unique needs of the student with disabilities.

4. The student with disabilities must be provided with counseling, guidance, and career development activities by professionally trained counselors.

5. The student with disabilities must be provided with counseling services that will facilitate the successful transition from school to postschool employment.

Source: Adapted from "Strategies for Transition to Employment Settings" by L. K. Elksnin and N. Elksnin in *Teaching Adolescents with Learning Disabilities: Strategies and Methods* (2nd ed.) (pp. 536–537) by D. D. Deshler, E. S. Ellis, & B. K. Lenz (Eds.), 1996, Denver: Love.

Scheiber and Talpers (1987) identified technical institutes, community colleges, and vocational-technical centers as public vocational education institutions. Private or proprietary programs include technical, trade, and business schools. Postsecondary vocational education is available in such fields as cosmetology, automotive service, food services, real estate, masonry, child care, medical technology, and horticulture. Such programs provide a viable alternative to college or university programs for students who are mildly disabled (Gajar et al., 1993).

In contrast to the college and university goals, the focus of **vocational rehabilitation** agency service providers is on employment. Any person can be referred to a technical education or vocational rehabilitation program. However, many state vocational rehabilitation agencies require that a diagnosis of learning disabilities be made by a licensed physician; they often do not accept a school's label. The diagnosis of a learning disability at the high school level does not automatically entitle a person to vocational rehabilitation services. Vocational rehabilitation, an eligibility rather than an entitlement program, has its own definition of learning disabilities and accompanying eligibility criteria. The agency defines persons with learning disabilities as "individuals who have a disorder in one or more of the psychological processes involved in understanding, perceiving, or expressing language or concepts." Three general criteria that most vocational rehabilitation agencies require are:

1. the presence of a physical or mental disability that constitutes or results in a substantial handicap to employment,
2. a reasonable expectation that vocational rehabilitative services may benefit the individual in terms of employability, and
3. that the psychological processing disorder be diagnosed by a licensed physician and/or a licensed or certified psychologist who is skilled in the diagnosis and treatment of such disorders.

Soon after a person is determined to be eligible for vocational rehabilitative services, an assigned counselor develops an Individualized Written Rehabilitation Program (IWRP) (Dowdy, Smith, & Nowell, 1992). Basic skill development, communication and interpersonal skill building, and specific on-the-job skills have been recognized as important parts of individual written rehabilitation programs (Okolo & Sitlington, 1986).

Many of the faculty and staff in postsecondary technical education settings do not have knowledge of the attributes of students with learning disabilities, nor do they understand the multiple ways in which instruction, materials, and other aspects of technical education can be modified to accommodate students with disabilities (Ryan & Price, 1992). Currently, few states have taken the initiative to train staff at vocational rehabilitation settings to work with students with disabilities (Ryan & Price, 1992).

Many secondary teachers are not aware of the vocational rehabilitation services available in their community. Special education teachers at the high school level need to develop a better understanding of the vocational rehabilitation system in order to access services more efficiently (Dowdy, Smith, & Nowell, 1992).

Supported Employment Models

Supported employment is paid employment for those with disabilities who need ongoing support on the job. We discuss this model in the postsecondary section because for some individuals with disabilities supported employment may present a transitional situation in preparation for an employed position without support. McLaughlin and Wehman (1992) outline four types of **supported employment models:**

1. *Individual placement model,* in which a job coach provides on-the-job training to individuals with disabilities.
2. *Mobile work crew model,* in which individuals with disabilities work in groups that travel from one work site to another.
3. *Enclave model,* in which employees work in an integrated setting at a business.
4. *Entrepreneurial model,* in which individuals with disabilities work with individuals without disabilities at a not-for-profit site.

Individuals with disabilities who are trained through a supported employment model may fare better in competitive employment than those who have worked only in sheltered situations (Wehman et al., 1989).

Assessment Issues

Although some students will enter postsecondary institutions with a high-quality assessment packet completed and their identity defined (i.e., student with learning disabilities), other students enter having never been identified as in need of special services. With little consensus on appropriate measures for identifying adults with mild disabilities (Blackburn & Iovacchini, 1982; Hoy & Gregg, 1986), assessment procedures vary considerably. Some of the variance is increased by the lack of consistency in admission criteria across postsecondary programs (Ostertag, Baker, Howard, & Best, 1982). Some programs serve only students who are designated as learning disabled; others serve a broad array of students with disabilities.

The goals for assessment of learning disabilities at the postsecondary level should resemble those at the secondary level, which are:

1. to identify the student's strengths and weaknesses,
2. to determine whether a discrepancy exists between aptitude and achievement,
3. to determine whether any medical conditions exist (e.g., vision, hearing), and
4. to determine the student's individual educational plans.

At the time of submission of materials (i.e., past assessment results) for entry into a postsecondary institution, many students with disabilities encounter their first major accommodation inquiry. Do their assessment materials reflect their potential, and if not, will the institution accept other materials? Because the high school GPA may not be an adequate reflection of academic performance if there is a wide range in grades attributable to a learning disability (Shaywitz & Shaw, 1988), other high school assessment results need to supplement grade scores. The SAT, when administered under standard test conditions, also may not reflect the full potential of a student with learning disabilities. Admissions office personnel cannot discriminate against a student with disabilities, but they can determine a student to be inadmissible based upon assessment information provided.

Mangrum and Strichart (1988) suggest students include materials other than the usual admission materials, such as letters of recommendation, an essay written by the student (e.g., statement of goals, a list of extracurricular activities), and a request for an interview. An interview may prove to be very helpful in the portrayal of a student's potential.

Some colleges have developed special admissions processes for those students who voluntarily identify themselves as learning disabled (Brinkerhoff, Shaw, & McGuire, 1992). Students who have been labeled prior to the completion of high school should review postsecondary institutions' admission policies in terms of assessment requirements.

At the completion of the admission process, some institutions develop an Individual College Plan (ICP) to address the academic and emotional needs of students with disabilities. According to Siperstein (1988), the ICP should assist students in (a) identifying their needs and delineating the most appropriate accommodations to meet these needs, (b) identifying coping skills necessary to learn effectively, (c) identifying available resources, (d) minimizing obstacles for learning, and (e) offering a plan of study and preparation. Not all colleges have the procedures in place to develop an ICP.

Another area of concern in terms of assessment issues at the postsecondary level is diagnosis of foreign language learning problems. Some students experience difficulty passing a foreign language course and have not previously been diagnosed as learning disabled. "Assessment and subsequent documentation of LD are difficult because these students often have done an excellent job of masking or compensating for their learning problems" (Sparks, Ganschow, & Javorsky, 1992, p. 153). Sparks et al. suggest assessing a foreign language learning problem by:

1. reviewing the student's developmental and family history;
2. reviewing the student's elementary and secondary learning history;
3. reviewing the student's foreign language learning history; and
4. administering specific tests such as *Woodcock-Johnson Psychological Battery, Tests of Written Language,* and/or *Tests of Adolescent Language* (pp. 153-154).

Preparing Students for Postsecondary Training

There are critical differences between secondary and postsecondary environmental demands; they differ both quantitatively and qualitatively (Brinkerhoff, Shaw, & McGuire, 1992). For example, college classroom instructional time is typically less than in high school; independent study time is greater. The emphasis on student responsibility is greater at the college level, which implies that the student with disabilities must possess a broad array of learning strategies (e.g., time management, study skills). The need for self-motivation and independence are also more critical at the postsecondary level than at the secondary level.

Dalke and Schmitt (1987) outlined four important differences between high school and college that often cause difficulty for students with mild disabilities:

- decrease in teacher-student contact
- greater academic competition
- different personal support network
- loss of protective environment

Many students arrive at postsecondary institutions unprepared. "Underpreparedness and limited awareness of postsecondary expectations may widen the gap between high school and college for many students" (Brinkerhoff et al., 1992, p. 418). Mangrum and Strichart (1988), among others, suggest that the gap may be closed by training students with disabilities to use effective study habits.

In addition, the recent emphasis on transition issues in the fields of both special and vocational education has encouraged secondary administrators to begin to prepare their students with disabilities for life after high school. In the mid-1980s, the Office of Special Education and Rehabilitative Services (OSERS) identified transition from school to work or higher education for individuals with disabilities as a major national priority for federal funding (Will, 1984). Transitional long-term goals and objectives now must be included in the IEPs of students with disabilities (age 16 and older). The next section discusses specific guidelines for preparing students with disabilities to make a successful transition.

Specific Guidelines for Preparing Students for Postsecondary Training

As more and more students with disabilities opt to continue their education beyond high school, secondary-school personnel must prepare these students to succeed. Many believe that individuals with disabilities will have a more successful transition to higher education settings if adequate preparation is received in their secondary schools.

A critical element of an effective high school program is the determination of which curricula and courses will be taken by students who may choose to enter postsecondary programs. Too frequently students are counseled into a general studies curriculum that later disqualifies them from admission to most four-year colleges. The following section discusses (1) skills that students with disabilities need to perfect during their secondary-level schooling and (2) suggestions for secondary personnel to ensure that these students are successful after exiting high school.

Skills students with mild disabilities need.   Students with mild disabilities who are contemplating entering postsecondary institutions need to prepare themselves academically and socially. Comprehensive secondary services for such students must include early transition planning and the development of independence and self-advocacy skills

(Shaw, Byron, Norlander, McGuire, & Anderson, 1987). In order for transition planning to be effective, the student must be fully involved in the decision-making process, and service providers must communicate with each other to ensure common and appropriate postsecondary goals.

Aune (1991) suggests the following key elements in a successful transition of students from high school to college:

1. self-understanding and self-advocacy,
2. completion of college preparatory coursework,
3. knowledge of accommodations,
4. active student participation, and
5. transition case management.

Students need to learn as much as possible about themselves and their strengths and weaknesses; this includes learning to self-advocate, developing self-confidence, and knowing their limits. Knowledge of one's own disability becomes a potent tool that empowers individuals with disabilities.

In preparing for postsecondary coursework, students should evaluate their organizational and time-management skills. If these skills prove difficult for them they should learn compensatory or study skill strategies that will assist in building these skills. Students with mild disabilities will be faced with the dual challenge of innate difficulties with organization skills combined with a sudden lack of overt supervision of their academic progress by others. Prior preparation in developing a system such as a comprehensive calendar (see Hildreth, Macke, & Carter, 1995) may keep students from becoming overwhelmed.

Students need to become aware of accommodations that may or may not be available to them at the postsecondary level. Some fail to identify themselves with the Disabled Student Service (DSS) office at their institution until after they begin to have trouble. Many institutions require identification with their DSS office before requesting professors to give accommodations. Students should be aware of the types of accommodations made at most institutions and the requirements for these accommodations.

Active student participation in program planning and self-awareness are pivotal in making a successful transition. Deshler, among others (see Deshler, Ellis, & Lenz, 1996), has suggested that active participation by the student in his or her planning increases the likelihood that the student will claim the plan as his or her own and be successful.

Ideally, students will have access to a case manager, teacher, or counselor who keeps the student on target in terms of the training in skills needed, the forms that need to be completed, and the assessment packets that may need to be updated. Not all schools provide this service.

Suggestions for secondary personnel.   As Aune (1991) suggested, designation of a person responsible for each student's transition assures that someone will feel responsible for that student's success. Such secondary personnel, either individually or as part of a team, should develop a four-year schedule for each student. Figure 12.3 illustrates a four-year schedule suggested by Shaw and Brinckerhoff (1990).

Figure 12.3
Four-year high school calendar for college planning and selection

---

Freshman Year

    Plan a college preparatory program of study
    Consider career options

Sophomore Year

    Explore interests
    Identify sources of college information
    Develop a tentative list of post-secondary schools
    Re-evaluate and adjust course of study

Junior Year

    Meet with counselor or college advisor
    Register and take PSAT
    Review sources of information on colleges
      with support programs for students with disabilities
    Discuss the need for special testing with counselor
    Discuss financial considerations
    Finalize list, write and obtain applications
    Call and arrange visits
    Prepare for SAT during summer

Senior Year

    Begin preparing applications
    Create a checklist of application deadlines
    Complete all financial aid forms
    Review college choices, if necessary visit again
    Once accepted, choose school and visit to meet with support personnel

---

Source: From *Training for Independence: Preparing Students with Learning Disabilities for Postsecondary Education* by S. F. Shaw and L. Brinckerhoff, 1990. Paper presented at the Twelfth International Conference of the Council for Learning Disabilities, Austin, TX.

Many secondary-school personnel have serious difficulties in developing effective instructional programs for students with mild disabilities, including those students who might succeed in postsecondary institutions. As a result, many such students who would like to continue their education find themselves unprepared for entry.

Little information is available in the literature that defines the specific roles required of key people involved in the transition process. Shaw and Brinckerhoff (1990) suggest that secondary personnel use the following guidelines to effectively prepare students with disabilities for life after high school:

    approach support services from a strategy perspective

    avoid subject matter tutoring

Figure 12.4
Critical checklist for preparing students with disabilities for postsecondary institutions

1. Make sure all testing (e.g., IQ) is current.
2. Obtain all special testing requirements.
3. Increase student's independent living skills.
4. Encourage student to work part-time or volunteer.
5. Encourage students to self-advocate.
6. Learn about Section 504 and Americans with Disabilities Act.
7. Obtain two copies of all college applications.
8. Visit colleges before making a choice.
9. Encourage students to have their own memberships in organizations for the disabled (e.g., LDA).
10. Make sure it is the student's choice to attend.

Source: From *Training for Independence: Preparing Students with Learning Disabilities for Postsecondary Education* by S. F. Shaw and L. Brinckerhoff, 1990, Paper presented at the Twelfth International Conference of the Council for Learning Disabilities, Austin, TX.

reinforce the importance of word processing skills

promote the development of student responsibility

work with postsecondary student support personnel in promoting awareness at the high school level of the demands of college

assist students to understand their learning styles and to be able to explain them in meaningful terms

Reviewing and understanding the student's level of academic performance in high school coursework as well as on standardized tests will help students and support personnel decide on the appropriateness of postsecondary options. Prior to completion of high school, several critical aspects of the student's materials and program should be reviewed by secondary personnel. Figure 12.4 provides a checklist for secondary personnel for preparing students with disabilities for postsecondary institutions.

Review of Commercial Curriculum Guides for Postsecondary Institutions

Since the passage of the Rehabilitation Act of 1973 and its accompanying Section 504 regulations, students with disabilities have been enrolling in postsecondary institutions in ever-increasing numbers (Mangrum & Strichart, 1988; Vogel, 1985). Because services vary from institution to institution, guides to postsecondary education services abound to assist students with disabilities in their search. Basic information about size, location,

Figure 12.5
Selected guides to postsecondary programs

Kravets, M., & Wax, I. F. (1993). *The K & W guide to colleges for the learning disabled*. New York: Harper Collins.

Mangrum, C. T., & Strichart, S. S. (1988). *College and the learning disabled student* (2nd ed.). Orlando, FL: Grune & Stratton.

Mangrum, C. T., & Strichart, S. S. (1992). *Peterson's guide to colleges with programs for students with learning disabilities*. Princeton, NJ: Peterson's Guides.

Sclafani, A. J., & Lynch, M. J. (1989). *College guide for students with learning disabilities 1988-1989*. Miller Place, NY: Laurel Publications.

Straughn, C. T., & Colby, S. C. (1985). *Lovejoy's college guide for the learning disabled*. New York: Monarch Press.

and housing can be obtained. Although such guides quickly become dated, they are useful in assisting students and teachers in making informed choices.

A comprehensive directory rapidly helps the student and his or her parents and counselor to target potentially appropriate programs and services, but even the most comprehensive directory will not have a complete listing of all institutions that offer services. After selection of an institution, contact should be made to find out about any changes that may have occurred. In addition, whether an institution of choice is not listed, a call should be made to that institution to inquire whether there are services available. Figure 12.5 offers a list of selected guides to postsecondary programs that offer services for students with disabilities.

Issues at the Postsecondary Level

Given the increase in the incidence of students with disabilities at postsecondary institutions, student service providers are faced frequently with the challenge of assuring them equal access, including special services that have not been clearly defined (McGuire, Hall, & Litt, 1991). Bursuck, Rose, Cowen, and Yahaya (1989) conducted a nationwide survey of postsecondary education services for students with learning disabilities. Their results suggest that in the late 1980s most institutions were in compliance with federal Section 504 regulations but that institutions varied considerably in the range of support services they offered. For example, deBettencourt, Bonero, and Sabornie (1995) examined the relationship between services for students with disabilities and career development centers at postsecondary institutions. The findings of deBettencourt et al. (1995) suggest that career development personnel have limited awareness of and little training in the characteristics and needs of students with LD. In addition, few students who are learning disabled use career centers.

On many campuses, students with disabilities are accessing generic support services such as writing centers, counseling services, and tutoring centers. Siperstein (1988) suggested that such service delivery systems have not worked for many students with disabilities and that as the numbers increase, so will the pressures on existing support services staff to make the services successful for these students. Successful interventions at this level must take into account individual student characteristics. As there is heterogeneity in school-age students with disabilities, so too is there among those at the college age.

Administrative Considerations

The literature on serving individuals with learning disabilities in higher education contains many suggestions on adjustments the administration and/or faculty can make in course or program requirements to compensate for a student's learning problem (Gajar, Murphy, & Hunt, 1982). Administrative accommodations usually include modifications in admissions policies and registration policies, reduced course loads, and course waivers.

For example, many colleges allow students with disabilities to register early and to take reduced course loads. Although the college experience may be difficult for such students, pacing of a course of study has proven to be an effective programming variable (Norlander, Shaw, Bloomer, & Czajkowski, 1986). A student with disabilities may not experience as much frustration and failure when taking only two or three courses as he or she might when taking a full college load.

Many colleges and universities require two years of a foreign language; for students with learning disabilities this requirement is often a major stumbling block. Some administrations allow program modifications that include the waiver of the foreign language requirement (Vogel, 1987). However, to obtain such a waiver, the diagnosis of learning disabilities is required (Ganshow, Myer, & Roeger, 1989).

Faculty members also have been instructed to modify their usual teaching and evaluating practices by allowing untimed tests or oral responses versus written ones; however, they need to be educated regarding the attributes of students with learning disabilities, their potential for success, and reasonable accommodations that should be made (Ryan & Price, 1992).

Service Delivery Issues

Higher-education officials have developed a number of support service programs including counseling, tutoring, peer mentoring, and instructional support in response to the increasing number of students with disabilities on their campuses (Mangrum & Strichart, 1988).

Counseling services are often cited as a component of a program for students with disabilities (Mangrum & Strichart, 1988; Vogel, 1987). Such services typically include personal or social counseling, career or vocational counseling, and academic or program counseling (Nelson & Lignugaris-Kraft, 1989).

Instructional accommodations include course modifications and support services such as tutoring, interpreters, taped textbooks, note takers, word processors, allowances for extra time on assignments and tests, copies of lecture notes, and alternative assignments.

Peer mentor systems provide direct support (e.g., guiding the mentee to accessing note takers and tutors) to students with disabilities for a designated number of semesters; then the students are trained to become peer mentors for new freshman or transfer students. The intention of such a system, as Ryan and Price (1992) suggest, is to "(a) lessen the dependence of students who have been previous recipients of services and (b) empower them to become proactive with respect to their own needs and the needs of others" (p. 13).

Technological Issues

Technology has enabled many individuals with mild disabilities to fully function in our society (Raskind & Scott, 1993). They can be trained to use technology to compensate for their disabilities and to help ensure their academic success. In addition, technology has assisted in decreasing students' anxiety about academic tasks and increasing their self-esteem. In this section we will discuss some of the most significant technologies for assisting students with mild disabilities at the postsecondary level. Refer to Table 12.2 for a matrix of technologies arranged according to disability areas.

Table 12.2
Technologies by area of disability

Technology	Written Language	Reading	Organization	Memory	Listening	Math
Word Processing	X					
Spell Checking	X					
Proofreading Programs	X					
Outlining/Brainstorming	X					
Abbreviation Expanders	X					
Speech Recognition	X					
Speech Synthesis/Screen Review	X	X				
Optical Character Recognition Systems		X				
Personal Data Managers			X	X		
Free-Form Databases			X	X		
Variable Speech Control Recorders		X		X	X	
Listening Aids					X	
Talking Calculators						X

Source: From "Technology for Postsecondary Students with Learning Disabilities" by M. H. Raskind and N. G. Scott in *Success for College Students with Learning Disabilities* (pp. 240–275) by S. A. Vogel and P. B. Adelman (Eds.), 1993, New York: Springer-Verlag.

Several researchers (Collins, 1990; MacArthur, Graham, Schwartz, & Schafer, 1995) have found word processors valuable in helping students with written language difficulties. In many college situations students pay for access to word processors on their campus as part of their student fees. The word processor allows a student to write freely without worrying about spelling and grammatical errors, which are easily corrected on the computer before printing. Handwriting difficulties can also be alleviated by the use of a word processor. Spell checkers permit the student to check for misspelled words within a document before a final copy is made. Most programs include a thesaurus and a dictionary; some programs include a speech synthesizer, so the word in question can be heard as well as seen.

There are also speech recognition computer systems; the student can speak to a computer and the computer writes down what is said. This technology may be a great asset to students whose oral language exceeds their written language capabilities.

Optical character recognition (OCR) systems are often available at service offices. Such systems allow a student to place written material (e.g., a page from a textbook) face down on a scanner. The computer scans the material and then it is read back to the student by means of a speech synthesizer. The use of OCR systems can help students compensate for reading difficulties (Raskind & Scott, 1993).

Hand-held personal organizers, which are easy to obtain and relatively inexpensive, assist students in scheduling classes and appointments and recording names, addresses, and phone numbers. Calendars, alarms, and memo lists are some additional features that may be helpful for students.

Technological advances have also been made with relatively common tape recorders and calculators, some of which are quite small and are voice controlled. The price range for such instruments varies from very inexpensive to quite costly.

Technology has important implications for students attending postsecondary institutions. It can assist them in compensating for their difficulties in the areas of mathematics, reading, organization, memory, written language, and listening. The possibilities seem endless as our technology continues to improve on a daily basis (Raskind & Scott, 1993).

Training and Research Needs

Students with disabilities can no longer be relegated to a less rigorous academic high school curriculum while at the same time be given encouragement to pursue college. If they are going to succeed in their postsecondary pursuits, they must be academically and socially prepared. Further research is needed that will look at various strategies and approaches to use with older students with disabilities and how these strategies must carry over to postsecondary environments such as college.

Students are actively seeking information about program options and their rights as matriculating students. Professionals are also interested in information that will enable them to provide appropriate services for students with disabilities (Walker, Shaw, & McGuire, 1992). There is little doubt that we need to continue to study how to program effectively for students with mild disabilities so they can be successful at postsecondary programs.

There is a paucity of research that college administrators might use to design a successful service program for students with mild disabilities; more is needed to determine program eligibility, to identify successful services and the effects of individual program components, to examine what students do after graduation, and to identify services that students find most useful.

Summary

As the 1990s have progressed, so has the development of programs and services provided by colleges and postsecondary settings for students with mild disabilities. A dramatic increase in the number of such students who attend postsecondary institutions has also occurred. We realize now that more postsecondary planning and preparation should begin in high school. We also know that postsecondary service providers need more training in special education and the implementation of services for this population and that we must continue to evaluate the programs that are currently in place to determine what works best so that students with mild disabilities can be more successful in postsecondary settings.

Key Terms

Section 504 of the Rehabilitation Act
program accessibility
vocational rehabilitation

supported employment model
optical character recognition (OCR) systems

References

Astin, A., Green, K., Korn, W., Schalit, M., & Berz, E. (1988). *The American freshman: National norms for 1988*. Los Angeles: University of California.

Aune, E. (1991). A transition model for postsecondary-bound students with learning disabilities. *Learning Disabilities Research and Practice, 6*, 177–187.

Blackburn, J. C., & Iovacchini, E. V. (1982). Student service responsibilities of institutions to learning disabled students. *College and University, 52*, 208–217.

Brinkerhoff, L. C., Shaw, S. F., & McGuire, J. M. (1992). Promoting access, accommodations, and independence for college students with learning disabilities. *Journal of Learning Disabilities, 25*, 417–429.

Brinkerhoff, L. C., Shaw, S. F., & McGuire, J. M. (1993). *Promoting postsecondary education for students with learning disabilities: A handbook for practitioners*. Austin, TX: PRO-ED.

Bursuck, W. D., Rose, E., Cowen, S., & Yahaya, M. A. (1989). Nationwide survey of postsecondary education services for students with learning disabilities. *Exceptional Children, 56*, 236–245.

Collins, T. (1990). The impact of microcomputer word processing on the performance of learning disabled students in a required first year writing course. *Computers and Composition, 8*(1), 49–68.

Dalke, C. L. (1991). *Support programs in higher education for students with learning disabilities*. Gaithersburg, MD: Aspen.

Dalke, C. L., & Schmitt, S. (1987). Meeting the transition needs of college-bound students with learning disabilities. *Journal of Learning Disabilities, 20,* 176–180.

deBettencourt, L. U., Bonero, D. A., & Sabornie, E. J. (1995). Career development services offered to postsecondary students with learning disabilities. *Learning Disabilities Research and Practice, 10,* 102–107.

Deshler, D. D., Ellis, E. S., & Lenz, B. K. (Eds.). (1996). *Teaching adolescents with learning disabilities: Strategies and methods* (2nd ed.) Denver: Love Publishing.

Dowdy, C. A., Smith, E. C., & Nowell, C. H. (1992). Learning disabilities and vocational rehabilitation. *Journal of Learning Disabilities, 25,* 442–447.

Gajar, A., Goodman, L., & McAfee, J. (1993). *Secondary schools and beyond: Transition of individuals with mild disabilities.* New York: Macmillan.

Gajar, A. H., Murphy, J. P., & Hunt, F. M. (1982). A university program for learning disabled students. *Reading Improvement, 19,* 282–288.

Ganshow, L., Myer, B., & Roeger, K. (1989). Implications of the foreign language policies and procedures for students with language learning disabilities. *LD Focus, 2,* 116–123.

Halpern, A. S., Yovanoff, P., Doren, B., & Benz, M. R. (1995). Predicting participation in postsecondary education for school leavers with disabilities. *Exceptional Children, 62,* 151–164.

Hildreth, B. L., Macke, R. A., & Carter, M. L. (1995). The comprehensive calendar: An organizational tool for college students with learning disabilities. *Intervention in School and Clinic, 20,* 306–308.

Hoy, C., & Gregg, N. (1986). Learning disabled students: An emerging population on college campuses. *The Journal of College Admissions, 112,* 10–14.

Kravets, M., & Wax, I. F. (1993). *The K & W Guide to colleges for the learning disabled.* New York: HarperCollins.

Mangrum, C., & Strichart, S. (1988). *College and the learning disabled student* (2nd ed.). Orlando, FL: Grune & Stratton.

Matthews, P., Anderson, D., & Skolnick, B. (1987). Faculty attitude toward accommodations for college students with learning disabilities. *Learning Disabilities Focus, 3,* 46–52.

MacArthur, C. A., Graham, S., Schwartz, S. S., & Schafer, W. D. (1995). Evaluation of a writing instruction model that integrated a process approach, strategy instruction, and word processing. *Learning Disability Quarterly, 18,* 278–291.

McGuire, J. M., Hall, D., & Litt, A. V. (1991). A field-based study of the direct service needs of college students with learning disabilities. *Journal of College Student Development, 32,* 101–108.

McGuire, J. M., Norlander, K. A., & Shaw, S. F. (1990). Postsecondary education for students with learning disabilities: Forecasting challenges for the future. *Learning Disabilities Focus, 5,* 69–74.

McGuire, J. M., & Shaw, S. F. (1987). A decision-making process for the college-bound learning disabled student: Matching learner, institution, and support program. *Learning Disability Quarterly, 10,* 106–111.

McLaughlin, J. A., & Wehman, P. (1992). *Developmental disabilities.* Boston, MA: Andover Medical.

Nelson, R., & Lignugaris-Kraft, B. (1989). Postsecondary education for students with learning disabilities. *Exceptional Children, 56,* 246–265.

Norlander, K. A., Shaw, S. F., & McGuire, J. M. (1990). Competencies of postsecondary education personnel serving students with learning disabilities. *Journal of Learning Disabilities, 23,* 426–432.

Norlander, K. A., Shaw, S. F., McGuire, J. M., Bloomer, R. H., & Czajkowski, A. (1986, October). *Diagnosis and program selection for learning disabled college students.* Paper presented at the Eighth International Conference of the Council for Learning Disabilities, Kansas City, MO.

Okolo, C. M., & Sitlington, P. L. (1986). The role of special education in LD adolescents' transition from school to work. *Learning Disability Quarterly, 9,* 141–155.

Ostertag, B. A., Baker, R. E., Howard, R. F., & Best, L. (1982). Learning disabled programs in California community colleges. *Journal of Learning Disabilities, 15,* 535–538.

Peterson's Guides. (1992). *Peterson's guide to colleges with programs for learning disabled students.* Princeton, NJ: Author.

Raskind, M. H., & Scott, N. G. (1993). Technology for postsecondary students with learning disabilities. In S. A. Vogel & P. B. Adelman (Eds.), *Success for college students with learning disabilities* (pp. 240-275). New York: Springer-Verlag.

Ryan, A. G., & Price, L. (1992). Adults with LD in the 1990s. *Intervention in School and Clinic, 28,* 6–20.

Scheiber, B., & Talpers, J. (1987). *Unlocking potential college and other choices for learning disabled people: A step-by-step guide.* Bethesda, MD: Adler & Adler.

Sclafani, A. J., & Lynch, M. J. (1989). *College guide for students with learning disabilities 1988–1989.* Miller Place, NY: Laurel Publications.

Shaw, S. F., & Brinckerhoff, L. (1990, October). *Training for independence: Preparing students with learning disabilities for postsecondary education.* Paper presented at the Twelfth International Conference of the Council for Learning Disabilities, Austin, TX.

Shaw, S. F., Byron, J., Norlander, K., McGuire, J., & Anderson, P. (1987, April). *Preparing learning disabled students for college.* Paper presented at the International Conference of the Council for Exceptional Children, Chicago, IL.

Shaw, S. F., & Norlander, K. A. (1986). The special educator's role in training personnel to provide assistance to college students with learning disabilities. *Teacher Education and Special Education, 9,* 77–81.

Shaywitz, S. E., & Shaw, R. (1988). The admissions process: An approach to selecting learning disabled students at the most selective colleges. *Learning Disabilities Focus, 3*(2), 81–86.

Siperstein, G. N. (1988). Students with learning disabilities in college: The need for a programmatic approach to critical transitions. *Journal of Learning Disabilities, 7,* 431–436.

Sparks, R., Ganschow, L., & Javorsky, K. L. (1992). Diagnosing and accommodating the foreign language learning difficulties of college students with learning disabilities. *Learning Disabilities Research and Practice, 7,* 150–160.

Straughn, C. T., & Colby, S. C. (1985). *Lovejoy's college guide for the learning disabled.* New York: Monarch Press.

Vogel, S. A. (1985). Learning disabled college students: Identification, assessment, and outcomes. In D. D. Duane & C. K. Leong (Eds.), *Understanding learning disabilities: International and multicultural views* (pp. 179–203). New York: Plenum Press.

Vogel, S. A. (1987). Issues and concerns in LD college programming. In D. Johnson & J. Blalock (Eds.), *Adults with learning disabilities* (pp. 239–275). New York: Grune & Stratton.

Vogel, S. A. (1993). A retrospective and prospective view of postsecondary education for adults with learning disabilities. In S. A. Vogel & P. B. Adelman (Eds.), *Success for college students with learning disabilities* (pp. 3–20). New York: Springer-Verlag.

Vogel, S. A., & Adelman, P. B. (1992). The success of college students with learning disabilities: Factors related to educational attainment. *Journal of Learning Disabilities, 25,* 430–441.

Vogel, S. A., & Adelman, P. B. (Eds.) (1993). *Success for college students with learning disabilities.* New York: Springer-Verlag.

Walker, J. K., Shaw, S. F., & McGuire, J. M. (1992). Concerns of professionals regarding postsecondary education for students with learning disabilities. *Learning Disabilities, 3*(1), 13–18.

Wehman, P., Parent, W., Wood, W., Talbert, C. M., Jasper, C., Miller, S., Marchant, J., & Walker, R. (1989). From school to competitive employment for young adults with mental retardation: Transition in practice. *Career Development for Exceptional Individuals, 12,* 97–105.

Will, M. C. (1984). Educating children with learning problems: A shared responsibility. *Exceptional Children, 52,* 411–415.

Appendix

Addresses

Access Unlimited, 3535 Briarpark Dr., Suite 102, Houston, TX 77042.

Association on Higher Education and Disability (AHEAD), P.O. Box 21192, Columbus, OH 43221-0192.

Center for Dropout Prevention, University of Miami, School of Education, Box 248065, Coral Gables, FL 33124.

Center for Early Adolescents, University of North Carolina at Chapel Hill, Suite 211, Car Mill Mall, Carboro, NC 27510.

Center on Postsecondary Education for Students with Learning Disabilities, The University of Connecticut, 249 Glenbrook Road, Storrs, CT 06269-2064.

Cities in Schools, Inc., 1023 15th Street, NW, Suite 600, Washington, DC 22005.

Council for Exceptional Children (CEC), 1920 Association Drive, Reston, VA 22091-1589.

Council for Learning Disabilities (CLD), P.O. Box 40303, Overland Park, KS 66204.

Division of Career Development, Council for Exceptional Children, 1920 Association Dr., Reston, VA 22091.

HEATH (Higher Education and Adult Training for People with Handicaps) Resource Center, One Dupont Circle, Suite 800, Washington, DC 20036-1193.

IBM National Support Center for Persons with Disabilities, 411 Northside Parkway, Atlanta, GA 30327.

Learning Disabilities Association of America (LDA), 4156 Library Road, Pittsburgh, PA 15234.

National Association of Private Schools for Exceptional Children (NAPSEC). 1522 K. Street N.W., Suite 1032, Washington, DC 20005.

National Center for Learning Disabilities (NCLD), 99 Park Avenue, New York, NY 10016.

National Center for Research in Vocational Education, University of California at Berkeley, 2150 Shattuck Ave., Berkeley, CA 94704.

National Center on Effective Secondary Schools, School of Education, University of Wisconsin—Madison, 1025 West Johnson Street, Madison, WI 53706.

National Clearinghouse for Professions in Special Education, Council For Exceptional Children, 1920 Association Dr., Reston, VA 22314.

National Council on Disability (NCD), 1331 F. Street N.W., Washington, DC 2004- 1107.

National Dropout Prevention Center, Clemson University, 393 College Ave., Clemson, SC 29634.

National Dropout Prevention Network, Ohio State University, 1960 Kenny Road, Columbus, OH 43210.

National Information Center for Children and Youth with Handicaps (NICHY), P.O. Box 1492, Washington, DC 20013.

Secondary Transition Intervention Institute, Transition Institute at Illinois, College of Education, University of Illinois at Urbana—Champaign, 110 Education Building, 1310 S. 6th St., Champaign, Il 61820.

Related Texts

Association on Higher Education and Disability. (1991). *College students with learning disabilities* (2nd ed.). Columbus, OH: Author.

Brinkerhoff, L. C., Shaw, S. F., & McGuire, J. M. (1993). *Promoting postsecondary education for students with learning disabilities: A handbook for practitioners.* Austin, TX: PRO-ED.

Clark, G. M., & Kolstoe, O. P. (1995). *Career development and transition education for adolescents with disabilities* (2nd ed.). Needham Heights, MA: Allyn & Bacon.

Daniels, H., & Anghileri, J. (1995). *Secondary mathematics and special educational needs.* London: Cassell.

Deshler, D. D., Ellis, E. S., & Lenz, B. K. (1996). *Teaching adolescents with learning disabilities: Strategies and methods* (2nd ed.). Denver, CO: Love.

Dowdy, C. A., Patton, J. R., Smith, T. E. C., & Polloway, E. A. (1996). *Attention-deficit/hyperactivity disorder in the classroom: A practical guide for teachers.* Austin, TX: PRO-ED.

Duhan-Sells, R. (Ed.). (1995). *Dealing with youth violence: What schools and communities need to know.* Bloomington, IN: National Educational Service.

Gajar, A., Goodman, L., & McAffee, J. (1993). *Secondary schools and beyond: Transition of individuals with mild disabilities.* New York: Macmillan.

Lenz, B. K., Ellis, E. S., & Scanlon, D. (1996). *Teaching learning strategies to adolescents and adults with learning disabilities.* Austin, TX: PRO-ED.

Mangrum, C. T., III., & Strichart, S. S. (1988). *College and the learning disabled student* (2nd ed.). Orlando, FL: Grune & Stratton.

Masters, L. F., Mori, B. A., & Mori, A. A. (1993). *Teaching secondary students with mild learning and behavior problems.* Austin, TX: PRO-ED.

Nolting, P. (1991). *Math and the learning disabled student: A practical guide for accommodations.* Pompano Beach, FL: Academic Success Press, Inc.

Patton, J. R., & Polloway, E. A. (Eds.) (1996). *Learning disabilities: The challenges of adulthood.* Austin, TX: PRO-ED.

Retish, P., Hitchings, W., Horvath, M., & Schmalle, B. (1991). *Students with mild disabilities in the secondary school.* New York: Longman.

Rooney, K. (1990). *Independent strategies for efficient study.* Richmond, VA: J. R. Enterprises.

Schloss, P. J., Smith, M. A., & Schloss, C. N. (1990). *Instructional methods for adolescents with learning and behavior problems.* Boston: Allyn & Bacon.

Vogel, S. A. (1990). *College students with learning disabilities: A handbook* (4th ed.). Pittsburgh: Learning Disabilities Association of America.

Vogel, S. A., & Adelman, P. B. (Eds.). (1993). *Success for college students with learning disabilities.* New York: Springer-Verlag.

Zigmond, N., Sansone, J., Miller, S. E., Donahoe, K. A., & Kohnke, R. (1986). *Teaching disabled students at the secondary level: What research and experience says to the teacher of exceptional children.* Reston, VA: Council for Exceptional Children.

College Guides

Dalke, C. (1991). *Support programs in higher education for students with disabilities: Access to all.* Gaithersburg, MD: Aspen.

Kravets, M., & Wax, I. F. (1993). *The K & W guide to college for the learning disabled.* New York: HarperCollins.

Mangrum, C. T., III, & Strichart, S. S. (Eds.). (1992). *Peterson's colleges with programs for learning disabled students* (3rd ed.). Princeton, NJ: Peterson's Guides.

Sclafani, A. J., & Lynch, M. J. (1989). *College guide for students with learning disabilities 1988–1989*. Miller Place, NY: Laurel Publications.

Straughn, C. T., & Colby, S. C. (1992). *Lovejoy's college guide for the learning disabled* (3rd ed.). New York: Monarch Press.

Vogel, S. A. (1985). *The college student with a learning disability: A handbook for college LD students, administrators*. Lake Forest, IL: Barat College.

Vogel, S. A., & Stattler, J. L. (1981). *The college student with a learning disability: A handbook for college and university officers, faculty, and administration*. Dekalb, IL: Council for Learning Disabilities.

Willingham, W. (1987). *Handicapped applicants to college: An analysis of admissions decisions*. New York: College Entrance Examination Board.

Classroom Resources

Alper, S. K., Schloss, P. J., & Schloss, C. N. (1994). *Families of students with disabilities: Consultation and advocacy*. Boston: Allyn & Bacon.

Cipani, E. *Non-compliance: Four strategies that work*. Reston, VA: Council for Exceptional Children.

Cipani, E. *Disruptive behavior: Three techniques that work*. Reston, VA: Council for Exceptional Children.

CSDC. *SMARTS: A study skills resource guide* (2nd ed.). Longmont, CO: Sopris West.

CSDC. *Exceptions: A handbook of inclusion activities for teachers of students at grades 6–12 with mild disabilities* (2nd ed.). Longmont, CO: Sopris West.

Culp, G. H., & Watkins, G. M. (1995). *The educator's guide to hypercard and hypertalk—Revised*. Boston: Allyn & Bacon.

Frender, G. *Learning to learn: Strengthening study skills and brain power*. Nashville, TN: Incentive Publications, Inc.

Hicks, B. B. *Youth suicide: A comprehensive manual for prevention and intervention*. Bloomington, IN: National Education Service.

Hoover, J. J. (1990). *Using study skills and learning strategies in the classroom*. Lindale, TX: Hamilton Publications.

Hoover, J. J., & Patton, J. R. (1995). *Teaching students with learning problems to use study skills*. Austin, TX: PRO-ED.

Hoppenstedt, E. M. (1991). *A teacher's guide to classroom management*. Springfield, IL: C. C. Thomas.

Siegel, M., Greener, K., Meyer, G., Halloran, W., & Gaylord-Ross, R. (1993). *Career ladders for challenged youth in transition from school to adult life*. Austin, TX: PRO-ED.

Sobel, M. A., & Maletsky, E. M. (1988). *Teaching mathematics: A source book of aids, activities, and strategies* (2nd ed.). Boston: Allyn & Bacon.

Strichart, S. S., & Mangrum, C. T., III. (1993). *Teaching study strategies to students with learning disabilities*. Boston: Allyn & Bacon.

Young, K. R., West, R. P., Smith, D. J., & Morgan, D. P. (1995). *Teaching self-management strategies to adolescents*. Longmont, CO: Sopris West.

Videos

ADHD—What do we know? An overview of ADHD. This video is specifically designed to help the teacher deal with the ADHD student, thereby providing a better environment for the entire class. Opportunities for Learning. (800) 243-7116. 36 min.

America's schools: Who gives a damn? New York: Columbia University, School for Journalism; Public Broadcasting System. 120 min.

Depression: Beating the blues. New York: Filmakers Library.

Effective schools for children at risk. (1991). Alexandria, VA: Association for School and Curriculum Development. 8 min.

Learning to change: Schools of excellence for at-risk students. (1990). Atlanta, GA: Southern Regional Council, Inc. 29 min.

Project Second Change: Dropouts in America. Arkansas Educational Television Network Foundation. 60 min.

Schools that work: Learning in America. (1990). Arlington, VA: MacNeil/Lehrer and WETA-TV. 120 min.

College: A viable option. HEATH Resource Center, Washington, DC. Produced by the University Bound LD Students Transition Project of the University of Utah, Disabled Student Services (Salt Lake City, UT) discusses what a learning disability is, learning strategies, and compensatory techniques. 20 min.

Degrees of success: Conversations with college students with learning disabilities. (1992). New York: The Access to Learning Program, New York University. (212) 998-4980. This videotape focuses on the experiences of college students with learning disabilities as described by the students themselves.

How difficult can this be? (1989). PBS Video, Alexandria, VA: FAT City Learning Disability Workshop. (703) 739-5380. Richard Lavoie demonstrates through simulation activities the frustration, anger, and anxiety children with learning disabilities encounter in the classroom. 70 min.

Learning disabilities and social skills: Last one picked . . . first one picked on. (1994). PBS Video. (703) 739-5380. This video addresses the social problems LD students face and offers some practical solutions for teachers. 68 min.

Learning disabilities: Coping in college. (1985). Dayton, OH: Handicapped Student Services, Wright State University. (513) 873-2141. This video presents a realistic overview of college life through the eyes of students with learning disabilities.

Understanding learning disabilities in higher education: A Georgetown University perspective. (1991). Washington, DC: Office of Student Affairs, Georgetown University. (202) 687-6985. This video presents the experiences of an accomplished faculty member with dyslexia and those of a student who needed assessment to determine if a learning disability exists.

Name Index

Achenbach, T. M., 39
Ackerman, G., 189
Adams, W. R., 221, 222
Adelman, H. S., 122
Adelman, P. B., 340, 355
Ager, C., 257
Agran, M., 309
Alberg, J., 266
Alberto, P. A., 73, 80, 84, 94
Algozzine, B., 3, 72, 134, 139, 276, 277, 278
Algozzine, R., 203, 300
Algozzine, R. F., 279–280
Allen-Hagen, B., 43
Allen, J., 208
Alley, G. R., 7, 11, 13, 52, 57, 64, 114, 189, 202, 203, 205, 214–215, 216, 234, 282, 302
Allinder, R. M., 160
Allred, R. A., 109
Alter, M., 57
Alvermann, D. E., 102
American Psychiatric Association, 6, 39
Ames, C., 193
Ames, R., 193
Ames, W., 189
Anders, P. L., 114, 115
Anderson, D., 340
Anderson, L. M., 132
Anderson, P., 350
Andrews, D. M., 311
Anthony, H. M., 132
Aponich, D. A., 7
Applegate, B., 176, 180, 182
Armbruster, B. B., 117
Armstrong, S., 155
Arnold, J., 44
Asher, S. R., 246
Astin, A., 340
Atwater, E., 24, 27, 36
Aune, E., 350
Ausubel, D. P., 24, 282
Auty, W. P., 260
Ayers, D., 245

Baer, D., 193
Baer, D. M., 74, 94
Bahr, C. M., 165, 166
Bailey, D. B., Jr., 93

Bak, J. J., 245
Baker, J. M., 2, 9, 11, 14
Baker, L., 102, 114
Baker, R. E., 347
Baker-Kroczynski, S., 156
Bakken, J. P., 156
Baldwin, R. S., 110, 112
Baldwin, W. K., 245
Ball, D. W., 204
Banikowski, A., 132
Banks, P. D., 301
Barcus, J. M., 299
Barenbaum, E., 133
Barry, 284
Bauman, R., 83
Bauwens, J., 290
Beals, V. L., 115, 215
Bean, T. W., 110, 112
Beardslee, W. R., 39
Beattie, J., 278
Beattie, S., 277, 278
Beatty, L., 158
Beck, A. T., 39, 40
Beck, I. L., 115
Becker, L. D., 155
Becker, W., 121
Becker, W. C., 118
Bedall, J. J., 278
Behrens, J. T., 62
Bell, E. D., 185
Bender, W. N., 63
Bennett, G. K., 311
Bennett, K., 166, 167
Benz, M. R., 64, 322, 341
Bereiter, C., 133, 143
Bergerud, D., 285
Berkell, D. E., 308, 313
Berz, E., 340
Best, L., 347
Billingsley, B., 12
Birch, J., 301
Birkimer, J. C., 83
Bishop, N., 276
Blackburn, J. C., 347
Black, F. L., 248
Blackorby, J., 53, 59, 61, 330
Block, J., 39
Bloomer, R. H., 354
Blos, P., 28–29

Bonero, D. A., 345, 353
Bopp, M. J., 245
Borakove, L. S., 164
Bormuth, J. R., 109
Bos, C., 155
Bos, C. S., 114, 115, 166, 167, 219, 257, 258
Botel, M., 106
Bottge, B. A., 283
Bourbeau, P. E., 74
Brakke, N. P., 246
Brammer, G., 301
Bridge, C., 139
Brigance, A. H., 107, 135, 137, 157, 316
Brinkerhoff, L. C., 340, 342, 348, 349, 350, 351, 352
Britt, C., 301
Broder, P. K., 64
Brolin, D. E., 103, 300, 302, 304, 314, 316, 317, 319, 320
Broome, K., 162, 164
Brophy, J., 74
Browder, P. M., 322
Brown, A., 140
Brown, A. L., 102, 114, 117, 118, 204
Brown, C., 301
Brown, G., 287
Brown, J. E., 308, 313
Brown, J. H., 83
Brown, V., 158
Brown, V. L., 106, 107, 108, 135, 209
Brown, W. F., 208
Browning, P. L., 156
Bruininks, R. H., 245, 301, 328
Bruininks, V. L., 245
Bryan, J. H., 45, 57, 245
Bryan, T., 65, 234, 245
Bryan, T. H., 45, 57
Bryant, B. R., 107, 1080
Bucher, D. E., 300
Buchwach, L., 10
Budoff, M., 245
Bulgren, J., 14, 124, 226, 281, 283, 284
Bulgren, J. A., 114, 115, 116
Bullis, M., 64
Bullock, L. M., 64
Burger, D. L., 310
Bursuck, B., 57
Bursuck, W., 65, 263

Bursuck, W. D., 279, 353
Bush, M. A., 33
Byron, J., 350

Calhoun, M. L., 278
Cameto, R., 53
Campbell, D. P., 310
Campbell, P., 260
Campbell, S., 38
Camp, B. W., 33
Campione, J. C., 118
Canfield, R. L., 38
Cantor, G. N., 44
Carey, L., 143
Cariglia-Bull, T., 201
Carman, R. A., 221, 222
Carnine, D., 104, 115, 118, 183, 184
Carpenter, C. D., 279
Carpenter, D., 278, 279
Carr, S., 156
Carson, R., 168, 300, 302
Carter, M. L., 223, 350
Cartledge, G., 242, 251, 257
Case, L., 177
Caspi, A., 36
Cassell, R., 208
Cawley, J., 156, 187
Cawley, J. F., 155, 156, 168, 173, 174,
   186, 187
Ceci, S. J., 38
Chadsey-Rusch, J., 193, 260, 306
Chaffin, J., 300
Chall, J. S., 101, 102
Chalmers, L., 191, 192
Charlesworth, R., 246
Christenson, S. L., 131, 139
Clark, F., 7, 57, 302
Clark, F. C., 212
Clark, F. L., 52, 202, 205
Clark, G. M., 313, 315, 316
Clements, B., 15
Clements, B. S., 78
Cline, B., 12
Close, D. E., 74
Cobb, R., 202
Coben, S. C., 245
Coffman, R. M., 234
Cognitive and Technology Group,
   Vanderbilt University, 283
Cohen, L. G., 302
Cohen, S., 209
Coie, J. D., 244, 245, 246
Colby, S. C., 353
Cole, C., 257
Collins, T., 356
Collins, W. A., 24, 25, 27, 31, 37, 38, 39,
   40, 41, 43
Colson, S. E., 193
Colvert, G., 132, 142, 146
Colvin, G., 43, 65, 77, 79, 234, 237
Colvin, J., 265

Combs, M. S., 235
Compton, C., 300
Conley, M. W., 102
Connolly, A. J., 157
Connolly, J., 246
Cooley, W., 114, 139
Cool, V., 300
Cooper, L., 300
Coppotelli, H., 244
Corcoran, J. R., 304
Corley, M. J., 74
Council for Exceptional Children, 304
Cowen, S., 353
Cox, P. D., 165, 166
Crealock, C. M., 143
Crews, W. B., 72, 134
Criswell, J. L., 164
Crowley, P. E., 286
Crump, W., 202
Csanyi, A. P., 87
Cullinan, D., 7, 52, 57, 62, 65, 155
Cullinan, D. A., 57, 245
Cummings, R. W., 317
Cuvo, A. J., 164
Czajkowski, A., 354

Dalke, C., 344, 349
Dalke, C. L., 341
D'Alonzo, B. J., 300
D'Amico, R., 53, 330
Darch, C., 282
Davidson, W. S., 74
Davila, R. R., 6
Davison, R., 300
Dawson, M. M., 204
Day, E., 64
deBettencourt, L. U., 10, 15, 102, 201,
   202, 202–203, 204, 209, 223, 300,
   345, 353
DeBlassie, R. R., 40
DeFries, J. C., 155
deFur, S., 297
Dehaven, E. D., 74
Dembo, M. H., 7
Deno, S. L., 2, 9, 10, 16, 17, 111, 112,
   132, 160
Denton, P. H., 119, 215, 216, 286
Deshler, D. D., 6, 7, 11, 13, 14, 52, 57,
   64, 103, 114, 115, 116, 119, 122,
   124, 143, 144, 201, 202, 203, 205,
   209, 212, 213, 214, 215, 216, 217,
   221, 226, 234, 257, 258, 276, 280,
   283, 284, 285, 286, 302, 345, 350
Destafano, L., 193, 260, 306
Dettmer, P., 289
Devlin, S. D., 65
DiGangi, S. A., 62
Dodge, K. A., 244, 246
Donahoe, K., 2, 102, 202
Donahoe, K. A., 122, 123
Doren, B., 64, 65, 341

Dorer, D. J., 39
Doucette, M., 155
Dowdy, C. A., 72, 346
Doyle, A., 246
Drew, C. J., 5, 45
Dunivant, N., 63, 64
Dunn, C., 297
Durand, R., 300
Dyck, N., 289

Eberhard, J. M., 74
Edelbrock, C. S., 39
Edgar, E., 15, 52, 168, 190, 277, 299,
   300, 301, 322, 331
Education, U.S. Department of, 9, 10,
   15, 16, 53, 55, 58, 59, 60, 61, 102,
   276, 279, 290
Education, U.S. Office of, 4
Educational Communications, 25, 96
Education Commission of the States,
   277
Egan, M. W., 5
Ehren, B. J., 287
Ekwall, E. E., 107, 109
Elbow, P., 146
Elias, M. J., 65
Elkind, D., 33, 34
Elksnin, L. K., 163, 245
Eller, A., 266
Ellett, L., 2, 276
Elliott, B., 302
Elliott, R. N., Jr., 65
Elliott, S. N., 236, 238, 246, 247, 248
Elliott, T. R., 304
Ellis, E., 74, 202, 226, 280
Ellis, E. E., 124
Ellis, E. S., 13, 103, 114, 115, 118, 120,
   123, 124, 132, 142, 145, 146, 201,
   205, 210, 217, 223, 224, 225, 226,
   245, 246, 284, 285, 345, 350
Emmer, E. T., 77, 78
Emshoff, J. G., 74
Enderle, J., 316
Englemann, S., 118, 121, 183, 184
Englert, C. S., 76, 132, 133, 140, 143
English, R. W., 156
Enright, B., 158, 159
Epstein, M. H., 52, 57, 62, 65, 155, 279,
   288
Erickson, E. H., 27–28
Espin, C. A., 2, 9, 10, 16, 17
Estes, T. H., 208
Evans, R. N., 303
Evers, R. B., 303, 330
Evertson, C. M., 78

Faas, L. A., 300
Fafard, M., 300
Fairweather, J. S., 300
Fanning, P. N., 301
Fardig, D., 203, 300

Farebrother, C., 260
Fawcett, S. B., 262
Fear, K. L., 132
Ferguson, C., 112
Ferrara, R. A., 118
Finck, K., 300
Finn, D. M., 72
Fisher, G. L., 65
Fitzmaurice-Hayes, A. M., 187
Flanders, J., 185
Flavell, J., 204
Flower, L., 133, 143
Foley, R. M., 288
Ford, M., 301
Fordyce, W. G., 245
Forgan, H. W., 218
Forness, S., 301
Forte, J., 322
Foss, G., 260, 262
Foster, S. L., 236
Foster, T. R., 185
Fourqurean, J. M., 300
Frank, A., 168, 300, 302
Frank, A. R., 16, 168
Franzini, L. R., 301
Fredrick, M. M., 186
Friend, M., 263, 290
Friend, P., 145
Fuchs, D., 112, 159, 160, 276
Fuchs, L. S., 111, 112, 159, 160, 165, 166, 276
Fulton, S. A., 299

Gable, R. A., 113, 138
Gajar, A. H., 2, 8, 14, 16, 17, 277, 303, 307, 320, 341, 346, 354
Ganshow, L., 348, 354
Gans, J., 23
Garcia, E., 74
Gardner, E., 158
Gardner, E. F., 107, 108
Gatlin, D., 245
Gaylord-Ross, C., 322
Gaylord-Ross, R., 262, 311, 322
Geist, H., 310
Gerardi, W. J., 185
Germann, G., 160
Gershaw, N. J., 250
Gersten, R., 282, 284
Gibbons, P. C., 43
Gilmore, E. C., 107, 108
Gilmore, J. V., 107, 108
Givens, A., 283
Gjerde, P. F., 39
Glascoe, L. G., 320, 321
Glazer, J. A., 246
Goldman, T., 204
Goldstein, A. P., 250
Gonso, J., 246
Gonzales, M. A., 87
Good, T., 77

Good, T. L., 74
Goodman, A. P., 33
Goodman, L., 2, 277, 303, 341
Gordon, L., 203
Gordon, L. R., 168, 300
Gordon, L. V., 310
Gottlieb, B. W., 57
Gottlieb, J., 57, 58, 245
Gottman, J. M., 244, 246
Graden, J. L., 139
Graham, S., 132, 133, 139, 140, 142, 143, 145, 146, 148, 177, 356
Grantham, L. B., 278
Graves, D., 132, 133, 139
Graves, D. H., 136
Gray, R., 132
Graybeal, N. L., 204
Green, K., 340
Greenan, J. P., 309, 310
Greenbaum, C. R., 135, 136
Greenstein, J., 158
Greenwood, C. R., 246, 249
Gregg, N., 62, 310, 311, 347
Gregg, S., 132, 133
Gregg, S. L., 132
Gregory, J. F., 72
Gresham, F., 6
Gresham, F. M., 51, 234, 235, 236, 238, 243, 245, 246, 247, 248, 257
Greuling, J. W., 40
Grise, P., 277, 278
Gross, J. C., 245
Grossman, H., 4, 5
Grove, M. K., 282

Hagborg, W. J., 59
Hall, D., 353
Hall, G. S., 24, 26–27, 45
Hallahan, D. P., 6, 52, 57, 92, 204
Halpern, A. S., 299, 304, 314, 322, 326, 341
Hamlett, C. L., 112, 159, 160
Hammill, D. D., 106, 107, 108, 135, 136
Haney, W., 277
Hanner, S., 121
Hansen, G., 301
Hansen, J., 310
Hardister, M. P., 278
Hardman, M. L., 5, 6, 45
Haring, K., 300
Harper, G. F., 166, 167, 286
Harris, A., 287
Harris, C. A., 195
Harris, F. C., 83
Harris, K., 132, 177
Harris, K. R., 91, 132, 133, 139, 140, 141, 142, 143, 145, 146
Hartmann, D. P., 83
Hartup, W. W., 246
Hartzell, H., 300
Hasazi, S., 203

Hasazi, S. B., 168, 300
Hasbrouck, J., 136, 137
Hasselbring, T. S., 112, 283
Haubrich, P. A., 300
Havinghurst, R. J., 30, 44
Havyren, M., 244
Hayes, J., 133
Hayes, J. R., 143
Hayes, M. L., 63
Haynes, H., 185
Hazel, J. S., 234, 236, 243, 249, 251, 256, 257
Hebbeler, K., 53, 59, 61
Heidi, E. F., 223, 287
Heller, H. B., 245
Hemingway, E., 131
Hendrickson, J. M., 138
Henley, M., 279–280
Hensel, J., 203, 300
Hensel, J. W., 260
Heron, T. E., 221
Herzog, A., 65
Hesselbrock, V., 301
Heward, W. L., 6
Hiebert, E., 139
Hildreth, B. L., 223, 350
Hill, J. P., 39
Hill, J. W., 301
Hill, M., 301
Hitchings, W., 277
Hofeling, D. V., 74
Hoffman, F. J., 260
Hofmeister, A. M., 195
Hoisch, S. A., 301
Holland, J., 310
Hollinger, J., 257
Holmes, D., 250
Holtzman, W. H., 208
Homme, L. E., 87
Hoover, J. J., 211, 212, 221, 223
Hops, H., 244, 246, 249
Horiuchi, C., 301
Horner, R. H., 74
Horton, G., 250
Horton, S., 164, 285
Horton, S. V., 187, 188, 189, 192, 283
Horvath, M., 277
Houck, D. G., 204
Hourcade, J., 290
Howard, R. F., 347
Howe, C. E., 245
Hoy, C., 62, 310, 311, 347
Hoyt, K. B., 303
Hudson, P., 260, 280, 281, 282, 283, 291
Hudson, P. J., 281
Hughes, C. A., 115, 220, 221
Hull, M., 300
Humes, C., 301
Hunt, F. M., 354

Huntington, D. D., 63
Husain, S. A., 40
Hutchinson, A., 143
Hutton, J. B., 245
Hymel, S., 244
Hynes, C., 185

Ianacone, R. N., 260, 301
Iano, R. P., 245
Idol, L., 115
Idol-Maestas, L., 221
Inhelder, B., 31
Iovacchini, E. V., 347
Iowa Department of Education, 301
Irvin, L. K., 260
Isaacson, S., 134, 139
Ishler, M., 74
Ivanic, M. T., 164, 165
Ivey, C., 204
Iwata, B. A., 164, 165

Jagota, M., 62
Janes, C., 301
Javorsky, K. L., 348
Jayanthi, M., 279
Jenkins, J. R., 276
Jenkins, L., 276
Jenkins, W. M., 304
Jewell, M., 276
Johansson, C. B., 310
Johns, J. L., 109
Johnson, C. J., 226
Johnson, D., 114, 115
Johnson, D. R., 328
Johnson, D. W., 287
Johnson, G., 121
Johnson, G. O., 245
Johnson, J. M., 302
Johnson, L. J., 291
Johnson, M. B., 135
Johnson, R. T., 287
Johnson, V. A., 262
Jones, W. L., 185
Jongsma, E., 1090
Joyce, K., 64

Kabideau, D. K., 223
Kahn, H., 155
Kaluger, G., 104
Kameenui, E. J., 78, 104, 115, 118
Kamm, K., 208
Karacostas, D. D., 65
Kardash, C. A., 63
Karen, R. L., 301
Karlsen, B., 107, 108, 158
Katchadourian, H., 37
Kauffman, J., 4, 7
Kauffman, J. M., 6, 52, 57, 58, 155, 204,
    208, 234, 245, 267
Kazdin, A., 52, 65
Kazdin, A. E., 83, 92

Keilitz, I., 63, 64
Keith, K. D., 315
Keller, C. E., 77
Keller, M. B., 39
Kerr, M. M., 223, 287, 289
Kiehl, W. S., 234
Kinder, D., 57
Kindsvatter, R., 74, 77, 78
King, J., 304
King, M., 62
King-Sears, M. E., 160
Kiraly, J., Jr., 278
Kirby, J. R., 155
Kirk, S. A., 109
Kirschner, B. W., 143
Kistner, J. A., 245
Klein, P., 250
Kliebhan, J. M., 109
Knackendoffel, E. A., 289, 290
Kohlberg, L., 31–32, 44
Kohler, F. W., 286
Kohler, P. D., 307
Kohnke, R., 122, 123
Kokaska, C. J., 103, 320, 321
Kolson, C. J., 104
Konke, J. L., 164
Korn, W., 340
Kounin, J., 76
Kozleski, E. B., 302
Kranstover, L. L., 301
Kravets, M., 345, 353
Kregel, J., 299, 301, 306, 324
Kress, J. S., 65
Krohn, M. D., 43
Kromer, K., 300
Kronick, D., 234
Kulp, S., 83
Kunce, J. T., 300

Labor, U. S. Department of, 310, 311
La Greca, A. M., 245
Lahey, B. B., 83
Lambert, D. L., 287, 289
Lancioni, G. E., 162, 164
Landrum, T. J., 92
Langress, L., 156
Lapp, E. R., 245
Larsen, S., 132
Larsen, S. C., 135, 136, 163
Laurie, T. E., 10, 278
Lavorie, P. W., 39
Leceister, N., 276
Ledford, R. R., 139, 144
Leinhardt, G., 114, 139
Leinwand, S. J., 186
Lenz, B. K., 13, 64, 103, 114, 115, 118,
    120, 122, 123, 124, 189, 201, 202,
    203, 205, 210, 212, 213, 214, 215,
    217, 225, 226, 280, 281, 282, 284,
    285, 287, 345, 350
Lenz, K., 14, 74, 124, 226

Lerner, J. W., 109, 276
Levin, E., 301
Levin, J. R., 190
Levine, E., 278
Levine, H., 156
Levine, P., 299, 300, 301
Lewin, K., 29–30
Lewin, L., 244, 246
Lewinsohn, P. M., 235
Lewis, R. B., 104, 105, 113, 207, 211
Libet, J. M., 235
Lichtenstein, S., 301
Light, J. G., 155
Lignugaris-Kraft, B., 260, 280, 281, 282,
    354
Linden, B., 301
Lipson, M. Y., 203
Litt, A. V., 353
Litt, I. F., 25, 43
Lloyd, J. W., 77, 92, 286
Logan, D. R., 45
Longstaff, H. P., 311
Loper, A. B., 204
Lovett, D., 300
Lovitt, T. C., 187, 188, 189, 192, 283,
    285
Lowe, M. L., 164
Lowrey, N., 11
Luckasson, R., 5
Luebke, J., 155
Luftig, R. L., 234
Luiten, T. C., 189
Lynch, M. E., 39
Lynch, M. J., 353
Lyon, R., 64

Maag, J. W., 62, 63
MacArthur, C., 132, 133, 143
MacArthur, C. A., 133, 139, 145, 148,
    356
MacDonald, J. T., 6
MacGinitie, W. H., 107
Macke, R. A., 223, 350
Mackin, J., 303
MacMillan, D. L., 51, 52, 57
Macro Systems, 256
Madaus, G., 277
Madden, R., 107, 108, 158
Maddux, C. D., 317
Maggs, A., 118
Maheady, L., 166, 167, 286
Malina, R. M., 37
Mandrum, C. T., 218
Mangrum, C., 340, 342, 348, 349, 352,
    354
Mangrum, C. T., 219, 353
Mangrum, C. T., III, 207
Mangum, C. T., 220
Mangum, G. L., 303
Mann, L., 12
Marder, C., 53, 330

Markwardt, F. C., 134
Marquard, K., 176, 180, 182
Marshall, K., 301
Marshall, K. J., 245
Marston, D., 132
Martin, J. E., 309, 310
Martin, S. M., 118
Martindale, A., 83
Martindale, B., 83
Martlett, L., 143
Masters, L. F., 3, 4, 7, 11, 17
Mastropieri, M. A., 74, 78, 156, 168, 190,
    219, 221, 223, 285
Mathews, R. M., 262
Matthews, P., 340
McAfee, J., 2, 277, 303, 341
McCarney, S. B., 314
McCarty, T., 308, 310
McConnell, S., 239, 243
McConnell, S. R., 247
McCoy, M., 41, 42
McCrowley, G., 301
McCuller, G. L., 260
McDonagh, E. C., 164
McDonnell, J., 303
McEntire, E., 158
McFall, R. M., 235
McGettigan, J. F., 245
McGill-Franzen, A., 114
McGinnis, E., 90
McGuire, J. M., 280, 340, 344, 348, 350,
    353, 356
McIlvane, W. J., 164
McIntosh, R., 257
McKenzie, R. G., 139, 149
McKeown, M. G., 115
McLaughlin, J. A., 347
McLeod, T., 155
McLoone, B., 190
McLoughlin, J. A., 104, 105, 113, 207,
    211
McNair, K., 78
McVicar, R., 131
Meadows, N., 301
Meers, G. D., 278
Mehring, T., 132
Mehring, T. A., 193
Meisgeier, C., 300
Melia, R., 304
Mental Retardation and Developmental
    Disabilities, Division on, 322
Menz, F. E., 301
Mercer, A. R., 10, 103, 105
Mercer, C. D., 6, 10, 103, 105, 190, 195,
    218, 219
Mesinger, J. R., 64
Meyen, E. L., 78, 249
Michael, J. J., 208
Michael, W. B., 208
Michenbaum, D., 33
Milburn, J. F., 242, 251, 257

Miller, D., 63
Miller, D. M., 162, 164
Miller, J., 155, 156, 168
Miller, L. S., 320, 321
Miller, R. J., 301
Miller, S. E., 122, 123
Miller, S. P., 195, 218, 219
Miller, T., 280, 281, 282
Millstein, S. G., 25, 43
Mirkin, P., 112
Mirkin, P. K., 132, 160
Mithaug, D. E., 301, 309, 310
Moffitt, T. E., 36
Monroe, J. D., 245
Montague, M., 155, 166, 167, 176, 180,
    182, 260
Moore, D. W., 102
Moreland, C., 62
Morgan, D. J., 63
Mori, A. A., 3
Mori, B. A., 3
Morsink, C. V., 113
Muller, P., 300
Murphy, D., 63, 64
Murphy, H. A., 204
Murphy, J. P., 354
Murtaugh, M., 234
Muuss, R. E., 24, 25, 31, 32
Myer, B., 354
Myers, D., 301

Nagel, D. R., 285
Nania, P. A., 186
National Commission on Excellence in
    Education, 2
National Council of Teachers of
    Mathematics, 193, 194
National Longitudinal Transition Study,
    301
Neel, R., 90, 301
Nelson, C. M., 287, 289
Nelson, J. S., 279
Nelson, R., 283, 354
Neubert, D. A., 260, 301
Newcomer, P., 133
Newman, L., 53, 330
Nigro, G., 38
Nodine, B. F., 133
Nolan, S. M., 143
Nolet, V., 10, 11
Norlander, K., 350
Norlander, K. A., 280, 340, 354
Nowacek, E. J., 290
Nowell, C. H., 346
Nuzum, M., 166, 167

Odom, S. L., 239, 243
Oka, E. R., 114, 117, 120, 122, 203
Okolo, C. M., 328, 346
O'Shea, D. J., 72, 134
Osnes, P., 266

Ostertag, B. A., 347
Otis-Wilborn, A., 136, 137
Owings, J., 14

Page, T. J., 164, 165
Palincsar, A., 140
Palincsar, A. S., 117, 118, 119, 204
Parent, W. S., 324
Paris, S. G., 114, 117, 120, 122, 203
Park, H. S., 262
Parker, J. G., 246
Parker, R., 134, 136
Parker, R. M., 304
Parmar, R. S., 168, 173, 174, 186,
    187
Parnell, G. G., 139, 144
Pasternack, R., 64
Paterson, D. G., 311
Patton, J. R., 103, 148, 156, 211, 288,
    315
Pauk, W., 208
Payne, J. S., 103, 148
Payne, R., 148
Payne, R. A., 103
Pearl, R., 65
Pearson, P. D., 104, 114, 115
Peck, M. L., 63
Pederson, C. S., 249, 256
Peery, J. C., 244
Peiper, E. L., 57
Pendleton, P., 301
Penniman, J., 301
Peraino, J. M., 169, 299
Perfetti, C., 115
Perlmutter, B., 234
Perotti, F., 302
Peters, C. W., 102
Peterson, K., 302
Petry, C., 266
Phelps, L. A., 193, 260, 306, 308, 310
Piaget, J., 31
Pollard, R. R., 278
Polloway, E. A., 57, 103, 148, 156, 190,
    211, 278, 279, 280, 288
Polo, L., 245
Polonsky, L., 185
Poplin, M., 132, 133
Porter, S., 185
Posthill, S. M., 302
Postman, R. D., 186
Powell, J., 83
Prescott, M., 64
Pressley, M., 119, 141, 201, 226
Price, L., 342, 343, 346, 354
Prillaman, D., 245
Prout, H. T., 63
Psychological Corporation, 107, 108,
    136
Pugach, M. C., 291
Putnam, M. L., 14, 226
Puttalaz, M., 244

Ramsey, E., 43, 65, 77, 79, 234, 237, 265
Ramsey, R. S., 279–280
Raphael, T. E., 132, 133, 143
Raskind, M. H., 355, 356
Rasmussen, B., 246
Raths, L., 245
Rayfield, R., 306
Raygor, A. L., 208
Readence, J. E., 110, 112
Rechs, J. R., 87
Redd, W. H., 74
Reeve, R. A., 118
Reeve, R. E., 204
Regan, C., 300
Reiff, H. B., 297
Reilly, T. F., 64
Reith, H. J., 165, 166
Reschly, D. J., 245
Retish, P., 277
Revell, W. G., 306
Reynolds, W. M., 63
Risley, T. R., 74
Ritchey, W. L., 236
Ritter, S., 221
Rivera, D. H., 165, 166
Rizzo, J. V., 155
Robinson, F. G., 282
Roe, B. D., 109
Roe, C., 203
Roe, C. A., 168, 300
Roeger, K., 354
Roessler, R. T., 262, 302
Roffman, A. J., 302
Roit, M. L., 139, 149
Rojewski, J. W., 278, 297
Rooney, K., 223
Rose, E., 353
Rosenshine, B., 72, 74, 75, 280
Rosenshine, B. V., 203
Ross, I., 302
Rousseau, M. K., 137
Rucker, C. N., 245
Ruhl, K. L., 221
Rusch, F. R., 193, 260, 306
Rutherford, R. B., 63
Ryan, A. G., 342, 343, 346, 354
Ryckman, D., 245
Rye, J., 109
Rynders, J. E., 245
Rzonca, C., 301

Sabatino, D. A., 12
Sabornie, E. J., 7, 57, 65, 74, 120, 123,
    205, 225, 234, 235, 236, 245, 246,
    247, 262, 267, 299, 345, 353
Sacca, M. K., 166, 167, 286
Salembier, G., 300
Salend, S. J., 283, 287
Salzberg, C. L., 260, 262, 264
Sands, D. J., 302
Sansone, J., 11, 12, 122, 123

Sargent, L. R., 257, 259, 260, 261, 262,
    264
Savage, R. C., 6
Sawyer, R., 132, 140, 142
Scardamalia, M., 133, 143
Schaeffer, A. L., 223, 287
Schafer, W. D., 356
Schalit, M., 340
Schalock, R., 302
Schalock, R. L., 299, 315
Scheiber, B., 346
Schenck, S. J., 139
Schloss, C. N., 234
Schloss, P. J., 62, 93, 94, 95, 234, 236
Schmalle, B., 277
Schmitt, S., 344, 349
Schonert, K. A., 44
Schonert-Reichl, K. A., 65
Schriver, J., 143
Schultz, J. B., 279
Schumaker, J. B., 6, 7, 13, 52, 57, 103,
    114, 115, 116, 119, 122, 124, 142,
    143, 189, 202, 203, 205, 212, 214,
    215, 216, 217, 221, 226, 234, 236,
    243, 249, 251, 256, 257, 258, 276,
    280, 282, 283, 284, 285, 286, 302
Schunk, D. H., 165, 166
Schwartz, S., 132, 203, 300
Schwartz, S. E., 260
Schwartz, S. S., 139, 145, 356
Sclafani, A. J., 353
Scott, C. S., 277
Scott, N. G., 355, 356
Scott-Miller, D., 90
Scranton, T., 245
Scruggs, T. E., 74, 78, 156, 168, 190,
    219, 221, 223, 285
Scuccimarra, D., 302
Seabaugh, G. O., 122
Sealander, K., 260
Seashore, H. G., 311
Selman, R. L., 32, 33
Senate, U. S., 2
Severson, S., 316
Seyfarth, J., 301
Shanahan, T., 72
Shaver, D. M., 11
Shaw, R., 187, 348
Shaw, S. F., 280, 340, 342, 344, 348,
    350, 351, 352, 354, 356
Shaywitz, S. E., 348
Sheehan, M., 303
Sheehan, M. R., 74
Sheinker, A., 202
Sheinker, J. M., 202
Sheldon, J., 142, 143, 216
Sheldon-Wildgen, J., 7, 251
Sherman, J. A., 7, 251
Shiah, S., 168
Shields, J., 221
Shinn, M. R., 160

Shriner, J. G., 2
Shulte, A. P., 185
Shure, M. B., 33
Silbert, J., 104, 115, 118
Silvaroli, N. J., 107, 109
Silverman, R., 10
Simmons, D. C., 78
Siperstein, G. N., 51, 245, 348, 353
Sitko, C., 143
Sitko, M. C., 143
Sitlington, P., 168, 300, 302, 328
Sitlington, P. L., 13, 16, 168, 297, 346
Skolnick, B., 340
Slaby, D. A., 235
Sloat, R. S., 63
Smeenge, M. E., 164, 165
Smeets, P. M., 162, 164
Smiley, L. R., 287
Smith, C., 90
Smith, C. R., 190
Smith, D., 300
Smith, D. D., 165, 166
Smith, E. C., 64, 346
Smith, H., 301
Smith, J. D., 5, 57
Smith, M. A., 93, 94, 95
Smith, T. E. C., 72, 211
Snider, B., 245, 301
Snyder, B. L., 201
Sols, D. K., 208
Sowers, J., 74
Spache, G. D., 106, 107
Sparks, R., 348
Spaulding, C. L., 77
Speece, D., 302
Spellman, C., 300
Spivack, G., 33
Spooner, F., 260
Sprafkin, R. P., 250
Sprinthall, N. A., 24, 25, 27, 31, 37, 38,
    39, 40, 41, 43
Spruill, J. A., 302
Stark, K. D., 63
Stearns, M. S., 300
Stecker, P. M., 112, 159
Steely, D., 183
Steely, D. G., 183
Steinberg, L., 36, 38
Stephens, T. M., 240, 242, 250, 251,
    255
Sternberg, R., 38
Stevens, L. J., 202
Stevens, R., 72, 75, 280
Stewart, D. M., 208
Stile, S. W., 300
Stockling, C., 14
Stoddard, B., 145
Stoddard, K., 72, 134
Stoddard, L. T., 164
Stodden, R. A., 322
Stokes, T., 193, 266

Stokes, T. E., 74, 94
Stone, W. L., 245
Stowitschek, J. J., 262, 264
Strain, P. S., 158, 239, 249, 286
Stratman, J., 143
Straughn, C. T., 353
Strichart, S., 340, 342, 348, 349, 352, 354
Strichart, S. S., 207, 219, 220, 353
Striefel, S., 162, 164
Strong, E. K., 310
Sucher, F., 109
Sugai, G. M., 93
Sullivan, H. S., 34–35
Sunstein, B. S., 136
Suritsky, S. K., 220
Sutton, L. P., 64
Swank, P. R., 300
Swanson, H. L., 201
Sylvester, B. T., 64
Symons, J., 226
Symons, S., 201
Szymanski, E., 193, 260, 306
Szymanski, E. M., 304

Takaishi, M., 36
Talpers, J., 346
Tanner, J. M., 36, 37
Tarver, S. G., 183, 204
Taylor, A. R., 246
Taylor, L., 122
Taylor, R., 157
Tedesco, A., 155
Test, D. W., 260
Thomas, C. C., 76, 132, 133, 140
Thomas, V., 234, 247
Thornton, H., 10, 15, 203, 300, 302
Thornton, H. S., 102, 202
Thurlow, M. L., 2, 3, 131, 139, 164, 165, 186, 301, 328
Thurston, L. P., 289
Tilson, G. P., 260, 301
Tindal, G., 10, 11, 134, 136, 137, 160
Todd, N. M., 246, 249
Todis, B., 250
Torgesen, J. K., 6, 7, 204
Trace, M. W., 164
Troutman, A. C., 73, 80, 84, 94
Troutner, N., 276
Tucker, J. A., 111, 160

Turnbull, A. P., 279
Turnure, J. E., 164, 165

Urban, A., 156
Usiskin, Z., 185

Vaca, J. L., 282
Vaca, R. T., 282
Valdes, K. A., 53, 54, 55, 56, 58, 60
Valencia, S. W., 104
Vallecorsa, A. L., 139, 143, 144
Vandiver, T., 40
Van Houten, E., 64
Van Reusen, A. K., 257, 258
Vaughan, J. L., Jr., 208
Vaughn, S., 219, 257
Veitch, V. D., 164
Vergason, G. A., 78
Viktora, S., 185
Vitello, S. J., 2, 277
Vogel, S. A., 220, 340, 352, 354, 355

Wagner, M. M., 2, 6, 9, 11, 14, 15, 16, 53, 55, 56, 58, 59, 60, 61, 299, 300, 302, 330
Walberg, H., 72
Walker, H. M., 43, 65, 77, 78, 79, 88, 234, 236, 237, 246, 247, 249, 250, 263, 265
Walker, J. E., 78
Walker, J. K., 356
Walker, V. S., 245
Wallace, G., 163, 208
Wambold, C. L., 162, 164
Wantuck, L. R., 186
Warger, C. L., 260
Warger, M., 278, 279
Warner, M., 7, 302
Warner, M. M., 6, 52, 57, 64, 202, 203, 234
Warrenfeltz, R. B., 262
Wax, I. F., 345, 353
Wehman, P. H., 193, 260, 299, 301, 304, 305, 306, 322, 323, 324, 325, 326, 327, 328, 329, 347
Weiner, I. B., 39
Weithorn, L. A., 38
Wells, R. L., 264
Werbel, G., 302

Wesman, A. G., 311
Wesson, C., 136, 137
West, M., 306
Westling, D., 203, 300
Wetzel, J. R., 25
Whang, P. L., 262
Whelan, R. J., 78
White, J. L., 39, 40, 41, 42
White, O. R., 192
White, W., 302
White, W. J., 203, 234
Whitehouse, R., 36
Wiederholt, J. L., 106, 107, 108, 135, 1080
Wilcox, B., 303
Wilen, W., 74
Will, M., 297, 299, 349
Willemsen, R. J., 162, 164
Williams, M. L., 6
Williams, R. E., 300
Williamson, C. L., 53, 55, 56
Wimmer, D., 326
Wishner, J., 57
Witt, J. C., 248
Wittrock, M. C., 78
Wixson, K. K., 102, 203
Wolery, M., 93, 94
Wolf, M. M., 74
Wolzen, B., 302
Wong, B. Y. L., 102, 119
Wood, C. E., 234
Woodcock, R. W., 106, 107, 108, 135
Woodward, J., 284
Worsham, M. E., 78
Wotruba, J. W., 186

Yahaya, M. A., 353
Yauck, W. A., 245
Yovanoff, P., 341
Ysseldyke, J. E., 2, 3, 131, 139, 186, 276

Zabel, R. H., 155
Zaragoza, N., 257
Zetlin, A. G., 234
Zigmond, N., 2, 9, 10, 11, 12, 14, 15, 16, 52, 65, 102, 103, 114, 122, 123, 139, 202, 203, 223, 225, 245, 278, 287, 300, 301, 302
Zimmerman, W. S., 208

Subject Index

AAMR (American Association on Mental Retardation), 4, 5
Absenteeism, 15, 59, 61, 287, 288–289
Abstract thinking, 31, 34
Academic deficits, 6, 11, 52, 62, 280
Academic engaged time (AET), 76–77
Academic remediation, 10, 11, 16, 103
Academic Skill Builders in Language Arts, 122
Academic skills, 308, 310
Academic traits, of adolescents with mild disabilities, 57–61
Acceptance, 246
Access Program, The, 250
Accommodation, 9
Acquisition learning, 73, 86
Activity reinforcement, 85
ADA. *See* Americans with Disabilities Act of 1990 (PL 101-336)
Adaptability, 309, 310
Adaptations, 186–190, 289, 303
Adaptive behavior scale, 309
ADD (attention deficit disorder), 6, 9
ADD/ADHD (attention deficit disorder/attention deficit hyperactivity disorder), 3–4
ADHD (attention deficit hyperactivity disorder), 6
Adjustment, 63, 277, 309, 312, 329
Adolescence and adolescents. *See also* Adolescents with mild disabilities
    Aristotle's theory of, 25–26
    Blos's theory of, 28–29
    challenges of, 17
    cognitive development and, 31, 33–34, 37–38, 45
    Comenius' theory of, 26
    conflicts of, 24–25, 30
    definition of, 24
    depression and, 39, 40, 41
    developmental changes of, 3
    early adolescence, 34–35
    Elkind's theory of adolescent egocentrism, 33–34
    Erickson's theory of identity development and, 27–28, 29
    Freud's theory of, 27, 28, 29
    Hall's theory of, 26–27

Havinghurst's developmental tasks of, 30, 44
    juvenile delinquency and, 41–43
    Kohlberg's theory of adolescent morality and, 31–32, 44
    late adolescence, 34, 35
    Lewin's theory of, 29–30, 37
    personal identity and, 23
    perspectives of, 96
    physical development and, 35–37
    Piaget's cognitive theory of, 31, 33–34, 37, 45
    preadolescence, 34
    primary reinforcers and, 85
    psychological disorders of, 38–43
    Selman's theory of social cognition and, 32–33, 45
    special education labels and, 3
    suicide and, 39–41
    Sullivan's theory of adolescent interpersonal development, 34–35
    teachers and, 96–97
    thinking and, 37–38
Adolescents with mild disabilities. *See also* Classroom management
    academic deficits of, 280
    applications to, 24, 43–45
    behavioral characteristics of, 61–66
    behavior disorders and, 52
    characteristics of, 6–7, 51–53
    content-area instruction and, 290
    curriculum and, 11, 16, 280
    demographics of, 53–56
    depression and, 62–63
    dropout phenomenon among, 14–16, 202–203, 277, 299
    formal operational thinking and, 31
    functional reading skills and, 103–104
    functional writing skills and, 133–134
    general classroom instruction and, 2–3, 11, 276
    grading and, 278–280
    heterogeneity of, 234
    inclusion of, 14, 275
    intellectual and academic traits of, 57–61, 62
    juvenile delinquency and, 63–66
    labels for, 51

minimum competency tests and, 277
    personal characteristics of, 53–56
    programs for, 10, 11–13
    reading instruction and, 102–104
    resource room pull-out and, 276
    secondary school educational reforms and, 2–3
    self-management techniques and, 92–93, 250, 266
    social skills and, 280, 299, 307
    sociometric rating scales and, 245
    suicide and, 63
    supported employment and, 306
    transition and, 300–302
    vocational education and, 60, 61, 330
    written language instruction problems and, 132–134
Adrenal cortex, 35–36
Adult basic education programs, 341, 343
Adulthood. *See also* Young adults with mild disabilities
    assimilation into adult society and, 34, 66
    community-based instruction and, 322
    early adulthood, 303
    generalization of behavior and, 94
    learning disabilities and, 16
Adult Services Supporting Instruction Survival Tactics (ASSIST), 344–345
Advanced Reading Inventory: Grades Seven Through College, The, 109
Advanced Reading Skill Builders, 120
Advance organizers (AO), 74, 167, 188–189, 281, 282–283
AET (academic engaged time), 76–77
African Americans, 42, 43, 54, 59, 96
Age-appropriate content, 76
Age-appropriate skills, 30
AIDS, 9
Alcohol consumption, 65
Algebra, 190, 191
American Association on Mental Retardation (AAMR), 4, 5
American Council on Education, 340
Americans with Disabilities Act of 1990 (PL 101-336), 8, 9, 340, 352

Androgen, 36
Anecdotal recording, 80, 81
Annual Report to Congress on the Implementation of the Education for All Handicapped Children Act (1988), 15
Annual Report to Congress on the Implementation of The Individuals with Disabilities Act (1992), 15
Antecedents, manipulation of, 257
Antecedent variables, 94
Anticipation guides, 282, 283
AO (advance organizers), 74, 167, 188–189, 281, 282–283
Aptitude tests, 309, 311
Aristotle's theory of adolescence, 25–26
Arithmetic, definition of, 156
Arrest status, 64–65
Asian Americans, 96
Assessment. *See also* Social skills assessment
    of adaptability, 310
    of cognitive learning strategies, 207–212
    community-based on-the-job assessment, 313
    curriculum-based assessment, 109, 111–112, 309
    of mathematics skills, 157–162
    postsecondary instruction and, 347–348
    of reading skills, 104–113, 280, 312, 329
    of study skills, 208–212
    for transition-related instruction, 308–316
    of written language skills, 134–139, 280, 312, 329
ASSET Program, The, 251
Assignments, and mathematics instruction, 192
ASSIST (Adult Services Supporting Instruction Survival Tactics), 344–345
Attendance, 15, 59, 61, 287, 288–289
Attention deficit disorder (ADD), 6, 9
Attention deficit disorder/attention deficit hyperactivity disorder (ADD/ADHD), 3–4
Attention deficit hyperactivity disorder (ADHD), 6
Audio recordings, 124, 281, 282, 286, 354
Autism, 3, 9
Automobile mathematics skills, 170–171
Average duration, 80–81
Aversive consequences, 90
Aversive stimuli, 86, 90
Avoidance behaviors, 86

Bank Street Writer Plus, 147
Basic skills program model, 11, 202
BDIES (*Brigance Diagnostic Inventory of Essential Skills*), 107, 135, 139, 157
Behavioral characteristics, of adolescents with mild disabilities, 61–66
Behavioral definition of social skills, 236, 238
Behavioral excesses, 234, 239
Behavioral objectives, 72
Behavior disorders
    academic-related characteristics of, 58–60
    adolescents with mild disabilities and, 52
    appearance of student and, 51
    demographics and, 54
    depression and, 62
    IQ and, 57
    juvenile delinquency and, 64
    mathematics skills and, 155
    moral development of adolescents and, 44
    physical therapy and, 56
    postsecondary instruction and, 60, 341
    sociometric rating scales and, 245–246
    teacher rating scales and, 247
    transition-related assessment and, 309
Behaviorism, 88
Behavior Problem Checklists, 65
Behavior rehearsal, 262
Behaviors
    avoidance behaviors, 86
    cognitive-verbal behavior, 235
    decreasing behaviors, 88–92
    defining behaviors, 72–73
    direct observation of, 79–84
    effective teaching behaviors, 73–74, 78, 183, 280–281
    environmental behaviors, 252
    escape behaviors, 86
    generalization of, 93–95
    increasing behaviors, 84–88
    independent study behaviors, 209
    interfering responses, 234, 235
    interpersonal behaviors, 252–253
    maladaptive behavior, 5, 66
    prosocial behaviors, 240, 263, 264
    self-management techniques and, 92–93
    self-related behaviors, 254–255
    teacher-pleasing behaviors, 287
Blacks. *See* African Americans
Blos's theory of adolescence, 28–29
Botel Reading Inventory, 106
Brigance Diagnostic Comprehensive Inventory, 107, 135

Brigance Diagnostic Inventory of Basic Skills, 107, 135
Brigance Diagnostic Inventory of Essential Skills (BDIES), 107, 135, 139, 157
Burns/Roe Informal Reading Inventory, The, 109
Business schools, 346

Calculators
    commercial mathematics curricula and, 185, 186
    computation instruction and, 156
    mathematics instruction and, 192
    problem solving and, 164
California Achievement Test, 208
Career Assessment Inventory, 310
Career development, 148–149
Career education
    adolescents with mild disabilities and, 10
    career-related instructional programs, 103, 168
    definition of, 303–304
    employment and, 304
    learning disabilities and, 304, 353
    transition-related instruction and, 317–322
Carl D. Perkins Vocational and Applied Technology Education Acts of 1984 and 1990 (PL 98-254), 8, 298, 306, 345
Catcher in the Rye, The, 45
CBM (curriculum-based measurement), 159–160
CEC (Council for Exceptional Children), 5
Cerebral palsy, 51
CETA (Comprehensive Employment and Training Act), 8
Checklists, 112–113, 137
Chemical dependency, 65
Childhood, 3, 38
Chronic adolescent syndrome, 35
Chumships, 34
Citizenship, 307
Classification categories, for special education assistance, 3–7
Classification-diagnosis social skills assessment, 238
Classroom-based instruction, 327
Classroom management
    adolescents with mild disabilities and, 78–95
    decreasing behaviors, 88–92
    direct instruction and, 76
    direct observation and, 79–84
    generalization enhancement and, 93–95
    increasing behaviors, 84–88
    self-management techniques, 92–93

Classroom Reading Inventory, The, 107, 109
Classwide peer tutoring (CWPT), 286
Clinical depression, 39
Cloze-plus, 121
Cloze procedure, 109–110
Coaching, 260
Cocaine, 43, 65
COG-MET (cognitive-metacognitive strategy), 176, 180–182
Cognitive deficits, 6
Cognitive development, 31, 33–34, 37–38, 45
Cognitive learning strategies
  assessment of, 207–212
  curriculum development, 212–215
  definition of, 205
  direct instruction and, 202
  mathematics instruction and, 167, 176–183, 218–219
  reading instruction and, 215–216
  study skills and, 219–225
  written language instruction and, 216–218
Cognitive-metacognitive strategy (COG-MET), 176, 180–182
Cognitive models, 140–145
Cognitive patterns of depression, 39, 40
Cognitive strategy training
  cognitive learning strategies assessment, 207–212
  cognitive learning strategies curriculum, 212–215
  content-area instruction and, 226
  generalization of, 225–226
  instruction of, 202–207
  study skills and, 201, 204–207
Cognitive-verbal behavior, 235
College placement tests, 51, 348
Colleges, 341, 343, 344–345
Colors, as discrimination tool, 162
Comenius' theory of adolescence, 26
Community adaptation, and transition, 303
Community-based instruction, 94, 193, 307, 322–325
Community-based on-the-job assessment, 313
Community colleges, 341, 344–345, 346
Compensatory program model, 13
Competitive employment, 304, 307
Complementary instruction, 290
Comprehension, 102–103
Comprehension instruction, 117–120
Comprehension Power, 121
Comprehensive Employment and Training Act (CETA), 8
Computation instruction, 156, 165, 173–174, 187. *See also* Mathematics instruction

Computer-assisted instruction, 165, 281, 282, 283–284, 286. *See also* Microcomputers
Computer software, 121–122, 147–148
Concept diagrams, 115, 116
Concrete operational thinking, 45
Conditioned reinforcement, 85
Confederates, 257
Consequences, 90, 257, 289
Consumer mathematics skills, 168–169
Content-area instruction. *See also* General classroom instruction
  adolescents with mild disabilities' success in, 290
  cognitive strategy training and, 226
  content enhancements, 280–289
  content reading inventory and, 110
  curriculum and, 276–277
  curriculum-based reading assessment and, 111
  departmentalization of, 2
  effective content-area instruction, 280–289
  grading modification and, 279
  instruction speed and, 276–277
  reading instruction and, 102, 123–124, 215
  responsibility for teaching of, 14
  social skills instruction and, 263, 264
  special education teachers and, 187
  standards for, 2
  study skills and, 219
  transition-related instruction and, 329
  vocabulary development and, 114–115
Content enhancements, 280–289
Content reading inventory, 109, 110–112
Contextual analysis, 115
Contingency contracting, 87–88, 122
Continuous reinforcement, 86
Conventional level of moral development, 31
Cooperative learning, 10, 167, 286–287
Cooperative teaching, 289–290
COPS, 143, 217–218, 285
Cornell Learning and Study Skills Inventory, The, 208
Corrective Mathematics, 183–185
Corrective Reading Program, 119, 121
Council for Exceptional Children, 5
Crack cocaine, 43
Crawford Small Parts Dexterity Test, 311
Criterion-referenced tests, 106–108, 134–139, 157–159, 208
Cues, 124
Curriculum
  adaptations of, 186–190
  for adolescents with mild disabilities, 11, 16, 280
  for cognitive learning strategies, 212–215

  content-area instruction and, 276–277
  curriculum alignment, 10
  functional curriculum, 103, 104–105
  functional skills curriculum, 326
  of general classroom instruction, 9–10, 11
  Life-Centered Career Education and, 318–319
  mathematics curricula and, 183–190
  for postsecondary instruction, 352–353
  reading curricula, 120–121
  of secondary schools, 2
  for social skills instruction, 250–256, 264–265
  standards for, 276
  transition-related instruction and, 326–327
  for vocational education, 13
  written language curricula, 147
Curriculum-based assessment, 109, 111–112, 309
Curriculum-based measurement (CBM), 159–160
Curriculum Evaluation Standards for School Mathematics (National Council of Teachers of Mathematics), 193
CWPT (classwide peer tutoring), 286

Decision making, 38, 309
Decreasing behaviors, 88–92
DEFENDS, 145, 217
Defining Issues Test, 44
Definition teaching, 115
Demographics, of adolescents with mild disabilities, 53–56
Depression, 39, 40, 41, 62–63
Descriptive procedures, 257
Developmentally disabled, 297, 306, 309
Diagnostic and Statistical Manual of Mental Disorders (DSM IV), 6, 39
Diagnostic mathematics interview, 162
Diagnostic Reading Scales, 106–107
Diagnostic tests, 106–108, 134–136, 157–159, 208
Differential Aptitude Test, 311
Differential reinforcement, 88–89
  of alternative behavior (DRA), 89
  of incompatible behavior (DRI), 89
  of low rates of behavior (DRL), 89
  of other behavior (DRO), 88–89
Direct instruction
  academic engaged time and, 76–77
  as accommodation, 9
  cognitive learning strategies and, 202
  comprehension instruction and, 118–119
  lesson pace and, 76
  lesson structure and, 74

mathematics instruction and, 165, 167
modeling and, 75
note-taking and, 219–221
performance feedback with correction,
75–76
positive climate and, 77–78
review with reteaching, 75
task-related questions and, 74
vocabulary development and, 115
Directive teaching, 251
Direct observation
classroom management and, 79–84
generalizable skills and, 309, 312–313
social skills assessment and, 238–243,
249, 267
transition-related assessment and, 308
Disabled Student Services (DSS), 342,
350
DISSECT word identification strategy,
115, 215
Down syndrome, 51
DRA (differential reinforcement of
alternative behavior), 89
DRAW, 219
DRI (differential reinforcement of
incompatible behavior), 89
Drift, 243
DRL (differential reinforcement of low
rates of behavior), 89
DRO (differential reinforcement of other
behavior), 88–89
Dropouts
adolescents with mild disabilities as,
14–16, 202–203, 277, 299
cognitive strategy training and, 225
education reforms and, 2
Drug use, 43, 65
DSM IV (*Diagnostic and Statistical
Manual of Mental Disorders*), 6,
39
DSS (Disabled Student Services), 342,
350
Duration recording, 80–81, 240, 242, 313

Early adolescence, 34–35
Early adulthood, 303
EB (environmental behaviors), 252
ED. *See* Emotional disturbance (ED)
Edibles, as primary reinforcement, 84–85
Educable mentally retarded (EMR), 3
Education, U. S. Department of, 9, 297
Education Amendments of Vocational
Education Act (PL 94-482), 7
Education for All Handicapped Children
Act (PL 94-142), 7, 8, 9, 91, 340
Education for the Handicapped Act (PL
94-142), 3, 4–5
Education of the Handicapped Act
Amendments of 1983 (PL 98-
199), 8, 298

Education of the Handicapped
Amendments of 1990 (PL 101-
476), 5–6, 8, 9. *See also*
Individuals with Disabilities
Education Act (PL 101-476)
Education reforms, 2–3, 11
Effective content-area instruction,
280–289
Effective instruction, 72
Effective teaching behaviors, 73–74, 78,
183, 280–281
Egocentrism, Elkind's theory of, 33–34
Ekwall Reading Inventory, The, 107, 109
Elementary schools
instruction and, 2, 71, 276
intelligence testing and, 57
special education and, 15, 52
Elkind's theory of adolescent
egocentrism, 33–34
Emotional disturbance (ED)
academic-related characteristics and,
59–61
definition of, 4
demographics and, 54
depression and, 62
dropout rate and, 15
drug use and, 65
empathy and, 65–66
IQ and, 55, 58
juvenile delinquency and, 63–64
mathematics skills and, 155
postsecondary instruction and, 341
transition-related assessment and, 309
tutors, readers, interpreters and, 56
Empathy, 65–66
Employers, 311–312, 327
Employment
career education and, 304
cognitive strategy training and, 225
commercial mathematics curricula
and, 185, 186
competitive employment, 304, 307
job-related writing tasks and, 134
mathematical process instruction and,
174–176, 178–179
pre-employment employment, 343
social skills instruction and, 260–262
supported employment, 304, 306–307,
347
tracking systems and, 280
transition and, 303, 304, 306–307
unemployment rates, 299
vocational mathematics skills and,
172–173
vocational program model and, 13
EMR (educable mentally retarded), 3
Enclave model of supported
employment, 347
*Enderle-Severson Transition Rating
Scale,* 316

Endocrine system, 35
*Enright Inventory of Basic Arithmetic
Skills* (IBAS), 158–159
Entrepreneurial model of support
employment, 347
Environmental behaviors (EB), 252
Environmental conflicts, 62
Environmental modifications, 277, 313
Environmental variables, Lewin's theory
of, 30
Erickson's theory of identity
development, 27–28, 29
Error analysis
mathematics skills assessment and,
159, 162, 163
reading skills assessment and, 113
written language assessment and, 137,
138
Error-monitoring strategy, 143
Escape behaviors, 86
*Essentials of Mathematics:
Consumer/Career Skills
Applications,* 185
Estradiol, 36
Estrogen, 36
Event recording, 80, 241
Exclusionary time-out, 91
Executive strategies, 223, 224
Extinction, 90, 236
Extrinsic motivation, 122, 123

Fair Labor Standards Act of 1938,
322–323
Family characteristics, 43, 54, 55
Family-living skills list, 358
Females. *See also* Gender
academic-related characteristics of, 59
adolescent suicide and, 40
Blos's views of, 29
depression and, 39, 62
Hall's views on, 26–27
juvenile delinquency and, 42–43,
64–65
morbidity and mortality statistics of,
25
physical development of, 25, 36
physical growth and, 36–37
transition and, 299
Fidelity, 28
Field theory, 29–30, 37
Fixed-ratio (FR) schedule of
reinforcement, 87
Flexible pacing, 277
Foreign languages, 348, 354
Formal operational thinking, 31, 34, 45
Formal Reading Inventory, 107
Four-year college programs, 344–345
Free writing exercises, 146
Frequency recording, 80, 239–240, 312
Freud's theory of adolescence, 27, 28, 29

Frustration level (reading), 109, 110
Full inclusion. *See* Inclusion;
  Mainstream classrooms
Functional curriculum, 103, 104–105
Functional mathematics, 156, 168–173
Functional reading skills, 103–104
Functional skills curriculum, 326
Functional skills program model, 10, 13,
  76
Functional writing skills, 133–134

Gangs, 43, 96
Gangsta rap music, 43
Gapper Reading Lab, The, 121
Gates-MacGinitie Reading Tests, The,
  107
Geist Picture Interest Inventory, 310
Gender. *See also* Females; Males
  adolescent suicide and, 40
  adolescents with mild disabilities and,
    54, 55
  depression and, 62
  transition and, 299
General Aptitude Test Battery, 311
General classroom instruction. *See also*
    Content-area instruction;
    Mainstream classrooms
  adaptations of, 186–190
  adolescents with mild disabilities and,
    2–3, 11, 276
  curricular emphasis of, 9–10, 11
  dropouts and, 16
  grading and, 279
  mathematics instruction and, 190–192
  National Longitudinal Transition
    Study and, 10
  percentage of time spent in, 60, 61
  social skills instruction and, 262–264,
    267
  special education teachers and, 10
  transition-related instruction and, 329
General classroom teachers
  career education and, 320, 322
  career-related instructional programs
    and, 103
  classroom management and, 78
  collaborative relationship with special
    education teachers, 10, 11, 280
  effective teaching behaviors and, 78
  functional mathematics instruction
    and, 168
  grading and, 280
  in-service training for, 16
  reading instruction and, 124
  responsibilities of, 276
  social skills instruction and, 263
  special education teachers'
    collaboration with, 10, 11, 14,
    262, 276, 280, 289–290, 329
  transition and, 297, 327

  transition-related instruction and, 329
  vocational curriculum and, 13
Generalizable skills, 309–310, 312–313,
  327
Generalization
  classroom management and, 93–95
  of cognitive strategy training, 225–226
  effective teaching behaviors and, 74
  mathematics instruction and, 165, 193
  reading instruction and, 123–124
  social skills instruction and, 259, 262,
    265, 266, 267
  transition-related assessment and,
    309–310, 312
  work samples and, 312
Generalized learning disability, 52
Gilmore Oral Reading Test, 107, 108
Goal setting, 122, 165, 287–288
Goals 2000: Educate America Act, 2
Gonads, 35–36
Gordon Occupational Checklist, 310
GORT-R (*Gray Oral Reading Test—
  Revised*), 108
Grades and grading
  adolescents with mild disabilities and,
    58, 59, 278–280
  alternative grading policies, 9
  poor grade performance, 15
  postsecondary instruction and, 60
  postsecondary instruction assessment
    and, 348
  secondary schools and, 278–280
Graduation, 2, 13, 277
Graphic organizers, 124, 190
Gray Oral Reading Test—Revised
  (GORT-R), 108
Gray Oral Reading Tests—3rd edition,
  107
Growth of Logical Thinking, The
  (Inhelder and Piaget), 31
Guidance counselors, 327
Guided notes, 221
Guided practice, 164, 167, 283
Guided rehearsal, 75

Hall's theory of adolescence, 26–27
Hallucinogens, 65
Havinghurst's developmental tasks of
  adolescence, 30, 44
Health-care mathematics skills, 170
Higher education, 343. *See also* Colleges;
    Community colleges;
    Postsecondary instruction
Hint, 122
Hispanics, 54, 96
HIV, 9
Home care mathematics skills, 171–172
Homemaking mathematics skills,
  169–170
Homework, 288–289

Hormones, 35–36, 39
HOW, 218
Hunt, 122
Hyperactivity, 62
Hypothalamus, 35
Hypothetical thinking, 31

IBAS (*Enright Inventory of Basic
  Arithmetic Skills*), 158–159
ICP (Individual College Plan), 348
IDEA. *See* Individuals with Disabilities
  Education Act (PL 101-476)
Idealism, 33
Identity, 23, 26, 27–28, 29
IEP. *See* Individual educational program
  (IEP)
Inclusion. *See also* Mainstream
    classrooms
  adolescents with mild disabilities and,
    14, 275
  collaborative approach and, 290
  postsecondary instruction and, 340
  social skills and, 234, 245, 247, 249,
    263–264
  transition-related instruction and, 329
Increasing behaviors, 84–88
Independent community living
  career education and, 317
  functional mathematics instruction
    and, 169
  functional skills curriculum and, 326
  postsecondary instruction and, 352
  tracking systems and, 280
  transition and, 303
Independent level (reading), 109, 110
Independent performance, 309, 312, 329
Independent practice, 75, 283
Independent study behaviors, 209
Indirect instruction, 9
Individual College Plan (ICP), 348
Individual educational program (IEP)
  community-based instruction and,
    307
  defining behaviors and, 73
  effective instruction and, 72
  generalization and, 94
  grading and, 279
  graduation standards and, 277
  Individuals with Disabilities Education
    Act and, 299
  mathematics instruction and, 186
  mathematics skills assessment and, 159
  medical profiles and, 308
  minimum competency tests and, 2
  social skills assessment and, 247
  social skills instruction and, 260, 264
  transition and, 9, 325, 349
  vocational education and, 298, 345
  written language assessment and, 136
  written language instruction and, 139

Individualized instruction, 51, 72, 309
Individualized Written Rehabilitation Program (IWRP), 346
Individual placement model of supported employment, 347
Individual planning, 10
Individuals with Disabilities Education Act (PL 101-476)
  career education and, 322
  demographics and, 53
  Education for the Handicapped Act and, 3
  emotional disturbance and, 63
  transition and, 3, 299, 327
  transition-related instruction and, 298–299, 306
Informal inventories, 137, 160
Informal reading inventories (IRIs), 109
Information-processing skills, 38, 219
In-service training, 16
Instruction. *See also* Direct instruction; Mathematics instruction; Reading instruction; Social skills instruction; Transition-related instruction
  for adolescents with mild disabilities, 72–78
  classroom-based instruction, 327
  of cognitive strategy training, 202–207
  community-based instruction, 94, 193, 307, 322–325
  complementary instruction, 290
  comprehension instruction, 117–120
  computation instruction, 156, 165, 173–174, 187
  computer-assisted instruction, 165, 281, 282, 283–284, 286
  cooperative teaching, 290
  defining behaviors, 72–73
  effective content-area instruction, 280–289
  effective instruction, 72
  effective teaching behaviors, 73–74, 78, 183, 280–281
  elementary schools and, 2, 71, 276
  indirect instruction, 9
  individualized instruction, 309
  metacognitive strategy instruction, 140, 203
  modifications in, 278, 340, 354
  reciprocal teaching, 117–119
  speed of, 276–277
  strategic teaching, 124
  supportive instruction, 10
  team teaching, 290
Instructional cycle, 280, 281
Instructional level (reading), 109, 110
Insurance
  community-based instruction and, 325
  social skills instruction and, 264

Intellectual traits, of adolescents with mild disabilities, 57–61, 62
Intelligence quotient. *See* IQ (intelligence quotient)
Intelligence tests, 5, 38, 57
Interaction quality, naturalistic observation and, 243
Interactive Unit, 187
Interagency collaboration, 327
Interagency cooperation, 307, 325, 327–328, 329
Interagency service agreements, 325, 329
Interdisciplinary transition teams, 307
Interest Checklist, 310
Interest inventories, 309, 310
Interfering responses, 234, 235
Intermittent schedules of reinforcement, 87
Internalizing effect, 62
Interobserver agreement, 83–84
Interpersonal behaviors (IP), 252–253
Interpersonal concordance orientation, 32
Interpersonal development, Sullivan's theory of, 34–35
Interpersonal relations, 312, 317, 329. *See also* Social skills
Interpersonal understanding, 32
Interpreters, 16, 55, 56, 304, 354
Interval recording, 82–83
Interval schedules of reinforcement, 87
Intervention-therapy social skills assessment, 238
Interviewing, 310–312
Intrinsic motivation, 122
Iowa Silent Reading Tests, 107
IP (interpersonal behaviors), 252–253
IQ (intelligence quotient)
  adolescence and, 38
  of adolescents with mild disabilities, 55, 57–58
  mental retardation and, 5, 55, 57, 58
  postsecondary instruction and, 352
  transition-related assessment and, 309
IRIs (informal reading inventories), 109
IWRP (Individualized Written Rehabilitation Program), 346

Job coaches, 304, 307, 327
Juvenile court system, 43
Juvenile delinquency, 41–43, 63–66

Kansas Institute for Research, 214
Keymath—Revised (KM-R), 157–158
Kohlberg's theory of adolescent morality, 31–32, 44

Labels, and special education, 3, 51
Labor, U. S. Department of, 322
Late adolescence, 34, 35

Latency recording, 82
Latinos, 54, 96
LCCE (*Life-Centered Career Education*), 317–321
LCCE Knowledge Battery, 314
LCCE Performance Battery, 316
LCD (Lifelong Career Development) Model, 320
LD. *See* Learning disabilities (LD)
LDA (Learning Disabilities Association), 340, 352
Leading, and direct instruction, 75
Learned helplessness, 7
Learning. *See also* Cognitive learning strategies
  acquisition learning, 73, 86
  cooperative learning, 10, 167, 286–287
  learning strategies, 119–120, 205, 214–215, 349
  learning strategies program model, 10, 13
  proficiency learning, 73–74
  rote learning, 168, 173, 187
Learning disabilities (LD)
  academic-related characteristics of, 58–61
  adulthood and, 16
  appearance of student and, 51
  career education and, 304, 353
  chemical dependency and, 65
  cognitive learning strategies and, 214–215
  demographics and, 54
  depression and, 62
  diagnosis of, 346
  dropout rate and, 15
  federal definitions of, 3, 4
  IQ and, 55, 57, 58
  juvenile delinquency and, 64
  mathematics instruction and, 165–168
  mild mental retardation compared with, 52, 57
  minimum competency tests and, 277
  physical therapy and, 56
  postsecondary instruction and, 60, 341
  postsecondary instruction assessment and, 348
  selective attention and, 204
  social cognition and, 45
  sociometric rating scales and, 245–246
  suicide and, 63
  supported employment and, 306
  teacher rating scales and, 247
  transition-related instruction and, 297, 328
Learning Disabilities Association (LDA), 340, 352
Learning strategies, 119–120, 205, 214–215, 349
Learning strategies program model, 10, 13

Legislation. *See also specific laws*
classification categories and, 3
education reforms and, 2
individualization of instruction and, 51
postsecondary instruction and,
341–342
special education and, 7–11
transition-related instruction and,
298–299, 306
Leisure skills, 307, 326
Lesson pace, 76
Lesson plans, 73
Lessons for Better Writing, 147
Lesson structure, 74
Lewin's theory of adolescence, 29–30, 37
Liability issues, 264, 325
Life-Centered Career Education (LCCE),
317–321
Lifelong Career Development (LCD)
Model, 320
Life Skills Inventory, 316
Life Skills Writing Skillbooks, 147
Life space, 29–30
Literacy, 11, 16, 102

Mainstream classrooms. *See also*
Inclusion
cognitive strategy training and, 226
grading practices, 278–280
graduation standards and, 277
in-service training on, 16
instruction speed and, 276–277
reading instruction and, 122–124
social skills assessment and,248
written language instruction and,
148–149
Maintenance
cognitive strategy training and, 225
colors as discrimination tool and, 162
effective teaching behaviors and, 74
mathematics instruction and, 176
social skills instruction and, 262, 265,
267
Maladaptive behavior, 5, 66
Males. *See also* Gender
academic-related characteristics of, 59
as adolescents with mild disabilities, 54
Blos's views on, 29
depression and, 39, 62
drug use and, 65
Hall's views on, 26
juvenile delinquency and, 42–43,
64–65
morbidity and mortality statistics of,
25
physical development of, 25, 36–37
suicide and, 40
Manipulatives, 173–174
Marijuana, 65
Mathematics, definition of, 156

Mathematics diagnostic interview, 162
*Mathematics for the Mildly
Handicapped: A Guide to
Curriculum and Instruction,* 187
Mathematics instruction
cognitive learning strategies and, 167,
176–183, 218–219
commercial mathematics curricula
and, 183–190
defining behaviors and, 73
functional mathematics instruction
and, 156, 168–173
general classroom instruction and,
190–192
generalization and, 165, 193
mathematical process instruction and,
173–176, 178–179
mathematics skills assessment and,
157–162
motivation and, 192–193
research validated instruction,
162–168
Mathematics Modules, 183
Mathematics skills
adolescents with mild disabilities and,
155–156, 280
assessment of, 157–162
functional mathematics instruction
and, 168–173
generalizable skills and, 312
informal assessment, 159–162
interagency service agreements and,
329
standardized, criterion-referenced and
diagnostic tests, 157–159
vocational mathematics skills,
172–173
Mathematics Skills for Daily Living,
185–186
MCT (minimum competency test), 2,
105, 277, 278
Medical profiles, 308–309
Melatonin, 35
Memorization, 168, 173
Memory, 38, 203, 204
Memory skills, 2, 6
Menarche, 36
Menstrual cycle, 36
Mental retardation (MR). *See also* Mild
mental retardation
academic-related characteristics of,
58–61
definition of, 4–5
demographics and, 54
dropout rate and, 15
IQ and, 5, 55, 57, 58
Piaget's cognitive stages of
development and, 45
postsecondary instruction and, 60
severity levels of, 5

supported employment and, 306
transition-related assessment and, 309
transition-related instruction and, 297
tutors, readers, interpreters and, 56
Mental Retardation and Developmental
Disabilities Division (MRDD), 5
Metacognition, and cognitive strategy
training, 203, 204
Metacognitive problem solving methods,
33
Metacognitive strategy instruction, 140,
203
Microcomputers, 121–122, 124,
147–148, 165. *See also*
Computer-assisted instruction
Middle schools, 2, 15, 57, 261
Mild disabilities, 3–7. *See also*
Adolescents with mild disabilities;
Young adults with mild
disabilities
Mild mental retardation. *See also* Mental
retardation (MR)
appearance of student and, 51
depression and, 62
IQ and, 57
juvenile delinquency and, 64
learning disabilities compared with,
52, 57
as level of mental retardation, 5
mathematics instruction and, 162–165
mathematics skills and, 156
postsecondary instruction and, 341
social cognition and, 45
sociometric rating scales and, 245–246
Minimum competency tests (MCT), 2,
105, 277, 278
Minnesota Clerical Test, 311
Minnesota Multiphasic Inventory - 2, 62
Minorities, 42, 57. *See also specific
minorities*
Misdemeanor offenses, 42
Mnemonic devices, 190, 205, 281, 282,
285–286
Mobile work crew model of supported
employment, 347
Modeling
direct instruction and, 75
mathematics instruction and, 164,
165, 167
note-taking and, 221
social skills instruction and, 250, 257,
259, 260
vocabulary development and, 115
Moderate developmental disabilities, 297
Momentary time sampling, 82
Mood-emotive-affective cluster of
depression, 39, 40
Moral autonomy, 31
Moral development, 31–32, 44
Moral education, 32

Morbidity statistics, 25
Morphemic analysis, 115
Mortality statistics, 25
Motivation
  cognitive strategy training and, 203
  direct instruction, 77
  extrinsic motivation, 122, 123
  intrinsic motivation, 122
  mathematics instruction and, 192–193
  motivation problems, 7
  postsecondary instruction and, 349
  reading instruction and, 114, 122
  social skills instruction and, 250
  written language instruction and, 148
Motivational-behavioral clusters of
    depression, 40
Motivational empowerment, 122
MRDD (Mental Retardation and
    Developmental Disabilities
    Division), 5
Multipass strategy, 216
Music as reinforcement, 162
Mutual perspective-taking skills, 33

National Council of Teachers of
    Mathematics (NCTM), 193–195
National Joint Committee on Learning
    Disabilities, 4
National Longitudinal Transition Study
    of Special Education Students
    (NLTS), 10, 15–16, 17, 53, 58–59
Nation at Risk, A (National Commission
    on Excellence in Education), 2
Naturalistic observation, and social skills,
    236, 243
NCTM (National Council of Teachers of
    Mathematics), 193–195
Negative nominations, 243–244
Negative reinforcement, 85
NLTS (National Longitudinal Transition
    Study of Special Education
    Students), 10, 15–16, 17, 53,
    58–59
Noncontingent reinforcement, 88
Nonexclusion time-out, 91
Nonreading Aptitude Test Battery, 311
Norm-referenced tests, 132
Note-taking, 219–221, 304, 354
Numeracy, 11

Observation. *See also* Direct observation
  naturalistic observation, 236, 243
  reading skills assessment and, 112–113
  reliability of, 83–84
  written language skills assessment
    and, 139
Observer bias, 243
Occupational therapy, 55, 56
Occupation training, 16. *See also* Career
    education; Vocational education

OCR (optical character recognition)
    systems, 356
Office of Special Education and
    Rehabilitative Services (OSERS),
    6, 297, 306, 349
Office of Special Education Programs
    (OSEP), 15, 53, 306
Office of Vocational and Adult Education,
    306
Ohio Social Acceptance Scale (OSAS),
    245–246
Optical character recognition (OCR)
    systems, 356
Oral edit, 137
Organizational skills, 2, 287, 350
Orientation and mobility training, 304
Orientation toward authority, law, and
    duty, 32
OSAS (*Ohio Social Acceptance Scale*),
    245–246
OSEP (Office of Special Education
    Programs), 15, 53, 306
OSERS (Office of Special Education and
    Rehabilitative Services), 6, 297,
    306, 349
Out-of-classroom application, 74
Overcorrection, 90–91
Overt-motoric behavior, 235

Paraphrasing, 124
Paraprofessionals, 79
Parents
  communication with, 289
  parental consent, 91
  single-parent homes, 54
  social skills instruction and, 264
  transition and, 327, 328, 330
Partial interval recording, 82
*Peabody Individual Achievement Test—
    Revised,* 134–135
Peer acceptance definition of social skills,
    236
Peer-assisted learning, 124
Peer groups
  adolescents with mild disabilities and,
    51
  community based-instruction and,
    323
  depression and, 62
  identity establishment and, 26, 27, 29
  peer acceptance definition of social
    skills, 236
  social-behavioral competence and, 237
  social skills instruction and, 234, 250
  sociometry and, 243–246, 249, 267
Peer-mediated instruction, 281, 282,
    286–287
Peer mentor systems, 354–355
Peer nomination, 243–244, 246
PENS, 142–143, 216–217

Performance adjustments, 277
Performance deficits, 234
Performance feedback, 75–76, 250, 257
Performance levels, 76
Perkins Acts. *See* Carl D. Perkins
    Vocational and Applied
    Technology Education Acts of
    1984 and 1990 (PL 98-254)
Permanent product recording, 83
Personal characteristics, of adolescents
    with mild disabilities, 53–56
Personal health, 307
Personal identity, 23
Personality development, 29
Personal management, 307
Personal value systems, 44–45
Perspective-taking skills, 33, 45
Physical development, 25, 35–37, 45
Physical therapy, 55–56
Physical-vegetative clusters of
    depression, 40
Physiological-emotional behavior, 235
Piaget's cognitive theory of adolescence,
    31, 33–34, 37, 45
Pineal gland, 35
PIRATES, 221, 223
Pituitary gland, 35–36
PL 93-112 (Vocational Rehabilitation Act,
    Section 504), 7, 8, 340, 341, 352
PL 93-203 (Comprehensive Employment
    and Training Act), 8
PL 94-142. *See* Education for All
    Handicapped Children Act (PL
    94-142); Education for the
    Handicapped Act (PL 94-142)
PL 94-482 (Education Amendments of
    Vocational Education Act), 7
PL 98-199 (Education of the
    Handicapped Act Amendments of
    1983), 8, 298
PL 98-254 (Carl D. Perkins Vocational
    and Applied Technology
    Education Acts of 1984 and
    1990), 8, 298, 306, 345
PL 99-506 (Rehabilitation Act as
    Amended), 306
PL 101-336 (Americans with Disabilities
    Act of 1990), 8, 9, 340, 352
PL 101-476. *See* Education of the
    Handicapped Amendments of
    1990 (PL 101-476); Individuals
    with Disabilities Education Act
    (PL 101-476)
PL 482 (Vocational Education Act of
    1976), 298
PLEASE, 217
Point-by-point procedure, 84
Positive practice overcorrection, 90–91
Positive reinforcement, 84, 91–92
Postconventional moral development, 32

Postsecondary instruction
  administrative considerations, 354
  assessment issues, 347–348
  college programs, 344–345
  commercial curriculum guides for,
    352–353
  legal foundations for, 341–342
  preparation for, 348–352
  research on, 356–357
  scope of programs, 342–344
  service delivery issues, 354–355
  supported employment and, 347
  support services for, 340, 342–344,
    353–354
  technical education and, 345–346
  technological issues, 355–356
  vocational rehabilitation and, 345–346
  young adults with mild disabilities
    and, 60–61, 299, 331, 340–347
*Practical Mathematics: Consumer
  Applications,* 186
Preadolescence, 34
Pre-employment employment, 343
PREP, 224
Previewing, 74
Primary reinforcement, 84–85
Principals, 78, 264
Principled stage of moral development,
  32
Prior history, naturalistic observation
  and, 243
Privileges, removal of, 90–91
Problem solving
  calculators and, 164
  computation instruction and, 173–174
  cooperative teaching and, 290
  mathematics instruction and, 167,
    168, 176, 187
  mathematics skills and, 156
  metacognitive methods of, 33
  social skills instruction and, 262
  visual displays and, 283
  written language instruction and, 133
Process approach to writing instruction,
  145
Proficiency learning, 73–74
Progesterone, 36
Program accessibility, 342
Program models, 10, 11–13, 76
Progression, 29
Prosocial behaviors, 240, 263, 264
Prosocial skills, 250, 267. *See also* Social
  skills
Psychological disorders, 38–43
Psychosexual development, 27
Psychosocial development, 27
Puberty, 24, 28, 35, 36
Pubescence, 24, 25. *See also* Adolescence
  and adolescents
Punishment, 86, 90, 236

Quality of Life Questionnaire, 315
Quality of Student Life Questionnaire,
  315

Race, 54, 55, 57, 96
RAP strategy, 119–120, 215
Rate recording, 80, 312
Ration schedules of reinforcement, 87
Reactivity to measurement, 34, 92–93
Readers, 16, 55, 56
Reading for Understanding, 120
Reading instruction. *See also* Reading
  skills assessment
  adolescents with mild disabilities and,
    102–104
  cognitive learning strategies and,
    215–216
  commercial reading curricula, 120–121
  comprehension instruction, 117–120
  computer software and, 121–122
  critical features of, 120
  defining behaviors, 73
  functional reading skills and, 103–104
  generalization and, 123–124
  in mainstream classrooms, 122–124
  reading as complex process, 102–103
  vocabulary development and, 114–116
Reading Report Card (U.S. Department
  of Education), 102
Reading skills assessment
  adolescents with mild disabilities'
    deficiencies and, 280
  complexity of, 104
  generalizable skills and, 312
  informal procedures, 108–113
  interagency service agreements and,
    329
  reasons for, 105
  standardized, criterion-referenced and
    diagnostic tests, 105–108
Reading Visual Aids Strategy (RVAS),
  284–285
Reasoning, 312, 329
Recapitulation, 26, 27, 29
Reciprocal peer editing, 145–146
Reciprocal teaching, 117–119
Recording procedures
  anecdotal recording, 80, 81
  duration recording, 80–81, 240, 242,
    313
  event recording, 80, 241
  frequency recording, 80, 239–240, 312
  time sampling procedures, 82–83, 242
Regression, 29
Regular classroom instruction. *See*
  Content-area instruction; General
  classroom instruction;
  Mainstream classrooms
Regular classroom teachers. *See* General
  classroom teachers

Rehabilitation Act as Amended (PL 99-
  506), 306
Rehabilitation counseling, 9
Rehabilitation engineering, 304
Rehabilitation Services Administration,
  306
Rehearsal, 75, 257, 259, 262
Reinforcement
  decreasing behaviors and, 88–92
  direct instruction and, 77
  extrinsic motivation and, 122, 123
  increasing behaviors and, 84–88
  mathematics instruction and, 167
  music as, 162
  social skills instruction and, 236, 257
Rejection, 246
Reliability of observation, 83–84
Removing desirables and privileges,
  90–91
Research
  mathematics instruction and, 162–168
  postsecondary instruction and,
    356–357
  transition-related instruction and, 299
Resource room pull-out, 276
Response cost, 90
Restitutional overcorrection, 91
Review with reteaching, 75
Role diffusion, 27, 28
Role-plays, 250, 251, 259
Rote learning, 168, 173, 187
RVAS (Reading Visual Aids Strategy),
  284–285

Scholastic Aptitude Test (SAT), 51, 348
School administration, 78, 264, 354
School-based training, 326–327
School survival skills, 287–289
Schoolwide discipline programs, 78, 79
Sciences, 102, 280
SCORER, 221–223
SDMT (*Stanford Diagnostic Mathematics
  Test*), 158
Seclusionary time-out, 91
Secondary Education and Transitional
  Services for Handicapped Youth,
  8
Secondary reinforcement, 84–85
Secondary schools. *See also* Classroom
  management
  cognitive strategy training and,
    202–207
  community-based instruction and,
    322–325
  creation of, 24
  curriculum of, 2
  demands of, 3
  educational program models of, 11–13
  education reforms and, 2–3, 11
  grading and, 278–280

graduation and, 2, 13, 277
instructional techniques and, 71
program development, 2–3
social skills instruction and, 261
transition and, 350–352
transition-related instruction and, 297
Secondary sex characteristics, 36
Secondary students with mild disabilities.
    See Adolescents with mild
    disabilities
Second individuation process, 29
Section 504 of the Rehabilitation Act, 7,
    8, 340, 341–342, 352
Secular trends, and puberty, 24, 36
Selective attention, 203, 204
*Self-Advocacy Strategy for Educational
    and Transition Planning, The,* 257
Self-control, 34, 122, 262
Self-deprecating humor, 77
Self-Directed Search, The, 310
Self-evaluation, 309, 312, 329
Self-instructional strategy training,
    140–145
Self-management techniques, 92–93,
    250, 266
Self-related behaviors (SR), 254–255
Self-reports, 309
Selman's theory of social cognition,
    32–33, 45
Semantic mapping, 115, 216, 223
Service delivery issues, 306, 354–355
Setting variable, 94
*Seventeenth Annual Report to Congress
    on the Implementation of The
    Individuals with Disabilities
    Education Act,* 53
Severe developmental disabilities, 297, 306
Shaping, 86
Short-term interventions, 52
Single-parent homes, 54
Skillstreaming the Adolescent, 250
SLANT, 224
*Social and Prevocational Information
    Battery—Revised,* 314
Social-behavioral competence, 237
Social cognition
    deficiencies in, 234
    Selman's theory of, 32–33, 45
Social competence, 235, 236, 237, 247,
    249
Social contract orientation, 32
Social impact, 244
Social intelligence, 32
Social maladjustment, 63
Social praise, 85
Social preference, 244
Social reinforcement, 85
Social skills
    adolescents with mild disabilities and,
        280, 299, 307

classroom-based instruction and,
    327
deficits in, 6–7, 234, 249
definition of, 235–238
inclusion and, 234, 245, 247, 249,
    263–264
Life-Centered Career Education and,
    317
lists of, 242, 248, 252–255, 258, 261
Social skills assessment
    direct observation and, 238–243, 249,
        267
    importance of, 267
    sociometry and, 243–246, 249, 267
    teacher rating scales, 247–249, 267
Social Skills for Daily Living, 256
Social Skills for School and Community,
    257, 259–260, 261
Social skills instruction. *See also* Social
    skills assessment
    considerations concerning, 264–266
    curricula for, 250–256, 265–265
    defining behaviors and, 73
    definitions of, 235–238
    employment and, 260–262
    general classroom instruction and,
        262–264, 267
    generalization and, 259, 262, 265, 266,
        267
    intervention methods, 249–250
    noncommercial social skills training
        procedures, 256–260
    purpose of, 233–234
    rationale for, 234–238, 264
Social Skills in the Classroom, 250–251
Social Skills on the Job, 256
Social Skills Rating System (SSRS),
    247–248
Social validity definition of social skills,
    238
Social work services, 9
Societal perspective-taking skills, 33
Socioeconomic status, 42, 54, 55, 57
Sociometry, 243–246, 249, 267
SOLVE, 219
Special education
    age-appropriate skills and, 30
    certification for, 52
    classification categories for, 3–7
    definition of, 9
    dropouts and, 15
    education reform and, 2–3
    funding for, 3
    history of, 52
    labels of, 3, 51
    legislation and, 7–11
    service delivery systems and, 306
    social skills instruction and, 267
Special Education for Adolescents
    (Cullinan and Epstein), 52

Special education teachers
    career education and, 320, 322
    career-related instructional programs
        and, 103
    classroom management and, 78
    content-area instruction and, 187
    effective teaching behaviors and, 78
    functional mathematics instruction
        and, 168
    functional skills program model and,
        13
    general classroom teachers'
        collaborative relationship with,
        10, 11, 14, 262, 276, 280,
        289–290, 329
    general education classes and, 10
    grading and, 280
    interagency collaboration and, 327
    teacher rating scales and, 247
    transition-related instruction and, 328
    tutorial program model and, 12
    vocational rehabilitation system and,
        346
Specific Skill Builders, 120–121
Speech impairments, 15
Speech-language therapy, 55, 56
Spelling, 137
Spelling Blizzard, 148
Spelling Jungle, 148
Spelling Wiz, 147–148
*Spellmaster Assessment and Teaching
    System, The,* 135, 136
SPUR, 185
SQRQCQ, 218–219
SQ3R method, 216
SR (self-related behaviors), 254–255
SRA Achievement Series, 208
SRI (Stanford Research Institute), 53
SSRS (*Social Skills Rating System*),
    247–248
Stages of Man theory, 27
Standardized tests
    generalizable skills and, 309
    mathematics skills assessment and,
        157–159
    reading skills assessment, 106–108
    study skills and, 208, 223
    transition-related assessment and,
        313–316
    written language skills assessment
        and, 134–136
Stanford Diagnostic Mathematics Test
    (SDMT), 158
*Stanford Diagnostic Reading Test (3rd
    ed.),* 107, 108
Stanford Research Institute (SRI), 53
Star Paperbacks, 121
Status offenses, 41–42
Storm and stress, of adolescence, 26, 45
Storybook Weaver, 148

Strategic teaching, 124
Strong-Campbell Interest Inventory, 310
Students with mild disabilities. *See*
    Adolescents with mild disabilities;
    Young adults with mild
    disabilities; Young children with
    mild disabilities
Study Attitudes and Methods Survey,
    208
Study guides, 124, 189, 281, 282, 285
Study skills
    adolescents with mild disabilities and,
        280
    assessment of, 208–212
    cognitive learning strategies and,
        219–225
    cognitive strategy training and, 201,
        204–207
    deficits in, 7
    inventory of, 210–212
    postsecondary instruction and, 349
    standardized tests and, 208, 223
Study Skills Checklist, 208
*Study Skills Test: McGraw-Hill Basic
    Skills System,* 208
Sturm and Drang, 26, 45
Sublimation, 27
Suburban schools, 57
Successive approximations, 86, 87
*Sucher-Allred Reading Placement
    Inventory, The,* 109
Suicide
    adolescents and, 39–41
    adolescents with mild disabilities and,
        63
    depression and, 40, 62–63
    early warning signs of, 41, 42
    identity and, 28
Sullivan's theory of adolescent
    interpersonal development, 34–35
Supplementary learning activities, 290
Supported employment, 304, 306–307,
    347
Supportive instruction, 10
Support services, and postsecondary
    instruction, 340, 342–344,
    353–354
Survey of Study Habits and Attitudes,
    208
Survival skills, 223, 287–289
Synonym teaching, 115

Tabula rasa, 72
Target behaviors, 82, 83
Task analysis, 165
Task-analyzed measurement, 159
Task-related questions, 74
TBI (traumatic brain injury), 3, 5–6, 9
Teacher-directed activities, 288
Teacher-made tests, 160, 278

Teacher-pleasing behaviors, 287
Teacher rating scales
    generalizable skills and, 309
    social skills assessment and, 247–249,
        267
Teachers. *See also* General classroom
    teachers; Instruction; Special
    education teachers
    adolescents and, 96–97
    collaboration of, 10, 11, 14, 262, 276,
        280, 289–290, 329
    cooperative teaching, 289–290
    employer interviewing and, 311–312
    extinction, and 90
    in-service training on mainstreaming,
        16
    instructional planning process of, 10
    measuring behavior and, 78
    recording behavior and, 78–79
    school accountability and, 2
    social-behavioral competence and, 237
    social reinforcement and, 85
    social skills assessment and, 242–243
    sociometric assessment and, 246
    teacher preparation, 10–11
    teacher rating scales, 247–249
    time-out and, 91
    transition-related instruction role and,
        325–330
Teacher training institutions, 10–11, 52
Teaching. *See* Instruction
*Teaching Competence in Written
    Language,* 147
Team teaching, 290
Technical education, 345–346
Technical institutes, 341, 346
Technological issues, in postsecondary
    instruction, 355–356
TEENS, 285
Television, 43
Testing (independent practice), 75
Test of Adolescent Language—3 (TOAL-
    3), 135, 348
Test of Mathematical Abilities (TOMA),
    158
*Test of Reading Comprehension—
    Revised* (TORC-R), 106, 107, 108
Test of Written Language—2 (TOWL-2),
    136
Test of Written Language—3, 135, 348
Test of Written Spelling—2 (TWS-2), 135
Testosterone, 36
Tests. *See also* Standardized tests; *and
    specific tests*
    aptitude tests, 309–311
    college aptitude tests, 51, 348
    criterion-referenced tests, 106–108,
        134–139, 157–159, 208
    diagnostic tests, 106–108, 134–136,
        157–159, 208

intelligence tests, 5, 38, 57
minimum competency tests, 2, 105,
    277, 278
norm-referenced tests, 132
teacher-made tests, 160, 278
Tests for Everyday Living, 314
Test taking
    adolescents with mild disabilities and,
        7
    modified testing procedures and, 277,
        354
    study skills and, 221, 223
Thinking, 31, 34, 37–38, 45
Thinning (reinforcement), 88
Third-person perspective-taking skills, 33
Thyroid, 35–36
Time management, 206–207, 349, 350
Time-out from positive reinforcement,
    91–92
Time sampling procedures, 82–83, 242
TOAL-3 (*Test of Adolescent Language—
    3*), 135, 348
Tokens, 85, 90, 122, 162
TOMA (*Test of Mathematical Abilities*),
    158
TORC-R (*Test of Reading
    Comprehension—Revised*), 106,
    107, 108
Total duration, 81
TOWER, 144–145, 217
TOWL-2 (*Test of Written Language—2*),
    136
Tracking systems, 280
Trade schools, 341, 346
Training centers, 9
Transenvironmental programming, 94
Transition
    adolescents with mild disabilities and,
        300–302
    definitions of, 299, 303–304
    employment and, 303, 304, 306–307
    gender and, 299
    individual education programs and, 9,
        325, 349
    Individuals with Disabilities Education
        Act and, 3, 299, 327
    interdisciplinary transition teams and,
        307
    mathematics skills and, 156
    parents and, 327, 328, 330
    postsecondary instruction and, 340,
        349–350
    Secondary Education and Transitional
        Services for Handicapped Youth
        and, 8
    secondary schools and, 350–352
    social skills instruction and, 260
    teacher's role in, 325–330
Transition Behavior Scale, 314
Transition Mathematics, 185

Transition Planning Inventory, 315
Transition-related instruction
  assessment for, 308–316
  career education and, 317–322
  collateral areas, 307
  community-based instruction and, 307, 322–325
  Education of the Handicapped Act Amendments and, 298
  inclusion and, 329
  Individuals with Disabilities Education Act, 298–299, 306
  rationale for, 298–307
  research on, 299
  secondary schools and, 297
  service delivery systems and, 306
  special education teachers and, 328
  teacher's role in, 325–330
Transportation issues, 264, 325, 327
Transportation mathematics skills, 170–171
Traumatic brain injury (TBI), 3, 5–6, 9
TREE, 142
Troubled Adolescent, The (White), 39
Tutorial program model, 12
Tutors, 16, 55, 56, 344, 354
Two-year college programs, 344–345
TWS-2 (*Test of Written Spelling—2*), 135–136

Unemployment rates, 299
Universal ethical principles orientation, 32
Universities, 341, 343
University of Wisconsin-Whitewater, 344
Urban schools, 57

Valence issues, 30
Value patterns, 44–45
Variable-ratio (VR) schedule of reinforcement, 87
Verbal feedback, 122
Verbal format, 188–189, 190
Verbal rehearsal, 257, 259
Verb Viper, 148
Vicarious reinforcement, 89, 263
Violence, 43, 96
Visual-spatial displays, 190, 281, 282, 283–285
Visual-verbal format, 190
VITAL checklist, 310

Vocabulary development, 114–116, 190, 191
Vocational education
  adolescents with mild disabilities and, 60, 61, 330
  curriculum for, 13
  definition of, 303
  Education Amendments of Vocational Education Act and, 7
  individual educational program and, 298, 345
  legislation for, 298
  postsecondary, 60
  service delivery systems and, 306
  support services of, 343
  transition-related instruction and, 328–329
Vocational Education Act of 1976 (PL 482), 298
Vocational mathematics skills, 172–173
Vocational outcomes, 16
Vocational program model, 13
Vocational rehabilitation (VR), 304, 305, 306, 327, 345–346
Vocational Rehabilitation Act (PL 93-112), Section 504, 7, 8, 340, 341, 352
Vocational skills, 310–313
Vocational technical schools, 341, 346
Vocational training, 323–325
VR (variable-ratio) schedule of reinforcement, 87
VR (vocational rehabilitation), 304, 305, 306, 327, 345–346

Walker-McConnell Scale of Social Competence and School Adjustment (WMC), 247
Webbing, 115, 216
Wechsler Individual Achievement Test (WIAT), 107, 108, 136
White Americans, 54, 59, 96
Whole interval recording, 82–83
WIAT (*Wechsler Individual Achievement Test*), 107, 108, 136
Wisconsin Tests of Reading Skill Development Study Skills, 208
WISE, 224
"Withitness," 76
WMC (*Walker-McConnell Scale of Social Competence and School Adjustment*), 247

Woodcock Johnson Psycho-Educational Battery—Revised, 135, 348
Woodcock Reading Mastery Test— Revised (WRMT-R), 106, 107, 108
Word identification strategy, 215
Word Invasion, 148
Word Man, 122
Word Master, 148
Word Radar, 122
Word recognition, 102–103
Work experience, 60, 61
Work samples, 312–313
WRITER, 218
Writing Adventure, The, 148
Writing portfolios analysis, 136–137
Writing Skills for the Adolescent, 147
Writing with a Point, 147
Written language instruction
  adolescents with mild disabilities' problems with, 132–134
  assessment and, 134–139, 280, 312, 329
  cognitive learning strategies and, 216–218
  cognitive models and, 140–145
  commercial written language curricula, 147
  as complex process, 133
  computer software and, 147–148
  importance of, 139–140
  mainstream classrooms and, 148–149
  reciprocal peer editing, 145–146
Written language skills assessment
  adolescents with mild disabilities' deficiencies and, 280
  generalizable skills and, 312
  informal assessment, 136–139
  interagency service agreements and, 329
  standardized, criterion-referenced and diagnostic tests, 134–136
WRMT-R (*Woodcock Reading Mastery Test—Revised*), 106, 107, 108

Young adults with mild disabilities
  assessment of, 347
  postsecondary instruction and, 60–61, 299, 331, 340–347
  supported employment and, 306
  transition and, 300–302
Young children with disabilities, 3